GW01048710

The K Club (Palmer Course), County Kildare.

Golf – Never Enough Time…

You can play a different golf course in Ireland every day of the year and still have more than a few left over!

After sixteen years of publishing Golfdays we still haven't been able to play them all – so, thankfully, the adventure continues.

This year we launch the revised Internet site for Golfdays.com in support of the book and using the new media's ability to give us exciting interactive view's of Ireland's golf courses. Log on and take a trip down a few courses and explore Ireland's rich golf heritage.

Start young – 387 courses to play.

William Campbell
Publisher

The EMBASSY ROOMS

Grill Restaurant ~ Niteclub
Lounge & Bar ~ Snooker & Pool

BAR & GRILL RESTAURNT

TOFFS
MEZZANINE

THE BELFRY
Award Winning Bar Food

THOMAS STREET

Open 6.00pm - 10.00pm
Sunday Lunch Only
Open 12.30pm - 2.30pm

Niteclub open
Thur, Fri, Sat & Sun

Food Served till 9pm every day
5 Championship Snooker Tables
& 4 American Pool Tables
Heated Smoking area available

John F. Kennedy Parade, Sligo Tel: 071-9161250 / 9161258

Ireland is divided into four ancient Provinces and these are applied in the administration of golf by the Golfing Union of Ireland. Golfdays has adopted the same geographical division. The courses in this book are grouped in Provinces, sub-divided into Counties and then listed alphabetically. The Province appears on the top centre and the County name at the top left of each page, with the name of the course on the top right.

Druids Glen

LOCATION: Twenty-three miles south of Dublin City. Two miles east Newtownmountkennedy off the N1

COURSE DESIGNER
Pat Ruddy
Tom Craddo

PROFESSION
Eamonn D

SCORE CARD

Some course cards are marked in metres, some in yards and some have both. Whatever method of distance that is currently used by each course, the same has been adopted in Golfdays to maintain the same standard of measurement. Some course lengths differ in text from course cards depending on whether Championship or Medal tees are on the score card.

COURSE INFORMATION

This information has been provided by each club and readers are advised to check details in advance as the publishers cannot guarantee the accuracy. Most clubs will be only too glad to answer queries and telephone numbers for all the courses listed have been included for this purpose. **A telephone call can save a wasted journey.**
There are different area dialing codes when calling from the Republic of Ireland to Northern Ireland and vice versa. From N.Ireland dial 00 353 and then the code omitting the first zero. From the Republic of Ireland replace the Northern Ireland 028 code with 048.

Course Description:
Druids Glen situated on the ancestral estate of Sir Thomas Wentworth is already an acknowledged masterpiece and had the honour of hosting the Murphy's Irish Open Championship in 1996, 1997, 1998 and 1999.

Course Information:
Par 71; Length 7,026 yards. Visitors: Welcome – tee times by arrangement. Opening Hours: 8.00am – Sunset. Green Fees: Mid October – mid April €85, €95 includes breakfast. €125 with dinner. Early Bird mid April – mid October €150. Clubhouse Hours: 8.00am – onwards. Dress: Neat Casual. Clubhouse Facilities: Lunch, Dinner and conference facilities available. ...es available by prior arrangement. ...on site.

CURRENCY

All green fees for Northern Ireland (Counties: Down, Armagh, Antrim, Londonderry, Fermanagh and Tyrone) are in £ Sterling. Those for the Republic of Ireland are in € Euro. The currencies exchange rate between £ Sterling and € Euro will fluctuate, although as a general rule € 1 is worth between £0.65 and £0.70 sterling.

COURSE MAP

Maps are produced as a general guide to assist familiarity of the course. They should not be taken as accurate representations for play but as an overview of the course layout. Some items, such as clubhouse illustrations are for approximate position and do not represent the actual structure.

Published by

Tudor Journals Ltd

97 Botanic Avenue,
Belfast BT7 1JN, N. Ireland.
Tel: (028) 9032 0088.
Fax: (028) 9032 3163.
Also: 74 Amiens Street Dublin1.
Email: info@tudorjournals.com
Web: www.tudorjournals.com

Code from Republic of Ireland replace (028) with (048)

Original Editorial Committee 1990
Leinster:
Kenneth W. Haughton
Ulster:
Brendan Edwards.
Munster:
J. Percy Shannon.
Connacht:
Michael P. O'Donoghue.

Provincial Introductions
Jack Magowan

Sales Team
Kimmo Proudfoot, Billy Spence

Sales Support
Galyna Murphy

Production Team
Marc Bell, Michael Bratton,
Nuala Hagan, Una Martin,
Michael McAnea, Damian Platek.

Publishing Manager
Paula Pavis

Assistant Publisher
Lori Somerville

Production Director
Charlene Devine

Publisher
Bill Campbell

Printed by
W&G Bairds Ltd.

Golf Clubs in Ireland – Locations

All courses are affiliated to the Golfing Union of Ireland.

PORTRUSH 239 - 240

BELFAST CITY 252 - 263

NORTH DOWN 290, 291, 293 294, 295, 297 299, 300, 305

COUNTY DUBLIN 49-82

DUBLIN CITY 83-103

WICKLOW 184 – 193, 195, 197

WEXFORD 174, 175

WATERFORD 433, 437 - 439

CORK 369, 371

ULSTER

CONNACHT

LEINSTER

MUNSTER

Numbers on the page opposite are colour coded in provinces with approximate geographical location shown on the map above, they also refer to the page number of each course.

LEINSTER

CARLOW
46 Borris
47 Carlow
48 Mount Wolseley
DUBLIN
49 Balbriggan
50 Balcarrick
51 Beaverstown
52 Beechpark
53 Christy O'Connor
54 City West
55 City West (Executive)
56 Corballis
57 Corrstown
58 Donabate
59 Dublin Mountain
60 Dun Loaghaire
61 Forrest Little
62 Grange Castle
63 Glencullen
64 Hermitage
65 Hollystown
66 Hollywood Lakes
67 Island
68 Killiney
69 Lucan
70 Malahide
71 Palmerstown House
72 Portmarnock
73 Portmarnock Links
74 Rush
75 Roganstown
76 Skerries
77 Slade Valley
78 South County
79 Stepaside
80 St Margarets
81 Swords
82 Turvey
DUBLIN CITY
83 Carrickmines
84 Castle
85 Clontarf
86 Deer Park
87 Dublin City
88 Edmondstown
89 Elmgreen
90 Elm Park
91 Foxrock
92 Grange
93 Hazel Grove
94 Howth
95 Luttrellstown
96 Milltown
97 Newlands
98 Rathfarnham
99 Royal Dublin
100 St Annes
101 Stackstown
102 Sutton
103 Westmanstown
KILDARE
104 Athy
105 Bodenstown
106 Carton House O'Meara
107 Carton House Montgomery
108 Castlewarden
109 Celbridge
110 Cill Dara
111 Craddockstown
112 The Curragh
113 Dunmurry Springs
114 Highfield
115 Kilkea Castle
116 Killeen
117 The 'K' Club
118 The 'K' Club
119 Knockanally
120 Millicent
121 Naas
122 Newbridge
123 Woodlands
KILKENNY
124 Callan
125 Castlecomer

126 Gowran Park
127 Kilkenny
128 Mountain View
129 Mount Juliet
130 Waterford
LAOIS
131 Abbeyleix
132 Heath
133 Mountrath
134 Portarlington
135 Rathdowney
136 The Heritage
LONGFORD
137 Longford
LOUTH
138 Ardee
139 Carnbeg
140 Co Louth
141 Dundalk
142 Greenore
143 Killin
144 Seapoint
MEATH
145 Ashbourne
146 Black Bush
147 Headfort (old)
148 Headfort (new)
149 Kilcock
150 Knightsbrook
151 Laytown & Bettystown
152 Meath County
153 Navan
154 Royal Tara
OFFALY
155 Birr
156 Castle Barna
157 Edenderry
158 Esker Hills
159 Tullamore
WESTMEATH
160 Delvin Castle
161 Glasson
162 Moate
163 Mullingar
164 Mount Temple
WEXFORD
165 Courtown
166 Enniscorthy
167 New Ross
168 Rosslare
169 St. Helen's Bay
170 Tuskar Rock
171 Wexford
WICKLOW
172 Arklow
173 Baltinglass
174 Blainroe
175 Bray
176 Charlesland
177 Coollattin
178 Delgany
179 Djouce Mountain
180 Druid's Glen
181 Druids Heath
182 European Club
183 Glenmalure
184 Glen of the Downs
185 Greystones
186 Kilcoole
187 Old Conna
188 Powerscourt
189 Powerscourt (west)
190 Rallsallagh
191 Roundwood
192 Tulfarris
193 Wicklow
194 Woodbrook
195 Woodenbridge

ULSTER

ANTRIM
221 Allen Park
222 Ballycastle
223 Ballyclare
224 Ballymena
225 Bushfoot

226 Cairndhu
227 Carrickfergus
228 Cushendall
229 Down Royal
230 Galgorm Castle
231 Gracehill
232 Greenacres
233 Greenisland
234 Hilton
235 Lambeg
236 Larne
237 Lisburn
238 Massereene
239 Royal Portrush
240 Royal Portrush Valley
241 Temple
242 Whitehead
ARMAGH
243 Co Armagh
244 Ashfield
245 Cloverhill
246 Edenmore
247 Loughall
248 Lurgan
249 Portadown
250 Silverwood
251 Tandragee
BELFAST CITY
252 Balmoral
253 Belvoir
254 City of Belfast
255 Cliftonville
256 Dunmurry
257 Fortwilliam
258 Knock
259 Mount Ober
260 Malone
261 Ormeau
262 Rockmount
263 Shandon
CAVAN
264 Belturbet
265 Blacklion
266 Cabra Castle
267 Co Cavan
268 Slieve Russell
269 Virginia
DONEGAL
270 Ballybofey & Stranorlar
271 Ballyliffen (Old)
272 Ballyliffen (Glashedy)
273 Buncrana
274 Bundoran
275 Cloughaneely
276 Cruit Island
277 Donegal
278 Dunfanaghy
279 Greencastle
280 Gweedore
281 Letterkenny
282 Narin & Portnoo
283 North West
284 Portsalon
285 Redcastle
286 Rosapenna Golf Links
287 Rosapenna Sandyhill Links
DOWN
288 Ardglass
289 Banbridge
290 Bangor
291 Blackwood
292 Bright Castle
293 Carnalea
294 Clandeboye (Ava)
295 Clandeboye (Dufferin)
296 Crossgar
297 Donaghadee
298 Downpatrick
299 Helen's Bay
300 Holywood
301 Kilkeel
302 Kirkistown
303 Mahee Island
304 Ringdufferin
305 Royal Belfast
306 Royal Co Down
307 Scrabo

308 Spa
309 Warrenpoint
FERMANAGH
310 Castlehume
311 Enniskillen
LONDONDERRY
312 Brown Trout
313 Castlerock
314 City of Derry
315 Foyle
316 Kilrea
317 Moyola
318 Portstewart
319 Roe Park
MONAGHAN
320 Castleblayney
321 Clones
322 Nuremore
323 Rossmore
TYRONE
324 Aughnacloy
325 Benburb
326 Dungannon
327 Fintona
328 Killymoon
329 Newtownstewart
330 Omagh
331 Strabane

MUNSTER

CLARE
352 Doonbeg
353 Dromoland Castle
354 East Clare
355 Ennis
356 Kilkee
357 Kilrush
358 Lahinch Old Course
359 Lahinch
360 Shannon
361 Spanish Point
362 Woodstock
CORK
363 Bandon
364 Bantry
365 Berehaven
366 Blarney
367 Charleville
368 Cobh
369 Cork
370 Doneraile
371 Douglas
372 Dunmore
373 East Cork
374 Fermoy
375 Fernhill
376 Fota Island
377 Frankfield
378 Glengarriff
379 Harbour Point
380 Kanturk
381 Kinsale
382 Lee Valley
383 Lisellan
384 Macroom
385 Mahon
386 Mallow
387 Mitchelstown
388 Monkstown
389 Muskerry
390 Old Head
391 Raffeen Creek
392 Skibbereen
393 Youghal
KERRY
394 Ardfert
395 Ballybunion
396 Ballybunion Cashen
397 Beaufort
398 Castlegregory
399 Castleisland
400 Ceann Sibeal
401 Dooks
402 Kenmare
403 Killarney Killeen
404 Killarney Mahony's

405 Killarney Lackbane
406 Killorglin
407 Listowel
408 Parknasilla
409 Ring of Kerry
410 Ross
411 Tralee
412 Waterville
LIMERICK
413 Abbeyfeale
414 Adare
415 Adare Manor
416 Castletroy
417 Limerick
418 Limerick County
419 Newcastle West
420 Rathbane
TIPPERARY
421 Ballykisteen
422 Cahir Park
423 Carrick-on-Suir
424 Clonmel
425 Nenagh
426 Roscrea
427 Slievenamon
428 Templemore
429 Thurles
430 County Tipperary
WATERFORD
431 Dungarvan
432 Dunmore East
433 Faithlegg
434 Gold Coast
435 Lismore
436 Tramore
437 Waterford Castle
438 West Waterford
439 Williamstown

CONNACHT

GALWAY
451 Athenry
452 Ballinasloe
453 Bearna
454 Connemara
455 Connemara Isles
456 Dunmore Demesne
457 Galway
458 Galway Bay
459 Glenlo Abbey
460 Gort
461 Loughrea
462 Mountbellew
463 Oughterard
464 Portumna
465 Tuam
LETRIM
466 Ballinamore
MAYO
467 Achill
468 Ashford Castle
469 Ballina
470 Ballinrobe
471 Ballyhaunis
472 Belmullet
473 Castlebar
474 Claremorris
475 Mulranny
476 Swinford
477 Westport
ROSCOMMON
478 Athlone
479 Ballaghaderreen
480 Boyle
481 Carrick-on-Shannon
482 Castlerea
483 Roscommon
484 Strokestown
SLIGO
485 Ballymote
486 Castle Dargon
487 Co Sligo
488 Enniscrone
489 Strandhill
490 Tubbercurry

Ryder Cup Match Results From 1927

Year	Venue		
2006	The K Club, Co. Kildare, Ireland	**Europe 18**1/2	U.S. 9 1/2
2004	Oakland Hills Country Club, Mich.	**Europe 18**1/2	U.S. 8 1/2
2002	The Belfry, Colfield, England	**Europe 15**1/2	U.S. 12 1/2
2001	Cancelled due to the tragic events of September 11th.		
1999	The Country Club, Brookline, MA	**U.S. 14**1/2	Europe 13 1/2
1997	Valderrama GC, Sotogrande Spain	**Europe 14**1/2	U.S. 13 1/2
1995	Oak Hill CC, Rochester, NY	**Europe 14**1/2	U.S. 13 1/2
1993	The Belfry, Sutton Coldfield, England	**U.S. 15**	Europe 13
1991	The Ocean Course, Kiawah Islnd, S.C.	**U.S. 14**1/2	Europe 13 1/2
1989	The Belfry, Sutton Coldfield, England	**Europe 14**	U.S. 14
1987	Muirfield Village GC, Dublin, Ohio	**Europe 15**	U.S. 13
1985	The Belfry, Sutton Coldfield, England	**Europe 16**1/2	U.S. 11 1/2
1983	PGA Ntnl GC, Plm Beach Gdns, Fla.	**U.S. 14**1/2	Europe 13 1/2
1981	Walton Health GC, Surrey, England	**U.S. 18**1/2	Europe 9 1/2
1979	The Greenbrier, W. Va.	**U.S. 17**	Europe 11
1977	Royal Lytham & St. Annes, England	**U.S. 12**1/2	GB & Ire 7 1/2
1975	Laurel Valley GC, Ligonier, Pa.	**U.S. 21**	GB & Ire 11
1973	Muirfield, Scotland	**U.S. 19**	GB & Ire 13
1971	Old Warson CC, St. Louis, Mo.	**U.S. 18**1/2	Britain 13 1/2
1969	Royal Birkdale GC, Southport, England	**U.S. 16**	Britain 16
1967	Champions GC, Houston, Texas	**U.S. 23**1/2	Britain 8 1/2
1965	Royal Birkdale GC, Southport, England	**U.S. 19**1/2	Britain 12 1/2
1963	East Lake CC, Atlanta, Ga.	**U.S. 23**	Britain 9
1961	Royal Lytham & St. Annes, England	**U.S. 14**1/2	Britain 9 1/2
1959	Eldorado CC, Palm Desert, Calif.	**U.S. 8**1/2	Britain 3 1/2
1957	Lindrick GC, Yorkshire, England	**Britain 7**1/2	U.S. 4 1/2
1955	Thunderbird CC, Plm Springs, Calif.	**U.S. 8**	Britain 4
1953	Wentworth GC, Wentworth, England	**U.S. 6**1/2	Britain 5 1/2
1951	Pinehurst CC, Pinehurst, N.C.	**U.S. 9**1/2	Britain 2 1/2
1949	Ganton GC, Scarborough, England	**U.S. 7**	Britain 5
1947	Portland GC, Portland, Ore.	**U.S. 11**	Britain 1
1939-1945	No Matches played due to World War II		
1937	Southport & Ainsdale GC, England	**U.S. 8**	Britain 4
1935	Ridgewood CC, Ridgewood, N.J.	**U.S. 9**	Britain 3
1933	Southport & Ainsdale GC, England	**Britain 6**1/2	U.S. 5 1/2
1931	Scioto CC, Columbus, Ohio	**U.S. 9**	Britain 3
1929	Moortown GC, Leeds, England	**Britain 7**	U.S. 5
1927	Worcester CC, Worcester, Mass.	**U.S. 9**1/2	Britain 2 1/2

GOLF
CENTRE

'Northern Ireland's Premier Golf Store'

163 York Street
Belfast, BT15 1AL
Tel: 028 9035 2000

also at

Riverside Centre,
Young Street, Lisburn.
Tel: 028 9260 5999

Ring Shops For opening hours.

Irish Open Results From 1927

Year	Venue	Winner	Score
2007	Adare Manor Hotel, Co. Limerick	**Padraig Harrington**	Score - 283
2006	Carton House, Co. Kildare	**Thomas Bjorn**	Score - 283
2005	Carton House, Co. Kildare	**Stephen Dodd**	Score - 279
2004	Baltry, Co. Louth	**Brett Rumford**	Score - 274
2003	Portmarnock, Co. Dublin	**Michael Campbell**	Score - 277
2002	Fota Island, Co. Cork	**Soren Hansen**	Score - 270
2001	Fota Island, Co. Cork	**Colin Montgomerie**	Score - 266
2000	Ballybunion, Co. Kerry	**Patrick Sjoland**	Score - 270
1999	Druids Glen, Co. Wicklow	**Sergio Garcia**	Score - 268
1998	Druids Glen, Co. Wicklow	**David Carter**	Score - 278
1997	Druids Glen, Co. Wicklow	**Colin Montgomerie**	Score - 269
1996	Druids Glen, Co. Wicklow	**Colin Montgomerie**	Score - 279
1995	Mount Juliet, Co. Kilkenny	**Sam Torrance**	Score - 277
1994	Mount Juliet, Co. Kilkenny	**Bernhard Langer**	Score - 275
1993	Mount Juliet, Co. Kilkenny	**Nick Faldo**	Score - 276
1992	Killarney, Co. Kerry	**Nick Faldo**	Score - 274
1991	Killarney, Co. Kerry	**Nick Faldo**	Score - 283
1990	Portmarnock, Co. Dublin	**Jose Maria Olazabal**	Score - 282
1989	Portmarnock, Co. Dublin	**Ian Woosnam**	Score - 278
1988	Portmarnock, Co. Dublin	**Ian Woosnam**	Score - 278
1987	Portmarnock, Co. Dublin	**Bernhard Langer**	Score - 269
1986	Portmarnock, Co. Dublin	**Seve Ballesteros**	Score - 285
1985	Royal Dublin, Co. Dublin	**Seve Ballesteros**	Score - 278
1984	Royal Dublin, Co. Dublin	**Bernhard Langer**	Score - 267
1983	Royal Dublin, Co. Dublin	**Seve Ballesteros**	Score - 271
1982	Portmarnock, Co. Dublin	**John O'Leary**	Score - 287
1981	Portmarnock, Co. Dublin	**Sam Torrance**	Score - 276
1980	Portmarnock, Co. Dublin	**Mark James**	Score - 284
1979	Portmarnock, Co. Dublin	**Mark James**	Score - 282
1978	Portmarnock, Co. Dublin	**Ken Brown**	Score - 281
1977	Portmarnock, Co. Dublin	**Hubert Green**	Score - 283
1976	Portmarnock, Co. Dublin	**Ben Crenshaw**	Score - 284
1975	Woodbrook, Co. Dublin	**Christy O'Connor Jr**	Score - 275
1974 - 1954 **Not Held**			
1953	Belvoir Park, Co. Antrim	**E.Brown**	Score - 272
1952 - 1951 **Not Held**			
1950	Royal Dublin, Co. Dublin	**H.Pickworth**	Score - 287
1949	Belvoir Park, Co. Antrim	**H.Bradshaw**	Score - 286
1948	Portmarnock, Co. Dublin	**D.Rees**	Score - 295
1947	Royal Portrush, Co. Antrim	**H.Bradshaw**	Score - 290
1946	Portmarnock, Co. Dublin	**F.Daly**	Score - 288
1945 - 1940 **Not Held**			
1939	Royal Co. Down, Co. Down	**A.Lees**	Score - 287
1938	Portmarnock, Co. Dublin	**A.Locke**	Score - 292
1937	Royal Portrush, Co. Antrim	**B.Gadd**	Score - 284
1936	Royal Dublin, Co. Dublin	**R.Whitcombe**	Score - 281
1935	Royal Co. Down, Co. Down	**E.Whitcombe**	Score - 292
1934	Portmarnock, Co. Dublin	**S.Easterbrook**	Score - 284
1933	Malone, Co. Antrim	**E.Kenyon**	Score - 286
1932	Cork, Co. Cork	**A.Padgham**	Score - 283
1931	Royal Dublin, Co. Dublin	**E.Kenyon**	Score - 291
1930	Royal Portrush, Co. Antrim	**C.Whitcombe**	Score - 289
1929	Portmarnock, Co. Dublin	**A.Mitchell**	Score - 309

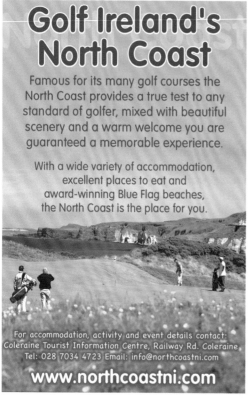
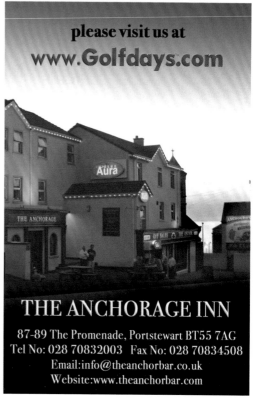

Walker Cup Match Results From 1922

Year	Venue	Result 1	Result 2
2007	Royal County Down, N. Ireland	To Be Played	To Be Played
2005	Chicago Golf Club, U.S.	United States, 12 1/2	Britain-Ireland, 11 1/2
2003	Ganton, England	Britain-Ireland, 12 1/2	United States, 11 1/2
2001	Ocean Forest, Sea Island G.A	Britain-Ireland, 15	United States, 9
1999	Nairn, Scotland	Britain-Ireland, 15	United States, 9
1997	Quaker Ridge, N.Y.	United States, 18	Britain-Ireland, 6
1995	Royal Portcawl, Wales	Britain-Ireland, 14	United States, 10
1993	Interlachen, Minnesota	United States, 19	Britain-Ireland, 5
1991	Portmarnock, Ireland	United States, 14	Britain-Ireland, 10
1989	Peachtree, N.J.	Britain-Ireland, 12 1/2	United States, 11 1/2
1987	Sunningdale, England	United States, 16 1/2	Britain-Ireland, 7 1/2
1985	Pine Valley, N.J.	United States, 13	Britain-Ireland, 11
1983	Hoylake, England	United States, 13 1/2	Britain-Ireland, 10 1/2
1981	Cypress Point, U.S	United States, 15	Britain-Ireland, 9
1979	Muirfield, Scotland	United States, 15 1/2	Britain-Ireland, 8 1/2
1977	Shinnecock Hills, N.Y.	United States, 16	Britain-Ireland, 8
1975	St Andrews, Scotland	United States, 15 1/2	Britain-Ireland, 8 1/2
1973	Brookline, Massachusetts	United States, 14	Britain-Ireland, 10
1971	St Andrews, Scotland	Britain-Ireland, 13	United States, 11
1969	Milwalkee, Wisconsin	United States, 13	Britain-Ireland, 11
1967	Sandwich, England	United States, 15	Britain-Ireland, 9
1965	Baltimore, U.S.	Draw, 12-12	
1963	Turnberry, Scotland	United States, 14	Britain-Ireland, 10
1961	Seattle, Washington	United States, 11	Britain-Ireland, 1
1959	Muirfield, Scotland	United States, 9	Britain-Ireland, 3
1957	Minikahda, U.S.	United States, 8 1/2	Britain-Ireland, 3 1/2
1955	St Andrews, Scotland	United States, 10	Britain-Ireland, 2
1953	Kittansett, Massachusetts	United States, 9	Britain-Ireland, 3
1951	Royal Birkdale, England	United States, 7 1/2	Britain-Ireland, 4 1/2
1949	Winged Foot, N.Y.	United States, 10	Britain-Ireland, 2
1947	St Andrews, Scotland	United States, 8	Britain-Ireland, 4
1940-1946	NOT HELD		
1938	St Andrews, Scotland	Britain-Ireland, 7 1/2	United States, 4 1/2
1936	Pine Valley N.J.	United States, 10 1/2	Britain-Ireland, 1 1/2
1934	St Andrews, Scotland	United States, 9 1/2	Britain-Ireland, 2 1/2
1932	Brookline, Massachusetts	United States, 9 1/2	Britain-Ireland, 2 1/2
1930	Sandwich, England	United States, 10	Britain-Ireland, 2
1928	Chicago, U.S.	United States, 11	Britain-Ireland, 1
1926	St Andrews, Scotland	United States, 6 1/2	Britain-Ireland, 5 1/2
1924	Garden City, N.Y.	United States, 9	Britain-Ireland, 3
1923	St Andrews, Scotland	United States, 6 1/2	Britain-Ireland, 5 1/2
1922	Long Island, N.Y.	United States, 8	Britain-Ireland, 4

tri®

the future of golf bag design

carry it or cart it ...

... wherever, whenever

www.tri-bag.com

telephone:
01525 704420

email:
enquiries@tri-bag.com

► Magnificent views over the North Atlantic Ocean form the par 4, 17th at Co. Sligo Golf Club, County Sligo.

► Trees are a real feature on Beaverstown Golf Course, County Dublin, especially on the 435 metre, par 5 fifth.

Golf days™

INTERACTIVE COMPUTER GENERATED 3D COURSE MAPS

MEASURE FROM TEE TO HOLE OR ZOOM IN

OVER 380 COURSES TO CHOOSE FROM – UP CLOSE AND PERSONAL!

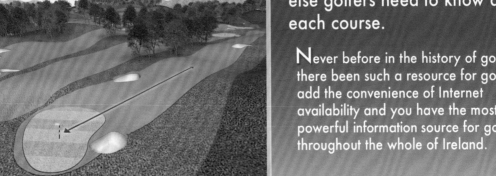

The European Club, County Wicklow.

Leinster

A Provincial Introduction by Jack Magowan

Jack's Hole is where a foxy old rum-runner called Jack White met a sticky end for trying to outwit the law once too often. He was hanged on the beach at Brittas Bay, near Wicklow, only a good four-iron shot from where Pat Ruddy realised his dream of building one of Ireland's great links courses, the European Club.

That was back in the late 1980's. Pat was 43 at the time, restless and overweight, and first to bid at auction for nearly 200 acres of sandhill and scrub that nobody else wanted.

"Build a golf course on this? You must be crazy", friends told him. "Mission impossible..... it's moon-crater country."

Happily, Ruddy wasn't listening. But new golf courses cost millions. Where would the big guy get that kind of money ?

▲
Water is a feature on many holes at The K Club (Palmer Course), Co. Kildare, and here on the 170 yard par 3, 3rd a good club selection is required to seek out the pin on the left hand side of the green.

"I'll make haste slowly; design and dig myself," was part of his master-plan.

"I cashed in my insurance policy, sold the car, re-mortaged the family home, and learned to drive a JCB. The job took five-years to complete, one hole at a time, even on the coldest of winter days, but look at the result. Tiger Woods has been here, and will be back."

Trust Ruddy to be different. Not content with a king-sized gem stretching over 7,000 yards from the tips, Pat the visionary has added two devious par-3 holes for good measure, making 20 holes in all for those who want to linger a bit and enjoy an almost unbroken string of wonderful sea views.

"No hole is less than very good," writes a Golf Odyssey

Photograph courtesy of Roganstown Golf Club.

critic. "Six or seven can fairly be labelled great, and three of these – one short, one long, and the par-four 7th – are truly among the world's greatest holes."

It was in millennium year 2000 that a posse of wealthy Dubliners offered Ruddy a cool £20/€29 million for the European Club. Naturally, he turned it down!

Ireland can now boast of having over 400 of the world's 32,000 golf courses, close to seventy of them within an hour's drive of Dublin's city centre, so visitors are spoiled for choice.

Portmarnock will always be the flagship of Leinster golf. Once a refuge for the elite, few outside the Royal and Ancient game had ever heard of the place until a couple of high-fliers called Alcock and Brown landed their Vickers-Vimy on the nearby strand, both fuel tanks empty, after taking off from Newfoundland 16 hours before.

It was the summer of 1919, and the quickest way to get to the Portmarnock links was across the estuary from

▲
Water comes into play on all but 6 holes creating a challenge for every standard of golfer at Roganstown Golf Club, Swords, County Dublin.

▲
Superb birds eye view of Esker
Hills course near Tullamore in
County Offaly. It plays over a
series of valleys and plateaux
with four lakes coming into play.
The 10th approach is particularly
well guarded.

Baldoyle in a row boat or horse and trap, depending
on the tide.

In those days, no stranger, they say, ever left the club. He
may have arrived as a stranger, but by the time a ship's bell
rang to signal the departure of the last boat back to the
mainland, he would have been everybody's friend.

All the big names in golf have played Portmarnock. From
Bobby Locke as winner of the Irish Open at the age of 21,
to Arnold Palmer and Sam Snead as a triumphant Canada

▲

The 340 yard par four 7th at Blainroe Golf Club in County Wicklow. This is a very pleasant parkland course overlooking the Irish Sea.

Cup duo, to Ballesteros, Langer, Olazabal, Crenshaw, Faldo, Daly and O'Connor.

Like so many great links, this Dublin Bay pearl without wind can be like Samson shorn of his hair, but how often do we ever get it bereft of wind? Even when Sandy Lyle broke a 30 year old record there with a sun-kissed 64 in an Irish Open, the mighty Scot was in cashmere and cords. And Palmer, too, when he hit that career-best 3-iron out over the beach and back to four feet on the short 15th. Arnie missed the putt, but bore the hole no grudge !

There are many permutations for a rewarding, if not inexpensive, tour of Leinster's finest courses, but for those in the know, it would begin at The Island, for so long Malahide's best kept secret, and span Royal Dublin and Portmarnock Links as well as St. Margaret's, the K-Club and both courses, too, at Carton House.

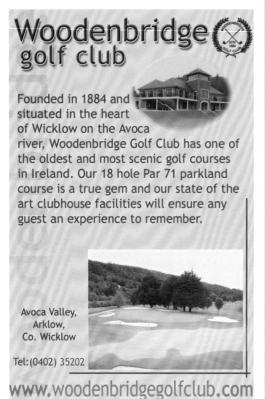

▲

Appealing green on the par four 7th at Druid's Heath in County Wicklow. Superb variety on this championship course includes lakes, pot bunkers, streams and natural rock quarries.

The K-Club is where green fees are probably the highest in Europe, and you have to own an island or two in the Caribbean to be a member there, but if the 2006 Ryder Cup course is the most beguiling American course outside the United States, as somebody once said, the new course is every bit as seductive.

Water adds greatly to the charm and challenge of both courses, and there's enough at the K-Club to refloat the Titanic.

It's behind five miles of stone walls at Maynooth that the new home of the oldest national body in the game is located, the Golfing Union of Ireland, plus two magnificent courses designed by, and named after, players of Ryder Cup fame, Montgomerie and O'Meara.

Conor Mallaghan was only eight years old when his dad, Lee, a major player in the sand and gravel business in Co. Tyrone, bought the 1,000-acre Carton House estate.

Built in the 1740's and about the size of the Mansion House in Dublin or half the size of Belfast City Hall, the House is where the first Duke of Leinster fathered 23 children, one of whom led the '98 rebellion.

Montgomerie's course is the longer of the two, and has a

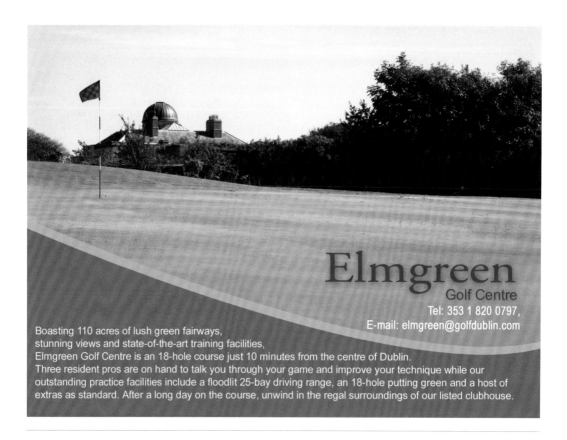

Elmgreen
Golf Centre

Tel: 353 1 820 0797,
E-mail: elmgreen@golfdublin.com

Boasting 110 acres of lush green fairways,
stunning views and state-of-the-art training facilities,
Elmgreen Golf Centre is an 18-hole course just 10 minutes from the centre of Dublin.
Three resident pros are on hand to talk you through your game and improve your technique while our
outstanding practice facilities include a floodlit 25-bay driving range, an 18-hole putting green and a host of
extras as standard. After a long day on the course, unwind in the regal surroundings of our listed clubhouse.

CORBALLIS GOLF LINKS

Excellent conditions and a demanding course make Corballis Golf Links one of Ireland's most popular pay and
play facilities. It is also the only public links course in the country but, because it's open throughout the year, we
can ensure that the timesheet is always accessible so that golfers can enjoy their game in comfort.

Corballis Golf Links, Tel: 353 1 843 6583, E-mail: corballislinks@golfdublin.com

distinct links' feel. Darren Clarke once came within a short putt of holing the K-Club's not-so-old course in 59 shots, but the odds would be heavily against him ever doing that score on Monty's masterpiece.

Mount Juliet is the brainchild of Jack Nicklaus, and, like Druids Glen at Newtownmountkennedy, has been host to the Irish Open.

Magnificent – that's the only word for Druids Glen, where the key is not just to play all four short holes in par, but without getting that Titleist wet.

The 17th to an island green is a spectacular hole, a carbon copy of No.17 on Florida's famous Tournament Players' course, only longer.

Statistics show that 70 per cent of people in the Republic have never ventured North, but golfers are not like that. Out of every ten in Ulster, seven go South on a regular basis to sample the charms of courses like County Louth, Woodenbridge, Rosslare, Faithlegg and Carlow.

Drink it in deeply with big, hungry gulps. Drink it all in, the brisk sea air, moody skies, and greenness, wrote Michael Konik in a delightful piece in *SKY* magazine. Then, as a punch-line, he adds:

Tell me, Lord, I need to know,
Why days like these must end;
Haste me back to Ireland,
And send along a friend.

▲
Picturesque views from
Corballis Golf Links,
County Dublin.

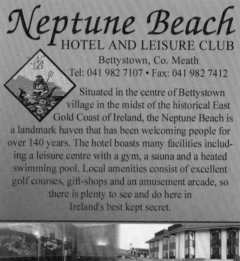

Padraig Harrington
by Jack Magowan

Padraig Harrington must surely be ranked among Irish golf's all-time greats, but this policeman's son has never been seduced by fame. His hat size remains constant. Ego and Padraig are not compatible.

Could we have his brothers to thank for that, all four of them?

"Their goal in life is to keep me grounded," grins Padraig. "The first text message I got after pipping Eduardo Romero in a play-off for the Dunhill read: 'Congrats on managing to wear the pensioner down.' They were taking the mickey about needing extra holes to beat a guy who was almost 50. To them, I'm just another Joe!"

Padraig's popularity and charm stem from his friendly, easy-going manner and rolling gait. He's never crusty or cantankerous, and leaves temper tantrums to somebody else.

It was a cruel body blow to be disqualified from the Benson and Hedges classic when five shots clear of the field going into final round, yet the mature way he

> "Padraig's popularity and charm stem from his friendly, easy-going manner and rolling gait."

▲
Padraig Harrington plays from the bunker on to the 6th green during round two of the American Express World Golf Championship at Mount Juliet Golf Club, Thomastown, Co. Kilkenny.

Ireland's Ryder Cup Region

This region, which encompasses counties Kildare, Laois, Longford, Louth, Meath, North Offaly, Westmeath and Wicklow, is a microcosm of all the delights you can find in Ireland. This sporting countryside has everything to offer the enthusiast - walking, fishing, hunting, mountain climbing, cycling, touring, but most of all, the East and Midlands has golf.

More European Tour Golf events have been played at East and Midlands Region golf clubs than in any other part of Ireland. The K Club has been the annual venue for the European Open since 1995, and the Irish Open has been held at Druids Glen in 1996-1999, County Louth Golf Club in 2004, and Carton in 2005. And of course the pinnacle of all Golfing competitions – The Ryder Cup was an outstanding success in this golfing region in 2006.

Everywhere you travel in the East & Midlands region of Ireland you will find golf courses of the highest quality yet affordable prices. With almost 100 golf courses in the East & Midlands region of Ireland it's difficult to highlight them all.

To obtain your FREE 'Ireland's Ryder Cup Region' golf guide log on to

www.eastcoastmidlands.ie

or contact:
Fáilte Ireland East & Midlands Region
Dublin Road, Mullingar
Co. Westmeath
Ireland

Tel: +353 (0) 44 93 48650
Fax: +353 (0) 44 93 40413

email: eastandmidlandsinfo@failteireland.ie
web: www.eastcoastmidlands.ie   www.ireland.ie/golf

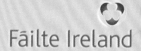

Kildare - Laois - Longford - Louth - Meath - Offaly - Westmeath - Wicklow

accepted the ruling was an example to all. It probably won him more friends around the world than success in the tournament might have done.

"That's him alright," says older brother Tadhg, a Dublin bookmaker. "He has always reacted well to adversity. He never moans about bad luck, or the run of the ball."

It was as a three-time Walker Cup player that Harrington first made his mark before graduating with a degree in accountancy, then turning professional at the age of 24.

"He has always reacted well to adversity. He never moans about bad luck, or the run of the ball."

Since then, he has won more than a dozen mainstream tournaments, two of them in America and in the same year. His storybook, last-gasp victory in the 2006 European Order of Merit was another feather in the cap of a player whose career earnings already top £15 million.

His dream home in Dublin has everything from a games' room with a bar and Guinness on tap (yet he doesn't drink) to jukebox, snooker table, cinema screen and space invaders machine.

It was after winning over £300,000 in his rookie year of '96 that Padraig – pronounced 'Pour-rig' – married Caroline, herself a delightful person and illuminating influence in her husband's neon-lit career. "I have to be," she teases. "If it were left to Padraig to make dinner reservations, we'd never eat." To which this prince among sporting giants responds: "I try not to bring a bad score home from the office, but Caroline is a good psychologist. She's there for me when things go wrong, and when I need a kick up the backside."

▲

Ireland's Darren Clarke, left, Paul McGinley, centre, and Padraig Harrington celebrate with the Ryder Cup trophy after victory over America. The 36th Cup Match was hosted by the K Club.

Silloge Park
Public Golf Course
Ballymun, Co Dublin

A challenging 5900 metres, par 71, 18 hole parkland course, which is situated 6 miles north of the centre of Dublin City, beside the M50 Motorway at the Ballymun junction and adjacent to Dublin Airport.

Green Fees: €18 to €25,
Mid Week early bird €12
Twilight €16
Off Peak and Concession
Rates available
Booking/Pay as you Play:
(01) 842 9956

Dublin City
Baile Átha Cliath

Dublin City Council
Parks and Landscape Services

Proudstown Road,
Navan, Co. Meath.
Tel: 046 9072888
Fax: 046 9076722
info@navangolfclub.ie
www.navangolfclub.ie

NAVAN GOLF CLUB
Your golfday starts here

Located at Navan Racecourse, Navan Golf Club is a golfing venue that provides you with an enjoyable yet challenging golfing experience. Friendly, helpful staff who will give you a warm welcome and effecient service, while our talented chefs will satisfy your appetite with delicious, home cooked meals. Just 30 miles north of Dublin, easily accessible from the North, it's central location in Meath's Royal County, makes it an ideal choice to visit.

Christy O'Connor Senior

by Jack Magowan

Christy O'Connor Senior putts on the 1st green during the AIB Irish Golf Masters Open at Mount Juliet, Kilkenny.

It will always be part of Irish folklore – Christy O'Connor's electrifying finish of eagle, birdie, eagle at Royal Dublin. With three holes to play in this Carroll's International, O'Connor trailed Ryder Cup teammate Eric Brown's target of 14-under-par by one stroke. Brown has just birdied the 16th and 18th holes, so Christy faced an uphill task. Uphill, yes, but not impossible; not to one of the greatest golfers of his day.

First O'Connor rifled a big drive 20 feet past the flag on the short par-4 16th and holed a slippery downhiller for a 'two'. Then, a bold 12-footer for birdie on seventeen hoisted 'Himself' into the lead before he

Stepaside
Public Golf Course

This beautifully mature course is situated approximately 25 minutes from Dublin's City Centre, just outside the small village of Stepaside.

With lush greens, excellent layout and easy accessibility from the Stillorgan Dual Carriageway, Stepaside Golf Course is the ideal venue for a round of golf.

Stepaside, Co. Dublin
stepaside@golfdublin.com
Tel +353 1 295 2859 • Fax +353 1 295 2639

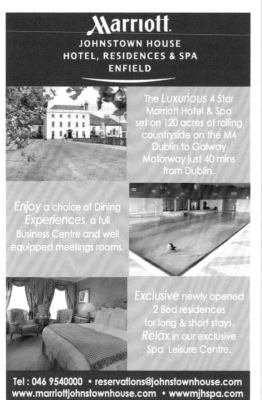

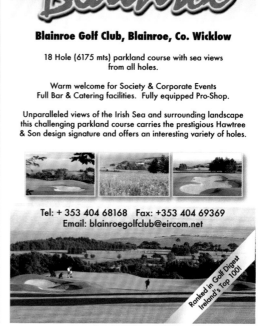

scorned safety with a superb long iron over the dreaded garden at the 18th that almost ripped out the flag.

Two putts from three yards were all Christie needed for his first (and only) major victory on his home course, but to the delight of a 5,000 gallery, he single-putted here, too, for a final round 66 that could easily have been 63. Had he holed from 6 feet on both the 14th and 15th greens, he would have been home in a never-to-be-repeated 28 shots, or eight-under-par!

Happily, Roy Lindsay's brilliant oil-painting of Christy playing the last hole will remain a potent reminder of the most spectacular climax to a round in the history of Irish golf.

Christy would practice until his hands bled and he had all the shots. His long-iron game could be majestic and even at 80-plus, he still drives it long and straight.

It was after watching O'Connor take his 10th, and final, Ryder Cup appearance that the late Peter Dobereiner wrote, 'without a major championship under his belt, O'Connor is a difficult man to place in the pecking order of golfing greats, yet you only have to see that rhythmic, self-taught swing to realise that this is no first-class second-rater....'

Chris had already chalked up SEVEN top-six finishes in the 'Open' and banked the biggest ever cheque of the day in world golf (£25,000) after winning the John Player classic in Nottingham. So why did he never win the Open? 'It's not that he isn't good enough,' Fred Daly used to say, 'he probably wants it too much and tries too hard. He is singed by the heat of his own desire.' Christy would practice until his hands bled and he had all the shots. His long-iron game could be majestic and even at 80-plus, he still drives it long and straight. 'I've always been in awe of O'Connor's genius,' confesses Norman Drew, a former World Cup partner. 'As a rough-weather and wind player, there have been none better and it doesn't matter how badly the ball is lying, Chris will hit it clean as a whistle. His swing is a gift from God!'

In company with Daly and the loveable Harry Bradshaw, O'Connor was first to put golf on the front page here, and there, we know, it will remain.

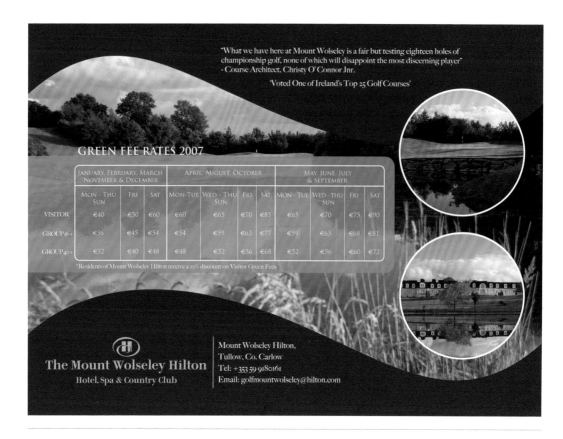

Mary McKenna

by Jack Magowan

It's not what Mary McKenna owes golf; it's what golf owes Mary McKenna, now in her fourth decade of playing the game she says she took up late in life. She was 14.

Joe Carr was always a McKenna fan. "The girl has done for women's golf what Christy O'Connor did for the men's game." Carr once commented. "She set standards with a pitching wedge that inspired all who saw her play."

Miss McKenna has more Curtis Cup blazers in her Malahide wardrobe than party dresses – nine in all, the last one from the 1986 match at Prairie Dunes, Kansas, which Britain won in a canter.

Mary had still to be crowned Irish champion for the eighth time, but that would come at the age of 40, nearly a decade after failing by only a couple of short putts to make the final of the U.S. Amateur.

Her job with the Bank of Ireland was a passport to golfing freedom, and she couldn't have represented her employers with more flair or panache.

As Lewine Mair wrote in the *Daily Telegraph:* "It's not so much her power and skill as the spirit in which she plays the game that makes Mary special in the eyes of the gallery."

"The girl has done for women's golf what Christy O'Connor did for the men's game"

It was after winning the British Stroke-play championship, and losing only one match out of sixteen at international level that Miss McKenna was voted DAKS' Women Golfer of the Year in '79, a time for celebration at her old school, Dublin's Loreto College.

Four years as boss of the bank's sports department had cost her valuable time on the practice range, but who would have guessed it. In her first brief spell of retirement, she won the British Seniors' championship, plus two other big events, a unique treble her club, Donabate, happily didn't over look.

"They honoured me with a dinner and presentation," she says with pride. "The buzz was great. It was just like old times..."

▲
Mary McKenna is one of Ireland's top female golfers.

Beaverstown
Golf Club
Donabate, Co. Dublin

Beaverstown Golf Club in North County Dublin,

what golf is all about.

Enjoy a *true test of golf* in friendly Surrounds.

Top Class Golf & dining within 15 mins of Dublin Airport.

For Reservations or enquiries please contact
our reservations desk on +353 1 8436439 or email us at info@beaverstown.com

www.beaverstown.ie

▶
The Island Golf Club
lives up to its name with
the sea on three sides.
One of Malahide's best
kept secrets, this links
course has many
spectacular holes.

▶
Portmarnock is the
flagship of Leinster golf
and is one of the
premium links courses in
the country. All the big
names in world golf have
played Portmarnock and
all have sang its praise.

Photograph courtesy of Druids Glen Golf Resort.

Druids Glen

by Jack Magowan

..the Glen is a pearl in an oyster setting,

L ord Ponsonby Tottenham Loftus was an extravagant party-goer, but stood for no hanky panky. When he caught his butler re-bottling and selling the wine in which he bathed regularly for a skin disorder, he sacked the rascal and told him to leave town.

Otherwise, his lordship, then Bishop of Clogher, was a

generous employer who paid his farmhands one shilling and tuppence (about 6p) a day, with strict orders that they were not to use any of the main entrances, front or rear, of the 30 room mansion in which he entertained lavishly.

It might offend "guests of the right social standing" to see staff leave by the front door, so they had to use a tunnel from the house to their quarters.

The tunnel at stately old Woodstock House is still there, but not much else to remind you of the 400 acre richly - wooded estate for which Bishop Loftus paid the princely sum of £12,000 back in the 1820's. Multiply this a thousand times and it still wouldn't buy a corner of what is now one of the finest golfing oasis in Europe – Druids Glen in Co.Wicklow, and its sister course, Druids Heath.

Tough – yes. Exciting – most definitely. Here is where you don't see a target green as much as discover it as if on a treasure hunt!

Host to four Irish Opens, the last of them won by a gifted 19 year old called Sergio Garcia, the Glen is a pearl in an oyster setting, arguably the most magical of Ireland's great inland courses.

You have had the main course; now for the dessert, a links' style heathland lay-out carved from the same rolling landscape and full of the same saber-toothed surprises.

Nobody learns to play good golf on an easy course any more than a jump-jockey acquires his skills on a rocking horse, and neither of these two parkland gems is for the fainthearted.

Tough – yes. Exciting – most definitely. Here is where you don't see a target green as much as discover it as if on a treasure hunt!

Mr Nice Guy, Denis Kane, is director of the Druids Glen resort, where the award winning Marriott Hotel matches the five star rating of both great courses. Go there via Newtownmountkennedy, just off the N11 about 30 miles south of Dublin.

▲
The 12th green looking back to the tee above the distinctive Celtic Cross. The tee shot has to avoid the water both behind the bushes to the right and in front of the green.

Numbers above refer to the page number of each course with approximate geographical location shown on the map beside.

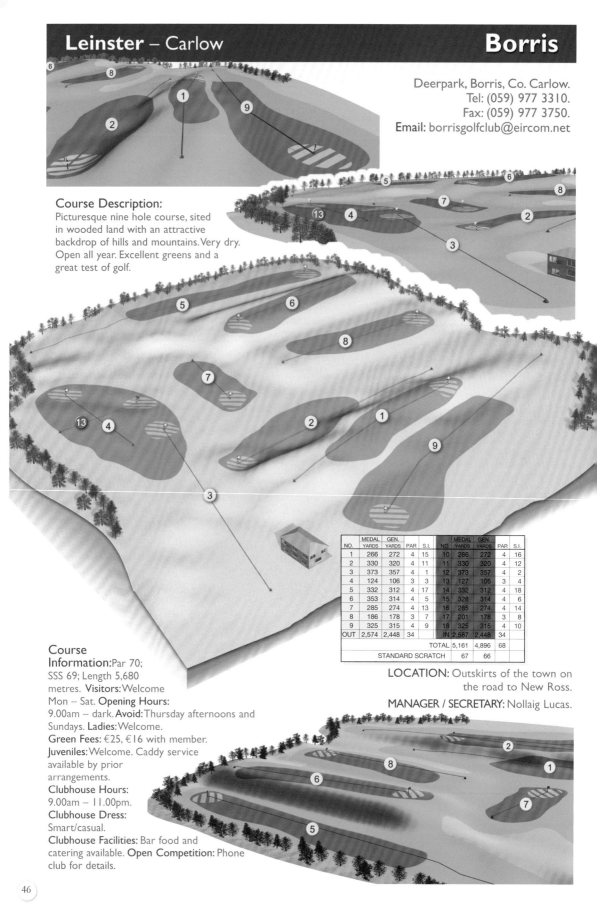

Deerpark, Borris, Co. Carlow.
Tel: (059) 977 3310.
Fax: (059) 977 3750.
Email: borrisgolfclub@eircom.net

Course Description:

Picturesque nine hole course, sited in wooded land with an attractive backdrop of hills and mountains. Very dry. Open all year. Excellent greens and a great test of golf.

NO.	MEDAL YARDS	GEN. YARDS	PAR	S.I.	NO.	MEDAL YARDS	GEN. YARDS	PAR	S.I.
1	266	272	4	15	10	266	272	4	16
2	330	320	4	11	11	330	320	4	12
3	373	357	4	1	12	373	357	4	2
4	124	106	3	3	13	127	106	3	4
5	332	312	4	17	14	332	312	4	18
6	353	314	4	5	15	328	314	4	6
7	285	274	4	13	16	285	274	4	14
8	186	178	3	7	17	201	178	3	8
9	325	315	4	9	18	325	315	4	10
OUT	2,574	2,448	34		IN	2,587	2,448	34	
					TOTAL	5,161	4,896	68	
					STANDARD SCRATCH		67	66	

Course Information:

Par 70; SSS 69; Length 5,680 metres. **Visitors:** Welcome Mon – Sat. **Opening Hours:** 9.00am – dark. **Avoid:** Thursday afternoons and Sundays. **Ladies:** Welcome. **Green Fees:** €25, €16 with member. **Juveniles:** Welcome. Caddy service available by prior arrangements. **Clubhouse Hours:** 9.00am – 11.00pm. **Clubhouse Dress:** Smart/casual. **Clubhouse Facilities:** Bar food and catering available. **Open Competition:** Phone club for details.

LOCATION: Outskirts of the town on the road to New Ross.

MANAGER / SECRETARY: Nollaig Lucas.

Deerpark, Dublin Road, Co. Carlow. Tel: (059) 913 1695 Fax: (059) 914 0065
E-mail: carlowgolfclub@eircom.net **Web:** www.carlowgolfclub.com

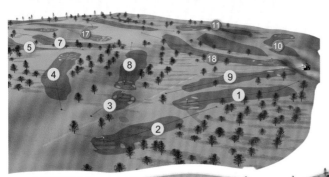

NO.	MEDAL YARDS	GEN. YARDS	PAR	S.I.	NO.	MEDAL YARDS	GEN. YARDS	PAR	S.I.
1	401	393	4	4	10	279	276	4	11
2	292	269	4	14	11	393	376	4	3
3	131	122	3	17	12	344	335	4	7
4	354	342	4	9	13	152	147	3	16
5	503	460	5	15	14	416	411	4	5
6	165	162	3	12	15	354	340	4	10
7	398	389	4	1	16	401	377	4	2
8	397	390	4	6	17	139	132	3	18
9	373	334	4	8	18	482	467	5	13
OUT	3,014	2,861	35		IN	2,960	2,861	35	
					TOTAL	5,974	5,722	70	
					STANDARD SCRATCH	70	70		

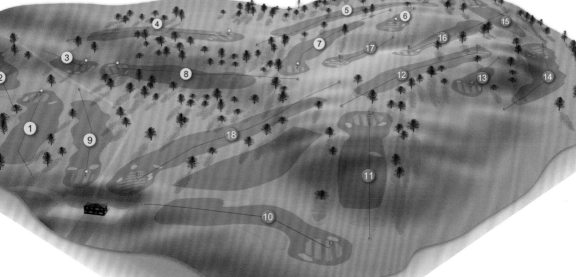

LOCATION:
Two miles north of
Carlow Town on main
Dublin Road (N9).

GENERAL MANAGER:
Donard MacSweeney

PROFESSIONAL:
Andrew Gilbert.
Tel: (059) 914 1745.

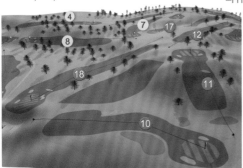

Course Information:
Par 70; SSS 71; Length 5,974 metres.
Visitors: Welcome. **Opening Hours:** Sunrise – Sunset. **Avoid:**
Tuesday, Saturday and Sunday. **Ladies:** Welcome. **Green Fees:** Mon
–Fri €50, Groups (20+) €45. Weekends €60, Groups (20+) €50.
Juveniles: Restricted. Lessons available by prior
arrangements. Caddy service available by prior
arrangement. Handicap certificate required. **Clubhouse
Hours:** 8.00am – 11.30pm. Full Clubhouse Facilities.
Clubhouse Dress: Casual. **Clubhouse Facilities:** Breakfast
(summer), lunches, evening meals, snacks all day. Menu
available on request. **Open Competitions:** Open Week: 2nd
-9th June; Midland Scratch Cup: 16th & 17th June.

Course Description: Considered one of the best inland
courses with fair but tight fairways and good greens. Its fine
springy turf earns the reputation of "inland links". The
course has extensive mature woods and many scenic views.

Mount Wolseley

Tullow, Co. Carlow.
Tel: (059) 9180161. Fax: (059) 9152123.
golfmountwolseley@hilton.com

Course Description:
A Christy O'Connor Jnr Designed Championship Golf Course. The Mature parkland course, with picturesque lakes filled with wildlife and fish. Water comes into play on eleven of the 18 holes. Heralded as one of the top twenty-five courses in Ireland by 'Golfing Ireland'

NO.	BLUE YARDS	WHITE YARDS	PAR	S.I.	NO.	BLUE YARDS	WHITE YARDS	PAR	S.I.
1	411	383	4	7	10	553	525	5	14
2	447	417	4	3	11	207	191	3	6
3	447	435	4	1	12	519	504	5	16
4	345	338	4	9	13	427	409	4	8
5	520	499	5	15	14	339	319	4	18
6	210	187	3	13	15	466	438	4	2
7	542	521	5	11	16	226	204	3	12
8	440	418	4	5	17	457	397	4	10
9	203	184	3	17	18	413	358	4	4
OUT	3,565	3,382	36		IN	3,633	3,381	36	
					TOTAL	7,172	6,763	72	
	STANDARD SCRATCH					74	73		

LOCATION: 1/2 mile from Tullow. 10 miles from Carlow town. One hour from Dublin

Course
Information: Par 72; SSS 74; Length 7,172 yards. **Avoid:** Each day before 10.30am (members only). **Green Fees:** €60 -€90 **Clubhouse Facilities:** Breakfast from 10am. Bar Menu from 11.30am. Hotel Restuarant & Lounge open from 7am **Open Competitions:** Mens open day 23rd May , 5th Sept & 8th Oct. Ladies 19th Sept. Open 15th August. Junior Scratch Cup 4th June. Intermediate Scratch Cup 24th June.
SECRETARY / MANAGER: Daniel Kearney.

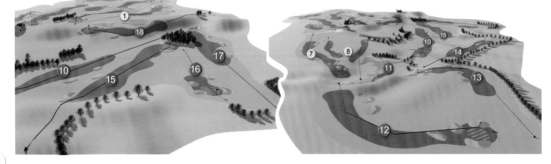

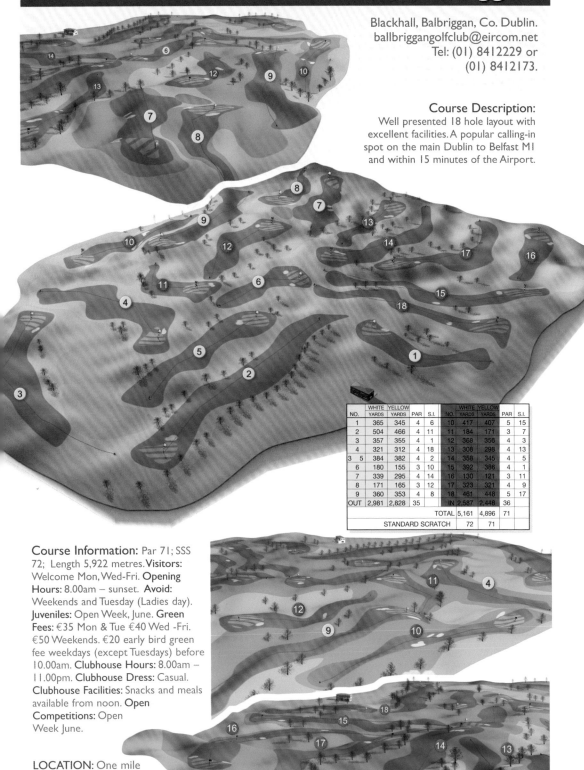

Blackhall, Balbriggan, Co. Dublin.
ballbriggangolfclub@eircom.net
Tel: (01) 8412229 or
(01) 8412173.

Course Description:
Well presented 18 hole layout with excellent facilities. A popular calling-in spot on the main Dublin to Belfast M1 and within 15 minutes of the Airport.

NO.	WHITE YARDS	YELLOW YARDS	PAR	S.I.	NO.	WHITE YARDS	YELLOW YARDS	PAR	S.I.
1	365	345	4	6	10	417	407	5	15
2	504	466	4	11	11	184	171	3	7
3	357	355	4	1	12	368	356	4	3
4	321	312	4	18	13	308	298	4	13
5	384	382	4	2	14	358	345	4	5
6	180	155	3	10	15	392	386	4	1
7	339	295	4	14	16	130	121	3	11
8	171	165	3	12	17	323	321	4	9
9	360	353	4	8	18	461	448	5	17
OUT	2,981	2,828	35		IN	2,587	2,448	36	
					TOTAL	5,161	4,896	71	
					STANDARD SCRATCH	72	71		

Course Information: Par 71; SSS 72; Length 5,922 metres. **Visitors:** Welcome Mon, Wed-Fri. **Opening Hours:** 8.00am – sunset. **Avoid:** Weekends and Tuesday (Ladies day). **Juveniles:** Open Week, June. **Green Fees:** €35 Mon & Tue €40 Wed -Fri. €50 Weekends. €20 early bird green fee weekdays (except Tuesdays) before 10.00am. **Clubhouse Hours:** 8.00am – 11.00pm. **Clubhouse Dress:** Casual. **Clubhouse Facilities:** Snacks and meals available from noon. **Open Competitions:** Open Week June.

LOCATION: One mile south of Balbriggan on Dublin / Belfast road.

SECRETARY: Jeanette McKenna

Balcarrick Golf Club, Corballis, Donabate, Co. Dublin.
Tel: (01) 8436957

COURSE DESIGNER: Barry Langan.

OFFICE ADMINISTRATOR: Patricia Fennelly.
Tel: (01) 843 6957 / 843 6228

Course Description:
A relatively new club, founded in 1992. In 1995 it was converted to a fine 18 hole course featuring deceptive holes and water hazards creating quite a challenge. In 1997 a clubhouse was built situated on course.

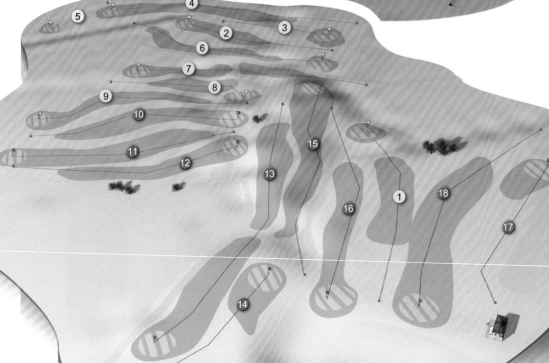

NO.	WHITE METRES	BLUE METRES	PAR	S.I.	NO.	WHITE METRES	BLUE METRES	PAR	S.I.
1	363	343	4	7	10	372	349	4	12
2	335	325	4	17	11	357	347	4	10
3	177	167	3	11	12	374	356	4	8
4	485	476	5	9	13	501	473	5	4
5	137	130	3	15	14	153	135	3	16
6	479	465	5	5	15	453	444	5	14
7	403	387	4	1	16	397	347	4	6
8	222	197	3	3	17	233	224	4	18
9	372	357	3	13	18	378	361	4	2
OUT	2,973	2,847	35		IN	3,218	3,036	37	
					TOTAL	6,191	5,883	72	
					STANDARD SCRATCH	72	72		

Course Information:
Par 72; SSS 72; Length 5,383 metres. **Visitors:** Welcome. **Opening Hours:** Sunrise – sunset. **Ladies:** Welcome. **Green Fees:** Weekdays €32; weekends €40. **Juveniles:** Must be accompanied by an adult. Early bird including breakfast for €28. **Clubhouse Hours:** 12am –11pm summer time. **Clubhouse Dress:** Neat & Tidy. No denims or trainers on course or in clubhouse. **Clubhouse Facilities:** Full catering facilities. Fully licenced. **Open Competitions:** Every Thursday and Bank Holidays, Summertime.

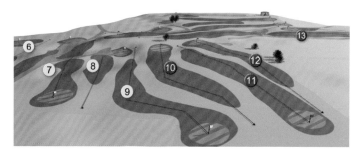

LOCATION: 6 miles north of Dublin Airport.

ARCHITECT: Eddie Hackett. Redesigned by Peter McEvoy.

MANAGER: Stephen Ennis.

PROFESSIONAL: Marcus Casey P.G.A.
Tel: (01) 8434655.

Beaverstown,
Donabate,
Co. Dublin.
Tel: (01) 8436439.
Fax: (01) 8435059.

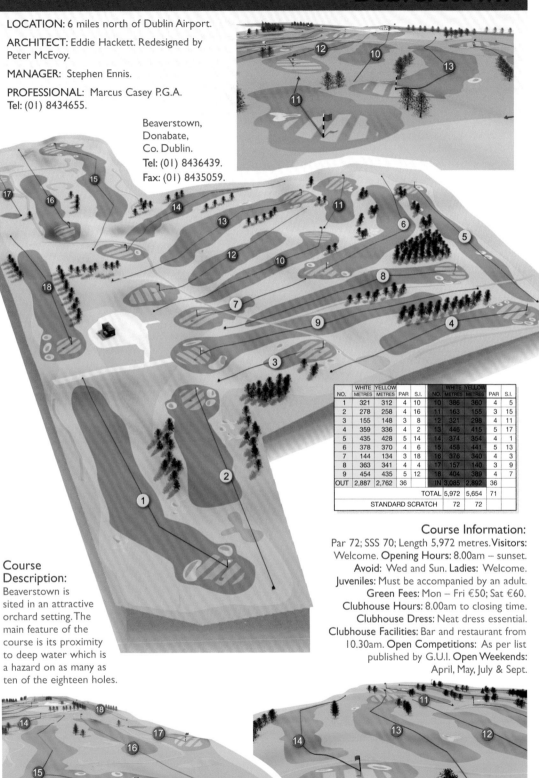

NO.	WHITE METRES	YELLOW METRES	PAR	S.I.	NO.	WHITE METRES	YELLOW METRES	PAR	S.I.
1	321	312	4	10	10	386	360	4	5
2	278	258	4	16	11	163	155	3	15
3	155	148	3	8	12	321	298	4	11
4	359	336	4	2	13	446	415	5	17
5	435	428	5	14	14	374	354	4	1
6	378	370	4	6	15	458	441	5	13
7	144	134	3	18	16	376	340	4	3
8	363	341	4	4	17	157	140	3	9
9	454	435	5	12	18	404	389	4	7
OUT	2,887	2,762	36		IN	3,085	2,892	36	
					TOTAL	5,972	5,654	71	
					STANDARD SCRATCH	72	72		

Course Description:
Beaverstown is sited in an attractive orchard setting. The main feature of the course is its proximity to deep water which is a hazard on as many as ten of the eighteen holes.

Course Information:
Par 72; SSS 70; Length 5,972 metres. **Visitors:** Welcome. **Opening Hours:** 8.00am – sunset. **Avoid:** Wed and Sun. **Ladies:** Welcome. **Juveniles:** Must be accompanied by an adult. **Green Fees:** Mon – Fri €50; Sat €60. **Clubhouse Hours:** 8.00am to closing time. **Clubhouse Dress:** Neat dress essential. **Clubhouse Facilities:** Bar and restaurant from 10.30am. **Open Competitions:** As per list published by G.U.I. **Open Weekends:** April, May, July & Sept.

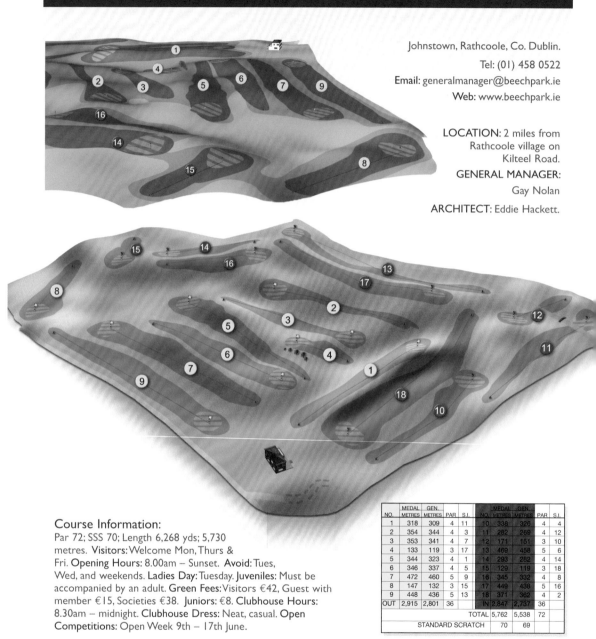

Johnstown, Rathcoole, Co. Dublin.

Tel: (01) 458 0522

Email: generalmanager@beechpark.ie

Web: www.beechpark.ie

LOCATION: 2 miles from Rathcoole village on Kilteel Road.

GENERAL MANAGER: Gay Nolan

ARCHITECT: Eddie Hackett.

Course Information:

Par 72; SSS 70; Length 6,268 yds; 5,730 metres. **Visitors:** Welcome Mon, Thurs & Fri. **Opening Hours:** 8.00am – Sunset. **Avoid:** Tues, Wed, and weekends. **Ladies Day:** Tuesday. **Juveniles:** Must be accompanied by an adult. **Green Fees:** Visitors €42, Guest with member €15, Societies €38. **Juniors:** €8. **Clubhouse Hours:** 8.30am – midnight. **Clubhouse Dress:** Neat, casual. **Open Competitions:** Open Week 9th – 17th June.

NO.	MEDAL METRES	GEN. METRES	PAR	S.I.	NO.	MEDAL METRES	GEN. METRES	PAR	S.I.
1	318	309	4	11	10	338	326	4	4
2	354	344	4	3	11	282	269	4	12
3	353	341	4	7	12	171	151	3	10
4	133	119	3	17	13	469	458	5	6
5	344	323	4	1	14	293	282	4	14
6	346	337	4	5	15	129	119	3	18
7	472	460	5	9	16	345	332	4	8
8	147	132	3	15	17	449	438	5	16
9	448	436	5	13	18	371	362	4	2
OUT	2,915	2,801	36		IN	2,847	2,737	36	
					TOTAL	5,762	5,538	72	
					STANDARD SCRATCH		70	69	

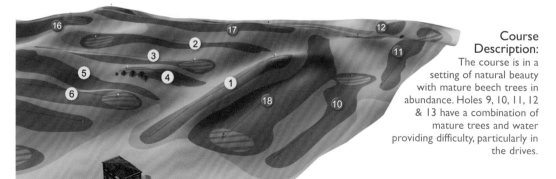

Course Description:

The course is in a setting of natural beauty with mature beech trees in abundance. Holes 9, 10, 11, 12 & 13 have a combination of mature trees and water providing difficulty, particularly in the drives.

Christy O'Connor

Silloge Park Golf Course,
Ballymun Road, Swords,
Co. Dublin.
Tel: (01) 8620 464/8620 440
christyoconnorgolf@gmail.com
www.christyoconnorgolf.com

LOCATION: Co. Dublin

NO.	METRES	PAR	S.I.	NO.	METRES	PAR	S.I.
1	381	4	4	10	392	4	2
2	162	3	10	11	360	4	8
3	424	5	7	12	508	5	3
4	347	4	12	13	156	3	13
5	505	5	5	14	317	4	14
6	296	4	16	15	351	4	11
7	124	3	15	16	374	4	9
8	411	4	1	17	307	4	18
9	120	3	17	18	370	4	6
OUT	2,770	35		IN	3,135	36	
				TOTAL	5,924	71	
		STANDARD SCRATCH			69		

Course Description:

18 hole parkland. Inland tree-lined course. SS of 70 makes this a long demanding course. Mostly flat over undulating hills. The feature hole is the 8th, 411 metres Par 4, index 1 over a small river and uphill dog-leg left. This course is very mature with tall tree features on numerous holes on the golf course.

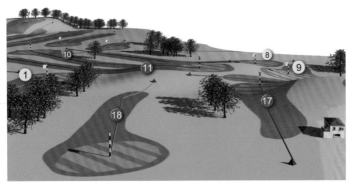

Course Information:

Par 71; SSS 70; Length 5,924 metres. **Ladies Day:** Monday. **Green Fees:** €18 weekdays, €25 weekends. **Juveniles:** Welcome. **Clubhouse Dress:** Casual **Clubhouse Facilities:** Changing rooms, showers, soup/sandwiches etc, caddy cars available.

HON SECRETARY:
Leo Lennon Maher.

PROFESSIONAL:
Peter & Christopher O'Connor.

Leinster – Co. Dublin **Citywest** (Championship Course)

Citywest Hotel & Golf Resort, Saggart, Co. Dublin.
Tel: (01) 401 0500
Fax: (01) 458 0945
Web: www.citywesthotel.com

LOCATION: On N7, off M50, 20 mins from Dublin Airport & Dublin City.

GOLF OPERATIONS MANAGER: Chris Patey.

ARCHITECT: Christy O'Connor.

NO.	CHAMP YARDS	MEDAL YARDS	PAR	S.I.	NO.	CHAMP YARDS	MEDAL YARDS	PAR	S.I.
1	350	345	4	9	10	192	186	3	10
2	193	173	3	13	11	365	339	4	12
3	538	512	5	3	12	398	380	4	8
4	206	200	3	11	13	555	540	5	4
5	388	366	4	15	14	154	154	3	18
6	447	420	4	1	15	510	487	5	14
7	372	351	4	17	16	392	385	4	6
8	182	177	3	7	17	157	137	3	16
9	430	416	4	5	18	437	416	4	2
OUT	3,106	2,960	34		IN	3,160	3,024	35	
					TOTAL	6,266	5,984	69	
					STANDARD SCRATCH		71	70	

Course Description:

The Championship Course is a first class test of golf in a wonderful parkland setting and the combination of perfectly manicured fairways, superb putting surfaces and beautiful mature trees offers the golfer a wonderful and inspiring golf experience. With so many sensational holes it would be difficult to decide on a specific signature hole and it is flattering to hear that with his global golf experience Christy O'Connor Junior reckons that "The 16th, 17th and 18th holes represent one of the best finishing stretches in Europe".

Course Information: The facilities at Citywest include two four star hotels, international conference & banqueting facilities, an excellent leisure centre and, lively bars and restaurants. Par 69; Length 6,266 yards. **Visitors:** Always welcome. **Opening Hours:** 7am – Sunset. **Green Fees:** Weekend from €45 - 70, Midweek from €35-55. Weekend golf breaks available. **Juveniles:** Welcome – €25. Golf clubs, trolleys, buggies, locker and caddies available. Professional tuition and golf schools available by appointment. **Clubhouse Dress:** Casual/Neat. **Clubhouse Facilities:** Restaurant, bar food, grill room, carvery. Conference facilities up to 6,500, banqueting 2000. Deluxe guestrooms, Health & Leisure Club with 20m pool. Golf Academy.

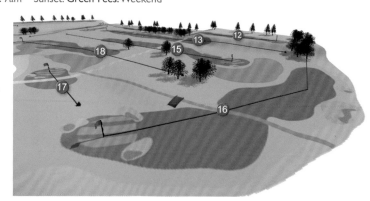

ARCHITECT: Christy O'Connor Jnr.

LOCATION: On N7, off M50, 20 mins from Dublin Airport & Dublin City.

Citywest Hotel & Golf Resort,
Saggart, Co. Dublin.
Tel: (01) 401 0500. **Fax:** (01) 458 0945.

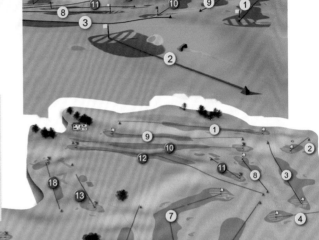

NO.	MEDAL YARDS	GEN. YARDS	PAR	S.I.	NO.	MEDAL YARDS	GEN. YARDS	PAR	S.I.
1	340	327	4	4	10	374	363	4	3
2	131	125	3	18	11	137	122	3	17
3	323	312	4	12	12	406	392	4	1
4	142	131	3	16	13	187	158	3	7
5	495	449	5	8	14	376	293	4	13
6	180	164	3	10	15	210	168	3	11
7	393	382	4	2	16	383	299	4	15
8	161	154	3	14	17	375	361	4	9
9	346	315	4	6	18	195	152	3	5
OUT	2,511	2,359	33		IN	2,643	2,308	32	
					TOTAL	5,164	4,667	65	
					STANDARD SCRATCH	65	65		

Course Information: The facilities at Citywest include two four star hotels, international conference & banqueting facilities, an excellent leisure centre and, lively bars and restaurants. Par 65; Length 5,154 yards. **Visitors:** Always welcome. **Opening Hours:** 7am – Sunset.
Green Fees: Weekends from €45, Midweek from €30-40, rates can vary due to time of the year and packages can be tailored for large groups. **Juveniles:** Welcome – €20. Golf clubs, trolleys, buggies, locker and caddies available. Professional tuition and golf schools available by appointment.
Clubhouse Dress: Casual/Neat. **Facilities:** Restaurant, bar food, grill room, carvery. Conference facilities up to 6,500, banqueting 2000. Deluxe guestrooms, Health & Leisure Club with 20m pool. Golf Academy.

Course Description: If you were to describe the Lakes course in two words it would be 'hidden gem'. The course is beautifully manicured to the highest standards, and with its various water features, magnificent rolling greens, and impressive bunkering it offers golferís a memorable and enjoyable round of golf. Golf enthusiasts regard The Lakes Course highly for both its layout and its contoured greens, which are considered to be amongst the best in Ireland.

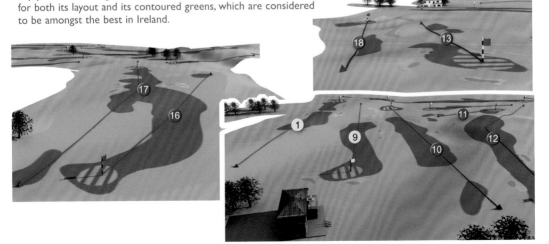

Corballis

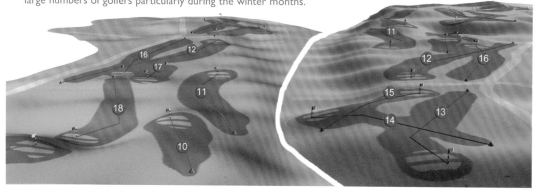

Corballis Public Golf Course,
Donabate, Co. Dublin.
Tel: (01) 8436583.
www.golfdublin.com
corballis@golfclub.com

MANAGER: A. Levins.
Tel: (01) 843 6583 / 843 6781.

ARCHITECT: Dublin County Council.

LOCATION: North County
Dublin on the coast.

NO.	YARDS	PAR	S.I.	NO.	YARDS	PAR	S.I.
1	155	3	12	10	132	3	15
2	251	4	18	11	374	4	9
3	465	4	2	12	405	4	3
4	155	3	16	13	264	4	17
5	389	4	4	14	191	3	11
6	183	3	6	15	196	3	5
7	188	3	8	16	392	4	1
8	264	4	14	17	140	3	13
9	494	5	10	18	333	4	7
OUT	2,544	33		IN	2,427	32	
				TOTAL	4,971	65	
				STANDARD SCRATCH	64		

Course Information:
Par 65; SSS 64; Length 4,971 yards. **Visitors:** Welcome. **Opening Hours:**
Weekends 7.00am; Weekdays 8.00am. **Ladies:** Welcome. **Green Fees:** €20
Mon – Fri; €25 Sat/Sun; Juveniles, Senior Citizens and unemployed €14
(Mon–Fri before 2.30pm). **Juveniles:** Welcome. **Clubhouse Hours:** Open
till 4pm in Winter and 7pm in Summer. **Clubhouse Dress:** Casual/neat.
Open Competitions: Phone club for details.

Course Description:
A links course situated adjacent to Corballis Beach, Donabate. Aquired and redeveloped by
Dublin County Council in 1973. A very popular and challenging Par 65 course which attracts
large numbers of golfers particularly during the winter months.

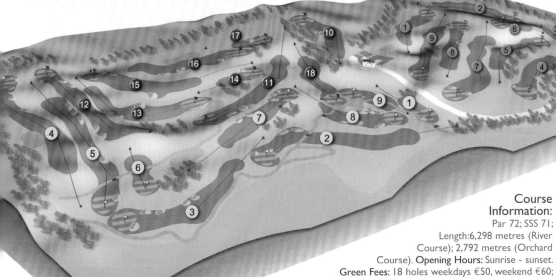

Corrstown Golf Club, Kilsallaghan, Co Dublin
Tel: (01) 864 0533 Fax: (01) 864 0537.
LOCATION: 6 minutes North of Dublin Airport
Email: info@corrstowngolfclub.com
Web: www.corrstowngolfclub.com

Course Information:

Par 72; SSS 71;
Length:6,298 metres (River Course); 2,792 metres (Orchard Course). **Opening Hours:** Sunrise - sunset. **Green Fees:** 18 holes weekdays €50, weekend €60; 9 holes weekdays €25, weekend €30. **Midweek Special Green Fee Rates:** Early Bird Special - sunrise to 10am; 18 holes €30 inc. breakfast. Night Owl Special - 4pm to sunset: 9 holes €17.50 inc. bar snack. **Visitors:** Welcome, ring for bookings. **Juveniles:** Welcome with an adult. **Societies:** €30 - €50 depending on numbers. **Clubhouse Hours:** 11.30am-11.30pm, pub hours in the Summer. **Clubhouse Dress:** Informal. **Clubhouse Facilities:** Full catering and bar. **Open Competitions:** Junior and Intermediate Scratch Cup - Saturday 9th June 2007. Seniors Open - phone for details.

Course Description:

27 holes – 9 hole course (Orchard Course) 18 hole course (River Course). Both parkland courses. 18 hole course contains a river with island green and water features throughout the course.

PROFESSIONAL: Pat Gittens.
ARCHITECT: Eddie Connaughton B. Sc. – Designer Agronomist. Course: Grass Technology International.
CAPTAIN: Jim Cowley.
LADIES CAPT: Catherine Fitzgerald.
Jnr CAPT: Kris Mc Grane

RIVER COURSE

NO.	MEDAL METRES	GEN. METRES	PAR	S.I.	NO.	MEDAL METRES	GEN. METRES	PAR	S.I.
1	144	138	3	10	10	319	314	4	15
2	518	504	5	2	11	538	526	5	5
3	372	361	4	12	12	476	463	5	17
4	507	497	5	6	13	415	387	4	1
5	454	446	5	16	14	176	189	3	13
6	153	144	3	18	15	410	384	4	7
7	395	388	4	4	16	421	395	4	9
8	292	286	4	14	17	174	163	3	11
9	150	141	3	8	18	382	371	4	3
OUT	2,985	2,905	36		IN	3,313	3,172	36	
					TOTAL	6,298	6,077	72	
					STANDARD SCRATCH		72	71	

ORCHARD COURSE

NO.	GENTS	PAR	S.I.	NO.	LADIES	PAR	S.I.
1	298	4	16	10	278	4	16
2	356	4	2	11	328	4	2
3	125	3	18	12	105	3	18
4	323	4	12	13	300	4	12
5	387	4	4	14	365	5	4
6	140	3	8	15	130	3	8
7	448	5	10	16	400	5	10
8	332	4	14	17	310	4	14
9	383	4	6	18	318	4	6
OUT	2,792	35		IN	2,532	36	
			TOTAL	5,324	72		
		STANDARD SCRATCH		71			

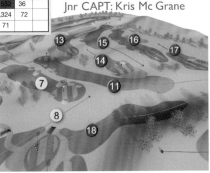

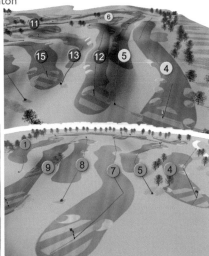

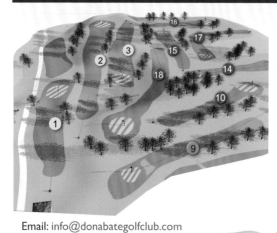

Balcarrick, Donabate, Co. Dublin. Tel: (01) 8436346.
LOCATION: 12 miles north of Dublin City.

Email: info@donabategolfclub.com
Web: www.donabategolfclub.com

Course Description:
Flat parkland with tree lined fairways
all 27 greens now reconstructed to
USPGA spec.

NO.	BLUE	PAR	S.I.	NO.	BLUE	PAR	S.I.
1	375	4	1	10	375	4	1
2	450	5	17	11	450	5	17
3	154	3	11	12	154	3	11
4	385	4	3	13	385	4	3
5	360	4	7	14	360	4	7
6	375	4	9	15	375	4	9
7	195	3	5	16	195	3	5
8	315	4	13	17	315	4	13
9	442	5	15	18	442	5	15
OUT	3,051	36		IN	3,051	36	
				TOTAL	3,051	70	
				STANDARD SCRATCH		72	

NO.	WHITE METRES	YELLOW METRES	PAR	S.I.	NO.	WHITE METRES	YELLOW METRES	PAR	S.I.
1	298	305	4	7	10	322	335	4	6
2	155	164	3	13	11	362	380	4	4
3	268	273	4	17	12	261	310	4	10
4	316	324	4	3	13	139	147	3	16
5	283	281	4	15	14	250	257	4	18
6	188	198	3	9	15	280	346	4	8
7	440	467	5	11	16	116	135	3	14
8	348	377	4	1	17	385	390	4	2
9	483	506	5	5	18	471	484	5	12
OUT	2,779	2,895	36		IN	2,585	2,743	35	
					TOTAL	5,364	5,638	71	
					STANDARD SCRATCH		73	71	

PROFESSIONAL: Hugh Jackson.

GOLF ADMINISTRATOR:
Dermot Dalton. Tel: (01) 8436346.

Course Information:
Par 72; SSS 72; Length 6,534 yards.
(red/yellow) **Visitors:** Everyday provided
advanced bookings are made. **Opening
Hours:** 7.30am – Sunset. **Green Fees:**
Winter Rates; Weekday €35, Weekend
€40. Summer Rates; Weekday €40,
Weekend inc. B/Hol €50. Society and group
rates available. **Juveniles:** Welcome if
accompanied by an adult. Club hire, Caddy
carts and Golf Buggies available by prior
arrangements. **Clubhouse Hours:** 8.00am –
11.30pm.
Clubhouse Dress: Casual / neat (no jeans
or trainers). **Clubhouse Facilities:** Snacks
available at all times; a la carte from 11am.
Open Competitions: Cotter Cup - June 23:
Open Week - August 7-12.

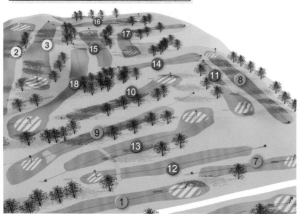

Gortlum, Brittas, Co. Dublin
Tel: (01) 458 2622. Fax: (01) 458 2048.

Email: dmgc@dublin.ie
Web: www.dublinmountaingolf.com

LOCATION: Just outside the village of Brittas, on the main N81.10 mins from Tallaght, South Dublin.

HON. SECRETARY: Brian Cruise.
SECRETARY MANAGER: Fiona Carolan.

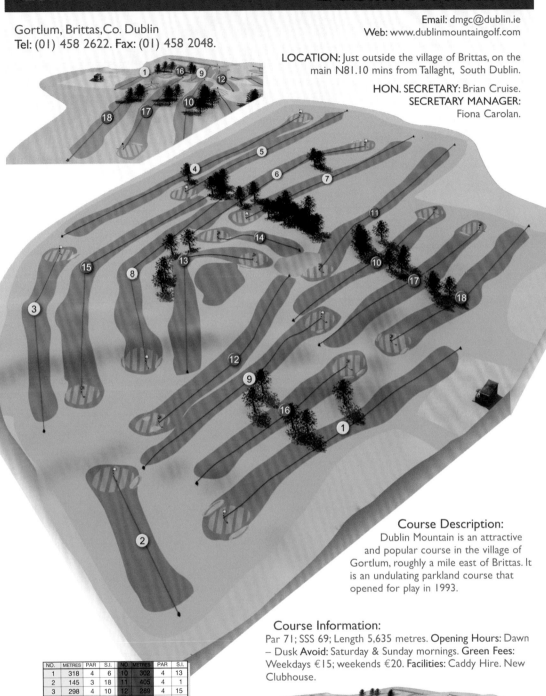

Course Description:

Dublin Mountain is an attractive and popular course in the village of Gortlum, roughly a mile east of Brittas. It is an undulating parkland course that opened for play in 1993.

Course Information:

Par 71; SSS 69; Length 5,635 metres. **Opening Hours:** Dawn – Dusk **Avoid:** Saturday & Sunday mornings. **Green Fees:** Weekdays €15; weekends €20. **Facilities:** Caddy Hire. New Clubhouse.

NO.	METRES	PAR	S.I.	NO.	METRES	PAR	S.I.
1	318	4	6	10	302	4	13
2	145	3	18	11	405	4	1
3	298	4	10	12	289	4	15
4	450	5	2	13	326	4	9
5	333	4	8	14	123	3	17
6	310	4	12	15	511	5	3
7	307	4	14	16	209	3	5
8	386	4	4	17	325	4	7
9	293	4	16	18	305	4	11
OUT	2,840	36		IN	2,795	36	
				TOTAL	5,635	71	
				STANDARD SCRATCH		69	

LOCATION: 7 miles South of Dublin.

GENERAL MANAGER: Dermot Murphy.
Tel: (01) 2803916

PROFESSIONAL: Vincent Carey.
Tel: (01) 280 3916

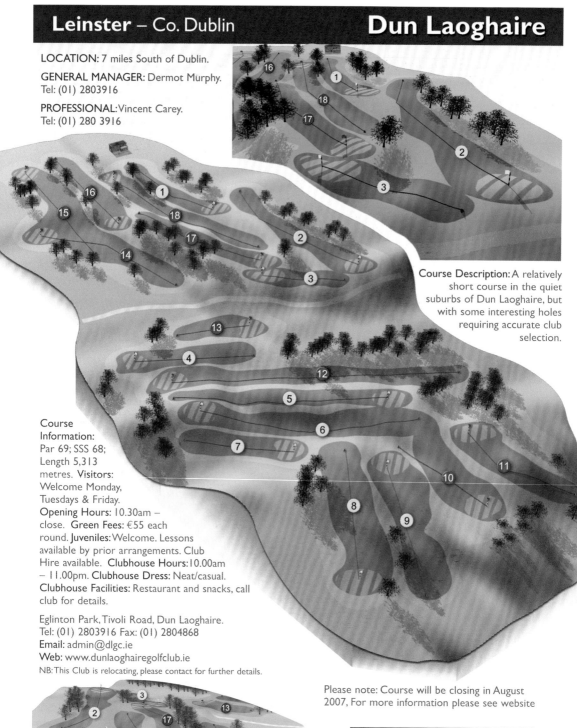

Course Description: A relatively short course in the quiet suburbs of Dun Laoghaire, but with some interesting holes requiring accurate club selection.

Course Information:
Par 69; SSS 68; Length 5,313 metres. **Visitors:** Welcome Monday, Tuesdays & Friday.
Opening Hours: 10.30am – close. **Green Fees:** €55 each round. **Juveniles:** Welcome. Lessons available by prior arrangements. Club Hire available. **Clubhouse Hours:** 10.00am – 11.00pm. **Clubhouse Dress:** Neat/casual. **Clubhouse Facilities:** Restaurant and snacks, call club for details.

Eglinton Park, Tivoli Road, Dun Laoghaire.
Tel: (01) 2803916 Fax: (01) 2804868
Email: admin@dlgc.ie
Web: www.dunlaoghairegolfclub.ie
NB: This Club is relocating, please contact for further details.

Please note: Course will be closing in August 2007, For more information please see website

NO.	MEDAL METRES	GEN. METRES	PAR	S.I.	NO.	MEDAL METRES	GEN. METRES	PAR	S.I.
1	304	291	4	11	10	183	174	3	8
2	332	323	4	5	11	241	233	4	16
3	148	139	3	9	12	440	430	5	18
4	173	164	3	7	13	149	137	3	14
5	392	376	4	1	14	368	359	4	2
6	284	275	4	15	15	331	323	4	12
7	114	107	3	17	16	337	329	4	6
8	367	360	4	3	17	328	318	4	4
9	343	336	4	13	18	479	471	5	10
OUT	2,457	2,371	33		IN	2,856	2,774	36	
					TOTAL	5,313	5,145	69	
					STANDARD SCRATCH	72	71		

Cloghran. Co. Dublin.
Tel: (01) 840 1183 or (01) 840 1763

LOCATION: Beside Dublin Airport.

PROFESSIONAL: Tony Judd.
Tel: 01 8407670

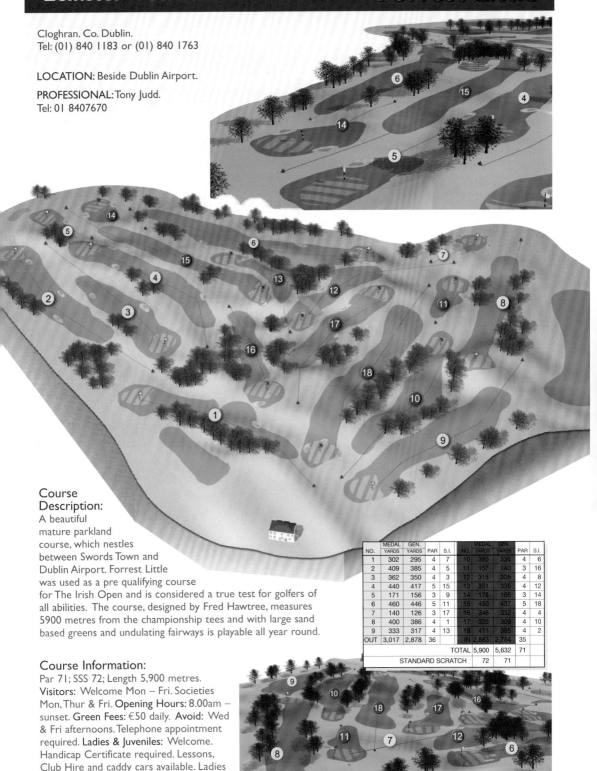

Course Description:

A beautiful mature parkland course, which nestles between Swords Town and Dublin Airport. Forrest Little was used as a pre qualifying course for The Irish Open and is considered a true test for golfers of all abilities. The course, designed by Fred Hawtree, measures 5900 metres from the championship tees and with large sand based greens and undulating fairways is playable all year round.

NO.	MEDAL YARDS	GEN. YARDS	PAR	S.I.	NO.	MEDAL YARDS	GEN. YARDS	PAR	S.I.
1	302	295	4	7	10	350	336	4	6
2	409	385	4	5	11	157	140	3	16
3	362	350	4	3	12	315	305	4	8
4	440	417	5	15	13	351	335	4	12
5	171	156	3	9	14	178	165	3	14
6	460	446	5	11	15	450	437	5	18
7	140	126	3	17	16	346	332	4	4
8	400	386	4	1	17	325	309	4	10
9	333	317	4	13	18	411	395	4	2
OUT	3,017	2,878	36		IN	2,883	2,754	35	
					TOTAL	5,900	5,632	71	
					STANDARD SCRATCH	72	71		

Course Information:

Par 71; SSS 72; Length 5,900 metres.
Visitors: Welcome Mon – Fri. Societies Mon, Thur & Fri. **Opening Hours:** 8.00am – sunset. **Green Fees:** €50 daily. **Avoid:** Wed & Fri afternoons. Telephone appointment required. **Ladies & Juveniles:** Welcome. Handicap Certificate required. Lessons, Club Hire and caddy cars available. Ladies day Tuesday. Juveniles must be off the course by 3pm. **Clubhouse Hours:** 8.00am – midnight. **Clubhouse Dress:** neat dress **Clubhouse Facilities:** Each day from 12 noon, full catering and bar.

Nangor Road, Clondalkin, Dublin 22
Tel: (01) 464 1043 Fax: (01) 464 1039
Web: www.grange-castle.com
Email: info@grange-castle.com

LOCATION: Situated only minutes
from the Naas Rd and M50 motorway.
An ideal location for a relaxing
game of golf.

HON. SECRETARY: Colm Tyndall.

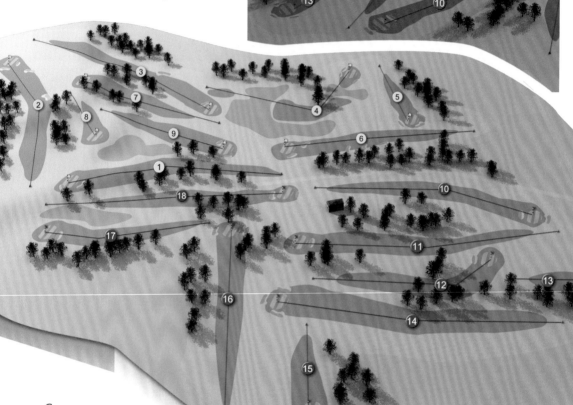

Course

Description: One of
Europe's foremost course
designers Paddy Merrigan has
designed a golf course of the very
highest standard in Grange Castle. The
course measures over 6,500 yards from
the back tees and will test both the novice
and seasoned golfer alike. The course has
matured considerably in the time since its
establishment, with a new clubhouse already
completed and a further nine holes are currently
under construction. Grange Castle is managed by
P.G.A. Sports Management LTD.

Course Information: Par 71; SSS 72; Length 5,966 metres.
Visitors: Welcome, booking required. **Juveniles:** Welcome.
Opening Hours: Daylight hours. **Ladies:** Welcome. **Green Fees:**
Weekdays €21; Weekends €30. **Facilities:** Motorised Buggies,
Motorised Caddy Carts, Club hire and snacks available. **Club
House Dress:** Neat.

NO.	MEDAL METRES	GEN. METRES	PAR	S.I.	NO.	MEDAL METRES	GEN. METRES	PAR	S.I.
1	412	393	4	1	10	302	296	4	12
2	437	418	5	15	11	350	344	4	6
3	395	379	4	5	12	268	253	4	16
4	386	357	4	3	13	147	131	3	14
5	162	139	3	17	14	395	375	4	4
6	353	333	4	7	15	183	95	3	18
7	452	448	5	13	16	380	375	4	2
8	168	148	3	11	17	330	306	4	8
9	363	344	4	9	18	430	408	5	10
OUT	3,128	2,959	36		IN	2,765	2,746	35	
					TOTAL	5,893	5,707	71	
					STANDARD SCRATCH		71	70	

Glencullen Golf Course, Glencullen, Co. Dublin.
Tel: (01) 2940898 Fax: (01) 2952895
E-mail: admin@glencullengolfclub.ie
Web: glencullengolfclub.ie

LOCATION: Set high in the Dublin Mountains, overlooked only by the Giants Grave.

HON. SECRETARY: Brendan O'Connor.

PROFESSIONAL: Paul McLoughlin

Course Description:

Glencullen Golf Course is a 9 hole parkland course located at the top of the Dublin Wicklow Mountains. It boasts panoramic views of the countryside, together with Dublin Bay and Howth Head. Although a 9 hole course, Glencullen has alternating tee boxes, giving the golfer the distinct impression that they have played 18 different holes. The signature hole is undoubtedly the 9th where the water hazards come into play.

Course Information:

Par 69; SSS 66; Length 4,925 metres.
Visitors: Welcome. **Opening Hours:** Daylight hours. **Ladies:** Welcome.
Green Fees: Weekdays, €17; Weekday with a member, €10, Weekends, €22; Weekends with a member, €10.
Facilities: Trolley hire and snacks available. **Course Dress:** Denims, training shoes, football jerseys and sleeveless shirts are forbidden on the golf course.

NO.	METRES	PAR	S.I.	NO.	METRES	PAR	S.I.
1	154	3	11	10	178	3	12
2	276	4	14	11	283	4	16
3	317	4	2	12	317	4	1
4	104	3	18	13	135	3	13
5	327	4	4	14	335	4	3
6	274	4	6	15	252	4	8
7	255	4	15	16	131	3	17
8	513	5	5	17	489	5	7
9	306	4	9	18	299	4	10
OUT	2,526	35		IN	2,419	34	
				TOTAL	4,945	69	
				STANDARD SCRATCH		67	

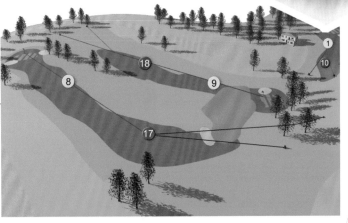

Ballydowd, Lucan, Co. Dublin. Tel: (01) 623 8881.
Email: hermitagegolf@eircom.net
Web: www.hermitagegolf.ie

LOCATION: 8 miles from Dublin city, on the N4.

GENERAL MANAGER: Eddie Farrell. Tel: (01) 6268491.

PROFESSIONAL: Simon Byrne. Tel: (01) 6268072.

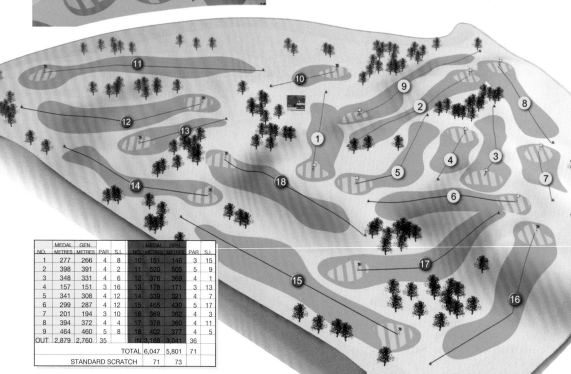

NO.	MEDAL METRES	GEN. METRES	PAR	S.I.	NO.	MEDAL METRES	GEN. METRES	PAR	S.I.
1	277	266	4	8	10	151	146	3	15
2	398	391	4	2	11	520	505	5	9
3	348	331	4	6	12	376	369	4	1
4	157	151	3	16	13	178	171	3	13
5	341	308	4	12	14	339	321	4	7
6	299	287	4	12	15	465	430	5	17
7	201	194	3	10	16	369	362	4	3
8	394	372	4	4	17	378	360	4	11
9	464	460	5	8	18	402	377	4	5
OUT	2,879	2,760	35		IN	3,168	3,041	36	
					TOTAL	6,047	5,801	71	
					STANDARD SCRATCH	71	73		

Course Description: This course has a fairly flat front nine and an undulating back nine. The 10th hole is the most scenic, followed by an extremely difficult par 5, bordered on right by the River Liffey and on the left by woodland. USPGA specification greens.

Course Information:
Par 71; SSS 71; Length 6,032 metres.
Visitors: Welcome Monday – Friday mornings (except Tuesday). **Opening Hours:** 8.00am – Sunset. **Avoid:** Weekends. **Ladies Day:** Tuesday. **Juveniles:** Must be accompanied by an adult, tel. appointment required. Caddy cars for hire; club hire and lessons available by prior arrangement. **Green Fees:** €80 Mon – Fri, €45 before 9am, €85 weekends. **Clubhouse Hours:** 9.00am – midnight. **Clubhouse Dress:** Casual. No jeans or shorts, no denims or trainers. Collar and tie in dining room after 8pm. **Clubhouse Facilities:** Snacks from 10am; full restaurant from 12.30pm – 9.30pm everyday.

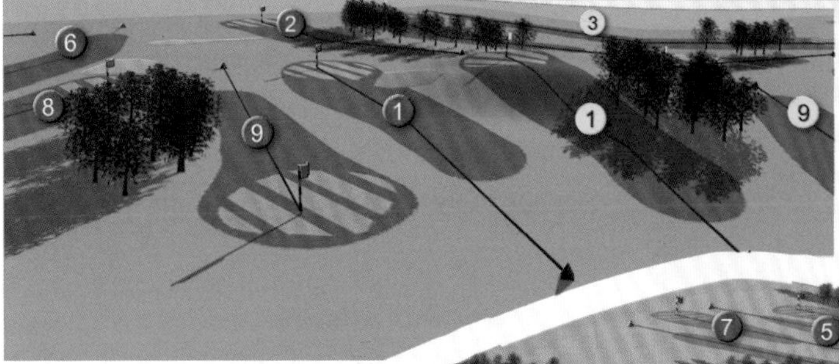

Hollystown Golf Club,
Hollystown,
Holywood Rath, Dublin 15.
Tel: (01) 8207444
Fax: (01) 8207447
Web: www.hollystown.com
Email: info@hollystown.com

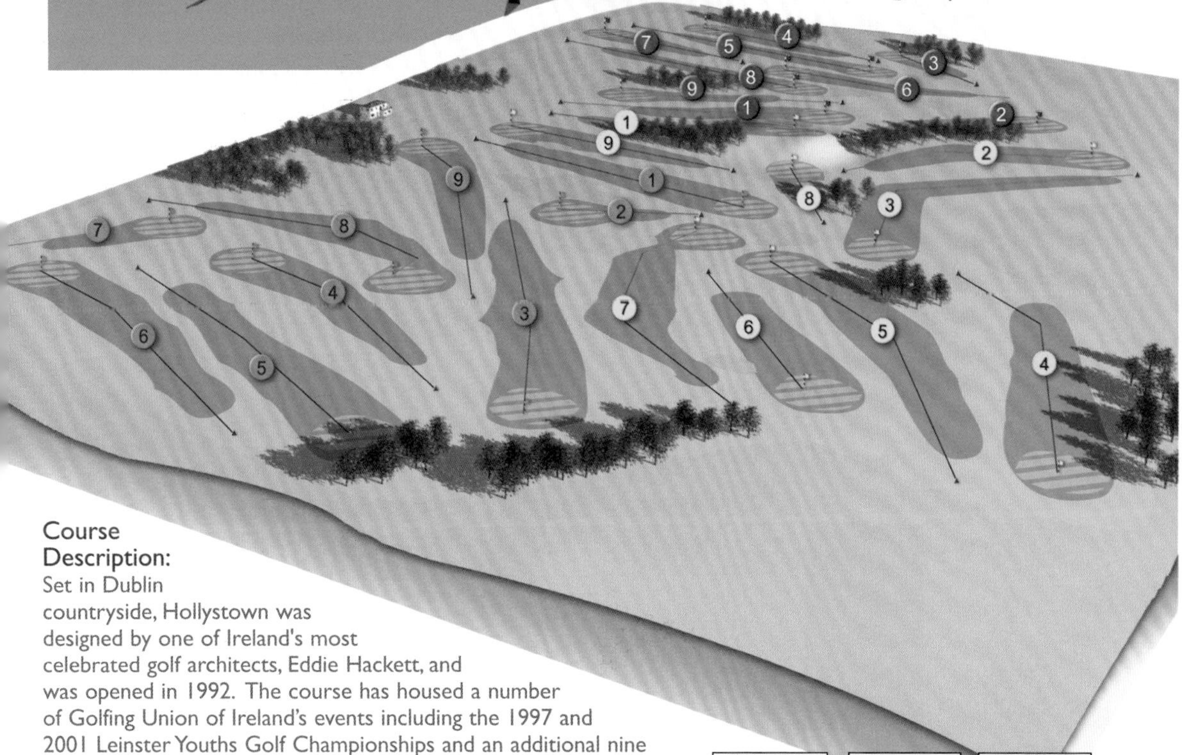

Course Description:

Set in Dublin countryside, Hollystown was designed by one of Ireland's most celebrated golf architects, Eddie Hackett, and was opened in 1992. The course has housed a number of Golfing Union of Ireland's events including the 1997 and 2001 Leinster Youths Golf Championships and an additional nine holes 'Blue' was opened in August 1999 to complement the course existing, and providing three challenging eighteen hole combinations. "The 4th on the red course at 234 yards is one of the best Par 3 in any part of the country" said Christy O'Connor Snr who also singled out the 1st on the blue course. The facilities include a fine new pavilion and is 20 minutes from Dublin's city centre.

Course Information: Visitors: Welcome.
Opening Hours: Daylight Hours. **Ladies:**
Welcome. **Green Fees:** €30 weekdays, €40 weekends. **Juveniles:** Welcome. **Clubhouse Hours:** Daylight Hours. **Clubhouse Dress:** Casual/Smart. **Clubhouse Facilities:** Full facilities including bar and catering.

PROFESSIONAL: Joe Murray.

MANAGER: Oliver Barry

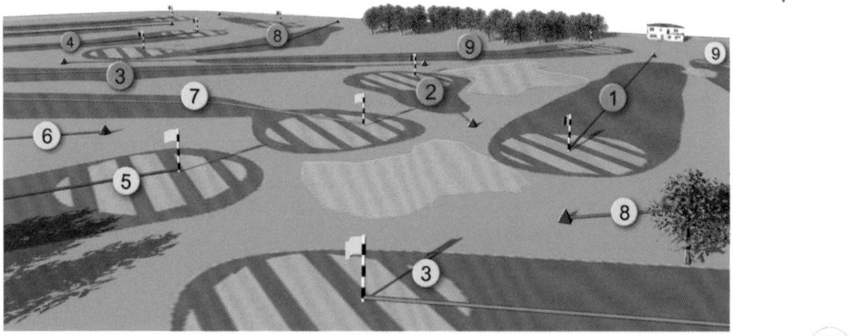

YELLOW COURSE			RED COURSE			BLUE COURSE		
NO.	YARDS	PAR	NO.	YARDS	PAR	NO.	YARDS	PAR
1	318	4	1	404	4	1	390	4
2	318	4	2	354	4	2	173	3
3	488	5	3	147	3	3	564	5
4	390	4	4	347	4	4	395	4
5	377	4	5	511	5	5	405	4
6	199	3	6	335	4	6	424	4
7	431	4	7	234	3	7	164	3
8	161	3	8	416	4	8	371	4
9	390	4	9	309	4	9	558	5
TOTAL	3,072	35	TOTAL	3,057	35	TOTAL	3,444	35

LOCATION: 10km from Dublin City.

ARCHITECT: Eddie Hackett/Joseph Bedford.

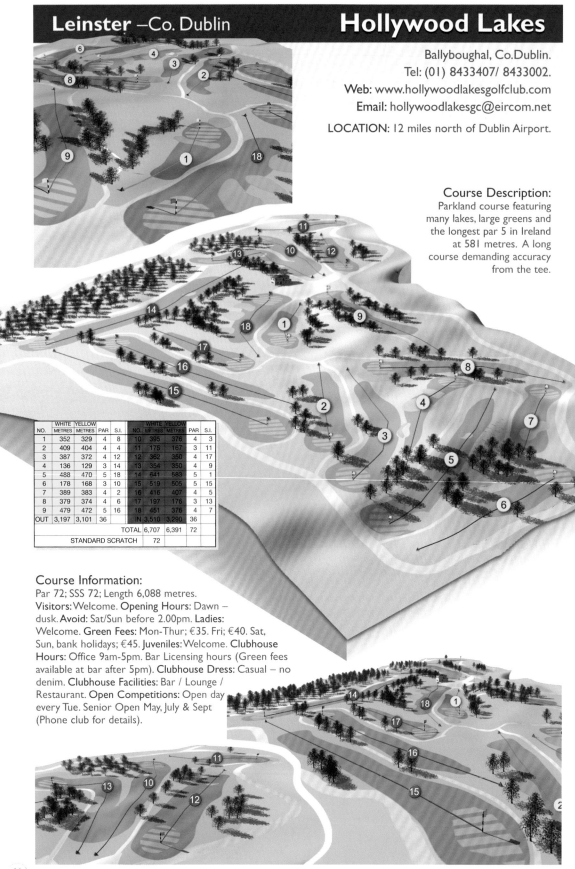

Ballyboughal, Co.Dublin.
Tel: (01) 8433407/ 8433002.
Web: www.hollywoodlakesgolfclub.com
Email: hollywoodlakesgc@eircom.net

LOCATION: 12 miles north of Dublin Airport.

Course Description:

Parkland course featuring many lakes, large greens and the longest par 5 in Ireland at 581 metres. A long course demanding accuracy from the tee.

NO.	WHITE METRES	YELLOW METRES	PAR	S.I.	NO.	WHITE METRES	YELLOW METRES	PAR	S.I.
1	352	329	4	8	10	395	376	4	3
2	409	404	4	4	11	175	167	3	11
3	387	372	4	12	12	362	350	4	17
4	136	129	3	14	13	354	350	4	9
5	488	470	5	18	14	641	583	5	1
6	178	168	3	10	15	519	505	5	15
7	389	383	4	2	16	416	407	4	5
8	379	374	4	6	17	197	176	3	13
9	479	472	5	16	18	451	376	4	7
OUT	3,197	3,101	36		IN	3,510	3,290	36	
					TOTAL	6,707	6,391	72	
					STANDARD SCRATCH		72		

Course Information:

Par 72; SSS 72; Length 6,088 metres.
Visitors: Welcome. **Opening Hours:** Dawn – dusk. **Avoid:** Sat/Sun before 2.00pm. **Ladies:** Welcome. **Green Fees:** Mon-Thur; €35. Fri; €40. Sat, Sun, bank holidays; €45. **Juveniles:** Welcome. **Clubhouse Hours:** Office 9am-5pm. Bar Licensing hours (Green fees available at bar after 5pm). **Clubhouse Dress:** Casual – no denim. **Clubhouse Facilities:** Bar / Lounge / Restaurant. **Open Competitions:** Open day every Tue. Senior Open May, July & Sept (Phone club for details).

Island Golf Club, Corballis,
Donabate, Co. Dublin
Tel: (01) 8436205
Fax: (01) 8436860
Email: info@theislandgolfclub.com

LOCATION: Corballis, 15 mins from
Dublin Airport.

ARCHITECT: 1990 Redesign,
F. Hawtree & E. Hackett.

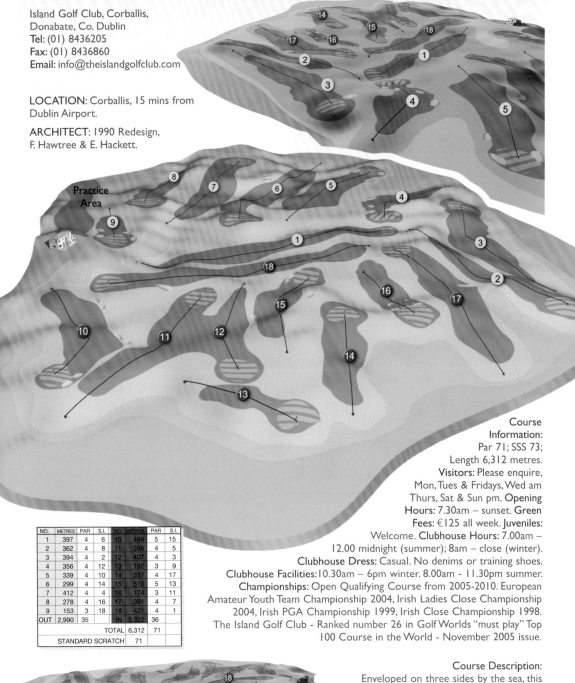

NO.	METRES	PAR	S.I.	NO.	METRES	PAR	S.I.
1	397	4	6	10	489	5	15
2	362	4	8	11	396	4	5
3	394	4	2	12	407	4	3
4	356	4	12	13	192	3	9
5	339	4	10	14	337	4	17
6	299	4	14	15	515	5	13
7	412	4	4	16	174	3	11
8	278	4	16	17	391	4	7
9	153	3	18	18	421	4	1
OUT	2,990	35		IN	3,322	36	
				TOTAL	6,312	71	
				STANDARD SCRATCH		71	

Course Information: Par 71; SSS 73; Length 6,312 metres. **Visitors:** Please enquire, Mon, Tues & Fridays, Wed am Thurs, Sat & Sun pm. **Opening Hours:** 7.30am – sunset. **Green Fees:** €125 all week. **Juveniles:** Welcome. **Clubhouse Hours:** 7.00am – 12.00 midnight (summer); 8am – close (winter). **Clubhouse Dress:** Casual. No denims or training shoes. **Clubhouse Facilities:** 10.30am – 6pm winter. 8.00am - 11.30pm summer. **Championships:** Open Qualifying Course from 2005-2010. European Amateur Youth Team Championship 2004, Irish Ladies Close Championship 2004, Irish PGA Championship 1999, Irish Close Championship 1998. The Island Golf Club - Ranked number 26 in Golf Worlds "must play" Top 100 Course in the World - November 2005 issue.

Course Description:
Enveloped on three sides by the sea, this is a naturally true links course. The 1st, 3rd and 7th are probably the best holes on the outward nine but the most spectacular are to be found on the inward half. The 12th needs an excellent drive while the 13th is a superb par 3 of 190 metres, requiring a long iron or wood shot to reach a naturally well protected green. The 425 metre par 4 18th offers an excellent challenge with imposing sandhills on both sides.

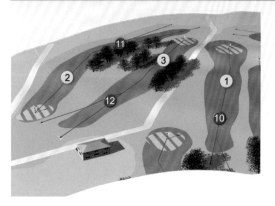

Killiney Golf Club, Balinclea Road,
Killiney, Co. Dublin.
Tel: (01) 2852823. Fax: (01) 2852861.
Email: killineygolfclub@eircom.net
Web: www.killineygolfclub.ie

NO.	YARDS	PAR	S.I.	NO.	YARDS	PAR	S.I.
1	354	4	7	10	354	4	8
2	402	4	3	11	353	4	14
3	308	4	13	12	348	4	4
4	333	4	5	13	383	4	2
5	143	3	15	14	104	3	18
6	429	5	17	15	451	5	16
7	159	3	11	16	165	3	12
8	407	4	1	17	372	4	10
9	314	4	9	18	338	4	6
OUT	2,855	35		IN	2,868	35	
				TOTAL	5,723	70	
				STANDARD SCRATCH		69	

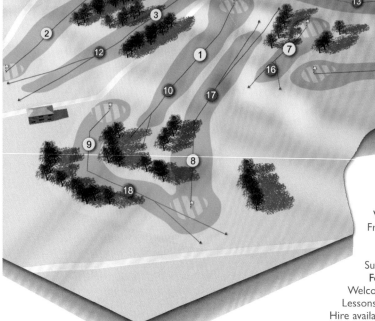

Course Information:
Par 70; SSS 70; Length 5,723 metres.
Visitors: Welcome Monday; Wednesday,
Friday and Sunday afternoons subject to
availability. **Opening Hours:** 8.30am –
sunset. Avoid: Thursdays, Saturdays,
Sunday mornings and Tuesday pm. **Green
Fees:** €50 (€25 with member). **Juveniles:**
Welcome. Must be accompanied by an adult.
Lessons available by prior arrangements; Club
Hire available. **Clubhouse Hours:** 8.30am – Dark.
Clubhouse Dress: Casual / Neat (no jeans, T-
shirts or trainers). **Clubhouse Facilities:** Bar &
bar snacks available 10am – 11pm.

Course Description:
This parkland course is on the southern side
of Killiney Hill, the most scenic area of Co.
Dubin. The local terrain while hilly is not too
difficult.

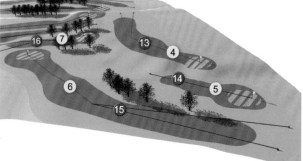

SECRETARY: Michael Walsh.

PROFESSIONAL: Paddy O'Boyle.

LOCATION: Killiney, South County Dublin.

Lucan, Co. Dublin. Tel: (01) 628 0246
Email: lucangolf@eircom.net
Web: www.lucangolfclub.com

LOCATION: 10 miles from Dublin City
on Cellbridge Road.

SECRETARY / MANAGER: Tom O'Donnell.
Tel: (01) 6282106

CADDYMASTERS: Martin Furey &
Christy Dobbs. Tel: (01) 6280246

Course Description:
Lucan Golf Course has an
undulating first nine. The first and
seventh providing a good test.
The back nine which was
added in 1988 is fairly
flat and has a fine
finishing 18th hole
of 530 metres.

**Course
Information:**
Par 71; SSS
71; Length 5,888
metres. **Visitors:**
Monday, Tuesday,
Fridays. **Ladies Day:**
Thursday. **Opening
Hours:** Sunrise – sunset.
Avoid: Weekends. **Green
Fees:** €45. **Juveniles:** Must be
accompanied by a member.
Telephone appointment required.
Clubhouse Hours: 9.00am – 12.00
midnight. Full clubhouse facilities.
Clubhouse Dress: No denims on
Course. Neat dress in clubhouse.
Clubhouse Facilities: Full bar & restaurant
facilities. Bar food available. **Open
Competition:** Phone club for details.

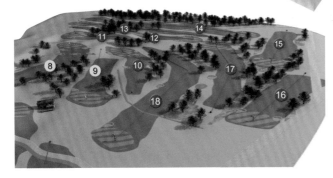

NO.	MEDAL METRES	GEN. METRES	PAR	S.I.	NO.	MEDAL METRES	GEN. METRES	PAR	S.I.
1	364	369	4	6	10	358	371	4	3
2	304	332	4	8	11	156	169	3	7
3	411	416	4	4	12	279	292	4	15
4	143	107	3	12	13	317	330	4	11
5	431	435	5	16	14	402	415	4	1
6	268	279	4	18	15	321	334	4	13
7	124	138	3	10	16	172	185	3	9
8	346	366	4	2	17	426	439	5	17
9	310	344	4	14	18	518	531	5	5
OUT	2,701	2,786	35		IN	2,949	3,066	36	
					TOTAL	5,650	5,852	71	
					STANDARD SCRATCH			71	70

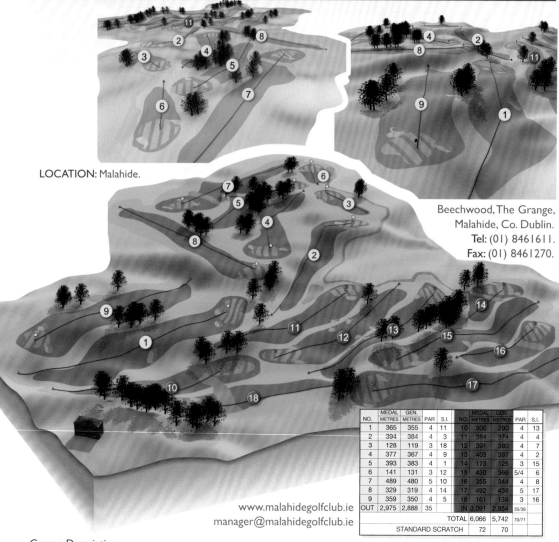

LOCATION: Malahide.

Beechwood, The Grange,
Malahide, Co. Dublin.
Tel: (01) 8461611.
Fax: (01) 8461270.

NO.	MEDAL METRES	GEN. METRES	PAR	S.I.	NO.	MEDAL METRES	GEN. METRES	PAR	S.I.
1	365	355	4	11	10	300	290	4	13
2	394	384	4	3	11	384	374	4	4
3	128	119	3	18	12	391	380	4	7
4	377	367	4	9	13	405	397	4	2
5	393	383	4	1	14	173	125	3	15
6	141	131	3	12	15	430	366	5/4	6
7	489	480	5	10	16	355	344	4	8
8	329	319	4	14	17	492	439	5	17
9	359	350	4	5	18	161	139	3	16
OUT	2,975	2,888	35		IN	3,091	2,854	35/36	
					TOTAL	6,066	5,742	70/71	
					STANDARD SCRATCH	72	70		

www.malahidegolfclub.ie
manager@malahidegolfclub.ie

Course Description:
A championship standard course, which opened to 27
holes in 1990. This parkland course has water as a
feature of a number of the holes.

GENERAL MANAGER: Mark Gannon.
PROFESSIONAL: John Murray.
ARCHITECT: E. Hackett

Course Information:
Par 71; SSS 72; Length 6,066 metres. **Visitors:** Welcome.
except Sat/Sun **Opening Hours:** Sunrise – sunset. **Ladies:**
Welcome. Telephone appointment required. **Green Fees:**
€55. **Clubhouse Hours:** Normal licensing hours.
Clubhouse Facilities: Full catering and bar facilities.
Clubhouse Dress: Neat dress essential. **Open
Competitions:** August Bank
Holiday week.

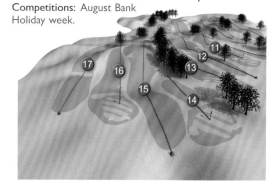

LOCATION: On N7, off M50, 30 mins from
Dublin Airport & Dublin City centre.
GROUP DIRECTOR OF GOLF:
Chris Patey.
PROFESSIONAL: Donal
Gleeson

ARCHITECT:
Christy O'Connor Jnr.

Palmerstown House, Johnstown. Tel: (045)
906 901 Fax: (045) 906 922
Web: www.palmerstownhouse.com

NO.	CHAMP. YARDS	MEDAL YARDS	PAR	S.I.	NO.	MEDAL YARDS	GEN. YARDS	PAR	S.I.
1	422	401	4	9	10	178	174	3	18
2	408	386	4	11	11	447	404	4	10
3	198	184	3	13	12	183	154	3	16
4	428	406	4	7	13	477	437	4	6
5	465	442	4	5	14	588	563	5	2
6	565	539	5	1	15	409	372	4	12
7	427	398	4	17	16	560	543	5	4
8	205	188	3	15	17	431	396	4	14
9	580	563	5	3	18	448	406	4	8
OUT	3,698	3,507	36		IN	3,721	3,449	36	
					TOTAL	7,419	6,956	72	
					STANDARD SCRATCH		72		

Course Description:

In the seclusion and
beauty of a once world
famous stud farm just 30
minutes from Dublin's city centre
lies an extraordinary golfing retreat
called The PGA National Ireland at
Palmerstown House. The golf course is set
amidst a myriad of stunning mature trees,
impressive bunkering and exquisite use of
water. Indeed accolades have already been
bestowed upon Palmerstown House and
this is highlighted by its inclusion in Golf
World's top 4 new courses of 2005.

Course Information:

Par 72; Length 7,419 yards. **Visitors:** Always welcome.
Opening Hours: 7am – Sunset. **Green Fees:** €150-185.
Golf clubs, trolleys, buggies, and locker facilities
available. Professional tuition and golf schools available
by appointment. **Clubhouse Dress:** Casual/Neat.
Facilities: Gourmet Restaurant, Spike Bar and Lounge
Bar, Bar food available, and excellent locker room
facilities. Practice ground, pitching green and four
practice putting greens.

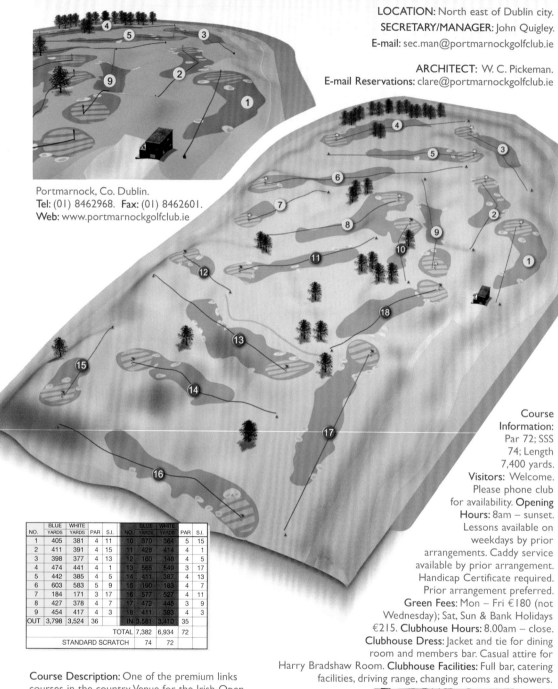

LOCATION: North east of Dublin city.
SECRETARY/MANAGER: John Quigley.
E-mail: sec.man@portmarnockgolfclub.ie

ARCHITECT: W. C. Pickeman.
E-mail Reservations: clare@portmarnockgolfclub.ie

Portmarnock, Co. Dublin.
Tel: (01) 8462968. **Fax:** (01) 8462601.
Web: www.portmarnockgolfclub.ie

Course Information:
Par 72; SSS 74; Length 7,400 yards.
Visitors: Welcome. Please phone club for availability. **Opening Hours:** 8am – sunset. Lessons available on weekdays by prior arrangements. Caddy service available by prior arrangement. Handicap Certificate required. Prior arrangement preferred.
Green Fees: Mon – Fri €180 (not Wednesday); Sat, Sun & Bank Holidays €215. **Clubhouse Hours:** 8.00am – close.
Clubhouse Dress: Jacket and tie for dining room and members bar. Casual attire for Harry Bradshaw Room. **Clubhouse Facilities:** Full bar, catering facilities, driving range, changing rooms and showers.

NO.	BLUE YARDS	WHITE YARDS	PAR	S.I.	NO.	BLUE YARDS	WHITE YARDS	PAR	S.I.
1	405	381	4	11	10	370	364	5	15
2	411	391	4	15	11	428	414	4	1
3	398	377	4	13	12	160	148	4	5
4	474	441	4	1	13	565	549	3	17
5	442	385	4	5	14	411	387	4	13
6	603	583	5	9	15	190	183	4	7
7	184	171	3	17	16	577	527	4	11
8	427	378	4	7	17	472	445	3	9
9	454	417	4	3	18	411	393	4	3
OUT	3,798	3,524	36		IN	3,581	3,410	35	
					TOTAL	7,382	6,934	72	
					STANDARD SCRATCH	74	72		

Course Description: One of the premium links courses in the country. Venue for the Irish Open Championship and given world championship ranking by many critics. The sandy soil of the Portmarnock peninsula makes it ideal for golf. Now has 27 holes with room for more. Its potential as a golf links was realised in 1894. Within two years of the opening of the 18 hole course, Portmarnock hosted its first tournament, the Irish Open Amateur Championship and has hosted the prestigious Irish Open Championship many times since then and was also host for the Walker Cup.

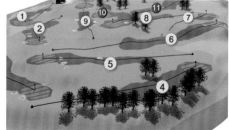

Portmarnock Hotel & Golf Links,
Strand Road, Portmarnock,
Co. Dublin.
Tel: (01) 8461800.
Fax: (01) 8461077.
E-mail: golfres@portmarnock.com
Web: www.portmarnock.com

Course Description:

Portmarnock Hotel & Golf Links is the venue for a good golf break. You will enjoy the formidable challenge of a Bernhard Langer championship links and a deluxe hotel (Golf Hotel of the year 1999) offering great comfort and the best of traditional hospitality. Course cover 180 acres of classic terrain. Widely recognised as one of Ireland's premier golf resorts. The links course takes full advantage of a natural setting.

NO.	MEDAL YARDS	GEN. YARDS	PAR	S.I.	NO.	MEDAL YARDS	GEN. YARDS	PAR	S.I.
1	320	320	4	14	10	342	329	4	7
2	341	329	4	10	11	150	135	3	17
3	178	172	3	16	12	419	406	4	1
4	549	512	5	6	13	507	467	5	15
5	431	409	4	2	14	317	312	4	13
6	486	462	5	18	15	392	364	4	5
7	412	405	4	4	16	383	360	4	9
8	374	342	4	8	17	185	171	3	11
9	156	145	3	12	18	408	365	4	3
OUT	3,247	3,096	36		IN	3,103	2,909	35	
					TOTAL	6,350	6,005	70	
	STANDARD SCRATCH						73	72	

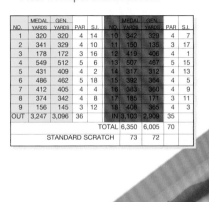

LOCATION:
15 minutes from Dublin Airport, 25 minutes from Dublin City Centre.

Course information: Par 71; SSS 73; Length 6,350 yards.
Visitors: Welcome **Opening Hours:** 7.30am-sunset. **Green Fees:** Hotel Residents: Apr-Oct €90, Nov-Dec €65. Non Residents: Apr-Oct, Mon-Sun €125. Nov-Dec, Mon-Fri €80, Sat/Sun €100. **Juveniles:** Must be accompanied by an adult. **Clubhouse Hours:** Dawn to dusk. **Clubhouse Facilities:** Catering facilities all day. Club Hire €25 to €55; Trolley Hire €4; Caddy service available by prior arrangement. Ride on buggy €40, electric cart €15.

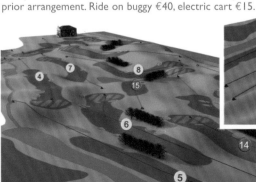

GOLF DIRECTOR: Moira Cassidy.

DESIGNER: Bernhard Langer.

ARCHITECT: Stan Eby.

GOLF SHOP MANAGER: Joe Connolly

Rush, Dublin.
Tel: (01) 8437548.
Fax: (01) 8438177.

LOCATION: Seaside.

SEC. MANAGER: Noeline Quirke.

HON. SECRETARY: Tom McNally.

Course Description:

Links course which is playable all year round. Good greens protected by pot bunkers, with undulating fairways. Alternate tees except on two par 3's.

NO.	BLUE METRES	WHITE METRES	PAR	S.I.	NO.	BLUE METRES	WHITE METRES	PAR	S.I.
1	283	279	4	13	10	295	293	4	14
2	340	333	4	3	11	363	358	4	1
3	535	522	5	2	12	527	519	5	5
4	352	348	4	6	13	347	343	4	10
5	330	328	4	12	14	366	357	4	11
6	192	188	3	9	15	192	188	3	8
7	370	366	4	4	16	363	359	4	7
8	141	134	3	15	17	136	134	3	16
9	243	230	4	18	18	268	265	4	17
OUT	2,786	2,728	35		IN	2,857	2,816	35	
					TOTAL	5,643	5,544	70	
					STANDARD SCRATCH	71	70		

Course Information:

Par 70; SSS 70; Length 5,643 metres.
Visitors: Welcome Monday - Friday.
Opening Hours: 8.00am – sunset. **Avoid:** weekends. **Ladies:** Welcome. **Green Fees:** €32 (€15 with member). **Clubhouse Hours:** 11.00am – 11.00pm. **Clubhouse Dress:** Smart Casual. **Clubhouse Facilities:** Available on request. **Open Competitions:** Seniors only on 4th Friday in May each year and on every Tuesday during the winter months.

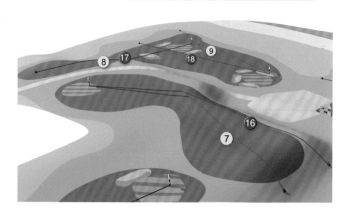

Roganstown

Course Information:
Par 71; SSS 74; Length 7,000 yards. **Visitors:** Welcome **Opening Hours:** 7.30am – Dusk. **Ladies:** Welcome. **Juveniles:** Permitted with Adult. **Green Fees:** Mon-Thurs €60, Fri-Sat and Bank Holidays €70. Winter and early bird specials available on request. **Clubhouse Dress:** Smart casual (no jeans). **Clubhouse Facilities:** Restaurant, bars, hotel accommodation, conference facilities, leisure club and swimming pool.

Roganstown, Swords, Co. Dublin
Tel: (01) 843 3118 **Email:** info@roganstown.com
Web: www.roganstown.com

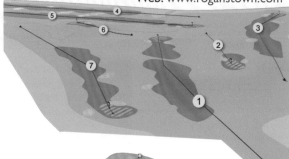

Course Description:
Renowned as one of Ireland's legendary golfers and now one of the world's most established golf course designers, Christy O'Connor Jnr, has created a masterpiece of skill and tactical design at Roganstown Golf & Country Club. Set among peaceful lakes, rolling hills and picturesque homes, this sanctuary for golf lovers has blended an exciting challenge and pure pleasure into a layout of outstanding beauty. The Broadmeadow River flows beside the course and water comes into play on all but 6 holes. From the first drive to the last put, the course is designed for the players maximum enjoyment.

NO.	MEDAL YARDS	GEN. YARDS	PAR	S.I.	NO.	MEDAL YARDS	GEN. YARDS	PAR	S.I.
1	434	413	4	4	10	532	489	5	11
2	195	170	3	14	11	419	401	4	7
3	441	414	4	8	12	206	180	3	15
4	544	522	5	16	13	446	414	4	1
5	519	504	5	6	14	409	390	4	13
6	196	182	3	10	15	417	398	4	9
7	445	428	4	2	16	446	417	4	3
8	388	372	4	12	17	199	175	3	17
9	172	154	3	18	18	592	565	5	5
OUT	3,334	3,159	35		IN	3,666	3,429	36	
					TOTAL	7,000	6,588	71	
					STANDARD SCRATCH			74	

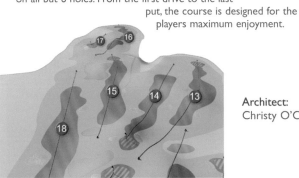

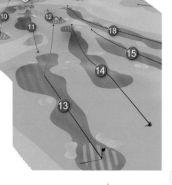

Architect:
Christy O'Connor Jnr.

Hacketstown, Skerries, Co. Dublin.
Tel: (01) 8491567/8491204
Fax: (01) 8491591

LOCATION: 20 miles north of Dublin.

PROFESSIONAL: Bobby.
Tel: (01) 8490925

www.skerriesgolfclub.ie
admin@skerriesgolfclub.ie

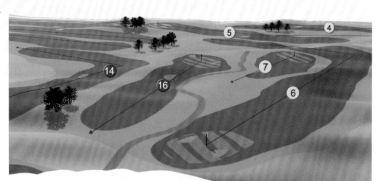

Course Information:

Par 73; SSS 72; Length 6,097 metres.
Visitors: Welcome Mon – Fri. **Avoid:**
Wednesday, Saturday and Sunday. **Opening
Hours:** Sunrise – sunset. **Ladies Day:** Tuesday. **Green
Fees:** €50 weekdays and €60 weekends, contact for
specials. Members Time is from 12.30pm - 2.00pm.
Juveniles: Must be accompanied by an adult.
Clubhouse Hours: 9.00am – 11.30pm. **Clubhouse
Dress:** Neat/Casual. No denims. **Clubhouse Facilities:**
Snacks lunches, dinner available daily. **Open
Competitions:** Junior Scratch Cup – May; Intermediate
Scratch Cup – June; Open Week – July.

Course Description:

A rolling parkland course with splendid views
of the coastline. Many of the holes demand
accuracy from the tee to the green. The
12th (par 3) and 18th (par 4)
are particularly attractive holes.
The newer 4th (par 5), 6th (par
5) and 7th (par 3) have
enhanced the course as a good
test of golf.

NO.	MEDAL METRES	GEN. METRES	PAR	S.I.	NO.	MEDAL METRES	GEN. METRES	PAR	S.I.
1	370	369	4	3	10	354	346	4	6
2	154	147	3	15	11	267	256	4	18
3	393	386	4	1	12	131	122	3	16
4	419	410	5	17	13	366	357	4	4
5	393	383	4	5	14	449	438	5	14
6	470	465	5	7	15	144	133	3	12
7	144	135	3	13	16	372	362	4	8
8	479	470	5	9	17	485	481	5	10
9	320	311	4	11	18	371	362	4	2
OUT	3,142	3,076	37		IN	2,939	2,857	36	
				TOTAL		6,081	5,933	73	
				STANDARD SCRATCH		72	71		

Lynch Park, Brittas,
Co. Dublin.
Tel: (01) 4582183.

SECRETARY:
Dermot Clancy.
Tel: 01 4582183.

ARCHITECT: W. Sullivan
& D. O'Brien.

NO.	MEDAL METRES	GEN. METRES	PAR	S.I.	NO.	MEDAL METRES	GEN. METRES	PAR	S.I.
1	390	421	4	4	10	383	395	4	5
2	164	176	3	8	11	371	373	4	1
3	324	330	4	10	12	320	334	4	15
4	248	252	4	16	13	112	123	3	17
5	114	123	3	14	14	282	288	4	13
6	251	276	4	6	15	320	335	4	9
7	423	440	5	2	16	363	375	4	7
8	275	280	4	12	17	164	170	3	11
9	390	395	4	2	18	372	382	4	3
OUT	2,579	2,693	35		IN	2,687	2,775	34	
TOTAL						5,266	5,468		
STANDARD SCRATCH						69	67		

Course Description:

Not a particularly demanding course, but the scenic views make for a very pleasant and relaxing game with some interesting holes. A "take it easy" course.

Course Information:

Par 69; SSS 68; Length 5,412 Metres. **Visitors:** Welcome Monday to Friday. **Opening Hours:** Sunrise – Sunset. **Avoid:** Weekends. **Ladies Day:** Tuesday. **Green Fees:** Weekdays – €30 (€15 with a member). **Juveniles:** Welcome. **Clubhouse Hours:** 8.30am – 12.00 midnight, peak season; Full clubhouse facilities. **Clubhouse Dress:** Neat dress. **Clubhouse Facilities:** All day.

PROFESSIONAL: John Dignam.

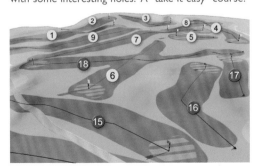

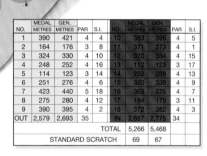

Lisheen Road, Brittas Village, Co Dublin
Tel: (01) 458 2965. Fax: (01) 458 2842
Pro Shop: 014583300 Bar: 014583302
E-mail: info@southcountygolf.ie
Web: www.southcountygolf.ie

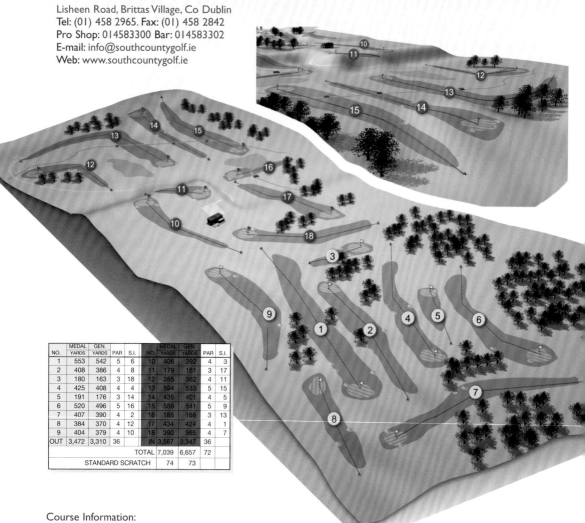

NO.	MEDAL YARDS	GEN. YARDS	PAR	S.I.	NO.	MEDAL YARDS	GEN. YARDS	PAR	S.I.
1	553	542	5	6	10	406	392	4	3
2	408	386	4	8	11	179	161	3	17
3	180	163	3	18	12	385	362	4	11
4	425	408	4	4	13	594	533	5	15
5	191	176	3	14	14	435	401	4	5
6	520	496	5	16	15	559	541	5	9
7	407	390	4	2	16	185	168	3	13
8	384	370	4	12	17	434	424	4	1
9	404	379	4	10	18	390	365	4	7
OUT	3,472	3,310	36		IN	3,567	3,347	36	
					TOTAL	7,039	6,657	72	
					STANDARD SCRATCH	74	73		

Course Information:

Par 72; SSS 73; Length 7,050 metres. Visitors: Sat and Sun,
not before 12.00pm. Opening Hours: 8:00am – 6:00pm. Ladies
Day: Tuesday 9:00am – 11:00pm. Green Fees: €50 Mon to Fri,
Early bird - before 10.00am, Mon to Fri, €30 (green fees are
subject to change). Juveniles: Welcome. Clubhouse Hours:
11:30pm during the week, 12:00pm at weekends. Clubhouse
Dress: Smart Casual. Denium not allowed, limited use of
mobiles. Clubhouse Facilities: Bar and Restaurant. Open
Competitions: Invitation competition only.

Course Description:

The quality of a golf course is very
dependant on the site one has been
given. At the South County all the
attributes were there, including adequate
area, wonderful surroundings, water and
undulating terrain.

LOCATION: Brittas village on the
Blessington Road only 7 miles from
the M50.

GENERAL MANAGER:

Vincent O' Reilly

SECRETARY: Olivia Molloy.

ARCHITECT:
Dr Nick Bielenberg.

Kilternan, Co. Dublin.
Tel: (01) 2952859
E-mail: stepaside@golfdublin.com
Web: www.golfdublin.com

LOCATION: Eight miles south of Dublin City.

SECRETARY: Mark Keogh.
Tel: (01) 2952859

ARCHITECT: E. Hackett.

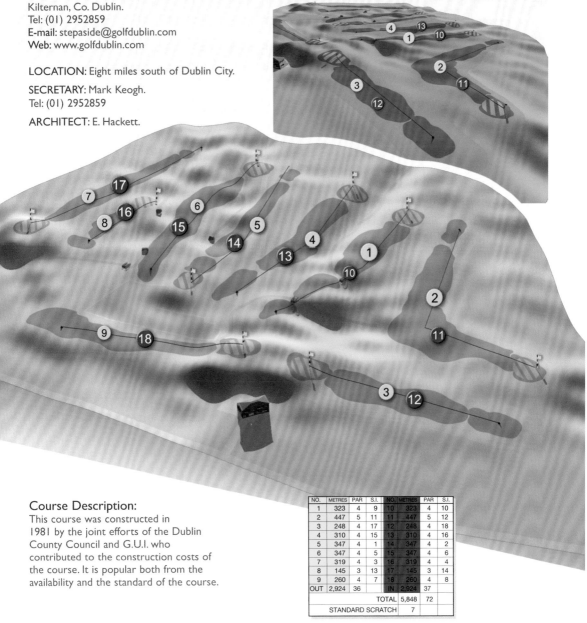

Course Description:

This course was constructed in
1981 by the joint efforts of the Dublin
County Council and G.U.I. who
contributed to the construction costs of
the course. It is popular both from the
availability and the standard of the course.

NO.	METRES	PAR	S.I.	NO.	METRES	PAR	S.I.
1	323	4	9	10	323	4	10
2	447	5	11	11	447	5	12
3	248	4	17	12	248	4	18
4	310	4	15	13	310	4	16
5	347	4	1	14	347	4	2
6	347	4	5	15	347	4	6
7	319	4	3	16	319	4	4
8	145	3	13	17	145	3	14
9	260	4	7	18	260	4	8
OUT	2,924	36		IN	2,924	37	
				TOTAL	5,848	72	
				STANDARD SCRATCH		7	

Course Information:

Par 72; SSS 70; Length 5,492 metres.
Visitors: Welcome. Opening Hours: 8.00am
– sunset. Green Fees: €17 Mon – Fri; €12
concession Mon-Fri 8.00am-2.00pm; €24
Weekend, bank and public holidays.
Juveniles: Welcome. Clubhouse Hours:
8.00am – sunset. Clubhouse Dress: Casual.
Clubhouse Facilities: Snacks available.

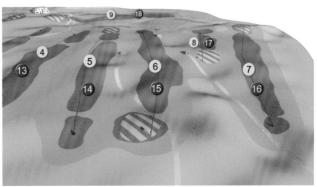

LOCATION: Eight miles north of city centre.
PROFESSIONAL : John Kelly.
ARCHITECT: Tom Craddock & Pat Ruddy
Email: reservations@stmargaretsgolf.com
www.stmargaretsgolf.com

St Margarets Golf & Country Club, St. Margarets,
Co. Dublin. Tel: (01) 864 0400. Fax: (01) 864 0408.

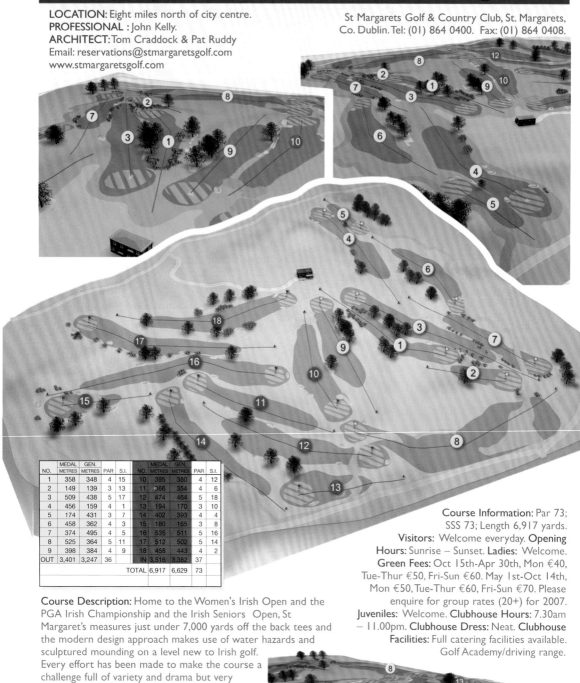

NO.	MEDAL METRES	GEN. METRES	PAR	S.I.	NO.	MEDAL METRES	GEN. METRES	PAR	S.I.
1	358	348	4	15	10	395	380	4	12
2	149	139	3	13	11	366	354	4	6
3	509	438	5	17	12	474	464	5	18
4	456	159	4	1	13	194	170	3	10
5	174	431	3	7	14	402	393	4	4
6	458	362	4	3	15	180	165	3	8
7	374	495	4	5	16	535	511	5	16
8	525	364	5	11	17	512	502	5	14
9	398	384	4	9	18	458	443	4	2
OUT	3,401	3,247	36		IN	3,516	3,382	37	
					TOTAL	6,917	6,629	73	

Course Information: Par 73;
SSS 73; Length 6,917 yards.
Visitors: Welcome everyday. **Opening
Hours:** Sunrise – Sunset. **Ladies:** Welcome.
Green Fees: Oct 15th-Apr 30th, Mon €40,
Tue-Thur €50, Fri-Sun €60. May 1st-Oct 14th,
Mon €50, Tue-Thur €60, Fri-Sun €70. Please
enquire for group rates (20+) for 2007.
Juveniles: Welcome. **Clubhouse Hours:** 7.30am
– 11.00pm. **Clubhouse Dress:** Neat. **Clubhouse
Facilities:** Full catering facilities available.
Golf Academy/driving range.

Course Description: Home to the Women's Irish Open and the
PGA Irish Championship and the Irish Seniors Open, St
Margaret's measures just under 7,000 yards off the back tees and
the modern design approach makes use of water hazards and
sculptured mounding on a level new to Irish golf.
Every effort has been made to make the course a
challenge full of variety and drama but very
playable by all standards of player. 15 mins from
city centre.

Swords Open Golf Course, Balheary Avenue, Swords, Co. Dublin.
Tel: (01) 840 9819
Email: info@swordsopengolfcourse.com
www.swordsopengolfcourse.com

SECRETARY: Orla McGuinness.
ARCHITECT: Tommy Halpin.

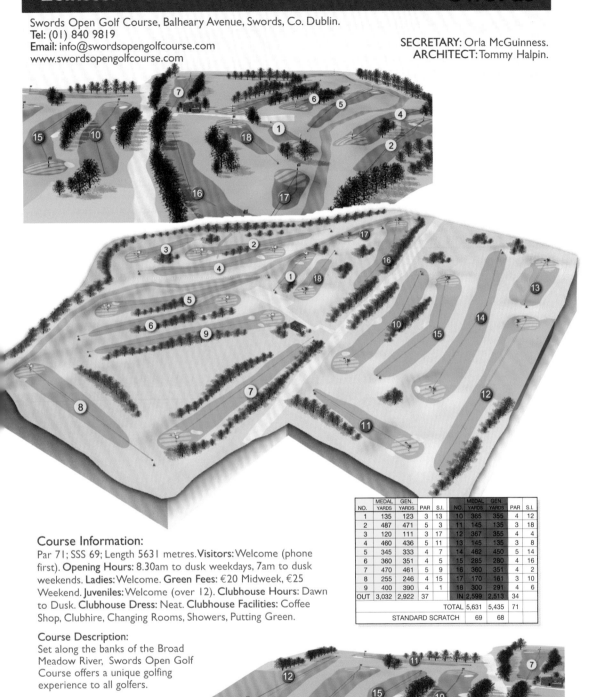

Course Information:

Par 71; SSS 69; Length 5631 metres. **Visitors:** Welcome (phone first). **Opening Hours:** 8.30am to dusk weekdays, 7am to dusk weekends. **Ladies:** Welcome. **Green Fees:** €20 Midweek, €25 Weekend. **Juveniles:** Welcome (over 12). **Clubhouse Hours:** Dawn to Dusk. **Clubhouse Dress:** Neat. **Clubhouse Facilities:** Coffee Shop, Clubhire, Changing Rooms, Showers, Putting Green.

Course Description:

Set along the banks of the Broad Meadow River, Swords Open Golf Course offers a unique golfing experience to all golfers.

NO.	MEDAL YARDS	GEN. YARDS	PAR	S.I.	NO.	MEDAL YARDS	GEN. YARDS	PAR	S.I.
1	135	123	3	13	10	365	355	4	12
2	487	471	5	3	11	145	135	3	18
3	120	111	3	17	12	367	355	4	4
4	460	436	5	11	13	145	135	3	8
5	345	333	4	7	14	462	450	5	14
6	360	351	4	5	15	285	280	4	16
7	470	461	5	9	16	360	351	4	2
8	255	246	4	15	17	170	161	3	10
9	400	390	4	1	18	300	291	4	6
OUT	3,032	2,922	37		IN	2,599	2,513	34	
					TOTAL	5,631	5,435	71	
					STANDARD SCRATCH	69	68		

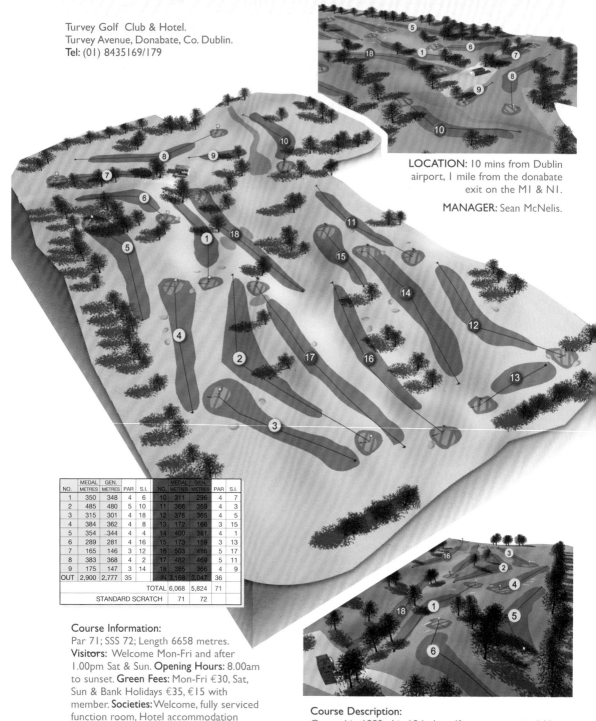

Turvey Golf Club & Hotel.
Turvey Avenue, Donabate, Co. Dublin.
Tel: (01) 8435169/179

LOCATION: 10 mins from Dublin airport, 1 mile from the donabate exit on the M1 & N1.

MANAGER: Sean McNelis.

NO.	MEDAL METRES	GEN. METRES	PAR	S.I.	NO.	MEDAL METRES	GEN. METRES	PAR	S.I.
1	350	348	4	6	10	311	296	4	7
2	485	480	5	10	11	366	359	4	3
3	315	301	4	18	12	376	365	4	5
4	384	362	4	8	13	172	166	3	15
5	354	344	4	4	14	400	381	4	1
6	289	281	4	16	15	173	159	3	13
7	165	146	3	12	16	503	486	5	17
8	383	368	4	2	17	482	469	5	11
9	175	147	3	14	18	385	366	4	9
OUT	2,900	2,777	35		IN	3,168	3,047	36	
					TOTAL	6,068	5,824	71	
					STANDARD SCRATCH		71	72	

Course Information:
Par 71; SSS 72; Length 6658 metres.
Visitors: Welcome Mon-Fri and after 1.00pm Sat & Sun. **Opening Hours:** 8.00am to sunset. **Green Fees:** Mon-Fri €30, Sat, Sun & Bank Holidays €35, €15 with member. **Societies:** Welcome, fully serviced function room, Hotel accommodation available. **Clubhouse Hours:** 8.00am – 10.00pm. **Clubhouse Dress:** Casual. **Clubhouse Facilities:** Snacks and meals available in clubhouse, further facilities & accommodation available in Hotel.

Course Description:
Opened in 1993, this 18 hole golf course is set in 144 acres of beautiful north County Dublin countryside. The tree lined course provides a good challenge for golfers of all standards to test their skills and improve their game. Clubhouse opened in August 1999 provides many welcome features.

Carrickmines, Dublin 18.
Tel: (01) 295 5972/295 5941.

LOCATION: Carrickmines.
HON. SECRETARY: C.R. Bailey.
Tel: (01) 490 3400.

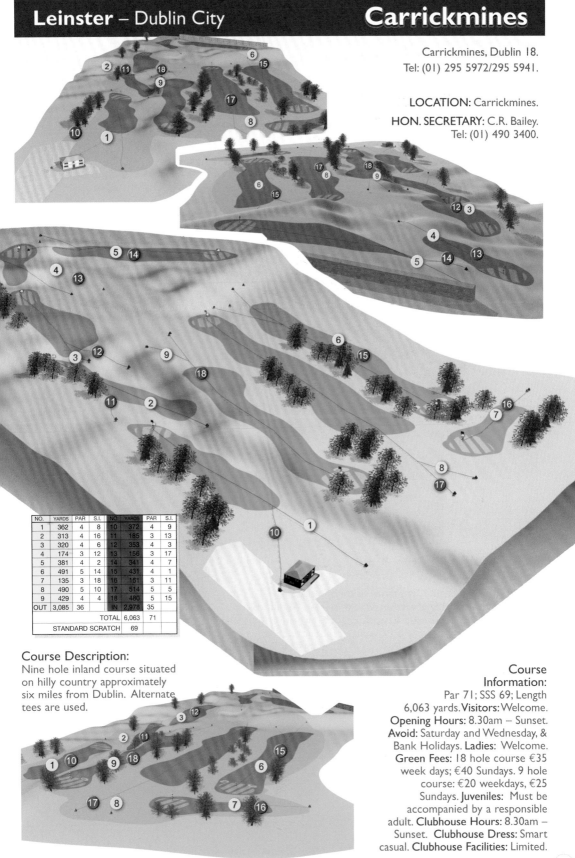

NO.	YARDS	PAR	S.I.	NO.	YARDS	PAR	S.I.
1	362	4	8	10	372	4	9
2	313	4	16	11	185	3	13
3	320	4	6	12	353	4	3
4	174	3	12	13	156	3	17
5	381	4	2	14	341	4	7
6	491	5	14	15	431	4	1
7	135	3	18	16	161	3	11
8	490	5	10	17	514	5	5
9	429	4	4	18	480	5	15
OUT	3,085	36		IN	2,978	35	
				TOTAL	6,063	71	
	STANDARD SCRATCH				69		

Course Description:
Nine hole inland course situated on hilly country approximately six miles from Dublin. Alternate tees are used.

Course Information:
Par 71; SSS 69; Length 6,063 yards. **Visitors:** Welcome. **Opening Hours:** 8.30am – Sunset. **Avoid:** Saturday and Wednesday, & Bank Holidays. **Ladies:** Welcome. **Green Fees:** 18 hole course €35 week days; €40 Sundays. 9 hole course: €20 weekdays, €25 Sundays. **Juveniles:** Must be accompanied by a responsible adult. **Clubhouse Hours:** 8.30am – Sunset. **Clubhouse Dress:** Smart casual. **Clubhouse Facilities:** Limited.

PROFESSIONAL: D. Kinsella.
Tel: (01) 492 0272

ARCHITECT: Harry Colt.

LOCATION: Between Rathfarnham &
Churchtown.

SECRETARY: J. McCormack.
Tel: (01) 490 4207

E-mail: info@castlegc,ie
Web: www.castlegc.ie

Castle Golf Club, Woodside Drive, Rathfarnham, Dublin 14. Tel:
(01) 490 4207

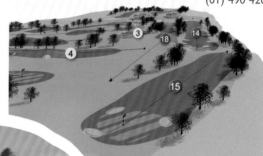

NO.	MEDAL YARDS	GEN. YARDS	PAR	S.I.	NO.	MEDAL YARDS	GEN. YARDS	PAR	S.I.
1	492	482	5	9	10	190	175	3	16
2	433	420	4	5	11	401	391	4	2
3	149	130	3	17	12	348	333	4	12
4	317	307	4	15	13	132	122	3	18
5	372	362	4	7	14	391	378	4	8
6	418	401	4	1	15	187	180	3	14
7	177	157	3	13	16	529	509	5	6
8	347	326	4	11	17	500	487	5	10
9	452	440	4	3	18	411	403	4	4
OUT	3,157	3,025	35		IN	3,089	2,978	35	
					TOTAL	6,246	6,003	70	
	STANDARD SCRATCH					71	70		

Course Information:

Par 70; SSS 71; Length 6,246 Yards. **Visitors:** Welcome.
Opening Hours: Sunrise - Sunset. **Avoid:** Tuesday, Wednesday
afternoons. **Ladies:** Tuesdays. Lessons available by prior
arrangements; Caddy trolleys available; telephone appointment required
(01) 492 2000. **Green Fees:** Visitor, €85. Members 1st guest, €20. Castle
Pavilion member, €22. Clergy, €22. Student, €30. Juvenile with member, €7.
Societies, €65. **Juveniles:** As Visitors, €20. Lessons available by prior arrangements;
Caddy trolleys available; telephone appointment required 01 492 2000. **Clubhouse Hours:**
8.30am - 11.30pm; Full clubhouse facilities. **Clubhouse Dress:** Casual dress in clubhouse.
Clubhouse Facilities: 10.00am - 10.30pm,
lunch, dinner, snacks & bar everyday. **Open
Competitions:** See website. Father & Son - July.

Course Description:

Very tight fairways – the Par 4 6th hole
regarded as one of the most difficult and
yet attractive golf holes. Spectacular views
from the Clubhouse.

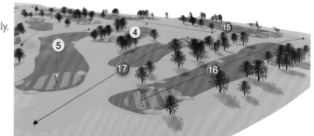

Clontarf Golf Club, Donnycarney House, Malahide Road, Dublin 3.
Tel: (01) 8331892.

LOCATION: Two miles from city centre.

PROFESSIONAL: Mark Callan.
Tel: (01) 8331877.

Club. SECRETARY:
Jerome Clancy.

ARCHITECT: Harry Colt.

Course Information:

Par 69; SSS 68; Length 5,345 metres. **Visitors:** Welcome Mon – Fri
(telephone first). **Avoid:** Monday. **Ladies:** Welcome. **Ladies Day:**
Monday. **Green Fees:** €30 Winter, €60 Weekends, €50 Summer, €60
Weekends. **Juveniles:** Must be accompanied by an adult member
if not before 10.00am. **Clubhouse Hours:** 9.00am – 12.00pm;
full clubhouse facilities. **Clubhouse Dress:** Casual (no
jeans). **Clubhouse Facilities:** Catering facilities:
meals and snacks everyday. **Open Competitions:**
AIB Lord Mayor's Cup (junior Matchplay)
August; Open Week – May;
Seniors Apr/May/Jun/Aug.

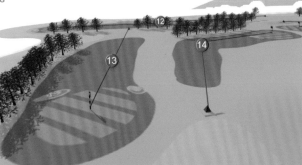

Course Description:

A pleasant
parkland course with
a quarry hole as a special
feature. Convenient city course with
good access.

NO.	CHAMP BLUE	SOCIETY GREEN	PAR	S.I.	NO.	CHAMP BLUE	SOCIETY GREEN	PAR	S.I.
1	305	297	4	10	10	363	356	4	7
2	410	401	4	2	11	183	176	3	11
3	288	281	4	14	12	332	326	4	1
4	139	124	3	12	13	247	247	4	13
5	343	334	4	6	14	326	320	4	3
6	130	118	3	18	15	147	135	3	17
7	336	349	4	8	16	352	344	4	5
8	353	347	4	4	17	351	343	4	9
9	290	279	4	16	18	450	442	5	15
OUT	2,594	2,504	34		IN	2,751	2,689	35	
					TOTAL	5,345	5,193	69	
					STANDARD SCRATCH	68	67		

Deer Park Hotel, Howth, Co. Dublin.
Tel: (01) 8322624/8320273. Fax: (01) 8392405.
Email: sales@deerpark.iol.ie Web: www.deerpark-hotel.ie

Course Information:
Par 72; SSS 73; Length 6,174 Metres.
Visitors: Welcome. Opening Hours:
8am – Sunset (Mon-Fri) & 6.30 –
Sunset (weekends). Ladies: Welcome.
Green Fees: €18 Mon – Fri; €27
Sat / Sun (18 holes). Juveniles:
Welcome. Club Hire and caddy
trolleys available. Clubhouse
Hours: Sunrise – Sunset.
Clubhouse facilities: Full catering
and bar facilities available at
Hotel – other leisure facilities
also.

MANAGER: David Tigne.
LOCATION: Howth Head.
SECRETARY: David Tighe.

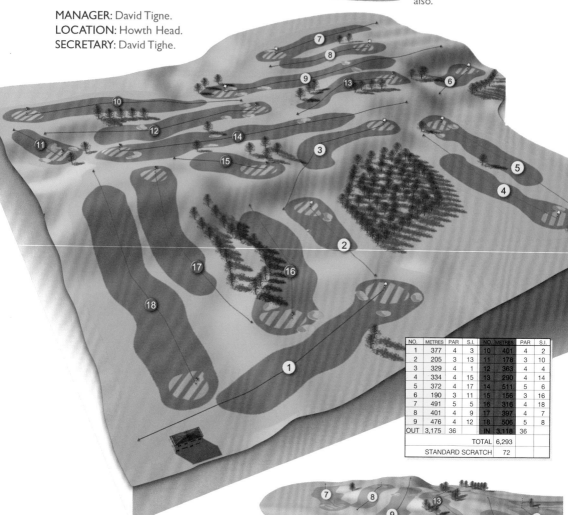

NO.	METRES	PAR	S.I.	NO.	METRES	PAR	S.I.
1	377	4	3	10	401	4	2
2	205	3	13	11	178	3	10
3	329	4	1	12	363	4	4
4	334	4	15	13	290	4	14
5	372	4	17	14	511	5	6
6	190	3	11	15	156	3	16
7	491	5	5	16	316	4	18
8	401	4	9	17	397	4	7
9	476	4	12	18	506	5	8
OUT	3,175	36		IN	3,118	36	
				TOTAL	6,293		
				STANDARD SCRATCH		72	

Course Description:
A busy course with both visitors and
holiday makers, especially during August,
well served by the adjacent Deer Park
Hotel – another 18 hole and a 9 hole
course are also included as part of
the hotel facilities.

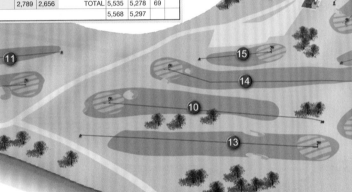

Ballinascorney, Dublin 24,
Tel: (01) 451 6430 / 451 2028
Fax: (01) 459 8445
Email: info@dublincitygolf.com
Web: www.dublincitygolf.com

LOCATION: Approx. ten miles south west of Dublin. 10mins from M50 motorway.

MANAGER: Frank Bagnall. Tel: (01) 4516430

NO.	WHITE YARDS	GREEN YARDS	PAR	S.I.	NO.	WHITE YARDS	GREEN YARDS	PAR	S.I.
1	405	329	4	5	10	378	364	4	2
2a/2b	116/149	116/135	3	15	11	272	250	4	8
3	319	285	4	3	12	292	273	4	18
4	207	202	3	7	13	427	411	4	4
5	484	470	5	9	14	460	447	5	10
6	338	324	4	13	15	150	135	3	14
7	198	185	3	11	16	348	338	4	12
8	274	265	4	17	17	123	112	3	16
9	415	400	3	1	18	329	311	4	6
OUT	2,756	2,637	34		IN	2,779	2,641	35	
	2,789	2,656			TOTAL	5,535	5,278	69	
						5,568	5,297		

Course Information:

Par 71; SSS 67; Length 5,464 metres. **Visitors:** Welcome 7 days a week (phone in advance) societies welcome. **Opening Hours:** Sunrise – sunset. **Green Fees:** €25 (weekdays) €36 (weekends) (subject to change). **Juveniles:** Welcome. **Clubhouse Hours:** 8.00am – 11.00pm. **Clubhouse Dress:** Smart / casual (no denim). **Clubhouse Facilities:** Snacks and full catering available. Trolly buggy & club hire available.

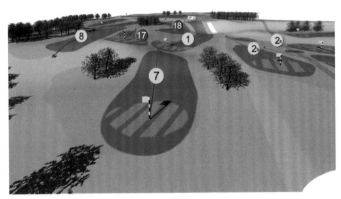

Course Description:

Dublin City Golf Club is set in the beautiful valley of Glen Na Smol (The valley of the thrush), overlooking the lakes and the River Dodder. The Course was originally designed by the late Eddie Hackett, with redesign work by Frank Clarke. The course would be described as parkland and the layout has been dictated by the terrain. The designers have taken full advantage of the varied terrain and produced a great variety of golf holes with very few parallel holes. Players never get bored with a new challange around every corner.

Edmondstown, Dublin 16. Tel: (01) 4931082.
Email: info@edmondstowngolfclub.ie
www.edmondstowngolfclub.ie
PRO SHOP: (01) 494 1049.
SECRETARY/MANAGER: Selwyn S. Davies.
HON. SECRETARY: R. Greenlee.

Course

Information:
Par 71; SSS 71;
Length 6,130 metres;
5,893 metres. Visitors:
Welcome to play Monday –
Friday. **Opening Hours:** 8.00am –
11.30pm. **Ladies:** Welcome. **Green
Fees:** Mon – Fri €55; Sat / Sun €65 (by
appointment). Lessons and electric caddy
service available by prior arrangement. 18th –
23th in July is Invitation Week. **Juveniles:** Welcome.
Must be accompanied by an adult. **Clubhouse Hours:**
8.00am – 11.30pm. **Clubhouse Dress:** Collar and tie in
restaurant. Neat casual dress on course. No denims.
Clubhouse Facilities: Coffee and snacks available 9.00am
onwards. Lunch: 12.30pm – 2.00pm. Dinner: 6.30pm –
11.00pm, to order if later.

Course Description:

Surrounded by beautiful countryside and
breathtaking scenery with hill and sea
views from golf course and newly
redeveloped Clubhouse. 30 minutes
from the centre of Dublin

NO.	WHITE METRES	YELLOW METRES	PAR	S.I.	NO.	WHITE METRES	YELLOW METRES	PAR	S.I.
1	376	365	4	3/7	10	310	287	4	14
2	338	318	4	9	11	338	319	4	10
3	153	143	3	15	12	477	460	5	4/2
4	494	480	5	7/3	13	140	110	3	16
5	391	366	4	1	14	358	329	4	6/4
6	382	366	4	5	15	275	257	4	18
7	451	426	5	13	16	322	309	4	12
8	160	138	3	17	17	166	140	3	8/6
9	330	312	4	11	18	380	366	4	2/8
OUT	3,075	2,914	36		IN	2,841	2,579	35	
					TOTAL	5,841	5,493		
					STANDARD SCRATCH		73	71	

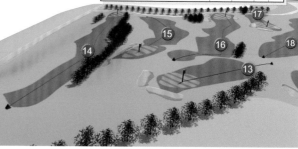

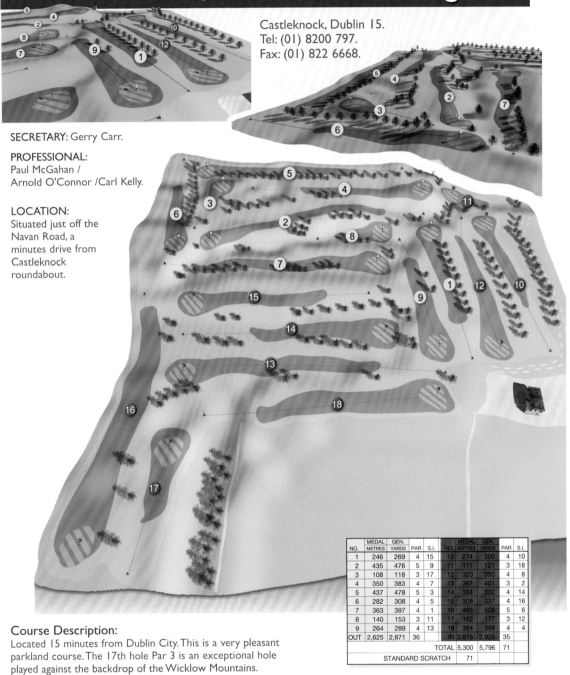

Castleknock, Dublin 15.
Tel: (01) 8200 797.
Fax: (01) 822 6668.

SECRETARY: Gerry Carr.

PROFESSIONAL:
Paul McGahan /
Arnold O'Connor /Carl Kelly.

LOCATION:
Situated just off the
Navan Road, a
minutes drive from
Castleknock
roundabout.

Course Description:
Located 15 minutes from Dublin City. This is a very pleasant
parkland course. The 17th hole Par 3 is an exceptional hole
played against the backdrop of the Wicklow Mountains.

NO.	MEDAL METRES	GEN. YARDS	PAR	S.I.	NO.	MEDAL METRES	GEN. YARDS	PAR	S.I.
1	246	269	4	15	10	274	300	4	10
2	435	476	5	9	11	111	121	3	18
3	108	118	3	17	12	320	350	4	8
4	350	383	4	7	13	367	401	3	2
5	437	478	5	3	14	304	332	4	14
6	282	308	4	5	15	308	337	4	16
7	363	397	4	1	16	465	509	5	6
8	140	153	3	11	17	162	177	3	12
9	264	289	4	13	18	364	398	4	4
OUT	2,625	2,871	36		IN	2,675	2,925	35	
					TOTAL	5,300	5,796	71	
					STANDARD SCRATCH		71		

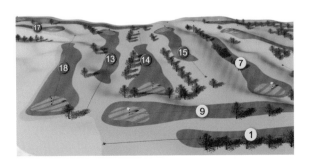

Course Information:
Par 71; SSS 68; Length 5,796 Yards. **Visitors:**
Welcome anytime. Telephone for booking.
Opening Hours: Dawn 'till Dusk. **Ladies:** Welcome
Anytime. **Green Fees:** €25 Weekdays. €32
Weekends. **Juveniles:** Welcome anytime.
Clubhouse Facilities: Changing Rooms / Showers.
Coffee Shop, restaurant. **Open Competitions:**
Varied contact club.

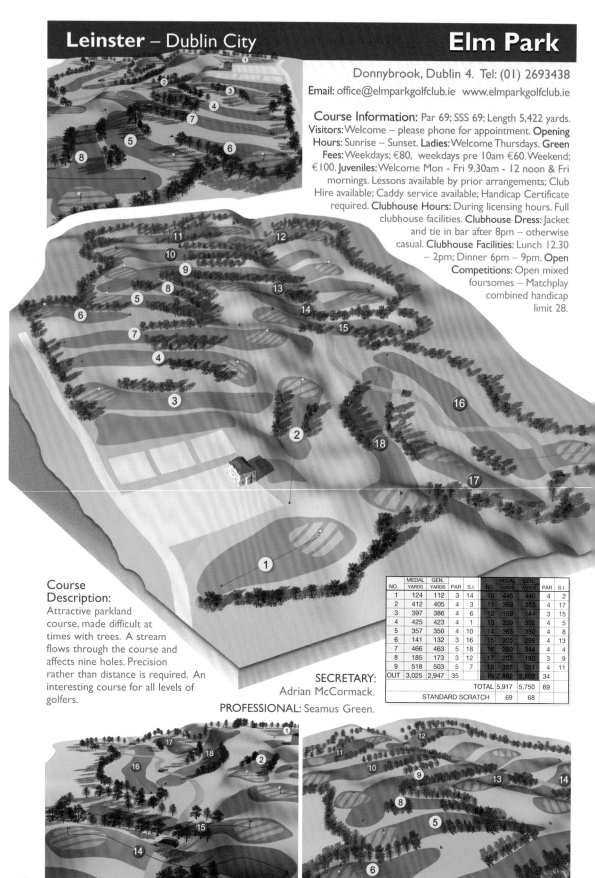

Donnybrook, Dublin 4. Tel: (01) 2693438
Email: office@elmparkgolfclub.ie www.elmparkgolfclub.ie

Course Information: Par 69; SSS 69; Length 5,422 yards.
Visitors: Welcome – please phone for appointment. **Opening Hours:** Sunrise – Sunset. **Ladies:** Welcome Thursdays. **Green Fees:** Weekdays; €80, weekdays pre 10am €60. Weekend; €100. **Juveniles:** Welcome Mon - Fri 9.30am - 12 noon & Fri mornings. Lessons available by prior arrangements; Club Hire available; Caddy service available; Handicap Certificate required. **Clubhouse Hours:** During licensing hours. Full clubhouse facilities. **Clubhouse Dress:** Jacket and tie in bar after 8pm – otherwise casual. **Clubhouse Facilities:** Lunch 12.30 – 2pm; Dinner 6pm – 9pm. **Open Competitions:** Open mixed foursomes – Matchplay combined handicap limit 28.

Course Description:

Attractive parkland course, made difficult at times with trees. A stream flows through the course and affects nine holes. Precision rather than distance is required. An interesting course for all levels of golfers.

SECRETARY: Adrian McCormack.

PROFESSIONAL: Seamus Green.

NO.	MEDAL YARDS	GEN. YARDS	PAR	S.I.	NO.	MEDAL YARDS	GEN. YARDS	PAR	S.I.
1	124	112	3	14	10	445	440	4	2
2	412	405	4	3	11	359	353	4	17
3	397	386	4	6	12	159	144	3	15
4	425	423	4	1	13	339	332	4	5
5	357	350	4	10	14	363	350	4	8
6	141	132	3	16	15	305	299	4	13
7	466	463	5	18	16	350	344	4	4
8	185	173	3	12	17	207	190	3	9
9	518	503	5	7	18	365	351	4	11
OUT	3,025	2,947	35		IN	2,892	2,803	34	
					TOTAL	5,917	5,750	69	
					STANDARD SCRATCH		69	68	

Torquay Road, Foxrock, Dublin 18.
Tel: (01) 2893992 /2895668.
www.foxrockgolfclub.com

LOCATION: South Dublin.
SEC/ MANAGER: Frank Hayes.
PROFESSIONAL: David Walker.
Tel: (01) 2893414. Fax: (01) 2894943.

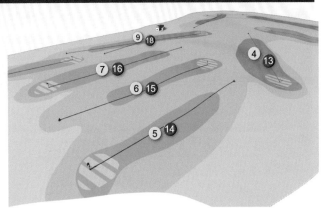

NO.	MEDAL METRES	GEN. METRES	PAR	S.I.	NO.	MEDAL METRES	GEN. METRES	PAR	S.I.
1	315	309	4	9	10	304	298	4	10
2	373	362	4	5	11	418	362	4	2
3	282	262	4	17	12	277	268	4	16
4	423	411	4	1	13	465	453	5	12
5	148	128	3	13	14	126	122	3	18
6	333	316	4	7	15	336	326	4	8
7	382	372	4	3	16	368	356	4	4
8	158	154	3	15	17	166	153	3	14
9	441	435	5	11	18	364	351	4	6
OUT	2,855	2,749	35		IN	2,812	2,890	35	
					TOTAL	5,667	5,439	70	
	STANDARD SCRATCH					69	68		

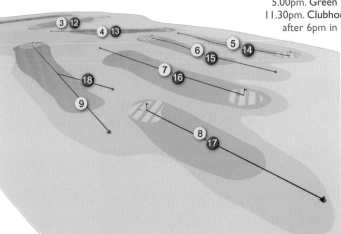

Course Information:
Par 70; SSS 69; Length 5,667 metres. Visitors:
Welcome Monday, Thursday and Friday mornings.
Opening Hours: 8.00am – Sunset. **Avoid:** Tues, Wed,
weekends. **Ladies:** Welcome. Lessons and Caddy service
available by prior arrangement; Club Hire available.
Juveniles: Welcome. Must be accompanied by an adult after
5.00pm. **Green Fees:** €65. **Clubhouse Hours:** 8.30am –
11.30pm. **Clubhouse Dress:** Smart/Casual. Jacket and tie
after 6pm in the Dining Room. **Clubhouse Facilities:**
Snacks in the bar; meals on
Wednesdays
and Saturdays.

Course Description:
Foxrock is a very flat course but it
nonetheless provides a reasonable
test of golf ability.

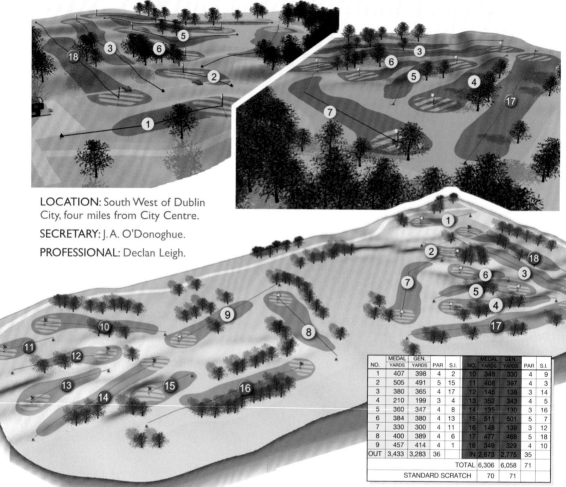

LOCATION: South West of Dublin City, four miles from City Centre.

SECRETARY: J. A. O'Donoghue.

PROFESSIONAL: Declan Leigh.

NO.	MEDAL YARDS	GEN. YARDS	PAR	S.I.	NO.	MEDAL YARDS	GEN. YARDS	PAR	S.I.
1	407	398	4	2	10	348	330	4	9
2	505	491	5	15	11	408	397	4	3
3	380	365	4	17	12	145	138	3	14
4	210	199	3	4	13	352	343	4	5
5	360	347	4	8	14	135	130	3	16
6	384	380	4	13	15	511	501	5	7
7	330	300	4	11	16	148	139	3	12
8	400	389	4	6	17	477	468	5	18
9	457	414	4	1	18	349	329	4	10
OUT	3,433	3,283	36		IN	2,873	2,775	35	
					TOTAL	6,306	6,058	71	
					STANDARD SCRATCH		70	71	

Course Information:
Par 69; SSS 70; Length 5,686 metres.
Visitors: Welcome to play during the week. **Opening Hours:** Sunrise – sunset. **Avoid:** Weekends (Members Only). **Ladies:** No green fees Tuesdays. **Green Fees:** €75 Mon – Fri. **Juveniles:** Welcome. Must be accompanied by an adult after 12.00 noon. Lessons available by prior arrangement; Caddy service available by prior arrangement; telephone appointment advisable. **Clubhouse Hours:** 8.00am – 12.30. **Clubhouse Facilities:** Full bar and catering facilities. **Clubhouse Dress:** Casual / neat (summer). Collar and tie (winter).

Whitechurch Road,
Rathfarnham, Dublin 16.
Tel: (01) 4932889.
Web: www.grangegolfclub.ie
Email: administration@grangegolfclub.ie

Course description:
Interesting and popular parkland course, with tree-lined fairways being a major feature, which is both attractive yet challenging.

Mount Seskin Road, Jobstown, Tallaght, Dublin 24. Tel: 4520911/4512010.

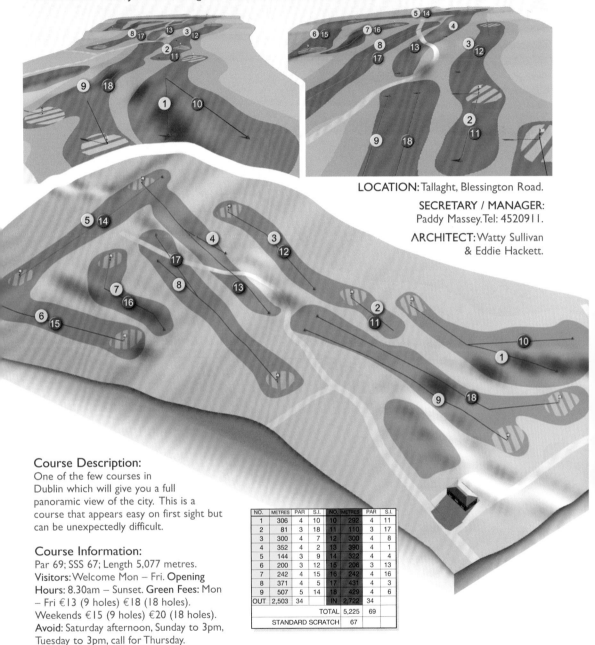

LOCATION: Tallaght, Blessington Road.

SECRETARY / MANAGER:
Paddy Massey. Tel: 4520911.

ARCHITECT: Watty Sullivan
& Eddie Hackett.

Course Description:
One of the few courses in
Dublin which will give you a full
panoramic view of the city. This is a
course that appears easy on first sight but
can be unexpectedly difficult.

Course Information:
Par 69; SSS 67; Length 5,077 metres.
Visitors: Welcome Mon – Fri. **Opening
Hours:** 8.30am – Sunset. **Green Fees:** Mon
– Fri €13 (9 holes) €18 (18 holes).
Weekends €15 (9 holes) €20 (18 holes).
Avoid: Saturday afternoon, Sunday to 3pm,
Tuesday to 3pm, call for Thursday.
Juveniles: Welcome. Lessons available by
prior arrangement; telephone
appointment required. **Clubhouse
Hours:** 8.30am – 11.30pm.
Clubhouse Dress: Neat / Casual.
Clubhouse Facilities: Full clubhouse
facilities. Catering facilities by prior
arrangement – Bar snacks throughout
the day. **Open Competitions:** Tuesday,
Fourballs from April – Sept; Open Week
June.

NO.	METRES	PAR	S.I.	NO.	METRES	PAR	S.I.
1	306	4	10	10	292	4	11
2	81	3	18	11	110	3	17
3	300	4	7	12	300	4	8
4	352	4	2	13	390	4	1
5	144	3	9	14	322	4	4
6	200	3	12	15	206	3	13
7	242	4	15	16	242	4	16
8	371	4	5	17	431	4	3
9	507	5	14	18	429	4	6
OUT	2,503	34		IN	2,722	34	
				TOTAL	5,225	69	
				STANDARD SCRATCH		67	

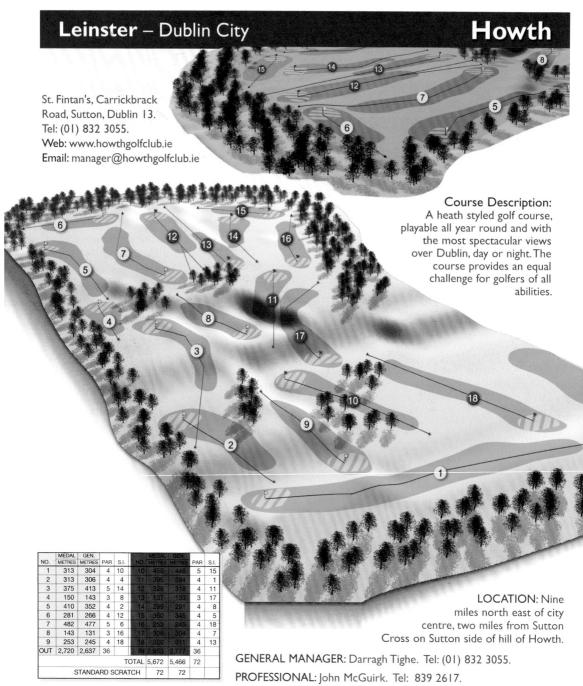

St. Fintan's, Carrickbrack
Road, Sutton, Dublin 13.
Tel: (01) 832 3055.
Web: www.howthgolfclub.ie
Email: manager@howthgolfclub.ie

Course Description:
A heath styled golf course,
playable all year round and with
the most spectacular views
over Dublin, day or night. The
course provides an equal
challenge for golfers of all
abilities.

NO.	MEDAL METRES	GEN. METRES	PAR	S.I.	NO.	MEDAL METRES	GEN. METRES	PAR	S.I.
1	313	304	4	10	10	455	446	5	15
2	313	306	4	4	11	395	384	4	1
3	375	413	5	14	12	326	318	4	11
4	150	143	3	8	13	137	133	3	17
5	410	352	4	2	14	299	291	4	8
6	281	266	4	12	15	360	345	4	5
7	482	477	5	6	16	253	245	4	18
8	143	131	3	16	17	308	304	4	7
9	253	245	4	18	18	320	311	4	13
OUT	2,720	2,637	36		IN	2,853	2,777	36	
					TOTAL	5,672	5,466	72	
					STANDARD SCRATCH	72	72		

LOCATION: Nine
miles north east of city
centre, two miles from Sutton
Cross on Sutton side of hill of Howth.

GENERAL MANAGER: Darragh Tighe. Tel: (01) 832 3055.

PROFESSIONAL: John McGuirk. Tel: 839 2617.

ARCHITECT: James Braid.

Course Information:
Par 71; SSS 69; Length 5,672 metres.
Visitors: Welcome weekdays except
Wednesday. **Opening Hours:** 8.30am –
Sunset. **Avoid:** 1.00pm – 2.00pm; All day
Wednesday, Thursday afternoons.
Lessons available by prior arrangements;
Golf buggies for hire €25. **Green Fees:**
€50 daily. **Clubhouse Hours:** 8.30am
–12.00pm. **Clubhouse Dress:** Informal.
No denim, training shoes or shorts in
Clubhouse. **Clubhouse Facilities:** Bar
snacks from 11.00am. **Open
Competitions:** Phone club for details.

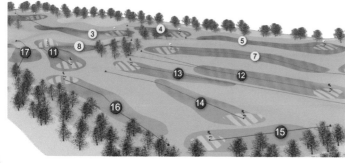

Luttrellstown Castle Golf & Country Club, Castleknock, Dublin 15.
Tel: (01) 808 9988
Email: golf@luttrellstown.ie
Web: www.luttrellstown.ie

Course Description:
Located just 20 minutes from Dublin city centre. This course is well manicured and regarded as having one of the best putting surfaces. "A Must" for the discerning golfer". Open Sept 2006, new Donald Steele designed course, new clubhouse, new restaurant, spike bar, well equipped shop, golf academy/driving range and practice area. Banqueting room available for group hire.

Course Information:
Par 72; SSS 74; Length 3,442 Yards. **Ladies Day:** Tuesday. **Visitors:** Welcome every day. **Green Fees:** €90 all week. **Juveniles:** €30. **Clubhouse Hours:** 8am-12am in Summer, Winter times vary. **Clubhouse Dress:** Neat dress - no denims. **Clubhouse facilities:** Spike bar, restaurant, pro shop, meeting facilities, function room.

LOCATION: West of Dublin City.

SECRETARY: Tony Weldon.

PROFESSIONAL: Edward Doyle.

ARCHITECT: Eddie Conaughton and Nick Bielenberg.

NO.	YARDS	PAR	S.I.	NO.	YARDS	PAR	S.I.
1	408	4	11	10	419	4	10
2	517	5	17	11	498	5	18
3	423	4	5	12	409	4	6
4	199	3	9	13	173	3	12
5	373	4	3	14	393	4	2
6	138	3	15	15	138	3	14
7	460	4	1	16	538	5	16
8	512	5	13	17	425	4	4
9	412	4	7	18	397	4	8
OUT	3,442	36		IN	3,390	36	
				TOTAL	6,832	72	
				STANDARD SCRATCH	70		

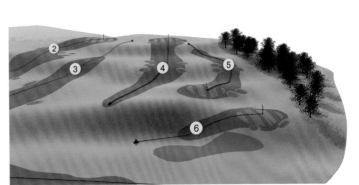

Lower Churchtown Road, Dublin 14.
Tel: (01) 4976090. **Fax:** (01) 4976008.

LOCATION: South Dublin three miles from the city centre.

GENERAL MANAGER: Eamonn Lawless.

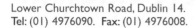

NO.	MEDAL YARDS	GEN. YARDS	PAR	S.I.	NO.	MEDAL YARDS	GEN. YARDS	PAR	S.I.
1	230	230	4	18	10	375	364	4	5
2	307	301	4	10	11	302	285	4	13
3	315	315	4	6	12	130	121	3	15
4	109	106	3	16	13	347	343	4	7
5	450	427	5	+1/12	14	434	433	5	+2/17
6	336	332	4	4	15	330	325	4	9
7	300	293	4	8	16	181	171	3	11
8	370	353	4	2	17	415	404	4	1
9	306	299	4	14	18	401	400	4	3
OUT	2,723	2,656	36		IN	2,915	2,846	35	
					TOTAL	5,638	5,502	71	
					STANDARD SCRATCH	70	69		

PROFESSIONAL: John Harnett.
Tel: (01) 4977072.

ARCHITECT: Freddie Davis.

Course Information:
Par 71; SSS 69;
Length 5,638 metres.
Visitors: Welcome.
Opening Hours: 8am – Sunset. **Avoid:** Weekends.
Ladies: Welcome. **Green Fees:** €85 Mon – Fri. **Juveniles:** Welcome. Lessons available by prior arrangement; club hire available. Telephone appointment is essential. Handicap Certificate required. **Clubhouse Hours:** 9.00am – 11.30pm. **Clubhouse Dress:** Neat/casual (no denim or training shoes). **Clubhouse Facilities:** Full clubhouse and catering facilities.

Course Description:
Well established parkland course on the suburbs of Dublin. One of the many Dublin clubs that provide convenient locations.

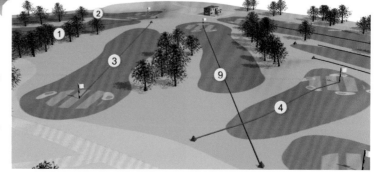

Newlands Cross, Dublin 22.
Tel: (01) 459 3157 / (01) 459 2903.
Fax: (01) 459 3498.

Course Information:

Par 71; SSS 70; Length 5,714 metres. **Visitors:** Welcome Monday, Thursday & Friday. Please contact office for full details. **Opening Hours:** Summer 7.30am-Sunset, Winter 9.00am – Sunset. **Avoid:** Tuesday, Saturday, Sunday. **Ladies Day:** Tuesdays. **Juveniles:** Must be accompanied by an adult after 6pm. Lessons and club hire available; telephone appointment required. **Green Fees:** €75 Mon – Fri (€20 with member). Societies: Negotiable please contact office for further details. **Clubhouse Hours:** 7.30am – 11.30pm (11pm on Sun). Full clubhouse facilities. **Clubhouse Dress:** Neat casual dress at all times in clubhouse and on course. **Clubhouse Facilities:** Full catering and bar; Summer 11.00am – 10.00pm; Winter 12.00pm – 6.00pm. **Open Competitions:** Husband and wife mixed foursomes – June.

NO.	BLUE METRES	GREEN METRES	PAR	S.I.	NO.	MEDAL METRES	GEN. METRES	PAR	S.I.
1	338	316	4	9	10	324	307	4	10
2	454	432	5	17	11	317	293	4	6
3	305	292	4	13	12	136	125	3	18
4	160	139	3	11	13	508	353	5	12
5	436	410	4	1	14	360	125	4	8
6	366	352	4	7	15	348	340	4	4
7	379	354	4	3	16	172	150	3	16
8	321	313	4	15	17	441	429	4	2
9	174	169	3	5	18	445	433	5	14
OUT	2,933	2,777	35		IN	3,049	2,906	36	
					TOTAL	5,982	5,683	71	
					STANDARD SCRATCH	70	69		

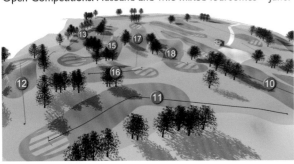

Course Description: Attractive, mature parkland course. The careful placing of trees, bunkers and other hazards soon dispels any feeling of complacency, even with the most accomplished of players.

GOLF OPERATIONS: Amber Dungan.

PROFESSIONAL: Karl O'Donnell.

ARCHITECT: James Braid.

Rathfarnham

Course Description:
Parkland course, with attractive scenery, mature trees and spinneys. Greens are built on the natural lie of the ground.

Newtown, Rathfarnham, Dublin 16.
Tel: (01) 4931201
LOCATION: Two miles from Rathfarnham Village.
SECRETARY/MANAGER: C Mc Inerny.
PROFESSIONAL: Brian O'Hara.
ARCHITECT: John Jacob..

NO.	WHITE METRES	YELLOW METRES	PAR	S.I.	NO.	WHITE METRES	YELLOW METRES	PAR	S.I.
1	310	302	4	8	10	282	301	4	5
2	137	135	3	18	11	297	345	4	11
3	464	460	5	14	12	89	417	3	17
4	375	368	4	2	13	227	170	4	9
5	307	301	4	12	14	370	363	4	1
6	350	345	4	4	15	336	328	4	3
7	450	434	5	16	16	154	135	3	15
8	180	170	3	6	17	461	449	5	13
9	292	284	4	10	18	343	340	4	7
OUT	2,865	2,799	36		IN	2,865	2,799	35	
					TOTAL	5,424	5,294	71	
					STANDARD SCRATCH	69	69		

Course Information:
Par 71; SSS 70; Length 5,815 metres. **Visitors:** Welcome Monday, Wednesday & Friday. **Opening Hours:** 8.30am – Sunset. Avoid: Tues, Sat, Sun & Bank Holidays. **Ladies:** Welcome (Handicap Certificate required). **Green Fees:** €40 Mon – Fri (€15 with member); €38 Sun. **Juveniles:** Welcome with member only. Lessons available by prior arrangements. **Clubhouse Hours:** 10.30am – 11.00pm. **Clubhouse Dress:** Jacket and tie after 7.30pm. **Clubhouse Facilities:** Light snacks daily; meals by prior arrangements.

Dollymount, Dublin 3. **Tel:** (01) 833 6346 **or** (01) 833 1262. **Fax:** (01) 833 6504
Email: info@theroyaldublingolfclub.com   www.theroyaldublingolfclub.com

LOCATION: Three miles north east from the city centre along the coast road.

CHIEF EXECUTIVE: Paul Muldowney

PROFESSIONAL: Leonard Owens.
Tel: (01) 833 6477

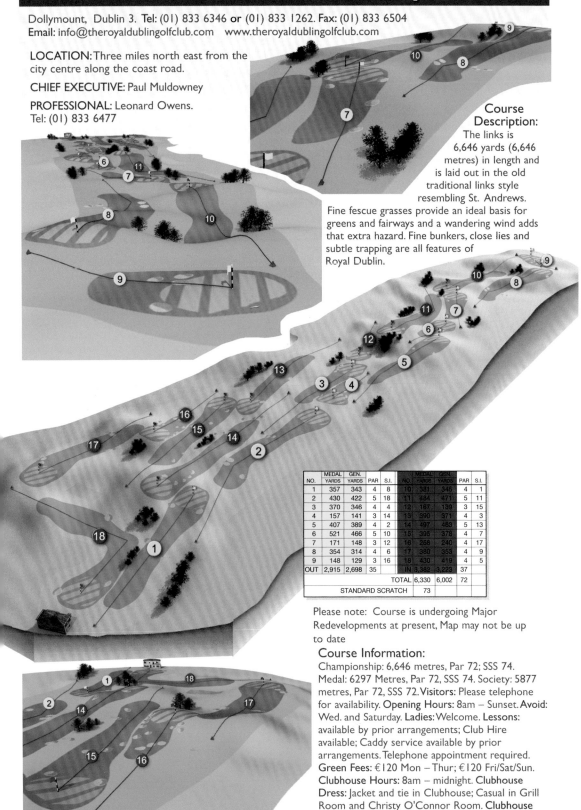

Course Description:
The links is 6,646 yards (6,646 metres) in length and is laid out in the old traditional links style resembling St. Andrews. Fine fescue grasses provide an ideal basis for greens and fairways and a wandering wind adds that extra hazard. Fine bunkers, close lies and subtle trapping are all features of Royal Dublin.

NO.	MEDAL YARDS	GEN. YARDS	PAR	S.I.	NO.	MEDAL YARDS	GEN. YARDS	PAR	S.I.
1	357	343	4	8	10	381	345	4	1
2	430	422	5	18	11	484	471	5	11
3	370	346	4	4	12	167	139	3	15
4	157	141	3	14	13	390	371	4	3
5	407	389	4	2	14	497	483	5	13
6	521	466	5	10	15	395	378	4	7
7	171	148	3	12	16	258	240	4	17
8	354	314	4	6	17	380	353	4	9
9	148	129	3	16	18	430	419	4	5
OUT	2,915	2,698	35		IN	3,382	3,223	37	
					TOTAL	6,330	6,002	72	
					STANDARD SCRATCH		73		

Please note: Course is undergoing Major Redevelopments at present, Map may not be up to date

Course Information:
Championship: 6,646 metres, Par 72; SSS 74. Medal: 6297 Metres, Par 72, SSS 74. Society: 5877 metres, Par 72, SSS 72. **Visitors:** Please telephone for availability. **Opening Hours:** 8am – Sunset. **Avoid:** Wed. and Saturday. **Ladies:** Welcome. **Lessons:** available by prior arrangements; Club Hire available; Caddy service available by prior arrangements. Telephone appointment required. **Green Fees:** €120 Mon – Thur; €120 Fri/Sat/Sun. **Clubhouse Hours:** 8am – midnight. **Clubhouse Dress:** Jacket and tie in Clubhouse; Casual in Grill Room and Christy O'Connor Room. **Clubhouse Facilities:** Full facilities available.

North Bull Island Nature Reserve,
North Bull Island, Dublin, 5.
Tel: (01) 833 6471 Fax: (01) 833 4618

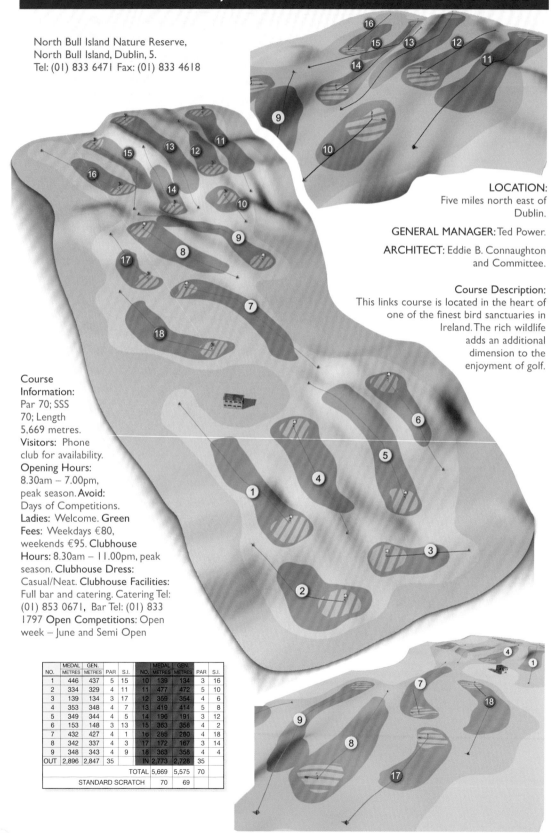

LOCATION:
Five miles north east of
Dublin.

GENERAL MANAGER: Ted Power.

ARCHITECT: Eddie B. Connaughton
and Committee.

Course Description:
This links course is located in the heart of
one of the finest bird sanctuaries in
Ireland. The rich wildlife
adds an additional
dimension to the
enjoyment of golf.

Course
Information:
Par 70; SSS
70; Length
5.669 metres.
Visitors: Phone
club for availability.
Opening Hours:
8.30am – 7.00pm,
peak season. Avoid:
Days of Competitions.
Ladies: Welcome. Green
Fees: Weekdays €80,
weekends €95. Clubhouse
Hours: 8.30am – 11.00pm, peak
season. Clubhouse Dress:
Casual/Neat. Clubhouse Facilities:
Full bar and catering. Catering Tel:
(01) 853 0671, Bar Tel: (01) 833
1797 Open Competitions: Open
week – June and Semi Open

NO.	MEDAL METRES	GEN. METRES	PAR	S.I.	NO.	MEDAL METRES	GEN. METRES	PAR	S.I.
1	446	437	5	15	10	139	134	3	16
2	334	329	4	11	11	477	472	5	10
3	139	134	3	17	12	359	354	4	6
4	353	348	4	7	13	419	414	5	8
5	349	344	4	5	14	196	191	3	12
6	153	148	3	13	15	363	358	4	2
7	432	427	4	1	16	285	280	4	18
8	342	337	4	3	17	172	167	3	14
9	348	343	4	9	18	363	358	4	4
OUT	2,896	2,847	35		IN	2,773	2,728	35	
					TOTAL	5,669	5,575	70	
	STANDARD SCRATCH					70	69		

Kellystown Road, Rathfarnham,
Dublin 16. Tel: (01) 494 1993.
Email: stackstowngc@eircom.net Web: www.stackstowngolfclub.ie

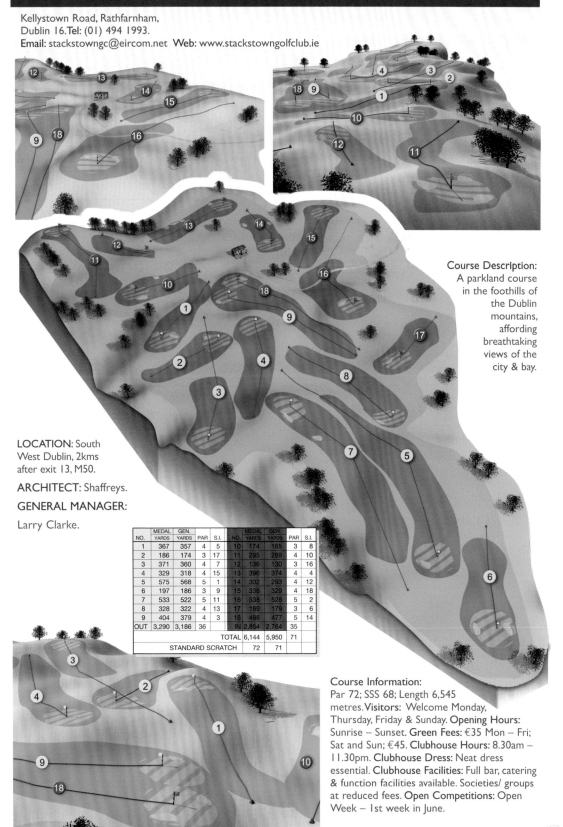

Course Description:
A parkland course in the foothills of the Dublin mountains, affording breathtaking views of the city & bay.

LOCATION: South West Dublin, 2kms after exit 13, M50.

ARCHITECT: Shaffreys.

GENERAL MANAGER:

Larry Clarke.

NO.	MEDAL YARDS	GEN. YARDS	PAR	S.I.	NO.	MEDAL YARDS	GEN. YARDS	PAR	S.I.
1	367	357	4	5	10	174	165	3	8
2	186	174	3	17	11	295	289	4	10
3	371	360	4	7	12	136	130	3	16
4	329	318	4	15	13	396	374	4	4
5	575	568	5	1	14	302	293	4	12
6	197	186	3	9	15	336	329	4	18
7	533	522	5	11	16	538	528	5	2
8	328	322	4	13	17	189	179	3	6
9	404	379	4	3	18	488	477	5	14
OUT	3,290	3,186	36		IN	2,854	2,764	35	
					TOTAL	6,144	5,950	71	
					STANDARD SCRATCH	72	71		

Course Information:
Par 72; SSS 68; Length 6,545 metres. **Visitors:** Welcome Monday, Thursday, Friday & Sunday. **Opening Hours:** Sunrise – Sunset. **Green Fees:** €35 Mon – Fri; Sat and Sun; €45. **Clubhouse Hours:** 8.30am – 11.30pm. **Clubhouse Dress:** Neat dress essential. **Clubhouse Facilities:** Full bar, catering & function facilities available. Societies/ groups at reduced fees. **Open Competitions:** Open Week – 1st week in June.

Cush Point, Sutton, Dublin 13. Tel: (01) 8323013.

LOCATION: Ten minutes from City centre.

HONORARY SECRETARY: Enda O'Brien.

PROFESSIONAL: Nicky Lynch.
Tel: (01)8321703.

MANAGER: Michael Healy.

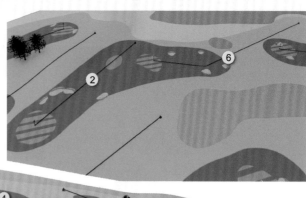

NO.	YARDS	PAR	S.I.	NO.	YARDS	PAR	S.I.
1	310	4	13	10	310	4	14
2	346	4	15	11	346	4	16
3	524	5	11	12	514	5	12
4	320	4	5	13	320	4	2
5	171	3	7	14	171	3	8
6	107	3	17	15	107	3	18
7	351	4	9	16	351	4	10
8	387	4	3	17	387	4	4
9	383	4	1	18	383	4	6
OUT	2,889	35		IN	2,889	35	
				TOTAL	5,778	70	
STANDARD SCRATCH							

Course Description:
Links course with very narrow fairways and one of the main features is that the course is surrounded by water.

Course Information:
Par 70; SSS 67; Length 5,718 yards. **Visitors:** Welcome. **Opening Hours:** Sunrise – sunset. **Avoid:** Tuesday and Saturday. **Green Fees:** €50 (€20 with member). **Juveniles:** Welcome no weekend play. Lessons by prior arrangments. Caddy cars available. **Clubhouse Hours:** 9.00am onwards. **Clubhouse Dress:** Casual, no denims or trainers. **Clubhouse Facilities:** Full clubhouse facilities, by arrangement.

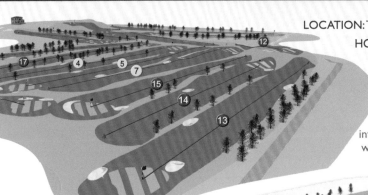

LOCATION: Two miles from Lucan Village.

HON. SECRETARY: John Doyle.

MANAGER: Brian Moran.
Tel: (01) 8205817.

ARCHITECT:
Mr Eddie Hackett.

info@westmanstowngolfclub.ie
www.westmanstowngolfclub.ie

Westmanstown,
Clonsilla, Dublin 15.
Tel: (01) 8205817.
Fax: (01) 8205858.

Course Description:
Flat parkland course
which has undergone
re-development and
an extensive drainage
programe making it
playable all year
round.

NO.	MEDAL METRES	GEN. METRES	PAR	S.I.	NO.	MEDAL METRES	GEN. METRES	PAR	S.I.
1	294	279	4	12	10	476	466	5	7
2	335	327	4	8	11	268	258	4	17
3	152	143	3	18	12	136	125	3	15
4	397	377	4	2	13	492	483	5	3
5	367	360	4	6	14	364	356	4	11
6	140	118	3	16	15	422	394	4	1
7	491	483	5	10	16	180	161	3	5
8	387	379	4	4	17	435	430	5	13
9	150	142	3	14	18	340	332	4	9
OUT	2,713	2,608	34		IN	3,113	3,005	37	
					TOTAL	5,826	5,613	71	
	STANDARD SCRATCH					71	71		

Course Information:
Par 71; SSS 70; Length 5,826
metres. **Visitors:** Welcome
Sat and Sun - phone for
appointment. **Opening Hours:** 8am – Sunset. **Ladies:** Welcome
Tuesdays. **Green Fees:** Weekdays €50; Sat, Sun & Bank Hols €60, €20
with member. **Clubhouse Hours:** 7.30am – 12.30pm. **Clubhouse Dress:**
Neat dress essential on course. **Clubhouse Facilities:** Full bar and catering
facilities all year round. **Semi Open Competitiions:** Invitation Four Ball
every Wednesday. **Open week:** 25th July – 31st July.

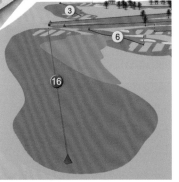

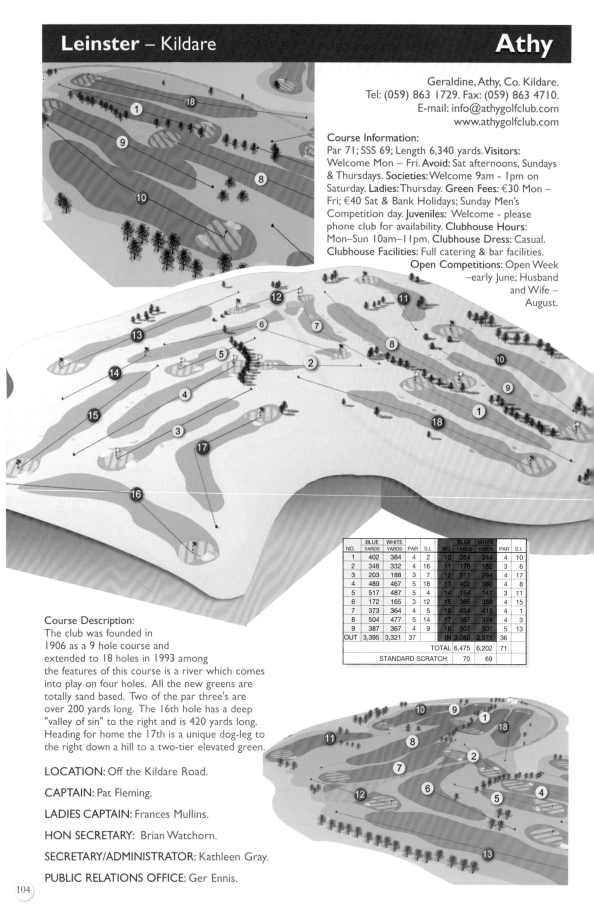

Geraldine, Athy, Co. Kildare.
Tel: (059) 863 1729. Fax: (059) 863 4710.
E-mail: info@athygolfclub.com
www.athygolfclub.com

Course Information:
Par 71; SSS 69; Length 6,340 yards. **Visitors:**
Welcome Mon – Fri. **Avoid:** Sat afternoons, Sundays
& Thursdays. **Societies:** Welcome 9am - 1pm on
Saturday. **Ladies:** Thursday. **Green Fees:** €30 Mon –
Fri; €40 Sat & Bank Holidays; Sunday Men's
Competition day. **Juveniles:** Welcome - please
phone club for availability. **Clubhouse Hours:**
Mon–Sun 10am–11pm. **Clubhouse Dress:** Casual.
Clubhouse Facilities: Full catering & bar facilities.

Open Competitions: Open Week
–early June; Husband
and Wife –
August.

NO.	BLUE YARDS	WHITE YARDS	PAR	S.I.	NO.	BLUE YARDS	WHITE YARDS	PAR	S.I.
1	402	384	4	2	10	354	344	4	10
2	348	332	4	16	11	176	162	3	6
3	203	188	3	7	12	311	294	4	17
4	489	467	5	18	13	402	380	4	8
5	517	487	5	4	14	154	147	3	11
6	172	165	3	12	15	365	356	4	15
7	373	364	4	5	16	424	413	4	1
8	504	477	5	14	17	387	374	4	3
9	387	367	4	9	18	507	501	5	13
OUT	3,395	3,321	37		IN	3,080	2,971	36	
					TOTAL	6,475	6,202	71	
				STANDARD SCRATCH		70	69		

Course Description:
The club was founded in
1906 as a 9 hole course and
extended to 18 holes in 1993 among
the features of this course is a river which comes
into play on four holes. All the new greens are
totally sand based. Two of the par three's are
over 200 yards long. The 16th hole has a deep
"valley of sin" to the right and is 420 yards long.
Heading for home the 17th is a unique dog-leg to
the right down a hill to a two-tier elevated green.

LOCATION: Off the Kildare Road.

CAPTAIN: Pat Fleming.

LADIES CAPTAIN: Frances Mullins.

HON SECRETARY: Brian Watchorn.

SECRETARY/ADMINISTRATOR: Kathleen Gray.

PUBLIC RELATIONS OFFICE: Ger Ennis.

Sallins, Co. Kildare.
Tel: (045) 897096 Fax: (045) 898126
Email: bodenstown@eircom.net

LOCATION: N7 south of Dublin, turn left at exit 7 for Straffan.

SECRETARY: Rita Mather.

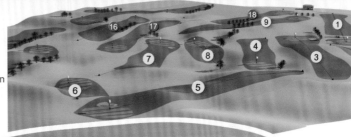

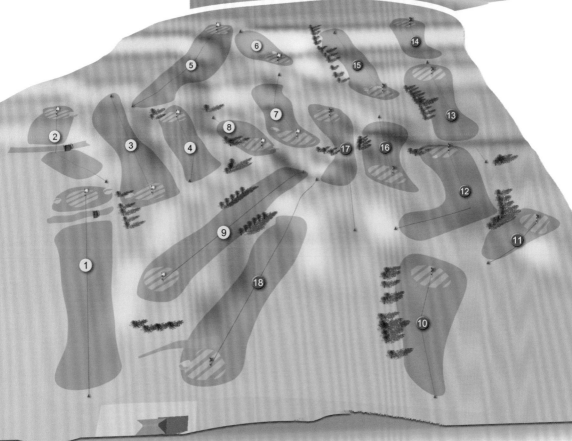

Course Information:

Par 72; SSS 70; Length 6,134 Metres (Old Course). **Visitors:** Welcome. **Opening Hours:** Sunrise – sunset. **Avoid:** Limited availability on Bodenstown course at weekends. Ladyhill course available. **Ladies:** Welcome Mondays. **Green Fees:** Bodenstown €20 Weekdays €25 Sat/Sun & Bank Holidays, Ladyhill all week. **Juveniles:** Welcome. **Clubhouse Hours:** 9am – Dusk. Full clubhouse facilities. **Clubhouse Dress:** Informal. **Clubhouse Facilities:** Full bar & catering available. **Open Competitions:** Open Week – June.

NO.	MEDAL METRES	GEN. METRES	PAR	S.I.	NO.	MEDAL METRES	GEN. METRES	PAR	S.I.
1	306	336	4	9	10	346	363	4	14
2	330	367	4	3	11	133	161	3	12
3	440	464	5	15	12	315	366	4	2
4	331	382	4	5	13	302	319	4	16
5	328	371	4	1	14	130	145	3	8
6	140	153	3	7	15	448	476	5	18
7	352	374	4	17	16	329	359	4	6
8	162	171	3	11	17	305	370	4	4
9	442	460	5	13	18	435	497	5	10
OUT	2,831	3,078	36		IN	2,741	3,056	36	
					TOTAL	5,572	6,134	72	
	STANDARD SCRATCH					70	72		

Course Description:

The Old Course in Bodenstown, with its ample fairways and large greens, some of which are raised, is one of the finest inland tests of golf in Leinster. The Ladyhill Course, also at Bodenstown, is a little shorter but still affords a fair challenge.

LOCATION: 14 miles west of Dublin city centre.

ARCHITECT: Mark O'Meara, in association with European Golf Design.

Maynooth, Co. Kildare
Tel: (01) 505 2000. **Fax:** (01) 628 6555.
Email: reservations@cartonhouse.com
Web: www.cartonhouse.com

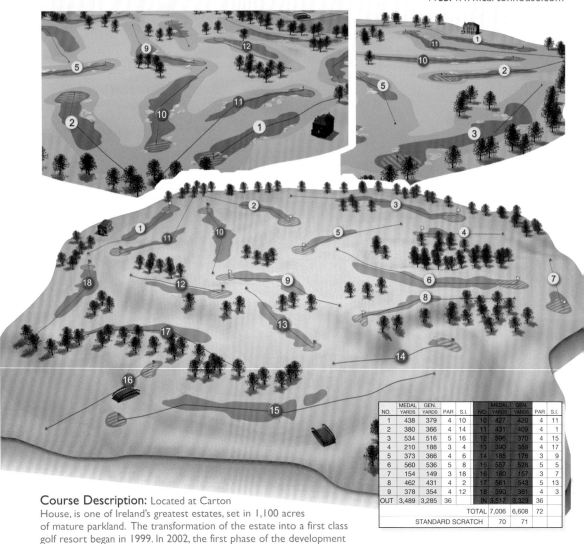

NO.	MEDAL YARDS	GEN. YARDS	PAR	S.I.	NO.	MEDAL YARDS	GEN. YARDS	PAR	S.I.
1	438	379	4	10	10	427	420	4	11
2	380	366	4	14	11	431	409	4	1
3	534	516	5	16	12	396	370	4	15
4	210	188	3	4	13	390	359	4	17
5	373	366	4	6	14	185	176	3	9
6	560	536	5	8	15	557	528	5	5
7	154	149	3	18	16	180	157	3	7
8	462	431	4	2	17	561	543	5	13
9	378	354	4	12	18	390	361	4	3
OUT	3,489	3,285	36		IN	3,517	3,323	36	
					TOTAL	7,006	6,608	72	
					STANDARD SCRATCH	70	71		

Course Description: Located at Carton House, is one of Ireland's greatest estates, set in 1,100 acres of mature parkland. The transformation of the estate into a first class golf resort began in 1999. In 2002, the first phase of the development saw the opening of the Mark O'Meara course that is demure rather than showy but with an overwhelming feel of subtle class. Home to the GUI National Academy.

Course Information: Par 72; SSS 74; Length 7,006 yards. **Visitors:** Always welcome. Advance booking is advisable. **Opening Hours:** 8am – Sunset. **2007 Green Fees:** €115 – €135 pp. Early Bird €75 pp before 9.30am Mon-Fri. **Clubhouse Hours:** 8am – 11.30pm. **Clubhouse Dress:** Neat/ Casual. **Clubhouse Facilities:** Full facilities available. 165 bedroom Hotel, Spa & Conference centre on site.

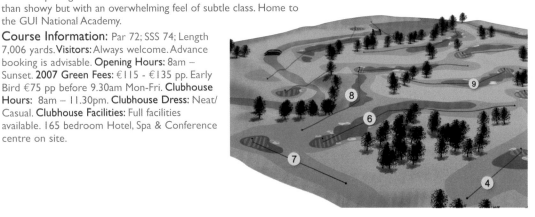

Carton House Golf Club. Maynooth, Co. Kildare
Tel: (01) 5052000 Fax: (01) 6286555.
Email: reservations@cartonhouse.com
Web: www.cartonhouse.com

LOCATION: 14 miles west of Dublin.

ARCHITECT: Colin Montgomerie in association with Stan Eby, European Golf Design.

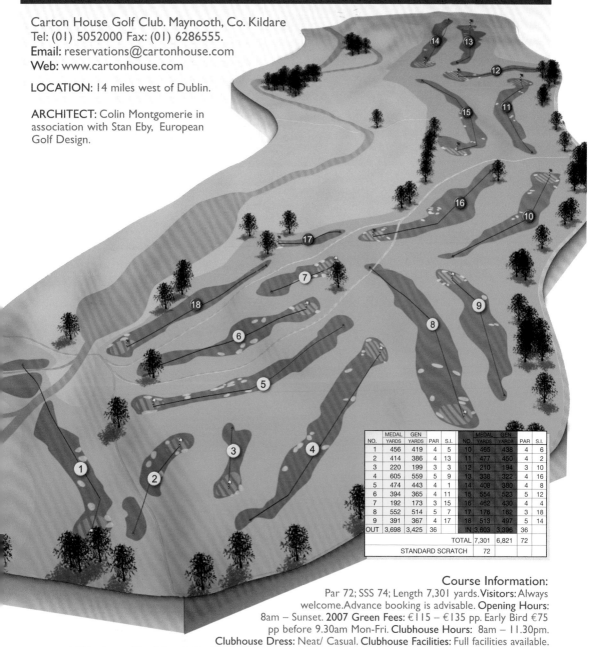

NO.	MEDAL YARDS	GEN YARDS	PAR	S.I.	NO.	MEDAL YARDS	GEN YARDS	PAR	S.I.
1	456	419	4	5	10	465	438	4	6
2	414	386	4	13	11	477	450	4	2
3	220	199	3	3	12	210	194	3	10
4	605	559	5	9	13	338	322	4	16
5	474	443	4	1	14	408	380	4	8
6	394	365	4	11	15	554	523	5	12
7	192	173	3	15	16	462	430	4	4
8	552	514	5	7	17	176	162	3	18
9	391	367	4	17	18	513	497	5	14
OUT	3,698	3,425	36		IN	3,603	3,396	36	
					TOTAL	7,301	6,821	72	
					STANDARD SCRATCH		72		

Course Information:

Par 72; SSS 74; Length 7,301 yards. **Visitors:** Always welcome. Advance booking is advisable. **Opening Hours:** 8am – Sunset. **2007 Green Fees:** €115 – €135 pp. Early Bird €75 pp before 9.30am Mon-Fri. **Clubhouse Hours:** 8am – 11.30pm. **Clubhouse Dress:** Neat/ Casual. **Clubhouse Facilities:** Full facilities available.

165 bedroom Hotel, Spa & Conference Centre on site **Events:** Host to the Nissan Irish Open 2006. Won "Best new Course Design", Golf World Magazine 2005. Ranked 10th in "U.S. Golf Digest" top 10 courses 2005. Home to the GUI National Academy.

Course Description: Located at Carton House, is one of Ireland's greatest estates offering the golfer today two magnificent courses. In July 2003 the second course, The Montgomerie opened for play. Quite different yet complimentary to The O'Meara course, this inland links style course features penal and strategically placed bunkers, run offs into cavernous swales and incredible contouring on and around the greens.

Castlewarden

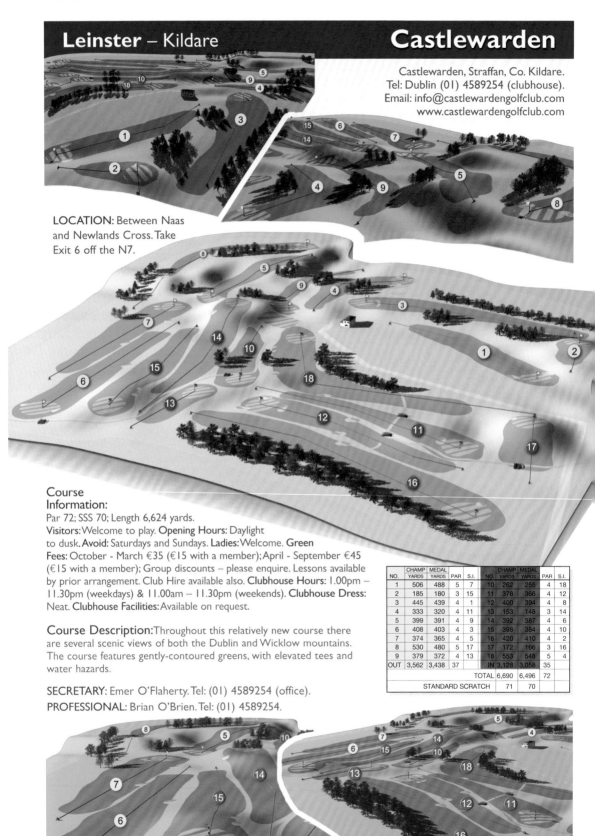

Castlewarden, Straffan, Co. Kildare.
Tel: Dublin (01) 4589254 (clubhouse).
Email: info@castlewardengolfclub.com
www.castlewardengolfclub.com

LOCATION: Between Naas and Newlands Cross. Take Exit 6 off the N7.

Course Information:

Par 72; SSS 70; Length 6,624 yards.
Visitors: Welcome to play. **Opening Hours:** Daylight to dusk. **Avoid:** Saturdays and Sundays. **Ladies:** Welcome. **Green Fees:** October - March €35 (€15 with a member); April - September €45 (€15 with a member); Group discounts – please enquire. Lessons available by prior arrangement. Club Hire available also. **Clubhouse Hours:** 1.00pm – 11.30pm (weekdays) & 11.00am – 11.30pm (weekends). **Clubhouse Dress:** Neat. **Clubhouse Facilities:** Available on request.

Course Description: Throughout this relatively new course there are several scenic views of both the Dublin and Wicklow mountains. The course features gently-contoured greens, with elevated tees and water hazards.

SECRETARY: Emer O'Flaherty. Tel: (01) 4589254 (office).
PROFESSIONAL: Brian O'Brien. Tel: (01) 4589254.

NO.	CHAMP YARDS	MEDAL YARDS	PAR	S.I.	NO.	CHAMP YARDS	MEDAL YARDS	PAR	S.I.
1	506	488	5	7	10	262	255	4	18
2	185	180	3	15	11	378	366	4	12
3	445	439	4	1	12	400	394	4	8
4	333	320	4	11	13	153	148	3	14
5	399	391	4	9	14	392	387	4	6
6	408	403	4	3	15	398	384	4	10
7	374	365	4	5	16	420	410	4	2
8	530	480	5	17	17	172	166	3	16
9	379	372	4	13	18	553	548	5	4
OUT	3,562	3,438	37		IN	3,128	3,058	35	
					TOTAL	6,690	6,496	72	
					STANDARD SCRATCH	71	70		

Celbridge Elm Hall Golf Club,
Celbridge, Co. Kildare.
Tel: (01) 628 8208

LOCATION: 1 km of the
Lucan/Celbridge Road.

GENERAL MANAGER: Seamus Lawless.
Tel: (01) 628 8208

NO.	YARDS	PAR	S.I.	NO.	YARDS	PAR	S.I.
1	161	3	13	10	161	3	16
2	475	5	12	11	424	4	2
3	407	4	4	12	407	4	18
4	352	4	11	13	352	4	12
5	419	4	1	14	462	5	4
6	380	4	6	15	360	4	8
7	361	4	8	16	361	4	10
8	136	3	17	17	136	3	14
9	315	4	16	18	315	4	6
OUT	3,006	35		IN	2,998	35	
				TOTAL	5,922	70	
				STANDARD SCRATCH		70	

Course Information:
Par 70; SSS 70; Length 6,004 yards.
Visitors: Welcome. **Opening Hours:** Sunrise –
Sunset. **Avoid:** Early Sat/Sun. **Ladies:** No restrictions.
Green Fees: Weekdays €16 (9 hole) & €30 (18 holes),
Weekends/Bank Holidays €18 (9 holes) & €33 (18
holes). Guests, Seniors and Juniors discounted. **Juveniles:**
Restricted. **Clubhouse Hours:** Weekdays 8am – sunset
& Weekends 7.30am – sunset. **Clubhouse Facilities:** Bar,
catering & showers etc. Also Available: 18 hole par, 3
and 18 hole pitch & putt.

Course Description:
Beautiful parkland course
with mature trees and outstanding
fairways. The excellent quality of the
greens at Celbridge Elm Hall are already
legendary amongst the golfing fraternity of
County Kildare and the
surrounding counties.

NO.	BLUE METRES	GREEN METRES	PAR	S.I.	NO.	BLUE METRES	GREEN METRES	PAR	S.I.
1	298	280	4	17	10	300	280	4	18
2	126	110	3	15	11	141	130	3	14
3	336	320	4	9	12	318	280	4	16
4	376	360	4	3	13	484	470	5	12
5	453	435	5	11	14	363	335	4	4
6	383	372	4	1	15	353	336	4	6
7	343	333	4	5	16	326	310	4	8
8	175	170	3	13	17	320	300	4	10
9	370	360	4	7	18	387	370	4	2
OUT	2,860	2,740	35		IN	2,992	2,811	36	
					TOTAL	5,852	5,571	71	
					STANDARD SCRATCH		70	69	

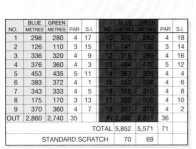

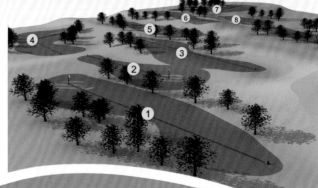

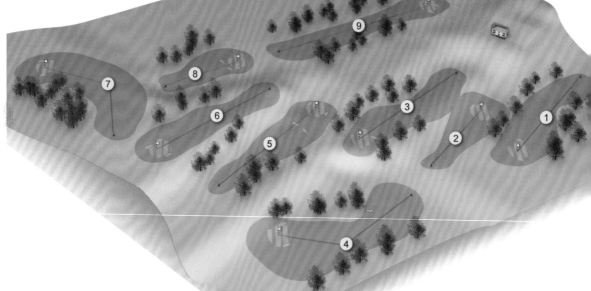

Course Information:
Par 71; SSS 70; Length 5,738 metres.
Visitors: Welcome. **Opening Hours:** Sunrise – sunset. **Avoid:** Wednesday, Sundays (Club Competitions). **Ladies Day:** Wednesday. **Green Fees:** €20 Weekday €10 with member; €25 Weekend €15 with member. **Juveniles:** Welcome. Club Hire available; telephone appointment required. **Clubhouse Hours:** 11.00am – 11.30pm. **Clubhouse Dress:** Casual. **Clubhouse Facilities:** 9.00am – 10.30pm daily (full facilities). **Open Competition:** 26th May - 4th June.

Course Description:
A course which is typical to many in the area with all the colour of the gorse and heather. Flat and relatively straight forward to play. A good choice for the middle and high handicappers.

Little Curragh, Kildare,
Co. Kildare.
Tel: (045) 521433

LOCATION: One mile west of Kildare town.

SECRETARY MANAGER:
Dan Doody.
cilldaragc@eircom.net

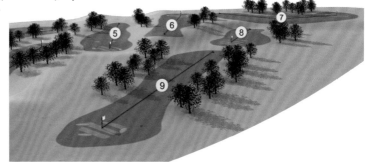

Craddockstown Golf Club, Blessington Road, Naas, Co. Kildare. Tel: (045) 897610.

LOCATION: 1.5 miles from Naas town.

MANAGER: Gay Nolan.

ARCHITECT: A. Spring.

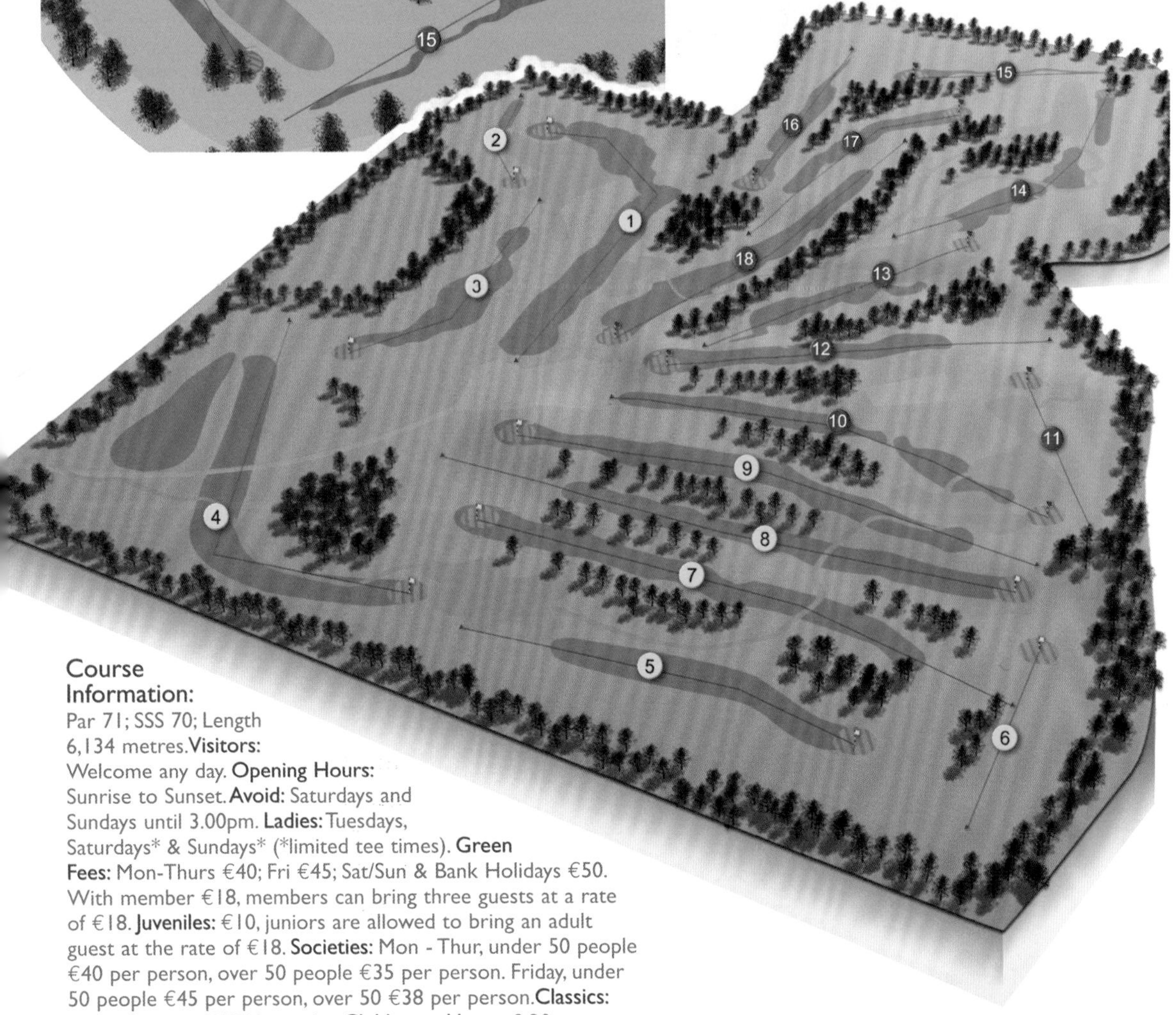

Course Information:

Par 71; SSS 70; Length 6,134 metres. **Visitors:** Welcome any day. **Opening Hours:** Sunrise to Sunset. **Avoid:** Saturdays and Sundays until 3.00pm. **Ladies:** Tuesdays, Saturdays* & Sundays* (*limited tee times). **Green Fees:** Mon-Thurs €40; Fri €45; Sat/Sun & Bank Holidays €50. With member €18, members can bring three guests at a rate of €18. **Juveniles:** €10, juniors are allowed to bring an adult guest at the rate of €18. **Societies:** Mon - Thur, under 50 people €40 per person, over 50 people €35 per person. Friday, under 50 people €45 per person, over 50 €38 per person. **Classics:** Classics all day, €3500 per day. **Clubhouse Hours:** 9.30am – 11.30pm. **Clubhouse Dress:** Smart and neat, casual. **Clubhouse Facilities:** Changing rooms, showers, bar and catering by arrangement. **Open Competitions:** Semi-Opens Wednesdays; Open Week July.

Course Description:

Testing, spacious course with young parkland trees, which when mature will increase accuracy needed. Greens well protected and some fairways include tricky water hazards.

NO.	MEDAL METRES	GEN. METRES	PAR	S.I.	NO.	MEDAL METRES	GEN. METRES	PAR	S.I.
1	473	447	5	15	10	340	323	4	2
2	131	121	3	7	11	175	146	3	16
3	317	310	4	17	12	317	308	4	12
4	416	378	4	1	13	324	304	4	4
5	373	334	4	3	14	467	456	5	6
6	174	164	3	11	15	183	162	3	14
7	381	365	4	9	16	325	301	4	18
8	475	453	5	13	17	358	350	4	8
9	391	356	4	5	18	513	470	5	10
OUT	3,131	2,928	36		IN	3,002	2,820	36	
					TOTAL	6,133	5,748	72	
					STANDARD SCRATCH		72	72	

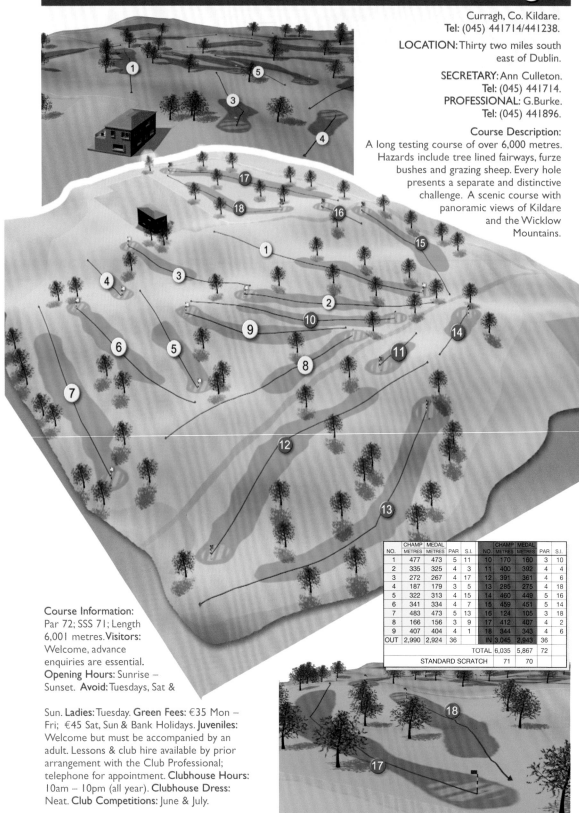

Curragh, Co. Kildare.
Tel: (045) 441714/441238.

LOCATION: Thirty two miles south east of Dublin.

SECRETARY: Ann Culleton.
Tel: (045) 441714.
PROFESSIONAL: G.Burke.
Tel: (045) 441896.

Course Description:
A long testing course of over 6,000 metres. Hazards include tree lined fairways, furze bushes and grazing sheep. Every hole presents a separate and distinctive challenge. A scenic course with panoramic views of Kildare and the Wicklow Mountains.

NO.	CHAMP METRES	MEDAL METRES	PAR	S.I.	NO.	CHAMP METRES	MEDAL METRES	PAR	S.I.
1	477	473	5	11	10	170	160	3	10
2	335	325	4	3	11	400	392	4	4
3	272	267	4	17	12	391	361	4	6
4	187	179	3	5	13	285	275	4	18
5	322	313	4	15	14	460	449	5	16
6	341	334	4	7	15	459	451	5	14
7	483	473	5	13	16	124	105	3	18
8	166	156	3	9	17	412	407	4	2
9	407	404	4	1	18	344	343	4	6
OUT	2,990	2,924	36		IN	3,045	2,943	36	
					TOTAL	6,035	5,867	72	
					STANDARD SCRATCH	71	70		

Course Information:
Par 72; SSS 71; Length 6,001 metres. Visitors: Welcome, advance enquiries are essential. Opening Hours: Sunrise – Sunset. Avoid: Tuesdays, Sat & Sun. Ladies: Tuesday. Green Fees: €35 Mon – Fri; €45 Sat, Sun & Bank Holidays. Juveniles: Welcome but must be accompanied by an adult. Lessons & club hire available by prior arrangement with the Club Professional; telephone for appointment. Clubhouse Hours: 10am – 10pm (all year). Clubhouse Dress: Neat. Club Competitions: June & July.

Dunmurry Springs

Dunmurry Hill, Kildare, Co. Kildare
Tel: (045) 531 400 Fax: (045) 520 203
E-mail: info@dunmurrysprings.ie
Web: www.dunmurrysprings.ie

LOCATION: 2 miles north of Kildare Town on R401 to Rathangan. Exit M7 at Kildare/Nurney Exit. Follow signs for town centre and then signs for Dunmurry Springs.

GENERAL MANAGER: Simon Holohan.

ARCHITECTS: Mel and Melvyn Flanagan, Irish Golf Design.

Course Description: Golf holes meander around the lakes and hollows of the land, enjoying spectacular views and scenery across seven counties. Dunmurry Springs is emerging as a truly breathtaking golf course, not only in relation to Ireland but comparable to those throughout Europe.

Course Information: Par 71; SSS 72; Length 6,757 yards. **Opening Hours:** From 1st May 2006; 7.30am – dusk. **Visitors:** Always Welcome. **Ladies:** No restrictions. **Green Fees:** €65 Mon-Tue, €80 Wed-Sun. **Clubhouse Facilities:** Golf reception, lounge (serving light snacks), boutique golf shop, luxurious changing rooms. Full bar and restaurant.

NO.	MEDAL YARDS	GEN. YARDS	PAR	S.I.	NO.	MEDAL YARDS	GEN. YARDS	PAR	S.I.
1	365	331	4	-	10	571	505	5	-
2	375	333	4	-	11	185	159	3	-
3	471	386	4	-	12	485	430	4	-
4	374	311	4	-	13	502	481	5	-
5	391	316	4	-	14	368	360	4	-
6	477	472	5	-	15	130	125	3	-
7	191	152	3	-	16	426	401	4	-
8	437	388	4	-	17	180	175	3	-
9	407	401	4	-	18	422	370	4	-
OUT	3,488	3,090	36		IN	3,269	3,006	35	
					TOTAL	6,757	6,096	71	
	STANDARD SCRATCH					-	-		

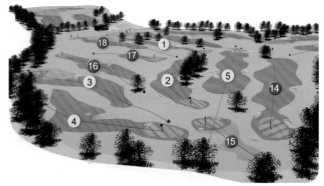

Highfield Golf Club, Carbury, Co. Kildare. Tel: (046) 973 1021.
Email: highfieldgolf@eircom.net
Web: www.highfield-golf.ie

LOCATION: North Kildare. Within one hour of Dublin, via M4 motorway.

GENERAL MANAGER: Denis Peacock.

ARCHITECT: Alan Duggan.

Course Information:
Par 70; SSS 69; Length 6,277 yards. **Visitors:** Welcome. **Opening Hours:** Sunrise – sunset. **Avoid:** Early Saturday & Sunday. **Ladies:** Welcome. **Green Fees:** Mon – Fri €35; Sat / Sun / Bank Holidays €45. Group Rates (12 or more) Mon – Fri €25 to €30; Sat / Sun / Bank Holidays €35 to €40. **Juveniles:** Must be accompanied by an adult. **Clubhouse Hours:** 8.30am – sunset. **Clubhouse Dress:** Smart / casual. **Clubhouse Facilities:** Available every day – reception; Restaurant. Accommodation available. **Open Competitions:** Contact club for details.

NO.	CHAMP METRES	MEDAL METRES	PAR	S.I.	NO.	CHAMP METRES	MEDAL METRES	PAR	S.I.
1	319	310	4	11	10	214	168	3	4
2	327	317	4	13	11	390	380	4	8
3	132	123	3	17	12	523	517	5	2
4	509	498	5	3	13	140	137	3	16
5	316	293	4	9	14	274	264	4	12
6	442	421	4	1	15	423	420	4	6
7	498	492	5	5	16	132	118	3	18
8	137	127	3	15	17	365	332	4	10
9	340	335	4	7	18	316	294	4	14
OUT	3,020	2,889	36		IN	2,777	2,630	34	
					TOTAL	5,797	5,546	70	
					STANDARD SCRATCH	69	67		

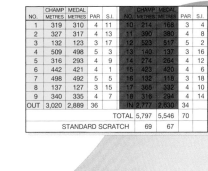

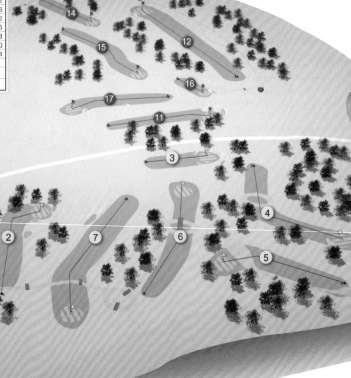

Course Description:
Attractive 18 hole parkland course, set in a quiet country area, featuring leisurely fairways and mature sycamore, beech & chestnut trees.

Kilkea Castle

Kilkea Castle, Castledermot, Co. Kildare.
Tel: (059) 914 5555. Fax: (059) 914 5505.
Email: kilkeagolfclub@eircom.net
Web: www.kilkeacastlehotelgolf.com

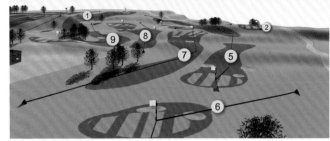

GOLF MANAGER: John Kissane.
LOCATION: 40 miles from Dublin.

NO.	MEDAL METRES	GEN. METRES	PAR	S.I.	NO.	MEDAL METRES	GEN. METRES	PAR	S.I.
1	369	362	4	11	10	138	133	3	17
2	499	483	5	4	11	385	379	4	10
3	339	326	4	12	12	489	478	5	14
4	160	152	3	6	13	414	401	4	8
5	499	491	5	13	14	168	161	3	16
6	148	141	3	18	15	413	402	4	7
7	390	382	4	2	16	173	161	3	5
8	415	402	4	3	17	344	333	4	1
9	364	351	4	15	18	384	352	4	9
OUT	3,189	3,091	36		IN	2,908	2,800	34	
					TOTAL	6,098	5,891	70	
					STANDARD SCRATCH	72	71		

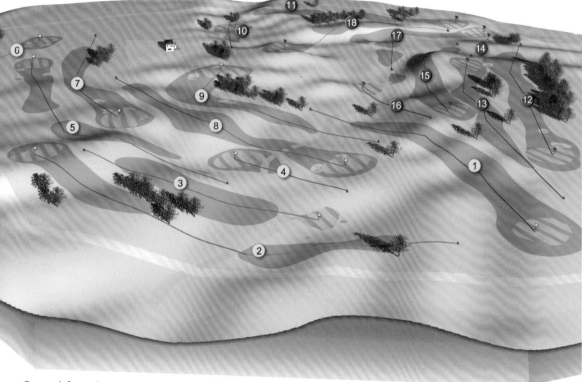

Course Information:
Par 70; SSS 71; Length 6,128 Metres. **Visitors:** Welcome to play every day.
Phone to book tee times. **Opening Hours:** Sunrise – Sunset. **Ladies:** Welcome.
Green Fees: €40 Mon-Thur, €50 Fri-Sun. **Hotel Residents:** €35 Mon-Thur,
€40 Fri-Sun. **Juveniles:** Welcome only when accompanied by adults. **Clubhouse
Hours:** 10.00am -11.30pm. **Clubhouse Dress:** Neat. **Clubhouse Facilities:** Bar,
restaurant, pro-shop, putting green, practice range and pitching green.
Conference facilities. **Open Competition:** Phone club for details.

Course Description:
A parkland course which
surrounds the oldest
inhabited castle in Ireland.
The River Griese comes into
play on ten of the holes.

Killeen Golf Club, Kill, County Kildare,
Tel: (045) 866003. Fax: (045) 875881.
Email: admin@kilkeengc.ie **Web:** www.killeengolf.com

LOCATION: Two miles west of Kill village, off N7 Dublin – Cork Road.

ARCHITECT:
Tom Craddock
& Pat Ruddy.

SECRETARY / MANAGER:
Maurice Kelly.

NO.	MEDAL YARDS	GEN. YARDS	PAR	S.I.	NO.	MEDAL YARDS	GEN. YARDS	PAR	S.I.
1	512	500	5	18	10	510	504	5	15
2	411	401	4	6	11	390	382	4	7
3	386	372	4	4	12	416	406	4	3
4	402	376	4	10	13	369	360	4	13
5	402	390	4	2	14	167	160	3	9
6	208	198	3	14	15	429	402	4	1
7	366	356	4	8	16	468	458	5	17
8	139	129	3	16	17	416	390	4	5
9	566	511	5	12	18	176	142	3	11
OUT	3,391	3,233	36		IN	3,341	3,204	36	
					TOTAL	6,732	6,437	72	
					STANDARD SCRATCH	71	70		

Course Information:
Par 71; SSS 71; Length 6,732 yards. **Visitors:** Welcome weekdays and at weekends. **Opening Hours:** Summer 7.00am – 12.00pm; winter 8.00am – 6.00pm. **Avoid:** Sat / Sun up to 4.00pm. At weekends telephone, appointments essential. **Ladies:** Welcome Tuesday and Thursday. **Green Fees:** €40 weekdays; €50 weekends. Caddy car hire available. **Clubhouse Hours:** Summer 9.00am – 12 midnight; winter 9.00am – 6.00pm. **Clubhouse Dress:** Neat. **Clubhouse Facilities:** Golf shop open everyday. Licensed restaurant and bar.

Course Description:

First laid in 1980, Kileen has undergone continuous development and improvement. In 1994 the purchase of additional land and the redesign by Tom Craddock and Pat Ruddy (of Druids Glen Fame) was a significant milestone for the Golf Course. Since the purchase by the recent owners in 1998 – the course has again been redesigned and brought up to Championship standard by Maurice Kelly. The course features state-of-the-art drainage and irrigation on all greens and tee boxes, and the greens themselves have been sown with Providence creeping bent grass, ensuring year-round playability.

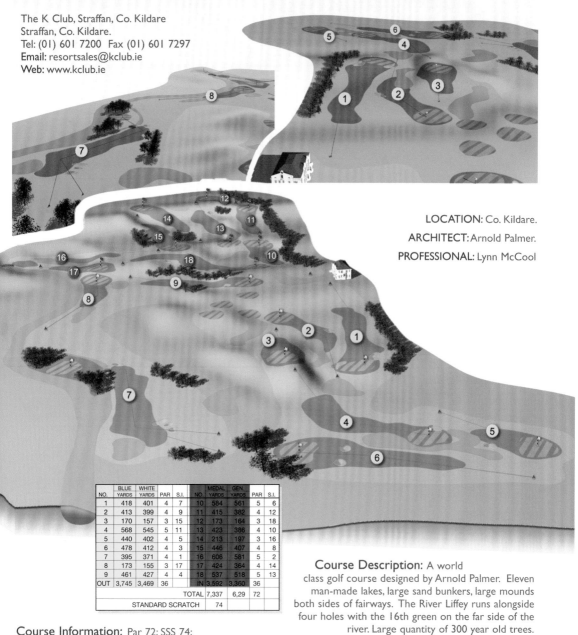

The K Club, Straffan, Co. Kildare
Straffan, Co. Kildare.
Tel: (01) 601 7200 Fax (01) 601 7297
Email: resortsales@kclub.ie
Web: www.kclub.ie

LOCATION: Co. Kildare.
ARCHITECT: Arnold Palmer.
PROFESSIONAL: Lynn McCool

NO.	BLUE YARDS	WHITE YARDS	PAR	S.I.	NO.	MEDAL YARDS	GEN. YARDS	PAR	S.I.
1	418	401	4	7	10	584	561	5	6
2	413	399	4	9	11	415	382	4	12
3	170	157	3	15	12	173	164	3	18
4	568	545	5	11	13	423	386	4	10
5	440	402	4	5	14	213	197	3	16
6	478	412	4	3	15	446	407	4	8
7	395	371	4	1	16	606	581	5	2
8	173	155	3	17	17	424	364	4	14
9	461	427	4	4	18	537	518	5	13
OUT	3,745	3,469	36		IN	3,592	3,360	36	
					TOTAL	7,337	6,29	72	
					STANDARD SCRATCH	74			

Course Description: A world
class golf course designed by Arnold Palmer. Eleven
man-made lakes, large sand bunkers, large mounds
both sides of fairways. The River Liffey runs alongside
four holes with the 16th green on the far side of the
river. Large quantity of 300 year old trees.

Course Information: Par 72; SSS 74;
Length 7,212 yards. **Visitors:** Welcome.
Opening Hours: 8.00am (summer), 8.30am
(winter). **Ladies:** Welcome. **Green Fees:** €370
(summer), €160 (winter) Group rates
available. Lessons available by prior
arrangement. Club Hire and Caddy service
available. No Open Competitions. **Juveniles:**
Must be accompanied by an adult. **Clubhouse
Dress:** Smart casual. **Clubhouse Hours:**
7.30am – 10 pm (summer), 9 pm (winter).
Clubhouse Facilities: Snack bar, Legends
Restaurant & Bar. Snack bar 9am–9pm. Bar &
Restaurant 11 am–9 pm everyday.

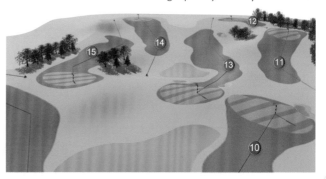

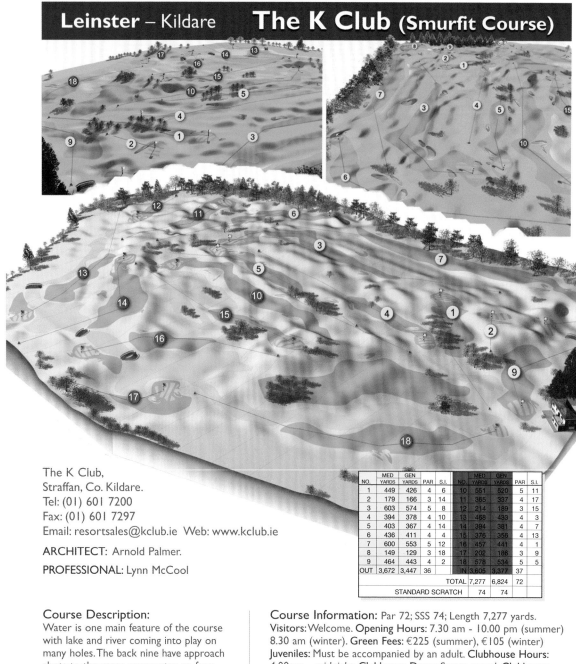

The K Club,
Straffan, Co. Kildare.
Tel: (01) 601 7200
Fax: (01) 601 7297
Email: resortsales@kclub.ie Web: www.kclub.ie

ARCHITECT: Arnold Palmer.

PROFESSIONAL: Lynn McCool

NO.	MED YARDS	GEN YARDS	PAR	S.I.	NO.	MED YARDS	GEN YARDS	PAR	S.I.
1	449	426	4	6	10	551	520	5	11
2	179	166	3	14	11	365	337	4	17
3	603	574	5	8	12	214	189	3	15
4	394	378	4	10	13	468	433	4	3
5	403	367	4	14	14	394	381	4	7
6	436	411	4	4	15	376	356	4	13
7	600	553	5	12	16	457	441	4	1
8	149	129	3	18	17	202	186	3	9
9	464	443	4	2	18	578	534	5	5
OUT	3,672	3,447	36		IN	3,605	3,377	37	
					TOTAL	7,277	6,824	72	
					STANDARD SCRATCH	74	74		

Course Description:

Water is one main feature of the course with lake and river coming into play on many holes. The back nine have approach shots to the green over water on four holes. A real test of accurate play.

Course Information: Par 72; SSS 74; Length 7,277 yards.

Visitors: Welcome. **Opening Hours:** 7.30 am - 10.00 pm (summer) 8.30 am (winter). **Green Fees:** €225 (summer), €105 (winter) **Juveniles:** Must be accompanied by an adult. **Clubhouse Hours:** 4.00pm – midnight. **Clubhouse Dress:** Smart casual. **Clubhouse Facilities:** Bar, Monza Restaurant, Oriental Restaurant.

Donadea, North Kildare.
Tel: (045) 869322.
Email: golf@knockanally.com

LOCATION: North Kildare.

SECRETARY: Declan Monaghan.
Tel: (045) 869671 (Proshop)
Fax: (045) 869322

ARCHITECT: Noel Lyons.

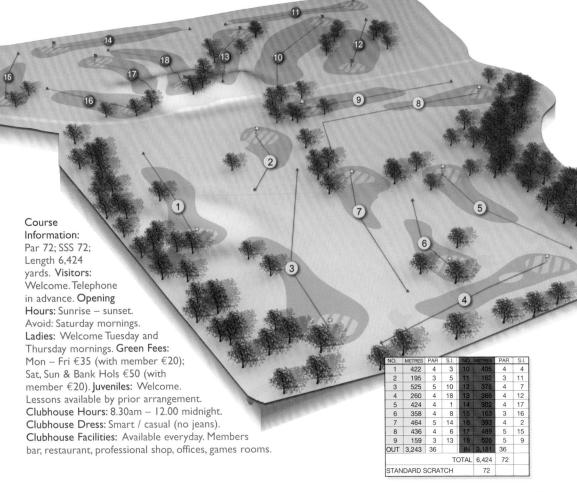

Course Information:

Par 72; SSS 72; Length 6,424 yards. **Visitors:** Welcome. Telephone in advance. **Opening Hours:** Sunrise – sunset. Avoid: Saturday mornings. **Ladies:** Welcome Tuesday and Thursday mornings. **Green Fees:** Mon – Fri €35 (with member €20); Sat, Sun & Bank Hols €50 (with member €20). **Juveniles:** Welcome. Lessons available by prior arrangement. **Clubhouse Hours:** 8.30am – 12.00 midnight. **Clubhouse Dress:** Smart / casual (no jeans). **Clubhouse Facilities:** Available everyday. Members bar, restaurant, professional shop, offices, games rooms.

NO.	METRES	PAR	S.I.	NO.	METRES	PAR	S.I.
1	422	4	3	10	405	4	4
2	195	3	5	11	162	3	11
3	525	5	10	12	375	4	7
4	260	4	18	13	366	4	12
5	424	4	1	14	302	4	17
6	358	4	8	15	163	3	16
7	464	5	14	16	393	4	2
8	436	4	6	17	489	5	15
9	159	3	13	18	526	5	9
OUT	3,243	36		IN	3,181	36	
				TOTAL	6,424	72	
STANDARD SCRATCH						72	

Course Description:

A popular parkland course which is basically flat, and has several water hazards. Christy O'Connor Senior once described the first hole as "the most difficult opening hole in golf". Home of the Irish International Professional Matchplay Championship. Palladian old world clubhouse is also an interesting feature.

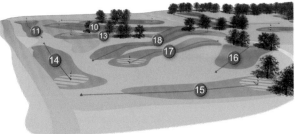

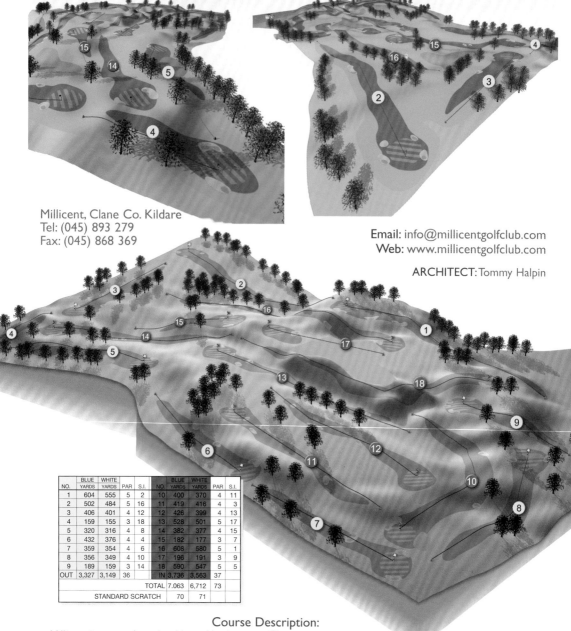

Millicent, Clane Co. Kildare
Tel: (045) 893 279
Fax: (045) 868 369

Email: info@millicentgolfclub.com
Web: www.millicentgolfclub.com

ARCHITECT: Tommy Halpin

NO.	BLUE YARDS	WHITE YARDS	PAR	S.I.	NO.	BLUE YARDS	WHITE YARDS	PAR	S.I.
1	604	555	5	2	10	400	370	4	11
2	502	484	5	16	11	419	416	4	3
3	406	401	4	12	12	426	399	4	13
4	159	155	3	18	13	528	501	5	17
5	320	316	4	8	14	382	377	4	15
6	432	376	4	4	15	182	177	3	7
7	359	354	4	6	16	608	580	5	1
8	356	349	4	10	17	196	191	3	9
9	189	159	3	14	18	590	547	5	5
OUT	3,327	3,149	36		IN	3,736	3,563	37	
					TOTAL	7.063	6,712	73	
					STANDARD SCRATCH		70	71	

Course Description:

Millicent is a true championship parklands course. The greens are sand based and the fairways are laid on gravel, making it a true all season course. The greens are very large and well contoured and the course enjoys extensive bunkering and trees, both young and semi mature.

Course Information:

Par 73; SSS 72; Length in yards and metres 7,045; 6,748, 6559; Visitors: Welcome. **Opening Hours:** Dawn – Dusk. **Ladies:** Welcome. **Green Fees: From** €27 – €45. Weekends & Bank Holidays €45. **Juveniles:** With adult supervision. **Clubhouse Hours:** Dawn – Dusk. **Clubhouse Dress:** Neat dress, no denims. **Clubhouse Facilities:** New Clubhouse open. Full bar and catering facilities, snack bar and full changing facilities. **Open Competitions:** See GUI website.

Kerdiffstown, Naas, Co. Kildare.
Tel: (045) 897509.

MANAGER: Denis Mahon.

ARCHITECT: Jeff Howes.

NO.	YARDS	PAR	S.I.	NO.	YARDS	PAR	S.I.
1	425	4	4	10	178	3	9
2	361	4	16	11	394	4	3
3	160	3	12	12	382	4	11
4	404	4	2	13	518	5	7
5	381	4	6	14	175	3	13
6	383	4	8	15	500	5	17
7	493	5	14	16	401	4	1
8	132	3	18	17	178	3	5
9	315	4	10	18	498	5	15
OUT	3,054	35		IN	3,224	36	
				TOTAL	6,278	35	
				STANDARD SCRATCH	68	71	

LOCATION: Beside Naas/Dublin dual carriageway on Johnstown /Sallins road.

Course Information:
Par 71; SSS 69; Length 6,278 yards. **Visitors:** Welcome Mon, Wed, Fri and Sat. **Opening Hours:** Sunrise – Sunset. **Ladies:** Welcome. **Green Fees:** €40 Weekdays; €45 Weekends & Bank Holidays. **Juveniles:** Welcome. **Clubhouse Hours:** 8.00am – 11.30pm. **Clubhouse Dress:** Neat. **Clubhouse Facilities:** Catering. **Open Competitions:** April, June & August.

Course Description:
A pleasant parkland course where each hole has its features providing a keen golfing challenge.

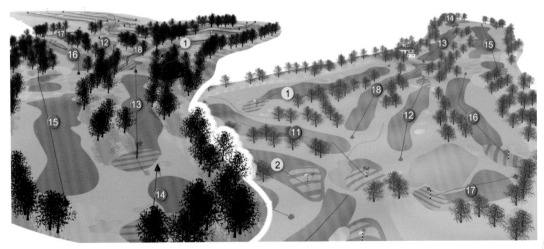

Barretstown, Newbridge. Co. Kildare.
Tel: (045) 486110. Tel/Fax: (045) 446840.
Email: info@newbridgegolfclub.com
OWNER: Eddie Stafford. **MANAGER:** Jamie Stafford.

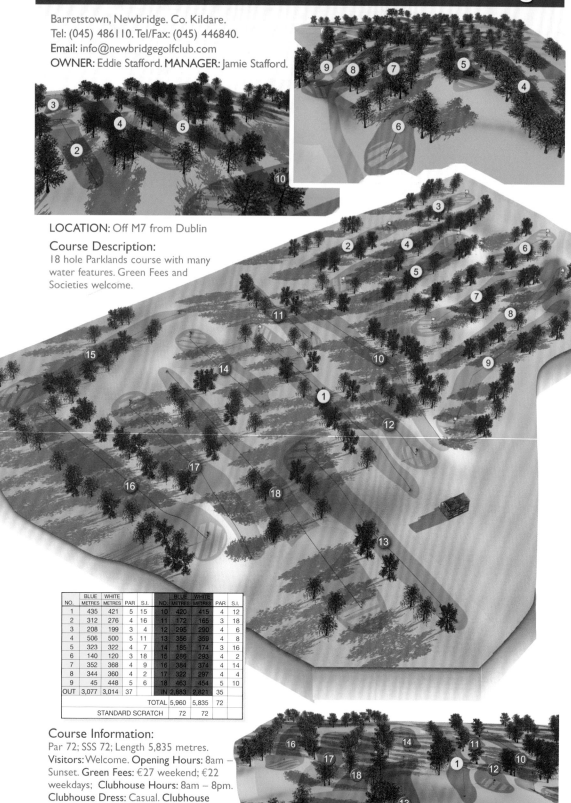

LOCATION: Off M7 from Dublin

Course Description:

18 hole Parklands course with many water features. Green Fees and Societies welcome.

NO.	BLUE METRES	WHITE METRES	PAR	S.I.	NO.	BLUE METRES	WHITE METRES	PAR	S.I.
1	435	421	5	15	10	420	415	4	12
2	312	276	4	16	11	172	165	3	18
3	208	199	3	4	12	295	290	4	6
4	506	500	5	11	13	356	359	4	8
5	323	322	4	7	14	185	174	3	16
6	140	120	3	18	15	286	293	4	2
7	352	368	4	9	16	384	374	4	14
8	344	360	4	2	17	322	297	4	4
9	45	448	5	6	18	463	454	5	10
OUT	3,077	3,014	37		IN	2,883	2,821	35	
					TOTAL	5,960	5,835	72	
					STANDARD SCRATCH	72	72		

Course Information:

Par 72; SSS 72; Length 5,835 metres.
Visitors: Welcome. **Opening Hours:** 8am – Sunset. **Green Fees:** €27 weekend; €22 weekdays; **Clubhouse Hours:** 8am – 8pm. **Clubhouse Dress:** Casual. **Clubhouse Facilities:** Snack all the time. **Open Competitions:** Various throughout year.

Course Description:
Woodlands Golf Course offers an attractive setting with a reasonable golf challenge.

Woodlands Golf Club, Coill Dubh, Naas, Co. Kildare
Tel: (045) 860 777. Fax: (045) 860 988.
E-mail: woodlandsgolf@eircom.net
www.woodlandsgolf.ie

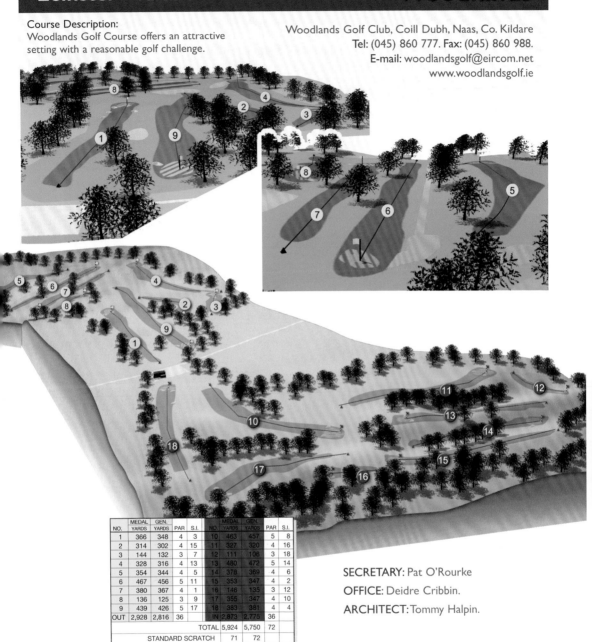

NO.	MEDAL YARDS	GEN. YARDS	PAR	S.I.	NO.	MEDAL YARDS	GEN. YARDS	PAR	S.I.
1	366	348	4	3	10	463	457	5	8
2	314	302	4	15	11	327	320	4	16
3	144	132	3	7	12	111	106	3	18
4	328	316	4	13	13	480	472	5	14
5	354	344	4	5	14	378	369	4	6
6	467	456	5	11	15	353	347	4	2
7	380	367	4	1	16	146	135	3	12
8	136	125	3	9	17	355	347	4	10
9	439	426	5	17	18	383	381	4	4
OUT	2,928	2,816	36		IN	2,873	2,775	36	
				TOTAL	5,924	5,750	72	
				STANDARD SCRATCH	71	72		

SECRETARY: Pat O'Rourke

OFFICE: Deidre Cribbin.

ARCHITECT: Tommy Halpin.

Course Information:
Par 72; SSS 72; Length 5,924 metres.
Avoid: Saturday and Sunday mornings - green fees normally available from 2.30pm onwards. **Green Fees:** Mon-Fri €30, Weekend/Bank hols €35. **Clubhouse Dress:** Neat. **Clubhouse Facilities:** Dressing/ Locker Rooms, Shower facilities. Bar and food available at weekends.
Clubhouse Hours: 11am to closing. **Open Competitions:** Open week 29th July-6th August inclusive. Wednesday Men's Open Singles starting 1st June - 29th September.

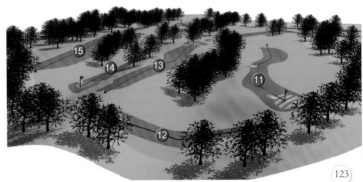

Geraldine, Callan, Co. Kilkenny.
Tel: (056) 7725136/7725949.
Fax: (056) 7755155.

HONORARY SECRETARY:
Murt Duggan.

SEC/MANAGER:
Liam Duggan
Tel: (056) 7755875

LOCATION: One mile
from town of Callan on Knocktopher road.

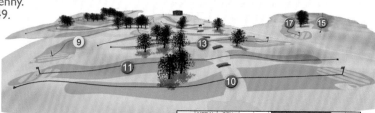

NO.	MEDAL YARDS	GEN. YARDS	PAR	S.I.	NO.	MEDAL YARDS	GEN. YARDS	PAR	S.I.
1	407	398	4	5	10	348	330	4	4
2	505	491	5	17	11	408	397	4	3
3	404	380	4	15	12	145	138	3	14
4	210	199	3	7	13	352	343	4	8
5	360	347	4	13	14	135	130	3	16
6	384	380	4	11	15	511	501	5	6
7	330	300	4	9	16	148	139	3	10
8	432	415	4	1	17	477	468	5	18
9	457	414	4	2	18	349	329	4	12
OUT	3,489	3,324	36		IN	2,873	2,775	35	
					TOTAL	6,362	6,099	71	
					STANDARD SCRATCH	70	71		

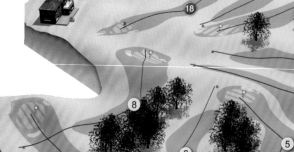

Course Description:
Stream comes into play on six holes with the par 3 10th requiring 155 yard carry over water to the green. In addition there are well placed spinneys to catch wayward drives. There is also a pond left of line of drive on the 9th. All greens are bunkered and well protected.

Course Information:
Par 71; SSS 69; Length 6,422 yards.
Visitors: Welcome to play. **Opening Hours:**
Daylight hours. **Avoid:** Sundays a.m, Saturdays p.m. Prior arrangement preferred. **Green Fees:** €30 weekdays, €35 weekends & Bank Holidays. Discount for groups of 20+. Caddy service and Club Hire available. **Juveniles:** Welcome if accompanied by an adult. Must be off the course by 6.00pm. Allocated days for juveniles, phone clubhouse for details. **Clubhouse Hours:** 9am-11pm. **Clubhouse Dress:** Neat/Casual. **Clubhouse Facilities:** Bar open 9.00am – 11.00pm. Full catering facilities. Golf Shop open everyday. **Open Week:** 9th - 17th June.

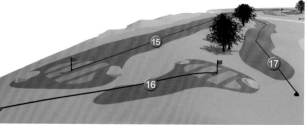

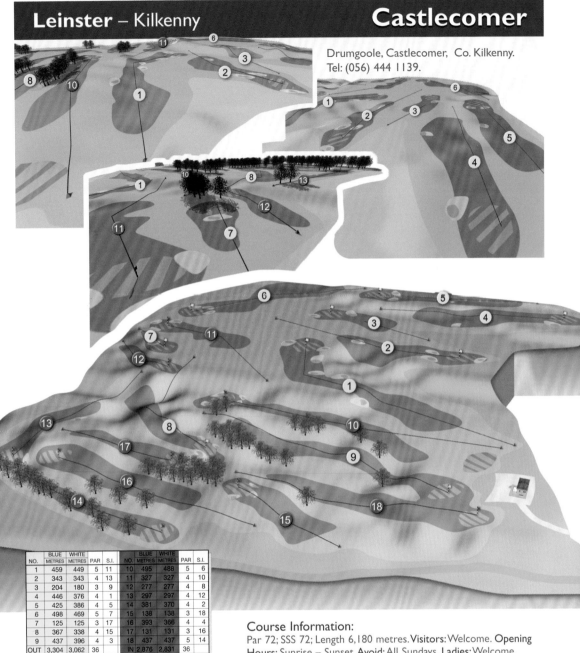

Drumgoole, Castlecomer, Co. Kilkenny.
Tel: (056) 444 1139.

NO.	BLUE METRES	WHITE METRES	PAR	S.I.	NO.	BLUE METRES	WHITE METRES	PAR	S.I.
1	459	449	5	11	10	495	488	5	6
2	343	343	4	13	11	327	327	4	10
3	204	180	3	9	12	277	277	4	8
4	446	376	4	1	13	297	297	4	12
5	425	386	4	5	14	381	370	4	2
6	498	469	5	7	15	138	138	3	18
7	125	125	3	17	16	393	366	4	4
8	367	338	4	15	17	131	131	3	16
9	437	396	4	3	18	437	437	5	14
OUT	3,304	3,062	36		IN	2,876	2,831	36	
					TOTAL	6,180	5,893	72	
					STANDARD SCRATCH		72	72	

Course Description:

Castlecomer Golf Club has joined the ranks of rare golfing gems to be designed by Pat Ruddy. The course is crafted out of beautiful mature forest terrain providing not just wonderful golf but stunning views of the surrounding countryside as well. In 2006 Castlecomer was voted into the top 100 golf courses in Ireland which in itself is a testimony to this prestigious layout.

Without doubt Castlecomer has arrived as a must play venue in the South East.

Course Information:

Par 72; SSS 72; Length 6,180 metres. Visitors: Welcome. Opening Hours: Sunrise – Sunset. Avoid: All Sundays. Ladies: Welcome. Green Fees: €35 Mon – Fri, €40 Weekends & Bank Holidays. Juveniles: Welcome. Clubhouse Hours: Sunrise – Sunset. Clubhouse Dress: Casual. Clubhouse Facilities: Full clubhouse facilities (by request for groups). Open Competitions: Open Week July / Aug.

HON. SECRETARY: Matt Dooley. Tel: (056) 444 1139.

ARCHITECT: Pat Ruddy.

LOCATION: Edge of town on Kilkenny road.

Email: info@castlecomergolf.com
Web: www.castlecomergolf.com

Gowran, Co. Kilkenny.
Tel: (056) 772 6699 Fax: (056) 772 6173
E-mail: gowranparkltd@eircom.net
Web: www.gowranpark.ie

SECRETARY/ MANAGER:
Michael O' Sullivan.

Course Description:
Incorporating a mixture of old established woodland and lakes, this par 71, 18 hole golf course provides an excellent test for the low handicap golfer whilst also being very enjoyable for the middle to high handicappers. The newly developed club house and corporate entertainment facilities are especially suited to large corporate groups and societies.

Course Information:
Par 71; SSS 72; Length 6,110 metres.
Visitors: Book in advance. **Opening Hours:** Daylight hours. **Avoid:** Sunday mornings.
Green Fees: Weekend €50, Weekdays €40.
Clubhouse Hours: 8.00am – Close (depends on time of year). **Clubhouse Dress:** No denims. Neat. **Clubhouse Facilities:** Full bar & restaurant facilities. Bar food available.

NO.	METRES	PAR	S.I.	NO.	METRES	PAR	S.I.
1	482	5	18	10	174	3	17
2	350	4	8	11	368	4	7
3	383	4	6	12	540	5	1
4	403	4	2	13	150	3	13
5	160	3	16	14	482	5	11
6	334	4	12	15	360	4	3
7	356	4	4	16	193	3	9
8	447	5	14	17	377	4	15
9	147	3	10	18	404	4	5
OUT	3,082	36		IN	3,048	35	
				TOTAL	6,110	71	
				STANDARD SCRATCH		72	

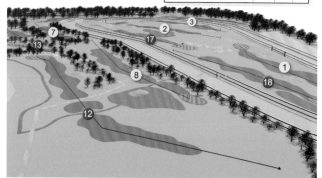

Glendine, Kilkenny. Tel: (056) 776 5400.

LOCATION: One mile outside the city – off Castlecomer Road.

NO.	BLUE METRES	WHITE METRES	PAR	S.I.	NO.	BLUE METRES	WHITE METRES	PAR	S.I.
1	375	353	4	2	10	192	183	3	7
2	304	295	4	10	11	399	395	4	1
3	390	358	4	5	12	460	447	5	16
4	327	320	4	14	13	388	354	4	4
5	275	273	4	17	14	458	441	5	18
6	145	133	3	13	15	181	172	3	9
7	364	357	4	8	16	355	350	4	3
8	367	353	4	6	17	162	153	3	11
9	443	435	5	12	18	323	310	4	15
OUT	2,990	2,877	36		IN	2,918	2,805	35	
					TOTAL	5,908	5,682	71	
				STANDARD SCRATCH		70	69		

Course Information:
Par 71; SSS 70; Length 5,933 metres.
Visitors: Welcome to play Mon – Fri, weekends by prior arrangement. **Opening Hours:** Daylight hours. **Avoid:** Saturday and Sunday – prior arrangement preferred. **Ladies:** Welcome. **Green Fees:** €35 - €45. Club hire and Lessons available. **Clubhouse Hours:** As per licensing law. **Clubhouse Dress:** Neat. **Clubhouse Facilities:** Bar, food snooker and pool.

PROFESSIONAL: Jimmy Bolger.

Course Description:
Parkland course with plenty of trees throughout the fairways which provide a good test of golf. GUI Irish finals are held here from time to time.

SECRETARY MANAGER:
Sean Boland

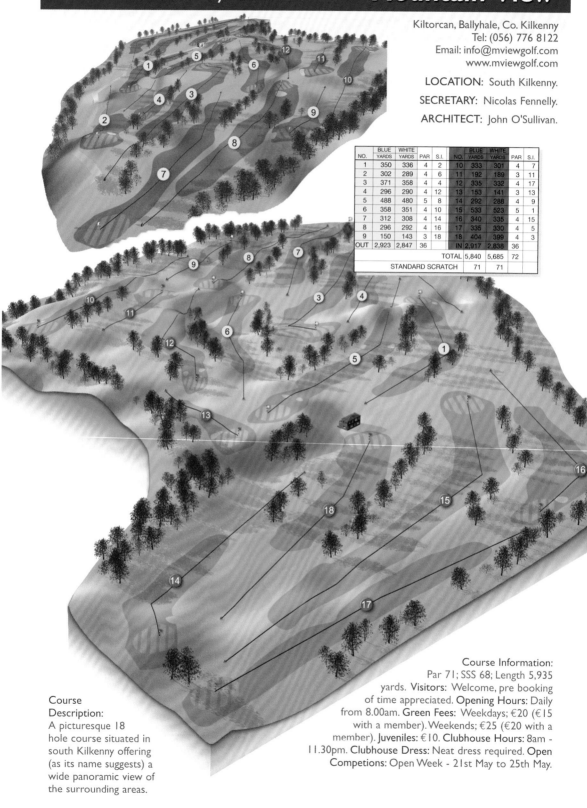

Kiltorcan, Ballyhale, Co. Kilkenny
Tel: (056) 776 8122
Email: info@mviewgolf.com
www.mviewgolf.com

LOCATION: South Kilkenny.

SECRETARY: Nicolas Fennelly.

ARCHITECT: John O'Sullivan.

NO.	BLUE YARDS	WHITE YARDS	PAR	S.I.	NO.	BLUE YARDS	WHITE YARDS	PAR	S.I.
1	350	336	4	2	10	333	301	4	7
2	302	289	4	6	11	192	189	3	11
3	371	358	4	4	12	335	332	4	17
4	296	290	4	12	13	153	141	3	13
5	488	480	5	8	14	292	288	4	9
6	358	351	4	10	15	533	523	5	1
7	312	308	4	14	16	340	335	4	15
8	296	292	4	16	17	335	330	4	5
9	150	143	3	18	18	404	399	4	3
OUT	2,923	2,847	36		IN	2,917	2,838	36	
					TOTAL	5,840	5,685	72	
					STANDARD SCRATCH	71	71		

Course Description:
A picturesque 18 hole course situated in south Kilkenny offering (as its name suggests) a wide panoramic view of the surrounding areas.

Course Information:
Par 71; SSS 68; Length 5,935 yards. **Visitors:** Welcome, pre booking of time appreciated. **Opening Hours:** Daily from 8.00am. **Green Fees:** Weekdays; €20 (€15 with a member). Weekends; €25 (€20 with a member). **Juveniles:** €10. **Clubhouse Hours:** 8am - 11.30pm. **Clubhouse Dress:** Neat dress required. **Open Competitions:** Open Week - 21st May to 25th May.

Thomastown, Co. Kilkenny.
Tel: (056) 777 3000 Fax: (056) 777 3078
Email: info@mountjuliet.ie
Web: www.mountjuliet.com

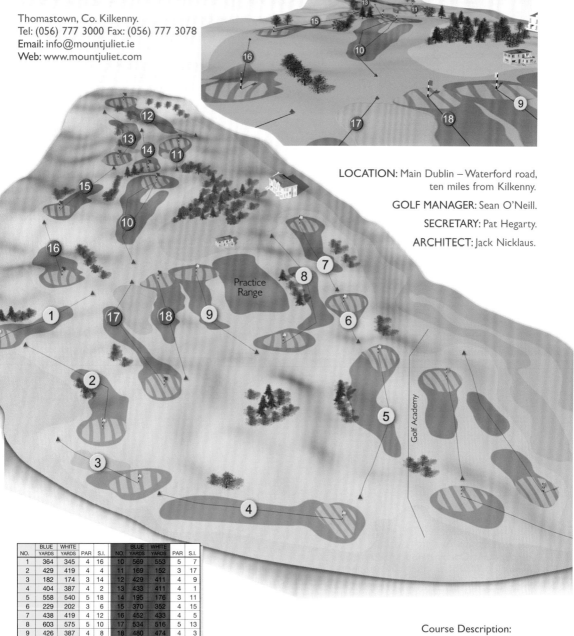

LOCATION: Main Dublin – Waterford road, ten miles from Kilkenny.

GOLF MANAGER: Sean O'Neill.

SECRETARY: Pat Hegarty.

ARCHITECT: Jack Nicklaus.

NO.	BLUE YARDS	WHITE YARDS	PAR	S.I.	NO.	BLUE YARDS	WHITE YARDS	PAR	S.I.
1	364	345	4	16	10	569	553	5	7
2	429	419	4	4	11	169	152	3	17
3	182	174	3	14	12	429	411	4	9
4	404	387	4	2	13	433	411	4	1
5	558	540	5	18	14	195	176	3	11
6	229	202	3	6	15	370	352	4	15
7	438	419	4	12	16	452	433	4	5
8	603	575	5	10	17	534	516	5	13
9	426	387	4	8	18	480	474	4	3
OUT	3,633	3,448	36		IN	3,631	3,478	36	
					TOTAL	7,264	6,926	72	
					STANDARD SCRATCH	75	73		

Course Information:
Par 72; SSS 72;
Length 7,264 yards.
Visitors: Welcome.
Prior arrangement required. Handicap certificate not required but desirable. **Opening Hours:** Daily from 7.30am – 8.00pm. **Ladies:** Welcome. **Green Fees:** November - March; €85 - €105. April, August and October; €100 - €130. May, June, July, September; €125 - €185 (depending on day required). **Juveniles:** Welcome (no reduction in green fees). **Clubhouse Hours:** 8.00am – 11.30pm. **Clubhouse Facilities:** Changing rooms, Bar, Restaurant. 8.00am – 9.00pm (Must be booked in advance).

Course Description:
The only Jack Nicklaus designed course in Ireland, it features old specimen trees, water hazards and bunkers. It is set in a beautiful old 1500 acre estate and appeals to all levels and standards of golfers. Accommodation is available in both Mount Juliet House and the clubhouse. New 18 hole putting course featuring par 2, 3 and 4, also with water features and bunkers.

Newrath, Waterford. Tel: (051) 876 748 Fax: (051) 853 405
Email: info@.waterfordgolfclub.com
www.waterfordgolfclub.com

LOCATION: Newrath.

NO.	BLUE METRES	WHITE METRES	PAR	S.I.	NO.	BLUE METRES	WHITE METRES	PAR	S.I.
1	384	372	4	5	10	270	253	4	14
2	334	314	4	11	11	452	438	5	10
3	119	110	3	17	12	443	435	5	6
4	380	368	4	1	13	178	170	3	12
5	370	360	4	7	14	398	390	4	2
6	361	340	4	3	15	439	435	5	8
7	164	151	3	15	16	128	115	3	18
8	494	470	5	9	17	270	260	4	16
9	170	150	3	13	18	368	360	4	4
OUT	2,776	2,635	34		IN	2,946	2,856	37	
					TOTAL	5,722	5,491	71	
	STANDARD SCRATCH					70	69		

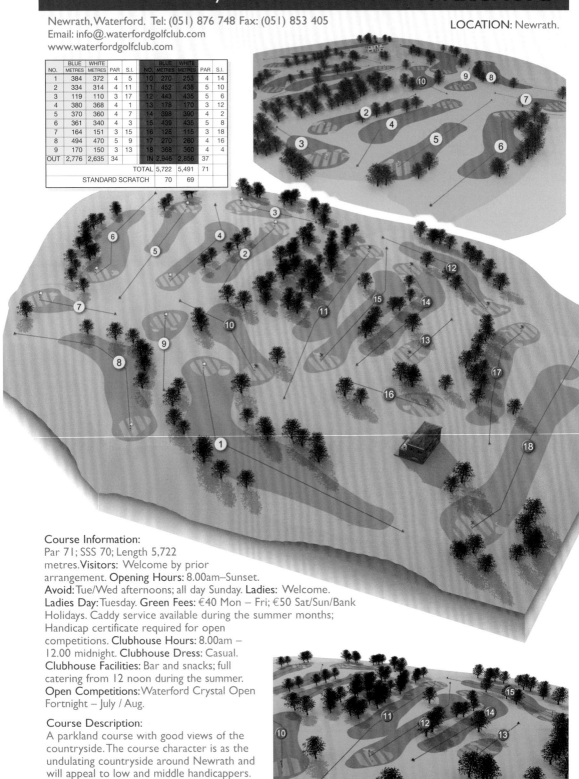

Course Information:
Par 71; SSS 70; Length 5,722
metres. **Visitors:** Welcome by prior
arrangement. **Opening Hours:** 8.00am–Sunset.
Avoid: Tue/Wed afternoons; all day Sunday. **Ladies:** Welcome.
Ladies Day: Tuesday. **Green Fees:** €40 Mon – Fri; €50 Sat/Sun/Bank
Holidays. Caddy service available during the summer months;
Handicap certificate required for open
competitions. **Clubhouse Hours:** 8.00am –
12.00 midnight. **Clubhouse Dress:** Casual.
Clubhouse Facilities: Bar and snacks; full
catering from 12 noon during the summer.
Open Competitions: Waterford Crystal Open
Fortnight – July / Aug.

Course Description:
A parkland course with good views of the
countryside. The course character is as the
undulating countryside around Newrath and
will appeal to low and middle handicappers.

SECRETARY: Damien Maguire.
Tel: (051) 876748

ARCHITECT: James Braid / Willie Park.

Rathmoyle, Abbeyleix, Co. Laois
Tel: (057) 8731450
Fax: (057) 8730108
info@abbeyleixgolfclub.ie
www.abbeyleixgolfclub.ie

LOCATION: Less than one mile north of the town on Stradbally road.

SECRETARY: Malachy Fogarty.
Tel: (057) 8731305.

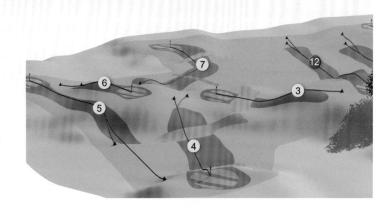

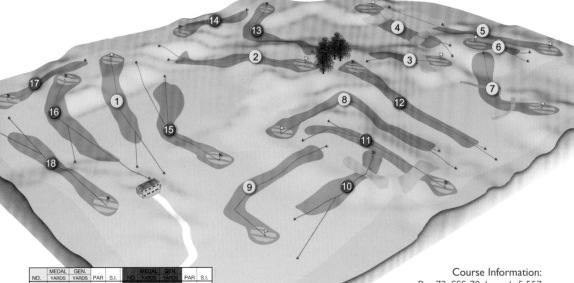

NO.	MEDAL YARDS	GEN. YARDS	PAR	S.I.	NO.	MEDAL YARDS	GEN. YARDS	PAR	S.I.
1	570	517	5	11	10	406	348	4	6
2	515	477	5	7	11	412	382	4	8
3	121	121	3	15	12	267	212	4	18
4	307	307	4	9	13	376	376	4	4
5	379	379	4	3	14	136	136	3	16
6	145	145	3	17	15	499	468	5	14
7	262	262	4	5	16	495	495	5	12
8	467	412	4	1	17	235	210	3	10
9	347	347	4	13	18	426	426	4	2
OUT	3,113	2,967	36		IN	3,252	3,053	36	
					TOTAL	6,365	6,020	72	
		STANDARD SCRATCH				74	72		

Course Information:
Par 72; SSS 70; Length 5,557 metres. **Visitors:** Welcome to play on weekdays. **Opening Hours:** Sunrise – Sunset. **Ladies:** Welcome. **Green Fees:** €25 Weekdays, €30 Weekends. **Juveniles:** Only when accompanied by adults. **Clubhouse Hours:** Winter: Mon/Tues/Fri evening 7pm - close; Summer: 1pm - Close; All day Sat/Sun. **Clubhouse Dress:** Informal but respectable. **Clubhouse Facilities:** General. Catering facilities and times by prior arrangement. **Open Competitions:** Open Week 13th - 22nd July.

Course Description:
Abbeyleix constructed a new 9 hole extension which opened on 1st April 2001. The new course features some great water hazards and natural contours which make it challenging to any golfer. Visitors are most welcome to play this new amenity and will come away enriched by the experience.

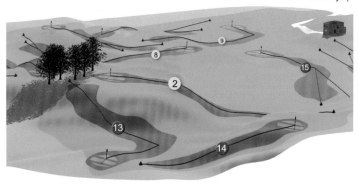

The Heath, Portlaoise, Co. Laois.
Tel: (0502) 46533. Fax: (0502) 46866

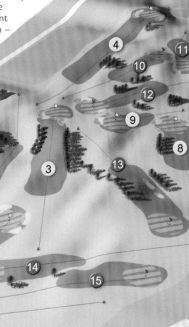

Course Information:
Par 71; SSS 70; Length 5,854 metres. **Visitors:** Welcome, please book. **Opening Hours:** Sunrise – sunset. **Avoid:** Weekends unless with advance booking. **Ladies:** Welcome. **Green Fees:** €20 Mon – Fri; €30 Sat / Sun / Bank Hols. Societies welcome. **Juveniles:** Welcome. Lessons available by prior arrangement; Club Hire available; Caddy service available by prior arrangement; telephone appointment required. **Clubhouse Hours:** 10.30am – 11.30pm Mon – Sat; 10.30am – 11.00pm Sundays. **Clubhouse Dress:** Casual (Neat). **Clubhouse Facilities:** Full catering facilities. Floodlit 10 bay driving range. **Open Competitions:** Open Week August. Other various days. Contact Administrator for details.

Course Description:
This Par 71 course is playable all year round and is exceptionally dry in wintertime. Set in picturesque surroundings with views of the rolling hills of Laois, the course incorporates three natural lakes. Noted for its rough of heather and gorse furze it is a challenge for any golfer. The Heath Golf Club is the seventh oldest Golf Club in Ireland, founded in November 1889.

NO.	MEDAL METRES	GEN. METRES	PAR	S.I.	NO.	MEDAL METRES	GEN. METRES	PAR	S.I.
1	450	442	5	16	10	341	330	4	7
2	160	150	3	12	11	139	132	3	17
3	350	339	4	4	12	341	332	4	11
4	458	452	5	10	13	388	381	4	1
5	286	286	4	14	14	352	346	4	9
6	359	341	4	6	15	367	344	4	3
7	347	330	4	8	16	482	473	5	15
8	351	334	4	2	17	171	162	3	13
9	167	148	3	18	18	345	335	4	5
OUT	2,928	2,820	36		IN	2,926	2,835	35	
					TOTAL	5,854	5,655	71	
		STANDARD SCRATCH				70	69		

ADMINISTRATOR:
Gaye Aston.
PROFESSIONAL:
Mark O'Boyle.

LOCATION: Two miles Limerick side of Mountrath – just off the main Dublin/ Limerick road.

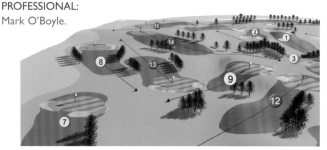

Knockinina, Mountrath, Co. Laois.
Tel: (0502) 32558

LOCATION: Two miles Limerick side of Mountrath – just off the main Dublin/Limerick road.

SECRETARY: Dinah Kingsley.

NO.	MEDAL YARDS	GEN. YARDS	PAR	S.I.	NO.	MEDAL YARDS	GEN. YARDS	PAR	S.I.
1	390	380	4	4	10	167	151	3	13
2	169	141	3	10	11	487	438	5	7
3	345	336	4	2	12	381	357	4	1
4	348	334	4	8	13	473	441	5	11
5	448	428	5	16	14	181	174	3	5
6	118	108	3	12	15	324	288	4	9
7	270	255	4	18	16	382	367	4	3
8	350	325	4	6	17	276	262	4	17
9	306	290	4	14	18	317	296	4	15
OUT	2,744	2,597	35		IN	2,988	2,774	36	
					TOTAL	5,732	5,371	71	
					STANDARD SCRATCH	69	68		

Course Information:

Par 71; SSS 69; Length 5,643 metres.
Visitors: Welcome.
Ladies: Welcome. **Opening Hours:** Sunrise – sunset. **Avoid:** Saturday or Sunday mornings (check in clubhouse). **Green Fees:** €20 per round Monday – Friday; Sat/Sun €30. **Clubhouse Hours:** Evening service available full time. **Clubhouse Dress:** Casual. **Clubhouse Facilities:** Catering facilities by prior arrangment.

Course Description:

This is an 18 hole course set on gently rolling land with the river Nore and an old Mill stream flowing through and coming into play on a number of holes. Lush fairways and good greens which are well bunkered make it an excellent test of golf.

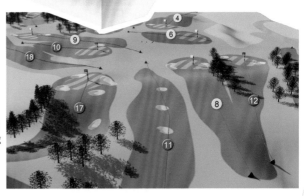

Portarlington Golf Club, Garryhinch,
Portarlington, Co. Laois.
Tel: (0502) 23115. Fax: (0502) 23044.
Email: portarlingtonc@eircom.net.
Web: www.portarlingtongolf.com

Course Description:
The course has recently undergone extensive development from a nine hole course to an eighteen hole course. The new course was completed in November 1992 and provides a fresh test of skill and ability.

NO.	MEDAL Metres	GEN. Metres	PAR	S.I.	NO.	MEDAL Metres	GEN. Metres	PAR	S.I.
1	337	322	4	11	10	462	456	5	16
2	395	384	4	3	11	149	146	3	14
3	168	158	3	9	12	409	396	4	2
4	375	371	4	5	13	413	404	4	18
5	134	123	3	17	14	363	356	4	4
6	331	325	4	13	15	307	292	4	10
7	411	403	4	1	16	319	304	4	6
8	435	420	5	15	17	169	160	3	8
9	351	339	4	7	18	344	340	4	12
OUT	2,937	2,845	35		IN	2,935	2,854	36	
					TOTAL	5,872	5,699	71	
					STANDARD SCRATCH	71	70		

Course Information:
Par 71; SSS 71; Length 5,872 metres. Visitors: Welcome as members of societies and as individuals. Opening Hours: 8.00am – sunset. Avoid: Weekends. Ladies: Tuesday. Handicap Cert. required for open competition. Green Fees: Mon – Fri, €25 Saturday / Sunday / holidays €30. 50% discount with member. Juveniles: Welcome. Clubhouse Hours: Early – sunset. Clubhouse Dress: Neat/Casual. Clubhouse Facilities: By prior arrangement. Golf Shop Tel: (0502) 42916.

LOCATION:
3 miles from Portarlington.

Coulnaboul West, Rathdowney, Co. Laois. Tel: (0505) 46170 Fax: (0505) 46065

Location: Less than 1 mile east of Rathdowney.

SECRETARY: Sean Bolger.

Course Description:
This inland course was redeveloped to eighteen holes in 1997 and provides the golfer with a varied game, testing flexibility.

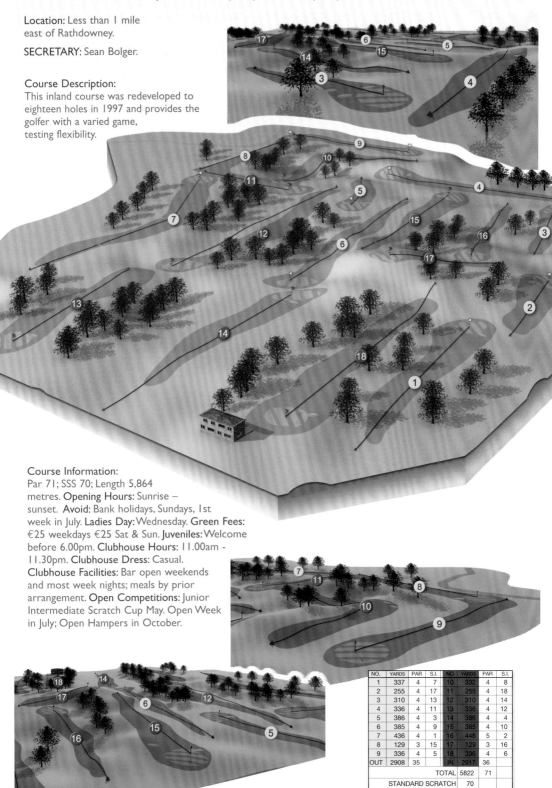

Course Information:
Par 71; SSS 70; Length 5,864 metres. **Opening Hours:** Sunrise – sunset. **Avoid:** Bank holidays, Sundays, 1st week in July. **Ladies Day:** Wednesday. **Green Fees:** €25 weekdays €25 Sat & Sun. **Juveniles:** Welcome before 6.00pm. **Clubhouse Hours:** 11.00am - 11.30pm. **Clubhouse Dress:** Casual. **Clubhouse Facilities:** Bar open weekends and most week nights; meals by prior arrangement. **Open Competitions:** Junior Intermediate Scratch Cup May. Open Week in July; Open Hampers in October.

NO.	YARDS	PAR	S.I.	NO.	YARDS	PAR	S.I.
1	337	4	7	10	332	4	8
2	255	4	17	11	255	4	18
3	310	4	13	12	310	4	14
4	336	4	11	13	336	4	12
5	386	4	3	14	386	4	4
6	385	4	9	15	385	4	10
7	436	4	1	16	448	5	2
8	129	3	15	17	129	3	16
9	336	4	5	18	336	4	6
OUT	2908	35		IN	2917	36	
				TOTAL	5822	71	
				STANDARD SCRATCH		70	

Killenard, Co. Laois.
Tel: (057) 8645500 Fax: (057) 8642392
Email: info@theheritage.com www.theheritage.com

LOCATION: 40 miles from Dublin and Dublin Airport in the charming village of Killenard just off the Dublin to Cork Road and the new M7 motorway.

GOLF OPERATIONS MANAGER: Niall Carroll.

HEAD PROFESSIONAL: Eddie Doyle.

Course Information: Par 72; SSS 75; Length 7,319 Yards. Visitors: Always welcome. **Opening Hours:** 8am to sunset. **Ladies:** Welcome. **Green Fees:** Mon-Fri €115, Sat-Sun and Bank Holidays €130. **Clubhouse Facilities:** Full clubhouse facilities. Golf clubs, buggies, electric trolleys available for hire. Professional tuition available by appointment Seve Ballesteros 'natural' school of golf available. Hotel, Resort Spa & Leisure Centre on site. Indoor and outdoor bowling facilities.

NO.	WHITE METRES	GREEN METRES	PAR	S.I.	NO.	WHITE METRES	GREEN METRES	PAR	S.I.
1	406	386	4	18	10	526	502	5	15
2	572	543	5	8	11	332	305	4	11
3	431	410	4	12	12	491	468	4	1
4	214	191	3	10	13	473	449	4	3
5	460	430	4	2	14	572	532	5	7
6	455	434	4	6	15	175	164	3	17
7	189	179	3	14	16	397	379	4	13
8	533	498	5	16	17	225	202	3	9
9	421	394	4	4	18	447	423	4	5
OUT	3,681	3,465	36		IN	3,638	3,424	36	
					TOTAL	7,319	6,889	72	
					STANDARD SCRATCH	75	74		

ARCHITECTS: Seve Ballesteros & Jeff Howes.

Course Description: Par 72 championship course set in the beautiful rolling countryside of County Laois with the Slieve Bloom Mountains as a backdrop. It provides a most enjoyable experience for golfers of all standards. Five lakes and a stream that meanders through the course brings water into play on 10 holes. Beautifully shaped bunkers and trees adorn the landscape which is very gently undulating without any climbing involved. Venue for 2005 AIB Irish Seniors Open. Host Venue to Seve Trophy 2007 & 2009. The Heritage has been selected by *Golf World* (June issue) as No. 1 of the best new golf courses (parkland & links) in Great Britain & Ireland.

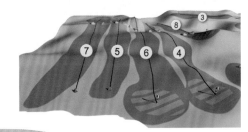

Glack, Dublin Road, Longford, Co. Longford.
Tel: (043) 46310. Fax: (043) 47082
Email:colonggolf@eircom.net
Web: countylongfordgolfclub.com

LOCATION: Dublin Road, Longford.

SECRETARY: Mark Glancy.

ARCHITECT: Mel Flanagan.

Course Description:
An elevated parkland course, overlooking Longford town and surrounding countryside.

Course Information:
Par 70; SSS 69; Length 6,044 yards. **Visitors:** Welcome.
Opening Hours: Sunrise – Sunset (closed mon. in winter) **Avoid:** Weekends and Tuesdays. **Ladies Day:** Tuesday. **Green Fees:** €25 Mon – Fri (€15 with member); €30 Sat/Sun (€20 with member on a one to one basis). **Juveniles:** Welcome. Lessons available; Club Hire and caddy cars also available. **Clubhouse Hours:** 12noon – 11pm.
Clubhouse Dress: Neat / Casual. **Clubhouse Facilities:** Meals snacks and bar. **Open Competitions:** Open week July / August.

NO.	YARDS	PAR	S.I.	NO.	YARDS	PAR	S.I.
1	330	4	9	10	435	4	1
2	133	3	18	11	377	4	11
3	415	4	2	12	192	3	7
4	372	4	14	13	405	4	3
5	350	4	6	14	305	4	8
6	339	4	15	15	495	5	13
7	362	4	4	16	478	5	10
8	161	3	17	17	127	3	16
9	358	4	12	18	410	4	5
OUT	2,820	34		IN	3,224	36	
				TOTAL	6,044	70	
				STANDARD SCRATCH	69		

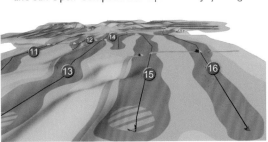

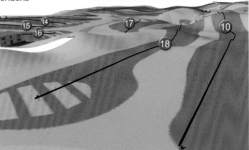

Townparks, Ardee,
Co. Louth. Tel: (041) 6853227.

LOCATION: Just north of Ardee town.

SECRETARY MANAGER: Seamus Rooney.
ARCHITECT: Declan Branagan.

Course Description:
A very fair test of golf and also a very pleasant walk with some beautiful old trees on this parkland course.

Course Information:
Par 71; SSS 69/71; Length 6,467 yards. **Visitors:** Welcome. **Avoid:** Sundays. **Societies:** Welcome. **Ladies:** Welcome. **Green Fees:** €35 Mon – Fri. Sat €50. No Green Fees Sun. **Clubhouse Hours:** 10.00am – 11.30pm. **Clubhouse Dress:** Neat, Casual. **Clubhouse Facilities:** Catering facilities available at all times. **Open Competitions:** Several dates throughout year. Open Week – June.

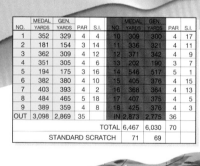

NO.	MEDAL YARDS	GEN. YARDS	PAR	S.I.	NO.	MEDAL YARDS	GEN. YARDS	PAR	S.I.
1	352	329	4	4	10	309	300	4	17
2	181	154	3	14	11	336	321	4	11
3	362	309	4	12	12	371	342	4	9
4	351	305	4	6	13	202	190	3	7
5	194	175	3	16	14	546	517	5	1
6	382	380	4	10	15	405	376	4	15
7	403	393	4	2	16	368	364	4	13
8	484	465	5	18	17	407	375	4	5
9	389	359	4	8	18	425	376	4	3
OUT	3,098	2,869	35		IN	2,873	2,775	36	
					TOTAL	6,467	6,030	70	
					STANDARD SCRATCH	71	69		

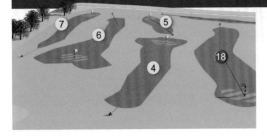

Armagh Road, Dundalk, Co. Louth.
Tel: (042) 9332518. Fax: (042) 9395731.

Course Information:

Par 72; SSS 70; Length 6,321 yards. **Visitors:** Welcome.
Opening Hours: Daylight hours. **Ladies:** Welcome.
Green Fees: Midweek €15 for 9 holes or €20 for 18
holes; Weekends €18 for 9 holes or €28 for 18 holes.
Special group rates available on request. **Juveniles:**
Welcome. **Clubhouse Hours:** Sunrise – sunset.
Clubhouse Dress: Casual. **Clubhouse Facilities:**
Full clubhouse facilities. Restaurant and
fully licensed Bar. Radison Hotel
and Leisure Centre.

LOCATION: Just a few minutes from
Dundalk town centre. Located on the R177
(Dundalk-Armagh Road), the course is just 1
hour from both Dublin and Belfast.

NO.	BLUE YARDS	GREEN YARDS	PAR	S.I.	NO.	BLUE YARDS	GREEN YARDS	PAR	S.I.
1	357	345	4	9	10	266	256	4	18
2	204	198	3	7	11	594	584	5	4
3	265	254	4	17	12	131	124	3	14
4	473	462	5	5	13	422	411	4	2
5	160	154	3	15	14	372	360	4	8
6	336	325	4	1	15	471	460	5	10
7	327	315	4	11	16	150	142	3	12
8	322	310	4	13	17	277	265	4	16
9	370	360	4	3	18	481	470	5	6
OUT	2,814	2,723	35		IN	3,164	3,072	37	
					TOTAL	5,978	5,795	70	
					STANDARD SCRATCH		70	70	

Course Description:

The course, designed by the late Eddie
Hackett (PGA Architect of the century), is full of
undulating dips and mounds, combined with over 90
bunkers, a stern test of golf awaits even the strongest
golfer. A par 72 course, Carnbeg has it all. 6321 yards in
total, the 600 yard par 5 11th hole, and the panoramic
setting with the Cooley peninsula providing a stunning
backdrop to this gem. There are four par 5's, four par 3's
and ten par 4's along the way. Carnbeg is the North
East's 'Premier Pay-As-You-Play Course'.

HON. SECRETARY:
Patrick McCaffrey.

HON. TREASURER: Brian Kirk.

ARCHITECT: Eddie Hackett.

County Louth

Balltray, Co. Louth. Tel: (041) 9881530.

SECRETARY: Michael Delany.
PROFESSIONAL: Paddy McGuirk. Tel: (041) 9881536.
ARCHITECT: Tom Simpson.

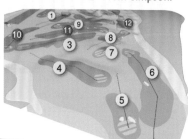

Course Description:
A championship links which can be enjoyed by every category of golfer. Not as well known as some of the other links courses. Baltray's demands are stern but its rewards are many, not least in the fun and enjoyment it evokes and the sense of freshness that prevails.

LOCATION: Five miles north east Drogheda.

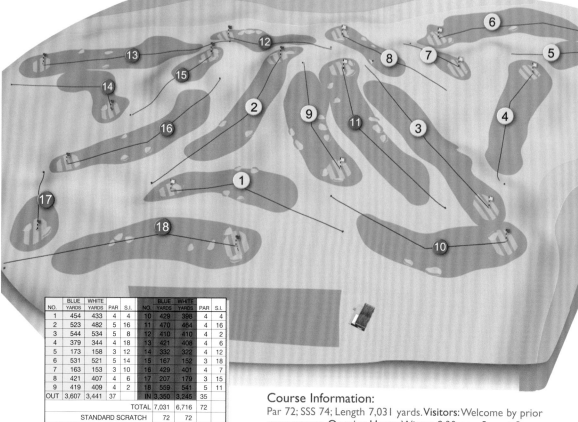

NO.	BLUE YARDS	WHITE YARDS	PAR	S.I.	NO.	BLUE YARDS	WHITE YARDS	PAR	S.I.
1	454	433	4	4	10	429	398	4	4
2	523	482	5	16	11	470	464	4	16
3	544	534	5	8	12	410	410	4	2
4	379	344	4	18	13	421	408	4	6
5	173	158	3	12	14	332	322	4	12
6	531	521	5	14	15	167	152	3	18
7	163	153	3	10	16	429	401	4	7
8	421	407	4	6	17	207	179	3	15
9	419	409	4	2	18	559	541	5	11
OUT	3,607	3,441	37		IN	3,350	3,245	35	
					TOTAL	7,031	6,716	72	
		STANDARD SCRATCH					72	72	

reservations@countylouthgolfclub.com
www.countylouthgolfclub.com

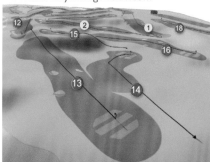

Course Information:
Par 72; SSS 74; Length 7,031 yards. Visitors: Welcome by prior arrangement. Opening Hours: Winter 8.30am – Sunset; Summer 7.30am – Sunset. Avoid: Weekends and Tuesdays. Ladies: Welcome at all times. Green Fees: €115 midweek; €135 weekends. Juveniles: Restrictions apply - please phone club for details. Lessons available by prior arrangement; Club Hire available; Caddy service available by prior arrangement; telephone appointment required. Clubhouse Hours: 8.00am – 12.00 midnight. Clubhouse Dress: Casual.

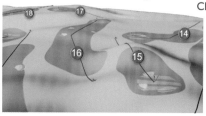

Clubhouse Facilities: Bar & Restaurant 8.00am – 8.30pm (winter); 8.00am – 10.30pm (summer). Open Competitions: Please phone club for details.

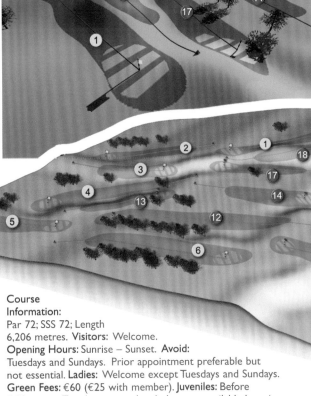

Blackrock, Dundalk, Co. Louth.
Tel: (042) 932 1731 Fax: (042) 932 2022
Email: manager@dundalkgolfclub.ie
Web: www.dundalkgolfclub.ie

LOCATION: Three miles south of Dundalk at Blackrock Village.

SECRETARY: Terry Sloane.

PROFESSIONAL: Leslie Walker.
Tel: (042) 932 2102

ARCHITECTS: Dave Thomas.

Course Information:
Par 72; SSS 72; Length 6,206 metres. **Visitors:** Welcome.
Opening Hours: Sunrise – Sunset. **Avoid:** Tuesdays and Sundays. Prior appointment preferable but not essential. **Ladies:** Welcome except Tuesdays and Sundays.
Green Fees: €60 (€25 with member). **Juveniles:** Before 6.00pm, not Tuesdays or weekends. Lessons available by prior arrangement; Club hire and Caddy service available by prior arrangement. **Clubhouse Hours:** Sunrise to midnight.
Clubhouse Dress: Informal. **Clubhouse Facilities:** Snacks and full meals any time. **Open Competitions:** May 14th-20th, July 22nd-29th.

Course Description:
Top ranking course with excellent facilities and catering. Hosted all Ireland finals in 1997 and 2000. Attracts country's top players to senior Scratch Cup. Hosts major PGA pro-Am.

NO.	MEDAL YARDS	GEN. YARDS	PAR	S.I.	NO.	MEDAL YARDS	GEN. YARDS	PAR	S.I.
1	218	199	3	2	10	154	147	3	18
2	562	547	5	15	11	523	506	5	14
3	409	393	4	17	12	424	359	4	4
4	409	396	4	4	13	436	418	4	6
5	420	403	4	8	14	149	140	3	12
6	130	115	3	13	15	360	342	4	10
7	419	393	4	11	16	438	429	4	2
8	412	398	4	6	17	492	478	5	16
9	323	316	4	1	18	369	358	4	8
OUT	3,302	3,160	35		IN	3,345	3,177	36	
					TOTAL	6,645	6,337		
	STANDARD SCRATCH						71	70	

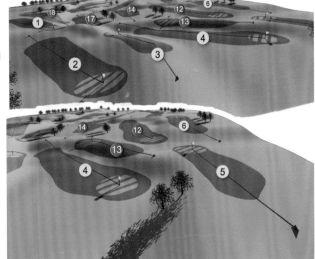

Greenore, Co. Louth. Tel: (042) 9373212/ 9373678. Fax: (042) 9383898.

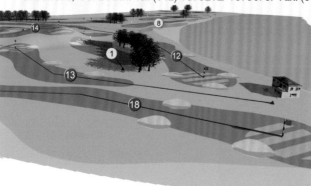

Email: greenoregolfclub@eircom.net
Web: www.greenoregolfclub.com

Course Information: Par 71; SSS 73; Length 6,647 yards. **Visitors:** Welcome to play weekdays and weekends, but appointment is recommended for weekends. **Opening Hours:** 8.00am (or earlier by appointment) – Sunset. **Green Fees:** €40 Mon – Fri (€20 with a member); €50 Sat & Sun & Bank Holidays (€25 with a member). Students half price. **Clubhouse Hours:** 9am – 6pm (winter); 8am – 11.30pm (summer). **Clubhouse Dress:** Informal. **Clubhouse Facilities:** All days. **Open Competitions:** Open Week – 6th/15th July

NO.	MEDAL YARDS	GEN. YARDS	PAR	S.I.	NO.	MEDAL YARDS	GEN. YARDS	PAR	S.I.
1	218	199	3	2	10	154	147	3	18
2	562	547	5	15	11	523	506	5	14
3	409	393	4	17	12	424	359	4	4
4	409	396	4	4	13	436	418	4	6
5	420	403	4	8	14	149	140	3	12
6	130	115	3	13	15	360	342	4	10
7	419	393	4	11	16	438	429	4	2
8	412	398	4	6	17	492	478	5	16
9	323	316	4	1	18	369	358	4	8
OUT	3,302	3,160	35		IN	3,345	3,177	36	
					TOTAL	6,645	6,337		
					STANDARD SCRATCH		71	70	

LOCATION: Travelling form Dublin – proceed through Drogheda and Dundalk and take the first turn right on the Newry road out of Dundalk and proceed to Greenore – 15 mins.

SECRETARY: Linda Clarke.

ARCHITECT: Eddie Hackett.

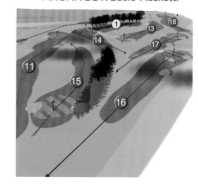

Course Description: An inland course with a links nature on the shores of Carlingford Lough. The course enjoys scenic views of both the Lough and the Mountains of Mourne. An unusual feature are the tall pine trees, a rare sight on a semi-links course, which come into play on seven holes. The 14th or "pigs back" is the most famous hole in Greenore, a par 3 to an elevated green.

Killin Park Golf & Country Club, Killin,
Dundalk, Co. Louth.
Tel: (042) 9339303.

LOCATION: Three miles from Dundalk town centre, off the Castleblayney road.

Course Information:

Par 69; SSS 65; Length 5,388 yards. **Visitors:** Welcome all times. **Ladies:** Welcome. **Green Fees:** €22 Mon – Fri; €27 weekends & public holidays. **Juveniles:** Welcome any time Mon - Fri, after 2pm Sat, Sun & Bank Holidays. **Clubhouse Hours:** Sunrise – sunset. **Clubhouse Dress:** Neat dress. **Clubhouse Facilities:** Bar snacks available everyday from 8.30am. Full catering facilities by prior arrangement. Club hire available. Buggie hire available – €25. **Open Competitions:** Various Open Days throughout the year, telephone Club for details.

NO.	CHAMP YARDS	MEDAL YARDS	PAR	S.I.	NO.	CHAMP YARDS	MEDAL YARDS	PAR	S.I.
1	114	109	3	16	10	280	277	4	17
2	360	351	4	3	11	161	161	3	4
3	196	177	3	5	12	177	160	3	6
4	358	354	4	1	13	476	473	5	8
5	310	305	4	14	14	396	382	4	2
6	312	307	4	9	15	310	310	4	11
7	492	487	5	10	16	291	291	4	7
8	280	268	4	18	17	160	160	3	15
9	261	244	4	13	18	359	342	4	12
OUT	2,682	2,602	35		IN	2,610	2,556	34	
					TOTAL	5,293	5,158	69	
					STANDARD SCRATCH		65	64	

Course Description:

Killin Park is a privately owned course situated in rolling parkland with mature trees and scenic views of the Mourne Mountains. Bordered by Killin Wood and the Castletown River, this exceptionally free-draining course has American style greens. Noted for its 6th hole which resembles the 10th at the Belfry, this course offers a challenge even to the most experienced golfer.

MANAGER: Pat Reynolds.

ARCHITECT: Eddie Hacket.

Termonfeckin, Co. Louth. Tel: (041) 982 2333. Fax: (041) 982 2331.
Email: golflinks@seapoint.ie www.seapointgolfclub.com

LOCATION: Seapoint lies by the mouth of the Boyne, near to the historic town of Drogheda, just 40 mins from Dublin on the M1.

SECRETARY/MANAGER:
Kevin Carrie.
PROFESSIONAL:
David Carroll
Tel: (041) 9881066.

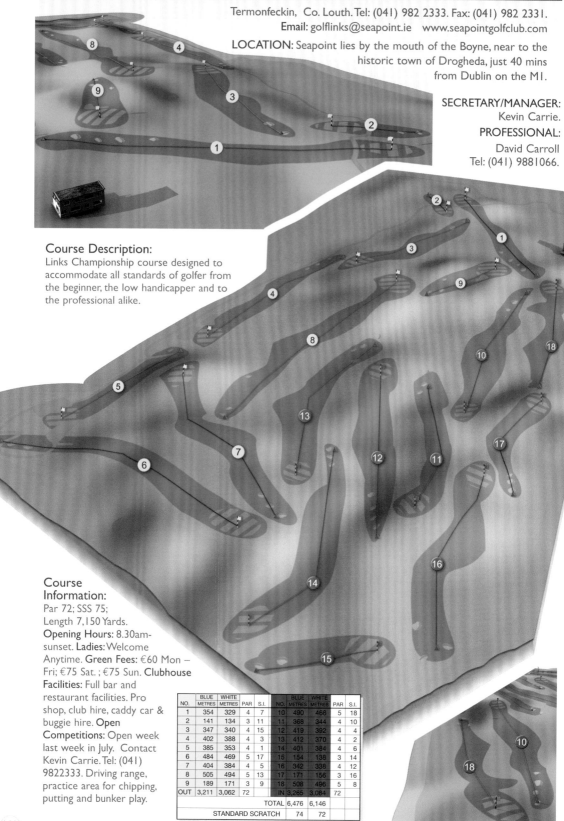

Course Description:

Links Championship course designed to accommodate all standards of golfer from the beginner, the low handicapper and to the professional alike.

Course Information:

Par 72; SSS 75; Length 7,150 Yards.
Opening Hours: 8.30am-sunset. **Ladies:** Welcome Anytime. **Green Fees:** €60 Mon – Fri; €75 Sat. ; €75 Sun. **Clubhouse Facilities:** Full bar and restaurant facilities. Pro shop, club hire, caddy car & buggie hire. **Open Competitions:** Open week last week in July. Contact Kevin Carrie. Tel: (041) 9822333. Driving range, practice area for chipping, putting and bunker play.

NO.	BLUE METRES	WHITE METRES	PAR	S.I.	NO.	BLUE METRES	WHITE METRES	PAR	S.I.
1	354	329	4	7	10	490	468	5	18
2	141	134	3	11	11	368	344	4	10
3	347	340	4	15	12	419	392	4	4
4	402	388	4	3	13	412	370	4	2
5	385	353	4	1	14	401	384	4	6
6	484	469	5	17	15	154	138	3	14
7	404	384	4	5	16	342	338	4	12
8	505	494	5	13	17	171	156	3	16
9	189	171	3	9	18	508	496	5	8
OUT	3,211	3,062	72		IN	3,265	3,084	72	
					TOTAL	6,476	6,146		
					STANDARD SCRATCH	74	72		

Ashbourne, Co Meath.
Tel: (01) 835 2005. Fax: (01) 835 2561.

LOCATION: One mile from Ashbourne, 12 miles (20 mins drive) from Dublin.

NO.	MEDAL METRES	GEN. METRES	PAR	S.I.	NO.	MEDAL METRES	GEN. METRES	PAR	S.I.
1	274	270	4	10	10	170	149	3	9
2	155	147	3	16	11	362	347	4	3
3	330	322	4	2	12	358	350	4	1
4	450	440	5	6	13	140	133	3	15
5	144	136	3	18	14	471	454	5	5
6	487	477	5	12	15	322	314	4	11
7	356	346	4	8	16	138	131	3	17
8	405	396	4	4	17	489	481	5	7
9	346	334	4	14	18	320	314	4	13
OUT	2,947	2,868	36		IN	2,770	2,673	35	
					TOTAL	5,717	5,541	71	
					STANDARD SCRATCH	70	69		

Course

Information: Par 71; SSS 70;
Length 5,884 metres. **Visitors:** Welcome Mon – Fri and Sat/Sun afternoons. **Opening Hours:** 9.00am – dusk. **Ladies:** No restrictions. **Green Fees:** Mon-Fri €40 Sat./Sun/Bank Holidays €50. **Juveniles:** Must be accompanied by an adult. **Clubhouse Hours:** Normal licensing hours. **Clubhouse Dress:** Neat casual dress required. **Clubhouse Facilities:** Lounge bar, bar food and full restaurant.
Open Competitions: Regularly during summer months – Open Week mid June.

Course Description:

Undulating parkland course with great variety incorporated in design. Water comes into play at eight holes. A fine blend of trees contributes to the players overall enjoyment.

MANAGER: Paul Wisniewski.

ARCHITECT: Des Smyth & Declan Branigan (Design).

Thomastown, Dunshaughlin,
Co. Meath.
Tel: (01) 8250021.
Fax: (01) 8250400.

LOCATION:
1 mile from Dunshaughlin off
the Ratoath road.

ARCHITECT:
R. J. Browne.

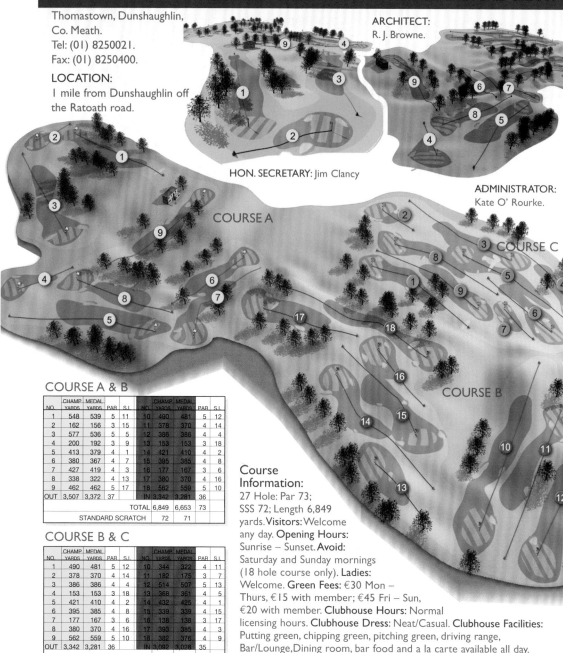

COURSE A

HON. SECRETARY: Jim Clancy

ADMINISTRATOR:
Kate O' Rourke.

COURSE C

COURSE B

COURSE A & B

NO.	CHAMP YARDS	MEDAL YARDS	PAR	S.I.	NO.	CHAMP YARDS	MEDAL YARDS	PAR	S.I.
1	548	539	5	11	10	490	481	5	12
2	162	156	3	15	11	378	370	4	14
3	577	536	5	5	12	386	386	4	4
4	200	192	3	9	13	153	153	3	18
5	413	379	4	1	14	421	410	4	2
6	380	367	4	7	15	395	385	4	8
7	427	419	4	3	16	177	167	3	6
8	338	322	4	13	17	380	370	4	16
9	462	462	5	17	18	562	559	5	10
OUT	3,507	3,372	37		IN	3,342	3,281	36	
					TOTAL	6,849	6,653	73	
					STANDARD SCRATCH	72	71		

COURSE B & C

NO.	CHAMP YARDS	MEDAL YARDS	PAR	S.I.	NO.	CHAMP YARDS	MEDAL YARDS	PAR	S.I.
1	490	481	5	12	10	344	322	4	11
2	378	370	4	14	11	182	175	3	7
3	386	386	4	4	12	514	507	5	13
4	153	153	3	18	13	368	361	4	5
5	421	410	4	2	14	432	425	4	1
6	395	385	4	8	15	339	339	4	15
7	177	167	3	6	16	138	138	3	17
8	380	370	4	16	17	393	385	4	3
9	562	559	5	10	18	382	376	4	9
OUT	3,342	3,281	36		IN	3,092	3,028	35	
					TOTAL	6,434	6,309	71	
					STANDARD SCRATCH	70	69		

COURSE C & A

NO.	CHAMP YARDS	MEDAL YARDS	PAR	S.I.	NO.	CHAMP YARDS	MEDAL YARDS	PAR	S.I.
1	344	322	4	12	10	548	539	5	11
2	182	175	3	8	11	162	156	3	15
3	514	507	5	14	12	577	536	5	5
4	368	361	4	6	13	200	192	3	9
5	432	425	4	2	14	413	379	4	1
6	339	339	4	16	15	380	367	4	7
7	138	138	3	18	16	427	419	4	3
8	393	385	4	4	17	338	322	4	13
9	382	376	4	10	18	462	462	5	17
OUT	3,092	3,028	35		IN	3,507	3,372	37	
					TOTAL	6,599	6,400	72	
					STANDARD SCRATCH	71	70		

Course Information:
27 Hole: Par 73;
SSS 72; Length 6,849
yards. **Visitors:** Welcome
any day. **Opening Hours:**
Sunrise – Sunset. **Avoid:**
Saturday and Sunday mornings
(18 hole course only). **Ladies:**
Welcome. **Green Fees:** €30 Mon –
Thurs, €15 with member; €45 Fri – Sun,
€20 with member. **Clubhouse Hours:** Normal
licensing hours. **Clubhouse Dress:** Neat/Casual. **Clubhouse Facilities:**
Putting green, chipping green, pitching green, driving range,
Bar/Lounge, Dining room, bar food and a la carte available all day.
Function room, Pro Shop, golf lessons etc. Tel: 825 0793. **Open
Competitions:** Regularly Mar-Oct, Open Week early August.

Course Description:
27 hole parkland, playable all year. Luscious fairways bounded by
maturing trees lead to well protected excellent sand based
greens. Strategic bunkering, water features and wildlife habitats
add to the enjoyment of golf here. Excellent value. M50 15 mins.

Email: golf@blackbush.iol.ie
Web: www.blackbushgolf.ie

Kells, Co. Meath. Tel: (046) 92 40146.
Fax: (046) 92 49282.

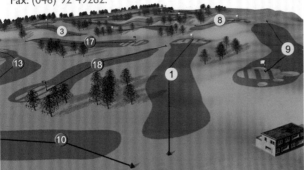

LOCATION: Kells/Navan road – within one mile of town.

Course Information:
Par 72; SSS 71; Length 5,780 metres. **Visitors:** Welcome. **Opening Hours:** Sunrise – Sunset. **Ladies:** Welcome. Ladies day: Tuesday (mostly old course) **Green Fees: Old Course** Mon-Thur €50 (Early Bird Mon-Thur 8-11am €40) Fri - Sun and Bank Holidays €55, With member €20. **Juveniles:** Must be accompanied by an adult (adults with juveniles must give way). Lessons available by prior arrangement; Club hire available; Buggies available; Telephone appointment required. **Clubhouse Hours:** 9.00am – 11.30pm. **Clubhouse Dress:** Casual. **Clubhouse Facilities:** Full facilities in new clubhouse.

Course Description:
Generally accepted as a first class parkland course, the Headfort Club is set in the rolling countryside of Kells. Two 18-hole Courses. New course designed by Christy O' Connor Jnr.

HON. SECRETARY: Brian Mungovan
Tel: (046) 92 40146.
PROFESSIONAL: Brendan McGovern.
Tel: (046) 92 40639.
E-mail: hgcadmin@eircom.net

NO.	MEDAL METRES	GEN. METRES	PAR	S.I.	NO.	MEDAL METRES	GEN. METRES	PAR	S.I.
1	438	426	5	17	10	171	160	3	16
2	173	164	3	12	11	491	483	5	13
3	369	362	4	5	12	356	332	4	4
4	444	433	5	8	13	351	341	4	6
5	394	377	4	1	14	171	165	3	11
6	381	363	4	3	15	301	298	4	15
7	436	427	5	18	16	372	352	4	2
8	144	139	3	14	17	326	320	4	7
9	318	308	4	10	18	337	330	4	9
OUT	3,097	2,999	37		IN	2,876	2,781	35	
					TOTAL	5,973	5,780	72	
					STANDARD SCRATCH	70	69		

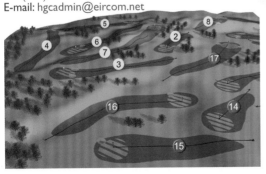

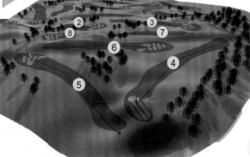

Navan Road, Kells, Co. Meath.
Tel: (046) 9240146. Fax: (046) 9249282.
E-mail: hgcadmin@eircom.net Web: headfortgolfclub.ie

Course Information: Par 72; SSS 71; Length 6,515 metres. **Visitors:** Welcome. **Opening hours:** Sunrise-Sunset. **Ladies:** Welcome. Ladies day; Tuesday (mostly old course). **Green Fees:** Mon-Thur €65 Fri-Sun and Bank holidays €70 (Early Bird Mon-Thur 8am-11am €50) **Juveniles:** Must be accompanied by an adult (adults with juveniles must give way). Lessons available by prior arrangement; Club hire available; Buggies available; Telephone appointment required. **Clubhouse Hours:** 9.00am-11.30pm. **Clubhouse Dress:** Casual. **Clubhouse Facilities:** Full facilities in new clubhouse.

LOCATION: Kells/Navan road, within one mile of town.

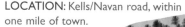

Course Description:
Generally accepted as a first class parkland course, the Headfort club is set in the rolling countryside of Kells. Two 18 hole courses, new course designed by Christy O'Connor Jnr.

HON. SECRETARY: Brian Mungovan

PROFESSIONAL: Brendan McGovern. Tel: (046) 9240639.

NO.	MEDAL METRES	GEN. METRES	PAR	S.I.	NO.	MEDAL METRES	GEN. METRES	PAR	S.I.
1	400	370	4	6	10	378	342	4	9
2	480	465	5	18	11	163	155	3	11
3	345	330	4	10	12	366	346	4	5
4	157	145	3	14	13	392	370	4	1
5	400	383	4	2	14	510	490	5	15
6	516	506	5	8	15	398	383	4	3
7	170	155	3	16	16	508	500	5	17
8	384	372	4	4	17	180	152	3	13
9	377	334	4	12	18	391	366	4	7
OUT	3,229	3,060	36		IN	3,286	3,104	36	
					TOTAL	6,515	6,164	72	
					STANDARD SCRATCH	75	74		

Course Information:
Par 72; SSS 70; Length 5,801 metres.
Visitors: Welcome except Sunday morning. Saturday by prior arrangement.
Opening Hours: Sunrise – sunset. **Ladies:** Welcome.
Green Fees: €25 Mon – Thur; €35 Fri / Sun / Bank Holidays, €10 Juveniles and students. **Juveniles:** Welcome (must be accompanied by an adult).
Clubhouse Dress: Neat. **Clubhouse Facilities:** Full bar and catering during high season. Catering by appointment off season. **Open Competitions:** Open Weekends – April. Various other Open Days throughout the summer. Available on club website.

Gallow, Kilcock, Co. Meath. Tel: (01) 6287592 Fax: (01) 6287283
Email: kilcockgolfclub@eircom.net **Web:** www.kilcockgolfclub.com

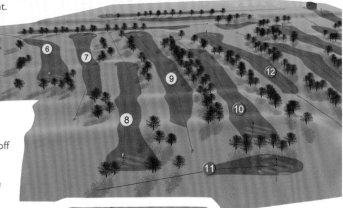

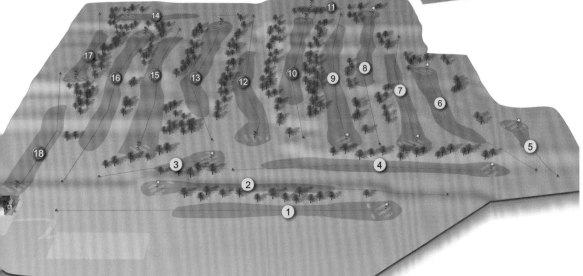

Course Description:
A relatively easy opening which will tie in with the warm welcome to all visitors to our golf club. Generally flat with some beautiful mature trees which add to the enjoyment of your game. The greens, by todays standards, are small but undulating and will be a test for even the best golfers. After upgrading from 9 to 18 holes, the course is now more challenging. Streams rolling through the course come into play on the 4th, 5th, 6th, 8th, 9th, 10th, 12th, 13th, 15th, 16th and 18th. Other recently added features are the mounding and bunkering.

NO.	WHITE METRES	GREEN METRES	PAR	S.I.	NO.	WHITE METRES	GREEN METRES	PAR	S.I.
1	293	288	4	16	10	397	382	4	2
2	320	290	4	7	11	147	137	3	15
3	130	125	3	18	12	461	454	5	9
4	335	330	4	8	13	419	414	4	1
5	135	129	3	14	14	172	153	3	11
6	368	360	4	3	15	366	358	4	5
7	310	300	4	10	16	437	427	5	13
8	456	451	5	12	17	272	262	4	17
9	478	408	5	4	18	320	306	4	6
OUT	2,725	2,681	36		IN	2,991	2,893	36	
					TOTAL	5,716	5,574	72	
					STANDARD SCRATCH	68	67		

LOCATION: South Meath.

HON. SECRETARY: Kevin O'Connor.

MANAGER: Seamus Kelly.

ARCHITECT: Eddie Hackett.

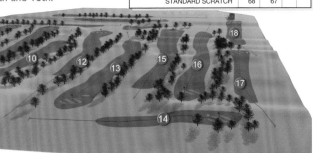

Course Description: 18 hole championship course which has been designed by former Ryder Cup player Christy O'Connor Jnr. A challenging and creative course, golfers will enjoy views over mature undulating parkland. They will be intrigued by 14 demanding water features with 9 lakes and the Knightsbrook River incorporated into the course.

Knightsbrook Hotel & Golf Resort, Dublin Road, Trim, Co. Meath.
Tel: (046) 948 2101.
Email: golf@knightsbrook.com
Web: www.knightsbrook.com

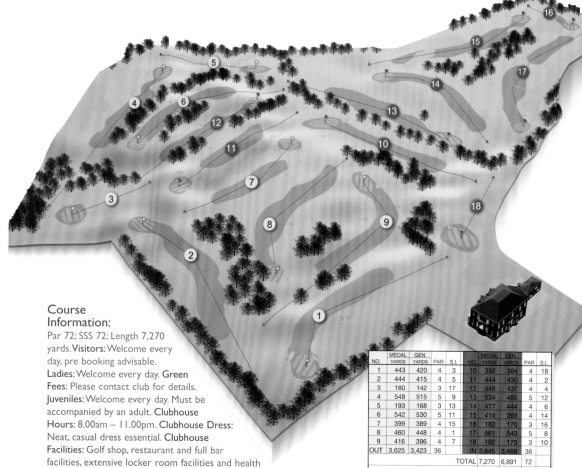

Course Information:

Par 72; SSS 72; Length 7,270 yards. **Visitors:** Welcome every day, pre booking advisable. **Ladies:** Welcome every day. **Green Fees:** Please contact club for details. **Juveniles:** Welcome every day. Must be accompanied by an adult. **Clubhouse Hours:** 8.00am – 11.00pm. **Clubhouse Dress:** Neat, casual dress essential. **Clubhouse Facilities:** Golf shop, restaurant and full bar facilities, extensive locker room facilities and health spa. Practice chipping and putting green, trolley hire, club hire and electric buggy hire. **Open Competitions:** Open programme updated on www.knightsbrook.com.

NO.	MEDAL YARDS	GEN. YARDS	PAR	S.I.	NO.	MEDAL YARDS	GEN. YARDS	PAR	S.I.
1	443	420	4	3	10	392	384	4	18
2	444	415	4	5	11	444	430	4	2
3	180	142	3	17	12	449	437	4	4
4	548	515	5	9	13	534	495	5	12
5	193	168	3	13	14	477	444	4	6
6	542	530	5	11	15	414	393	4	14
7	399	389	4	15	16	182	170	3	16
8	460	448	4	1	17	561	540	5	8
9	416	396	4	7	18	192	175	3	10
OUT	3,625	3,423	36		IN	3,645	3,468	36	
					TOTAL	7,270	6,891	72	
					STANDARD SCRATCH		72		

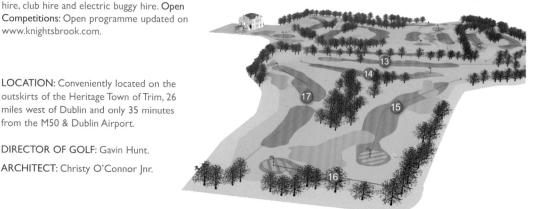

LOCATION: Conveniently located on the outskirts of the Heritage Town of Trim, 26 miles west of Dublin and only 35 minutes from the M50 & Dublin Airport.

DIRECTOR OF GOLF: Gavin Hunt.

ARCHITECT: Christy O'Connor Jnr.

Bettystown, Co. Meath.
Tel: (041) 982 7170.
www.landb.ie
links@landb.ie

LOCATION: Thirty miles north of Dublin.

SECRETARY: Helen Finnegan.
Tel: (041) 982 7170

PROFESSIONAL:
Robert J Browne.
Tel: (041) 982 8793

Course Information:
Par 71; SSS 72; Length 5,852 metres. **Visitors:** Welcome all week. **Opening Hours:** 8.30am – Sunset. **Avoid:** Weekends am. **Ladies:** Welcome. **Ladies Days:** Mon. and Thurs. **Green Fees:** €60 Mon – Fri; €75 Weekend. Ring for societiy rates. **Juveniles:** Welcome – must be accompanied by an adult before 6pm. Lessons available by prior arrangement; Club Hire available. **Clubhouse Hours:** 10.30am – licencing hours. **Clubhouse Dress:** Neat Dress. **Clubhouse Facilities:** Full bar and catering facilities available everyday. **Open Competitions:** Various competitions - phone club for details.

Course Description:
This is a traditional links course with the reputation of being a good test of golf skills with a par of 71. It has produced many fine players, the best known of whom is Des Smyth.

NO.	WHITE METRES	GREEN METRES	PAR	S.I.	NO.	WHITE METRES	GREEN METRES	PAR	S.I.
1	294	288	4	12	10	382	375	4	3
2	309	290	4	13	11	347	337	4	7
3	372	362	4	4	12	421	410	4	1
4	443	434	5	17	13	354	345	4	6
5	333	325	4	9	14	312	307	4	16
6	153	142	3	10	15	361	352	4	8
7	361	350	4	2	16	176	172	3	11
8	361	353	4	5	17	278	271	4	18
9	163	153	3	14	18	432	423	5	15
OUT	2,799	2,703	35		IN	3,063	2,994	36	
					TOTAL	5,862	5,697	71	
					STANDARD SCRATCH		72		

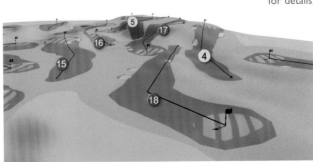

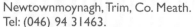

Newtownmoynagh, Trim, Co. Meath.
Tel: (046) 94 31463.

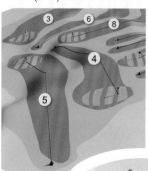

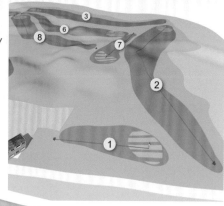

Course Description: Originally a pleasing nine hole course which has been recently developed into eighteen holes. Work was completed on the course in 1990.

LOCATION: Three miles from Trim on Longwood road.

SECRETARY: Jerry Kearney.
ARCHITECT: E. Hackett and Tom Craddock.
PROFESSIONAL: Robin Machin.

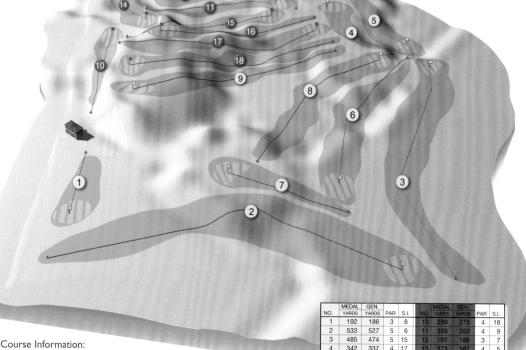

Course Information:
Par 73; SSS 72; Length 6,720 yards. Visitors: Welcome. **Opening Hours:** 8.00am – Sunset. **Avoid:** Thursday. **Ladies:** Welcome. **Ladies Day:** Thursday. **Green Fees:** €30 Mon – Thurs; €35 Fri/Sat/Sun. **Juveniles:** Welcome. **Clubhouse Hours:** 10.30am – 11.30pm. **Clubhouse Dress:** Casual. **Clubhouse Facilities:** Full catering facilities. Driving range on site.

NO.	MEDAL YARDS	GEN. YARDS	PAR	S.I.	NO.	MEDAL YARDS	GEN. YARDS	PAR	S.I.
1	192	186	3	8	10	289	275	4	18
2	533	527	5	6	11	359	353	4	9
3	485	474	5	15	12	197	186	3	7
4	342	337	4	17	13	373	367	4	5
5	418	411	4	2	14	3345	334	4	11
6	385	378	4	4	15	350	344	4	16
7	160	158	3	12	16	428	419	4	3
8	368	360	4	10	17	466	456	4	1
9	537	530	5	13	18	493	486	5	14
OUT	3,420	3,361	37		IN	3,300	3,220	36	
					TOTAL	6,720	6,581	73	
					STANDARD SCRATCH		72		

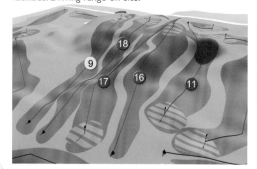

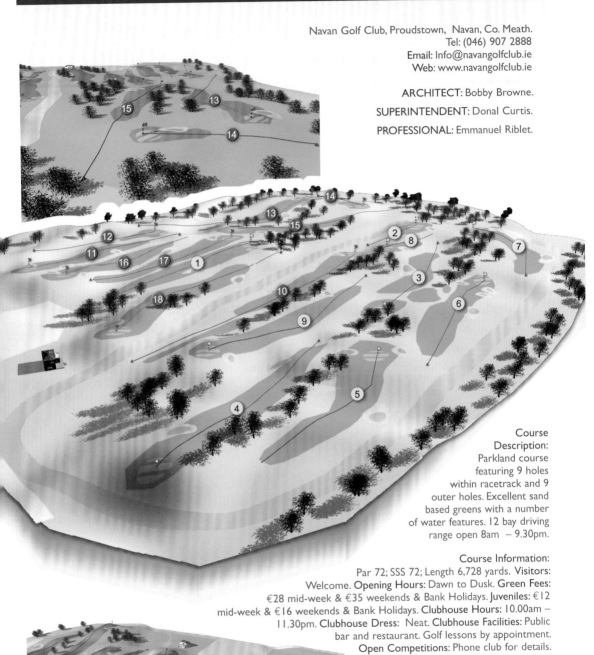

Navan Golf Club, Proudstown, Navan, Co. Meath.
Tel: (046) 907 2888
Email: Info@navangolfclub.ie
Web: www.navangolfclub.ie

ARCHITECT: Bobby Browne.

SUPERINTENDENT: Donal Curtis.

PROFESSIONAL: Emmanuel Riblet.

Course Description:
Parkland course featuring 9 holes within racetrack and 9 outer holes. Excellent sand based greens with a number of water features. 12 bay driving range open 8am – 9.30pm.

Course Information:
Par 72; SSS 72; Length 6,728 yards. Visitors: Welcome. Opening Hours: Dawn to Dusk. Green Fees: €28 mid-week & €35 weekends & Bank Holidays. Juveniles: €12 mid-week & €16 weekends & Bank Holidays. Clubhouse Hours: 10.00am – 11.30pm. Clubhouse Dress: Neat. Clubhouse Facilities: Public bar and restaurant. Golf lessons by appointment. Open Competitions: Phone club for details.

NO.	MEDAL METRES	GEN. METRES	PAR	S.I.	NO.	MEDAL METRES	GEN. METRES	PAR	S.I.
1	396	378	4	3	10	471	459	5	8
2	166	159	3	12	11	375	370	4	5
3	381	375	4	4	12	157	150	3	17
4	470	440	5	18	13	359	353	4	16
5	341	335	4	10	14	163	155	3	9
6	403	398	4	1	15	358	352	4	11
7	344	337	4	6	16	376	370	4	2
8	162	153	3	16	17	363	358	4	7
9	480	474	5	14	18	457	440	5	15
OUT	3,143	3,049	36		IN	3,078	3,007	36	
					TOTAL	6,221	6,056	72	
					STANDARD SCRATCH	72	73		

Bellinter, Navan, Co. Meath.
Tel: (046) 9025508/ 9026684.
Fax: (046) 9026684

LOCATION: Twenty miles north of Dublin off National Primary Route N3.

E-mail: info@royaltaragolfclub.com.
www.royaltaragolfclub.com

BELLINTER		
NO.	YARDS	PAR
1	334	4
2	183	3
3	472	5
4	344	4
5	372	4
6	280	4
7	150	3
8	398	4
9	349	4
TOTAL	2,882	35

CLUIDE		
NO.	YARDS	PAR
1	433	5
2	374	4
3	447	5
4	274	4
5	127	3
6	309	4
7	401	4
8	166	3
9	459	5
TOTAL	2,990	37

GENERAL MANAGER:
Francis Duffy.
HON. SECRETARY: Damien Usher.
Tel: (046) 9025508.
PROFESSIONAL: Mr John Byrne.
Tel:(046) 9026009.
ARCHITECT: Des Smyth Golf Design Ltd.

Course Description:
Parkland course situated in the heart of Co. Meath adjacent to the Hill of Tara, ancient home of the high kings of Ireland. A pleasant tree-lined course of average length with various degrees of difficulty.

TARA		
NO.	YARDS	PAR
1	395	4
2	159	3
3	366	4
4	160	3
5	468	5
6	176	3
7	388	4
8	376	4
9	500	5
TOTAL	2,988	35

Course Information:
Par 72; SSS 71; **Length** 5,904 metres. **Visitors:** Welcome. **Opening Hours:** 8.00am – 4.00pm. **Avoid:** Ladies Day (Tuesday). **Ladies:** Welcome. **Green Fees:** Mon – Thur €45; Fri €50; Sat / Sun €55. **Juveniles:** Welcome. Lessons available by prior arrangement. **Club Hire:** Available. **Caddy Service:** Available by prior arrangement. Telephone appointment required. **Clubhouse Hours:** 10.30am –11.00pm. **Clubhouse Dress:** Neat / smart. **Clubhouse Facilities:** 10.00am – 10.30pm (summer); 12.00 noon – 6.00pm (winter). Full catering

The Glenns, Birr, Co. Offaly. Tel: (05791) 20082.

Web: www.birrgolfclub.com
Email: birrgolfclub@ercom.net

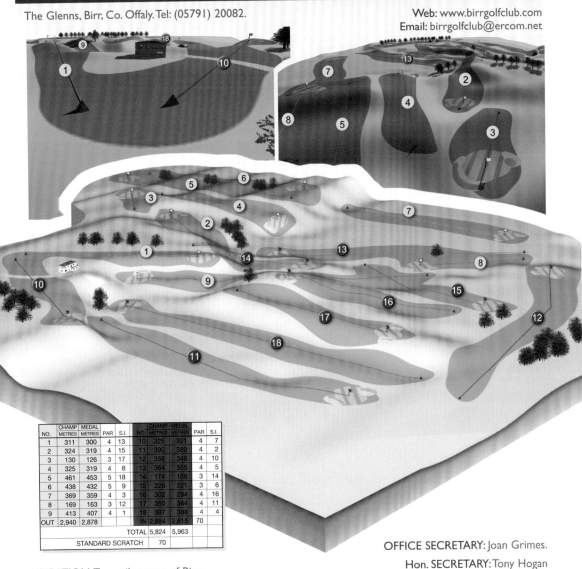

NO.	CHAMP METRES	MEDAL METRES	PAR	S.I.	NO.	CHAMP METRES	MEDAL METRES	PAR	S.I.
1	311	300	4	13	10	325	321	4	7
2	324	319	4	15	11	390	380	4	2
3	130	126	3	17	12	358	346	4	10
4	325	319	4	8	13	364	355	4	5
5	461	453	5	18	14	174	166	3	14
6	438	432	5	9	15	226	221	3	6
7	369	359	4	3	16	302	294	4	16
8	169	163	3	12	17	350	344	4	11
9	413	407	4	1	18	397	388	4	4
OUT	2,940	2,878			IN	2,884	2,615	70	
					TOTAL	5,824	5,963		
	STANDARD SCRATCH					70			

OFFICE SECRETARY: Joan Grimes.

Hon. SECRETARY: Tony Hogan

PROFESSIONAL: Kevin Mc Grath

LOCATION: Two miles west of Birr.

Course Description:
Undulating parkland course with sandy sub-soil, the greatest difficulties being "blind" shots and the strategic placing of pines.

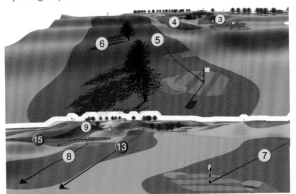

Course Information:
Par 70; SSS 70; Length 5,824 metres. **Visitors:** Welcome, limited to 11.00am – 12.00 noon on Sundays. **Opening Hours:** Sunrise – sunset. **Avoid:** Weekends if possible. **Green Fees:** €30. **Juveniles:** Welcome. **Clubhouse Hours:** 10.00am – 12.00 midnight. **Clubhouse Dress:** Neat/Casual. **Clubhouse Facilities:** Food available every day. **Opens:** Open singles every Tuesday.

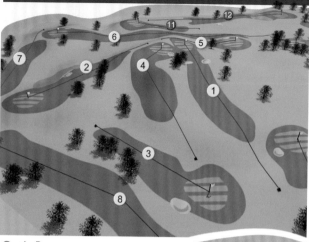

LOCATION: 8 miles south of main Dublin to Galway road (N6). One hour from Dublin. Only 30 miles from The "K" Club, Ryder Cup venue.

SECRETARY: Evelyn Mangan.

Tel: (057) 9353384.

ARCHITECT: Alan Duggan.

Email: info@castlebarna.ie

Web: www.castlebarna.ie

Course Description:
18 hole parkland course, with rolling parkland and natural water hazards making it an interesting course to play.

Castle Barna
Golf Club,
Daingean,
Co. Offaly.
Tel: (057) 9353384

NO.	MEDAL METRES	F/WARD METRES	PAR	S.I.	NO.	MEDAL METRES	F/WARD METRES	PAR	S.I.
1	347	332	4	3	10	422	418	5	18
2	275	272	4	13	11	175	151	3	14
3	178	161	3	7	12	346	341	4	10
4	262	258	4	9	13	282	250	4	16
5	167	164	3	11	14	333	330	4	8
6	474	449	5	5	15	374	372	4	2
7	402	398	5	17	16	459	424	5	12
8	375	373	4	1	17	383	371	4	6
9	143	137	3	15	18	401	379	4	4
OUT	2,623	2,544	35		IN	3,175	3,036	37	
					TOTAL	5,798	5,580	72	
					STANDARD SCRATCH		69	68	

Course Information:
Par 72; SSS 69; Length 6,200 yards.
Visitors: Welcome. **Opening Hours:** Sunrise – sunset. **Ladies:** Welcome every day. **Green Fees:** Weekdays €25; Sat, Sun & Bank Holidays €35. Juniors and juveniles €10. **Clubhouse Hours:** 8.00am – sunset. **Clubhouse Dress:** Neat. **Clubhouse Facilities:** Coffee shop, golf clubs for hire, golf shop, bar. **Open Competitions:** June, July and August.

Kishawanny, Edenderry, Co. Offaly.
Tel: (04697) 31072. Fax: (04697) 33911.
Web: www.edenderrygolfclub.com

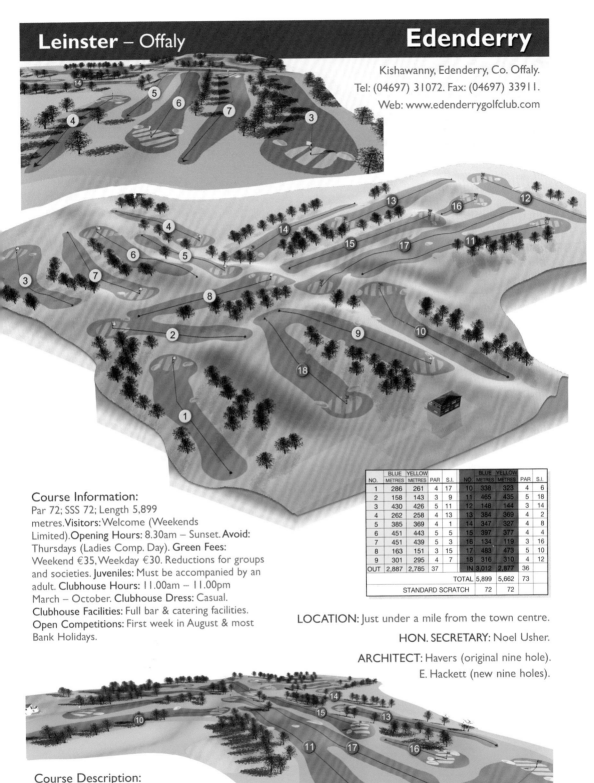

Course Information:

Par 72; SSS 72; Length 5,899
metres. **Visitors:** Welcome (Weekends
Limited). **Opening Hours:** 8.30am – Sunset. **Avoid:**
Thursdays (Ladies Comp. Day). **Green Fees:**
Weekend €35, Weekday €30. Reductions for groups
and societies. **Juveniles:** Must be accompanied by an
adult. **Clubhouse Hours:** 11.00am – 11.00pm
March – October. **Clubhouse Dress:** Casual.
Clubhouse Facilities: Full bar & catering facilities.
Open Competitions: First week in August & most
Bank Holidays.

NO.	BLUE METRES	YELLOW METRES	PAR	S.I.	NO.	BLUE METRES	YELLOW METRES	PAR	S.I.
1	286	261	4	17	10	338	323	4	6
2	158	143	3	9	11	465	435	5	18
3	430	426	5	11	12	148	144	3	14
4	262	258	4	13	13	384	369	4	2
5	385	369	4	1	14	347	327	4	8
6	451	443	5	5	15	397	377	4	4
7	451	439	5	3	16	134	119	3	16
8	163	151	3	15	17	483	473	5	10
9	301	295	4	7	18	316	310	4	12
OUT	2,887	2,785	37		IN	3,012	2,877	36	
					TOTAL	5,899	5,662	73	
					STANDARD SCRATCH	72	72		

LOCATION: Just under a mile from the town centre.

HON. SECRETARY: Noel Usher.

ARCHITECT: Havers (original nine hole).
E. Hackett (new nine holes).

Course Description:

Unique, in so much that it is built almost
entirely on fen peat. An attractive 18
hole course, the par 3's in particular
being challenging. Trees and traps are
ideally located.

157

Esker Hills Golf Club, Ballykilmurray, Tullamore, Co. Offaly. Tel: (057) 935 5999. Fax: (057) 935 5021. Email: info@eskerhillsgolf.com Web: www.eskerhillsgolf.com

Course Description: The course has a series of valleys and plateaux, part of the Esker Riada which together with the natural lakes and woodlands makes for an amazing variety of challenging golf holes. "A great test of golf to all who care to challenge it." "Esker Hills is one of Ireland's finest Golf Courses. If you are a golfer, never ever pass this place" -David Walshe, The Sunday Times.

Course Information:
Par 71; SSS 71; Length 6,669 yards. **Visitors:** Welcome every day. Booking required. **Opening Hours:** Summer: 8am – sunset. Winter: 9am – 5pm. **Green Fees:** €35 weekdays; €45 weekends/Bank Holidays. **Clubhouse Dress:** Smart / Casual. **Open Competition:** Open week July 9th-16th. **Additional Facilities:** Full dining facilities. Esker Hills is situated in the heart of Ireland where a golfing paradise awaits you!

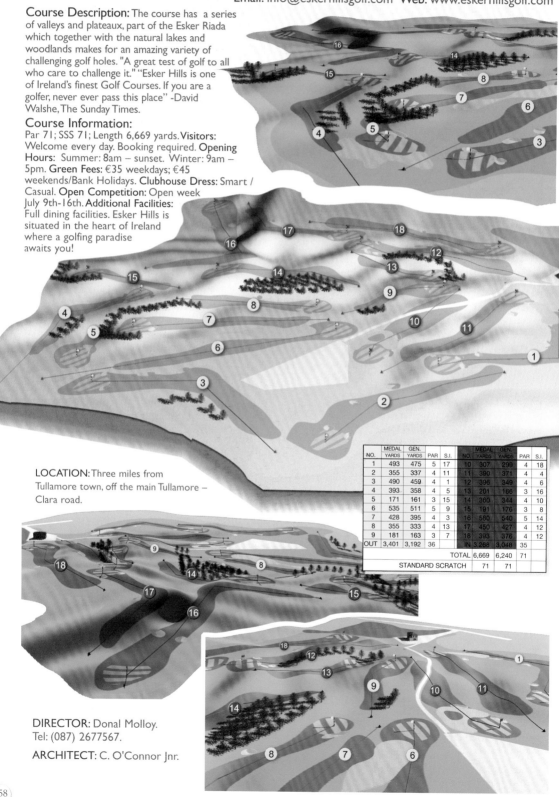

LOCATION: Three miles from Tullamore town, off the main Tullamore – Clara road.

NO.	MEDAL YARDS	GEN. YARDS	PAR	S.I.	NO.	MEDAL YARDS	GEN. YARDS	PAR	S.I.
1	493	475	5	17	10	307	299	4	18
2	355	337	4	11	11	390	371	4	4
3	490	459	4	1	12	396	349	4	6
4	393	358	4	5	13	201	166	3	16
5	171	161	3	15	14	360	344	4	10
6	535	511	5	9	15	191	176	3	8
7	428	395	4	3	16	580	540	5	14
8	355	333	4	13	17	450	427	4	12
9	181	163	3	7	18	393	376	4	12
OUT	3,401	3,192	36		IN	3,268	3,048	35	
					TOTAL	6,669	6,240	71	
					STANDARD SCRATCH	71	71		

DIRECTOR: Donal Molloy. Tel: (087) 2677567.

ARCHITECT: C. O'Connor Jnr.

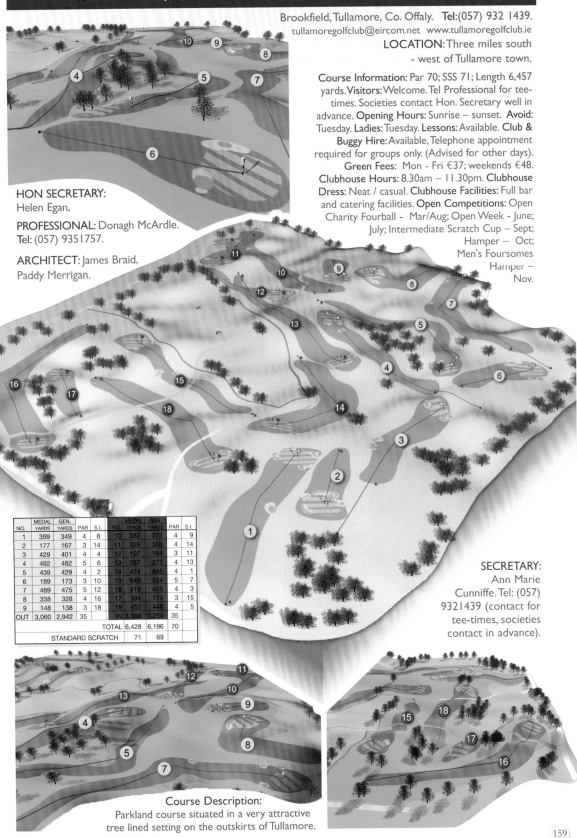

Brookfield, Tullamore, Co. Offaly. **Tel:**(057) 932 1439.
tullamoregolfclub@eircom.net www.tullamoregolfclub.ie

LOCATION: Three miles south - west of Tullamore town.

Course Information: Par 70; SSS 71; Length 6,457 yards. **Visitors:** Welcome. Tel Professional for tee-times. Societies contact Hon. Secretary well in advance. **Opening Hours:** Sunrise – sunset. **Avoid:** Tuesday. **Ladies:** Tuesday. **Lessons:** Available. **Club & Buggy Hire:** Available, Telephone appointment required for groups only. (Advised for other days). **Green Fees:** Mon - Fri €37; weekends €48. **Clubhouse Hours:** 8.30am – 11.30pm. **Clubhouse Dress:** Neat / casual. **Clubhouse Facilities:** Full bar and catering facilities. **Open Competitions:** Open Charity Fourball - Mar/Aug; Open Week - June; July; Intermediate Scratch Cup – Sept; Hamper – Oct; Men's Foursomes Hamper – Nov.

HON SECRETARY:
Helen Egan.

PROFESSIONAL: Donagh McArdle.
Tel: (057) 9351757.

ARCHITECT: James Braid,
Paddy Merrigan.

SECRETARY:
Ann Marie Cunniffe. Tel: (057) 9321439 (contact for tee-times, societies contact in advance).

NO.	MEDAL YARDS	GEN. YARDS	PAR	S.I.	NO.	MEDAL YARDS	GEN. YARDS	PAR	S.I.
1	359	349	4	8	10	382	372	4	9
2	177	167	3	14	11	325	305	4	14
3	429	401	4	4	12	197	194	3	11
4	492	482	5	6	13	387	377	4	13
5	439	429	4	2	14	474	455	4	1
6	189	173	3	10	15	548	524	5	7
7	489	475	5	12	16	419	405	4	3
8	338	328	4	16	17	184	174	3	15
9	148	138	3	18	18	452	448	4	5
OUT	3,060	2,942	35		IN	3,368	3,254	35	
					TOTAL	6,428	6,196	70	
					STANDARD SCRATCH	71	69		

Course Description:
Parkland course situated in a very attractive tree lined setting on the outskirts of Tullamore.

LOCATION: In the village of Delvin on the N52 road from the North. Dundalk is to the West.

Delvin, Co Westmeath. Tel: (044) 96 64671
www.devlincastlegolf.com
MANAGER: Fiona Dillon.
PROFESSIONAL: David Keenaghan.
ARCHITECT: John Day.

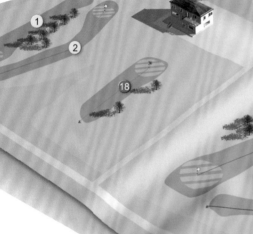

NO.	MEDAL YARDS	GEN. YARDS	PAR	S.I.	NO.	MEDAL YARDS	GEN. YARDS	PAR	S.I.
1	314	302	4	18	10	177	163	3	9
2	385	377	4	5	11	477	468	5	3
3	424	410	4	2	12	349	337	4	1
4	290	280	4	15	13	389	377	4	5
5	176	163	3	13	14	360	317	4	1
6	376	354	4	4	15	552	533	5	1
7	360	353	4	14	16	351	345	4	1
8	202	191	3	8	17	224	218	3	1
9	390	379	4	7	18	328	317	4	3
OUT	2,917	2,809	34		IN	3,207	3,074	36	
					TOTAL	6,124	5,883	70	
	STANDARD SCRATCH					68			

Course Description:

Set in the parkland of Clonyn Castle, this course provides a challenging test of Golf amid a unique historic setting. A ruined castle provides the focus of the back nine. The course opened in 1992 and has an active club membership.

Course Information:

Par 70; SSS 68; Length 6,124 yards. **Visitors:** Welcome, prior reservation at weekends necessary. **Opening Hours:** Daylight hours. **Ladies:** Welcome. **Green Fees:** €28 weekdays, €38 weekends and Bank Holidays. **Juveniles:** Welcome. **Clubhouse Hours:** Daylight hours. **Clubhouse Dress:** Casual. **Clubhouse Facilities:** Full bar and restaurant facilities.

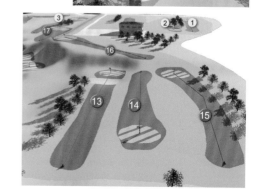

Glasson Golf Hotel and Country Club, Glasson, Athlone, Co. Westmeath.
Tel: (090) 64 85120 Fax: (090) 64 85444
Email: info@glassongolf.ie **Web:** www.glassongolf.ie

LOCATION: 6 miles north of Athlone Town on the N55.

SECRETARY: Fidelma Reid.
Tel: (090) 64 85120

ARCHITECT:
Christy O'Connor Jnr.

Course Description:
A Christy O'Connor Jnr. design that has golfers talking. Every hole is fascinating and measuring over 7000 yds from the championship tees it is a true test for all golfing standards. New on-site hotel with 'play and stay' offers.

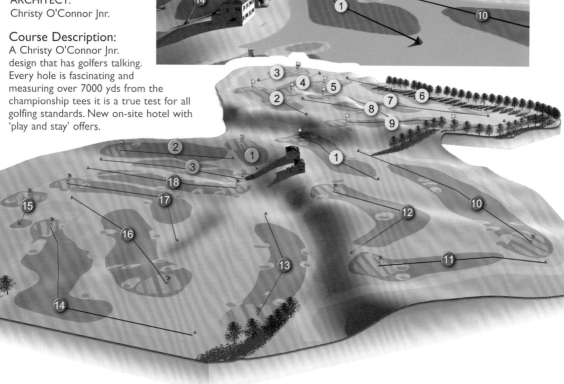

NO.	MEDAL YARDS	GEN. YARDS	PAR	S.I.	NO.	MEDAL YARDS	GEN. YARDS	PAR	S.I.
1	396	373	4	8	10	513	508	5	18
2	552	536	5	13	11	183	170	3	17
3	219	190	3	7	12	406	384	4	9
4	406	384	4	4	13	397	369	4	3
5	199	177	3	11	14	566	521	5	15
6	559	535	5	12	15	185	170	3	4
7	410	386	4	2	16	452	417	4	1
8	432	404	4	14	17	450	432	5	16
9	412	377	4	10	18	383	361	4	6
OUT	3,585	3,362	36		IN	3,630	3,474	37	
					TOTAL	7,215	6,836	73	
	STANDARD SCRATCH					76	74		

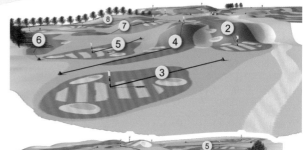

Course Information:
Par 76; SSS 76; Length 7,215 Yards.
Visitors: Welcome anyday. **Opening Hours:** Sunrise – Sunset. **Green Fees:** €60 Mon – Thur, €65 Fri & Sun, €75 Sat. Caddies available on request. **Clubhouse Facilities:** Bar Lounge & Restaurant, Full changing facilities. **Open Competitions:** Easter weekend. **Hotel:** 65 Bedrooms beautiful views, sauna, steam room, hot tub and fitness suite. Glasson is holding a European Challenge Tour Event in August 2007

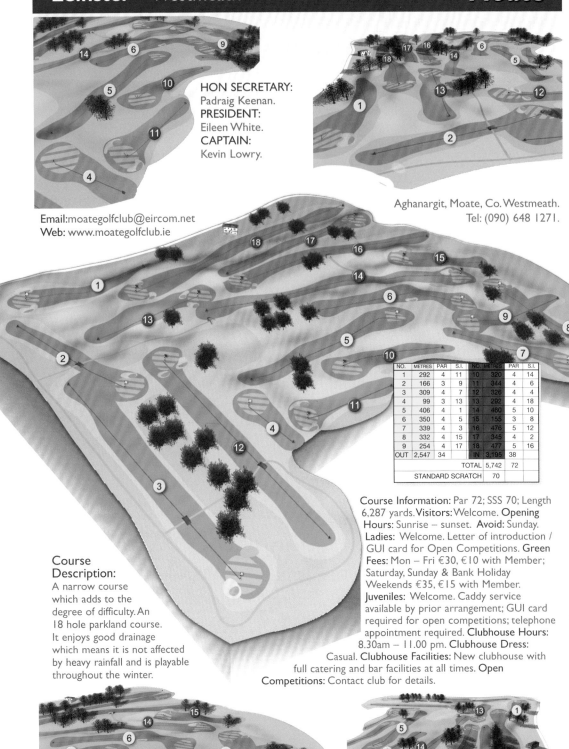

HON SECRETARY:
Padraig Keenan.
PRESIDENT:
Eileen White.
CAPTAIN:
Kevin Lowry.

Email: moategolfclub@eircom.net
Web: www.moategolfclub.ie

Aghanargit, Moate, Co. Westmeath.
Tel: (090) 648 1271.

NO.	METRES	PAR	S.I.	NO.	METRES	PAR	S.I.
1	292	4	11	10	320	4	14
2	166	3	9	11	344	4	6
3	309	4	7	12	326	4	4
4	99	3	13	13	292	4	18
5	406	4	1	14	460	5	10
6	350	4	5	15	155	3	8
7	339	4	3	16	476	5	12
8	332	4	15	17	345	4	2
9	254	4	17	18	477	5	16
OUT	2,547	34		IN	3,195	38	
				TOTAL	5,742	72	
			STANDARD SCRATCH		70		

Course Information: Par 72; SSS 70; Length 6,287 yards. **Visitors:** Welcome. **Opening Hours:** Sunrise – sunset. **Avoid:** Sunday. **Ladies:** Welcome. Letter of introduction / GUI card for Open Competitions. **Green Fees:** Mon – Fri €30, €10 with Member; Saturday, Sunday & Bank Holiday Weekends €35, €15 with Member. **Juveniles:** Welcome. Caddy service available by prior arrangement; GUI card required for open competitions; telephone appointment required. **Clubhouse Hours:** 8.30am – 11.00 pm. **Clubhouse Dress:** Casual. **Clubhouse Facilities:** New clubhouse with full catering and bar facilities at all times. **Open Competitions:** Contact club for details.

Course Description:
A narrow course which adds to the degree of difficulty. An 18 hole parkland course. It enjoys good drainage which means it is not affected by heavy rainfall and is playable throughout the winter.

Belvedere, Mullingar, Co. Westmeath. Tel: (044) 9340085.

Course Description:
Parkland golf at its most sublime. Generous, rolling fairways wind their paths through mature timbers. It hosts important amateur events annually such as the Mullingar Scratch Cup.

NO.	CHAMP YARDS	MEDAL YARDS	PAR	S.I.	NO.	CHAMP YARDS	MEDAL YARDS	PAR	S.I.
1	338	332	4	10	10	433	421	4	2
2	189	182	3	7	11	386	300	4	9
3	389	379	4	4	12	152	139	3	16
4	486	480	5	14	13	370	360	4	5
5	186	173	3	12	14	480	470	5	17
6	330	313	4	18	15	162	154	3	13
7	453	444	4	1	16	493	485	5	8
8	343	329	4	6	17	425	371	4	3
9	338	330	4	15	18	511	476	5	11
OUT	3,052	2,962	35		IN	3,406	3,236	37	
					TOTAL	6,466	6,198	72	
					STANDARD SCRATCH	72	72		

LOCATION: Three miles south of Mullingar.

Email: mullingargolfclub@hotmail.com
Web: www.mullingargolfclub.com

PROFESSIONAL: John Burns.
Tel: (044) 9348366.

Course Information:
Par 72; SSS 71; Length 6,198 metres. Visitors: Welcome. Prior arrangement required for weekends. **Opening Hours:** 8.00am – sunset. **Avoid:** Wednesday and weekends. **Green Fees:** €40 Mon – Fri; €45 weekends. Sun- members only. **Ladies:** Welcome. **Juveniles:** Welcome. **Clubhouse Hours:** 10.00am – 11.30pm peak season. **Clubhouse Dress:** Casual, no shorts. **Clubhouse Facilities:** Bar food.

SECRETARY / MANAGER: Anne McLoughlin.
Tel: (044) 9348366. Fax: (044) 41499.

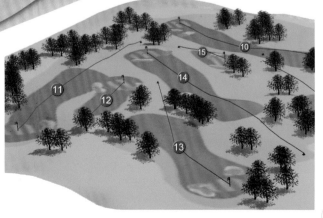

Mount Temple Golf Club, Mount Temple Village, Moate, Co. Westmeath.
Tel: (090) 648 1841. Web: www.mounttemplegolfclub.com
Email: mttemple@iol.ie

SECRETARY: Michelle Allen.
PROFESSIONAL: David Byrne.

Course Information:
Par 72; SSS 72; Length 5,972 metres. Visitors: Welcome. **Opening Hours:** Sunrise – sunset. **Avoid:** Playable all week, but check weekends. **Ladies:** Welcome. **Green Fees:** €30 weekdays; €40 weekends and public holidays. **Juveniles:** Welcome. Lessons and caddy service available by prior arrangement. **Clubhouse Hours:** 8.30am – 11.30pm. **Clubhouse Dress:** Neat and casual. **Clubhouse Facilities:** Farmhouse cuisine in oldtime clubhouse atmosphere. Golf Acadamy now open.

ARCHITECT: Michael Dolan.

NO.	MEDAL METRES	GEN. METRES	PAR	S.I.	NO.	MEDAL METRES	GEN. METRES	PAR	S.I.
1	161	125	3	17	10	397	260	4	1
2	326	300	4	12	11	458	458	5	15
3	348	320	4	4	12	372	310	4	5
4	435	415	5	14	13	363	320	4	2
5	364	320	4	6	14	118	300	4	7
6	320	320	4	13	15	453	118	3	18
7	350	300	4	3	16	143	435	5	9
8	183	183	3	8	17	450	120	3	11
9	288	230	4	16	18	381	395	5	10
OUT	2,775	2,513	35		IN	3,152	2716	37	
				TOTAL	5,229	5,927	72		
				STANDARD SCRATCH		72			

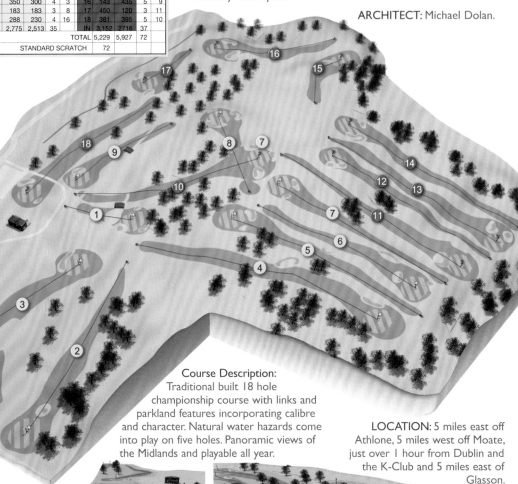

Course Description:
Traditional built 18 hole championship course with links and parkland features incorporating calibre and character. Natural water hazards come into play on five holes. Panoramic views of the Midlands and playable all year.

LOCATION: 5 miles east off Athlone, 5 miles west off Moate, just over 1 hour from Dublin and the K-Club and 5 miles east of Glasson.

Courtown Golf Club Kiltennel, Gorey, Co. Wexford
Tel: (055) 25166 Fax: (055) 25553

LOCATION: 3 miles from Gorey.

SECRETARY: Sharon O'Hara.
Tel: (053) 942 5166 / 942 5553

PROFESSIONAL: John Coone.

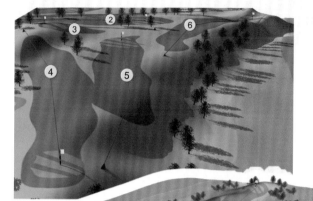

NO.	MEDAL METRES	GEN. METRES	PAR	S.I.	NO.	MEDAL METRES	GEN. METRES	PAR	S.I.
1	288	278	4	18	10	439	436	5	17
2	393	340	4	4	11	389	379	4	1
3	155	145	3	14	12	512	485	5	11
4	302	292	4	16	13	347	337	4	9
5	311	301	4	10	14	183	173	3	7
6	294	284	4	12	15	352	342	4	5
7	389	369	4	2	16	294	284	4	11
8	166	156	3	8	17	370	360	4	3
9	516	516	5	6	18	152	142	3	13
OUT	2,814	2,681	35		IN	3,038	2,938	36	
					TOTAL	5,898	5,619	71	
					STANDARD SCRATCH		70	69	

Course Information:
Par 71; SSS 71; Length 5,898
metres. **Visitors:** Welcome except on
major competition days and Tuesdays.
Opening Hours: Sunrise – sunset. **Ladies:**
Welcome. Lessons available; Club Hire
available; Caddy cars available. **Green Fees:**
Weekdays; Oct-Mar, €33, Apr-Sept €40.
Weekends/Bank hols; Oct-Mar, €36-€38,
Apr-Sept, €42-€45. **Clubhouse Hours:**
10.30am – 11.30pm. **Clubhouse Dress:**
Casual/Neat. **Clubhouse Facilities:** April –
October full catering available. **Open
Competitions:** Open Week June.

**Course
Description:**
This is a heavily wooded
parkland course. Features are the
four par 3's, particularly the nerve
wracking 18th. Top class bar and catering facilities
complement this excellent course. The newly
refurbished clubhouse has panoramic views across the
course and the Irish Sea.

Knockmarshall, Enniscorthy, Co. Wexford.
Tel: (053) 9233191
Fax: (054) 9237637
Email: info@enniscorthygc.ie
www.enniscorthygc.ie

LOCATION: 2 miles from Enniscorthy post office off main New Ross Road.

SECRETARY: Sean O'Leary.

PROFESSIONAL: Martin Sludds.

ARCHITECT: E. Hackett.

GENERAL MANAGER: A.P. Colley.

Course Description:
A course of the highest quality. Excellent Greens. Enjoyable for all handicap players.

Course Information:
Par 72; SSS 72;
Length 6,115 metres.
Visitors: Welcome. Opening Hours: Sunrise – Sunset. Avoid: Sundays (telephone first). Telephone appointment required for open competitions.
Green Fees: €30 Mon - Thur, €40 Fri - Sun.
Clubhouse Hours: 11.00am – 11.00pm; Full clubhouse facilities; Catering facilities up to 9pm daily.
Clubhouse Dress: Neat/casual.

NO.	MEDAL METRES	GEN. METRES	PAR	S.I.	NO.	MEDAL METRES	GEN. METRES	PAR	S.I.
1	159	154	3	14	10	486	460	5	13
2	349	339	4	6	11	504	495	5	17
3	129	126	3	18	12	162	158	3	15
4	492	472	5	14	13	339	334	4	7
5	461	453	5	10	14	347	340	4	5
6	167	160	3	12	15	401	395	4	1
7	394	388	4	4	16	324	321	4	11
8	354	347	4	2	17	360	355	4	3
9	331	321	4	8	18	312	307	4	9
OUT	2,836	2,760	35		IN	3,235	3,165	37	
					TOTAL	6,071	5,925	72	
					STANDARD SCRATCH	72	71		

Tinneranny, New Ross, Co. Wexford.
Tel: (051) 421433

LOCATION: Tinneranny.

HONORARY SECRETARY:
Jim Meggs.

SECRETARY / MANAGER:
Kathleen Daly.

NO.	MEDAL METRES	GEN. METRES	PAR	S.I.	NO.	MEDAL METRES	GEN. METRES	PAR	S.I.
1	334	329	4	6	10	475	465	5	12
2	171	160	3	4	11	173	173	3	10
3	290	272	4	15	12	301	293	4	17
4	420	408	4	1	13	495	485	5	13
5	332	309	4	14	14	166	152	3	8
6	330	309	4	9	15	363	343	4	3
7	335	321	4	11	16	331	313	4	16
8	366	350	4	7	17	357	347	4	5
9	148	139	3	18	18	408	400	4	2
OUT	2,726	2,597	34		IN	3,069	2,971	36	
					TOTAL	5,795	5,568	70	
					STANDARD SCRATCH	71	70		

Course Description:
Pleasent, well kept 18 hole golf course. Straight hitting and careful placing of shots is very important as the fairways are tight and allow little room for errors.

Course Information:
Par 70; SSS 70; Length 5,795 metres. **Visitors:** Welcome weekdays and saturdays. **Ladies Day:** Wednesday. **Juveniles:** Welcome - mornings. **Green Fees:** €30 Midweek; €40 Sat / Sun & Bank Holidays. **Clubhouse Hours:** 8am - 11:30pm (summer); 9am - 10:30pm (winter). **Clubhouse Dress:** Neat / Casual. **Clubhouse Facilities:** Full catering by arrangement and bar everyday. **Open competitions:** Open week 15th-18th June and 20th-25th June.

Rosslare, Co. Wexford. Tel: (053) 9132203. Fax: (053) 9132263.

Email: office@rosslaregolf.com
Web: www.rosslaregolf.com

Course Description:
Links land is known for its ability to absorb water and Rosslare is no exception with the course playable all year round. The prevailing south-westerly winds make the links both a challenging and an enjoyable test for golfers.

LOCATION: In the village of Rosslare.

SECRETARY: Roisin Doyle.
MANAGER: John P. Hanrick.
PROFESSIONAL: Johnny Young.

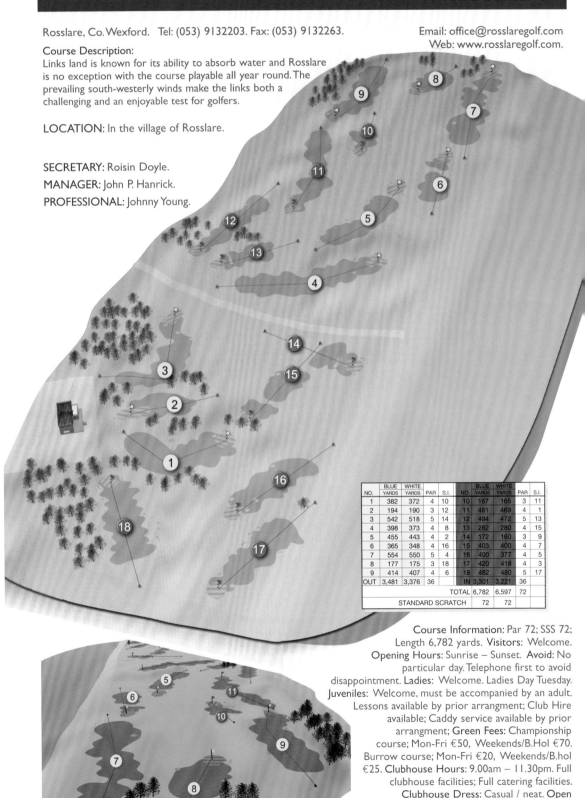

NO.	BLUE YARDS	WHITE YARDS	PAR	S.I.	NO.	BLUE YARDS	WHITE YARDS	PAR	S.I.
1	382	372	4	10	10	167	165	3	11
2	194	190	3	12	11	481	469	4	1
3	542	518	5	14	12	494	472	5	13
4	398	373	4	8	13	282	280	4	15
5	455	443	4	2	14	172	160	3	9
6	365	348	4	16	15	403	400	4	7
7	554	550	5	4	16	400	377	4	5
8	177	175	3	18	17	420	418	4	3
9	414	407	4	6	18	482	480	5	17
OUT	3,481	3,376	36		IN	3,301	3,221	36	
					TOTAL	6,782	6,597	72	
					STANDARD SCRATCH		72	72	

Course Information: Par 72; SSS 72; Length 6,782 yards. **Visitors:** Welcome. **Opening Hours:** Sunrise – Sunset. **Avoid:** No particular day. Telephone first to avoid disappointment. **Ladies:** Welcome. Ladies Day Tuesday. **Juveniles:** Welcome, must be accompanied by an adult. Lessons available by prior arrangment; Club Hire available; Caddy service available by prior arrangment; **Green Fees:** Championship course; Mon-Fri €50, Weekends/B.Hol €70. Burrow course; Mon-Fri €20, Weekends/B.hol €25. **Clubhouse Hours:** 9.00am – 11.30pm. Full clubhouse facilities; Full catering facilities. **Clubhouse Dress:** Casual / neat. **Open Competitions:** Most Saturdays & Sundays. In high season open to visitor paying green fees.

Kilrane, Rosslare Harbour, Co. Wexford.
Tel: (053) 9133234 Fax: (053) 9133803
Email: info@sthelensbay.com

Course Information:
Par 72; SSS 72; Length 6,091 Metres. **Type:** Parkland / Links course. **Opening Hours:** Daylight Hours. **Avoid:** None. **Green Fees:** Low Season – €25 Mon-Thur, €30 Fri-Sun; High Season – €40 Mon-Fri, €50 Fri-Sun. Club hire and Caddie Service available. **Clubhouse Hours:** Licencing Hours. **Clubhouse Dress:** Neat, casual dress. **Clubhouse Facilities:** Full catering and clubhouse facilities available. Accommodation available on site. **Open Competitions:** Various Open Days throughout the year and three Open Weeks.

LOCATION: 2 miles from Rosslare Europort; 10 miles from Wexford; 1 hour from Waterford Airport, 2 hours from Dublin.

GENERAL MANAGER: Barry Brennan

COURSE DESIGN / ARCHITECT: Philip Walton.

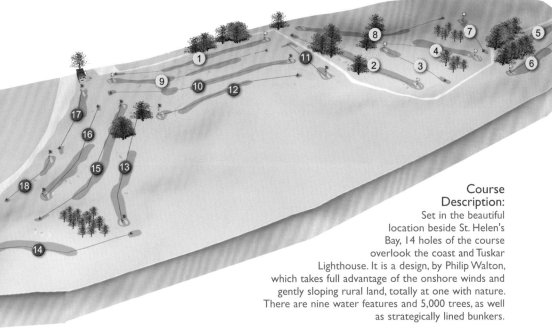

Course Description:
Set in the beautiful location beside St. Helen's Bay, 14 holes of the course overlook the coast and Tuskar Lighthouse. It is a design, by Philip Walton, which takes full advantage of the onshore winds and gently sloping rural land, totally at one with nature. There are nine water features and 5,000 trees, as well as strategically lined bunkers.

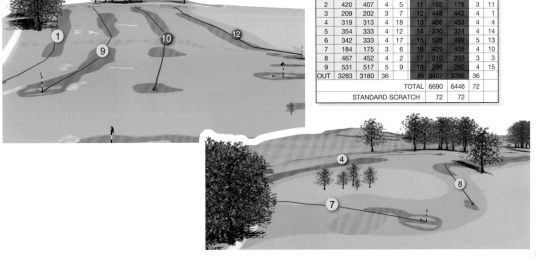

NO.	MEDAL YARDS	GEN. YARDS	PAR	S.I.	NO.	MEDAL YARDS	GEN. YARDS	PAR	S.I.
1	457	448	5	16	10	550	512	5	8
2	420	407	4	5	11	182	178	3	11
3	209	202	3	7	12	448	442	4	1
4	319	313	4	18	13	466	453	4	4
5	354	333	4	12	14	330	324	4	14
6	342	333	4	17	15	526	499	5	13
7	184	175	3	6	16	429	405	4	10
8	467	452	4	2	17	210	203	3	3
9	531	517	5	9	18	266	250	4	15
OUT	3283	3180	36		IN	3407	3266	36	
					TOTAL	6690	6446	72	
					STANDARD SCRATCH	72	72		

Kilrane, Rosslare Harbour, Co. Wexford.
Tel: (053) 9133234 Fax: (053) 9133803
Email: info@sthelensbay.com

COURSE DESIGN / ARCHITECT: Philip Walton.

LOCATION: 2 miles from
Rosslare Europort; 10 miles from Wexford;
1 hour from Waterford Airport,
2 hours from Dublin.

GENERAL MANAGER: Barry Brennan

Course Information:
Par 72; SSS 72; Length 6,091 Metres. **Type:** Parkland /
Links course. **Opening Hours:** Daylight Hours. **Avoid:**
None. **Green Fees:** Low Season – €25 Mon-Thur, €30
Fri-Sun; High Season – €40 Mon-Fri, €50 Fri-Sun.
Club hire and Caddie Service available. **Clubhouse
Hours:** Licencing Hours. **Clubhouse Dress:** Neat,
casual dress. **Clubhouse Facilities:** Full catering
and clubhouse facilities available.
Accommodation available on site. **Open
Competitions:** Various Open Days throughout
the year and three
Open Weeks.

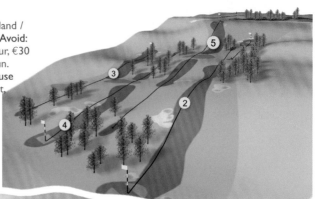

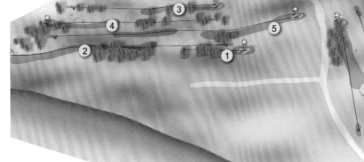

Course Description:
Set in the beautiful location beside St.
Helen's Bay, 14 holes of the course overlook the
coast and Tuskar Lighthouse. It is a design, by Philip Walton,
which takes full advantage of the onshore winds and gently sloping
rural land, totally at one with nature. There are nine water features
and 5,000 trees, as well as strategically lined bunkers.

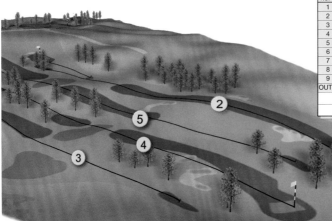

NO.	BLUE YARDS	WHITE YARDS	PAR	S.I.	NO.	MEDAL YARDS	GEN. YARDS	PAR	S.I.
1	130	124	3	5	10	130	124	3	5
2	479	467	5	4	11	479	467	5	4
3	344	334	4	9	12	344	334	4	9
4	372	364	4	3	13	372	364	4	3
5	546	539	5	7	14	546	539	5	7
6	336	322	4	2	15	336	322	4	2
7	148	136	3	1	16	148	136	3	1
8	320	312	4	8	17	320	312	4	8
9	319	307	4	6	18	319	307	4	6
OUT	2994	2905	36		IN	2994	2905	36	
					TOTAL	5998	5801	72	
					STANDARD SCRATCH	72	72		

Mulgannon, Co. Wexford.
Tel: (053) 91 42238.
Fax: (053) 91 42243.
Web: www.wexfordgolfclub.ie
Email: info@wexfordgolfclub.ie

Course Description:

Parkland course with many mature trees. The location has beautiful views of County Wexford, including the Saltee Islands, Bletchin Mountains and Wexford Harbour.

LOCATION: Wexford Town.

HON. SECRETARY: Roy Doyle.

ARCHITECT: H. Stutt & Co. D. Branigan.

PROFESSIONAL: Damien McGraine.
Tel: (053) 91 46300.

Please note: Course is being redesigned, Due to reopen August 2007.

Course Information:

Par 70; SSS 70; Length 6,306 yards, 5,734 metres.
Visitors: Welcome (except on Sundays). Should book in advance. **Opening Hours:** Sunrise – sunset. **Avoid:** Sunday.
Ladies Day: Thursday. **Juveniles:** Lessons available by prior arrangments; Club Hire available; Caddy service available by prior arrangments; Telephone appointment required. **Green Fees:** Weekdays €32, Weekends & Bank Holidays €38 (Summer); Weekdays €27, Weekends & Bank Holidays €38 (winter); €15 with a member, €55 husband & wife (Midweek only). **Clubhouse Hours:** 8am – 11.30pm (summer). **Clubhouse Dress:** Casual / Neat. **Clubhouse Facilities:** Bar snacks available all day every day. Full catering available by arrangement.

NO.	WHITE METRES	BLUE METRES	PAR	S.I.	NO.	WHITE METRES	BLUE METRES	PAR	S.I.
1	160	174	3	5	10	294	309	4	12
2	282	288	4	15	11	455	460	5	10
3	345	359	4	7	12	135	150	3	8
4	298	318	4	11	13	431	464	5	14
5	346	351	4	4	14	379	391	4	3
6	127	136	3	13	15	114	121	3	17
7	233	239	4	18	16	354	363	4	1
8	470	493	5	9	17	408	420	5	16
9	354	394	4	2	18	286	313	4	6
OUT	2,615	2,743	35		IN	2,856	2,991	37	
					TOTAL	5,471	5,734	72	
					STANDARD SCRATCH	69	70		

Abbeylands, Arklow, Co Wicklow. Tel: (0402) 32492 Fax: (0402) 91604
Email: arklowgolflinks@eircom.net

LOCATION: Just south of the town centre.

SECRETARY: Mr Philip Kavanagh.

ARCHITECT: Haughtry & Taylor.

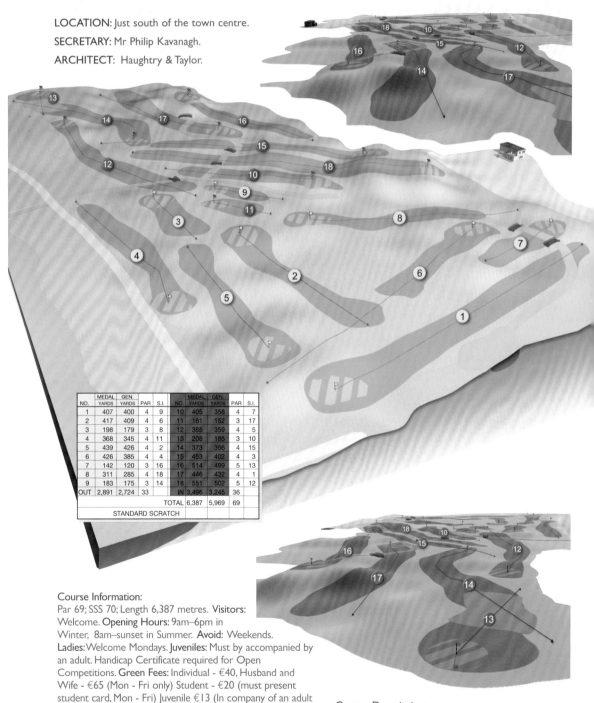

NO.	MEDAL YARDS	GEN. YARDS	PAR	S.I.	NO.	MEDAL YARDS	GEN. YARDS	PAR	S.I.
1	407	400	4	9	10	405	358	4	7
2	417	409	4	6	11	161	152	3	17
3	198	179	3	8	12	385	359	4	5
4	368	345	4	11	13	208	185	3	10
5	439	426	4	2	14	373	356	4	15
6	426	385	4	4	15	453	402	4	3
7	142	120	3	16	16	514	499	5	13
8	311	285	4	18	17	446	432	4	1
9	183	175	3	14	18	551	502	5	12
OUT	2,891	2,724	33		IN	3,496	3,245	36	
					TOTAL	6,387	5,969	69	
					STANDARD SCRATCH				

Course Information:
Par 69; SSS 70; Length 6,387 metres. **Visitors:**
Welcome. **Opening Hours:** 9am–6pm in
Winter, 8am–sunset in Summer. **Avoid:** Weekends.
Ladies: Welcome Mondays. **Juveniles:** Must by accompanied by
an adult. Handicap Certificate required for Open
Competitions. **Green Fees:** Individual - €40, Husband and
Wife - €65 (Mon - Fri only) Student - €20 (must present
student card, Mon - Fri) Juvenile €13 (In company of an adult
Mon - Fri) With Member €20 (Mon - Fri). **Clubhouse Hours:**
Winter: 9am – 6pm. Summer: 8am – Sunset. **Clubhouse
Dress:** No denims, shorts etc allowed. **Clubhouse Facilities:**
Full bar and restaurant open all year round. **Open
Competitions:** Open Week July / August.

Course Description:
A typical links course with majestic scenery and
the opportunity to play throughout the year.
Sited just outside the townland of Arklow.

Baltinglass

Stratford Lodge, Baltinglass, Co. Wicklow.
Tel: (059) 6481350 Fax: (059) 6482842
Email: baltinglassgc@eircom.net
Web: www.baltinglassgc.com

LOCATION: Baltinglass.

SECRETARY: Owen Cooney.

ARCHITECTS: Lionel Hewtson,

Eddie Connaughton.

NO.	WHITE METRES	GREEN METRES	PAR	S.I.	NO.	WHITE METRES	GREEN METRES	PAR	S.I.
1	369	359	4	3	10	456	444	5	10
2	152	137	3	9	11	347	334	4	12
3	454	444	5	11	12	137	127	3	18
4	295	285	4	15	13	399	394	4	4
5	147	137	3	13	14	364	356	4	6
6	344	334	4	7	15	421	413	4	1
7	366	356	4	5	16	157	147	3	16
8	538	528	5	5	17	338	332	4	8
9	315	309	4	17	18	313	301	4	14
OUT	2,980	2,889	36		IN	2,932	2,848	35	
					TOTAL	5,912	5,737		
					STANDARD SCRATCH			72	71	

Course Information:
Par 71; SSS 69; Length 5,912
metres. **Visitors:** Welcome.
Societies catered for everyday. **Opening
Hours:** 9.00am – Sunset. **Avoid:** Competition
dates, weekends & Thursdays. **Ladies:** Welcome. Ladies
Day Thursday. **Green Fees:** Mon–Fri €25/30; Sat/Sun/Bank
Holidays €35. **Juveniles:** Welcome. Caddy service available by prior
arrangement, telephone appointment required. **Clubhouse Dress:**
Neat/Casual. **Clubhouse Facilities:** Bar and catering available,
catering by previous arrangements except at weekends. For
summer months-all day. Buggies for hire by prior arrangement.
Open for membership. **Open Competitions:** Open Week June/July.

Course Description:
Old nine hole course opened in 1928.
(Architect Lionel Hewston) New nine
hole development added in 2002.
(Architect Eddie Connaughton) Situated
on N81 a half mile on the Dublin side of
Baltinglass town. The course is a scenic
parkland with stunning views of the
Wicklow Hills.

Blainroe

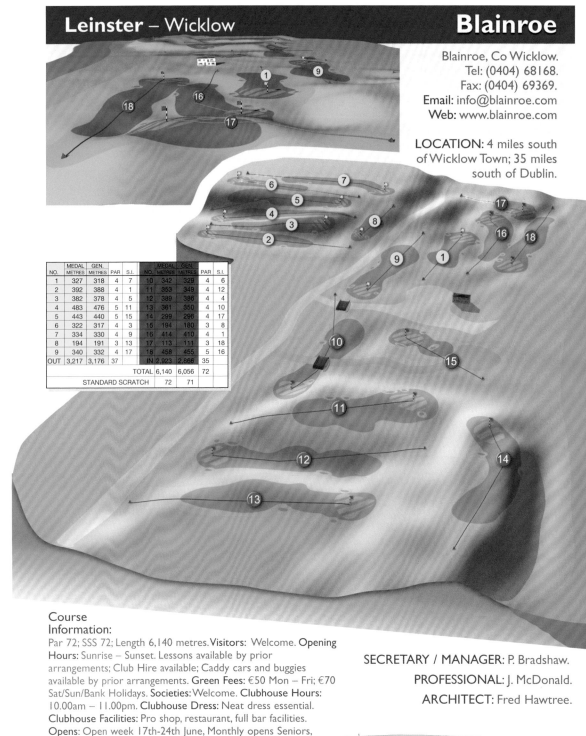

Blainroe, Co Wicklow.
Tel: (0404) 68168.
Fax: (0404) 69369.
Email: info@blainroe.com
Web: www.blainroe.com

LOCATION: 4 miles south
of Wicklow Town; 35 miles
south of Dublin.

NO.	MEDAL METRES	GEN. METRES	PAR	S.I.	NO.	MEDAL METRES	GEN. METRES	PAR	S.I.
1	327	318	4	7	10	342	329	4	6
2	392	388	4	1	11	353	349	4	12
3	382	378	4	5	12	389	386	4	4
4	483	476	5	11	13	361	350	4	10
5	443	440	5	15	14	299	296	4	17
6	322	317	4	3	15	194	180	3	8
7	334	330	4	9	16	414	410	4	1
8	194	191	3	13	17	113	111	3	18
9	340	332	4	17	18	458	455	5	16
OUT	3,217	3,176	37		IN	2,923	2,866	35	
					TOTAL	6,140	6,056	72	
		STANDARD SCRATCH					72	71	

Course Information:

Par 72; SSS 72; Length 6,140 metres. Visitors: Welcome. **Opening Hours:** Sunrise – Sunset. Lessons available by prior arrangements; Club Hire available; Caddy cars and buggies available by prior arrangements. **Green Fees:** €50 Mon – Fri; €70 Sat/Sun/Bank Holidays. **Societies:** Welcome. **Clubhouse Hours:** 10.00am – 11.00pm. **Clubhouse Dress:** Neat dress essential. **Clubhouse Facilities:** Pro shop, restaurant, full bar facilities. **Opens:** Open week 17th-24th June, Monthly opens Seniors, Sept-May Contact club for details

SECRETARY / MANAGER: P. Bradshaw.

PROFESSIONAL: J. McDonald.

ARCHITECT: Fred Hawtree.

Course Description:

This is a parkland course overlooking the sea. Two holes worth noting are the 14th, which is played from the cliff peninsula, and the par 3 15th hole over the lake. There are over 50 sand bunkers which makes it a very challenging test to all golfers.

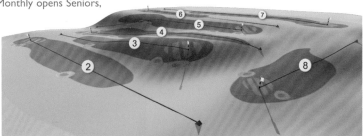

Greystones Road, Bray, Co Wicklow.
Tel: (01) 276 3200 Fax: (01) 276 3262

GENERAL MANAGER:
A Threadgold.

PROFESSIONAL :
Ciaron Carroll
Tel: (01) 276 3200
info@braygolfclub.com

LOCATION:
Bray Town.

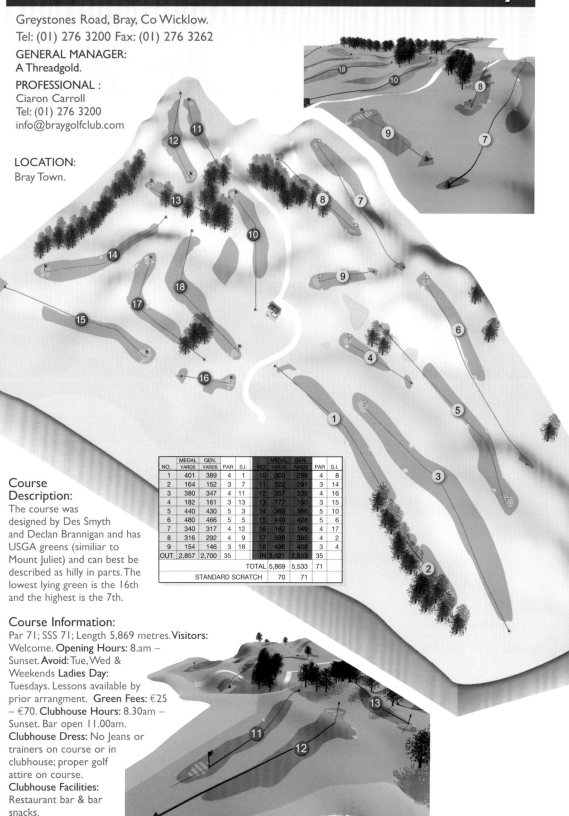

Course Description:

The course was designed by Des Smyth and Declan Brannigan and has USGA greens (similiar to Mount Juliet) and can best be described as hilly in parts. The lowest lying green is the 16th and the highest is the 7th.

NO.	MEDAL YARDS	GEN. YARDS	PAR	S.I.	NO.	MEDAL YARDS	GEN. YARDS	PAR	S.I.
1	401	389	4	1	10	300	288	4	8
2	164	152	3	7	11	322	291	4	14
3	380	347	4	11	12	357	338	4	16
4	182	161	3	13	13	177	150	3	15
5	440	430	5	3	14	360	366	5	10
6	480	466	5	5	15	440	428	5	6
7	340	317	4	12	16	162	149	4	17
8	316	292	4	9	17	398	385	4	2
9	154	146	3	18	18	496	468	3	4
OUT	2,857	2,700	35		IN	3,021	2,833	35	
					TOTAL	5,869	5,533	71	
					STANDARD SCRATCH		70	71	

Course Information:

Par 71; SSS 71; Length 5,869 metres. **Visitors:** Welcome. **Opening Hours:** 8.am – Sunset. **Avoid:** Tue, Wed & Weekends **Ladies Day:** Tuesdays. Lessons available by prior arrangment. **Green Fees:** €25 – €70. **Clubhouse Hours:** 8.30am – Sunset. Bar open 11.00am. **Clubhouse Dress:** No Jeans or trainers on course or in clubhouse; proper golf attire on course. **Clubhouse Facilities:** Restaurant bar & bar snacks.

Greystones, Co Wicklow.
Tel: (01) 2874350. Fax: (01) 2874360.
Email: info@charlesland.com
Web: www.charlesland.com

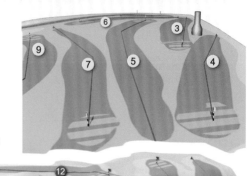

Course Information:

Par 72; SSS 72; Length 6,169 metres. **Visitors:** Welcome.
Opening Hours: Sunrise – Sunset. **Juveniles:** Welcome with
adult or handicap certificate. Lessons available by prior
arrangement. **Green Fees:** 1 Apr - 31 Oct Mon - Thurs €50;
Fri - Sun and bank holidays €60. **Clubhouse Dress:** Neat dress
essential. **Clubhouse Facilities:** Full facilities
available. Bar food menu and Dining room
available every day. Also 12 en-suite
bedrooms. **Competitions:** Open
Week – August.

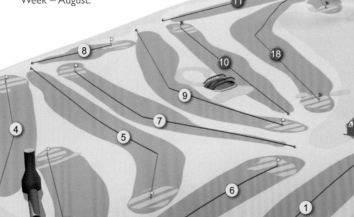

NO.	MEDAL METRES	GEN. METRES	PAR	S.I.	NO.	MEDAL METRES	GEN. METRES	PAR	S.I.
1	369	358	4	10	10	388	377	4	5
2	131	120	3	16	11	338	329	4	11
3	312	301	4	14	12	310	301	4	13
4	341	320	4	4	13	229	218	3	7
5	479	470	5	8	14	409	400	4	1
6	275	257	4	18	15	441	432	5	15
7	416	405	4	2	16	422	409	4	3
8	140	131	3	12	17	135	123	3	17
9	472	462	5	6	18	562	520	5	9
OUT	2,935	2,834	36		IN	3,234	3,129	36	
					TOTAL	6,169	5,963	72	
					STANDARD SCRATCH		72	71	

Course Description:

Parkland course in a superb setting on a delightfully rolling
terrain, sweeping towards the Irish Sea. Well bunkered, with
water hazards on seven of the holes. An all weather course
playable twelve months of the year.

LOCATION: 18 Miles south of Dublin.

GOLF ADMINISTRATION:
Rosaleen Casey.
Tel: (01) 2878200.

GENERAL MANAGER:
Mr. Patrick Bradshaw

PROFESSIONAL:
Peter Duignan

ARCHITECT:
Eddie Hackett.

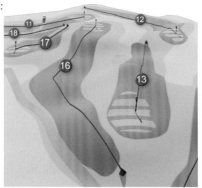

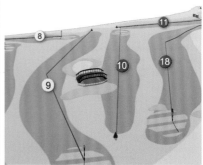

Shillelagh, Co. Wicklow.
Tel: (055) 29125.

LOCATION: South Wicklow.

HON. SECRETARY: Billy Stamp.

ARCHITECT: Peter McAvoy.

NO.	BLUE YARDS	WHITE YARDS	PAR	S.I.	NO.	BLUE YARDS	WHITE YARDS	PAR	S.I.
1	307	293	4	18	10	165	150	3	7
2	185	170	3	8	11	490	456	5	12
3	383	373	4	10	12	122	115	3	14
4	407	393	4	6	13	516	497	5	9
5	202	174	3	13	14	384	378	4	3
6	581	559	5	11	15	390	375	4	5
7	391	383	4	2	16	261	239	4	17
8	340	308	4	15	17	460	450	4	1
9	367	352	4	4	18	163	146	3	16
OUT	3,163	3,005	35		IN	2,951	2,806	35	
					TOTAL	6,114	5,811	70	
	STANDARD SCRATCH					69	68		

Course Description:

A picturesque parkland course with excellent fairways and greens. The large number of trees of different varieties add greatly to the character of the course. Part of the Old Fitzwilliam Solate, set in lovely countryside. New 18 hole course opened in March 1998, built to U.S.G.A. standards.

Course Information:

Par 70; SSS 68; Length 6,114 yards. **Visitors:** Welcome. **Opening Hours:** Sunrise – Sunset. **Avoid:** Weekends. **Green Fees:** €35 Mon – Fri; €45 weekends & bank holidays. 10% discount for groups of 20+, Pro shop fully stocked. **Clubhouse Hours:** 12.00pm – close, All day Saturday and Sunday. **Clubhouse Dress:** Casual. **Clubhouse Facilities:** Full house facilities. **Open Competitions:** Open Week end of June.

Delgany, Co Wicklow.
Tel: (01) 2874536. Fax: (01) 287 3977.
Email: delganygolf@eircom.net
Web: www.delganygolfclub.com.

LOCATION: Delgany Village.
GENERAL MANAGER: Peter Ribeiro.
Tel: (01) 2874536.
PROFESSIONAL: Gavin Kavanagh.
Tel: (01) 2874697.
CATERER: Stephan O'Neill.
Tel: (01) 2875426.

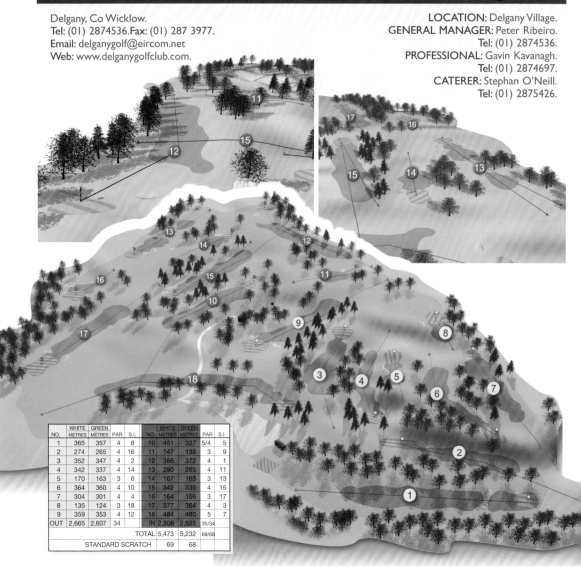

NO.	WHITE METRES	GREEN METRES	PAR	S.I.	NO.	WHITE METRES	GREEN METRES	PAR	S.I.
1	365	357	4	8	10	451	327	5/4	5
2	274	265	4	16	11	147	139	3	9
3	352	347	4	2	12	386	372	4	1
4	342	337	4	14	13	290	285	4	11
5	170	163	3	6	14	167	163	3	13
6	364	360	4	10	15	342	339	4	15
7	304	301	4	4	16	164	156	3	17
8	135	124	3	18	17	377	364	4	3
9	359	353	4	12	18	484	480	5	7
OUT	2,665	2,607	34		IN	2,808	2,625	35/34	
					TOTAL	5,473	5,232	69/68	
					STANDARD SCRATCH		69	68	

Course Information: Par 69; SSS 69; Length 5,473 metres. **Visitors:** Welcome Weekdays. Weekends by arrangement only. **Opening Hours:** 8.00am – Sunset. **Avoid:** Tuesday and Wednesday. **Ladies:** Welcome. **Juveniles:** Welcome. Lessons available by prior arrangement; Club hire available; Golf buggies available by prior arrangement; Caddy service available prior arrangement; **Green Fees:** €45 Mon – Fri; €55 Sat/Sun. **Clubhouse Hours:** 8.30am – close. **Clubhouse Dress:** Neat/ casual. **Clubhouse Facilities:** Snacks & bar food, Restaurant and bar facilities available. **Caterer:** Stephanie O Neill.
Tel (01) 2875426

Course Description:
Surrounded by beautiful countryside and breathtaking scenery with hill and sea views from golf course and newly redeveloped club house. 40 minutes from the centre of Dublin.

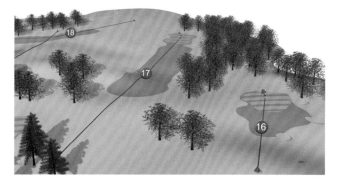

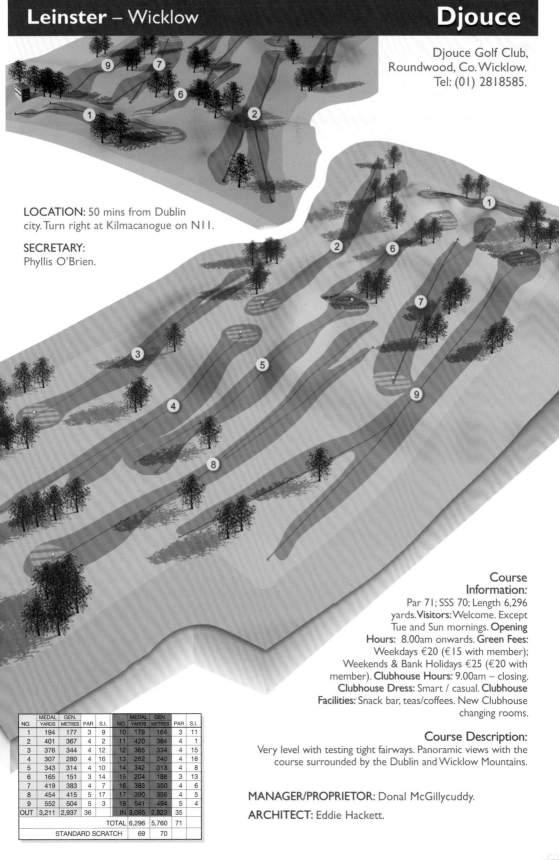

Djouce Golf Club,
Roundwood, Co. Wicklow.
Tel: (01) 2818585.

LOCATION: 50 mins from Dublin city. Turn right at Kilmacanogue on N11.

SECRETARY:
Phyllis O'Brien.

Course Information:

Par 71; SSS 70; Length 6,296 yards. **Visitors:** Welcome. Except Tue and Sun mornings. **Opening Hours:** 8.00am onwards. **Green Fees:** Weekdays €20 (€15 with member); Weekends & Bank Holidays €25 (€20 with member). **Clubhouse Hours:** 9.00am – closing. **Clubhouse Dress:** Smart / casual. **Clubhouse Facilities:** Snack bar, teas/coffees. New Clubhouse changing rooms.

Course Description:

Very level with testing tight fairways. Panoramic views with the course surrounded by the Dublin and Wicklow Mountains.

MANAGER/PROPRIETOR: Donal McGillycuddy.

ARCHITECT: Eddie Hackett.

NO.	MEDAL YARDS	GEN. METRES	PAR	S.I.	NO.	MEDAL YARDS	GEN. METRES	PAR	S.I.
1	194	177	3	9	10	179	164	3	11
2	401	367	4	2	11	420	384	4	1
3	376	344	4	12	12	365	334	4	15
4	307	280	4	16	13	262	240	4	18
5	343	314	4	10	14	342	313	4	8
6	165	151	3	14	15	204	188	3	13
7	419	383	4	7	16	383	350	4	6
8	454	415	5	17	17	390	356	4	5
9	552	504	5	3	18	541	494	5	4
OUT	3,211	2,937	36		IN	3,085	2,823	35	
					TOTAL	6,296	5,760	71	
					STANDARD SCRATCH	69	70		

Newtownmountkennedy, Co. Wicklow.
Tel: (01) 287 3600 Fax: (01) 287 3699
Email: info@druidsglen.ie
Web: www.druidsglen.ie

LOCATION: Twenty-three miles south of Dublin City. Two miles east of Newtownmountkennedy off the N11.

COURSE DESIGNERS: Pat Ruddy & Tom Craddock.

PROFESSIONAL: George Henry.

GENERAL MANAGER: Donal Flinn.

Course Information:
Par 71; Length 7,026 yards.
Visitors: Welcome – tee times by arrangement. **Opening Hours:** 8.00am – Sunset. **Green Fees:** October – May, €90 per person, (golf only). €100pp, breakfast and golf. €130pp, 5 course meal with wine and golf. May - Oct €180pp, golf only. Early bird Mon-Fri, 7.30am-9am €115pp, golf only. **Clubhouse Hours:** 8.00am – onwards. **Clubhouse Dress:** Neat Casual. **Clubhouse Facilities:** Snacks, Lunch, Dinner and conference facilities available. Buggy hire available (pre-book) €45 Caddies available by prior arrangement. Hotel on site.

Course Description:
Druids Glen situated on the ancestral estate of Sir Thomas Wentworth is already an acknowledged masterpiece and had the honour of hosting the Murphy's Irish Open Championship in 1996, 1997, 1998 and 1999.

NO.	MEDAL YARDS	GEN. YARDS	PAR	S.I.	NO.	MEDAL YARDS	GEN. YARDS	PAR	S.I.
1	445	427	4	3	10	440	401	4	9
2	190	174	3	7	11	522	512	5	12
3	339	330	4	16	12	174	155	3	11
4	446	417	4	6	13	471	461	4	1
5	517	492	5	17	14	399	333	4	13
6	476	456	4	2	15	456	395	4	8
7	405	392	2	5	16	538	481	5	18
8	166	152	3	10	17	203	178	3	4
9	389	369	4	15	18	450	422	4	14
OUT	3373	3209	35		IN	3653	3338	36	
					TOTAL	7026	6547	71	
					STANDARD SCRATCH				

Newtownmountkennedy, Co. Wicklow.
Tel: (01) 287 3600 Fax: (01) 287 3699
Email: druidsheath@druidsglen.ie

LOCATION: Twenty-three miles south of Dublin City. Two miles east of Newtownmountkennedy off the N11.

Course Information:

Par 71; Length 7,434 yards. **Visitors:** Welcome – tee times by arrangement.

Opening Hours: 8.00am – Sunset. **Green Fees:** October – May €70pp, golf only. €80pp includes breakfast. May - October, €130pp golf only. Early Bird Mon-Fri, 7.30am-9am (golf only) €80 pp. **Clubhouse Hours:** 8.00am – onwards. **Clubhouse Dress:** Neat Casual. **Clubhouse Facilities:** Snacks, Lunch, Dinner & conference facilities available. Buggy Hire available (Pre- Book) €45. Caddies available by prior arrangement. Hotel on site.

NO.	MEDAL YARDS	GEN. YARDS	PAR	S.I.	NO.	MEDAL YARDS	GEN. YARDS	PAR	S.I.
1	464	420	4	5	10	426	422	4	6
2	561	536	5	12	11	250	201	3	13
3	233	186	3	9	12	492	473	4	1
4	519	504	5	18	13	420	345	4	8
5	202	192	3	4	14	171	159	3	17
6	467	459	4	7	15	500	484	5	10
7	466	457	4	2	16	513	460	4	3
8	449	375	4	14	17	447	386	4	11
9	439	398	4	16	18	415	376	4	15
OUT	3,800	3,527	36		IN	3,634	3,306	35	
					TOTAL	7,434	6,833	71	
					STANDARD SCRATCH				

COURSE DESIGNERS: Pat Ruddy and Tom Craddock.

PROFESSIONAL: Eamonn Darcy.

Course Description:

Druids Heath championship course provides a unique and thrilling experience for all golfers. Maintained to tour standards, the golf course is carved from the natural landscape of Ireland's Garden County with rolling fairways, natural rock quarries, lakes, trees, streams, gorse, pot-bunkers and a testing sea breeze. In addition to a warm Irish welcome, golfers will experience breathtaking scenery throughout their round.

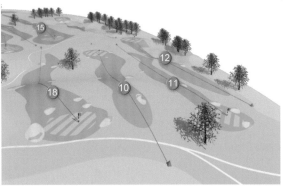

The European Club

Brittas Bay, Wicklow.
Tel: (0404) 47415 Fax: (0404) 47449.
Email: info@theeuropeanclub.com
Web: www.theeuropeanclub.com

LOCATION: 45 minutes from city centre via the Bray – Shankill Bypass on N11.

SECRETARY / MANAGER: Pat Ruddy.

ARCHITECT: Mr. Pat Ruddy.

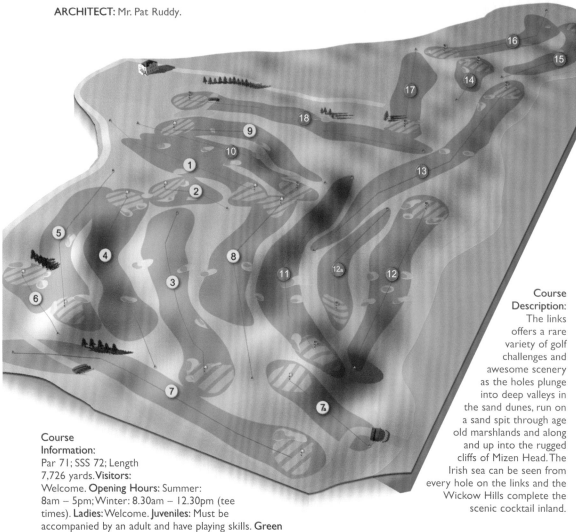

Course Description:
The links offers a rare variety of golf challenges and awesome scenery as the holes plunge into deep valleys in the sand dunes, run on a sand spit through age old marshlands and along and up into the rugged cliffs of Mizen Head. The Irish sea can be seen from every hole on the links and the Wickow Hills complete the scenic cocktail inland.

Course Information:
Par 71; SSS 72; Length 7,726 yards. Visitors: Welcome. **Opening Hours:** Summer: 8am – 5pm; Winter: 8.30am – 12.30pm (tee times). **Ladies:** Welcome. **Juveniles:** Must be accompanied by an adult and have playing skills. **Green Fees:** Nov-Mar €80 April-May €150, Jun- Oct weekdays €150, Sat&Sun €175
Clubhouse Hours: Open 8.00am until dusk. **Clubhouse Dress:** Smart / casual. **Clubhouse Facilities:** Full clubhouse and catering facilities. Caddy car hire available.

NO.	MEDAL YARDS	GEN. YARDS	PAR	S.I.	NO.	MEDAL YARDS	GEN. YARDS	PAR	S.I.
1	424	363	4	8	10	466	397	4	2
2	160	148	3	18	11	416	379	4	9
3	499	481	5	16	12	459	438	4	6
4	470	426	4	3	12a	205	160	3	19
5	409	398	4	5	13	596	503	5	15
6	210	177	3	14	14	195	165	3	17
7	470	449	4	1	15	415	379	4	13
7a	166	120	3	20	16	415	399	4	11
8	415	402	4	10	17	432	389	4	4
9	427	402	4	12	18	477	425	4	7
OUT	3,650	3,366	35		IN	4,076	3,634	36	
					TOTAL	7,726	7,000	71	
					STANDARD SCRATCH		72	71	

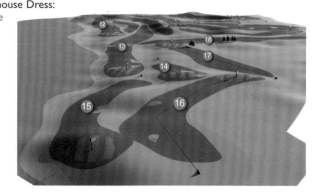

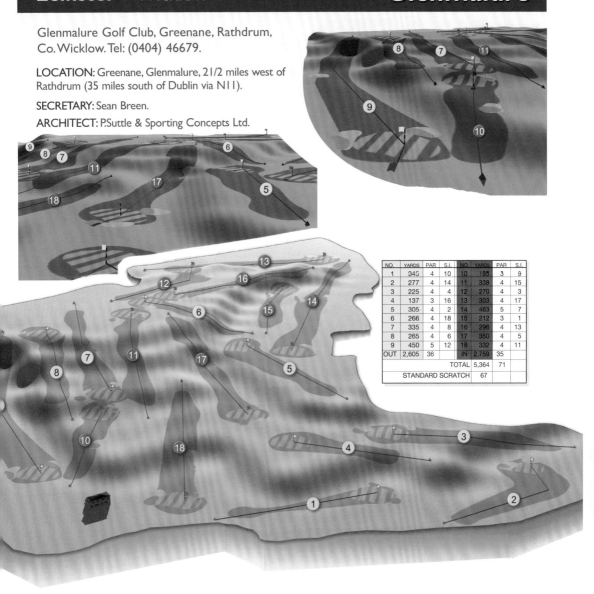

Glenmalure Golf Club, Greenane, Rathdrum,
Co. Wicklow. Tel: (0404) 46679.

LOCATION: Greenane, Glenmalure, 2 1/2 miles west of
Rathdrum (35 miles south of Dublin via N11).

SECRETARY: Sean Breen.

ARCHITECT: P.Suttle & Sporting Concepts Ltd.

NO.	YARDS	PAR	S.I.	NO.	YARDS	PAR	S.I.
1	345	4	10	10	195	3	9
2	277	4	14	11	338	4	15
3	225	4	4	12	270	4	3
4	137	3	16	13	303	4	17
5	305	4	2	14	463	5	7
6	266	4	18	15	212	3	1
7	335	4	8	16	296	4	13
8	265	4	6	17	350	4	5
9	450	5	12	18	332	4	11
OUT	2,605	36		IN	2,759	35	
				TOTAL	5,364	71	
				STANDARD SCRATCH		67	

Course Description:
Set in a beautiful location overlooking the
Glenmalure & Vale of Avoca in the Wicklow
Hills. Delightful course with inclines, a plateau
and downhill. Accommodation available in
lodges on site.

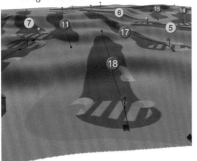

Course Information:
Par 71; SSS 66; Length 5,384 yards. **Visitors:** Welcome. **Opening
Hours:** 8.00am – dusk. **Ladies:** ILGU affiliated. **Green Fees:** €20
weekdays; €25 weekends. Juveniles: €15. **Clubhouse Hours:** Normal
licencing hours. **Clubhouse Dress:** No special requirements.
Clubhouse Facilities: Full bar and catering available. Buggy hire
available. **Open Competitions:** 14th-16th April, 9th-10th
September. Please phone club for details.

Coolnaskeagh, Delgany, Co. Wicklow.
Tel: (01) 2876240. Fax: (01) 2870063
Email: info@glenofthedowns.com
Web: www.glenofthedowns.com

LOCATION: Off the N11 Main Dublin,
Wexford Road. (approx. 30 mins from
Dublin Centre)

NO.	MEDAL YARDS	GEN. YARDS	PAR	S.I.	NO.	MEDAL YARDS	GEN. YARDS	PAR	S.I.
1	181	160	3	14	10	382	361	4	5
2	416	385	4	4	11	395	366	4	9
3	395	373	4	8	12	338	305	4	15
4	186	166	3	10	13	558	528	5	1
5	441	427	4	2	14	206	167	3	11
6	498	471	5	12	15	510	489	5	7
7	156	138	3	16	16	181	159	3	13
8	404	367	3	16	17	405	385	4	3
9	500	466	5	18	18	291	267	4	17
OUT	3,177	2,953	35		IN	3266	3027	36	
					TOTAL	6443	5980	71	
					STANDARD SCRATCH	71	70		

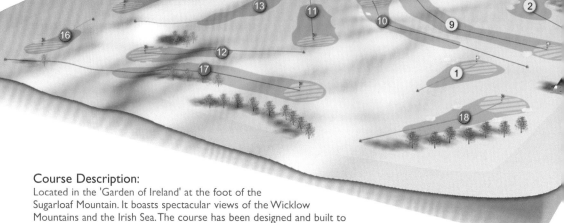

Course Description:

Located in the 'Garden of Ireland' at the foot of the
Sugarloaf Mountain. It boasts spectacular views of the Wicklow
Mountains and the Irish Sea. The course has been designed and built to
USGA standard with sand based greens and tees. Golfers will find Glen of the Downs a
challenge with its natural slopes and valleys combined with its fairway bunkering and lakes.

Course Information:

Par 71; SSS 70; Length 5,980 yards. **Green Fees:** €65 Midweek, €80 Weekend. €50 before
10am midweek. **Restrictions:** Soft spikes only. **Ladies:** Welcome. **Juveniles:** Welcome.
Clubhouse Hours: 8am - Sunset. **Clubhouse Dress:** Neat dress essential/ no denim.
Clubhouse Facilities: Bar, Spike Bar, Restaurant and a well stocked golf shop.

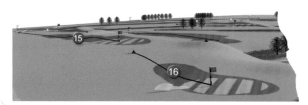

GENERAL MANAGER: James Murphy.
GOLF DIRECTOR: Derek Murphy
ARCHITECT:
Peter McEvoy/ Paddy Governey

Greystones, Co. Wicklow.
Tel: (01) 287 4136.
Email:
secretary@greystonesgc.com.
www.greystonesgc.com

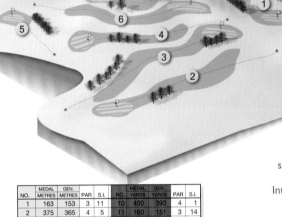

Course Information:
Par 69; SSS 69; Length 5,322
metres. Visitors: Welcome
Mon, Tues, Fri and Sun.
Opening Hours: 9.00am –
Sunset. Avoid: Wed, Thurs and Sat.
Green Fees: €45 weekdays – €50 weekends.
Clubhouse Hours: 9.00am – 12.00 midnight.
Clubhouse Dress: Casual. No jeans or
sneakers. Clubhouse Facilities: Full bar and Restaurant
available. Open Competitions: Open Week July;
Intermediate Scratch Cup July. Junior Scratch Cup; July.

Course Description:
A parkland course with considerable contrasts. The first nine
holes are hilly with some spectacular views, which are in stark
contrast to the more level second nine holes. A new Clubhouse,
incorporating an old Georgian Manor House, completes this very
attractive package.

NO.	MEDAL METRES	GEN. METRES	PAR	S.I.	NO.	MEDAL YARDS	GEN. YARDS	PAR	S.I.
1	163	153	3	11	10	400	393	4	1
2	375	365	4	5	11	160	151	3	14
3	363	353	4	3	12	374	360	4	4
4	308	298	4	15	13	321	315	4	8
5	101	96	3	17	14	148	128	3	16
6	338	328	4	1	15	449	437	5	10
7	276	266	4	7	16	127	125	3	18
8	326	321	4	13	17	364	362	4	6
9	402	397	5	9	18	327	315	4	12
OUT	2,652	2,577	35		IN	2,670	2,586	34	
					TOTAL	5,322	5,163	69	
	STANDARD SCRATCH					68	68		

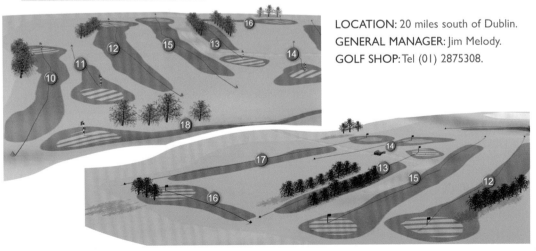

LOCATION: 20 miles south of Dublin.
GENERAL MANAGER: Jim Melody.
GOLF SHOP: Tel (01) 2875308.

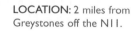

LOCATION: 2 miles from Greystones off the N11.

PRESIDENT: Ian Calton

HON SECRETARY: Eleanor Nelson.

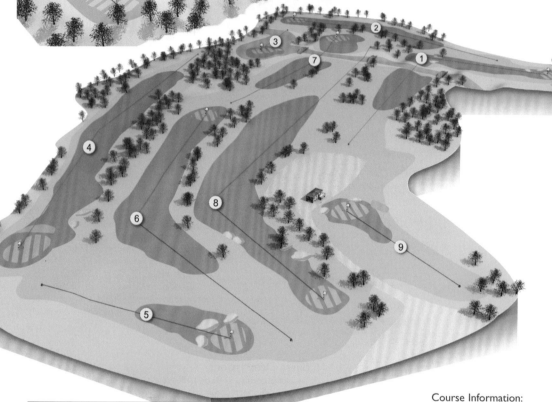

NO.	MEDAL METRES	GEN. METRES	PAR	S.I.	NO.	MEDAL METRES	GEN. METRES	PAR	S.I.
1	361	344	4	2	10	361	344	4	1
2	322	305	4	13	11	322	305	4	14
3	122	119	3	7	12	122	119	3	8
4	436	421	5	15	13	436	421	5	16
5	156	140	3	9	14	156	140	3	10
6	365	360	4	5	15	365	360	4	6
7	296	284	4	17	16	296	284	4	18
8	557	536	5	3	17	557	536	5	4
9	142	130	3	11	18	142	130	3	12
OUT	2,757	2,639	35		IN	2,757	2,639	35	
					TOTAL	5,514	5,278	70	
					STANDARD SCRATCH	70	71		

Course Information:
Par 70; SSS 69; Length 5,514 metres.
Visitors: Welcome. **Opening Hours:** Daylight hours. **Green Fees:** €30 - €40. **Clubhouse Dress:** Casual. **Clubhouse Facilities:** Bar and Restaurant.

Course Description:
A flat, manicured, challenging nine hole course with water on six of the holes, featuring our signature island third hole. A good test for all standards of golfer.

Newcastle Road, Kilcoole,
Co. Wicklow.
Tel: (01) 287 2066/ 201 0497
Email: adminkg@eircom.net
Web: www.kilcoolegolfclub.com

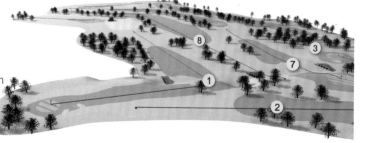

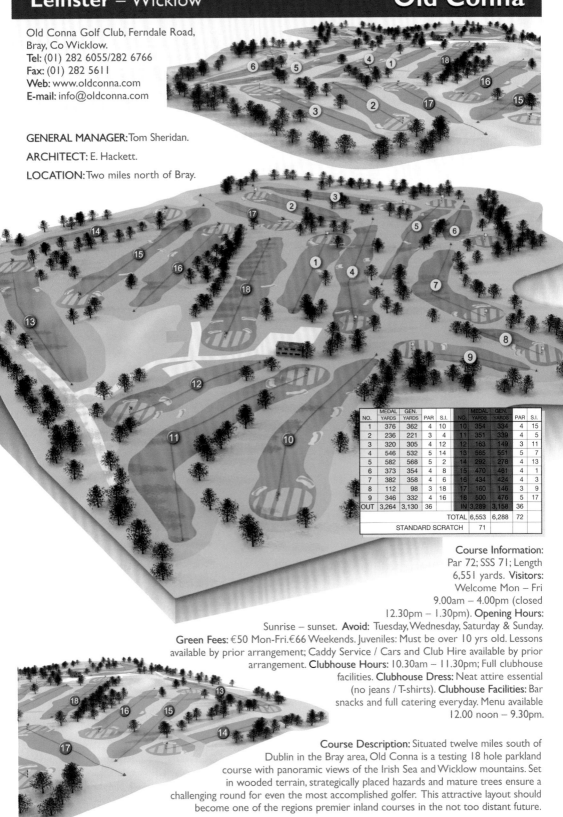

Old Conna Golf Club, Ferndale Road,
Bray, Co Wicklow.
Tel: (01) 282 6055/282 6766
Fax: (01) 282 5611
Web: www.oldconna.com
E-mail: info@oldconna.com

GENERAL MANAGER: Tom Sheridan.

ARCHITECT: E. Hackett.

LOCATION: Two miles north of Bray.

NO.	MEDAL YARDS	GEN. YARDS	PAR	S.I.	NO.	MEDAL YARDS	GEN. YARDS	PAR	S.I.
1	376	362	4	10	10	354	334	4	15
2	236	221	3	4	11	351	339	4	5
3	320	305	4	12	12	163	149	3	11
4	546	532	5	14	13	565	551	5	7
5	582	568	5	2	14	292	278	4	13
6	373	354	4	8	15	470	461	4	1
7	382	358	4	6	16	434	424	4	3
8	112	98	3	18	17	160	146	3	9
9	346	332	4	16	18	500	476	5	17
OUT	3,264	3,130	36		IN	3,289	3,158	36	
					TOTAL	6,553	6,288	72	
					STANDARD SCRATCH	71			

Course Information:
Par 72; SSS 71; Length
6,551 yards. **Visitors:**
Welcome Mon – Fri
9.00am – 4.00pm (closed
12.30pm – 1.30pm). **Opening Hours:**
Sunrise – sunset. **Avoid:** Tuesday, Wednesday, Saturday & Sunday.
Green Fees: €50 Mon-Fri.€66 Weekends. Juveniles: Must be over 10 yrs old. Lessons
available by prior arrangement; Caddy Service / Cars and Club Hire available by prior
arrangement. **Clubhouse Hours:** 10.30am – 11.30pm; Full clubhouse
facilities. **Clubhouse Dress:** Neat attire essential
(no jeans / T-shirts). **Clubhouse Facilities:** Bar
snacks and full catering everyday. Menu available
12.00 noon – 9.30pm.

Course Description: Situated twelve miles south of
Dublin in the Bray area, Old Conna is a testing 18 hole parkland
course with panoramic views of the Irish Sea and Wicklow mountains. Set
in wooded terrain, strategically placed hazards and mature trees ensure a
challenging round for even the most accomplished golfer. This attractive layout should
become one of the regions premier inland courses in the not too distant future.

Enniskerry, Co. Wicklow.
Tel: (01) 2046033.
Fax: (01) 2761303.

Course Information:
Par 72; SSS 74; Length 6,421 metres. Visitors: Welcome. Opening Hours: 8.00am – sunset. Ladies: Welcome. Juveniles: With handicap welcome, Caddies, club and trolley hire available, practice range and short game practice area also available. Green Fees: €140 all week, group rates on request; Clubhouse Hours: 8.00am – 12.00pm. Clubhouse Dress: Casual. No jeans. Clubhouse Facilities: Golf shop, restaurant and full bar facilities, dedicated visitor changing rooms, practice range.

MANAGER: Bernard Gibbons.

PROFESSIONAL: Paul Thompson.

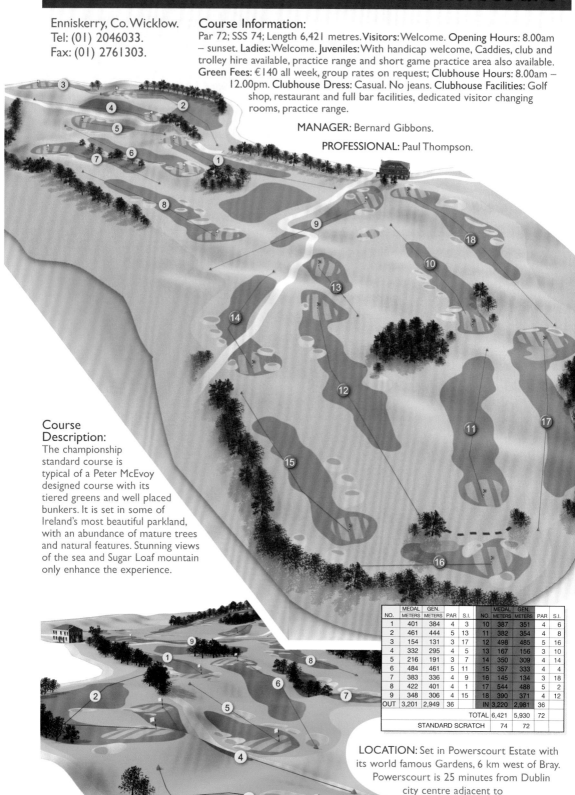

Course Description:
The championship standard course is typical of a Peter McEvoy designed course with its tiered greens and well placed bunkers. It is set in some of Ireland's most beautiful parkland, with an abundance of mature trees and natural features. Stunning views of the sea and Sugar Loaf mountain only enhance the experience.

NO.	MEDAL METERS	GEN. METERS	PAR	S.I.	NO.	MEDAL METERS	GEN. METERS	PAR	S.I.
1	401	384	4	3	10	387	351	4	6
2	461	444	5	13	11	382	354	4	8
3	154	131	3	17	12	498	485	5	16
4	332	295	4	5	13	167	156	3	10
5	216	191	3	7	14	350	309	4	14
6	484	461	5	11	15	357	333	4	4
7	383	336	4	9	16	145	134	3	18
8	422	401	4	1	17	544	488	5	2
9	348	306	4	15	18	390	371	4	12
OUT	3,201	2,949	36		IN	3,220	2,981	36	
TOTAL						6,421	5,930	72	
STANDARD SCRATCH							74	72	

LOCATION: Set in Powerscourt Estate with its world famous Gardens, 6 km west of Bray. Powerscourt is 25 minutes from Dublin city centre adjacent to Enniskerry village.

Powerscourt West

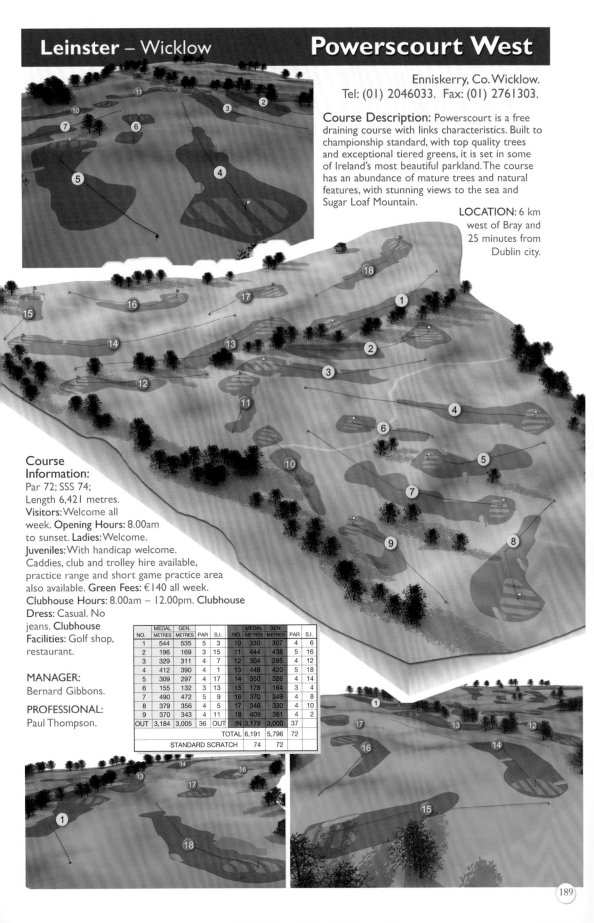

Enniskerry, Co. Wicklow.
Tel: (01) 2046033. Fax: (01) 2761303.

Course Description: Powerscourt is a free draining course with links characteristics. Built to championship standard, with top quality trees and exceptional tiered greens, it is set in some of Ireland's most beautiful parkland. The course has an abundance of mature trees and natural features, with stunning views to the sea and Sugar Loaf Mountain.

LOCATION: 6 km west of Bray and 25 minutes from Dublin city.

Course Information:

Par 72; SSS 74; Length 6,421 metres. **Visitors:** Welcome all week. **Opening Hours:** 8.00am to sunset. **Ladies:** Welcome. **Juveniles:** With handicap welcome. Caddies, club and trolley hire available, practice range and short game practice area also available. **Green Fees:** €140 all week. **Clubhouse Hours:** 8.00am – 12.00pm. **Clubhouse Dress:** Casual. No jeans. **Clubhouse Facilities:** Golf shop, restaurant.

MANAGER:
Bernard Gibbons.

PROFESSIONAL:
Paul Thompson.

NO.	MEDAL METRES	GEN. METRES	PAR	S.I.	NO.	MEDAL METRES	GEN. METRES	PAR	S.I.
1	544	535	5	3	10	330	307	4	6
2	196	169	3	15	11	444	438	5	16
3	329	311	4	7	12	304	285	4	12
4	412	390	4	1	13	448	420	5	18
5	309	297	4	17	14	350	326	4	14
6	155	132	3	13	15	178	164	3	4
7	490	472	5	9	16	370	349	4	8
8	379	356	4	5	17	346	330	4	10
9	370	343	4	11	18	409	381	4	2
OUT	3,184	3,005	36	OUT	IN	3,179	3,000	37	
				TOTAL		6,191	5,796	72	
			STANDARD SCRATCH			74	72		

Rathsallagh Golf Club, Dunlavin, Co. Wicklow.
Tel: 045 403316 Fax: 045 403295
Email: info@rathsallagh.com
Web: www.rathsallagh.com

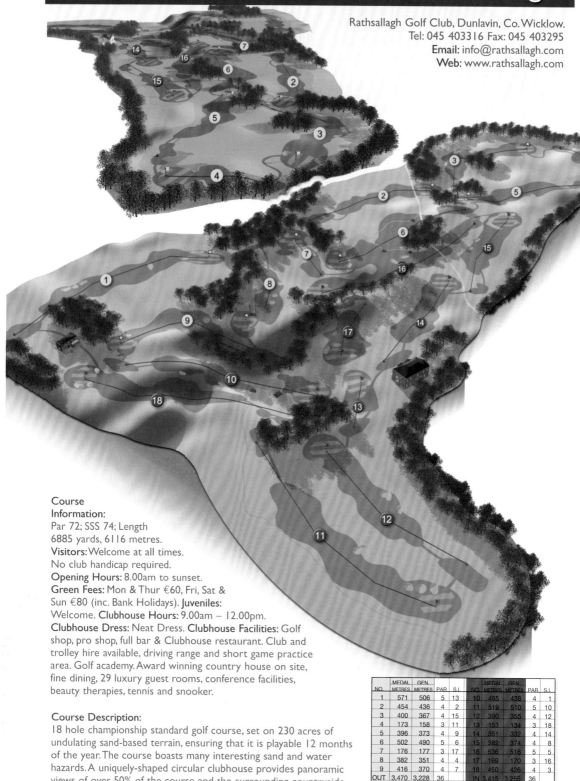

Course Information:

Par 72; SSS 74; Length
6885 yards, 6116 metres.
Visitors: Welcome at all times.
No club handicap required.
Opening Hours: 8.00am to sunset.
Green Fees: Mon & Thur €60, Fri, Sat &
Sun €80 (inc. Bank Holidays). **Juveniles:**
Welcome. **Clubhouse Hours:** 9.00am – 12.00pm.
Clubhouse Dress: Neat Dress. **Clubhouse Facilities:** Golf
shop, pro shop, full bar & Clubhouse restaurant. Club and
trolley hire available, driving range and short game practice
area. Golf academy. Award winning country house on site,
fine dining, 29 luxury guest rooms, conference facilities,
beauty therapies, tennis and snooker.

Course Description:

18 hole championship standard golf course, set on 230 acres of
undulating sand-based terrain, ensuring that it is playable 12 months
of the year. The course boasts many interesting sand and water
hazards. A uniquely-shaped circular clubhouse provides panoramic
views of over 50% of the course and the surrounding countryside.
Other facilities include driving range, three hole short-game area, 12
4 star luxury holiday cottage accommodation on site.

NO.	MEDAL METRES	GEN. METRES	PAR	S.I.	NO.	MEDAL METRES	GEN. METRES	PAR	S.I.
1	571	506	5	13	10	465	438	4	1
2	454	436	4	2	11	519	510	5	10
3	400	367	4	15	12	390	355	4	12
4	173	158	3	11	13	153	134	3	18
5	396	373	4	9	14	351	332	4	14
6	502	490	5	6	15	382	374	4	8
7	176	177	3	17	16	536	516	5	5
8	382	351	4	4	17	169	170	3	16
9	416	370	4	7	18	450	426	4	3
OUT	3,470	3,228	36		IN	3,415	3,255	36	
					TOTAL	6,885	6,483	72	
		STANDARD SCRATCH				74	72		

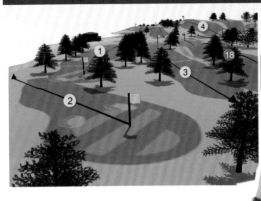

Roundwood Golf Club,
Newtownmountkennedy, Co. Wicklow.
Tel: (01) 281 8488. **Fax:** (01) 284 3642.
Email: rwood@indigo.ie
Web: www.roundwoodgolf.com

Course Description:

All sand greens built to U.S.P.G.A.
standards. Water hazards and forestry.
Heathland plays like links. Magnificent
views of coast, mountains and
Roundwood Lakes.

NO.	MEDAL YARDS	GEN. YARDS	PAR	S.I.	NO.	MEDAL YARDS	GEN. YARDS	PAR	S.I.
1	413	379	4	12	10	182	172	3	7
2	176	166	3	10	11	397	382	4	9
3	480	470	5	16	12	435	420	4	3
4	427	383	4	2	13	184	146	3	13
5	556	541	5	8	14	320	300	4	17
6	347	337	4	6	15	501	481	5	5
7	125	119	3	18	16	446	360	4	1
8	381	371	4	4	17	211	183	3	15
9	515	505	5	14	18	589	579	4	11
OUT	3,420	3,271	37		IN	3,265	3,023	35	
					TOTAL	6,685	6,294	72	
					STANDARD SCRATCH				

LOCATION: 2.5 miles from Newtownmountkennedy on
Glendalough/ Roundwood Road (N765).
SECRETARY: Mr Michael McGuirk and Angela Brady.
ARCHITECT: Consortium.

Course Information:

Par 72; Length 6,685 yards. **Visitors:**
Welcome. **Opening Hours:** 8am – sunset.
Juveniles: Restricted. **Green Fees:** €40
weekdays; €58 weekends & bank holidays.
Society Rates available. **Clubhouse Dress:**
Smart / Casual. **Clubhouse Facilities:** Bar
food available. **Tel:** (01) 2818500. Motorised
Buggy, Hand Cart, Trolley & Clubs available
for hire.

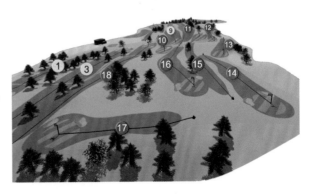

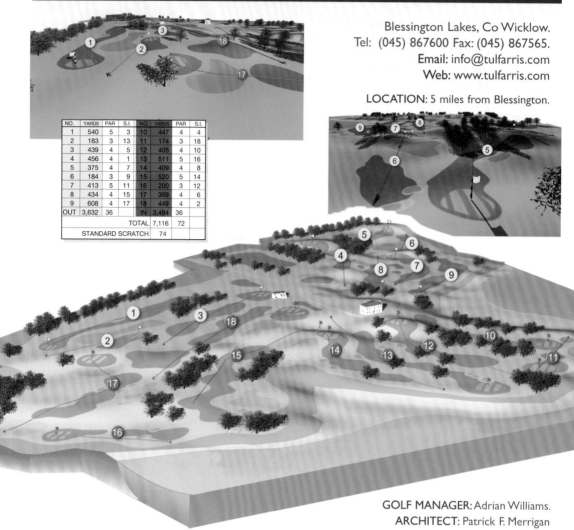

Blessington Lakes, Co Wicklow.
Tel: (045) 867600 Fax: (045) 867565.
Email: info@tulfarris.com
Web: www.tulfarris.com

LOCATION: 5 miles from Blessington.

NO.	YARDS	PAR	S.I.	NO.	YARDS	PAR	S.I.
1	540	5	3	10	447	4	4
2	183	3	13	11	174	3	18
3	439	4	5	12	405	4	10
4	456	4	1	13	511	5	16
5	375	4	7	14	409	4	8
6	184	3	9	15	520	5	14
7	413	5	11	16	200	3	12
8	434	4	15	17	369	4	6
9	608	4	17	18	449	4	2
OUT	3,632	36		IN	3,484	36	
				TOTAL	7,116	72	
				STANDARD SCRATCH	74		

GOLF MANAGER: Adrian Williams.
ARCHITECT: Patrick F. Merrigan

Course Information:
Par 72; SSS 74; Length 7,116 yards. Visitors:
Welcome. Opening Hours: Sunrise to
sunset. Ladies: Welcome. Juveniles: Welcome
but must be accompanied by an adult.
Green Fees: €80 weekdays. €100 Sat, Sun &
Bank Holidays. Clubhouse Hours: 6am -
10pm. Clubhouse Dress: Neat dress
essential. Clubhouse Facilities: Bar Snacks
10am - 10pm. Courtyard Restaurant 7pm –
10pm.

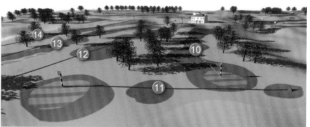

Course Description:
Designed by Patrick F. Merrigan (Old Head of Kinsale,
Slieve Russell, Woodenbridge) situated on a 200 acre
site overlooking Poulaphuca and Blessington Lakes at
the foothills of the Wicklow mountains. The course
which measures over 7100 yards from the back tees
has been designed to be challenging and enjoyable for
golfers of all levels. The tees, fairways, and sand based
greens have been manicured to a high standard.

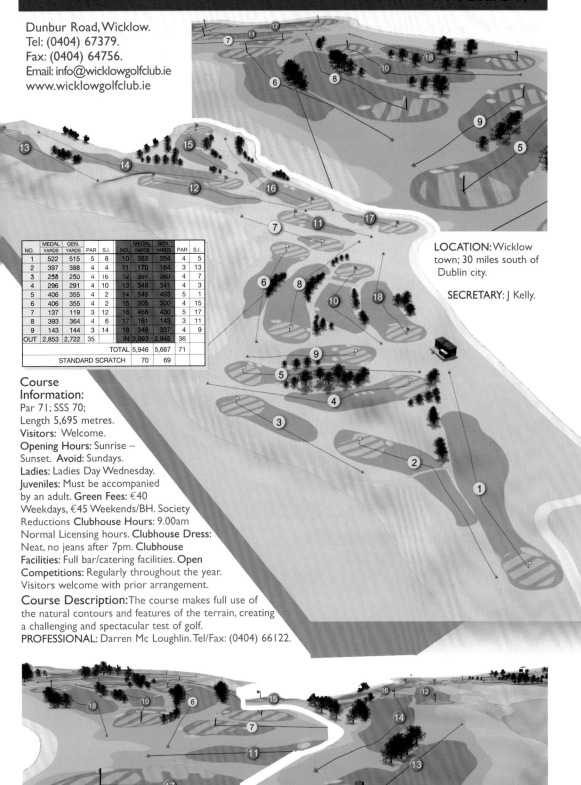

Dunbur Road, Wicklow.
Tel: (0404) 67379.
Fax: (0404) 64756.
Email: info@wicklowgolfclub.ie
www.wicklowgolfclub.ie

NO.	MEDAL YARDS	GEN. YARDS	PAR	S.I.	NO.	MEDAL YARDS	GEN. YARDS	PAR	S.I.
1	522	515	5	8	10	363	354	4	5
2	397	388	4	4	11	170	164	3	13
3	258	250	4	16	12	397	383	4	7
4	296	291	4	10	13	348	341	4	3
5	406	355	4	2	14	545	493	5	1
6	406	355	4	2	15	305	300	4	15
7	137	119	3	12	16	456	430	5	17
8	393	364	4	6	17	161	143	3	11
9	143	144	3	14	18	348	337	4	9
OUT	2,853	2,722	35		IN	3,093	2,945	36	
					TOTAL	5,946	5,667	71	
					STANDARD SCRATCH		70	69	

LOCATION: Wicklow town; 30 miles south of Dublin city.

SECRETARY: J Kelly.

Course Information:

Par 71; SSS 70;
Length 5,695 metres.
Visitors: Welcome.
Opening Hours: Sunrise – Sunset. **Avoid:** Sundays.
Ladies: Ladies Day Wednesday.
Juveniles: Must be accompanied by an adult. **Green Fees:** €40 Weekdays, €45 Weekends/BH. Society Reductions **Clubhouse Hours:** 9.00am Normal Licensing hours. **Clubhouse Dress:** Neat, no jeans after 7pm. **Clubhouse Facilities:** Full bar/catering facilities. **Open Competitions:** Regularly throughout the year. Visitors welcome with prior arrangement.

Course Description: The course makes full use of the natural contours and features of the terrain, creating a challenging and spectacular test of golf.
PROFESSIONAL: Darren Mc Loughlin. Tel/Fax: (0404) 66122.

Woodbrook

Woodbrook Golf Club, Dublin Road, Bray, Co. Wicklow
Tel: (01) 2824799.
Fax: (01) 2821950.

LOCATION: Eleven Miles south of Dublin City on N11.
GENERAL MANAGER: Patrick F. Byrne
Tel: (01) 282 4799 **Fax:** (01) 282 1950.
PROFESSIONAL: Mark Callan.
E-mail: golf@woodbrook.ie
Web: www.woodbrook.ie

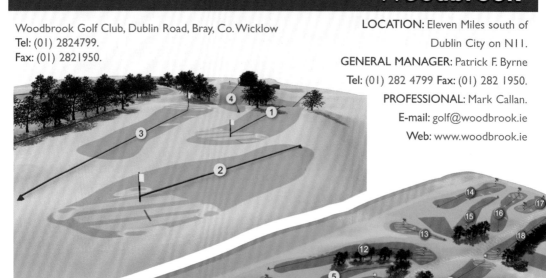

NO.	YARDS	PAR	S.I.	NO.	YARDS	PAR	S.I.
1	506	5	17	10	443	4	4
2	194	3	9	11	175	3	10
3	383	4	11	12	542	5	14
4	392	4	3	13	230	3	6
5	576	5	7	14	551	5	12
6	401	4	13	15	447	4	2
7	467	4	1	16	507	5	16
8	385	4	5	17	136	3	18
9	157	3	15	18	371	4	8
OUT	3,461	36		IN	3,402	36	
				TOTAL	6,863	72	
		STANDARD SCRATCH			72		

Course Information:
Par 72; SSS 72; Length 6,863 yards. **Visitors:** Welcome Mon, Thur & Fri only. **Opening Hours:** Sunrise – Sunset. **Avoid:** Tuesdays, Wednesdays and Bank Holidays. **Ladies:** Welcome. **Green Fees:** €75 midweek & Weekends **Juveniles:** Welcome. Lessons available; Club hire; Caddy service available by prior arrangement; Handicap certificate required. **Clubhouse Hours:** 8am-12 midnight. **Clubhouse Dress:** Smart casual wear in restaurant after 7pm. **Clubhouse Facilities:** 10am - 9pm (with some exceptions in winter); Full restaurant facilities. **Open Competitions:** Throughout July & August

Course Description:
Newly constructed layout with 18 new sand based greens and whilst beside the sea it is not a links course. The return of the course to Championship status will offer an excellent test of golf for all handicaps and with its traditional heritage, atmosphere and ambience, it is the perfect location for golf and hospitality.

NO.	YARDS	PAR	S.I.	NO.	YARDS	PAR	S.I.
1	362	4	9	10	455	4	2
2	419	4	3	11	194	3	4
3	377	4	13	12	353	4	16
4	186	3	11	13	386	4	10
5	410	4	5	14	295	4	18
6	437	4	1	15	500	5	12
7	324	4	15	16	357	4	14
8	123	3	17	17	167	3	6
9	502	5	7	18	553	5	8
OUT	3,140	35		IN	3,260	36	
				TOTAL	6,400	71	
				STANDARD SCRATCH		70	

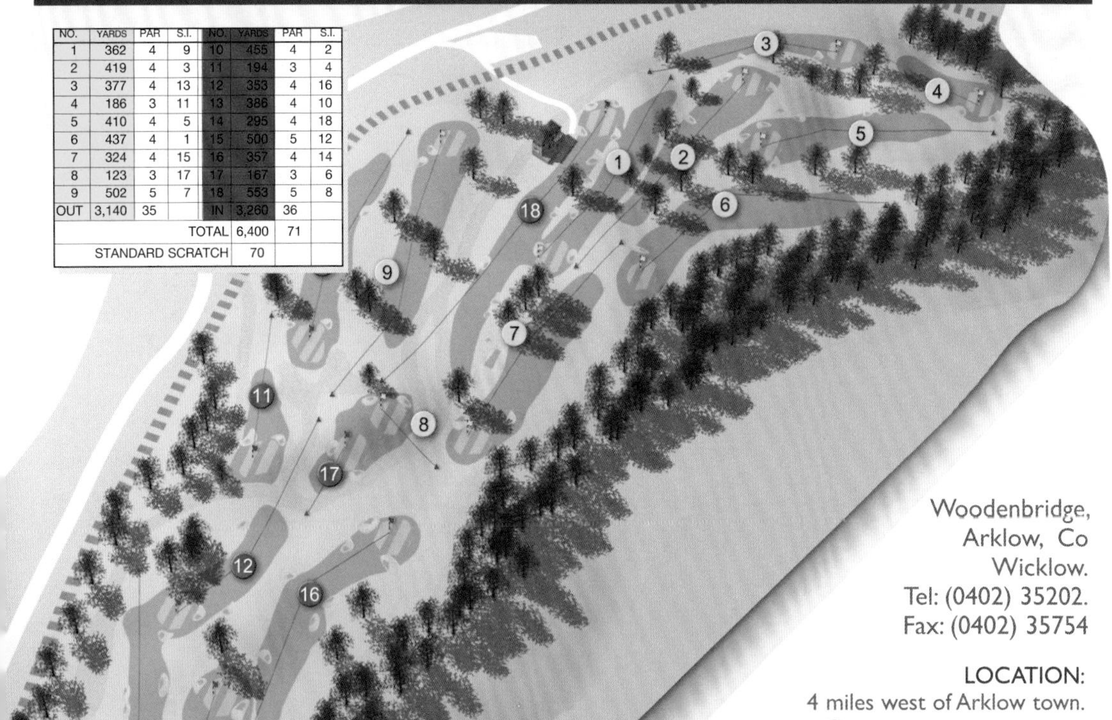

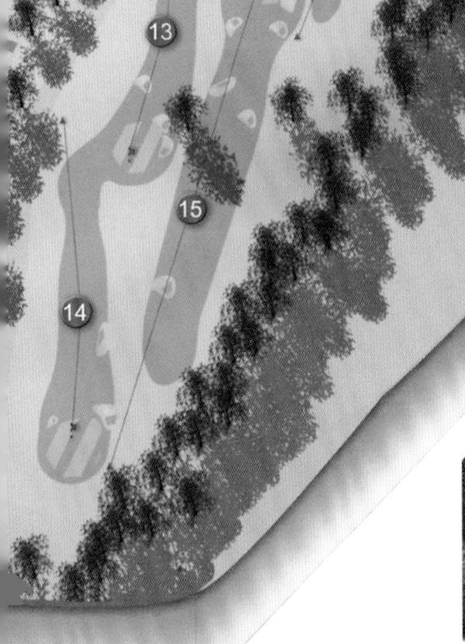

Woodenbridge,
Arklow, Co
Wicklow.
Tel: (0402) 35202.
Fax: (0402) 35754

LOCATION:
4 miles west of Arklow town.

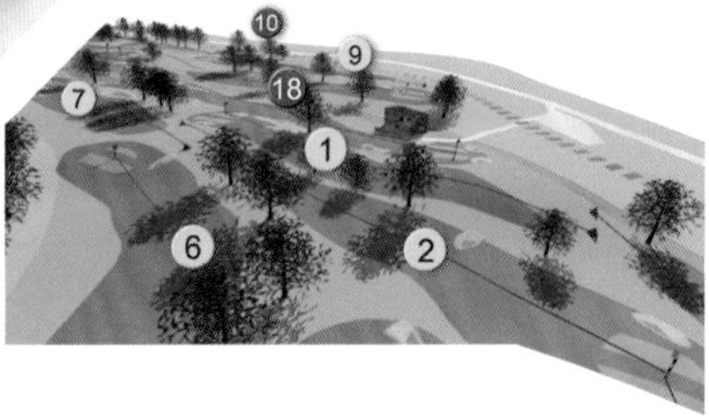

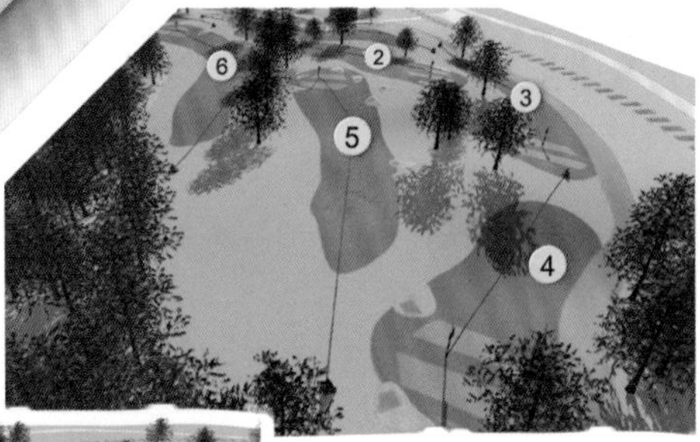

Course Description:

An 18 hole level parkland course, renowned for the quality of its greens. Carefully appointed trees and bunkers demand accurate shots. Sitting scenically in the beautiful Vale of Avoca, crouched under hills of magnificent forests and encircled by the meandering Rivers Avoca & Aughrim, it possesses a charm and character very special to Woodenbridge

Course Information: Par 71; SSS 70; Length 6,400 yards. **Visitors:** Welcome all week except Thursday and Saturday. **Opening Hours:** Sunrise – sunset. **Avoid:** Thursdays and Saturdays. **Ladies Day:** Thursdays. **Juveniles:** Welcome. **Green Fees:** €55 weekdays, €65 Sundays/ Bank Holidays. **Clubhouse Hours:** 8.00am – 11.00pm. **Clubhouse Dress:** Informal – neat and tidy. **Clubhouse Facilities:** Full clubhouse facilities. Mid-day – 9.00pm. Dinner menu and á la carte. Prior telephone call for special service. **Open Competitions:** Ladies open 2nd - 30th August contact club for details

SECRETARY/MANAGER: Kevin Mulcahy

Email: reception@woodenbridgegolfclub.com
Web: www.woodenbridgegolfclub.com

195

Photograph courtesy of North & West Coast Links. Portsalon Golf Club, County Donegal.

DONEGAL

L'DERRY

ANTRIM

TYRONE

FERMANAGH

ARMAGH

DOWN

MONAGHAN

CAVAN

A Provincial Introduction by Jack Magowan

Ulster's best golf courses are as tastily different as sirloin and salmon. Which might explain why the Province was given a prestigious No. 4 rating among the top 50 holiday destinations in the game.

The ranking marked an anniversary issue of *Golf Digest* whose editors compiled thumbnail sketches of nearly a hundred popular travel and hotel resorts, then invited over 600 prominent players and panellists to list them on a scale of one to ten.

Top of the poll was Monterey in California, followed by St. Andrews, Pinehurst in North Carolina, and Northern Ireland.

County Kerry and the South-West came in at No. 6 ahead of Myrtle Beach and Palm Springs, and County Dublin was at 15.

For American and European golfers, what best defines a rewarding destination ?

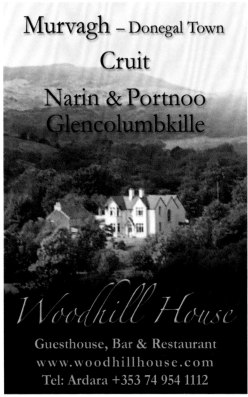

Royal Belfast is Ireland's oldest club, moving to its present scenic location, on the shores of Belfast Lough, in the mid-1920's.

• It has to have a strong mix of attractive and challenging courses.
• Hotel and guesthouse accommodation must be of good standard and value for money.
• Local attractions and amenities have to be highly recommended, and
• Friendly natives are as important as the proximity of the golf courses.

And it's here that Ulster scores a bull's eye.

If the two 'Royals', Portrush and County Down, rank among the jewels of links' golf, Portstewart and Castlerock are semi-precious stones. Unpolished gems, remote and primitive in some way as Atlantic breezes sting both cheeks and leave you with a feeling that this was how the game was meant to be played.

The Irish are always last to leave a good party, and no visitor is expected to leave before the Irish do.

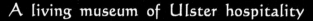

David Hamilton-Brown should know. He is the New York banker who was smitten so much by the charms of Royal Portrush that he bought a half-million dollar Causeway Coast apartment just to be near both courses. And there's a variety of other great courses within a 20-mile radius of the Hamilton-Browns, Ballyliffin among them.

Keep a sharp eye open for the Glashedy Rock, and there they are – two bright pearls in an oyster setting.

If it was anywhere else but in Donegal, this would be 'Royal Ballyliffin', can the club help it that Malin Head lacks a monarch to bestow a title of nobility.

Nick Faldo once sought a piece of the action there, and it's easy to understand why. Thirty-six holes in all, every one a separate experience as fairways twist and turn in every direction, and the wind is never an ally. Here, you're invited to play shots you never knew were in the bag.

Royal Belfast is Ireland's oldest club. Whisky was only 24 shillings (less than two euro or £1.20) a gallon when the game was played for the first time on a course at Carnalea, and no

▲
One of Ireland's top courses, Royal Portrush has played a virtuoso role in Irish golf as host to more major championships than they can count.

Loughgall
country park and golf course...

t: +44 [0] 28 3889 2900

Measured at 6,281 yards this 18 hole par 72 course was designed to produce a golfing experience that would present a fair challenge to golfers irrespective of their ability. Golfers will encounter every type of lie on the natural terrain and many of the magnificent mature trees have been brought into play. The front nine holes at 3542 yards will prove a challenge for even the very best golfers, culminating in a monster length par five over 600 yards long. The back nine is shorter with a par of 35 and will allow the golfer with good course management skills to put together a low score. For other members of the family facilities include a 37 acre Coarse Fishery, way marked walks, bridle paths, play area and trim trails.

City and District Council
Recreation & Leisure Facility

11-14 Main Street, Loughgall, Co. Armagh,
BT61 8HZ, Northern Ireland.
e: loughgallcountrypark@armagh.gov.uk
w: www.visitarmagh.com

▲
Venue for the 2007 Walker Cup, Royal County Down was voted by Tom Watson for the front nine holes 'close to perfection'. Another must-visit course for any golfer. Outstanding for its setting at the foot of the Mourne Mountains and noted for its five blind tee shots.

competition could begin until the 11 o'clock train arrived from the city.

The ladies of the club had their own cosy little clubhouse, but without the comfort of a warm shower. In those days, nobody complained. There were rocks nearby, so quite a few of the pretty young set would go bathing to cool off after their round.

Subject to one condition, that is: "Would ladies kindly refrain from passing the main clubhouse window in swim attire while the men are at lunch" read the notice bolted to the wooden fence.

It was in the mid-20's that Royal Belfast moved to Craigavad. For a handsome Victorian manor, plus 140-acre estate, now valued in eight figures, the club paid the princely sum of £6,000 and never looked back.

MARINE COURT HOTEL

The Marine Court Hotel is beautifully situated on the seafront at Bangor, Weekends buzz with entertainment, midweek is a comfort zone...

Central to 14 of N. Ireland's Premier Golf Clubs. Special packages Available upon request.

Marine Court Hotel, 18-20 Quay Street Bangor, Co. Down
Tel: (028) 9145 1100 Fax: (028) 9145 1200
E: marinecourt@btconnect.com

www.marinecourthotel.net

Photograph courtesy of Ballyliffin Golf Club.

▲
A tee shot at Galgorm Castle, Ballymena, County Antrim. A stimulating challenge for both novice and low handicap golfers.

First Royal Belfast, then Royal Dublin, Royal Curragh, Mullingar, Royal Portrush, Aughnacloy and Royal County Down.

By the time the Golfing Union was born, there were over 20 golf clubs in Ireland, half of them Ulster clubs. Indeed, the GUI is the grandfather of all national golf unions, older than the United States GA by three years, and the Welsh Union by four.

What a virtuoso role Royal Portrush has played in the game. Hosts to more major championships than they can count, the clubs' roll-call is dotted with players of distinction, names like Gary Player, Tom Watson, Fred Daly, Joe Carr, Catherine Lacoste and Garth McGimpsey, not forgetting such legends as the Hezlet sisters, Rhona Adair and Zara Bolton.

Malone was showered in kudos by Player, and so would Gracehill, Belvoir Park, Ardglass and Slieve Russell had he been able to play them. And lets pencil in Donegal (Murvagh) and dear little Cruit Island, too, for a visit.

▲
One of the best inland courses in Ireland, Malone has lush fairways in a sylvan setting with its lake providing several feature holes. Commodious and undulating greens are another feature.

Cruit spans only nine holes, so you'll play the sixth twice, and there can't be many more intimidating, or memorable, short holes anywhere.

There are some places that golfers know they must return to in order to discover them for the first time, and Royal County Down has always been one of them.

Tom Watson might not have won the British Seniors' Open there, as most of us thought he would, but felt that the front nine holes were 'close to perfection'. The Walker Cup is there in 2007, by which time the new 16th hole will have reached

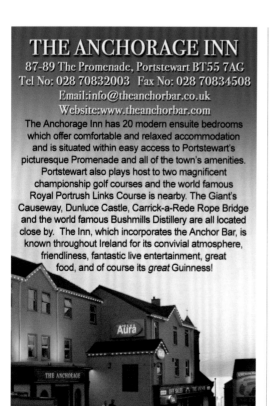
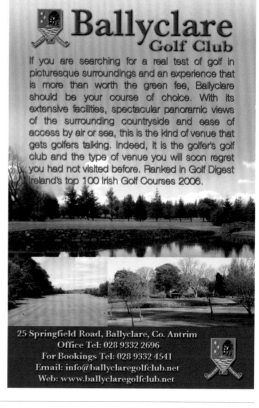

maturity. Like all 17 others, it's a superb test of links golf.

It was an American writer of hard-boiled detective stories who likened golf in Ireland to playing poker with nothing wild.

"It's the real thing," declared Larry Ferguson after a month-long safari here. "Ireland is not for players who like to be petted and protected. It's for pulling on a sweater, feeling the spray in your face, then boring long irons under winds that may keep the Coast Guard in port."

Is it possible that globe-trotter Ferguson could have played Portrush or Newcastle on a rough-weather day in March ? It's not that Irish weather can't be trusted. There's just so much of it, that's all!

Nobody in the Press tent has a longer lasting love-affair with the Emerald Isle than the late Peter Dobereiner.

"In Ireland, there are six days in the week," he used to say, "plus one for Guinness and golf. It's informal and welcoming, and the welcome is 100 per cent genuine."

Spectacular setting gives an edge to Donegal Golf Club in the south of the county near the famous Rossnowlagh beach.

Garth McGimpsey

by Jack Magowan

For over 20 years, Garth McGimpsey was one of Ireland's most professional looking amateur golfers. During that marathon spell, he won 14 championships, was capped over 150 times and never hit a shot he had not practiced a thousand times. Off the course, courteous and uncomplicated, but on it stern, unsmiling, a competitor to his finger-tips. It was inevitable that McGimpsey would succeed Peter McEvoy as captain of Britain's Walker Cup side and nobody could have been surprised when Garth led the team to a victory hat-trick at Ganton. It was only by a short putt that refused to drop that he failed to lead the team to a successful defence of the trophy before the match comes to Royal County Down in 2007, only the

How many players, amateur and professional, can say that they beat the great Jack Nicklaus

▲
Garth McGimpsey pictured during the Irish Amateur Close Championships at the Island Golf Club, County Dublin.

INISHOWEN GATEWAY
HOTEL

Gateway Health & Fitness Club
Seagrass Wellbeing Centre

This elegant, contemporary style hotel has 79 well appointed luxurious bedrooms and is situated on the sandy shores of Lough Swilly.

Close to **Ballyliffin** and **North West** Golf Clubs. The Hotel is the ideal location for golf enthusiasts who will enjoy the fine choice of either links or parkland golf. Complimentary golf is offered on the adjacent **Buncrana** 9 Hole course for residents, subject to availability. Local ferries makes **Portsalon, Castlerock, Royal Portrush** and **Portstewart** clubs all easily accessible.

The hotel boasts a fully equipped leisure centre complete with a 20 metre pool, gym sauna, steam room and spa bath.

The breathtaking views from The Peninsula Restaurant across Lough Swilly provide the perfect setting for dinner, where mouth-watering dishes are created from only the finest locally sourced produce.

An excellent Bar Food Menu is available daily in The Lisfannon Bar. Come and enjoy the live entertainment on weekends.

The Seagrass Wellbeing Centre offers a wide range of treatments for the weary golfer at the end of the day.

Golf, Fine Dining, Bar, Pool, Spa and Excellent Accommodation in one location.

Railway Road, Buncrana,
Inishowen, Co. Donegal
Tel: 00353 (0) 74 936 1144
Fax: 00353 (0) 74 936 2278
Email: info@inishowengateway.com
www.inishowengateway.com

Scrabo Golf Club
1907-2007

Scrabo boasts a unique, panoramic golfing challenge, to test the best of golfers and provide enjoyment for all who play and a warm welcome to all visitors.

Facilities

Our members have invested in a new clubhouse, construction of which completes in mid summer, in time for our major celebrations.
We have an excellent club shop, along with formal dining and bar services - all of which continue to operate during clubhouse construction.

Membership

Membership is currently open and in recognition of our centenary, the Club's Council have decided to extend the waiver on Entrance fees, for successful applicants to all categories joining this year. All prospective new members will be given the courtesy of a round of golf during the application process.

Come join us, whether as a visitor or as a prospective new member.

You will be most welcome.

email: admin.scrabogc@btconnect.com
Tel: (028) 9181 2355 Fax: (028) 9182 2919
www.scrabo-golf.org

second time on record it has been hosted by an Irish club.

McGimpsey and Ronan Rafferty might be labelled 'peas in a pod' and I remember the first time the pair shared a hotel room as international teammates. It was at St. Andrew's during the week of a European championship and Garth couldn't have been more impressed by how the precocious Rafferty handled pressure, not to speak of the teenager's rare gifts of concentration and course management. "Ronan was only 17 years old, but had the golfing brain of somebody twice his age," recalls the Bangor legend. It was in a force-9 gale that

It was in a force - 9 gale that McGimpsey holed moody old Ballybunion in 67 shots – arguably the greatest tournament round of his career

McGimpsey holed moody old Ballybunion in 67 shots – arguably the greatest tournament round of his career – but Royal Portrush has long been his favourite links, with Birkdale, he says, a close second. "Both wonderful golf courses; long on hazards and hard on accuracy," he grins.

How many players, amateur and professional, can say that they beat the great Jack Nicklaus over the course on which he would win a sixth US Masters only 5 days later? Garth can and has a framed four-dollar cheque to prove it!

The Highlight years in Garth McGimpsey's neon-lit career:

* Amateur Championship – won at Royal Dornoch 1985, semi finalist 1989
* Irish Amateur Championship – won at Royal Portrush 1988, beaten finalist 1996
* Walker Cup – played 1985, 1989 (Britain won at Peachtree) and 1991. Non-playing captain 2003 and 2005
* World Team Championship – played 1984, 1986 and 1988 (Britain won in Sweden)
* North of Ireland Amateur championship – won 1978, '84, '91, '92 and '93 at Royal Portrush.
* West of Ireland Amateur Championship – won 1984, '88, '93 and '96 at County Sligo
* East of Ireland Amateur Championship – won 1988, '94 and '98 at County Louth

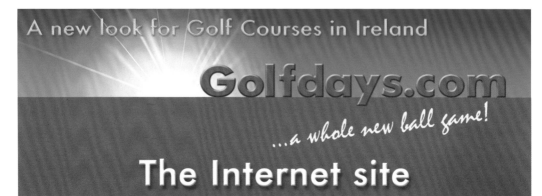

Hidden Gem at Rosapenna

by Jack Magowan

Martin Luther King had a dream, and so did Frank Casey only with this golfing visionary, it was more like an obsession – to build a links course so dramatically challenging that it would rank with the best in Ireland.

If the Rosapenna Hotel, on Donegal's north tip, gave the Emerald Isle its first holiday resort course over a century ago, the hidden gem of sandy hills will be Frank's legacy to the game.

..a thinking man's course, full of subtle twists and turns

It's a new and inviting cocktail of links' golf at its purest, or as Casey Junior so aptly put it, "a course that has conjured enough ballads to drain the repertoire of a good tenor".

There's no prize for guessing who designed this duneland masterpiece. Pat Ruddy's creative talents were already on show at Druid's Glen, Ballyliffin and his own beloved European Club, and this, too, is a thinking man's course full of subtle twists and turns, even on the putting surface.

Jack Green, a brother of Elm Park professional,

▲
6th green at Rosapenna (Sandy Hills) with picture-postcard views of Muckish Mountain straight ahead.

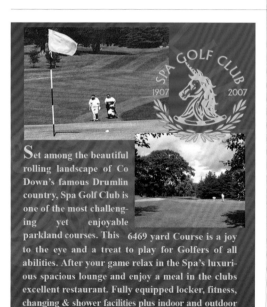

Seamus Green, supervised the spadework. He is a graduate of golf's old school, and tried hard to preserve what nature put there.

"All great links are fun to play, a pleasure not a penance, and this one is all of that", says Strabane's Enda Kennedy, the first man to hole Sandy Hills in 67 shots.

> **"All great links are fun to play, a pleasure not a penance, and this one is all of that"**

Nobody had much love for the 3rd Earl of Leitrim – otherwise he wouldn't have been assassinated – but the 4th Earl was a gentleman, and quick to see Donegal's tourist potential. He imported special timber from Sweden to build the original Rosapenna Hotel, but, sadly, never lived to welcome the first guest. He cut his hand badly in an accident, and died from blood poisoning.

Vardon, old Tom Morris, Herd, Duncan, Ball… all the top golfers of the day holidayed there and photographs to prove it are in the Casey collection happily rescued from the fire that gutted the hotel in 1962, about 20 years before Frank Casey bought what his wife, Hilary, a delightful Fermanagh girl, proudly calls "a resort for all seasons".

There are now two championship courses at Downings, plus an academy nine that was once part of the course on which Frank Senior found a 100 year old ball, small wonder the ghosts of Vardon and friends still tip-toe across these great links!

▲
All the golfers have retired as the sun sets on another challenging day at Rosapenna.

malone lodge HOTEL
& APARTMENTS

60 Eglantine Avenue
Malone Road,
Belfast BT9 6DY

Tel: (028) 9038 8000
Fax: (028) 9038 8088

info@malonelodgehotel.com
www.malonelodgehotelbelfast.com

- 65 Deluxe Hotel Bedrooms & Suites
- 22 Executive Self Catering Apartments
- Private Fitness Suite & Sauna
- 5 minutes from Belfast City centre
- 10 minutes from Belfast City Airport
- Complimentary Car Parking

Situated in the leafy suburbs of South Belfast between the
exclusive Malone Road and the ever increasing fashion-
able Lisburn Road lies this elegant four star Victorian
Townhouse Hotel.
Malone Lodge Hotel is an ideal base to play many of the
top courses in the Belfast area like
Malone, Dunmurry, Down Royal, Belvoir, Balmoral,
Rockmount and Shandon

The Best Reception in Belfast

Graeme McDowell

by Jack Magowan

G raeme McDowell's courtship with professional golf was invitingly brief. Within six weeks of joining the European Tour, this mild-mannered Portrush lad had won the Scandinavian Masters, and in only his third season of plundering the world's greenest fairways, he banked over £1 million in prize money as the sixth best player this side of the Atlantic.

Nobody will be surprised if McDowell scales the summit and soon. That's how gifted he is in a game that demands so much between the ears. And as the brightest of young students at Coleraine Institute and later the University of Alabama, Graeme must have had a head start on most.

"In a span of four great months, he won seven titles in all"

It was as a World Universities and Irish champion that McDowell first caught the eye. In a span of four great months, he won seven titles in all, then returned to the United States to better a Tiger Woods' college record before helping Britain win the Walker Cup at Sea Island, Georgia. Success as a rookie pro was instantaneous.

"That £200,000 Swedish windfall helped ease quite a few financial pressures but may have sparked others," confessed Graeme. "My second big win in the Italian Open of 2004 couldn't have come at a better time, and I played really well for the rest of the year."

Just how well can be judged from his second-place finish in the Diageo Gleneagles tournament, followed by rewarding rounds of 64 in France and Germany, not forgetting a spectacular best-of-the-week 62 in Munich – the overture to another brilliant 62, this time at St Andrews for a share of the record at the famous Old Course. He was runner-up there too, beaten in a Dunhill play-off, but still richer by nearly £300,000.

Confidence is the key word in McDowell's learning curve and a thrilling last-hole victory over Darren Clarke in the Accenture World match-play classic in California, plus a runner-up spot in the Bay Hill (Florida) classic has been a real feather in his cap.

▲
Graeme McDowell, watches his tee shot at the 3rd tee box during the first round at the Nissan Irish Open Golf Championship at Portmarnock Golf Club, Co. Dublin.

Numbers above refer to the page number of each course with approximate geographical location shown on the map above.

PORTRUSH
239 - 240

BELFAST CITY
252 - 263

NORTH DOWN
290, 291, 293
294, 295, 297
299, 300, 305

Allen Park, 45 Castle Road,
Antrim, BT41 4NA.
Tel: (028) 9442 9001.

MANAGER: Marie Agnew.

ARCHITECT: Mr T. McAuley.

LOCATION: 2 1/2 miles from Antrim town centre on the road from Antrim to Randalstown.

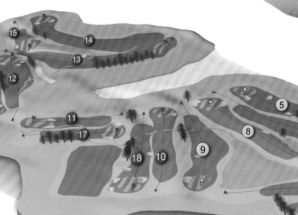

Course Description:

The course opened in Spring 1996. This gently undulating parkland course will test the skill and ability of even the more experienced golfer. The shortest hole is 129 yards with the longest being 562 yards. 3 lakes provide interesting features in the front nine holes.

Course Information:

Visitors: Welcome. **Opening Hours:** Dawn–Dusk **Green Fees:** Mon/Fri – Adults £16.50: Senior Citizen (Over 60) £10.50: Junior (Under 18) £7.50: Weekends & Holidays – Adults £18.50: Senior Citizen (Over 60) £12.50: Junior (Under 18) £8.50. **Juveniles:** Welcome. **Clubhouse Dress:** Casual. **Clubhouse Facilities:** Locker rooms and Snooker table. Licensed restaurant.

NO.	WHITE YARDS	YELLOW YARDS	PAR	S.I.	NO.	WHITE YARDS	YELLOW YARDS	PAR	S.I.
1	432	421	4	9	10	421	410	4	10
2	291	281	4	13	11	199	185	3	14
3	321	311	4	17	12	407	388	4	4
4	323	304	4	15	13	485	473	5	6
5	505	490	5	5	14	534	523	5	2
6	562	547	5	1	15	129	119	3	18
7	181	156	3	7	16	368	354	4	16
8	452	437	4	3	17	199	184	3	8
9	431	378	4	11	18	392	382	4	12
OUT	3,498	3,325	37		IN	3,134	3,018	35	
					TOTAL	6,632	6,343	72	
					STANDARD SCRATCH	72	71		

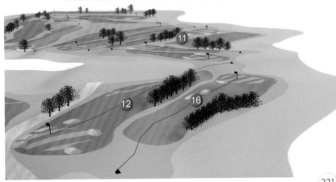

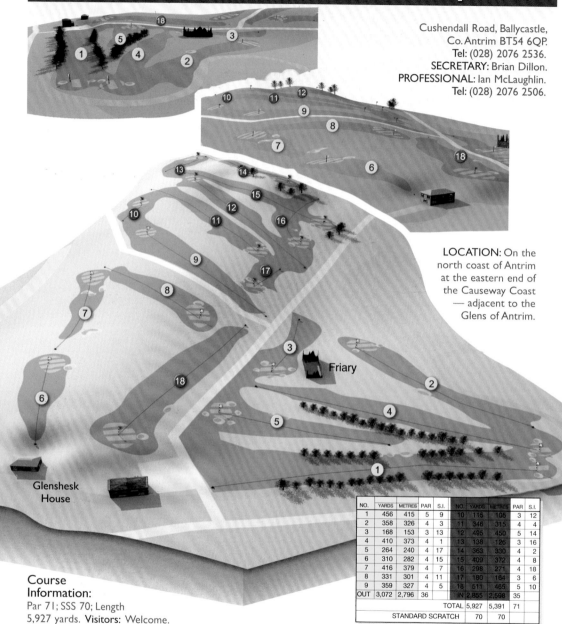

Cushendall Road, Ballycastle,
Co. Antrim BT54 6QP.
Tel: (028) 2076 2536.
SECRETARY: Brian Dillon.
PROFESSIONAL: Ian McLaughlin.
Tel: (028) 2076 2506.

Friary

Glenshesk
House

LOCATION: On the
north coast of Antrim
at the eastern end of
the Causeway Coast
— adjacent to the
Glens of Antrim.

NO.	YARDS	METRES	PAR	S.I.	NO.	YARDS	METRES	PAR	S.I.
1	456	415	5	9	10	115	105	3	12
2	358	326	4	3	11	346	315	4	4
3	168	153	3	13	12	495	450	5	14
4	410	373	4	1	13	138	126	3	16
5	264	240	4	17	14	363	330	4	2
6	310	282	4	15	15	409	372	4	8
7	416	379	4	7	16	298	271	4	18
8	331	301	4	11	17	180	164	3	6
9	359	327	4	5	18	511	465	5	10
OUT	3,072	2,796	36		IN	2,855	2,598	35	
					TOTAL	5,927	5,391	71	
					STANDARD SCRATCH		70	70	

Course Information:

Par 71; SSS 70; Length
5,927 yards. **Visitors:** Welcome.
Opening Hours: Summer 9.00am – 9.00pm;
Winter 9.00am – 3.00pm. **Avoid:** Sat and Sun
morning. **Ladies Day:** Friday. **Green Fees:** £25 (£10
with member) Mon – Fri; £35 (£15 with member)
Sat / Sun and public holidays. Juveniles under 18
years – 1/2 rates. **Juveniles:** Welcome before
6.00pm in July and August. Lessons by prior
arrangement; Club hire and Caddy service
available by prior arrangement. **Clubhouse Hours:**
11.30am – 11pm (July & August); Restricted in
winter. **Clubhouse Dress:** Casual. **Clubhouse
Facilities:** Bar snacks and meals throughout the
day. Evening meals by prior arrangement. **Open
Competitions:** Open Week – July; other
competitions throughout the season.

Course Description:

The opening five holes are parkland bordered by the
Margy and Carey Rivers and played around the ruins of a
13th Century Friary. The Warren area of four holes is
true links and the final nine are played in an adjacent
upland, giving panoramic views including Mull of Kintyre,
Rathlin Island and Ballycastle Bay. Accurate iron play is
essential for good scoring.

25 Springvale Road, Ballyclare, Co. Antrim.
Tel/Fax: (028) 9332 2696
Pro Shop: (028) 9332 4541
Restaurant: (028) 9332 4542
Web: www.Ballyclaregolfclub.net
Email: ballyclaregolfclub.net

Course Description:

Set in the rolling green countryside around the bustling, traditional market town of Ballyclare. This parkland course makes good use of its natural landscape with tree-lined fairways, lakes between the 3rd and 7th fairways and meandering river across the course, provide a number of challenges to skilled and amateur golfers alike.

ARCHITECT: T. McCauley.
LOCATION: Two miles north of Ballyclare - off the Rashee Road (at five corners).
PGA PROFESSIONAL: Colin Lyttle.

NO.	YARDS	METRES	PAR	S.I.	NO.	YARDS	METRES	PAR	S.I.
1	308	320	4	11	10	347	364	4	12
2	494	504	5	7	11	158	175	3	6
3	399	431	4	1	12	461	479	5	14
4	343	364	4	15	13	429	437	4	8
5	362	378	4	5	14	394	404	4	2
6	148	157	3	13	15	112	128	3	18
7	358	374	4	3	16	406	418	4	4
8	349	360	4	17	17	470	483	5	16
9	149	166	3	9	18	359	372	4	10
OUT	2,910	3,054	35		IN	3,136	3,260	36	
					TOTAL	6,046	6,314	71	
					STANDARD SCRATCH		69	71	

Course Information:

Par 71; SSS 71; Length 6,314 yds. **Visitors:** Societies & visitors welcome - except Saturdays and Sunday mornings (book through Pro-Shop). **Opening Hours:** Dawn–Dusk. **Avoid:** Sunday mornings, Thursdays from 1.30pm and Saturdays. **Ladies:** Welcome. **Green Fees:** £22 Mon – Fri; £28 Sunday/Bank Holidays. £18/£23 Low Season. **Juveniles:** Mon – Fri before 4.30pm; Sat/Sun after 4.30pm. **Clubhouse Hours:** 12.30 – 9.00 pm. Restaurant - 12 noon (closed Mondays). Bar - 12.30 to 11pm. **Clubhouse Dress:** Jacket and tie after 7.00pm. **Clubhouse Facilities:** Meals from 12.30pm unless by prior arrangement.

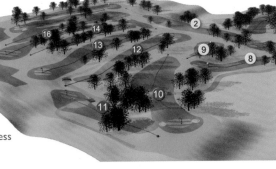

128 Raceview Road, Ballymena.
Tel: (028) 2586 1487.
Email: ballymena@golfnet.ie
www.ballymenagolfclub.co.uk

LOCATION: Three miles east of Ballymena.

Course Description:
A flat course comprised mainly of heathland with numerous bunkers. The Glens of Antrim lie to the northeast and Slemish Mountain is clearly visible to the east.

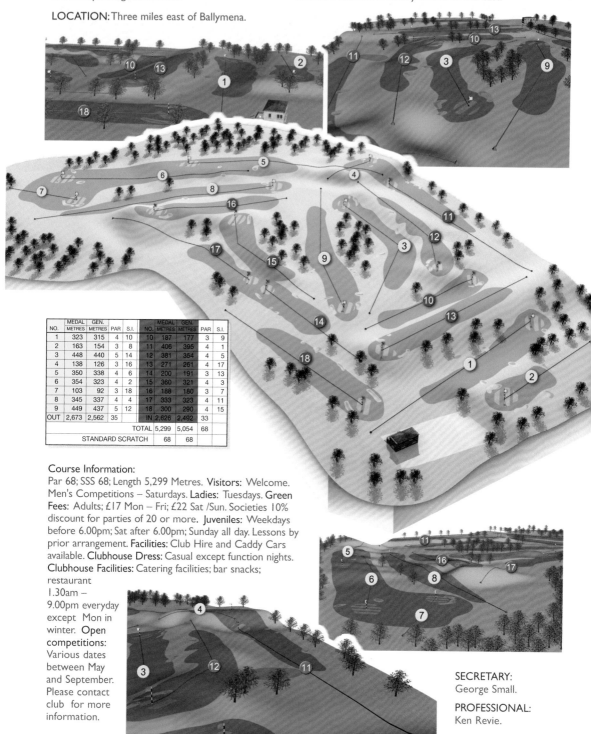

NO.	MEDAL METRES	GEN. METRES	PAR	S.I.	NO.	MEDAL METRES	GEN. METRES	PAR	S.I.
1	323	315	4	10	10	187	177	3	9
2	163	154	3	8	11	406	395	4	1
3	448	440	5	14	12	381	354	4	5
4	138	126	3	16	13	271	261	4	17
5	350	338	4	6	14	200	191	3	13
6	354	323	4	2	15	360	321	4	3
7	103	92	3	18	16	188	180	3	7
8	345	337	4	4	17	333	323	4	11
9	449	437	5	12	18	300	290	4	15
OUT	2,673	2,562	35		IN	2,626	2,492	33	
					TOTAL	5,299	5,054	68	
					STANDARD SCRATCH	68	68		

Course Information:
Par 68; SSS 68; Length 5,299 Metres. **Visitors:** Welcome. Men's Competitions – Saturdays. **Ladies:** Tuesdays. **Green Fees:** Adults; £17 Mon – Fri; £22 Sat /Sun. Societies 10% discount for parties of 20 or more. **Juveniles:** Weekdays before 6.00pm; Sat after 6.00pm; Sunday all day. Lessons by prior arrangement. **Facilities:** Club Hire and Caddy Cars available. **Clubhouse Dress:** Casual except function nights. **Clubhouse Facilities:** Catering facilities; bar snacks; restaurant 1.30am – 9.00pm everyday except Mon in winter. **Open competitions:** Various dates between May and September. Please contact club for more information.

SECRETARY:
George Small.

PROFESSIONAL:
Ken Revie.

50 Bushfoot Road, Portballintrae, Bushmills,
Co Antrim BT57 8RA.
Tel: (028) 2073 1317. **Fax:**(028) 2073 1852.
MANAGER: J. Knox Thompson.
HON. SECRETARY: Victor Freeman

LOCATION: Two miles from Bushmills
beside Portballintrae village.

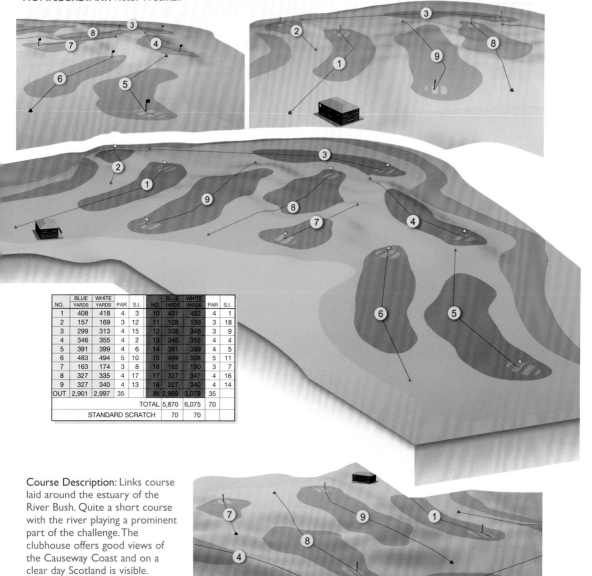

NO.	BLUE YARDS	WHITE YARDS	PAR	S.I.	NO.	BLUE YARDS	WHITE YARDS	PAR	S.I.
1	408	418	4	3	10	431	452	4	1
2	157	169	3	12	11	128	139	3	18
3	299	313	4	15	12	338	348	3	9
4	346	355	4	2	13	346	355	4	4
5	391	399	4	6	14	391	399	4	5
6	483	494	5	10	15	499	508	5	11
7	163	174	3	8	16	182	190	3	7
8	327	335	4	17	17	327	347	4	16
9	327	340	4	13	18	327	340	4	14
OUT	2,901	2,997	35		IN	2,969	3,078	35	
					TOTAL	5,870	6,075	70	
	STANDARD SCRATCH						70	70	

Course Description: Links course laid around the estuary of the River Bush. Quite a short course with the river playing a prominent part of the challenge. The clubhouse offers good views of the Causeway Coast and on a clear day Scotland is visible.

Course Information:
Par 70; SSS 70; Length 6,075 Yards. **Visitors:** Welcome Mon – Fri.
Avoid: Saturday or Sunday unless guest of a member. **Ladies:** Welcome any time. **Green Fees:** £16 Mon – Fri; £20 Bank & Public Holidays; Sat/Sun. **Juveniles:** Handicap Certificate required. Prior arrangement preferable. **Clubhouse Dress:** Acceptable Casual. **Clubhouse Facilities:** Full meals, bar snacks.

192 Coast Road, Ballygally, Larne.
Tel: (028) 2858 3324. Pro: (028) 2858 3954.

LOCATION: Four miles north of Larne.

SECRETARY: Kerry Craig.

PROFESSIONAL: Steven Hood.

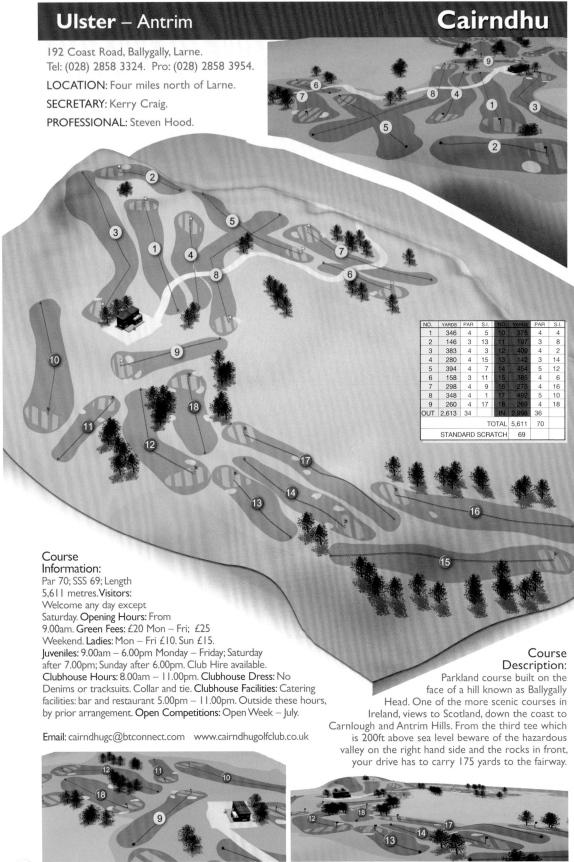

NO.	YARDS	PAR	S.I.	NO.	YARDS	PAR	S.I.
1	346	4	5	10	375	4	4
2	146	3	13	11	197	3	8
3	383	4	3	12	409	4	2
4	280	4	15	13	142	3	14
5	394	4	7	14	454	5	12
6	158	3	11	15	385	4	6
7	298	4	9	16	275	4	16
8	348	4	1	17	492	5	10
9	260	4	17	18	269	4	18
OUT	2,613	34		IN	2,998	36	
				TOTAL	5,611	70	
			STANDARD SCRATCH		69		

Course Information:

Par 70; SSS 69; Length 5,611 metres. Visitors: Welcome any day except Saturday. **Opening Hours:** From 9.00am. **Green Fees:** £20 Mon – Fri; £25 Weekend. **Ladies:** Mon – Fri £10. Sun £15. Juveniles: 9.00am – 6.00pm Monday – Friday; Saturday after 7.00pm; Sunday after 6.00pm. Club Hire available. **Clubhouse Hours:** 8.00am – 11.00pm. **Clubhouse Dress:** No Denims or tracksuits. Collar and tie. **Clubhouse Facilities:** Catering facilities: bar and restaurant 5.00pm – 11.00pm. Outside these hours, by prior arrangement. **Open Competitions:** Open Week – July.

Email: cairndhugc@btconnect.com   www.cairndhugolfclub.co.uk

Course Description:

Parkland course built on the face of a hill known as Ballygally Head. One of the more scenic courses in Ireland, views to Scotland, down the coast to Carnlough and Antrim Hills. From the third tee which is 200ft above sea level beware of the hazardous valley on the right hand side and the rocks in front, your drive has to carry 175 yards to the fairway.

35 North Road, Carrickfergus, BT38 8LP.
Tel: (028) 9336 3713.
Email: carrickfergusgc@btconnect.com
www.carrickfergusgc.com

SECETARY / MANAGER: Ian McLean.

PROFESSIONAL: Gary Mercer.

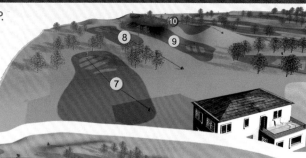

NO.	MEDAL YARDS	GEN. YARDS	PAR	S.I.	NO.	MEDAL YARDS	GEN. YARDS	PAR	S.I.
1	410	408	4	8	10	438	436	4	1
2	101	101	3	18	11	406	396	4	5
3	381	379	4	4	12	167	165	3	15
4	127	125	4	16	13	434	430	4	3
5	316	314	4	10	14	197	187	3	11
6	425	423	4	2	15	353	350	4	9
7	132	130	3	12	16	295	293	4	7
8	282	280	4	14	17	490	485	5	17
9	437	435	4	6	18	322	320	4	13
OUT	2,611	2,595	33		IN	3,102	3,062	35	
					TOTAL	5,713	5,657	68	
					STANDARD SCRATCH		68		

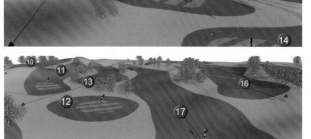

Course Description:

A parkland course with a spectacular first hole. The first drive, from an elevated tee is over the infamous dam which is full of water and quite intimidating! Although a reasonably flat course there are several demanding holes to be tackled. The par 4, 6th hole is a dog-leg left playing to a hidden green beside the dam. The course is well maintained throughout the year and there are some very pleasant views across the Belfast Lough to Co. Down.

Course Information:

Par 68; SSS 68; Length 5,713 Yards. Visitors: Welcome any day during the week. Sunday after 12 noon. Avoid: Tuesday, Saturday and Sunday. Ladies: Tuesdays. Green Fees: £19 Mon – Fri (£12 with member); £24 Sat / Sun/Bank Holidays (£15.00 with a member). Juveniles: Up to 4pm – restricted times at weekends. Clubhouse Dress: Casual. Clubhouse Facilities: Catering facilities: bar snacks, meals 12 noon – 9pm everyday except Mondays. Open Competitons: Open Week – July / Aug.

LOCATION: In Cushendall village on road to beach.

SECRETARY: Shaun McLaughlin. Tel: (028) 2175 8366.

ARCHITECT: Dan Delargy.

21 Shore Road, Cushendall, Co. Antrim.
Tel: (028) 2177 1318.

NO.	METRES	PAR	S.I.	NO.	METRES	PAR	S.I.
1	273	4	11	10	271	4	12
2	162	3	7	11	162	3	6
3	285	4	3	12	293	4	4
4	262	4	9	13	262	4	10
5	143	3	13	14	135	3	14
6	243	4	17	15	243	4	18
7	115	3	15	16	115	3	16
8	352	4	1	17	352	4	2
9	358	4	5	18	358	4	8
OUT	2,193	33		IN	2,191	33	
				TOTAL	4,384	66	
				STANDARD SCRATCH	63		

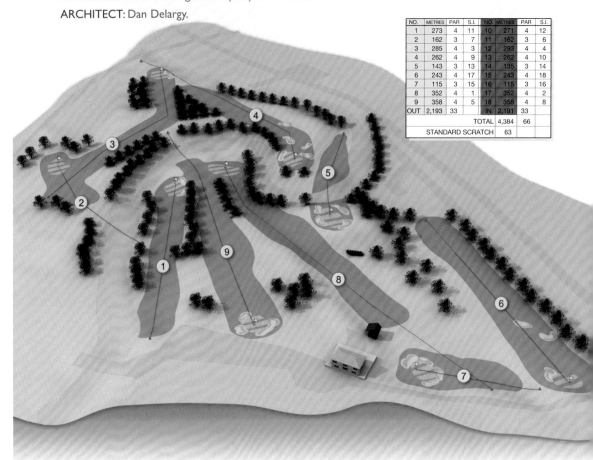

Course Information: Par 66; SSS 63; Length 4,386 metres. **Visitors:** Check with club in advance. **Avoid:** Sundays anytime (time sheet). **Ladies:** Any time but not Sunday before 1.00pm. Priority on Thursdays. **Green Fees:** £13 Mon – Fri; £18 Sat / Sun / Bank Holidays. **Juveniles:** Weekdays up to 5.00pm. Must be off course by 1.00pm Sat and no play on Sun. Lessons can be arranged. **Clubhouse Dress:** Casual. **Clubhouse Facilities:** Full bar and Catering available at all times during summer. **Open Competitions:** Glens of Antrim mixed foursomes – May / June most weekends. Handicap Certificate required for Open Competitions.

Course Description:
Beautifully situated course where the River Dall winds through the fairways in seven of the nine holes. Cushendall is quite a short course, it has three par 3's and no par 5's, but it requires great accuracy as it is possible to go out of bounds at every hole.

Dunygarton Road, Maze, Lisburn, BT27 5RT.

Tel: (028) 9262 1339/ 92622 370.

MANAGER: Miss S Moore.

Tel: (028) 9262 1339.

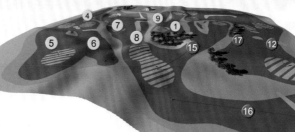

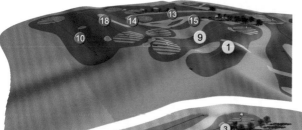

NO.	BLUE YARDS	WHITE YARDS	PAR	S.I.	NO.	BLUE YARDS	WHITE YARDS	PAR	S.I.
1	360	354	4	14	10	539	509	5	11
2	631	525	5	2	11	196	173	3	17
3	181	174	3	10	12	432	420	4	3
4	338	333	4	18	13	189	185	3	7
5	389	386	4	4	14	473	422	4	1
6	550	481	5	16	15	534	512	5	13
7	177	162	3	8	16	372	358	4	15
8	369	355	4	12	17	447	373	4	9
9	300	347	4	6	18	484	420	4	5
OUT	3,355		36		IN	3,666		36	
					TOTAL	7,021		72	
					STANDARD SCRATCH			72	

LOCATION: Within the Maze racecourse.

ARCHITECT: Golf Design Associates.

Course Information:

Par 72; SSS 72; Length 6,824 Yards. Visitors: Welcome. **Ladies:** Welcome. **Green Fees:** Mon – Fri £15; 2 for the price of 1 promotion available during Summer. Sat – Sun £20. Before 1.00pm. After 1.00pm £15. Juveniles: Must be accompanied by an adult. **Clubhouse Dress:** Smart **Clubhouse Facilities:** Licensed restaurant open to public.

Course Description:

Situated in the Lagan Valley amid pleasant rural surroundings the course is conveniently situated to many of the major provincial towns. Set in 150 acres of rolling heathland with gorse lined fairways within the Down Royal (Maze) Racecourse. The nature of the soil being sandy loam ensures the course is playable all year round. The course is in two loops of nine and a classical Par 72, with four Par 5's, four Par 3's and ten Par 4's.

Galgorm Castle

LOCATION: Galgorm, Ballymena. **SECRETARY:** Barbara McGeown.
ARCHITECT: Simon Gidman.

Galgorm Castle, Galgorm Road,
Ballymena, BT42 1HL.
Tel: (028) 256 46161.
Email: golf@galgormcastle.com
To book online, check availability and special offers visit:
www.galgormcastle.com

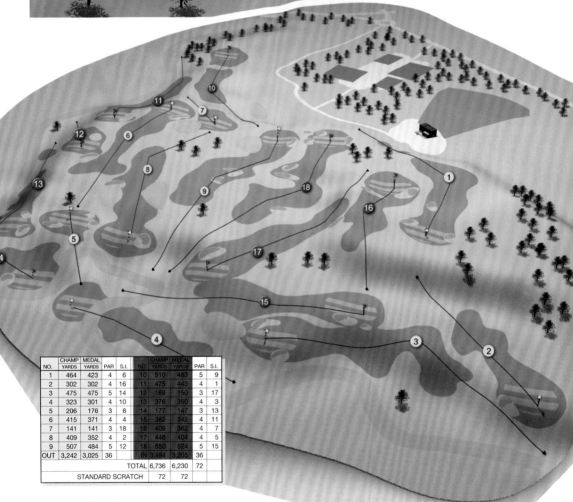

NO.	CHAMP YARDS	MEDAL YARDS	PAR	S.I.	NO.	CHAMP YARDS	MEDAL YARDS	PAR	S.I.
1	464	423	4	6	10	510	483	5	9
2	302	302	4	16	11	475	443	4	1
3	475	475	5	14	12	169	150	3	17
4	323	301	4	10	13	376	350	4	3
5	206	176	3	8	14	177	147	3	13
6	415	371	4	4	15	382	342	4	11
7	141	141	3	18	16	409	362	4	7
8	409	352	4	2	17	446	404	4	5
9	507	484	5	12	18	550	524	5	15
OUT	3,242	3,025	36		IN	3,494	3,205	36	
					TOTAL	6,736	6,230	72	
	STANDARD SCRATCH					72	72		

Course Information:
Par 72; SSS 72; Length 6,736 yards. **Visitors:** Welcome.
Opening Hours: 8am – 10pm. Saturday, ring to book.
Green Fees: Weekdays £32; weekends £40. Group rate
for 12+. No metal spikes. **Ladies:** Welcome. **Juveniles:**
Welcome, ring in advance. **Clubhouse Hours:** 8.00am –
10.00pm. **Clubhouse Dress:** Casual. **Facilities:** Pavilion
licenced bar and restaurant with wonderful views of
the course. P.G.A. staffed Academy. Floodlit covered
driving range. Golf School. Golf shop.

Course Description:
18 hole championship course set in 220 acres of
mature parkland in the grounds of Galgorm
Castle. The course is bordered by the rivers
Maine and Braid which come into play and include
a magnificent oxbow feature and five landscape
lakes. A stimulating challenge and memorable
round for both novice and low handicap golfers.

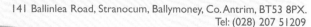

141 Ballinlea Road, Stranocum, Ballymoney, Co. Antrim, BT53 8PX.
Tel: (028) 207 51209
Email: gracehillgc@bigboo.net
Web: www.gracehillgolfclub.co.uk

LOCATION: Seven miles north of Ballymoney, forty five minutes from Belfast International Airport and ten minutes from the Causeway Coast.

PROPRIETORS: J&M Gillan.

ARCHITECT: Frank Ainsworth.

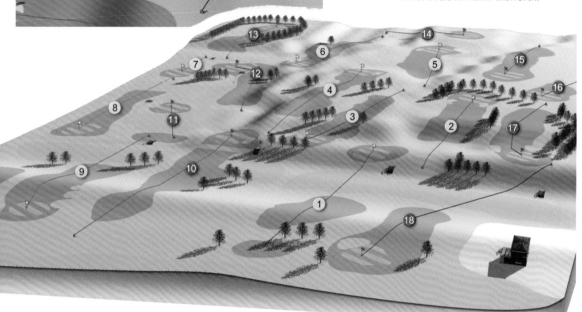

Course Description:

Gracehill opened in July 1995 and is a very challenging parkland course which will provide a stern test for even the best golfers. Some of the holes are played over water and many mature trees also come into play. Considered to be one of the best 18 hole golf courses in all of Ulster.

Course Information

Par 72; SSS 73; Length 6,531 yards. **Opening Hours:** 8am–Sunset. **Green Fees:** £25 Mon – Fri; £30 Sat, Sun & Public Holidays. **Juveniles:** Must be accompanied by an adult. **Clubhouse Hours:** 8am – Sunset. **Clubhouse Dress:** Smart / Casual. **Clubhouse Facilities:** Catering available from 12 noon - 5.30pm or later for party bookings (only available at weekends during Winter). **Open Competitions:** Mens Open, Easter Monday, May Day & end of May Bank Holiday.

NO.	BLUE YARDS	YELLOW YARDS	PAR	S.I.	NO.	BLUE YARDS	YELLOW YARDS	PAR	S.I.
1	344	329	4	10	10	455	402	4	3
2	348	331	4	18	11	163	150	3	13
3	378	346	4	16	12	467	450	5	7
4	492	480	5	6	13	415	400	4	1
5	448	438	4	2	14	211	200	3	5
6	374	360	4	14	15	471	460	5	11
7	183	173	3	8	16	146	120	3	15
8	386	372	4	4	17	359/273	329/265	4	17
9	486	461	5	12	18	405	385	4	9
OUT	3,439	3,290	37		IN	3,092	2,896	35	
					TOTAL	6,531	6,186	72	
					STANDARD SCRATCH		73	70	

Greenacres Golf Centre,
153 Ballyrobert Road,
Ballyclare, Co. Antrim.
Tel: (028) 9335 4111
Fax: (028) 9335 4166

Course Information:
Par 70; SSS 69;
Length 5,839
yards. Visitors:
Welcome.
Opening Hours:
8.00am – 10.00pm.
Avoid: Saturday mornings.
Green Fees: Mon – Fri £16, Weekends &
Bank holidays £22. Ladies: Welcome. Juveniles:
Welcome if accompanied by an adult. Clubhouse Dress:
Smart / Casual. Clubhouse Facilities: Full restaurant
facilities and bar. Weekend booking advisable. Tel.
Barnaby's (028) 9335 4151. 16 bay full flood-lit driving
range. Open Competitions: June.

Course Description: A challenging parkland
course designed to fit in with the
natural rolling countryside of
Co. Antrim.

LOCATION: 8 miles from Belfast city centre.

SECRETARY: Stephen Crawford
Tel: (028) 9335 4111

NO.	YARDS	PAR	S.I.	NO.	YARDS	PAR	S.I.
1	321	4	11	10	389	4	8
2	407	4	3	11	136	3	18
3	179	3	17	12	401	4	2
4	351	4	15	13	182	3	12
5	380	4	6	14	355	4	6
6	161	3	7	15	290	4	17
7	465	4	1	16	202	3	14
8	486	5	13	17	360	4	4
9	486	5	9	18	480	5	10
OUT	3,236	36		IN	2,795	34	
				TOTAL	6,031	70	
				STANDARD SCRATCH	69		

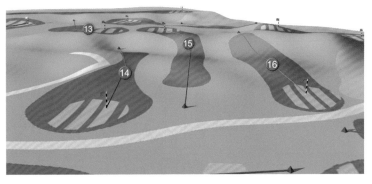

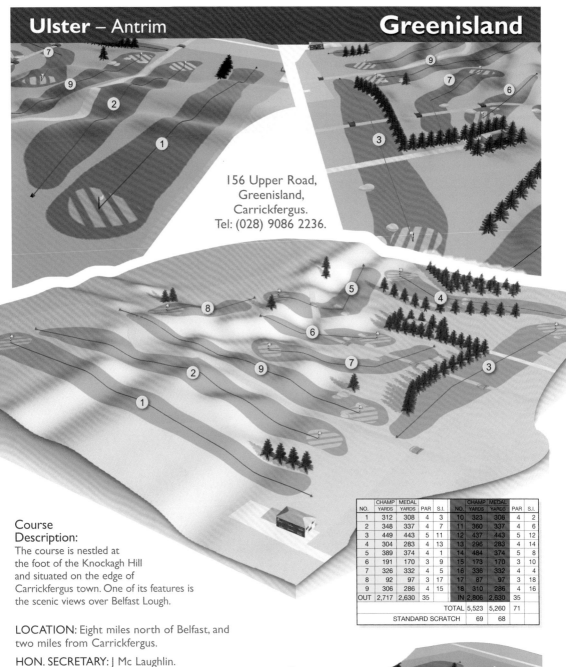

156 Upper Road,
Greenisland,
Carrickfergus.
Tel: (028) 9086 2236.

Course Description:

The course is nestled at the foot of the Knockagh Hill and situated on the edge of Carrickfergus town. One of its features is the scenic views over Belfast Lough.

LOCATION: Eight miles north of Belfast, and two miles from Carrickfergus.

HON. SECRETARY: J Mc Laughlin.

Course Information:

Par 71; SSS 68; Length 5,536 Metres. Visitors: Welcome. **Opening Hours:** Sunrise – Sunset. **Avoid:** Saturdays until 5.00pm and Thursdays. **Ladies Day:** Thursday. **Green Fees:** £12 Mon – Fri (£6 with a member); £18 Sat/Sun/All Public Holidays (£9 with a member). **Juveniles:** Saturdays after 5.30pm. Must be accompanied by an adult. Prior arrangement is required for societies. **Clubhouse Hours:** 12.00pm – 11.00pm (summer). Full clubhouse facilities. **Clubhouse Dress:** Bar area – casual; Dinning room – jacket, collar and tie. **Clubhouse Facilities:** Lunch and evening meals, bar snacks. **Open Competitions:** Contact club for details. Weather permitting.

NO.	CHAMP YARDS	MEDAL YARDS	PAR	S.I.	NO.	CHAMP YARDS	MEDAL YARDS	PAR	S.I.
1	312	308	4	3	10	323	308	4	2
2	348	337	4	7	11	360	337	4	6
3	449	443	5	11	12	437	443	5	12
4	304	283	4	13	13	296	283	4	14
5	389	374	4	1	14	484	374	5	8
6	191	170	3	9	15	173	170	3	10
7	326	332	4	5	16	336	332	4	4
8	92	97	3	17	17	87	97	3	18
9	306	286	4	15	18	310	286	4	16
OUT	2,717	2,630	35		IN	2,806	2,630	35	
					TOTAL	5,523	5,260	71	
					STANDARD SCRATCH	69	68		

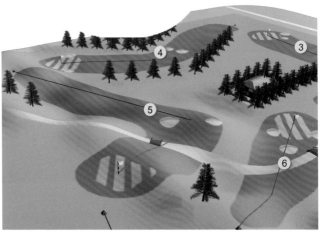

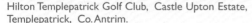

Hilton Templepatrick Golf Club, Castle Upton Estate,
Templepatrick, Co. Antrim.
Tel: (028) 94 435542
Email: eamon.logue@hilton.com

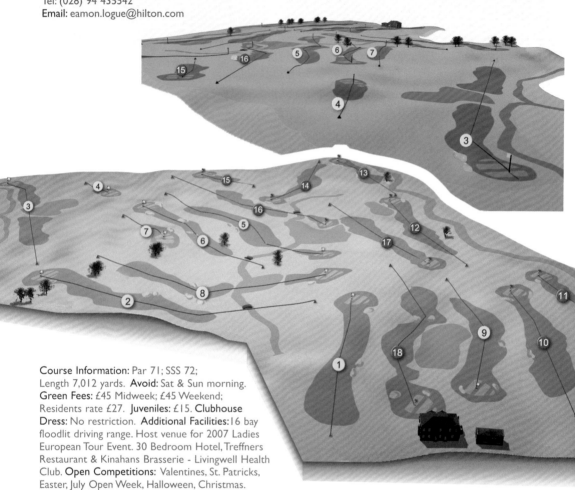

Course Information: Par 71; SSS 72;
Length 7,012 yards. **Avoid:** Sat & Sun morning.
Green Fees: £45 Midweek; £45 Weekend;
Residents rate £27. **Juveniles:** £15. **Clubhouse
Dress:** No restriction. **Additional Facilities:** 16 bay
floodlit driving range. Host venue for 2007 Ladies
European Tour Event. 30 Bedroom Hotel, Treffners
Restaurant & Kinahans Brasserie - Livingwell Health
Club. **Open Competitions:** Valentines, St. Patricks,
Easter, July Open Week, Halloween, Christmas.

Course Description:
220 acres of parkland provide the setting for an exciting course
in Co. Antrim. The mature woodlands of the Castle Upton
Estate come in to play, and also act as a backdrop to the
championship standard golf course. Water punctuates the
course with a number of lakes and rivers making shot and club
selection the key to the course. The 18th hole with the Hilton
Hotel as a backdrop allows the golfer to play safe or take on
the challenge of the lake in front of the green.

NO.	METRES	PAR	S.I.	NO.	METRES	PAR	S.I.
1	395	4	12	10	426	4	11
2	435	4	6	11	183	3	13
3	564	5	8	12	461	4	1
4	170	3	18	13	363	4	5
5	568	5	14	14	374	4	15
6	450	4	4	15	182	3	7
7	200	3	16	16	526	5	17
8	434	4	2	17	445	4	3
9	392	4	10	18	444	4	9
OUT	3,608	36		IN	3,404	35	
				TOTAL	7,012	71	
				STANDARD SCRATCH		72	

LOCATION: 5 miles from Int. Airport and
12 miles from Belfast.

MANAGER: Eamon Logue.

PROFESSIONAL:
Eamon Logue & Marcus
Twitchett.

ARCHITECT: David Jones & David Feherty.

Aberdelghy, Bells Lane, Lambeg,
Lisburn. **Tel:** (028) 9266 2738.
www.mmsportsgolf.com • info@mmsportsgolf.com

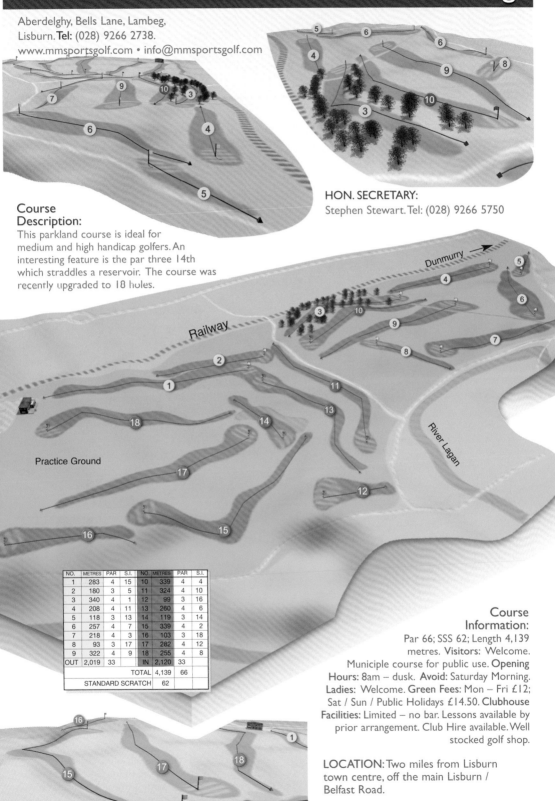

HON. SECRETARY:
Stephen Stewart. Tel: (028) 9266 5750

Course Description:
This parkland course is ideal for medium and high handicap golfers. An interesting feature is the par three 14th which straddles a reservoir. The course was recently upgraded to 18 holes.

NO.	METRES	PAR	S.I.	NO.	METRES	PAR	S.I.
1	283	4	15	10	339	4	4
2	180	3	5	11	324	4	10
3	340	4	1	12	99	3	16
4	208	4	11	13	260	4	6
5	118	3	13	14	119	3	14
6	257	4	7	15	339	4	2
7	218	4	3	16	103	3	18
8	93	3	17	17	282	4	12
9	322	4	9	18	255	4	8
OUT	2,019	33		IN	2,120	33	
				TOTAL	4,139	66	
				STANDARD SCRATCH		62	

Course Information:
Par 66; SSS 62; Length 4,139 metres. **Visitors:** Welcome. Municiple course for public use. **Opening Hours:** 8am – dusk. **Avoid:** Saturday Morning. **Ladies:** Welcome. **Green Fees:** Mon – Fri £12; Sat / Sun / Public Holidays £14.50. **Clubhouse Facilities:** Limited – no bar. Lessons available by prior arrangement. Club Hire available. Well stocked golf shop.

LOCATION: Two miles from Lisburn town centre, off the main Lisburn / Belfast Road.

PROFESSIONAL: Ian Murdock.

54 Ferris Bay Road, Islandmagee,
Larne, Co. Antrim BT40 3RT.
Tel: (028) 9338 2228.
internet@larnegolfclub.freeserve.co.uk

LOCATION: Six miles north of Whitehead.

HON SECRETARY:
Mr K. J. Healey.
Tel: (028) 9338 2228.

ARCHITECT: G. L. Bailie.

Course Information:

Par 70; SSS 70; Length 6,288 yards.
Visitors: Welcome. **Opening Hours:** Sunrise – sunset. Friday & Saturday by arrangement. **Ladies:** Welcome (Par 74 SSS 74). **Green Fees:** £15 Mon – Fri (with a member £10); £17.50 Sat / Sun / Bank Hols (w/m £12.50) Saturdays. Juveniles: Mon – Fri £4 before 5.00pm. Not weekends. **Clubhouse Hours:** Mon – Fri 1pm – 11.00pm; Sat 12 noon – 11pm, Sun 12.30pm – 2.30pm and 5.00pm – 8.00pm. Full clubhouse facilities. **Clubhouse Dress:** Casual. **Clubhouse Facilities:** Mon – Fri meals after 5.00pm by arrangement. Sunday – as bar hours.

NO.	YARDS	PAR	S.I.	NO.	YARDS	PAR	S.I.
1	514	5	13	10	514	5	14
2	295	4	15	11	295	4	16
3	435	4	5	12	435	4	6
4	370	4	9	13	370	4	10
5	395	4	7	14	395	4	8
6	440	4	1	15	440	4	2
7	102	3	17	16	102	3	18
8	417	3	3	17	417	4	4
9	192	4	11	18	192	3	12
OUT	3,160	35		IN	3,160	35	
				TOTAL	6,320	70	
				STANDARD SCRATCH		70	

Course Description:

This course is part links, meadowland with good views of Larne Lough and part Maidens. The first five holes are fairly 'open', and from the 6th the course becomes tighter with the 7th, 8th and 9th being 'sterner' tests along the shore. Greens are varied. The 8th is the most difficult, spoiling many good cards.

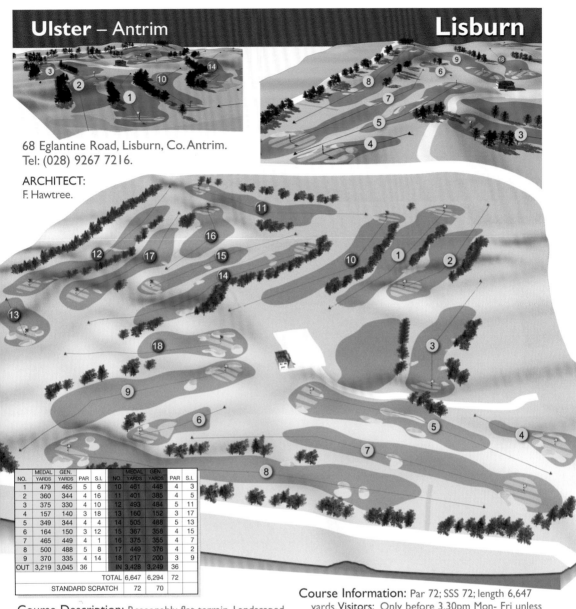

68 Eglantine Road, Lisburn, Co. Antrim.
Tel: (028) 9267 7216.

ARCHITECT:
F. Hawtree.

NO.	MEDAL YARDS	GEN. YARDS	PAR	S.I.	NO.	MEDAL YARDS	GEN. YARDS	PAR	S.I.
1	479	465	5	6	10	461	448	4	3
2	360	344	4	16	11	401	385	4	5
3	375	330	4	10	12	493	484	5	11
4	157	140	3	18	13	160	152	3	17
5	349	344	4	4	14	505	488	5	13
6	164	150	3	12	15	367	358	4	15
7	465	449	4	1	16	375	355	4	7
8	500	488	5	8	17	449	376	4	2
9	370	335	4	14	18	217	200	3	9
OUT	3,219	3,045	36		IN	3,428	3,249	36	
					TOTAL	6,647	6,294	72	
					STANDARD SCRATCH		72	70	

Course Description: Reasonably flat terrain. Landscaped in recent years, many shrubs are beginning to feature and enhance the course. A course of championship standard with a very difficult finish at 16, 17 and 18.

LOCATION: Two miles south of Lisburn off A1 to Hillsborough.

Course Information: Par 72; SSS 72; length 6,647 yards. Visitors: Only before 3.30pm Mon- Fri unless with member. Green Fees: £35 Mon – Fri (with member £13); £40 Sun / Bank Holidays (with member £15). Juveniles: Mon – Fri £12.50 (with member £5), Sun / Bank Holidays £15 (with member £6). Lessons by prior arrangements. Club Hire available. Caddy trolleys available prior arrangement required. Telephone club for details on restricted hours of play. Clubhouse Dress: Jacket and tie after 7.30pm. Clubhouse Facilities: Snacks & meals all day.

SECRETARY/MANAGER: Nicola Greene

PROFESSIONAL: S. Hamill

Course Description:
Established in 1895, Masserene Golf Club offers a challengng and picturesque 18 hole par 72 Parkland course. With Panoramic views over Lough Neagh it is suitable for golfers at all levels of skill and experience. Our welcome to individuals and groups is always genuine and warm.

SECRETARY/MANAGER: Gary Henry.

PROFESSIONAL: Jim Smyth
Tel: (028) 9446 4074.

51 Lough Road, Antrim BT41 4DQ.
Tel: (028) 9442 8096.
Email: info@massereene.com
Web: www.massereene.com

LOCATION: 1/4 mile from Antrim town centre.

ARCHITECT: Mr F. Hawtree.

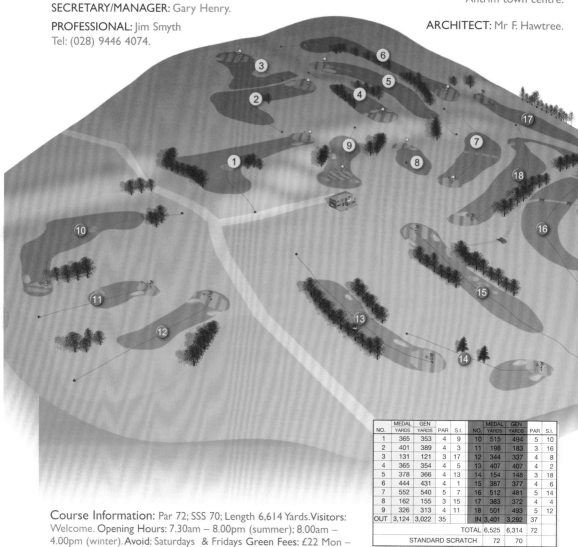

NO.	MEDAL YARDS	GEN YARDS	PAR	S.I.	NO.	MEDAL YARDS	GEN YARDS	PAR	S.I.
1	365	353	4	9	10	515	494	5	10
2	401	389	4	3	11	198	183	3	16
3	131	121	3	17	12	344	337	4	8
4	365	354	4	5	13	407	407	4	2
5	378	366	4	13	14	154	148	3	18
6	444	431	4	1	15	387	377	4	6
7	552	540	5	7	16	512	481	5	14
8	162	155	3	15	17	383	372	4	4
9	326	313	4	11	18	501	493	5	12
OUT	3,124	3,022	35		IN	3,401	3,292	37	
					TOTAL	6,525	6,314	72	
					STANDARD SCRATCH		72	70	

Course Information: Par 72; SSS 70; Length 6,614 Yards. Visitors: Welcome. **Opening Hours:** 7.30am – 8.00pm (summer); 8.00am – 4.00pm (winter). **Avoid:** Saturdays & Fridays **Green Fees:** £22 Mon – Fri; £30 Sat / Sun / Bank Holidays; **Clubhouse Hours:** 11.30am – 11.00pm. Full clubhouse facilities. **Clubhouse Dress:** Casual – no denims. **Clubhouse Facilities:** Catering facilities: Extensive Menus available (A la Carte/snacks/specials) Opening Hours (Winter) Mon-Thur 11am - 6.45pm; Fri- Sat 11am - 8.45pm. sun 11am - 7.45pm, (Summer) Mon-Sat 11am - 8.45 pm; Sun 11am - 7.45pm (breakfast served from 10.00am- 12 noon Sat & Sun) **Open Competitions:** Open Week: 5th -12th August Other Opens throughout the year.

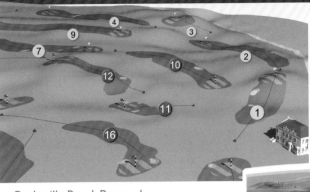

Course Description: One of Ireland's most famous links courses. The course is laid out in a marvellous stretch of natural golfing country. Through a tangle of sandhills the course threads its way, with the sweeping contours of dunes lending infinite variety of the game. Situated east of Portrush occupying a triangle of giant sandhills, from the highest point of which is an amazing varied prospect. The hills of Donegal in the west, the Isle of Islay and southern Hebrides in the north with the Giants Causeway and the Skerries to the east.

Bushmills Road, Portrush,
Co. Antrim BT56 8JQ.
Tel: (028) 7082 2311.
Fax: (028) 7082 3139.

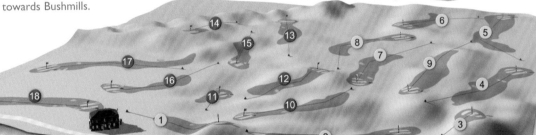

DUNLUCE COURSE

LOCATION: One mile from Portrush town towards Bushmills.

Course Information:
Par 72; SSS 73; Length 6,641 yards.
Visitors: Welcome on any week day. **Opening Hours:** Sunrise – sunset. **Avoid:** Mon am, Wed, Fri pm, Saturday. **Ladies:** Welcome. **Green Fees:** Mon – Fri £110 (£60 additional round); Sat / Sun / Bank Hols £125. **Juveniles:** Play with a member. Lessons by prior arrangements. Club Hire available; Caddy service available by prior arrangement. A letter of introduction is required and Handicap Certificate required.
Clubhouse Hours: 9am – 11pm. Full clubhouse facilities. **Clubhouse Dress:** Casual acceptable; jacket & tie for functions. **Clubhouse Facilities:** Limited snacks. **Open Competitions:** Antrim Cup: May (Mixed foursomes); Lifeboat Trophy: June; Irish Cup: August (Mixed foursomes); Scott Cup: Sept (Mixed foursomes).

PROFESSIONAL: Gary McNeill. Tel: (028) 7082 3335.

SECRETARY: Wilma Erskine.   **ARCHITECT:** Harry Colt.

Dunluce Course									
NO.	MEDAL YARDS	GEN. YARDS	PAR	S.I.	NO.	MEDAL YARDS	GEN. YARDS	PAR	S.I.
1	392	382	4	7	10	478	475	5	10
2	505	490	4	11	11	170	165	3	18
3	155	145	3	17	12	392	386	4	2
4	457	455	4	3	13	372	370	4	6
5	411	379	4	9	14	210	202	3	16
6	189	185	3	15	15	365	360	4	12
7	431	418	4	1	16	442	409	4	4
8	384	363	4	13	17	548	528	5	14
9	475	472	5	5	18	469	457	4	8
OUT	3,339	3,289	36		IN	3,446	3,352	36	
					TOTAL	6,845	6,641	72	
					STANDARD SCRATCH		73		

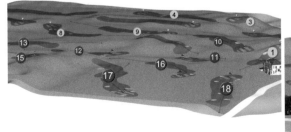

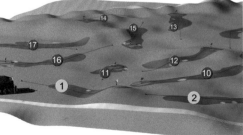

Royal Portrush

Bushmills Road, Portrush, Co. Antrim. BT56 8JQ.
Tel: (028) 7082 2311. Fax: (028) 7082 3139.

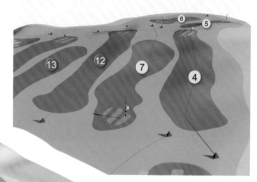

ARCHITECT: Harry Colt.

VALLEY COURSE

Male Clubhouse

Female Clubhouse

LOCATION: One mile from Portrush town towards Bushmills.

SECRETARY: Wilma Erskine.

PROFESSIONAL: Gary McNeill.
Tel: (028) 7082 3335.

Course Description:

The Valley lies between the East Strand and the Dunluce course. It is the home of Royal Portrush Ladies Club and the affiliated Rathmore Club. Its characteristics are very much that of a links, undulating sandhills, remarkably dry and in some places below sea level.

Course Information: Par 70; SSS 71: Length 6,273 Yards. **Visitors:** Welcome every day. **Opening Hours:** Dawn – Dusk. **Avoid:** Sat (am) & Sun (am). **Ladies:** Saturday mornings. **Green Fees:** £35 Mon – Fri (additional round £15); £40 Sat/Sun/Bank Hols. **Juveniles:** Play with a member. **Clubhouse Hours:** 9am – 11pm. **Clubhouse Dress:** Smart casual at all times. Jacket and tie required for functions. **Clubhouse Facilities:** Full clubhouse facilities. Catering facilities: snacks. R.P.G.C.

NO.	MEDAL YARDS	GEN. YARDS	PAR	S.I.	NO.	MEDAL YARDS	GEN. YARDS	PAR	S.I.
1	349	339	4	11	10	496	472	5	2
2	385	374	4	3	11	140	130	3	18
3	141	135	3	17	12	465	452	4	4
4	534	520	5	7	13	486	458	5	8
5	336	324	4	13	14	421	412	4	12
6	237	231	3	9	15	165	155	3	14
7	453	441	4	1	16	360	349	4	10
8	409	399	4	5	17	384	382	4	6
9	320	311	4	15	18	192	170	3	16
OUT	3,164	3,074	35		IN	3,109	2,980	35	
					TOTAL	6,273	6,054	70	
					STANDARD SCRATCH	71	70		

Valley Course

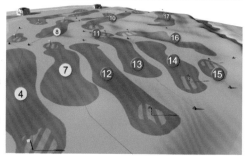

Temple Golf & Country Club, 60 Church Road, Boardmills, Lisburn. BT27 6UP. Tel: (028) 9263 9213. Fax: (028) 9263 8637. **Web:** www.templegolf.com **Email:** jude@templegolf.com

Course Description:
A 9 hole challenging golf course with a new innovation of 18 tees, designed to incorporate the panormic views of the Mourne Mountains and the Dromara Hills. Good natural drainage ensures all year round golf.

ADMINISTRATOR:
Brian Mc Connell

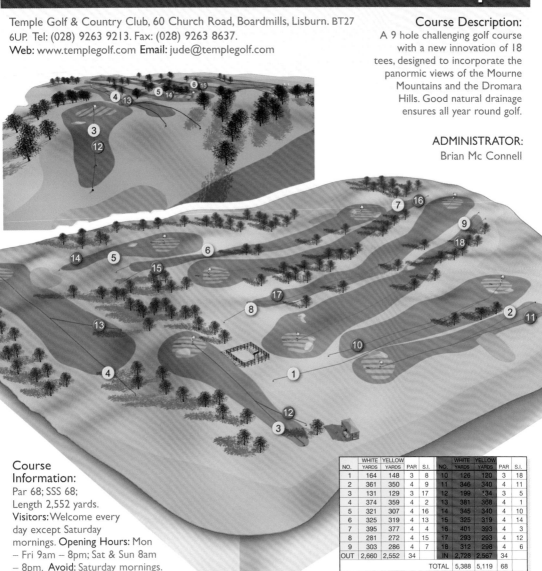

Course Information:
Par 68; SSS 68; Length 2,552 yards.
Visitors: Welcome every day except Saturday mornings. **Opening Hours:** Mon – Fri 9am – 8pm; Sat & Sun 8am – 8pm. **Avoid:** Saturday mornings. **Ladies:** Welcome. **Green Fees:** Mon – Fri £9 (9 holes), £13 (18 holes); weekends / Bank Holidays £11 (9 holes), £17 (18 holes). **Juveniles:** Permitted to play until 5.30pm Mon – Fri. **Clubhouse Hours:** Daily 9am – 9pm; Saturday night licenced bar hours. **Clubhouse Dress:** Smart / casual. **Clubhouse Facilities:** Tennis courts, licenced bar & restaurant with conference & function facilities and ensuite bedrooms now available. **Open Competitions:** Varies year to year. Contact club for details.

LOCATION: Situated within easy access to Belfast / Lisburn.

ARCHITECT: Frank Ainsworth.

NO.	WHITE YARDS	YELLOW YARDS	PAR	S.I.	NO.	WHITE YARDS	YELLOW YARDS	PAR	S.I.
1	164	148	3	8	10	126	120	3	18
2	361	350	4	9	11	346	340	4	11
3	131	129	3	17	12	199	134	3	5
4	374	359	4	2	13	381	368	4	1
5	321	307	4	16	14	345	340	4	10
6	325	319	4	13	15	325	319	4	14
7	395	377	4	4	16	401	393	4	3
8	281	272	4	15	17	293	293	4	12
9	303	286	4	7	18	312	298	4	6
OUT	2,660	2,552	34		IN	2,728	2,567	34	
					TOTAL	5,388	5,119	68	
					STANDARD SCRATCH	68	68		

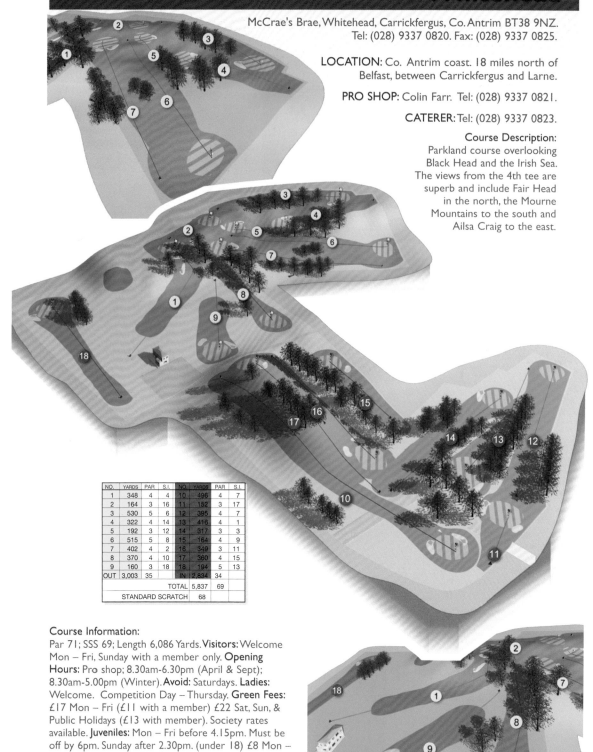

McCrae's Brae, Whitehead, Carrickfergus, Co. Antrim BT38 9NZ.
Tel: (028) 9337 0820. Fax: (028) 9337 0825.

LOCATION: Co. Antrim coast. 18 miles north of Belfast, between Carrickfergus and Larne.

PRO SHOP: Colin Farr. Tel: (028) 9337 0821.

CATERER: Tel: (028) 9337 0823.

Course Description:
Parkland course overlooking Black Head and the Irish Sea. The views from the 4th tee are superb and include Fair Head in the north, the Mourne Mountains to the south and Ailsa Craig to the east.

NO.	YARDS	PAR	S.I.	NO.	YARDS	PAR	S.I.
1	348	4	4	10	496	4	7
2	164	3	16	11	152	3	17
3	530	5	6	12	395	4	7
4	322	4	14	13	416	4	1
5	192	3	12	14	317	3	3
6	515	5	8	15	164	4	9
7	402	4	2	16	349	3	11
8	370	4	10	17	360	4	15
9	160	3	18	18	194	5	13
OUT	3,003	35		IN	2,834	34	
				TOTAL	5,837	69	
				STANDARD SCRATCH	68		

Course Information:
Par 71; SSS 69; Length 6,086 Yards. **Visitors:** Welcome Mon – Fri, Sunday with a member only. **Opening Hours:** Pro shop; 8.30am-6.30pm (April & Sept); 8.30am-5.00pm (Winter). **Avoid:** Saturdays. **Ladies:** Welcome. Competition Day – Thursday. **Green Fees:** £17 Mon – Fri (£11 with a member) £22 Sat, Sun, & Public Holidays (£13 with member). Society rates available. **Juveniles:** Mon – Fri before 4.15pm. Must be off by 6pm. Sunday after 2.30pm. (under 18) £8 Mon – Fri (£6 with a member); £11 Sat/Sun/All Public Holidays (with a member only). Parties 20 plus: £13 Mon – Fri; £18 Sat/Sun/All Public Holidays. **Clubhouse Hours:** 12am – 11.30pm. **Clubhouse Dress:** Casual, **Open Competitions:** August – McKenna Scratch & Open mixed foursomes. Open week June/July.

The Demense, Newry Road,
Armagh.
Tel: (028) 3752 2501.
Email: info@golfarmagh.co.uk
www.golfarmagh.co.uk

Course Information: Par 70; SSS 69; Length 6,212 Yards. **Visitors:** Welcome Mon – Fri (contact Secretary's office for weekends). **Opening Hours:** Sunrise – Sunset. **Avoid:** Tues evenings and Thurs (Ladies Day). **Green Fees:** £17 weekdays, (£14 with member) £22 weekends (£17 with member). Prior arrangement required if possible. Lessons available by prior arrangement. Caddy cars available. **Ladies Day:** Thursday. **Juveniles:** Monday – Friday with adult evenings and weekends. **Clubhouse Hours:** 9.30am – 11.30pm. **Clubhouse Dress:** Smart and neat (no denims or football garments). **Clubhouse Facilities:** Full catering and bar facilities except Monday, bar snacks and a la carte available until 9.00pm. **Open Competitions:** Numerous through the year, contact club for details.

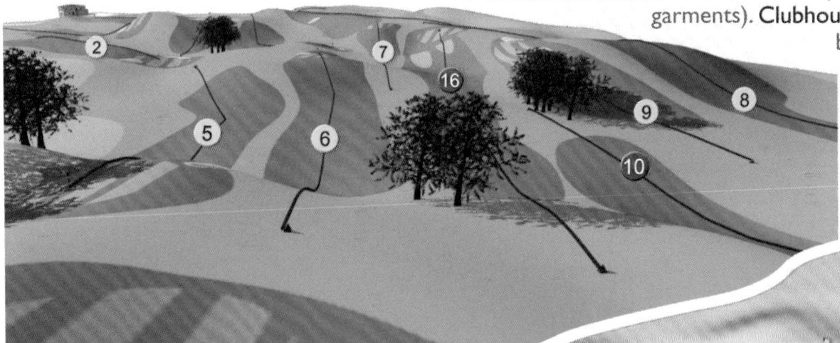

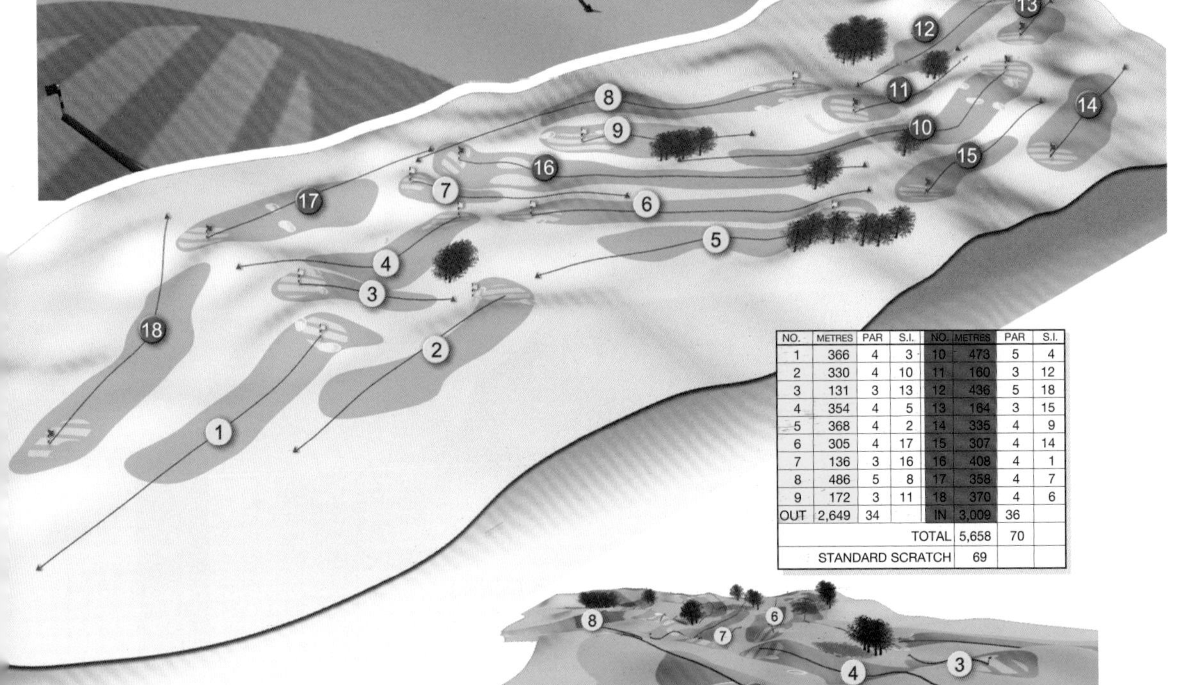

NO.	METRES	PAR	S.I.	NO.	METRES	PAR	S.I.
1	366	4	3	10	473	5	4
2	330	4	10	11	160	3	12
3	131	3	13	12	436	5	18
4	354	4	5	13	164	3	15
5	368	4	2	14	335	4	9
6	305	4	17	15	307	4	14
7	136	3	16	16	408	4	1
8	486	5	8	17	358	4	7
9	172	3	11	18	370	4	6
OUT	2,649	34		IN	3,009	36	
				TOTAL	5,658	70	
				STANDARD SCRATCH		69	

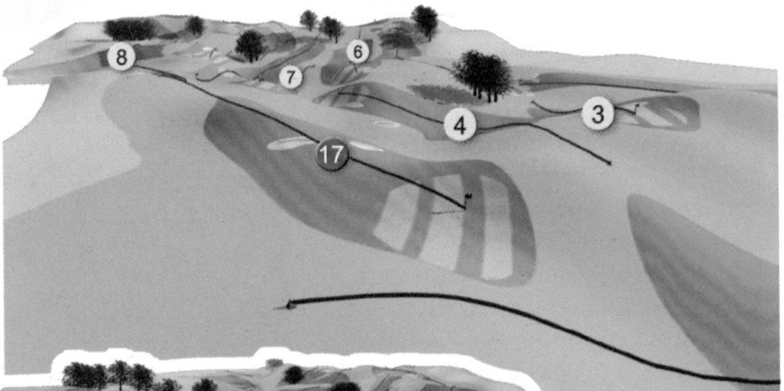

Course Description:

This wooded parkland course, established in 1893, has nice views from the Obelisk built by Primate Robinson in 1700's. While the 16th might be considered the most difficult, the fifth requires an accurate drive and then an even more accurate second shot down an alley of mature trees, which should be the most rewarding hole to play well.

SECRETARY: Lynne Fleming.
Tel: (028) 3752 5861.

PROFESSIONAL: Alan Rankin.
Tel: (028) 3752 5864.

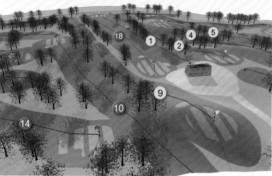

Freeduff, Cullyhanna, Co. Armagh.
Tel: (028) 3086 8180
Fax: (028) 3086 8611

LOCATION: Two miles from Crossmaglen, 1 hour from Belfast, 1.5 hours from Dublin.

SECRETARY: James and Elizabeth Quinn.

PROFESSIONAL: Erill Maney.

ARCHITECT: Frank Ainsworth.

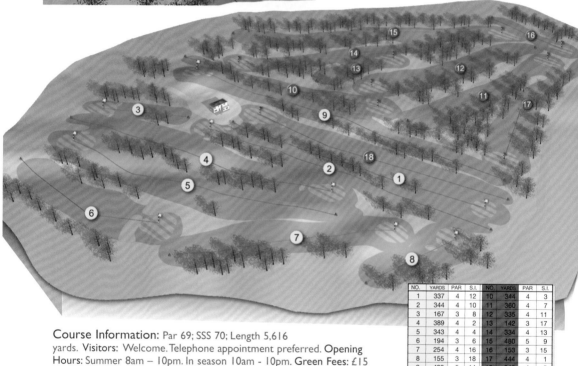

NO.	YARDS	PAR	S.I.	NO.	YARDS	PAR	S.I.
1	337	4	12	10	344	4	3
2	344	4	10	11	360	4	7
3	167	3	8	12	335	4	11
4	389	4	2	13	142	3	17
5	343	4	4	14	334	4	13
6	194	3	6	15	480	5	9
7	254	4	16	16	153	3	15
8	155	3	18	17	444	4	1
9	493	5	14	18	348	4	5
OUT	2,676	34		IN	2,940	35	
				TOTAL	5,616	69	
				STANDARD SCRATCH	70		

Course Information: Par 69; SSS 70; Length 5,616 yards. **Visitors:** Welcome. Telephone appointment preferred. **Opening Hours:** Summer 8am – 10pm. In season 10am - 10pm. **Green Fees:** £15 Mon – Fri; £20 Sat, Sun & bank holidays. Special reductions for juveniles, students, senior citizens, handicapped persons and unemployed persons (£10). Special rates for societies. **Juveniles:** Welcome. Lessons by prior arrangment. Club Hire available. **Clubhouse Hours:** 8am – 10pm. **Clubhouse Dress:** Informal. **Clubhouse Facilities:** Meals and snacks available. New state of the art clubhouse with gym and sauna facilities.

Course Description:

An interesting eighteen hole course situated in attractive rural surroundings. Advance notice is recommended before turning up at weekends. There are over one hundred new trees of mature variety and a man-made lake, and bunkers on the 17th, 4th, 1st 3rd and 8th.

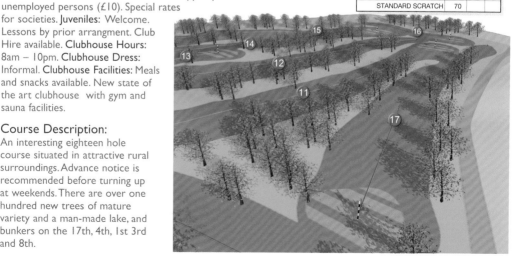

Mullaghbawn, Newry, Co. Armagh.
Tel: (028) 3088 8380/(028) 3088 9374
Email: info@cloverhillgc.com www.cloverhillgc.com

LOCATION: In scenic area of the Ring of Gullion in south Armagh.

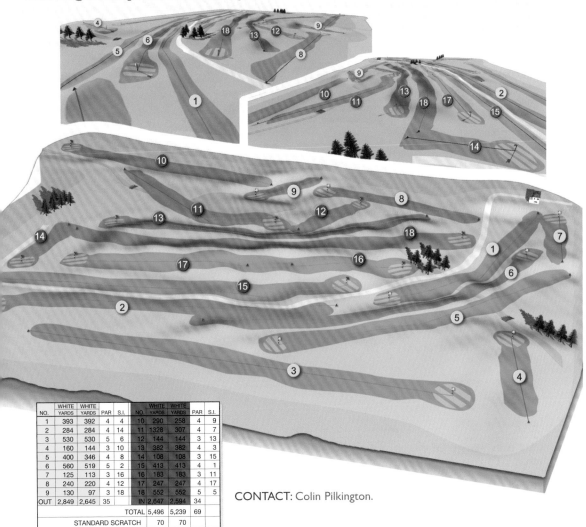

NO.	WHITE YARDS	WHITE YARDS	PAR	S.I.	NO.	WHITE YARDS	WHITE YARDS	PAR	S.I.
1	393	392	4	4	10	290	258	4	9
2	284	284	4	14	11	1328	307	4	7
3	530	530	5	6	12	144	144	3	13
4	160	144	3	10	13	382	382	4	3
5	400	346	4	8	14	108	108	3	15
6	560	519	5	2	15	413	413	4	1
7	125	113	3	16	16	183	183	3	11
8	240	220	4	12	17	247	247	4	17
9	130	97	3	18	18	552	552	5	5
OUT	2,849	2,645	35		IN	2,647	2,594	34	
					TOTAL	5,496	5,239	69	
					STANDARD SCRATCH	70	70		

CONTACT: Colin Pilkington.

Course Description:
18 hole golf course situated in the scenic area of the Ring of Gullion. 10 miles south of Newry, 8 miles from Dundalk. The course has very good greens and maintained to a high standard.

Course Information:
Par 69; SSS 69; Length 6,090 yards. **Green Fees:** £15 Weekdays, Weekends and Bank Holidays. **Juveniles:** £5. **Clubhouse Hours:** From 8:00am. Full club facilities. **Additional Dress:** Smart/ Casual. **Clubhouse Facilities:** Licensed club house with full changing facilities. Snacks available. Open 7 days. Golf clubs and trolleys for hire. Golfing societies welcome. Private partys catered for. Open days every second Friday.

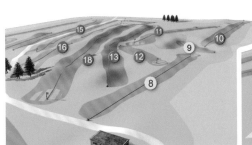

Edenmore House, Drumnabreeze Road,
Magheralin, Craigavon, Co. Armagh.
Tel: (028) 9261 9241 Fax: (028) 9261 3310
Web: www.edenmore.com

LOCATION: Twenty miles from Belfast, five
minutes from Moira roundabout.
Signposted from Magheralin
on main Moira - Lurgan Road.

SECRETARY MANAGER:
Kenneth Logan.

PROFESSIONAL:
Andrew Manson

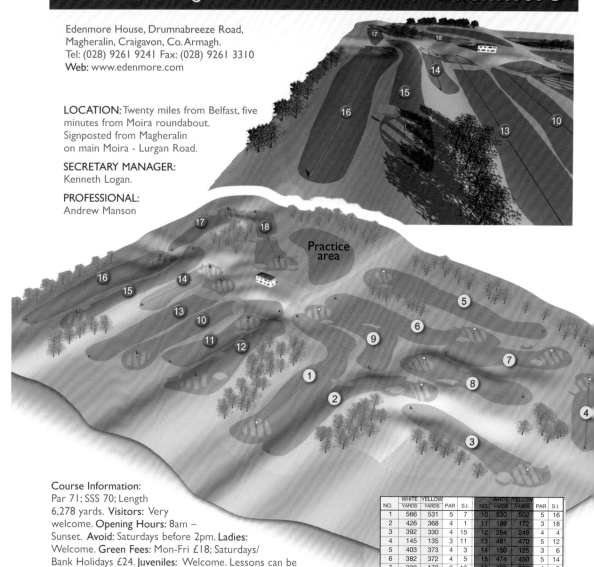

Course Information:
Par 71; SSS 70; Length
6,278 yards. **Visitors:** Very
welcome. **Opening Hours:** 8am –
Sunset. **Avoid:** Saturdays before 2pm. **Ladies:**
Welcome. **Green Fees:** Mon-Fri £18; Saturdays/
Bank Holidays £24. **Juveniles:** Welcome. Lessons can be
arranged, telephone for details. **Clubhouse Dress:** Smart.
Clubhouse Facilities: Bailies restaurant open 7 days, conference and
wedding facilities, full gym and health suite.
Open week: 24th-30th June.

NO.	WHITE YARDS	YELLOW YARDS	PAR	S.I.	NO.	WHITE YARDS	YELLOW YARDS	PAR	S.I.
1	566	531	5	7	10	530	502	5	16
2	426	368	4	1	11	199	172	3	18
3	392	330	4	15	12	284	249	4	4
4	145	135	3	11	13	481	470	5	12
5	403	373	4	3	14	150	125	3	6
6	382	372	4	5	15	474	450	5	14
7	200	170	3	13	16	407	380	4	2
8	311	285	4	17	17	192	155	3	8
9	363	322	4	9	18	373	334	4	10
OUT	3,188	2,886	35		IN	3,090	2,837	36	
					TOTAL	6,278	5,723	71	
					STANDARD SCRATCH	69	67		

Course Description:
The golf course at Edenmore has
seen many changes through the
recent years with three new holes in
play to maximise player enjoyment
and provide them with superb
playing conditions and the best
scenery available. The course is
renowned for its consistently good
condition and winter playability.

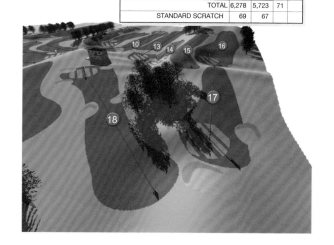

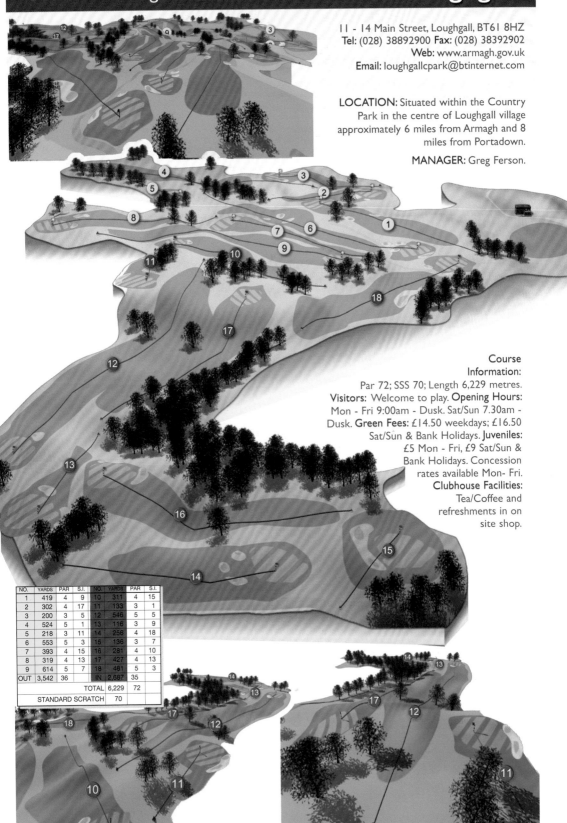

11 - 14 Main Street, Loughgall, BT61 8HZ
Tel: (028) 38892900 Fax: (028) 38392902
Web: www.armagh.gov.uk
Email: loughgallcpark@btinternet.com

LOCATION: Situated within the Country Park in the centre of Loughgall village approximately 6 miles from Armagh and 8 miles from Portadown.

MANAGER: Greg Ferson.

Course Information:
Par 72; SSS 70; Length 6,229 metres.
Visitors: Welcome to play. **Opening Hours:** Mon - Fri 9:00am - Dusk. Sat/Sun 7.30am - Dusk. **Green Fees:** £14.50 weekdays; £16.50 Sat/Sun & Bank Holidays. **Juveniles:** £5 Mon - Fri, £9 Sat/Sun & Bank Holidays. Concession rates available Mon- Fri.
Clubhouse Facilities: Tea/Coffee and refreshments in on site shop.

NO.	YARDS	PAR	S.I.	NO.	YARDS	PAR	S.I.
1	419	4	9	10	311	4	15
2	302	4	17	11	133	3	1
3	200	3	5	12	546	5	5
4	524	5	1	13	116	3	9
5	218	3	11	14	256	4	18
6	553	5	3	15	136	3	7
7	393	4	15	16	281	4	10
8	319	4	13	17	427	4	13
9	614	5	7	18	461	5	3
OUT	3,542	36		IN	2,687	35	
				TOTAL	6,229	72	
				STANDARD SCRATCH	70		

The Demense, Lurgan BT67 9BN. Tel: (028) 3832 2087.

Course Information: Par 70; SSS 70; Length 6,257 yards. **Visitors:** Welcome Mon – Fri. **Opening Hours:** 9.00am – 6.00pm. **Avoid:** Wednesday (playing by arrangement) and Saturday. **Ladies:** £14 (£8 with member). **Green Fees:** £17 Mon – Fri (£12 with member); £22 Sat / Sun / Bank Holidays (£14 with member). **Juveniles:** £6 Must give way to adult members and visitors. **Student:** £14 (£8 with member). **Clubhouse Hours:** 9.00am – 11.30pm. Professional shop open 9.00am – 6.00pm. **Clubhouse Dress:** Smart / casual. **Clubhouse Facilities:** Changing rooms with showers. Lounge and members bars. Restaurant offering bar snacks and full menu, open 12.00pm - 9pm everyday except Monday and Thursday, unless by special request. **Open Competitions:** Open week normally May. Handicap certificate required for Open Competition only.

Course Description:

Parkland course bordering on Lurgan Lake. Well wooded and greens well trapped. Pond on 7th fairways, internal out-of- bounds (on some holes), quite a few dog-legs, long straight driving essential. Considered an excellent course to all golfers.

LOCATION: Half a mile from the town centre.

HONORARY SECRETARY: Sean Mulvenna

SECRETARY / MANAGER: Mrs Muriel Sharpe.

PROFESSIONAL: Des Paul.

NO.	MEDAL YARDS	GEN. YARDS	PAR	S.I.	NO.	MEDAL YARDS	GEN. YARDS	PAR	S.I.
1	268	240	4	13	10	324	299	4	14
2	227	208	3	5	11	171	157	3	15
3	112	105	3	18	12	390	379	4	2
4	405	392	4	3	13	474	458	5	12
5	420	389	4	9	14	412	403	4	8
6	556	539	5	7	15	419	400	4	4
7	419	410	4	1	16	418	408	4	6
8	160	157	3	16	17	150	125	3	17
9	570	562	5	11	18	377	364	4	10
OUT	3,137	3,002	35		IN	3,135	2,993	35	
				TOTAL	6,272	5,995	70		
				STANDARD SCRATCH		70	69		

192 Gilford Road, Portadown.
Tel: (028) 3835 5356. Fax: (028) 3839 1394

GENERAL MANAGER:
Nicola Greene.

PROFESSIONAL:
Paul Stevenson.
Tel: (028) 3833 4655.

Course Description:
Situated on the edge of Portadown this parkland course has one of the holes actually played over the River Bann (9th). Trees come into play on many of the holes, and the course is generally flat.

LOCATION: On Gilford Road out of Portadown, approx. 34 miles from Belfast.

NO.	METRES	PAR	S.I.	NO.	METRES	PAR	S.I.
1	247	4	18	10	334	4	12
2	297	4	14	11	376	4	9
3	392	4	1	12	378	4	4
4	150	3	13	13	173	3	7
5	398	4	3	14	259	4	15
6	113	3	7	15	129	3	16
7	346	4	8	16	329	4	10
8	371	4	5	17	504	5	6
9	452	5	2	18	401	4	2
OUT	2,766	35		IN	288	35	
				TOTAL		3	70
			STANDARD SCRATCH	5,62			

Course Information:
Par 70; SSS 70; Length 5,621 Metres. **Visitors:** Welcome. **Opening Hours:** 9.00am – 9.30pm. **Ladies:** Tuesday (No green fees on Tuesdays). **Green Fees:** Mon – Fri £18 (£12 with member); Sat / Sun, Bank Holidays; £22 (£14 with member); Juveniles: 50% off listed price. **Juveniles:** Mon, Wed, Fri until 4pm; Thur after 12.00 noon Sat before 5pm; resricted on Sun. Club Hire available. **Clubhouse Hours:** Office: 9am – 5pm. Bar: 12 noon – 11pm. Full Clubhouse facilities. **Clubhouse Dress:** Neat dress essential. No jeans, shorts or sleeveless shirts both on the course or clubhouse. **Clubhouse Facilities:** Full catering, á la carte, snacks and functions 12 – 9pm. Closed Mondays. **Open Competitions:** Opens run from June to September. Societies welcome: £15 Mon-Fri £18 weekends (early booking advisable).

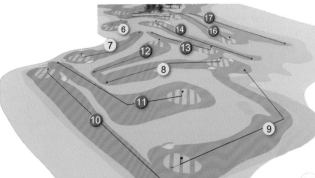

Tormoyra Lane, Silverwood,
Lurgan, BT66 6NG.
Tel: (028) 3832 6606.

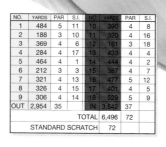

Course Description:
The course has sand-based, well irrigated greens making ideal winter putting conditions and is ideally suited for the middle and high handicap golfers. One of its main features are the lakes which are incorporated into the third and tenth holes. The course has already proved extremely popular with golfing societies for tournaments.

LOCATION: The Golf/Ski Centre is located at Silverwood, just off the M1 Lurgan roundabout.

MANAGER: Declan Brown.

PROFESSIONAL: Micheal Stanford PGA. Tel: (028) 3832 6606.

Course Information:
Par 72; SSS 72; Length 6,496 yards. **Visitors:** Welcome to play: municipal course for public use. **Opening Hours:** Daylight hours. **Green Fees** £17 Monday – Friday; £19.50 Saturday, Sunday & Bank Hols. Club Hire available. **Clubhouse Hours:** Mon – Fri 8.00am – 9.30pm. Sat/Sun 8am – 7pm. **Clubhouse Facilities:** Full restaurant available. Driving range Par 3 Course and Pitch and Putt. Ski centre on site. **Open Competitions:** June / July.

NO.	YARDS	PAR	S.I.	NO.	YARDS	PAR	S.I.
1	484	5	11	10	390	4	8
2	188	3	10	11	320	4	16
3	369	4	6	12	161	3	18
4	284	4	17	13	433	4	4
5	464	4	1	14	444	4	2
6	212	3	3	15	387	4	7
7	321	4	13	16	477	5	12
8	326	4	15	17	401	4	5
9	306	4	14	18	529	5	9
OUT	2,954	35		IN	3,542	37	
				TOTAL	6,496	72	
			STANDARD SCRATCH		72		

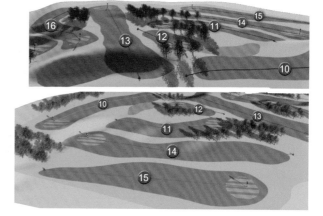

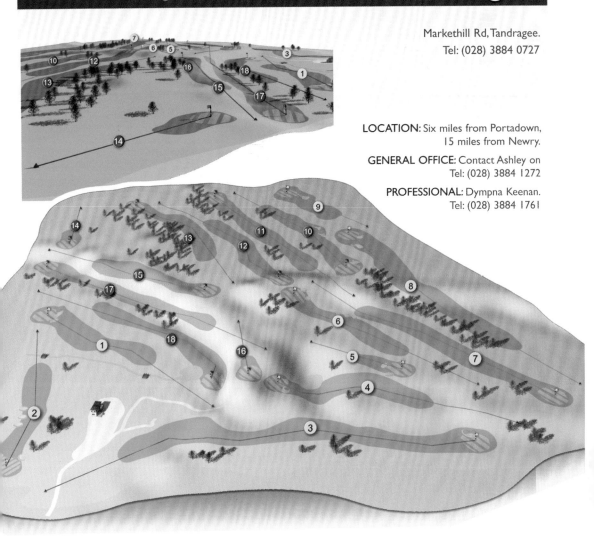

Markethill Rd, Tandragee.
Tel: (028) 3884 0727

LOCATION: Six miles from Portadown,
15 miles from Newry.

GENERAL OFFICE: Contact Ashley on
Tel: (028) 3884 1272

PROFESSIONAL: Dympna Keenan.
Tel: (028) 3884 1761

Course Information:

Par 71; SSS 70; Length 5,589 metres. **Visitors:** Welcome. **Opening Hours:** Dawn – dusk. **Avoid:** Thursdays and Saturdays. **Green Fees:** £16 weekdays; £21 Sat / Sun / Public Holidays. Ladies: £12 weekdays; £19 weekends. Juveniles: £6 daily. **Clubhouse Hours:** 9.00am – 11.00pm. Full clubhouse facilities. **Clubhouse Dress:** GUI dress code applies; jacket & tie on function nights. **Clubhouse Facilities:** Full catering from 12.30pm. Last orders 9pm. No catering on Monday. **Open Competitions:** Contact professional for details.

Course Description:

Parkland course — complete with beautiful old trees and pleasant views of the Mourne Mountains and South Armagh hills.

NO.	METRES	PAR	S.I.	NO.	METRES	PAR	S.I.
1	346	4	4	10	305	4	15
2	273	4	14	11	380	4	1
3	490	5	6	12	350	4	5
4	307	4	18	13	363	4	9
5	168	3	11	14	140	3	17
6	322	4	16	15	304	4	7
7	388	4	2	16	157	3	10
8	456	5	12	17	474	5	13
9	182	3	8	18	342	4	3
OUT	2,544	36		IN	2,815	35	
				TOTAL	5,747	71	
	STANDARD SCRATCH				70		

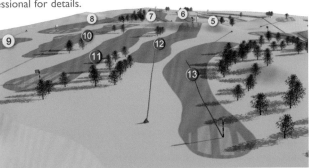

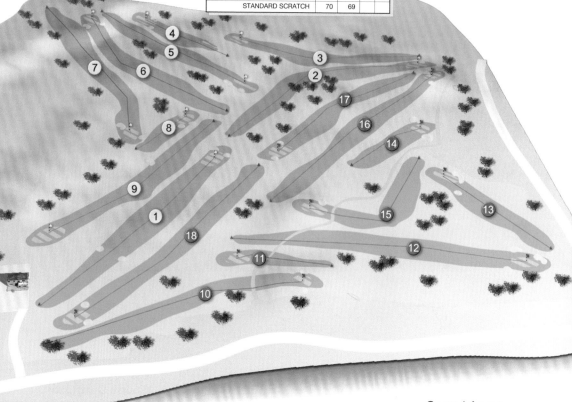

518 Lisburn Road, Belfast BT9 6GX. Tel: (028) 9038 1514
www.balmoralgolf.com

NO.	MEDAL YARDS	GEN. YARDS	PAR	S.I.	NO.	MEDAL YARDS	GEN. YARDS	PAR	S.I.
1	452	439	4	5	10	367	54	4	4
2	394	385	4	3	11	151	144	3	18
3	408	396	4	9	12	436	425	4	2
4	176	163	3	13	13	194	176	3	8
5	397	379	4	11	14	159	148	3	14
6	401	388	4	7	15	367	359	4	10
7	500	487	5	15	16	526	494	5	12
8	150	138	3	17	17	353	341	4	16
9	392	379	4	1	18	453	439	4	6
OUT	3,270	3,154	35		IN	3,006	2,880	34	
					TOTAL	6,276	6,034	69	
					STANDARD SCRATCH	70	69		

LOCATION: Three miles south of Belfast City Centre on main Lisburn Road, next to King's Hall.

MANAGER: Terry Graham.

PROFESSIONAL: G. Bleakley.

Tel: (028) 9066 7747

Course Information:
Par 69; SSS 70; Length 5,702 Metres. **Visitors:** Welcome.
Green Fees: £27 Mon – Fri (£15 with member) £40 weekends & public holidays (£20 with a member). **Ladies:** £16 Mon - Fri; £20 weekends; £9 with a member / Public holidays. **Juveniles:** £12 and restricted on weekends. **Lessons:** By prior arrangement. **Clubhouse Hours:** 9.00am - 11.00pm. **Clubhouse Dress:** Smart casual (no jeans) up to 8.00pm. After 7.30pm jacket and tie for gentlemen. **Catering Facilities:** Lunch 12.30pm - 2.30pm; Evening meal 6.30pm-10pm. Full á la carte menu. (Last orders 9.30pm). **Open Competitions:** Several throughout the golfing season.

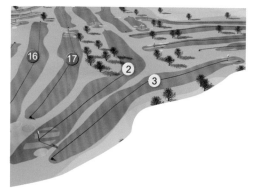

Course Description:
A flat undulating course with thirty plus bunkers, and a stream to contend with when playing. The greens are generally excellent and approached by tree-lined fairways. Situated beside the Royal Ulster Agricultural Society, the course is particularly convenient to Belfast city centre.

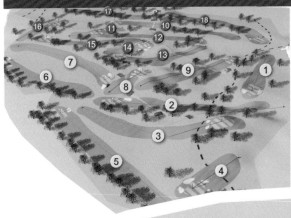

Newtownbreda, Belfast BT8 7AN.

Tel: (028) 9049 1693. Fax: (028) 9064 6113.

LOCATION: Four miles south of city centre.

SECRETARY: Ann Vaughan.

PROFESSIONAL: Michael McGivern.

Tel: (028) 9064 6714.

Course Description:

Considered one of the best inland courses with fair but tight fairways and good greens. Rarely closed due to water logging. The course has extensive mature woods and many scenic views.

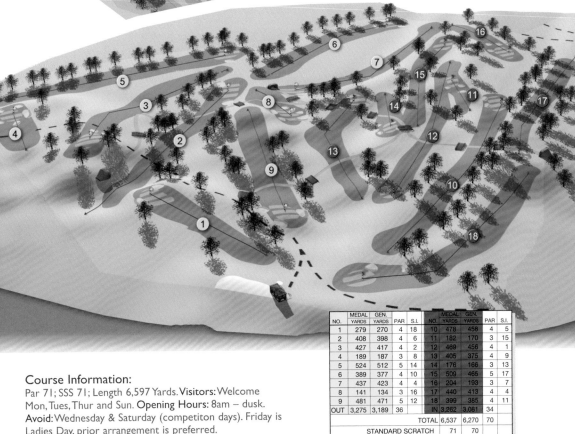

Course Information:

Par 71; SSS 71; Length 6,597 Yards. **Visitors:** Welcome Mon, Tues, Thur and Sun. **Opening Hours:** 8am – dusk. **Avoid:** Wednesday & Saturday (competiton days). Friday is Ladies Day, prior arrangement is preferred. **Green Fees:** Weekdays excluding Wed – £45. Weekends and Bank Hols – £55. **Clubhouse Dress:** Smart casual, no denims. **Clubhouse Facilities:** Catering facilities 10.30am – 9.30pm. **Open Competitions:** Open week – July. **Clubhouse Hours:** 10am – 11pm.

NO.	MEDAL YARDS	GEN. YARDS	PAR	S.I.	NO.	MEDAL YARDS	GEN. YARDS	PAR	S.I.
1	279	270	4	18	10	478	458	4	5
2	408	398	4	6	11	182	170	3	15
3	427	417	4	2	12	469	456	4	1
4	189	187	3	8	13	405	375	4	9
5	524	512	5	14	14	176	166	3	13
6	389	377	4	10	15	509	465	5	17
7	437	423	4	4	16	204	193	3	7
8	141	134	3	16	17	440	413	4	4
9	481	471	5	12	18	399	385	4	11
OUT	3,275	3,189	36		IN	3,262	3,081	34	
					TOTAL	6,537	6,270	70	
					STANDARD SCRATCH	71	70		

City of Belfast Golf Course, Mallusk, Antrim Road, Newtownabbey, Co. Antrim.
Tel: (028) 90 843799.
Fax: (028) 90 342383.
secretary@cityofbelfastgolfclub.com
www.cityofbelfastgolfclub.com

LOCATION:
From Belfast on the A8 to Antrim. The course is situated just before the Chimney Corner Hotel.

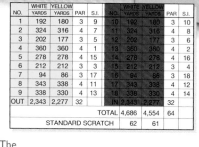

NO.	WHITE YARDS	YELLOW YARDS	PAR	S.I.	NO.	WHITE YARDS	YELLOW YARDS	PAR	S.I.
1	192	180	3	9	10	192	180	3	10
2	324	316	4	7	11	324	316	4	8
3	202	177	3	5	12	202	177	3	6
4	360	360	4	1	13	360	360	4	2
5	278	278	4	15	14	278	278	4	16
6	212	212	3	3	15	212	212	3	4
7	94	86	3	17	16	94	86	3	18
8	343	338	4	11	17	343	338	4	12
9	338	330	4	13	18	338	330	4	14
OUT	2,343	2,277	32		IN	2,343	2,277	32	
					TOTAL	4,686	4,554	64	
					STANDARD SCRATCH	62	61		

Course Description:
Attractive parkland course featuring some tricky holes, with water coming into play testing your short irons. Accuracy and not length should be the focus of your play and if you happen to be a dab hand with your short irons you may just score well. The club is owned and run by the Belfast City Council, who keep it in good condition all year round.

HON. SECRETARY:
Kevin McGlennon MBA.
Tel: (028) 90 843799.

Course Information:
Par 64; SSS 62; Length 4,686 Yds.
Visitors: Welcome. **Opening Hours:** Mon-Fri, 9.00am-Dusk. Weekends, 8.00am-Dusk. **Ladies:** No ladies club facilities available. **Juveniles:** Welcome. Under 10's to be accompanied by an adult. **Green Fees:** Mon-Fri, Adult £9.50, Senior citizen, £5.30, Juveniles, £5.00. Sat, Sun, Bank holidays, £7.50- £12.50 for all. **Clubhouse Dress:** Neat and tidy dress, no denim. **Course Facilities:** Caddy carts are available for hire.

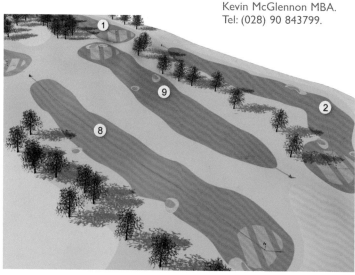

44 Westland Road, Belfast, BT146NH.
Tel: (028) 9074 4158

LOCATION: Situated between Cavehill
Road and Cliftonville Circus.

HON. TREASURER: Paul Adams.

SECRETARY: E. Lusty O.B.E. (028) 9074 6595

PRO-SHOP: Tel: (028) 9022 8585

Course Description:
Parkland course on rising ground with
extensive views of Belfast Lough.
Course is played around the
waterworks complex.

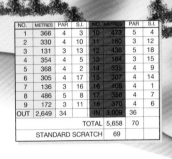

NO.	METRES	PAR	S.I.	NO.	METRES	PAR	S.I.
1	366	4	3	10	473	5	4
2	330	4	10	11	160	3	12
3	131	3	13	12	436	5	18
4	354	4	5	13	164	3	15
5	368	4	2	14	335	4	9
6	305	4	17	15	307	4	14
7	136	3	16	16	408	4	1
8	486	5	8	17	358	4	7
9	172	3	11	18	370	4	6
OUT	2,649	34		IN	3,009	36	
				TOTAL	5,658	70	
				STANDARD SCRATCH		69	

Course Information:
Par 70; SSS 70; Length 5,672 yards (medal).
Visitors: Welcome. **Opening Hours:** 8.30am – sunset. **Avoid:**
Tuesday afternoons and Sunday mornings. Members only – Saturday.
Ladies: Tuesdays. **Green Fees:** Mon-Fri; £14, Sunday £16 for visitors.
With a member £10, societies £12. Mon-Fri; £11 per player, Sunday
£14 per player. **Juveniles:** £7 weekdays only, until 6pm. Must be
accompanied by an adult. **Societies:** Mon-Fri £11,
Sun £13. **Clubhouse Hours:** 8.00am –
11.00pm. **Clubhouse Dress:** No
Denims. Jacket and tie in lounge
after 9pm. **Clubhouse Facilities:**
Snacks, meals 12 – 3pm and á la
carte 5pm – 9pm. No catering on
Monday except
by arrangement.

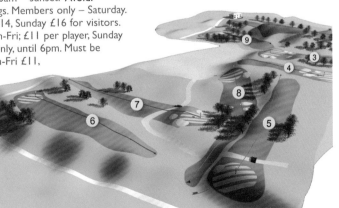

LOCATION: Between Upper
Malone Road and Lisburn Rd.

91 Dunmurry Lane, Dunmurry, Belfast.

Tel: (028) 9061 0834.

PROFESSIONAL: J. Dolan. Tel: (028) 9062 1314.

Course Description:

The course lies astride
Dunmurry Lane and consists
of rolling parkland in all
directions. Since its opening in
1983 it has matured well and
is a popular venue for many
golfers. The lake at the 8th and
9th fairways makes it a very
interesting hole.

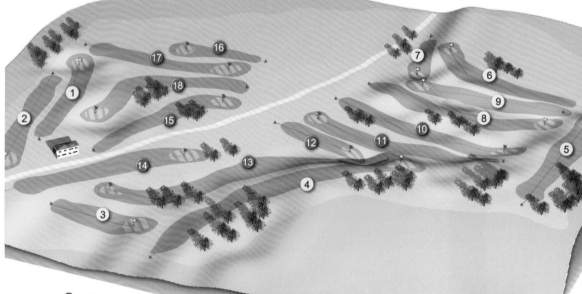

Course Information:

Par 70; SSS 68; Length 6,111 Yards.

Visitors: Welcome Mon – Thur by arrangement.

Opening Hours: Dawn to dusk. Ladies: Welcome Friday.

Green Fees: £27 weekdays; £37 weekends. Juveniles: Must be
accompanied by an adult. Lessons, Club Hire and Caddy trolleys
(limited) available. Clubhouse Dress: Jacket and tie all day Sunday
in restaurant, otherwise smart / casual. Clubhouse Facilities: Full
clubhouse facilities all week during summer months. Snacks and
meals: at certain times during the
winter. No catering on Mon during
the winter. Open Competitions:
Open Week: 26th July to 5th
August. Various other semi opens
during the summer.

NO.	MEDAL YARDS	GEN. YARDS	PAR	S.I.	NO.	MEDAL YARDS	GEN. YARDS	PAR	S.I.
1	364	346	4	7	10	345	344	4	10
2	354	344	4	13	11	389	370	4	4
3	168	150	3	15	12	168	153	3	12
4	529	519	5	9	13	522	502	5	8
5	366	356	4	11	14	281	271	4	14
6	426	410	4	1	15	365	340	4	2
7	161	146	3	17	16	180	170	3	16
8	400	390	4	3	17	311	301	4	18
9	388	368	4	5	18	370	345	4	6
OUT	3,156	3,029	35		IN	2,955	2,806	35	
					TOTAL	6,111	5,836	71	
					STANDARD SCRATCH		70	70	

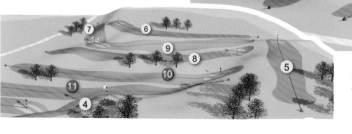

GOLF MANAGER: Tony Cassidy.

Tel: (028) 9061 0834.

Downview Avenue, Belfast BT15 4EZ.
Tel: (028) 9037 0770
Web: www.fortwilliam.co.uk

LOCATION: Off Antrim Road, Belfast.

HONORARY SECRETARY: Pat Toal.

Tel: (028) 9037 0770

PROFESSIONAL: Peter Hanna.

Tel: (028) 9077 0980

ARCHITECT: H. Colt.

Course Description:
The course is dominated by the picturesque and heavily wooded 'Cavehill' which rises to over 1,000 feet above sea level, making an attractive background to many shots throughout the round. There is quite a height difference between the top and bottom of the course, which in itself is divided into two parts by Grays Lane.

Course Information:
Par 70; SSS 69; Length 6,030 Yards. **Visitors:** Mon–Fri, Sunday.
Opening Hours: 8.30 – Dusk. **Ladies Green Fees:** £20 Mon – Fri
(£12 with a member) £22 Sat / Sun / Bank holidays (£14 with a member). Ladies Day: Monday & Friday. **Gents Green Fees:** £20 Mon – Fri (£13 with a member) £24 Sat / Sun / Bank holidays (£14 with a member). **Juveniles:** Can play all day Mon, Tues, Thur, Fri & Sun. Restricted hours Wed & Sat – telephone club for details. **Clubhouse Hours:** 9.00am – 11.30pm daily. **Clubhouse Dress:** October – March jacket and tie after 9.00pm. April - September casual smart dress (no denims). Societies welcome. **Open Competitions:** Open Week – August; plus various other open competitions. Golf buggies available at £20 per round.

NO.	MEDAL YARDS	GEN. YARDS	PAR	S.I.	NO.	MEDAL YARDS	GEN. YARDS	PAR	S.I.
1	421	412	4	7	10	195	168	3	10
2	329	298	4	9	11	381	362	4	8
3	437	418	4	5	12	146	120	3	18
4	330	306	4	17	13	377	358	4	2
5	474	442	5	1	14	502	491	5	12
6	186	153	3	15	15	321	315	4	14
7	311	292	4	11	16	345	331	4	4
8	421	402	4	3	17	150	140	3	16
9	272	260	4	13	18	432	404	4	6
OUT	3,181	2,983	36		IN	2,849	2,709	34	
					TOTAL	6,030	5,692	70	
	STANDARD SCRATCH						69	68	

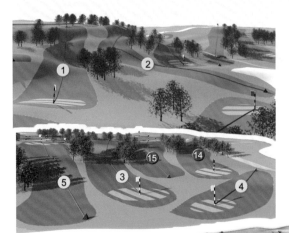

Summerfield, Dundonald, Belfast. BT16 2QX.

Tel: (028) 9048 2249.

LOCATION: Five miles east of Belfast onthe Upper Newtownards Road.

Course Description:

Parkland course with numerous large and small trees with the additional hazard of several deep bunkers. The 8th is an interesting hole with a river immediately fronting the green. The course is situated on the eastern suburbs of the city adjacent to Dundonald village.

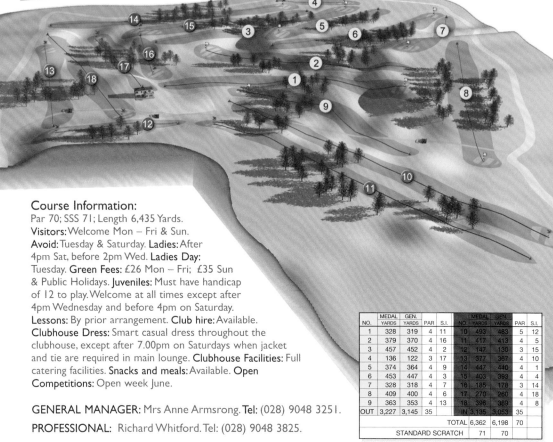

Course Information:

Par 70; SSS 71; Length 6,435 Yards.
Visitors: Welcome Mon – Fri & Sun.
Avoid: Tuesday & Saturday. **Ladies:** After 4pm Sat, before 2pm Wed. **Ladies Day:** Tuesday. **Green Fees:** £26 Mon – Fri; £35 Sun & Public Holidays. **Juveniles:** Must have handicap of 12 to play. Welcome at all times except after 4pm Wednesday and before 4pm on Saturday.
Lessons: By prior arrangement. **Club hire:** Available.
Clubhouse Dress: Smart casual dress throughout the clubhouse, except after 7.00pm on Saturdays when jacket and tie are required in main lounge. **Clubhouse Facilities:** Full catering facilities. **Snacks and meals:** Available. **Open Competitions:** Open week June.

GENERAL MANAGER: Mrs Anne Armsrong. **Tel:** (028) 9048 3251.

PROFESSIONAL: Richard Whitford. **Tel:** (028) 9048 3825.

NO.	MEDAL YARDS	GEN. YARDS	PAR	S.I.	NO.	MEDAL YARDS	GEN. YARDS	PAR	S.I.
1	328	319	4	11	10	493	483	5	12
2	379	370	4	16	11	417	413	4	5
3	457	452	4	2	12	147	130	3	15
4	136	122	3	17	13	377	367	4	10
5	374	364	4	9	14	447	440	4	1
6	453	447	4	3	15	403	393	4	4
7	328	318	4	7	16	185	178	3	14
8	409	400	4	6	17	270	260	4	18
9	363	353	4	13	18	396	389	4	8
OUT	3,227	3,145	35		IN	3,135	3,053	35	
					TOTAL	6,362	6,198	70	
					STANDARD SCRATCH		71	70	

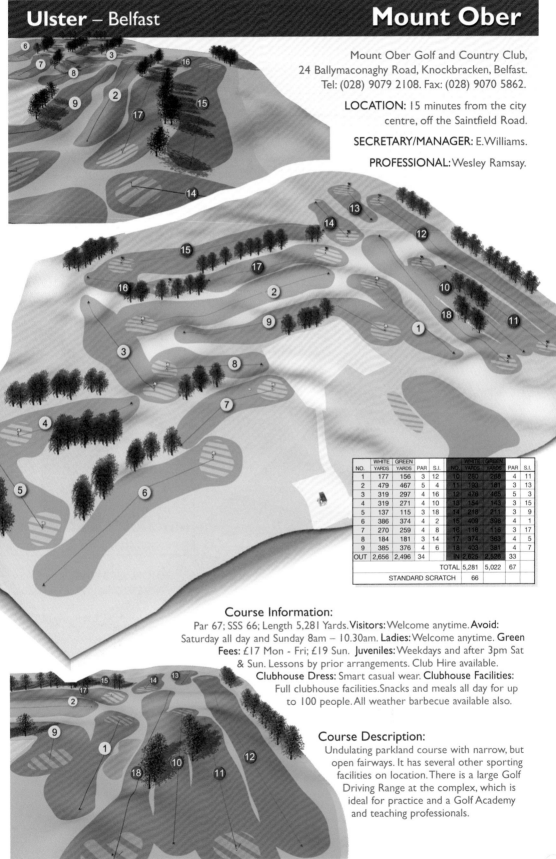

Mount Ober

Mount Ober Golf and Country Club,
24 Ballymaconaghy Road, Knockbracken, Belfast.
Tel: (028) 9079 2108. Fax: (028) 9070 5862.

LOCATION: 15 minutes from the city centre, off the Saintfield Road.

SECRETARY/MANAGER: E. Williams.

PROFESSIONAL: Wesley Ramsay.

NO.	WHITE YARDS	GREEN YARDS	PAR	S.I.	NO.	WHITE YARDS	GREEN YARDS	PAR	S.I.
1	177	156	3	12	10	280	268	4	11
2	479	467	5	4	11	193	181	3	13
3	319	297	4	16	12	476	465	5	3
4	319	271	4	10	13	154	143	3	15
5	137	115	3	18	14	218	211	3	9
6	386	374	4	2	15	409	398	4	1
7	270	259	4	8	16	118	116	3	17
8	184	181	3	14	17	374	363	4	5
9	385	376	4	6	18	403	381	4	7
OUT	2,656	2,496	34		IN	2,625	2,526	33	
					TOTAL	5,281	5,022	67	
					STANDARD SCRATCH		66		

Course Information:

Par 67; SSS 66; Length 5,281 Yards. **Visitors:** Welcome anytime. **Avoid:** Saturday all day and Sunday 8am – 10.30am. **Ladies:** Welcome anytime. **Green Fees:** £17 Mon - Fri; £19 Sun. **Juveniles:** Weekdays and after 3pm Sat & Sun. Lessons by prior arrangements. Club Hire available. **Clubhouse Dress:** Smart casual wear. **Clubhouse Facilities:** Full clubhouse facilities. Snacks and meals all day for up to 100 people. All weather barbecue available also.

Course Description:

Undulating parkland course with narrow, but open fairways. It has several other sporting facilities on location. There is a large Golf Driving Range at the complex, which is ideal for practice and a Golf Academy and teaching professionals.

LOCATION: Five miles from centre of Belfast.
MANAGER: Nick Agate.

240 Upper Malone Road, Dunmurry,
Belfast BT17 9LB.
Tel: (028) 9061 2758.

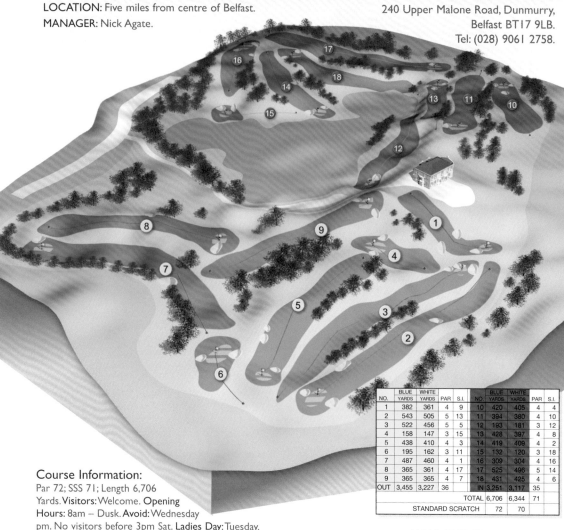

NO.	BLUE YARDS	WHITE YARDS	PAR	S.I.	NO.	BLUE YARDS	WHITE YARDS	PAR	S.I.
1	382	361	4	9	10	420	405	4	4
2	543	505	5	13	11	394	380	4	10
3	522	456	5	5	12	193	181	3	12
4	158	147	3	15	13	428	397	4	8
5	438	410	4	3	14	419	409	4	2
6	195	162	3	11	15	132	120	3	18
7	487	460	4	1	16	309	304	4	16
8	365	361	4	17	17	525	496	5	14
9	365	365	4	7	18	431	425	4	6
OUT	3,455	3,227	36		IN	3,251	3,117	35	
					TOTAL	6,706	6,344	71	
	STANDARD SCRATCH					72	70		

Course Information:

Par 72; SSS 71; Length 6,706
Yards. Visitors: Welcome. **Opening
Hours:** 8am – Dusk. **Avoid:** Wednesday
pm. No visitors before 3pm Sat. **Ladies Day:** Tuesday.
Green Fees: £65 Mon – Fri (£15 with member); £75
Sat / Sun & Bank Holidays (£17 with member). Lessons
by prior arrangements. Caddy trolleys available. Society
& Company book through office Mon & Thurs only.
Juveniles: Restricted on main course. **Clubhouse Hours:**
From 8.00am. **Clubhouse Dress:** Jacket and tie in upstairs
lounge, otherwise smart / casual. No denim, tee shirts or
training shoes on course. **Clubhouse Facilities:** Full
catering by arrangement with caterer. Lunch and bar
snacks. **Open Competitions:** Open Week: July. Open
Scratch Foursomes in September.

HON. SECRETARY: A N S Kirk.
PROFESSIONAL: Michael McGee.

Course Description: This course is of championship
standard with many mature trees and flowering shrubs. The
greens on the course are large with many undulations and
an exceptionally good putting surface. The course is quite
long and demanding and is classed as one of the best inland
courses in Ireland. A real pleasure to play.

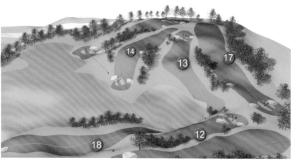

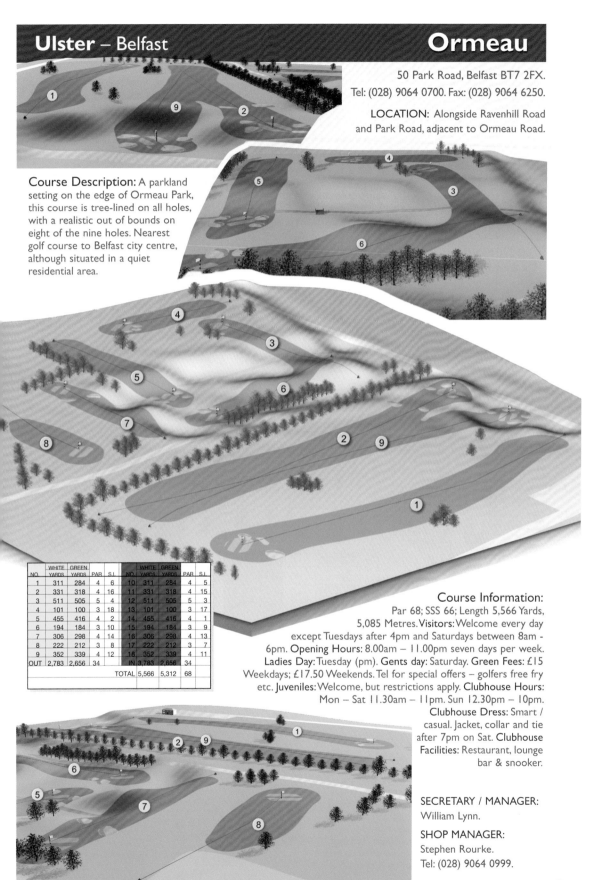

50 Park Road, Belfast BT7 2FX.
Tel: (028) 9064 0700. Fax: (028) 9064 6250.

LOCATION: Alongside Ravenhill Road and Park Road, adjacent to Ormeau Road.

Course Description: A parkland setting on the edge of Ormeau Park, this course is tree-lined on all holes, with a realistic out of bounds on eight of the nine holes. Nearest golf course to Belfast city centre, although situated in a quiet residential area.

NO.	WHITE YARDS	GREEN YARDS	PAR	S.I.	NO.	WHITE YARDS	GREEN YARDS	PAR	S.I.
1	311	284	4	6	10	311	284	4	5
2	331	318	4	16	11	331	318	4	15
3	511	505	5	4	12	511	505	5	3
4	101	100	3	18	13	101	100	3	17
5	455	416	4	2	14	455	416	4	1
6	194	184	3	10	15	194	184	3	9
7	306	298	4	14	16	306	298	4	13
8	222	212	3	8	17	222	212	3	7
9	352	339	4	12	18	352	339	4	11
OUT	2,783	2,656	34		IN	3,783	2,656	34	
					TOTAL	5,566	5,312	68	

Course Information:
Par 68; SSS 66; Length 5,566 Yards, 5,085 Metres. Visitors: Welcome every day except Tuesdays after 4pm and Saturdays between 8am - 6pm. **Opening Hours:** 8.00am – 11.00pm seven days per week. **Ladies Day:** Tuesday (pm). **Gents day:** Saturday. **Green Fees:** £15 Weekdays; £17.50 Weekends. Tel for special offers – golfers free fry etc. **Juveniles:** Welcome, but restrictions apply. **Clubhouse Hours:** Mon – Sat 11.30am – 11pm. Sun 12.30pm – 10pm. **Clubhouse Dress:** Smart / casual. Jacket, collar and tie after 7pm on Sat. **Clubhouse Facilities:** Restaurant, lounge bar & snooker.

SECRETARY / MANAGER:
William Lynn.

SHOP MANAGER:
Stephen Rourke.
Tel: (028) 9064 0999.

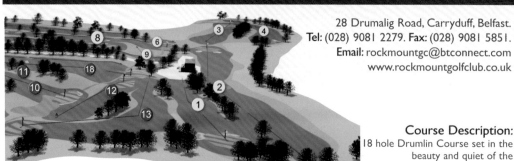

28 Drumalig Road, Carryduff, Belfast.
Tel: (028) 9081 2279. **Fax:** (028) 9081 5851.
Email: rockmountgc@btconnect.com
www.rockmountgolfclub.co.uk

Course Description:

18 hole Drumlin Course set in the beauty and quiet of the countryside with scenic views of the Mourne Mountains. The course has been designed to ensure that the land's natural features are incorporated throughout the 18 holes.

LOCATION: Seven miles south of Belfast.

NO.	MEDAL YARDS	GEN. YARDS	PAR	S.I.	NO.	MEDAL YARDS	GEN. YARDS	PAR	S.I.
1	301	289	4	12	10	358	345	4	5
2	496	485	5	4	11	397	361	4	2
3	213	199	3	6	12	157	147	3	15
4	324	305	5	16	13	353	340	4	9
5	541	513	5	8	14	361	343	4	11
6	489	473	5	18	15	554	511	5	7
7	410	384	4	1	16	193	157	3	17
8	349	338	4	10	17	360	338	4	13
9	129	121	3	14	18	425	412	4	3
OUT	3,215	3,082	37		IN	3,158	2,972	35	
					TOTAL	6,410	6,079	72	
		STANDARD SCRATCH					72	70	

SECRETARY:
R & D. Patterson.
Tel: (028) 9081 2279.

Course Information:

Par 72; SSS 72; Length 6,410 yards. **Opening Hours:** 8am – Dusk. **Avoid:** Saturday – (as it is members only). **Ladies:** Welcome. **Green Fees:** Mon – Fri £24 and Sunday £28. **Visitors:** Welcome any day (except Saturday). **Juveniles:** Must be accompanied by an adult. **Clubhouse Facilities:** Restaurant open to the public. Function room for hire. Shop. **Clubhouse Dress:** Smart casual, No Denims, no tracksuits.

73 Shandon Park,
Belfast, BT5 6NY.
Tel: (028) 90805030.
Fax: (028) 90805999.

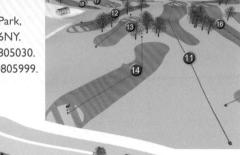

GENERAL MANAGER:
Greg Bailie.

PROFESSIONAL:
B. Wilson.

LOCATION: Three miles from Belfast city centre.

NO.	MEDAL YARDS	GEN. YARDS	PAR	S.I.	NO.	MEDAL YARDS	GEN. YARDS	PAR	S.I.
1	356	345	4	13	10	129	120	3	18
2	375	361	4	3	11	524	503	5	8
3	519	476	5	11	12	347	336	4	10
4	364	349	4	7	13	170	161	3	16
5	398	383	4	5	14	397	386	4	4
6	453	438	4	1	15	166	159	3	12
7	364	350	4	15	16	423	410	4	2
8	190	181	3	9	17	402	388	4	6
9	330	321	4	17	18	354	344	4	14
OUT	3,349	3,204	36		IN	2,912	2,807	34	
					TOTAL	6,261	6,011	70	
					STANDARD SCRATCH	70	69		

Course Description: Situated in eastern suburbs of Belfast this is a well known lush parkland course with true greens. Irrespective of handicap, golfers will find that it offers an enjoyable challenge to their golfing prowess. The course is generally flat and trees come into play on some of the holes.

Course Information:
Par 70; SSS 70; Length 6,282 yards. **Visitors:** Welcome.
Opening Hours: 8.30am – sunset. **Avoid:** Saturdays and Wednesdays. **Ladies:** Welcome. **Green Fees:** £27.50 Mon – Fri; £35 Weekends. **Juveniles:** Accompanied by a member. Lessons by prior arrangement. **Clubhouse Dress:** Casual. **Clubhouse Facilities:** Bar and Restaurant 12.00 – 11.00pm. **Open Competitions:** Open Week; 14th – 21st July.

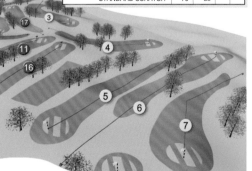

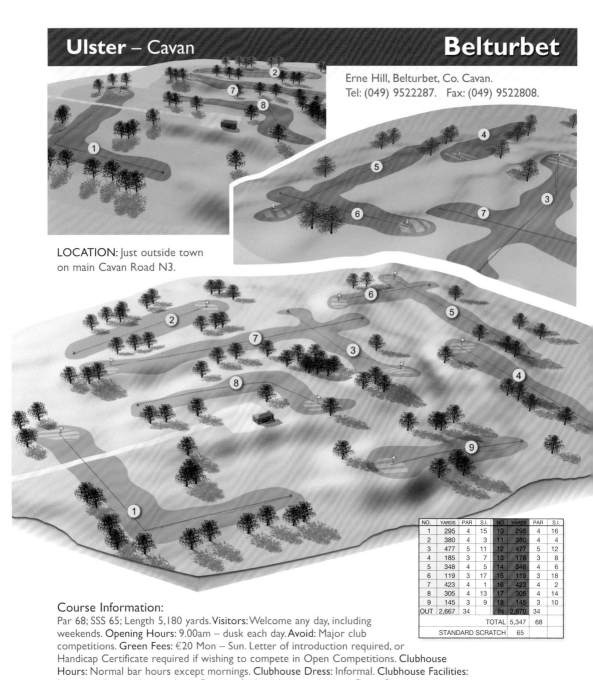

Erne Hill, Belturbet, Co. Cavan.
Tel: (049) 9522287.   Fax: (049) 9522808.

LOCATION: Just outside town on main Cavan Road N3.

NO.	YARDS	PAR	S.I.	NO.	YARDS	PAR	S.I.
1	295	4	15	10	295	4	16
2	380	4	3	11	380	4	4
3	477	5	11	12	477	5	12
4	185	3	7	13	178	3	8
5	348	4	5	14	348	4	6
6	119	3	17	15	119	3	18
7	423	4	1	16	423	4	2
8	305	4	13	17	305	4	14
9	145	3	9	18	145	3	10
OUT	2,667	34		IN	2,670	34	
				TOTAL	5,347	68	
				STANDARD SCRATCH		65	

Course Information:

Par 68; SSS 65; Length 5,180 yards. **Visitors:** Welcome any day, including weekends. **Opening Hours:** 9.00am – dusk each day. **Avoid:** Major club competitions. **Green Fees:** €20 Mon – Sun. Letter of introduction required, or Handicap Certificate required if wishing to compete in Open Competitions. **Clubhouse Hours:** Normal bar hours except mornings. **Clubhouse Dress:** Informal. **Clubhouse Facilities:** New members welcome, darts. Catering facilities by arrangement. **Open Competitions:** Contact club for details. **Company Dress:** Casual.

Course Description:

Most of the holes at Belturbet are played to elevated greens. Out of the eighteen holes the 5th, 7th and 9th holes are considered to be the toughest on the whole course.

SECRETARY: Nevin Traynor.

Tel: (049) 952 2287.

Web: www.belturbetgolfclub.com

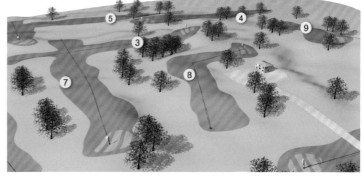

Toam, Blacklion, Co. Cavan.
Tel: (071) 98 53024 Fax: (071) 98 53481

LOCATION: At Blacklion Village
on the main
Enniskillen – Sligo Road
(A4 / N15).

HON. SECRETARY:
Pat Gallery.

ARCHITECT: E. Hackett.

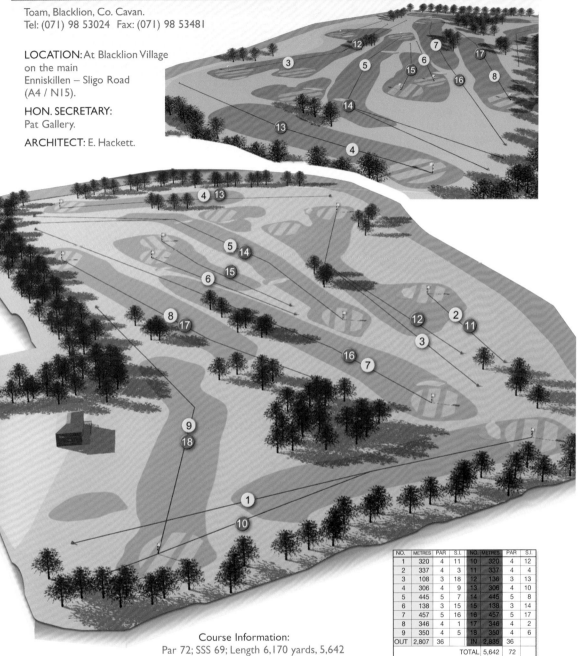

Course Information:

Par 72; SSS 69; Length 6,170 yards, 5,642
metres. Visitors: Welcome any day, but prior arrangement is preferred.
Limited at weekend. Opening Hours: Sunrise – sunset. Avoid: Sunday
morning and early afternoon. Certain club competitions, which are posted
in clubhouse. Ladies: Welcome Thursdays. Green Fees: €20 weekdays, €25
Sat / Sun and all public holidays. Juveniles: Welcome when accompanied
by an adult. Lessons available by prior arrangement. Clubhouse Hours:
Summer 10am - Close. Winter 12pm - Close. Clubhouse Dress: Informal.
Clubhouse Facilities: Snacks and meals available throughout the day. Open
Competitions: Open Week August, Blacklion Golf Classic, Bush Men &
Ladies Competitions, Singles Open, Ladies and Seniors Opens. Please call
club for details.

NO.	METRES	PAR	S.I.	NO.	METRES	PAR	S.I.
1	320	4	11	10	320	4	12
2	337	4	3	11	337	4	4
3	108	3	18	12	136	3	13
4	306	4	9	13	306	4	10
5	445	5	7	14	445	5	8
6	138	3	15	15	138	3	14
7	457	5	16	16	457	5	17
8	346	4	1	17	346	4	2
9	350	4	5	18	350	4	6
OUT	2,807	36		IN	2,835	36	
				TOTAL	5,642	72	
	STANDARD SCRATCH			69			

Course Description:
The course is bordered on two
sides by Lough McNean, which
can come into play on three
holes. Typical inland course that
is playable all year. Out of
bounds on two holes, some
thick shrubbery comes into play
on two holes. Reasonably easy
for the straight hitter!

Cabra Castle

Kingscourt, Co. Cavan.
Tel: (042) 966 7030.
Fax: (042) 966 7039.

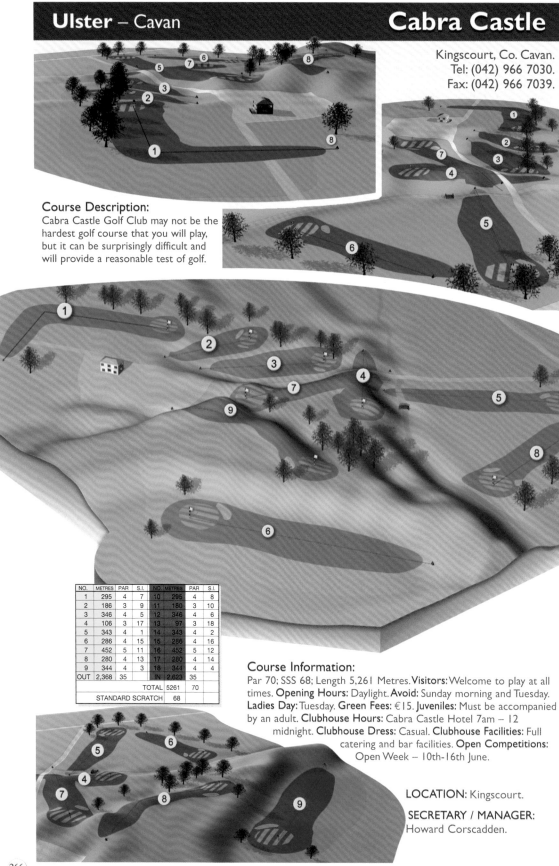

Course Description:

Cabra Castle Golf Club may not be the hardest golf course that you will play, but it can be surprisingly difficult and will provide a reasonable test of golf.

NO.	METRES	PAR	S.I.	NO.	METRES	PAR	S.I.
1	295	4	7	10	295	4	8
2	186	3	9	11	180	3	10
3	346	4	5	12	346	4	6
4	106	3	17	13	97	3	18
5	343	4	1	14	343	4	2
6	286	4	15	15	286	4	16
7	452	5	11	16	452	5	12
8	280	4	13	17	280	4	14
9	344	4	3	18	344	4	4
OUT	2,368	35		IN	2,623	35	
				TOTAL	5261	70	
				STANDARD SCRATCH	68		

Course Information:

Par 70; SSS 68; Length 5,261 Metres. **Visitors:** Welcome to play at all times. **Opening Hours:** Daylight. **Avoid:** Sunday morning and Tuesday. **Ladies Day:** Tuesday. **Green Fees:** €15. **Juveniles:** Must be accompanied by an adult. **Clubhouse Hours:** Cabra Castle Hotel 7am – 12 midnight. **Clubhouse Dress:** Casual. **Clubhouse Facilities:** Full catering and bar facilities. **Open Competitions:** Open Week – 10th-16th June.

LOCATION: Kingscourt.

SECRETARY / MANAGER: Howard Corscadden.

Arnmore House, Drumelis,
Cavan, Co. Cavan.
Tel: (049) 433 1388
E-mail: cavangc@iol.ie

LOCATION: One mile from
Cavan town, on the Killeshandra
Road.
HON. SECRETARY:
Seamus Mc Connon.
Tel: (049) 4331541

PROFESSIONAL: Bill Noble.
Tel: (049) 433 1388

Course Information:

Par 70; SSS 69;
Length 5,634 metres.
Visitors: Welcome to play at
any time. **Opening Hours:** Daylight
hours. **Avoid:** Sundays and Wednesdays.
Ladies: Welcome Wednesdays. **Green Fees:** €30 Mon - Thur; €35 Fri - Sun & Bank
Holidays. **Juveniles:** Must be accompanied by an adult. Club Hire and Caddy cars
available by prior arrangement. **Clubhouse Hours:** Normal licensing hours. **Clubhouse
Dress:** Casual. **Clubhouse Facilities:** Bar, meals. Catering facilities available any day May
– Sep. (prior arrangements may be made with resident steward or caterer). Newly
developed back nine opened in Spring 2006. **Open Competitions:** Open Day every
Thursday. Open Week – July; Open Junior Scratch Cup – Sep; Open Intermediate
Scratch Cup – Sept.

Course Description:
A Parkland course in the
suburbs of Cavan town
that offers a good test of
golf, with several
interesting holes a feature
of the course. Eight of the
holes have recently been
modified.

NO.	CHAMP YARDS	MEDAL YARDS	PAR	S.I.	NO.	CHAMP YARDS	MEDAL YARDS	PAR	S.I.
1	288	283	4	6	10	189	179	3	11
2	291	291	4	16	11	303	298	4	13
3	371	371	4	2	12	341	341	4	9
4	161	154	3	18	13	133	133	3	17
5	350	340	4	4	14	381	376	4	5
6	312	312	4	14	15	377	367	4	1
7	488	476	5	12	16	358	353	4	3
8	326	321	4	10	17	447	437	5	15
9	171	150	3	8	18	347	341	4	7
OUT	2,758	2,698	35		IN	2,758	2,698	36	
					TOTAL	5,634	5,525	72	
					STANDARD SCRATCH	74	72		

Slieve Russell

Ballyconnell, Co. Cavan. Tel: (049) 9525090. Fax: (049) 9526640

ARCHITECT: Paddy Merrigan.

HON. SECRETARY: Fergal McGuire.

GOLF DIRECTOR / PROFESSIONAL: Liam McCool.

Driving range

Course Description:

An 18 hole championship course is set in 300 acres of parkland including 50 acres of lake. The unique style of the Slieve Russell fits and compliments the Cavan Drumlin landscape multiple tee positions facilitate all categories of golfer.

Course Information: Par 72; SSS 72; Length 7,053 yards. **Visitors:** Welcome. **Opening Hours:** 8am –11pm (seasonal opening times). **Avoid:** Saturday. **Ladies:** Welcome. **Juveniles:** Over 12yrs discounted rates apply. **Green Fees:** Non-resident rates - €72 (Sun – Fri). €90 (Sat). **Clubhouse Hours:** 9am –11pm. **Clubhouse Dress:** Dress code in operation. **Clubhouse Facilities:** Restaurant & bar also available. **Additional Facilities:** 9 hole Par 3 course; Flood lit driving range; Golf Tuition available. Adjacent to Slieve Russell Hotel.

NO.	MEDAL YARDS	GEN. YARDS	PAR	S.I.	NO.	MEDAL YARDS	GEN. YARDS	PAR	S.I.
1	428	399	4	10	10	411	393	4	2
2	434	407	4	1	11	193	168	3	1
3	398	371	4	6	12	442	434	4	3
4	167	159	3	16	13	529	502	5	4
5	436	412	4	3	14	374	356	4	1
6	512	491	5	18	15	453	326	4	2
7	220	196	3	8	16	176	165	3	1
8	389	338	4	14	17	399	369	4	6
9	552	509	5	12	18	540	519	5	5
OUT	3,536	3,282	36		IN	3,517	3,332	36	
					TOTAL	7,053	6,614	72	
					STANDARD SCRATCH		74	72	

Virginia, Co Cavan.
Tel: (049) 8548066.
virginiagolfclub@eircom.net

LOCATION: Fifty miles N.W. of Dublin on Virginia – Ballyjamesduff Road on the grounds of the Park Hotel.
SECRETARY: Tom Hutchinson.

Course Information:

Par 64; SSS 62; Length 4,139 Metres. **Visitors:** Welcome to play on any day except Ladies Day on Thurs. **Opening Hours:** Daylight hours. **Avoid:** Sunday mornings – Men's competitions. **Ladies:** Welcome (except on Competition Days) Thursdays and Sundays. **Green Fees:** €15, €10 with a member. **Ladies day:** Thursday. **Juveniles:** Not allowed after 5.00pm or on Sun. or Thur. Club Hire and Caddy service available by prior arrangement. **Clubhouse Facilities:** Available in the Park Hotel. **Open Competitions:** Open Week: last week in June.

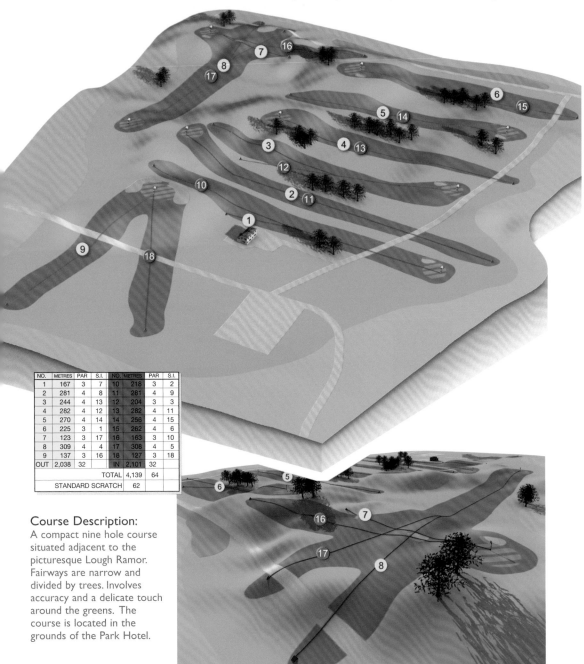

NO.	METRES	PAR	S.I.	NO.	METRES	PAR	S.I.
1	167	3	7	10	218	3	2
2	281	4	8	11	281	4	9
3	244	4	13	12	204	3	3
4	282	4	12	13	282	4	11
5	270	4	14	14	256	4	15
6	225	3	1	15	262	4	6
7	123	3	17	16	163	3	10
8	309	4	4	17	308	4	5
9	137	3	16	18	127	3	18
OUT	2,038	32		IN	2,101	32	
				TOTAL	4,139	64	
				STANDARD SCRATCH	62		

Course Description:

A compact nine hole course situated adjacent to the picturesque Lough Ramor. Fairways are narrow and divided by trees. Involves accuracy and a delicate touch around the greens. The course is located in the grounds of the Park Hotel.

Ballybofey, Co. Donegal. **Tel:** (074) 913 1093. **Fax:** (074) 913 0158.

LOCATION: Lough Alzlan, Stranorlar, off Strabane/Stranorlar main road.

HON SECRETARY: Patsy O'Donnell.

PRESIDENT: Phil Roddy.

ARCHITECT: P. C. Carr.

CAPTAIN: James Mc Allistar.

LADIES CAPTAIN: Eileen Boyce.

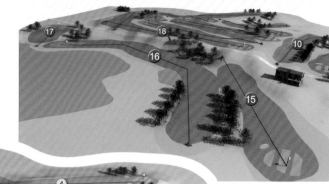

Lough Allan

NO.	MEDAL YARDS	GEN. YARDS	PAR	S.I.	NO.	MEDAL YARDS	GEN. YARDS	PAR	S.I.
1	377	371	4	6	10	392	387	4	5
2	359	349	4	12	11	151	141	3	7
3	283	273	4	14	12	278	272	4	17
4	307	297	4	16	13	320	320	4	11
5	157	147	3	4	14	337	327	4	13
6	346	335	4	10	15	185	175	3	3
7	421	411	4	8	16	450	435	5	1
8	137	127	3	18	17	140	130	3	15
9	361	351	4	2	18	375	360	4	9
OUT	2,750	2,673	35		IN	2,750	2,673	34	
					TOTAL	5,378	5,220	69	
					STANDARD SCRATCH	68	67		

Course Information: Par 68; SSS 69; Length 5,399 metres. **Visitors:** Welcome. Booking essential for weekends. Please telephone (074) 31093. **Opening Hours:** 9.00am – sunset. New shop. **Avoid:** Tue & Wed evenings from 4.30pm. **Green Fees:** €30 Weekends €25 Mon – Fri; Societies please call club for details. **Clubhouse Hours:** 12 noon – 11pm. **Clubhouse Dress:** Informal. **Clubhouse Facilities:** A new clubhouse with full facilities. **Open Competitions:** Please call club for details.

Course Description: Undulating parkland course with picturesque views of the Donegal Hills and Valley of River Finn. The course is located on the shores of Lough Allan yet follows the rolling contours of the surrounding countryside. A satisfying course and one that is popular with societies.

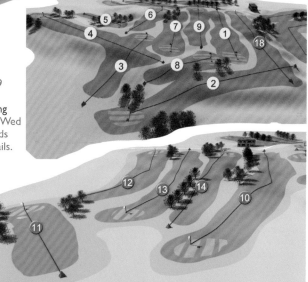

Ballyliffin Golf Club, Ballyliffin, Inishowen, Co. Donegal.
Tel: (074) 93 76119 Fax: (074) 93 76672
E-mail: info@ballyliffingolfclub.com
Web: www.ballyliffingolfclub.com

LOCATION: Exactly 10 miles due south of Malin Head.

MANAGER: John Farren.

ARCHITECT: Members and Mother Nature & Nick Faldo.

PROFESSIONAL:

John Dolan.

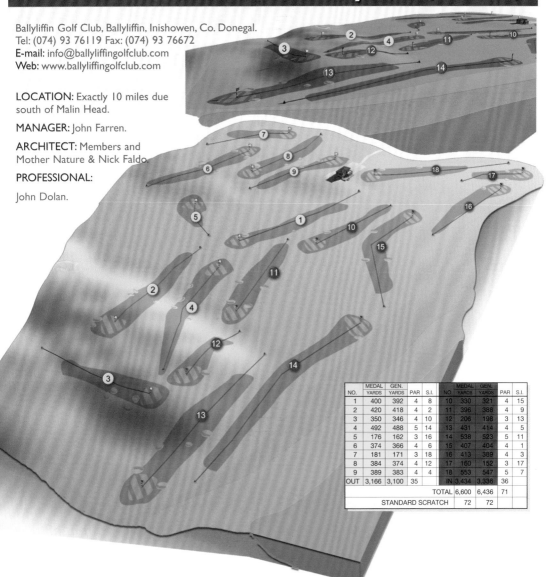

NO.	MEDAL YARDS	GEN. YARDS	PAR	S.I.	NO.	MEDAL YARDS	GEN. YARDS	PAR	S.I.
1	400	392	4	8	10	330	321	4	15
2	420	418	4	2	11	396	388	4	9
3	350	346	4	10	12	206	198	3	13
4	492	488	5	14	13	431	414	4	5
5	176	162	3	16	14	538	523	5	11
6	374	366	4	6	15	407	404	4	1
7	181	171	3	18	16	413	389	4	3
8	384	374	4	12	17	160	152	3	17
9	389	383	4	4	18	553	547	5	7
OUT	3,166	3,100	35		IN	3,434	3,336	36	
					TOTAL	6,600	6,436	71	
					STANDARD SCRATCH	72	72		

Course Description:

To play, The Old Links at Ballyliffin is to experience golf on one of Nature's most beautiful stages. All around are dramatic hills and mountains with magnificent views of the bay, the ocean and the course.

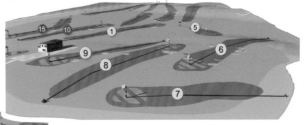

Course Information:

Par 71; SSS 72; Length 6,600 yards. **Visitors:** Welcome. **Opening Hours:** Daylight. **Avoid:** Not booking. **Ladies:** Welcome Tuesdays and 4.00pm – 6.00pm Sat & Sun. **Green Fees:** Mon – Fri €60. Weekend €65. **Juveniles:** By arrangement. Caddy service available by prior arrangement. **Clubhouse Hours:** 9.00am – 11.30pm. **Clubhouse Facilities:** Bar, snacks, showers. Catering facilities by arrangement and most weekends. **Open Competitions:** Contact Pro Shop (074) 937 8100.

Ballyliffin (Glashedy)

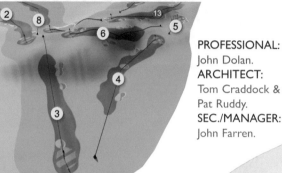

Ballyliffin Golf Club, Inishowen, Co. Donegal.
Tel: (074) 9376119 Fax: (074) 9376672.

PROFESSIONAL:
John Dolan.
ARCHITECT:
Tom Craddock &
Pat Ruddy.
SEC./MANAGER:
John Farren.

LOCATION: 6 miles from Carndonagh.

Course Information:

Par 72; SSS 73;
Length 6,897 yards.
Visitors: Welcome. **Opening Hours:** Daylight. **Avoid:** Sat & Sun afternoons. **Ladies:** Welcome Tuesdays and 4.00pm – 6.00pm Sat & Sun. **Green Fees:** Old Links: Mon – Fri €60. Weekend €65. Glashedy: Mon – Fri €70. Weekend €80. **Juveniles:** By arrangement. Caddy service available by prior arrangement.
Clubhouse Hours: 9.00am – 11.30pm. **Clubhouse Facilities:** Bar, snacks, Restaurant and showers. **Open Competitions:** Contact office for details.

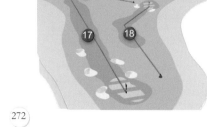

NO.	CHAMP YARDS	MEDAL YARDS	PAR	S.I.	NO.	CHAMP YARDS	MEDAL YARDS	PAR	S.I.
1	426	420	4	6	10	397	376	4	11
2	432	423	4	10	11	419	413	4	9
3	428	408	4	2	12	448	414	4	3
4	479	465	5	12	13	572	564	5	13
5	177	173	3	14	14	183	159	3	17
6	404	361	4	16	15	440	430	4	1
7	183	162	3	18	16	426	416	4	5
8	422	419	4	4	17	549	542	5	7
9	382	372	4	8	18	450	380	4	15
OUT	3,333	3,203	35		IN	3,884	3,694	37	
					TOTAL	7,217	6,897	72	
					STANDARD SCRATCH	74	73		

Course Description:

The Glashedy Links was opened in 1995, designed by Tom Craddock & Pat Ruddy is 7,000 yards of sweeping fairways, undulating greens and cavanous bunkers - a real professional test.

Email: info@ballyliffingolfclub.com
Web: www.ballyliffingolfclub.com

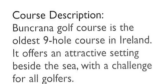

Railway Road, Buncrana, Co. Donegal.
Tel: (074) 93 62279

LOCATION: Buncrana Town.

SECRETARY: Francis McGrory.

Tel: (074) 932 0749

Course Description:
Buncrana golf course is the oldest 9-hole course in Ireland. It offers an attractive setting beside the sea, with a challenge for all golfers.

Course Information:
Par 62; SSS 60; Length 4,310 yards.
Visitors: Welcome any time - phone for teetimes at weekends. Opening Hours: Sunrise – sunset. Ladies: Welcome anytime, Ladies day Friday. Green Fees: €13 Gents, €8 Ladies, €5 Juveniles. Juveniles: Must be accompanied by an adult after 4pm and at weekends. Clubhouse Hours: 9am – closing. Clubhouse Dress: Casual. Clubhouse Facilities: Golf shop. Open Competitions: All year. Handicap certificate required for competitions.

NO.	YARDS	PAR	S.I.	NO.	YARDS	PAR	S.I.
1	280	4	7	10	280	4	8
2	159	3	15	11	159	3	16
3	240	3	9	12	240	3	10
4	176	3	11	13	176	3	12
5	357	4	3	14	357	4	4
6	128	3	13	15	128	3	14
7	335	4	5	16	335	4	6
8	385	4	1	17	369	4	2
9	95	3	17	18	95	3	18
OUT	2,155	31		IN	2,125	31	
				TOTAL	4,310	62	
				STANDARD SCRATCH	60		

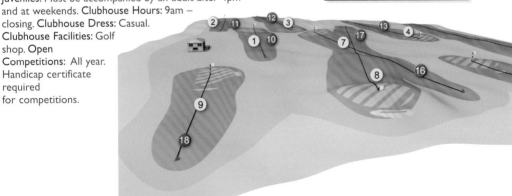

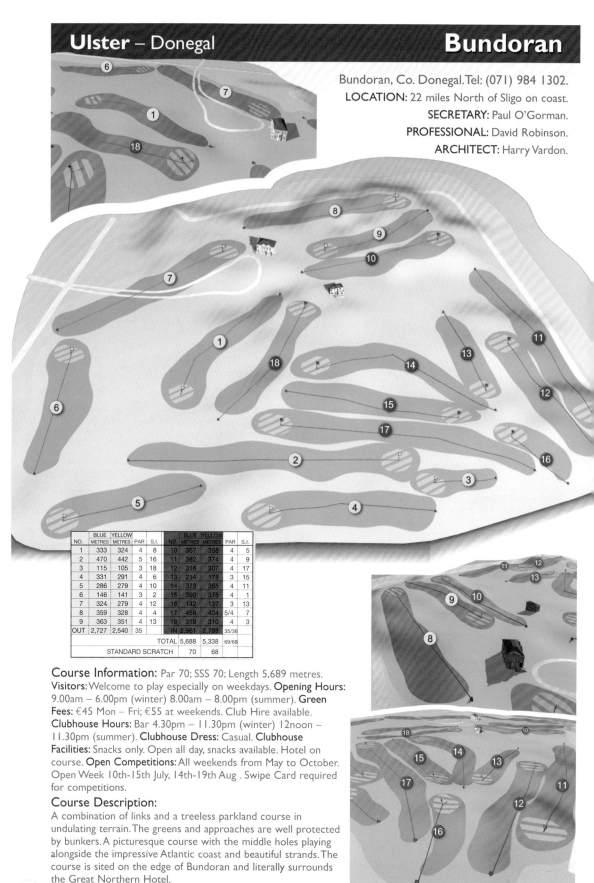

Bundoran, Co. Donegal. Tel: (071) 984 1302.
LOCATION: 22 miles North of Sligo on coast.
SECRETARY: Paul O'Gorman.
PROFESSIONAL: David Robinson.
ARCHITECT: Harry Vardon.

NO.	BLUE METRES	YELLOW METRES	PAR	S.I.	NO.	BLUE METRES	YELLOW METRES	PAR	S.I.
1	333	324	4	8	10	367	358	4	5
2	470	442	5	16	11	382	374	4	9
3	115	105	3	18	12	316	307	4	17
4	331	291	4	6	13	214	178	3	15
5	286	279	4	10	14	373	355	4	11
6	146	141	3	2	15	390	375	4	1
7	324	279	4	12	16	142	137	3	13
8	359	328	4	4	17	458	404	5/4	7
9	363	351	4	9	18	319	310	4	3
OUT	2,727	2,540	35		IN	2,961	2,798	35/36	
					TOTAL	5,688	5,338	69/68	
					STANDARD SCRATCH	70	68		

Course Information: Par 70; SSS 70; Length 5,689 metres.
Visitors: Welcome to play especially on weekdays. **Opening Hours:**
9.00am – 6.00pm (winter) 8.00am – 8.00pm (summer). **Green
Fees:** €45 Mon – Fri; €55 at weekends. Club Hire available.
Clubhouse Hours: Bar 4.30pm – 11.30pm (winter) 12noon –
11.30pm (summer). **Clubhouse Dress:** Casual. **Clubhouse
Facilities:** Snacks only. Open all day, snacks available. Hotel on
course. **Open Competitions:** All weekends from May to October.
Open Week 10th-15th July, 14th-19th Aug . Swipe Card required
for competitions.

Course Description:

A combination of links and a treeless parkland course in
undulating terrain. The greens and approaches are well protected
by bunkers. A picturesque course with the middle holes playing
alongside the impressive Atlantic coast and beautiful strands. The
course is sited on the edge of Bundoran and literally surrounds
the Great Northern Hotel.

Cloughaneely

Cloughaneely Golf Club,
Ballyconnell, Falcarragh,
Co. Donegal.
Tel: (074) 916 5416
salcarraghgolfclub@eircom.net

Course Description:
Opened in 1997 this is an
undulating inland course set in an
old estate with mature woodlands.
A pleasure to play regardless of
the score.

Course Information:
Par 70; SSS 69; Length 6,088 yards.
Visitors: Welcome. **Opening Hours:** 8.30am –
10.00pm. **Avoid:** Sunday mornings. **Green Fees:** Phone
club for information. **Juveniles:** Welcome. **Clubhouse Hours:**
9.00am – 11.00pm in summer. **Clubhouse Dress:** Informal.
Clubhouse Facilities: Tea, coffee, sandwiches and snacks by
arrangement in local hotels. Nearby accommodation in Ostan
Lough Altan Gortahork. **Open Competitions:** Bank Holiday
weekends / Open Week July.

NO.	YARDS	PAR	S.I.	NO.	YARDS	PAR	S.I.
1	408	4	1	10	408	4	2
2	195	3	15	11	195	3	16
3	334	4	13	12	334	4	14
4	345	4	9	13	345	4	10
5	381	4	11	14	381	4	12
6	362	4	5	15	362	4	6
7	147	3	17	16	147	3	18
8	501	5	7	17	501	5	8
9	371	4	3	18	371	4	4
OUT	3,044	34		IN	3,044	35	
				TOTAL	6,088	70	
				STANDARD SCRATCH		69	

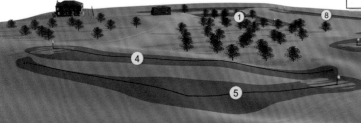

LOCATION: Ballyconnell,
Falcarragh,
Co. Donegal.

SECRETARY: Michael Murray.

ARCHITECT: Michael Doherty.

Course Description:

A breathtaking 9 hole links course perched precariously on the edge of the Atlantic Ocean and accessible only by a bridge which joins it to the mainland and the village of Kincasslagh. The crowning glory of the course is the magnificent Par 3 6th hole where nerves of steel are required to hit over a deep cove and land on a small green which has a sheer drop into the sea behind for anyone who overclubs it.

Kincasslagh, Co Donegal.
Tel: (074) 954 3296

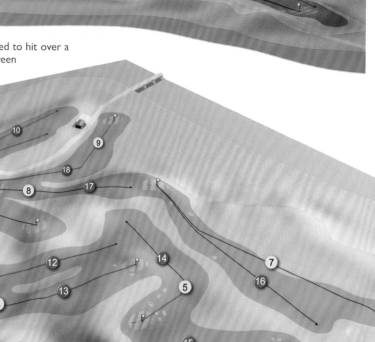

Course Information:

Par 68; SSS 66; Length 5,141 metres. **Visitors:** Welcome anytime. Prior arrangement required for parties in excess of 12 people. **Avoid:** Club Competitions Sunday mornings; Ladies Competitions Thursday. **Green Fees:** €25 weekdays and weekends; Groups €18. **Juveniles:** Welcome. No restrictions. **Clubhouse Hours:** June/Sept 10.00am – dusk. **Clubhouse Facilities:** Bar, locker rooms. Trolley hire. Catering facilities, meals available. Prior arrangement required for larger parties.

NO.	METRES	PAR	S.I.	NO.	METRES	PAR	S.I.
1	394	4	3	10	387	4	4
2	386	4	1	11	386	4	2
3	302	4	15	12	302	4	16
4	318	3	5	13	318	4	6
5	256	4	17	14	256	4	18
6	137	3	13	15	145	3	14
7	293	4	11	16	293	4	12
8	195	3	7	17	195	3	8
9	289	4	9	18	289	4	10
OUT	2,570	34		IN	2,571	34	
				TOTAL	5,141	68	
				STANDARD SCRATCH		68	

LOCATION: Two miles outside village of Kincasslagh.

SECRETARY: Joseph Gillespie.
Tel: (074) 954 8508

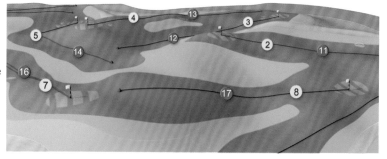

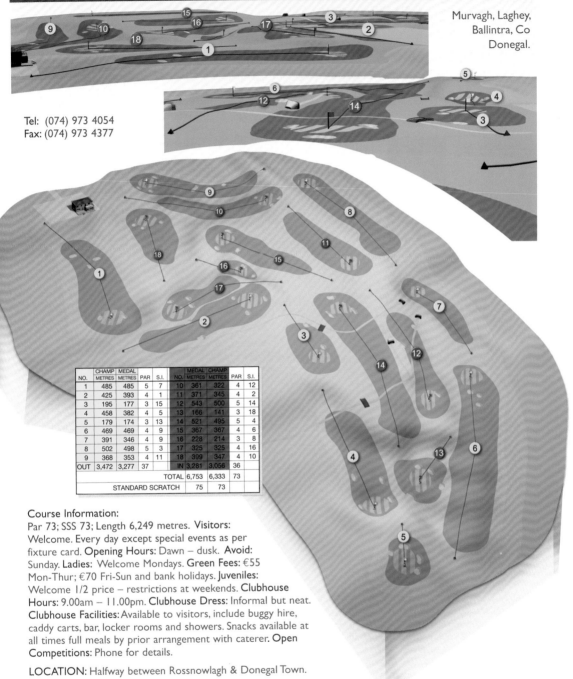

Murvagh, Laghey, Ballintra, Co Donegal.

Tel: (074) 973 4054
Fax: (074) 973 4377

NO.	CHAMP METRES	MEDAL METRES	PAR	S.I.	NO.	MEDAL METRES	CHAMP METRES	PAR	S.I.
1	485	485	5	7	10	361	322	4	12
2	425	393	4	1	11	371	345	4	2
3	195	177	3	15	12	543	500	5	14
4	458	382	4	5	13	166	141	3	18
5	179	174	3	13	14	521	495	5	4
6	469	469	4	9	15	367	367	4	6
7	391	346	4	9	16	228	214	3	8
8	502	498	5	3	17	325	325	4	16
9	368	353	4	11	18	399	347	4	10
OUT	3,472	3,277	37		IN	3,281	3,056	36	
					TOTAL	6,753	6,333	73	
					STANDARD SCRATCH	75	73		

Course Information:
Par 73; SSS 73; Length 6,249 metres. Visitors: Welcome. Every day except special events as per fixture card. Opening Hours: Dawn – dusk. Avoid: Sunday. Ladies: Welcome Mondays. Green Fees: €55 Mon-Thur; €70 Fri-Sun and bank holidays. Juveniles: Welcome 1/2 price – restrictions at weekends. Clubhouse Hours: 9.00am – 11.00pm. Clubhouse Dress: Informal but neat. Clubhouse Facilities: Available to visitors, include buggy hire, caddy carts, bar, locker rooms and showers. Snacks available at all times full meals by prior arrangement with caterer. Open Competitions: Phone for details.

LOCATION: Halfway between Rossnowlagh & Donegal Town.

ARCHITECT: Eddie Hackett, Pat Ruddy.

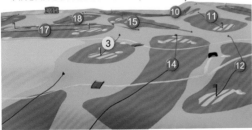

Course Description:
Challenging links course fit to test the best. Superbly scenic between sea and mountains. The holes are a mixture of testing Par 5's, tricky Par 4's and memorable Par 3's.

Kill, Dunfanaghy. Tel: (074) 913 6335 Fax: (074) 913 6684.
Email: dunfanaghygolf@eircom.net
Web: www.dunfanaghygolfclub.com

LOCATION: Within walking distance of the Village of Dunfanaghy on the main Letterkenny Road.

SECRETARY: Sandra McGinley.

NO.	WHITE METRES	YELL. METRES	PAR	S.I.	NO.	WHITE METRES	YELL. METRES	PAR	S.I.
1	316	310	4	11	10	284	275	4	16
2	148	143	3	13	11	298	290	4	18
3	363	355	4	3	12	355	340	4	4
4	347	340	4	5	13	147	142	3	14
5	330	325	4	9	14	331	325	4	2
6	392	338	4	1	15	364	358	4	6
7	209	205	3	7	16	467	467	5	8
8	283	277	4	15	17	171	160	3	10
9	124	120	3	17	18	338	330	4	12
OUT	2,512	2,413	33		IN	2,755	2,687	35	
					TOTAL	5,267	5,100	68	
					STANDARD SCRATCH		66	66	

Course Description:
Beautiful seaside links course located on the western shores of "Sheep Haven Bay". The course offers an enjoyable challenge for golfers of every ability. Memorable holes include the 7th, 9th, 10th and a superb finishing five holes.

Course Information:
Par 68; SSS 66; Length 5,267 metres. **Visitors:** Very welcome. Please check time sheet for weekends. **Opening Hours:** Dawn - Dusk. **Ladies:** Welcome. **Green Fees:** Mon – Fri €30; €40 Sat, Sun & Bank Hols. Special rates for societies and local hotel residents (including most weekends). **Juveniles:** Welcome. **Clubhouse Hours:** 9.00am onwards. **Clubhouse Dress:** Informal but neat. **Clubhouse Facilities:** Bar and snacks available all day. Clubs and trolleys available for hire. **Open Competitions:** The club organise open competitions throughout the year. Open week is held over the last week in July and first weekend in August. Please phone for further details.

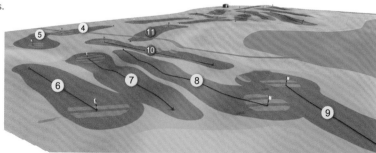

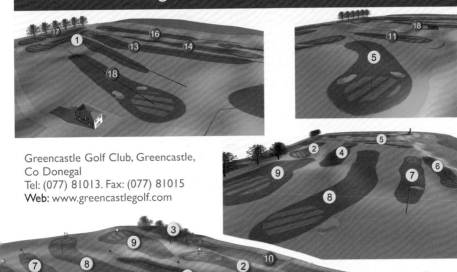

Greencastle Golf Club, Greencastle,
Co Donegal
Tel: (077) 81013. Fax: (077) 81015
Web: www.greencastlegolf.com

NO.	YARDS	PAR	S.I.	NO.	YARDS	PAR	S.I.
1	341	4	11	10	536	5	6
2	424	4	1	11	180	3	8
3	151	3	13	12	340	4	10
4	468	4	3	13	477	5	14
5	307	4	7	14	382	4	4
6	270	4	16	15	117	3	18
7	132	3	15	16	409	4	2
8	278	4	17	17	308	4	12
9	314	4	9	18	192	3	9
OUT	2,685	34		IN	2,941	35	
				TOTAL	5,626	69	
				STANDARD SCRATCH		67	

Course Description:

A very picturesque course with panoramic views
of Inishowen and Lough Foyle. Challenging
without being truly tiring.

LOCATION: 23 miles North of Derry on
Moville road.
HON. SECRETARY: Joe Mc Cafferty
ADMINISTRATOR: Billy Mc Caul
ARCHITECT: E. Hackett.

Course Information:

Par 69; SSS 67; Length 5,145 metres. **Visitors:**
Welcome. **Opening Hours:** 8am to dark. **Ladies
Day:** Thursday. **Green Fees:** £30 Mon-Fri, (£20
with member); £40 Sat / Sun & Bank Hols (£30
with member). **Juveniles:** Welcome. **Clubhouse
Hours:** 12 noon to after dark. **Clubhouse Dress:**
G.U.I. dress code. **Clubhouse Facilities:** Bar.
Catering Thur, Fri, Sat, Sun or by arrangement.
Open Competitions: Open Week - 2nd week in
June. Open Competitions on various weekends.

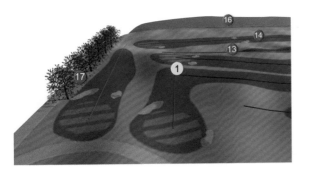

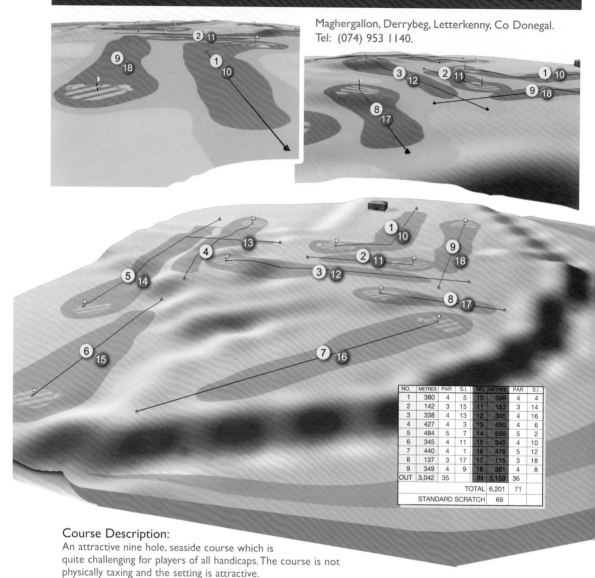

Maghergallon, Derrybeg, Letterkenny, Co Donegal.
Tel: (074) 953 1140.

NO.	METRES	PAR	S.I.	NO.	METRES	PAR	S.I.
1	380	4	5	10	398	4	4
2	142	3	15	11	153	3	14
3	338	4	13	12	305	4	16
4	427	4	3	13	450	4	6
5	484	5	7	14	556	5	2
6	345	4	11	15	345	4	10
7	440	4	1	16	476	5	12
8	137	3	17	17	115	3	18
9	349	4	9	18	361	4	8
OUT	3,042	35		IN	3,159	36	
					TOTAL	6,201	71
				STANDARD SCRATCH		69	

Course Description:

An attractive nine hole, seaside course which is
quite challenging for players of all handicaps. The course is not
physically taxing and the setting is attractive.

Course Information:

Par 71; SSS 69; Length 6,201 metres. Visitors: Welcome. Opening Hours:
All day. Ladies: Welcome. Green Fees: €20 everyday, €15 with a member.
Caddy service available by prior arrangement. Juveniles: Sat mornings.
Clubhouse Hours: Normally 10am – 12 midnight. Clubhouse Dress:
Informal. Clubhouse Facilities: Showers, Cloakrooms. Catering facilities;
daily during summer months. Weekends for remainder of the year.

LOCATION:
North west of Letterkenny.
SECRETARY / MANAGER:
Eric Campbell.

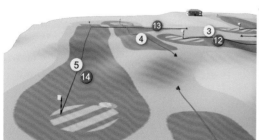

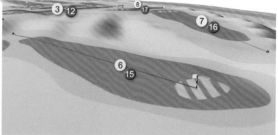

Letterkenny Co Donegal. Tel: (074) 91 21150 Fax: (074) 91 21175

LOCATION: 2km from outskirts of Letterkenny town on Ramelton Road.

Course Description:
An attractive eighteen hole parkland golf course in which the first eleven holes are played on relatively flat ground, the remaining seven holes are played on a plateau above the others. The course is a good challenge with a demanding finishing hole. The first five holes are wrapped around the shore of Lough Swilly. Hosted the 1999 European Ladies Professional Tournament.

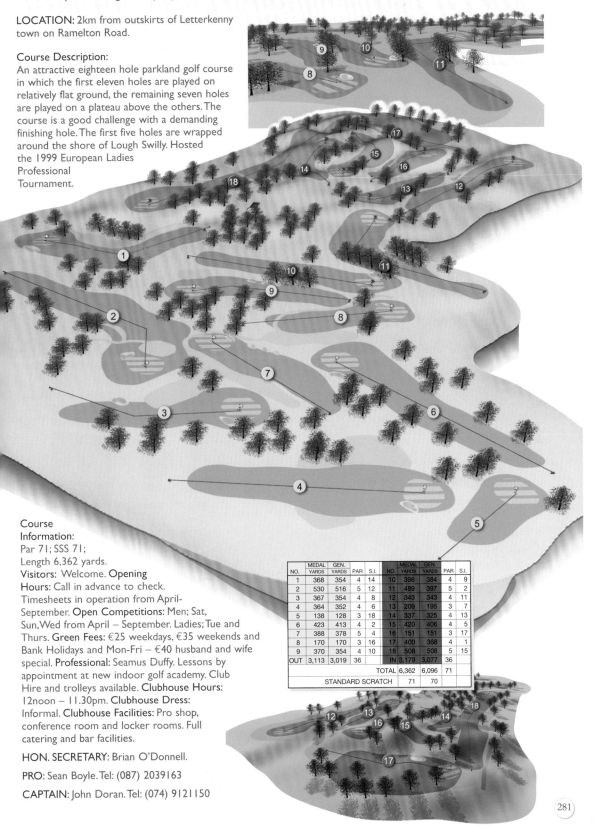

Course Information:
Par 71; SSS 71;
Length 6,362 yards.
Visitors: Welcome. **Opening Hours:** Call in advance to check. Timesheets in operation from April-September. **Open Competitions:** Men; Sat, Sun, Wed from April – September. Ladies; Tue and Thurs. **Green Fees:** €25 weekdays, €35 weekends and Bank Holidays and Mon-Fri – €40 husband and wife special. **Professional:** Seamus Duffy. Lessons by appointment at new indoor golf academy. Club Hire and trolleys available. **Clubhouse Hours:** 12noon – 11.30pm. **Clubhouse Dress:** Informal. **Clubhouse Facilities:** Pro shop, conference room and locker rooms. Full catering and bar facilities.

HON. SECRETARY: Brian O'Donnell.

PRO: Sean Boyle. Tel: (087) 2039163

CAPTAIN: John Doran. Tel: (074) 9121150

NO.	MEDAL YARDS	GEN. YARDS	PAR	S.I.	NO.	MEDAL YARDS	GEN. YARDS	PAR	S.I.
1	368	354	4	14	10	396	384	4	9
2	530	516	5	12	11	489	397	5	2
3	367	354	4	8	12	343	343	4	11
4	364	352	4	6	13	209	195	3	7
5	138	128	3	18	14	337	325	4	13
6	423	413	4	2	15	420	406	4	5
7	388	378	5	4	16	151	151	3	17
8	170	170	3	16	17	400	368	4	1
9	370	354	4	10	18	508	508	5	15
OUT	3,113	3,019	36		IN	3,179	3,077	36	
					TOTAL	6,362	6,096	71	
					STANDARD SCRATCH		71	70	

Narin & Portnoo

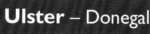

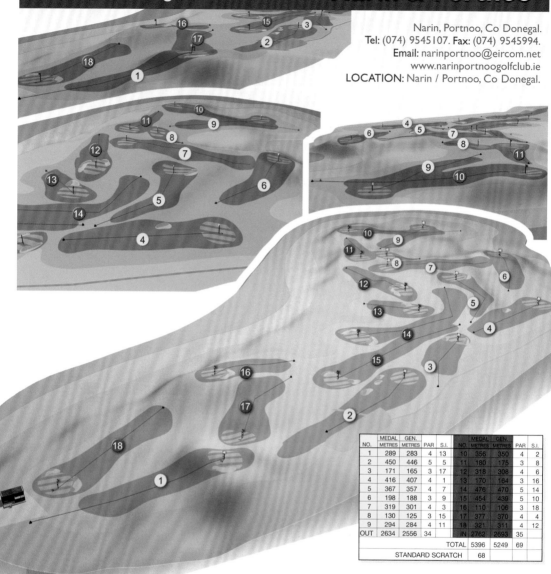

Narin, Portnoo, Co Donegal.
Tel: (074) 9545107. Fax: (074) 9545994.
Email: narinportnoo@eircom.net
www.narinportnoogolfclub.ie
LOCATION: Narin / Portnoo, Co Donegal.

NO.	MEDAL METRES	GEN. METRES	PAR	S.I.	NO.	MEDAL METRES	GEN. METRES	PAR	S.I.
1	289	283	4	13	10	356	350	4	2
2	450	446	5	5	11	180	175	3	8
3	171	165	3	17	12	318	308	4	6
4	416	407	4	1	13	170	164	3	16
5	367	357	4	7	14	476	470	5	14
6	198	188	3	9	15	454	439	5	10
7	319	301	4	3	16	110	106	3	18
8	130	125	3	15	17	377	370	4	4
9	294	284	4	11	18	321	311	4	12
OUT	2634	2556	34		IN	2762	2693	35	
					TOTAL	5396	5249	69	
					STANDARD SCRATCH		68		

Course Information:

Par 69; SSS 69; Length 5,930 yards. Visitors: Welcome.
Opening Hours: Daylight hours. Avoid: Sunday before 1pm.
Ladies: Welcome. Green Fees: €40 daily, €45 weekends.
Juveniles: Welcome. Clubhouse Hours: 9.00am – 12.00am.
Clubhouse Dress: Casual. Clubhouse Facilities: Bar and light
refreshments. Open Competitions: Open week from 18th –
26th of June. Open competitions regular during Summer..

SECRETARY: Willie Quinn.
ARCHITECT: Hughie McNeill and Leo Wallace.

Course Description:

Beautiful scenery and a quiet course,
although it is particularly popular in the
summer months as it is located in a Blue-
flag holiday area. Set amidst beautiful
scenery and historic landmarks on the
extreme west coast of Donegal, garnering
well deserved praise from both low and high
handicappers. A very popular location with
the best of links and inland characteristics.

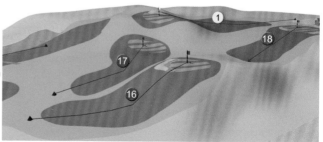

Lisfannon, Buncrana, Co. Donegal.   www.northwestgolfclub.com
Tel: (074) 936 1027 / 936 1715   Fax: (074) 936 3284

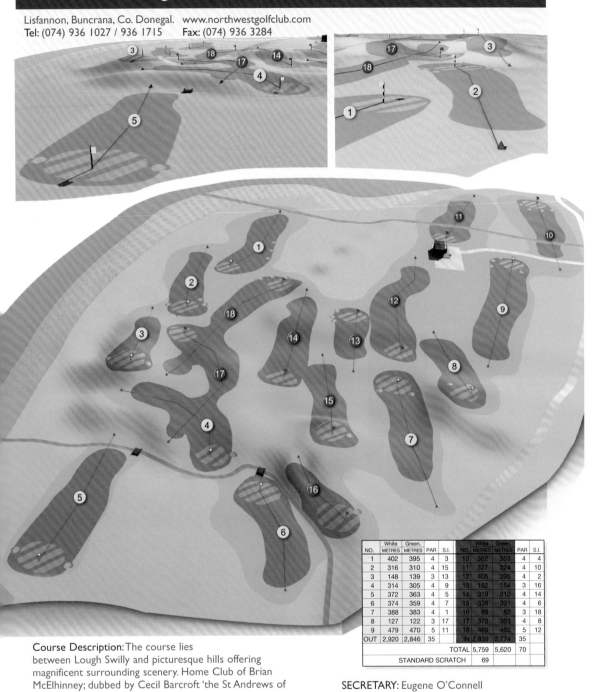

NO.	White METRES	Green. METRES	PAR	S.I.	NO.	White METRES	Green. METRES	PAR	S.I.
1	402	395	4	3	10	362	353	4	4
2	316	310	4	15	11	327	324	4	10
3	148	139	3	13	12	405	395	4	2
4	314	305	4	9	13	162	154	3	16
5	372	363	4	5	14	319	310	4	14
6	374	359	4	7	15	338	331	4	6
7	388	383	4	1	16	85	82	3	18
8	127	122	3	17	17	372	363	4	8
9	479	470	5	11	18	469	462	5	12
OUT	2,920	2,846	35		IN	2,839	2,774	35	
					TOTAL	5,759	5,620	70	
					STANDARD SCRATCH	69			

Course Description: The course lies between Lough Swilly and picturesque hills offering magnificent surrounding scenery. Home Club of Brian McElhinney; dubbed by Cecil Barcroft 'the St Andrews of Ireland' drawing comparisons with that famous links course.

SECRETARY: Eugene O'Connell

Tel: 086 66047299.

PROFESSIONAL: Seamus McBriarty.

Course Information:
Par 70; SSS 69; Length 5,759 metres. Visitors & Societies Welcome Mon-Fri and Weekends by arrangement.
Opening Hours: 8.00am till dark. (Links Course open all year round) **Avoid:** Weekends during October – March, 12.00 – 2.00pm Saturday and 8.30am – 11pm Sunday's. **Ladies:** Welcome. **Green Fees:** €30 weekdays (€15 with member), €30 weekends & Bank Hols (€25 with member). Societies: €25 weekdays, €30 weekends, Caddy cars always available. **Juveniles:** Welcome. **Clubhouse Dress:** Casual. **Clubhouse Facilities:** Locker room, showers. Full bar, catering facilities all week at 1.00pm. **Open Competitions:** Easter Open, Whit Open, Open week 15th July. Handicap certificate required.

Portsalon, Letterkenny, Co. Donegal.
Tel: (074) 915 9459. Fax: (074) 915 9919.
www.portsalongolfclub.ie
portsalongolfclub@eircom.net
LOCATION: Twenty miles north of Letterkenny
on western shore of Lough Swilly.
SECRETARY: Peter Doherty.

Course Information:
Par 72; SSS 72; Length 6,191 metres. **Visitors:** Welcome
(ring in advance). **Opening Hours:** Sunrise – Sunset.
Green Fees: €45 weekdays, €50 weekends & bank hols,
weekly tickets on request. **Ladies:** Welcome. **Juveniles:**
Should be accompanied by an adult. **Clubhouse Hours:**
8.30 – 11.30pm. **Clubhouse Facilities:** Bar snacks and
meals available everyday (April – October). Normal
clubhouse facilities. **Open Competitions:** Open Week
Sat. 30th June to Sun. 8th July inc.

NO.	MEDAL METRES	GEN. METRES	PAR	S.I.	NO.	MEDAL METRES	GEN. METRES	PAR	S.I.
1	349	333	4	13	10	141	133	3	18
2	396	361	4	3	11	497	485	5	4
3	327	325	4	15	12	166	159	3	14
4	470	450	5	11	13	322	313	4	12
5	180	171	3	9	14	387	366	4	2
6	408	406	4	1	15	140	131	3	16
7	343	332	4	7	16	355	342	4	10
8	467	456	5	17	17	477	469	5	8
9	409	406	4	5	18	364	358	4	6
OUT	3,349	3,240	37		IN	2,842	2,733	35	
					TOTAL	6,191	5,973	72	
	STANDARD SCRATCH					72	71		

Course Description:
A popular seaside links with quite narrow fairways. Greens are well
protected with bunkers, streams and natural sand dunes all coming
into play. Course runs in clockwise direction, so the out-of-bounds
is generally on left. The club celebrated its Centenary in 1991 and
in the same year built a new clubhouse. The entire course
has been modified.

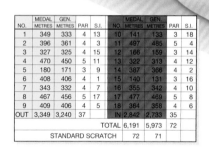

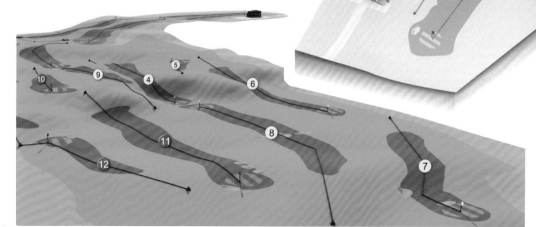

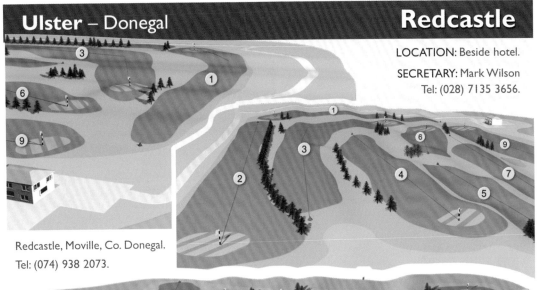

LOCATION: Beside hotel.

SECRETARY: Mark Wilson
Tel: (028) 7135 3656.

Redcastle, Moville, Co. Donegal.
Tel: (074) 938 2073.

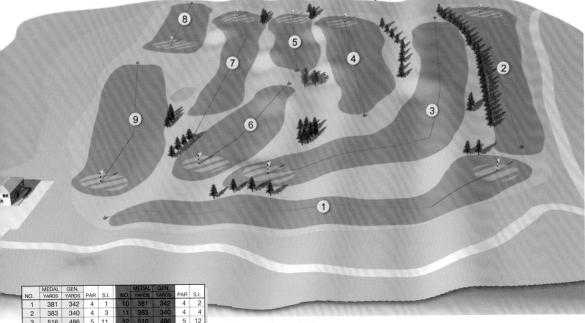

NO.	MEDAL YARDS	GEN. YARDS	PAR	S.I.	NO.	MEDAL YARDS	GEN. YARDS	PAR	S.I.
1	381	342	4	1	10	381	342	4	2
2	383	340	4	3	11	383	340	4	4
3	516	486	5	11	12	516	486	5	12
4	350	328	4	9	13	350	328	4	10
5	125	130	3	17	14	125	130	3	18
6	307	290	4	13	15	307	290	4	14
7	494	469	5	5	16	494	469	5	6
8	174	131	3	7	17	174	131	3	8
9	334	330	4	15	18	334	330	4	16
OUT	3,064	2,846	36		IN	3,064	2,846	36	
					TOTAL	6,128	5,692	72	
					STANDARD SCRATCH	71	72		

Course Description:
Difficult course set in a picturesque area on the shores of Lough Foyle, with the advantage of its own hotel. The two Par 3 holes are quite difficult and should be approached with the necessary respect.

Course Information:
Par 72; SSS 69; Length 6,128 yards. **Visitors:** Welcome to play midweek. **Opening Hours:** All day, all year. **Ladies:** Welcome. **Green Fees:** €20 Midweek, €25 Weekend. **Juveniles:** Welcome if accompanied by an adult. Half Price. **Open Competitions:** Various throughout the season. Information on request.

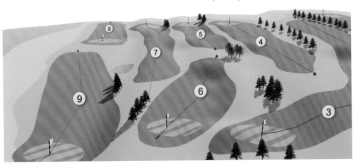

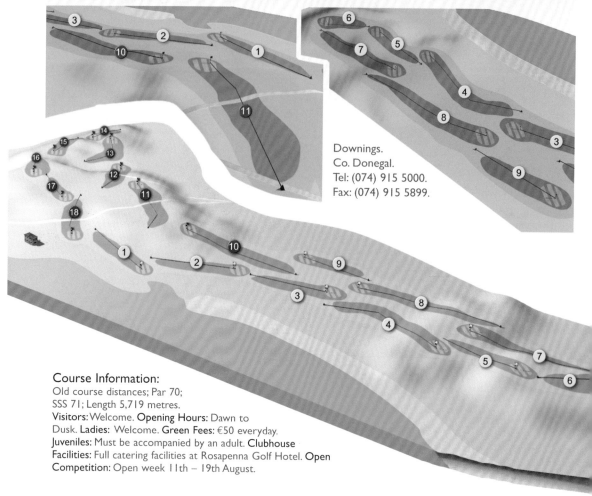

Downings.
Co. Donegal.
Tel: (074) 915 5000.
Fax: (074) 915 5899.

Course Information:

Old course distances; Par 70;
SSS 71; Length 5,719 metres.
Visitors: Welcome. **Opening Hours:** Dawn to
Dusk. **Ladies:** Welcome. **Green Fees:** €50 everyday.
Juveniles: Must be accompanied by an adult. **Clubhouse**
Facilities: Full catering facilities at Rosapenna Golf Hotel. **Open**
Competition: Open week 11th – 19th August.

Course Description:

This championship length links course is set in north west Donegal
at Downings. The first nine are played along a majestic stretch of
beach. Looping around a large bluff, the second nine have inland
characteristics. Very popular with visiting societies as the
Rosapenna Golf Hotel is situated on the course and and offers
special golf breaks.

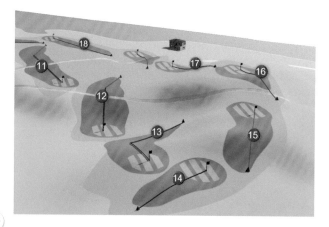

NO.	MEDAL METRES	MEDAL YARDS	PAR	S.I.	NO.	MEDAL METRES	MEDAL YARDS	PAR	S.I.
1	291	318	4	11	10	505	552	5	10
2	383	419	4	5	11	387	423	4	2
3	416	455	4	1	12	311	340	4	14
4	358	392	4	9	13	440	481	4	6
5	295	323	4	15	14	115	126	3	18
6	181	198	3	17	15	377	412	4	4
7	383	419	4	3	16	153	167	3	16
8	471	515	5	7	17	331	362	4	12
9	175	191	3	13	18	350	383	4	8
OUT	2,953	3,230	35		IN	2,969	3,246	35	
					TOTAL	5,922	6,476	70	
					STANDARD SCRATCH	71	71		

LOCATION: Two miles north of Carrigart.

SECRETARY: Frank Casey.

ARCHITECT: Original Course (1893) –
Old Tom Morris.

Email: golf@rosapenna.ie
Web: www.rosapenna.ie

Ulster – Donegal
Rosapenna (Sandy Hills)

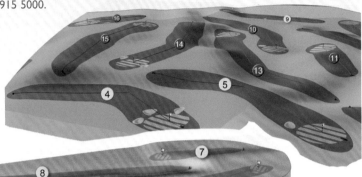

Downings. Co. Donegal. Tel: (074) 915 5000.
Fax: (074) 915 5899
Email: golf@rosapenna.ie
Web: www.rosapenna.ie

LOCATION: Two miles north
of Carrigart.
SECRETARY: Frank Casey.
ARCHITECT: Sandy Hills Links,
Pat Ruddy – 2003.

Course Information:
Par 71; SSS 73; Length 7,255
metres. **Visitors:** Welcome.
Opening Hours: Dawn to
Dusk. Ladies: Welcome.
Green Fees: €75 everyday.
Juveniles: Must be
accompanied by an adult.
Clubhouse Facilities: Full
catering facilities in season
or by arrangement. **Open
Competition:** Open
week 11th – 19th
August.

NO.	MEDAL YARDS	GEN. YARDS	PAR	S.I.	NO.	MEDAL YARDS	GEN. YARDS	PAR	S.I.
1	495	461	4	3	10	405	365	4	4
2	463	411	4	5	11	186	166	3	10
3	188	162	3	15	12	409	330	4	8
4	438	346	4	13	13	522	510	5	16
5	493	445	4	7	14	354	321	4	18
6	420	390	4	1	15	468	400	3	12
7	196	182	3	17	16	167	140	3	12
8	536	487	5	11	17	487	455	5	14
9	441	391	4	9	18	487	394	4	2
OUT	3,670	3,275	35		IN	3,485	3,081	71	
					TOTAL	7,155	6,356	71	
	STANDARD SCRATCH					73	70		

Course Description:
Almost every hole on Sandy Hills is in a subtly different
direction adding to the challenge in windy conditions. The
first six holes make an immediate impact. Each, except
the 3rd, is a par-4 that invites a well placed tee-shot
and not necessarily with the driver. The third hole
plays across a dune valley towards the ocean.
Hitting the greens at the par 3-7th and 11th is vital,
while the par 5-8th typifies the necessity for brain
rather than brawn to successfully negotiate the hole. The
final six holes maintain the incredibly high standard already
set. Accuracy, both off the tee and on the approach, are
the hallmark requirements of Sandy Hills.

Castle Place, Ardglass, Co. Down.
Tel: (028) 448 41219 Fax: (028) 448 41841
Email: info@ardglassgolfclub.com
Web: www.ardglassgolfclub.com

LOCATION:

Approx 7 miles from Downpatrick on B1.

CLUB MANAGER: Debbie Polly.
Tel: (028) 448 41219

PROFFESSIONAL: Philip Farrell.
Tel: (028) 448 41022

Course Description:

A seaside course with superb views over St. Johns Point, Killough Harbour and lying to the west, the Mourne Mountains. The 2nd (Howds) hole a 147 Metres, Par 3 is played over a gaping gorge to an elevated green. Another Par 3, the 12th is played from an elevated tee looking down to Coney Island. Both provide two memorable golf holes.

With the inclusion of three new challenging holes along Coney Island Bay with two of the new companion holes along the cliff and down to the sea, a little loop of beautiful challenging holes has been added to the charismatic links. This is a course not to be missed.

Course Information:

Par 70; SSS 70; Length 6,268 yards.
Visitors: Welcome Monday, Tuesday, Thursday & Friday. **Avoid:** Arrangement only Wednesday, Saturday, Sunday. **Green Fees:** £37 Mon – Fri; £52.50 weekends. **Ladies Day:** Wednesday. **Clubhouse Dress:** Smart dress. **Clubhouse Facilities:** Bistro menu available all day with the exception of Mondays, there is also a Practice area, Putting green, Shower facilities. **Open Competitions:** Phone club for details or visit club website.

NO.	MEDAL YARDS	GEN. YARDS	PAR	S.I.	NO.	MEDAL YARDS	GEN. YARDS	PAR	S.I.
1	335	292	4	10	10	205	181	3	13
2	167	160	3	14	11	488	465	4	3
3	334	269	4	16	12	198	187	3	7
4	375	351	4	6	13	397	333	4	1
5	151	135	3	18	14	400	362	4	11
6	414	394	4	4	15	491	480	5	15
7	219	205	3	12	16	422	384	4	5
8	439	430	4	2	17	361	356	4	9
9	527	503	5	8	18	345	304	4	17
OUT	2,739	2,752	34		IN	3,307	3,052	36	
				TOTAL	6,268	5,791	70		
		STANDARD SCRATCH			70	68			

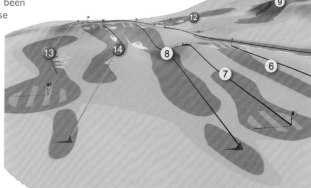

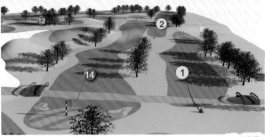

Course Description:
The course is a mature parkland course set in the rolling drumlins of Co. Down. Signature holes are the 6th hole with its menacing pond and the par 3, 210 yd. The 10th hole where playing for a safe 4 is usually the best option! The course provides a challenge to all golfers whether scratch or 24 handicaps, without being intimidating.

Huntly Road, Banbridge.
Co. Down. BT32 3UR
Tel: (028) 4066 2211.
banbridgegolf@btconnect.com

Course Information:
Par 69; SSS 67; Length 5,590 metres. Visitors: Contact Pro Shop (028) 4062 6189. Green Fees: £17 Mon – Fri (£10 with member); Weekends £22 (£12 with member). Ladies £14 (£10 with member) Juveniles £6. Students £10. Winter packages available, phone club for information. Ladies - Weekend £17 (£12 with member) **Ladies Day:** Tuesday. **Clubhouse Dress:** Casual. **Clubhouse Facilities:** Well stocked Pro Shop, superb luxurious clubhouse, restaurant & conference room. **Open Competitions:** Telephone Club for details.

LOCATION: 1 mile from town centre on Huntly Road.

HON SEC: Tom Mulholland.

GENERAL MANAGER: John McKeown

NO.	MEDAL YARDS	GEN. YARDS	PAR	S.I.	NO.	MEDAL YARDS	GEN. YARDS	PAR	S.I.
1	364	346	4	9	10	221	218	3	4
2	491	448	5	5	11	345	335	4	6
3	309	300	4	17	12	128	122	3	18
4	365	350	4	3	13	327	310	4	16
5	375	358	4	1	14	521	513	5	2
6	336	314	4	7	15	164	108	3	14
7	315	314	4	15	16	327	323	4	12
8	158	153	3	11	17	310	306	4	8
9	338	333	4	13	18	196	190	3	10
OUT	3,051	2,916	36		IN	2,539	2,425	33	
					TOTAL	5,590	5,341	69	
					STANDARD SCRATCH		69	68	

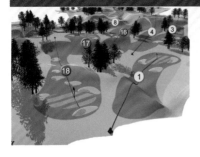

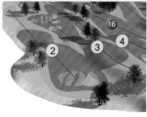

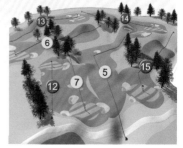

Broadway, Bangor, Co. Down.
Tel: (028) 9127 0922. Fax: (028) 9145 3394.
Email: bangorgolfclubni@btconnect.com
LOCATION: 1 mile from town centre off
Donaghadee Road.

PROFESSIONAL:
Michael Bannon.
Tel: (028) 9146 2164.
ARCHITECT:
James Braid.

Course Description:

Bangor Golf Course is a pleasant, well-groomed, scenic parkland course. The four 'pitch' holes balance the three Par 5's, and the long and difficult Par 4, 5th hole. Recent improvements in fairway drainage and in the treatment of greens have resulted in the course returning to its previous year-round excellence. A major tree planting programme has been undertaken. It remains a challenge and a pleasure to both 'single-figure' and less serious players.

Course Information:

Par 71; SSS 71; Length 6,410 yards. **Visitors:** Welcome, Monday, Wednesday, Thursday, Friday & Sunday. **Avoid:** 1.00pm – 2.00pm every day; Wednesday, Friday after 4.00pm; Sunday morning. Members only Tuesday and Saturday. **Green Fees:** £25 Mon – Fri (£15 with member); £33 Sun / all bank holidays. Weekends (£20 with member). For special rates contact the golf manager. **Ladies Day:** Tuesday. **Juveniles:** Weekdays up to 12 noon only. Lessons by prior arrangements. Golf trolleys & motorised buggies available. **Clubhouse Facilities:** Bar snacks up to 7.30pm. Lunch and evening meal – booking is essential. No catering on Mondays from Oct – Mar. Tel: (028) 9127 0483. **Clubhouse Dress:** Jacket and tie in dining room. No denim at any time.

NO.	MEDAL YARDS	GEN. YARDS	PAR	S.I.	NO.	MEDAL YARDS	GEN. YARDS	PAR	S.I.
1	351	341	4	9	10	438	417	4	4
2	493	482	5	13	11	319	309	4	16
3	359	339	4	15	12	194	175	3	8
4	471	461	5	7	13	384	374	4	6
5	463	455	4	1	14	175	163	3	12
6	354	344	4	17	15	408	398	4	2
7	192	182	3	5	16	510	482	5	18
8	409	391	4	11	17	159	149	3	10
9	392	384	4	3	18	339	323	4	14
OUT	3,484	3,379	37		IN	2,926	2,790	34	
					TOTAL	6,410	6,169	71	
					STANDARD SCRATCH	71	70		

LOCATION: Ten miles from Belfast – three miles from Bangor, Co. Down.

NO.	MEDAL YARDS	GEN. YARDS	PAR	S.I.	NO.	MEDAL YARDS	GEN. YARDS	PAR	S.I.
1	354	343	4	12	10	436	421	4	3
2	540	529	5	4	11	354	341	4	15
3	212	206	3	6	12	166	152	3	9
4	306	295	4	18	13	436	415	4	1
5	419	398	4	2	14	491	475	5	11
6	332	321	4	14	15	404	385	4	7
7	165	165	3	16	16	180	164	3	5
8	325	305	4	10	17	355	340	4	13
9	480	471	5	8	18	349	331	4	17
OUT	3,133	3,033	36		IN	3,171	3,024	35	
					TOTAL	6,304	6,057	71	
					STANDARD SCRATCH				

Crawfordsburn Rd.
Clandeboye, Co. Down.
Tel: (028) 9185 2706.
Fax: (028) 9185 3785.

PROFESSIONAL: Debbie Hanna.
ARCHITECT: Simon Gidman.
GENERAL MANAGER: Richard Gibson.
Tel: (028) 9185 2706.

Course Description:

Blackwood Golf Centre is Ulster's premier pay and play golf facility. Opened in 1994, the centre comprises Hamilton course – an eighteen hole championship standard course, Temple course – an eighteen hole, par 3 course, plus a twenty bay covered, floodlit driving range. The centre also boasts a bar & grill.

Course Information:

Par 71; SSS 70; Length 6,304 yards. **Visitors:** Welcome. **Opening Hours:** 8am – 10pm. **Green Fees:** £20 midweek & £25 weekends and Bank Holidays (booking advised). **Opening hours:** 8 a.m –10 p.m. **Driving Range:** 10am –10pm. **Golf Centre Dress:** Smart /casual. **Golf Centre Facilities:** Bar and grill (with lunch menu).

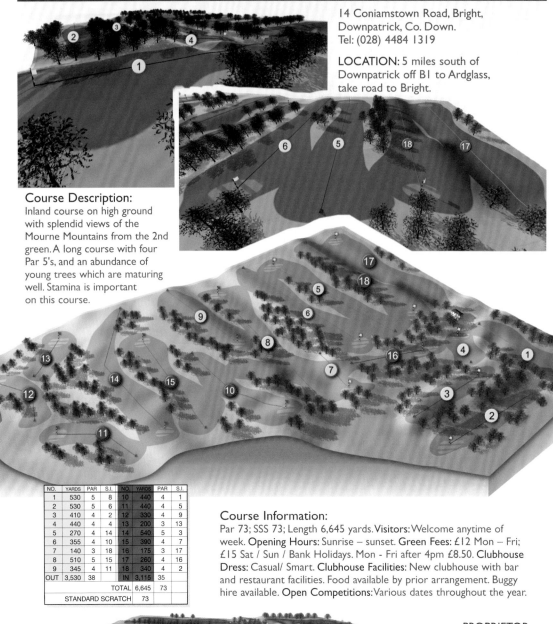

14 Coniamstown Road, Bright,
Downpatrick, Co. Down.
Tel: (028) 4484 1319

LOCATION: 5 miles south of
Downpatrick off B1 to Ardglass,
take road to Bright.

Course Description:

Inland course on high ground
with splendid views of the
Mourne Mountains from the 2nd
green. A long course with four
Par 5's, and an abundance of
young trees which are maturing
well. Stamina is important
on this course.

NO.	YARDS	PAR	S.I.	NO.	YARDS	PAR	S.I.
1	530	5	8	10	440	4	1
2	530	5	6	11	440	4	5
3	410	4	2	12	330	4	9
4	440	4	4	13	200	3	13
5	270	4	14	14	540	5	3
6	355	4	10	15	390	4	7
7	140	3	18	16	175	3	17
8	510	5	15	17	260	4	16
9	345	4	11	18	340	4	2
OUT	3,530	38		IN	3,115	35	
				TOTAL	6,645	73	
				STANDARD SCRATCH		73	

Course Information:

Par 73; SSS 73; Length 6,645 yards. Visitors: Welcome anytime of
week. **Opening Hours:** Sunrise – sunset. **Green Fees:** £12 Mon – Fri;
£15 Sat / Sun / Bank Holidays. Mon - Fri after 4pm £8.50. **Clubhouse
Dress:** Casual/ Smart. **Clubhouse Facilities:** New clubhouse with bar
and restaurant facilities. Food available by prior arrangement. Buggy
hire available. **Open Competitions:** Various dates throughout the year.

PROPRIETOR:
Gordan Ennis.
Tel: 07770 922943
SECRETARY:
Harry Scott.

ARCHITECT: Mr A. Ennis (Sen).

Station Road, Bangor, Co. Down.
Tel: (028) 9146 5004
Fax: (028) 9127 3989

LOCATION: 2 Miles West of Bangor.

SECRETARY: Gary Steele.
Tel: (028) 9127 0368

Course Information:
Par 69; SSS 67; Length 5,647 yards.
Visitors: Welcome any day. **Avoid:** Saturday.
Ladies: Welcome. **Green Fees:** £16.50 Mon – Fri; £21 Sat – Sun.
Juveniles: Must be accompanied by an adult. Lessons available by prior arrangement. Club Hire and trollys available. **Clubhouse Dress:** Informal except Saturday night. Jacket and tie after 8.00pm. **Clubhouse Facilities:** Full facilities. Lunches, snacks 11.30am – 2.30pm. Snacks, high tea, á la carte 5pm to 10pm.

NO.	YARDS	PAR	S.I.	NO.	YARDS	PAR	S.I.
1	265	4	7	10	296	4	2
2	346	4	17	11	157	3	1
3	200	3	13	12	328	4	0
4	454	5	11	13	176	3	1
5	406	4	3	14	276	4	4
6	344	4	9	15	182	3	1
7	293	4	1	16	513	5	6
8	409	4	15	17	336	3	1
9	141	3	5	18	434	4	8
OUT	2,908	35		IN	2,699	35	
				TOTAL	5,649	70	
				STANDARD SCRATCH		70	

Course Description:
The course is situated on rising ground by the shores of Belfast Lough and the turf is of inland variety. The railway line runs parallel and adjacent to the 1st hole so one has to be careful not to be playing three off the tee! If your game is not working on all cylinders you can enjoy the scenery instead.

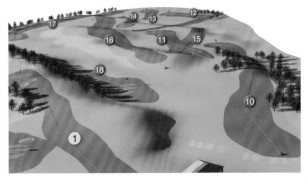

293

Clandeboye (Ava)

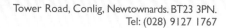

Tower Road, Conlig, Newtownards. BT23 3PN.
Tel: (028) 9127 1767

LOCATION: Above Conlig Village off A21 between Bangor and Newtownards.

GENERAL MANAGER: John W. Thomson.

PROFESSIONAL: Peter Gregory.
Tel: (028) 9127 1750

ARCHITECT: Dr Von Limburger, William Rennick Robinson .

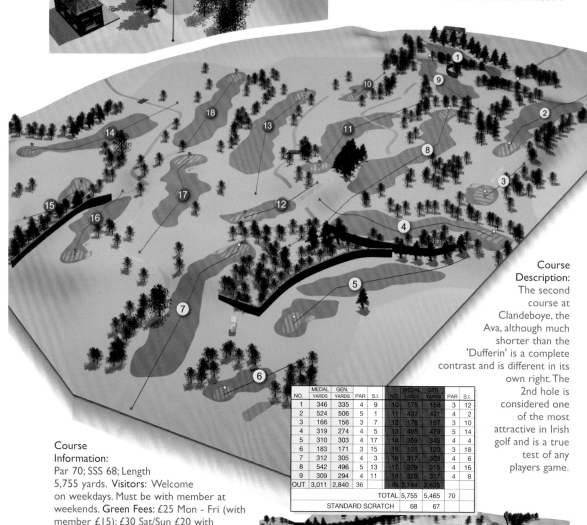

Course Description:
The second course at Clandeboye, the Ava, although much shorter than the 'Dufferin' is a complete contrast and is different in its own right. The 2nd hole is considered one of the most attractive in Irish golf and is a true test of any players game.

Course Information:
Par 70; SSS 68; Length 5,755 yards. **Visitors:** Welcome on weekdays. Must be with member at weekends. **Green Fees:** £25 Mon - Fri (with member £15); £30 Sat/Sun £20 with member. Club Hire and Caddy cars also available. **Clubhouse Dress:** Smart / Casual. **Clubhouse Facilities:** Full facilities (except during the winter closed on Mon). Prior arrangement required. Snacks, meals 10.00am - 10.00pm. **Open Competitions:** Numerous throughout the year. Letter of introduction required, if possible.

NO.	MEDAL YARDS	GEN. YARDS	PAR	S.I.	NO.	MEDAL YARDS	GEN. YARDS	PAR	S.I.
1	346	335	4	9	10	175	158	3	12
2	524	506	5	1	11	432	421	4	2
3	166	156	3	7	12	178	167	3	10
4	319	274	4	5	13	495	479	5	14
5	310	303	4	17	14	359	345	4	4
6	183	171	3	15	15	131	120	3	18
7	312	305	4	3	16	317	303	4	6
8	542	496	5	13	17	329	315	4	16
9	309	294	4	11	18	328	317	4	8
OUT	3,011	2,840	36		IN	2,744	2,625		
					TOTAL	5,755	5,465	70	
					STANDARD SCRATCH	68	67		

Clandeboye (Dufferin)

Tower Road, Conlig, Newtownards, BT23 3PN.
Tel: (028) 9127 1767

LOCATION: Above Conlig Village off A21 between Bangor and Newtownards.

GENERAL MANAGER: John W. Thomson.

PROFESSIONAL: Peter Gregory. Tel: (028) 9127 1750

ARCHITECT: William Rennick Robinson, Dr Von Limburger.

Course Information:
Par 71; SSS 71;
Length 6,559 yards.
Visitors: Welcome on weekdays. Must be with members at weekends. **Green Fees:** £30 Mon – Fri (with member £16). £35 Sat/Sun/Bank Holidays (£25 with member) Lessons available by prior arrangement. Club Hire and Caddy cars available. **Clubhouse Facilities:** Full facilities. Prior arrangement required. Snacks, meals 10.00am – 10.00pm. **Open Competitions:** Numerous throughout the year contact: (028) 9127 1767. Letter of introduction required, if possible, for open competitions.

NO.	MEDAL YARDS	GEN YARDS	PAR	S.I.	NO.	MEDAL YARDS	GEN YARDS	PAR	S.I.
1	388	378	4	7	10	415	403	4	2
2	172	162	3	5	11	153	142	3	12
3	417	403	4	9	12	490	481	5	16
4	389	378	4	1	13	360	350	4	10
5	183	169	3	13	14	167	153	3	8
6	521	509	5	17	15	495	483	5	18
7	360	349	4	15	16	392	381	4	4
8	452	440	4	3	17	375	351	4	14
9	397	385	4	11	18	433	418	4	6
OUT	3,279	3,173	35		IN	3,280	3,162	36	
					TOTAL	6,548	6,320	71	
					STANDARD SCRATCH		71	70	

Course Description:

One of North Down's most popular golf clubs, Clandeboye, has two courses – the Ava and the Dufferin. The latter being the Championship one, the short Par 4, 1st giving no indication of the stern test ahead. The course is laid out on the hills above Conlig village and has superb views over Belfast Lough and the Irish sea. The course is now recognised as one of the great inland golfing experiences in Ireland.

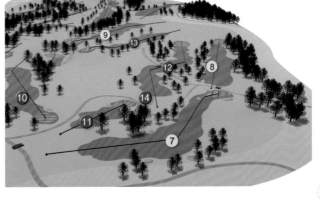

231 Derryboye Road,
Crossgar, Co. Down, BT30 9DL.
Tel: (028) 4483 1523

LOCATION: Close to the village of
Crossgar, Co. Down.

HON SECRETARY: Adrian Bell.
Tel: (028) 4483 1523

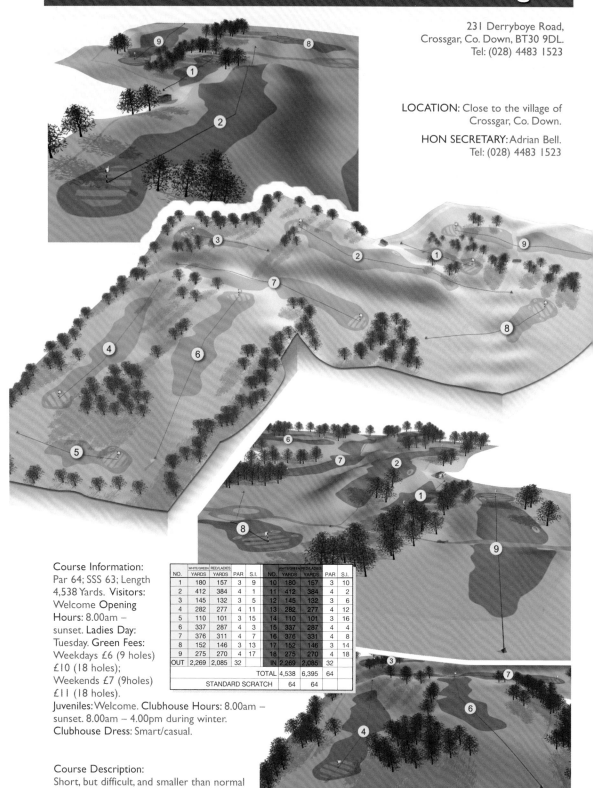

Course Information:
Par 64; SSS 63; Length
4,538 Yards. **Visitors:**
Welcome **Opening
Hours:** 8.00am –
sunset. **Ladies Day:**
Tuesday. **Green Fees:**
Weekdays £6 (9 holes)
£10 (18 holes);
Weekends £7 (9holes)
£11 (18 holes).
Juveniles: Welcome. **Clubhouse Hours:** 8.00am –
sunset. 8.00am – 4.00pm during winter.
Clubhouse Dress: Smart/casual.

NO.	WHITE/GREEN YARDS	RED/LADIES YARDS	PAR	S.I.	NO.	WHITE/GREEN YARDS	RED/LADIES YARDS	PAR	S.I.
1	180	157	3	9	10	180	157	3	10
2	412	384	4	1	11	412	384	4	2
3	145	132	3	5	12	145	132	3	6
4	282	277	4	11	13	282	277	4	12
5	110	101	3	15	14	110	101	3	16
6	337	287	4	3	15	337	287	4	4
7	376	311	4	7	16	376	331	4	8
8	152	146	3	13	17	152	146	3	14
9	275	270	4	17	18	275	270	4	18
OUT	2,269	2,085	32		IN	2,269	2,085	32	
					TOTAL	4,538	6,395	64	
					STANDARD SCRATCH		64	64	

Course Description:
Short, but difficult, and smaller than normal
greens. A test to all types of golfers.

Donaghadee

84 Warren Road, Donaghadee, Co. Down.

Tel: (028) 9188 3624.

Email: deegolf@freenet.co.uk

LOCATION: 5 miles south of Bangor on A2 on Coast Road.

GENERAL MANAGER: Gareth Boyd

Tel: (028) 9188 3624.

PROFESSIONAL: Gordon Drew.

Course Description:

A part links and part inland open course with little rough but several water hazards which can catch the unthinking shot. The 18th with out-of-bounds on both left and right can be intimidating. Lovely views over the Copeland Islands to the Scottish Coast, particularly from the 16th tee. Well appointed clubhouse.

NO.	MEDAL YARDS	GEN. YARDS	PAR	S.I.	NO.	MEDAL YARDS	GEN. YARDS	PAR	S.I.
1	268	251	4	16	10	371	354	4	1
2	435	383	5	10	11	317	302	4	11
3	369	360	4	4	12	429	421	5	17
4	362	322	4	8	13	140	115	3	13
5	337	310	4	2	14	364	353	4	3
6	333	305	4	12	15	322	308	4	7
7	299	291	4	14	16	303	290	4	15
8	299	293	4	6	17	169	156	3	5
9	116	100	3	18	18	337	327	4	9
OUT	2,818	2,615	36		IN	2,752	2,626	35	
					TOTAL	5,570	5,241	71	
					STANDARD SCRATCH	69	68		

Course Information:

Par 71; SSS 69;
Length 5,570 metres.
Visitors: Welcome on any weekday and Sunday.
Members only on Saturday.
Avoid: Saturdays. Green Fees: £23 Mon – Fri; £26 Sunday. Special rates for societies. Special offers to include food. Juveniles: Mon – Fri and Sun. Must be accompanied by an adult. Lessons available by prior arrangement. Club Hire available also. Clubhouse Facilities: Full facilities; 10.00am – 9.00pm Tues – Sun during winter; 7 days a week in summer. Open Competitions: Open week: June 14th - 18th; Youth Tournament: 13th–17th Aug. Various others throughout the season; telephone club for details.

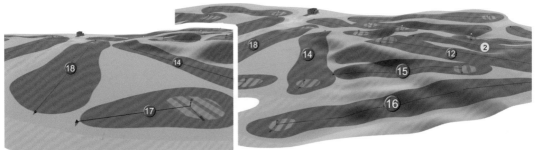

43 Saul Road, Downpatrick, Co. Down BT30 6PA
Tel: (028) 4461 2152
Email: office@downpatrickgolf.co.uk
Web: www.downpatrickgolf.co.uk

Course Description:
Recently upgraded, challenging parkland course. 5th hole particularly challenging. Excellent drainage so open all year round.

LOCATION: 25 miles south of Belfast on (A7) and 1.5 miles south east of Downpatrick town centre.

HON. SECRETARY: Joe McCoubrey.

COURSE MANAGER: Emmett Curran.
Tel: (028) 4461 5947

ARCHITECT: Martin Hawtree.

NO.	MEDAL METRES	GEN. METRES	PAR	S.I.	NO.	MEDAL YARDS	GEN. YARDS	PAR	S.I.
1	374	368	4	3	10	362	326	4	10
2	298	293	4	1	11	181	170	3	12
3	506	500	5	7	12	544	538	5	4
4	176	166	3	1	13	390	379	4	6
5	457	457	4	1	14	424	390	4	2
6	330	324	4	1	15	171	168	3	16
7	437	427	4	3	16	364	338	4	14
8	135	129	3	5	17	278	270	4	18
9	337	325	4	9	18	336	330	4	8
OUT	3,050	2,989	35		IN	3,050	2,909	34	
					TOTAL	6,100	5,898	69	
		STANDARD SCRATCH				69			

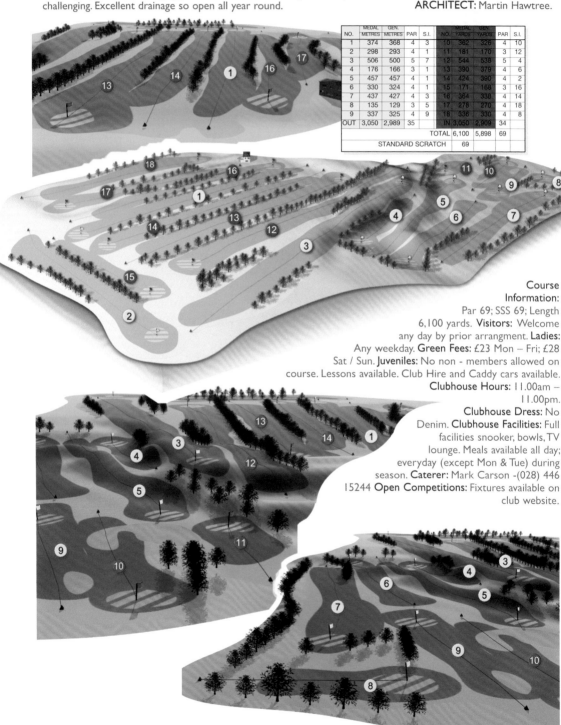

Course Information:
Par 69; SSS 69; Length 6,100 yards. **Visitors:** Welcome any day by prior arrangment. **Ladies:** Any weekday. **Green Fees:** £23 Mon – Fri; £28 Sat / Sun. **Juveniles:** No non - members allowed on course. Lessons available. Club Hire and Caddy cars available. **Clubhouse Hours:** 11.00am – 11.00pm. **Clubhouse Dress:** No Denim. **Clubhouse Facilities:** Full facilities snooker, bowls, TV lounge. Meals available all day; everyday (except Mon & Tue) during season. **Caterer:** Mark Carson -(028) 446 15244 **Open Competitions:** Fixtures available on club website.

Golf Road, Helen's Bay, Bangor, Co. Down.
Tel: (028) 9185 2601
Fax: (028) 91 852660

Web: www.helensbaygc.com
Email: mail@helensbaygc.com

LOCATION: 9 miles east of
Belfast on A2.

SECRETARY MANAGER: Alan

Briggs.

Course
Information:
Par 68; SSS 67;
Length 5,643 yards.
Visitors: Welcome to play;
Mon, Wed, Thurs up to 1.30pm.
Fri and Sun. (Fri Jul/Aug after
11.30am). **Avoid:** Tue, Thur (after 1.30pm)
Sat before 6.00pm. Tuesday – members only.
Green Fees: £19 Mon-Thurs; £22 Fri-Sun / Public
Holidays. **Juveniles:** Under 18's must be accompanied by an
adult and unable to play after 6.00pm Mon – Fri. **Clubhouse
Hours:** 9.00am – 11.30am. **Clubhouse Dress:** Smart casual
dress is permitted until 7.30pm. After 7.30pm gentlemen
must wear a jacket, collar and tie. Tee shirts or denim jeans
are not acceptable on the course or in the Clubhouse.
Clubhouse Facilities: Full facilities. Evening meals until
9.00pm. **Open Competitions:** Open week; July.
Numerous other competitions –
telephone for details.

NO.	MEDAL YARDS	GEN. YARDS	PAR	S.I.	NO.	MEDAL YARDS	GEN. YARDS	PAR	S.I.
1	266	272	4	15	10	286	272	4	16
2	330	320	4	11	11	330	320	4	12
3	373	357	4	1	12	373	357	4	2
4	124	106	3	3	13	127	106	3	4
5	332	312	4	17	14	332	312	4	18
6	353	314	4	5	15	328	314	4	6
7	285	274	4	13	16	285	274	4	14
8	186	178	3	7	17	201	178	3	8
9	325	315	4	9	18	325	315	4	10
OUT	2,574	2,448	34		IN	2,587	2,448	34	
					TOTAL	5,161	4,896	68	
	STANDARD SCRATCH					67	66		

Course Description:
This popular course is
compact with the layout encircling
the Clubhouse. The turf is of the inland
variety, greens are small making
scoring more difficult than first
impressions would suggest. There
are extensive views of the Antrim
Hills across Belfast Lough. The 4th
hole, a short pitch over trees to a
green protected by bunkers on three
sides, is a particularly interesting one.

Course Information: Par 69; SSS 68; Length 5,480 metres.
Opening hours: Sunrise - Sunset. **Visitors:**
Welcome to play. **Green Fees:** Mon-Fri £22
(18 holes) £11 (9 holes) £14 (with
menber), Sat- Sun £27 (18 holes) £13 (9
holes) £18 (with member), Juveniles £9 (18
holes) £5 (9 holes). **Juveniles:** Lessons
available by prior arrangments. Club Hire
and Caddy service available. Clubhouse Hours:
9.00am-11.30pm. **Clubhouse Dress:** Smart / casual,
no denims or training shoes on course or in Clubhouse.
Clubhouse Facilities: Full facilities. Snacks evening meals all
day everyday (except Monday). **Open Competitions:** Open
Week in August. Various other open competitions throughout the summer –
telephone club for details.

Demesne Road,
Holywood, Co Down.
Tel: (028) 9042 3135

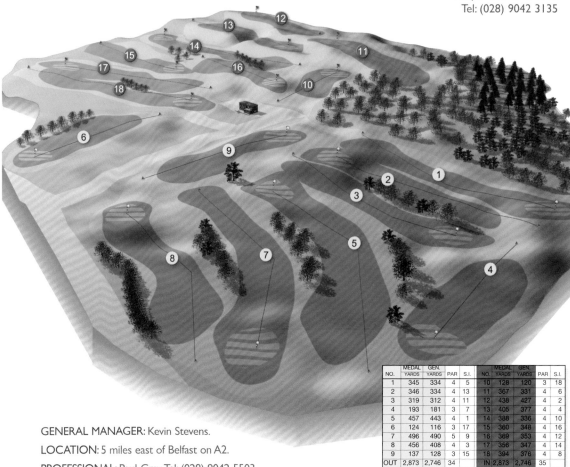

GENERAL MANAGER: Kevin Stevens.

LOCATION: 5 miles east of Belfast on A2.

PROFESSIONAL: Paul Gray. Tel: (028) 9042 5503.

NO.	MEDAL YARDS	GEN. YARDS	PAR	S.I.	NO.	MEDAL YARDS	GEN. YARDS	PAR	S.I.
1	345	334	4	5	10	128	120	3	18
2	346	334	4	13	11	367	331	4	6
3	319	312	4	11	12	438	427	4	2
4	193	181	3	7	13	405	377	4	4
5	457	443	4	1	14	388	336	4	10
6	124	116	3	17	15	360	348	4	16
7	496	490	5	9	16	369	353	4	12
8	456	408	4	3	17	356	347	4	14
9	137	128	3	15	18	394	376	4	8
OUT	2,873	2,746	34		IN	2,873	2,746	35	
					TOTAL	6,078	5,761	69	
					STANDARD SCRATCH	68	66		

Course Description:

Hilly parkland course over-looking Holywood, and
with excellent views over Belfast Lough. The first
nine play on the slopes of the Holywood Hills, whilst
the back nine are more varied with some interesting
tee shots and some steep hills and valleys. Most of
the greens run toward the sea.

Mourne Park, Kilkeel, Co Down.
Tel: (028) 4176 5095 Fax: (028) 4176 5579

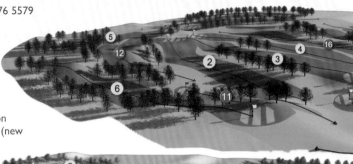

LOCATION: Three miles from Kilkeel on main Newry Road.

SECRETARY: S. C. McBride.

ARCHITECT: Lord Justice Babington (original nine holes); Mr. E. Hackett (new development).

NO.	YARDS	PAR	S.I.	NO.	YARDS	PAR	S.I.
1	314	4	12	10	314	4	12
2	340	4	5	11	340	4	5
3	170	3	9	12	170	3	9
4	280	4	18	13	280	4	18
5	380	5	6	14	380	5	6
6	165	3	16	15	165	3	16
7	282	4	14	16	282	4	14
8	425	5	13	17	425	5	13
9	165	3	3	18	165	3	3
OUT	2,521	35		IN	2,521	35	
				TOTAL	5,042	70	
	STANDARD SCRATCH					67	

Course Information:

Par 72; SSS 72; Length 6,579 yards. **Opening hours:** Sunrise – sunset. **Visitors:** Welcome Mon, Wed, Thurs, Fri and Sun. **Avoid:** Tues & Sat. Ladies Day: Tuesday. **Green Fees:** £23 Mon – Fri, £15 with member; £28 weekends, £18 with member. **Societies:** £20 weekday, £25 weekend. Juveniles: Up to 5.00pm. Caddy cars available by prior arrangment. **Clubhouse Dress:** Neat/casual. **Clubhouse Facilities:** Full facilities. Snacks, evening meals all day during summer or by prior arrangment. **Open Competitions:** Several throughout the year. Contact club for details.

Course Description:
Situated at the foot of Knockcree Mountain, the course is ringed by woodlands and masses of rhododendron shrubs in an area that might well be described as the Garden of Mourne. The course was enlarged in 1993 from 9 holes to 18 holes.

142 Main Road, Cloughey, Co Down, BT22 IJA.
Tel: (028) 4277 1233 Fax: (028) 4277 1699
Email: kirkstown@supanet.com
Web: www.linksgolfkirkistown.com

LOCATION: Approx. 45 mins. from Belfast, 16 miles from Newtownards on the A2.

HON. SECRETARY: Rosemary Coulter.

PROFESSIONAL: Richard Whitford. Tel: (028) 4277 1004.

ARCHITECT: J Braid.

Course Description:
This fine old links course, designed by the legendary course architect Jim Braid, on the coast of County Down, has a tremendous variety of holes. The long 398 metre par 4 10th, plays like a par 5 when into the wind. A true and fair test of golf catering for low and high handicappers alike. You will find a warm and friendly atmosphere in the clubhouse. This course dries so quickly after bad weather that it is usually open when other courses are closed.

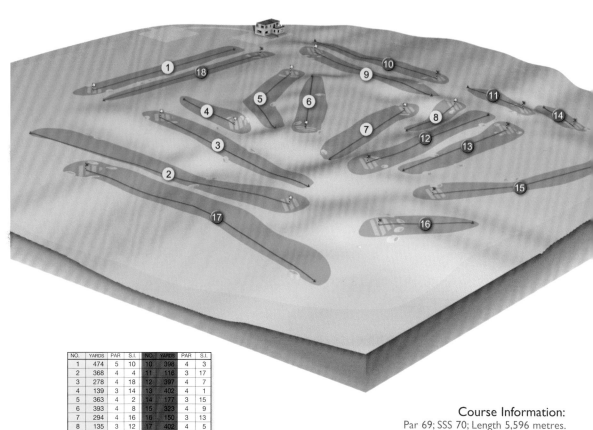

NO.	YARDS	PAR	S.I.	NO.	YARDS	PAR	S.I.
1	474	5	10	10	398	4	3
2	368	4	4	11	116	3	17
3	278	4	18	12	397	4	7
4	139	3	14	13	402	4	1
5	363	4	2	14	177	3	15
6	393	4	8	15	323	4	9
7	294	4	16	16	150	3	13
8	135	3	12	17	402	4	5
9	351	4	6	18	479	5	11
OUT	2,795	35		IN	2,844	34	
				TOTAL	5,639	70	
	STANDARD SCRATCH				70		

Course Information:
Par 69; SSS 70; Length 5,596 metres.
Opening hours: 8am - Dusk. **Visitors:** Welcome any day except Saturday.
Avoid: Friday mornings. **Green Fees:** £25 Mon – Fri; (£15 with a member); £30 Sat / Sun / All public holidays (£20 with a member).
Juveniles: £7 Mon – Fri; £8 – Sat / Sun, must be accompanied by an adult. Can play anytime. **Clubhouse Hours:** 9am – 10.30pm.
Clubhouse Dress: Casual, jacket and tie after 7.30pm.
Clubhouse Facilities: Trolleys and Golf Clubs for hire. Bar & catering facilities daily. Evening meals must be ordered before commencing play. **Open Competitions:** Throughout the season. Open Week June/July.

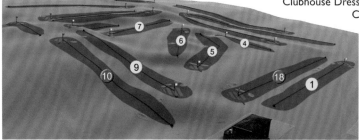

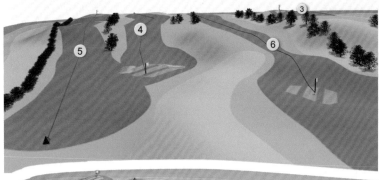

SECRETARY: Mr Marshall.

Tel: (028) 9754 1234.

SHOP: Mr Macaw.

Tel: (028) 9754 1234.

ARCHITECT: Mr Robinson, Bangor.

NO.	YARDS	PAR	S.I.	NO.	YARDS	PAR	S.I.
1	332	4	7	10	332	4	8
2	255	4	17	11	255	4	18
3	310	4	13	12	310	4	14
4	336	4	11	13	336	4	12
5	386	4	3	14	386	4	2
6	385	4	5	15	385	4	4
7	436	4	1	16	448	5	8
8	129	3	15	17	129	3	16
9	336	4	9	18	336	4	10
OUT	2,905	35		IN	2,917	36	
				TOTAL	5,822	71	
			STANDARD SCRATCH		68		

Course Information:
Par 71; SSS 70; Length 5,822 yards 5,108 metres. **Opening hours:** 9.00am – 9.00pm. **Visitors:** Welcome to play. **Avoid:** Sat before 4.30pm and Wed after 4.30pm. **Ladies day:** Mondays. **Green Fees:** £13 Mon – Fri; £18 Sat / Sun / Bank hols. **Juveniles:** Juveniles competition day Thursday. Handicap Certificate required for Open Competitions only. Prior arrangement required. **Clubhouse Hours:** 9.00am – 5.30pm. **Clubhouse Dress:** Casual. Jacket and tie at all functions. **Clubhouse Facilities:** Meals by prior arrangement. No bar. **Open Competitions:** Open week July.

Comber, Newtownards, Co Down.
Tel: (028) 9754 1234.

LOCATION: Take Killyleagh Road from Comber, in less than a mile take a road to left, signposted Mahee Island. Bear left for 6 miles to Mahee Island.

Course Description:
A nine hole course sited on an island in Strangford Lough with excellent views for 360 degrees. The course is parkland with luscious fairways and well manicured greens. The undulating fairways and tricky approach shots make this a good test of golf. The course record stands at 66 so it is no pushover. One to visit, not only for the golf enthusiast, but for the views.

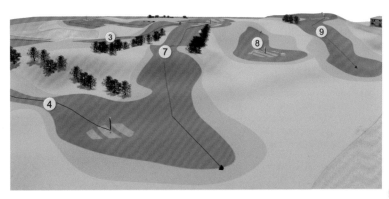

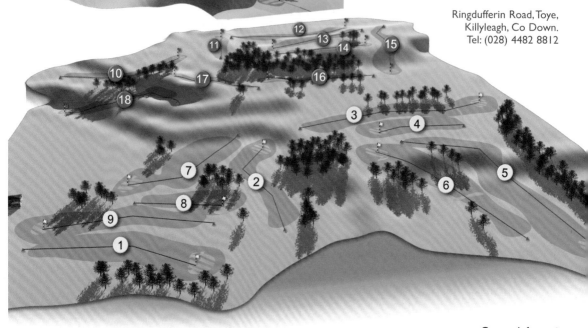

LOCATION: Three miles north of Killyleagh off Comber Road.

COURSE SECRETARY: Helen Lindsay.
Tel: (028) 4482 8812

MENS CLUB SECRETARY: Willis Marshall.

LADIES CLUB SECRETARY: Sharon Neill.

PRESIDENT: Raymond McGrory.

SECRETARY/MANAGER: Jim Lindsay.

Ringdufferin Road, Toye,
Killyleagh, Co Down.
Tel: (028) 4482 8812

Email: country-club@btconnect.com

Course Information:
Par 68; SSS 65; Length 5,302 metres. **Visitors:** Welcome at all times (some restrictions Jul & Aug). **Opening Hours:** Dawn – Dusk. **Ladies:** Welcome. **Green Fees:** Mid-week; £12, 18 holes, £8, 9 holes. Weekends, Public Holidays; £14, 18 holes, £9, 9 holes. Juniors and Senior Citizens; £5, 9 holes, £7, 18 holes, Mon-Fri before 12. £6, 9 holes, £14 18 holes, Weekends and Public Holidays. **Clubhouse Dress:** Casual. **Clubhouse Facilities:** Practice putting green, practice range, training bunker & training net. Restaurant & Bar, tennis courts & fitness suite, hairdressers & beauticians, fitness classes. **Open Competitions:** Contact club for details.

NO.	YARDS	PAR	S.I.	NO.	YARDS	PAR	S.I.
1	352	4	6	10	325	4	1
2	285	4	10	11	145	3	7
3	338	4	8	12	276	4	17
4	192	3	4	13	341	4	5
5	467	5	16	14	308	4	9
6	342	4	2	15	136	3	13
7	303	4	12	16	303	4	11
8	132	3	14	17	101	3	15
9	318	4	18	18	429	4	3
OUT	2,729	35		IN	2,364	33	
				TOTAL	5,093	68	
		STANDARD SCRATCH				65	

Course Description:
An 18 hole course with excellent views. The course runs over drumlins (rounded hills) with undulating fairways and tricky approach shots which make this a testing course to play on. Idyllic views over Strangford Lough from some of the elevated tees.

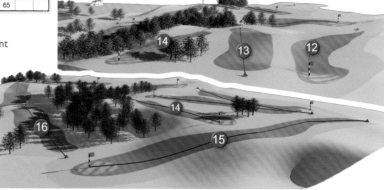

Station Road, Craigavad,
Holywood, Co Down.
Tel: (028) 9042 8165.

LOCATION:
7 miles east of Belfast on A2.

MANAGER: Susanna Morrison.
Tel: (028) 9042 8165

PROFESSIONAL: Andrew Ferguson.
Tel: (028) 9042 8586

ARCHITECT: H. C. Colt.

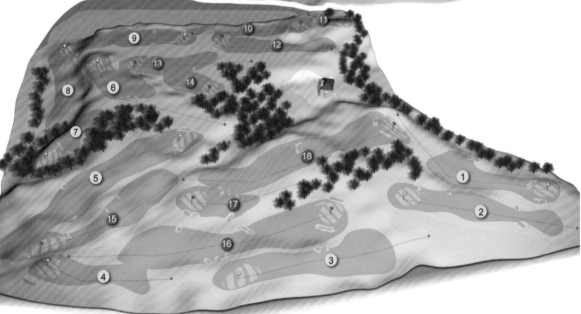

NO.	MEDAL YARDS	GEN. YARDS	PAR	S.I.	NO.	MEDAL YARDS	GEN. YARDS	PAR	S.I.
1	417	414	4	7	10	303	299	4	14
2	404	400	4	3	11	165	162	3	8
3	372	359	4	13	12	433	430	4	4
4	143	140	3	15	13	360	357	4	12
5	555	550	5	9	14	187	184	3	10
6	351	348	4	11	15	410	407	4	2
7	184	164	3	17	16	485	476	5	16
8	394	392	4	5	17	193	190	3	18
9	409	406	4	1	18	509	506	5	6
OUT	3,229	3,173	35		IN	3,045	3,011	35	
					TOTAL	6,274	6,184	70	
					STANDARD SCRATCH		71	70	

Course Information:
Par 70; SSS 71; Length 6,274 yards. **Visitors:** Welcome any day except Wednesday, Saturday before 4.30pm and Fridays after 1.00pm is members only. **Opening Hours:** 7.30am – 7.30pm. **Avoid:** Wednesday. **Green Fees:** £46 Mon – Fri; £56 Saturday / Sunday / all public holidays. Buggy hire £25 per round. **Clubhouse Dress:** Smart / casual. **Juveniles:** Must be accompanied by an adult. Lessons available by prior arrangement. **Clubhouse Facilities:** Changing Facilities, Full catering and bar.

Course Description:
Eighteen hole parkland course rolls gently to the shores of Belfast Lough. The course is very picturesque with many mature trees and many carefully placed bunkers. The greens are undulating and generally run towards the sea. A very pleasant course that presents a challenge to any handicap of golfer.

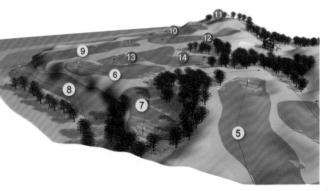

Newcastle, Co. Down. BT33 OAN Tel: (028) 43723314 Fax: (028) 4372 6281

Email: golf@royalcountydown.org
Web: www.royalcountydown.org

SECRETARY: J.H. Laidler.
Tel: (028) 4372 3314

PROFESSIONAL: Kevan J. Whitson.
Tel: (028) 4372 2419

ARCHITECT: Tom Morris

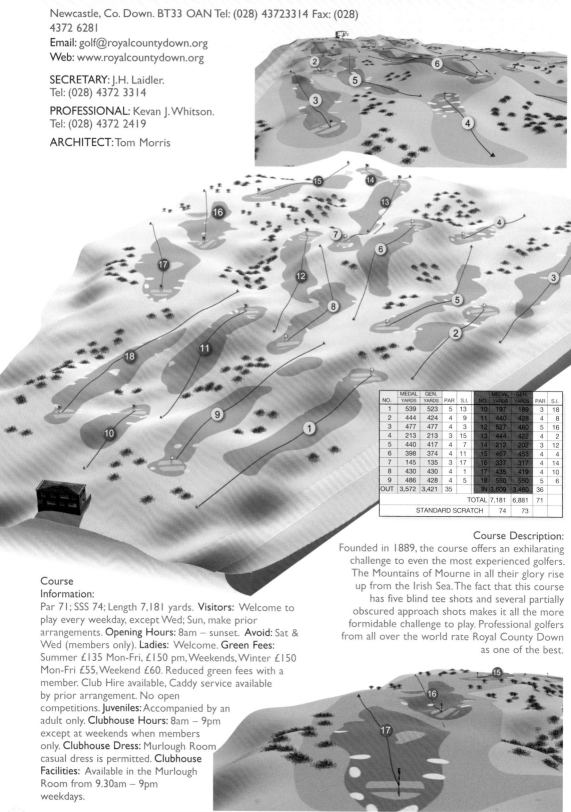

NO.	MEDAL YARDS	GEN. YARDS	PAR	S.I.	NO.	MEDAL YARDS	GEN. YARDS	PAR	S.I.
1	539	523	5	13	10	197	189	3	18
2	444	424	4	9	11	440	428	4	8
3	477	477	4	3	12	527	480	5	16
4	213	213	3	15	13	444	422	4	2
5	440	417	4	7	14	212	202	3	12
6	398	374	4	11	15	467	453	4	4
7	145	135	3	17	16	337	317	4	14
8	430	430	4	1	17	435	419	4	10
9	486	428	4	5	18	550	550	5	6
OUT	3,572	3,421	35		IN	3,609	3,460	36	
					TOTAL	7,181	6,881	71	
					STANDARD SCRATCH	74	73		

Course Description:
Founded in 1889, the course offers an exhilarating challenge to even the most experienced golfers. The Mountains of Mourne in all their glory rise up from the Irish Sea. The fact that this course has five blind tee shots and several partially obscured approach shots makes it all the more formidable challenge to play. Professional golfers from all over the world rate Royal County Down as one of the best.

Course Information:
Par 71; SSS 74; Length 7,181 yards. **Visitors:** Welcome to play every weekday, except Wed; Sun, make prior arrangements. **Opening Hours:** 8am – sunset. **Avoid:** Sat & Wed (members only). **Ladies:** Welcome. **Green Fees:** Summer £135 Mon-Fri, £150 pm, Weekends, Winter £150 Mon-Fri £55, Weekend £60. Reduced green fees with a member. Club Hire available, Caddy service available by prior arrangement. No open competitions. **Juveniles:** Accompanied by an adult only. **Clubhouse Hours:** 8am – 9pm except at weekends when members only. **Clubhouse Dress:** Murlough Room casual dress is permitted. **Clubhouse Facilities:** Available in the Murlough Room from 9.30am – 9pm weekdays.

233 Scrabo Road, Newtownards, Co Down.
Tel: (028) 9181 2355 Fax: (028) 9182 2919

LOCATION: 10 miles from Belfast off the main Belfast to Newtownards carriageway, (follow signs for Scrabo Country Pk).

MANAGER: Bill Brown.
Tel: (028) 9181 2355

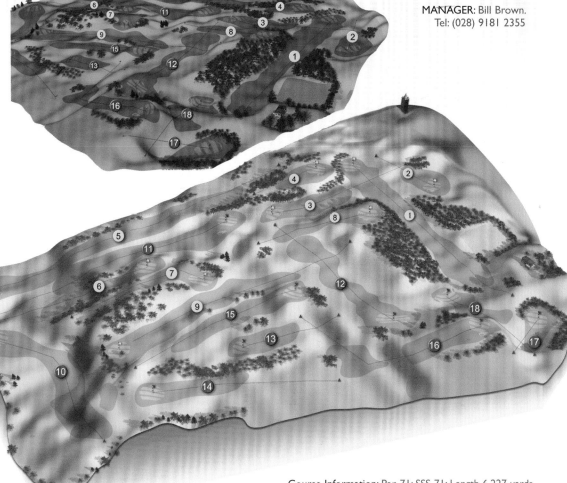

Course Information: Par 71; SSS 71; Length 6,227 yards. **Visitors:** Welcome. **Opening Hours:** 9am – sunset. **Avoid:** Saturday & Wednesday afternoons. **Ladies:** Anyday except Sat. **Green Fees:** £19 Mon – Fri; £24 weekend. **Juveniles:** Not to play after 5.30pm. Must be accompanied by an adult member. Lessons and Caddy service available by prior arrangements. Club Hire, motorised buggies available also by prior arrangements. **Clubhouse Hours:** 8.30am – 11pm. Full clubhouse facilities. **Clubhouse Dress:** Informal. Jacket & Tie after 7.30pm in Dining Room. No Denim. **Catering Facilities:** Excellent Cuisine, varied times, Tel: (028) 9181 5048

NO.	YARDS	PAR	S.I.	NO.	YARDS	PAR	S.I.
1	459	4	1	10	322	4	16
2	163	3	9	11	474	5	14
3	415	4	3	12	443	4	2
4	128	3	17	13	204	3	8
5	555	5	7	14	384	4	10
6	313	4	15	15	378	4	6
7	320	4	11	16	345	4	4
8	318	4	13	17	145	4	4
9	565	5	5	18	296	4	12
OUT	3,236	36		IN	2,991	35	
			TOTAL		6,227	70	
	STANDARD SCRATCH					71	

Course Description: The course winds its way around Scrabo Hill and Tower, one of the well-known Co. Down landmarks. Fabulous views over Strangford Lough and Mourne Mountains (the 2nd hole is called Mourne View). Narrow fairways bordered by heath and gorse call for accurate driving.

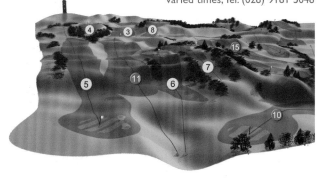

20 Grove Road, Ballynahinch, Co. Down.
Tel: (028) 9756 2365

LOCATION: 11 miles south of Belfast on the main road to Newcastle.

HON. SECRETARY: Brian Wilton.

Tel: (028) 9756 2365

SECRETARY / MANAGER: Terry Magee.

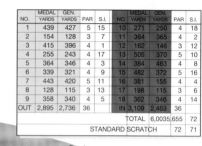

NO.	MEDAL YARDS	GEN. YARDS	PAR	S.I.	NO.	MEDAL YARDS	GEN. YARDS	PAR	S.I.
1	439	427	5	15	10	271	250	4	18
2	154	128	3	7	11	364	365	4	2
3	415	396	4	1	12	162	146	3	12
4	255	243	4	17	13	505	370	5	10
5	364	346	4	3	14	384	463	4	8
6	339	321	4	9	15	482	372	5	16
7	443	420	5	11	16	381	155	4	4
8	128	115	3	13	17	198	115	3	6
9	358	340	4	5	18	362	346	4	14
OUT	2,895	2,736	36		IN	3,109	2,463	36	
					TOTAL	6,003	5,655	72	
					STANDARD SCRATCH			72	71

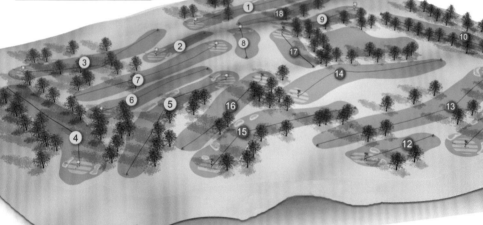

Course Description:

Each fairway is lined with trees, and several high points on the course give scenic views of the countryside. The 8th and 17th give panoramic views of the Mourne Mountains. This is a relatively new eighteen hole golf course which has been laid out adjacent to the Monalto Estate. Not physically demanding and many of the views on the course overlook the Mourne Mountains. Wildlife is also a great feature of the course.

Course Information:

Par 72; SSS 72; Length 6,003 metres. **Visitors:** Welcome any day except Saturdays. **Green Fees:** £20.00 Mon – Fri; £25.00 Sun / Bank Holidays. **Ladies:** Welcome. **Ladies:** Competition – Friday. **Juveniles:** Must be accompanied by an adult at weekends and off the course by 6.00pm during weekdays. **Clubhouse Hours:** 8.30am – 11.30pm. **Clubhouse Facilities:** Full clubhouse facilities all week. Bar snacks from 12noon – 3.00pm. Arrangements for parties. **Clubhouse Dress:** Casual – no denims. **Open Competitions:** Open Week; 4th – 11th Aug.

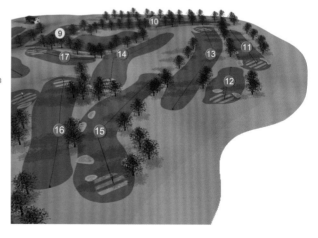

Warrenpoint

Lower Dromore Road,
Warrenpoint,
Co. Down.
Tel: (028) 4177 53695

SECRETARY / MANAGER:
Marian Trainor.
Tel: (028) 4175 3695

PROFESSIONAL: Nigel Shaw.
Tel: (028) 4175 2371

Course Information:

Par 71; SSS 70;
Length 5,618 metres.
Visitors: Welcome Mon, Thurs & Fri. By arrangement Wed & Sun. **Avoid:** Tues & Sat. **Green Fees:** £28 Mon – Fri; £34 Sat/Sun/ Bank Holidays. **Juveniles:** Must be accompanied by an adult. Lessons available. Club Hire and Caddy Cars available by prior arrangement. **Clubhouse Hours:** 8.30am – 12midnight. **Clubhouse Facilities:** Full clubhouse facilities everyday. Catering 10.30am – 9.30pm. **Clubhouse Dress:** Respectable dress essential. **Open Competitions:** Open Week June. Handicap certificate is required for open competitions.

NO.	MEDAL METRES	GEN. METRES	PAR	S.I.	NO.	MEDAL METRES	GEN. METRES	PAR	S.I.
1	471	466	5	5	10	180	175	3	12
2	165	159	3	3	11	258	250	4	16
3	458	450	5	7	12	307	294	4	10
4	482	468	5	17	13	339	329	4	2
5	305	300	4	11	14	137	127	3	18
6	140	130	3	9	15	466	461	5	8
7	374	368	4	1	16	158	151	3	14
8	318	309	4	13	17	402	399	4	4
9	270	260	4	15	18	388	364	4	6
OUT	2,983	2,910	37		IN	2,635	2,550	34	
TOTAL						5,618	5,460	71	
STANDARD SCRATCH						70	69		

Course Description:

The course is set in parkland with picturesque views of the Carlingford Mountains. Although not a long course, it demands from the golfer straight driving and skill around the greens. There are five par 3's and four par 5's so it offers plenty of variety.

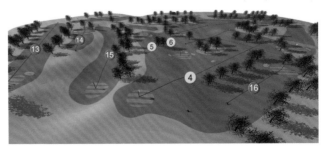

Castle Hume, Enniskillen, Co. Fermanagh.
Tel: (028) 6632 7077 Fax: (028) 6632 7076
info@castlehumegolf.com
www.castlehumegolf.com

LOCATION:
A few minutes drive from
Enniskillen on the A46
Belleek/Donegal Road.

OFFICE ADMINISTRATOR:
Wilma Connor.

MANAGER: Pat Duffy.

PROFESSIONAL:
Shaun Donnelly.

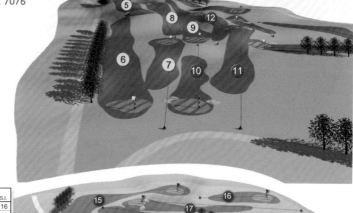

NO.	MEDAL METRES	GEN. METRES	PAR	S.I.	NO.	MEDAL METRES	GEN. METRES	PAR	S.I.
1	340	330	4	7	10	331	327	4	16
2	145	137	3	17	11	458	453	5	10
3	452	449	5	5	12	327	322	4	4
4	171	168	3	13	13	158	154	3	12
5	387	371	4	1	14	378	366	4	2
6	519	479	5	15	15	455	445	5	8
7	355	351	4	3	16	139	131	3	18
8	330	324	4	11	17	343	333	4	6
9	351	343	4	9	18	293	287	4	14
OUT	3,050	2,952	36		IN	2,882	2,818	36	
					TOTAL	5,932	5,770		
					STANDARD SCRATCH	71	70		

Course Description:
Castle Hume
championship golf course is
situated within the grounds of old
Ely Estate, surrounded by Castle Hume
Lake and Lower Lough Erne. It is one of
the most scenic parkland areas in
Fermanagh Lakelands. Hospitality service
for cruising golfers from local Carrick
Reagh Jetty. Castle Hume Golf Course has
hosted the Ulster Professional
Championship in 2003 and 2004.

Course Information:
Par 72; SSS 71;
Length 5,932 metres.
Visitors/Groups: Welcome.
Opening Hours: Dawn – Dusk. **Green Fees:** Mon – Fri £25; Weekends/Bank Holidays £35, Reduced rates for groups of 13+. **Clubhouse Facilities:** New 10,000 sq.ft Colonial style clubhouse, complete with full bar/catering facilities. Driving range and practice area. Hospitality Conference room available. **Open Competitions:** Open Week July 2nd-9th. Erne Waterways June 9th-10th. Lakeland Open July 21st-& 22nd. Wednesday Open Stablefords, April to October £15.

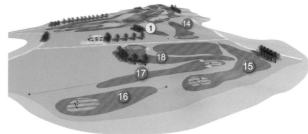

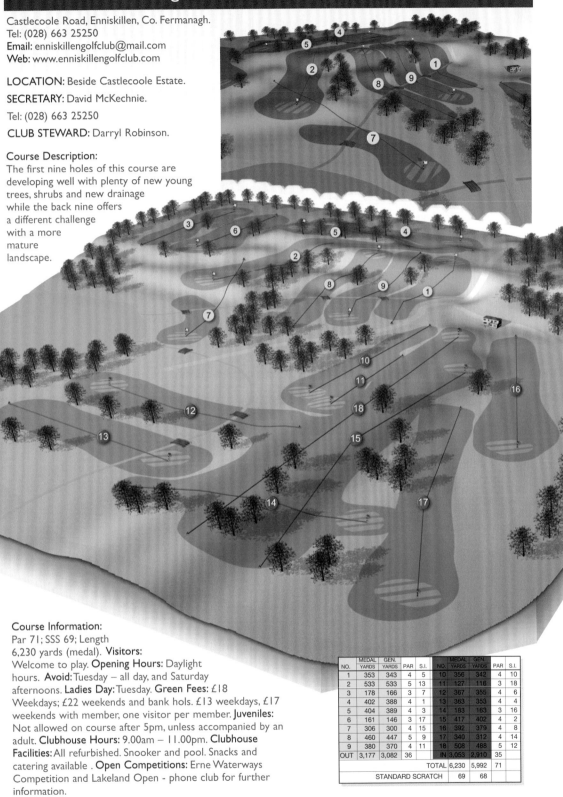

Castlecoole Road, Enniskillen, Co. Fermanagh.
Tel: (028) 663 25250
Email: enniskillengolfclub@mail.com
Web: www.enniskillengolfclub.com

LOCATION: Beside Castlecoole Estate.

SECRETARY: David McKechnie.

Tel: (028) 663 25250

CLUB STEWARD: Darryl Robinson.

Course Description:
The first nine holes of this course are developing well with plenty of new young trees, shrubs and new drainage while the back nine offers a different challenge with a more mature landscape.

Course Information:
Par 71; SSS 69; Length 6,230 yards (medal). **Visitors:** Welcome to play. **Opening Hours:** Daylight hours. **Avoid:** Tuesday – all day, and Saturday afternoons. **Ladies Day:** Tuesday. **Green Fees:** £18 Weekdays; £22 weekends and bank hols. £13 weekdays, £17 weekends with member, one visitor per member. **Juveniles:** Not allowed on course after 5pm, unless accompanied by an adult. **Clubhouse Hours:** 9.00am – 11.00pm. **Clubhouse Facilities:** All refurbished. Snooker and pool. Snacks and catering available . **Open Competitions:** Erne Waterways Competition and Lakeland Open - phone club for further information.

NO.	MEDAL YARDS	GEN. YARDS	PAR	S.I.	NO.	MEDAL YARDS	GEN. YARDS	PAR	S.I.
1	353	343	4	5	10	356	342	4	10
2	533	533	5	13	11	127	116	3	18
3	178	166	3	7	12	367	355	4	6
4	402	388	4	1	13	363	353	4	4
5	404	389	4	3	14	183	163	3	16
6	161	146	3	17	15	417	402	4	2
7	306	300	4	15	16	392	379	4	8
8	460	447	5	9	17	340	312	4	14
9	380	370	4	11	18	508	488	5	12
OUT	3,177	3,082	36		IN	3,053	2,910	35	
					TOTAL	6,230	5,992	71	
					STANDARD SCRATCH	69	68		

Brown Trout Golf Club, 209 Agivey Road, Aghadowey, Co. L/Derry.
TEL: (028) 7086 8209
FAX: (028) 7086 8878

Email: jane@browntroutinn.com
www.browntroutinn.com

Course Information:

Par 70; SSS 68; Length 5,510 yards. **Visitors:** Always welcome. **Opening Hours:** 7.00am – sunset. **Ladies:** No restrictions. **Green Fees:** Mon – Fri £10; weekends / holidays £15. **Juveniles:** Must be accompanied by an adult on weekends / holidays / Wednesday & Thursday evenings. **Clubhouse Hours:** 7.00am – midnight. **Clubhouse Dress:** Casual. **Clubhouse Facilities:** 15 bedroom hotel, gym and full bar / restaurant. Four 5 star cottages. **Open Competitions:** 1st Friday of month May – September.

NO.	YARDS	PAR	S.I.	NO.	YARDS	PAR	S.I.
1	466	5	15	10	466	5	16
2	189	3	3	11	189	3	4
3	286	4	9	12	286	4	10
4	155	3	11	13	155	3	12
5	492	5	1	14	492	5	2
6	313	4	7	15	313	4	8
7	345	4	5	16	345	4	14
8	345	4	13	17	345	4	14
9	164	3	17	18	164	3	18
OUT	2,755	35		IN	2,755	35	
				TOTAL	5,510	70	
				STANDARD SCRATCH		68	

Course Description:

A nine hole parkland course which crosses water seven times and is heavily wooded. The feature hole is the 2nd, a 170 yard carry across the Agivey River.

LOCATION: 7 miles from Coleraine on A54 / B66 intersection.

SECRETARY / MANAGER:
Bill O'Hara. Tel: (028)7086 8209

PROFESSIONAL: Ken Revie.

ARCHITECT: Bill O'Hara Snr.

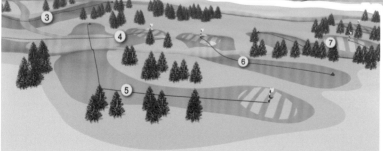

65 Circular Rd, Castlerock.
Tel: (028) 7084 8314

LOCATION: Six miles north-west of Coleraine.

SECRETARY: Mark Steen.

PROFESSIONAL: Ian Blair. Tel: (028) 7084 9424

ARCHITECT: Ben Sayers.

CATERER: Tel: (028)7084 9869.

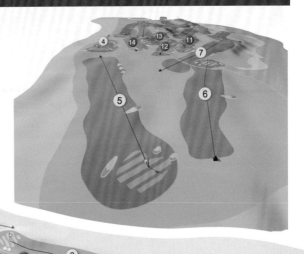

Course Information:

Par 73; SSS 72; Length 6,499
Yards. **Visitors:** Welcome. **Opening
Hours:** Sunrise – sunset. Weekends by
arrangement Sat/Sun from 3pm and Sun 9.30-
10.15 am. **Ladies Day:** Friday. **Green Fees:** Mon – Fri
£60, Weekends £75. **Juveniles:** Lessons by prior
arrangements; Club Hire available. Caddy service available by
prior arrangements. **Clubhouse Hours:** 8am – 12 midnight.
Clubhouse Facilities: Full clubhouse facilities; Snacks; meals by
arrangement. **Clubhouse Dress:** Neat (no denims / trainers)
jacket & tie for functions. **Open
Competitions:** Open Week – July.

NO.	MEDAL YARDS	GEN. YARDS	PAR	S.I.	NO.	MEDAL YARDS	GEN. YARDS	PAR	S.I.
1	343	348	4	5	10	386	391	4	4
2	366	375	4	13	11	485	509	5	16
3	493	509	5	11	12	420	430	4	1
4	184	200	3	8	13	363	379	4	14
5	472	477	5	15	14	182	192	3	9
6	336	347	4	7	15	510	518	5	6
7	407	409	4	2	16	145	157	3	18
8	400	411	4	3	17	485	493	5	12
9	193	200	3	17	18	330	342	4	10
OUT	3,194	3,276	36		IN	3,305	3,411	37	
					TOTAL	6,499	6,687	73	
					STANDARD SCRATCH		72	71	

Course Description:

A true links course, with two courses —
eighteen holes and nine holes. Main feature is
the 4th hole with a burn on left and a railway
on the right! The club claims the best greens
in Ireland twelve months of the year.
Castlerock can sometimes be underestimated,
or not appreciated for the magnificent links
course that it is. There are also superb views
to Donegal and over
to Scotland.

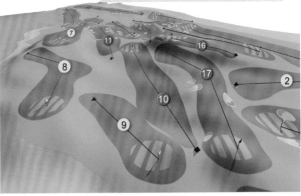

49 Victoria Road,
Londonderry, BT47 2PU.
Tel: (028) 71346369
Fax: (028) 7131 0008.
info@cityofderrygolfclub.com
www.cityofderrygolfclub.com

LOCATION: Three miles from city centre on A5 to Strabane, turn left.

HON. SECRETARY: Noreen Allen.
PROFESSIONAL: Michael Doherty.
Tel: (028) 7131 1496.

Course Information:

Par 71; SSS 71; Length 6,429 yards. **Visitors:** Welcome anytime. Weekends – please check with the club professional. Contact club for booking. **Opening Hours:** Sunrise – sunset. **Avoid:** Tuesday (ladies day). **Green Fees:** £25 Monday – Friday; Weekend & Bank Holidays £30. 9 hole course everyday, Adults £5, Juveniles £3. Members half price. 10% discount - GUI members. Handicap certificate required. **Juveniles:** Handicap, 12 and under anytime, otherwise with adult only. 9 hole course £3. Lessons by prior arrangement. Full clubhouse facilities. **Clubhouse Hours:** 8.00am – 12.00 midnight. **Clubhouse Dress:** Smart / casual (no jeans). **Clubhouse Facilities:** Bar snacks, full meals everyday except Monday. Handicap Certificate is required for Open competitions. Driveway and car park are on a steep slope up from below level 1. **Open Competitions:** Open Week - phone club for future information. Texaco Team Classic Weekend.

Course Description:

Parkland course overlooking River Foyle with views towards Donegal. Undulating terrain well lined by plenty of trees. There is also an easy nine hole course which is very suitable for those beginning golf.

NO.	MEDAL YARDS	GEN. YARDS	PAR	S.I.	NO.	MEDAL YARDS	GEN. YARDS	PAR	S.I.
1	222	212	3	12	10	362	342	4	13
2	381	374	4	4	11	507	495	5	7
3	540	516	5	8	12	175	166	3	11
4	441	431	4	2	13	412	404	4	3
5	370	362	4	6	14	435	427	4	1
6	338	328	4	16	15	142	130	3	17
7	488	478	5	10	16	299	289	4	15
8	165	154	3	18	17	401	393	44	5
9	379	369	4	14	18	349	341	35	9
OUT	3,324	3,224	36		IN	3,082	2,987	71	
					TOTAL	6,406	6,211		
					STANDARD SCRATCH	71	70		

12 Alder Road, Londonderry. BT48 8DB. Tel: (028) 7135 2222 Fax: (028) 7135 3967
Email: mail@foylegolf.club24.co.uk
Web: www.foylegolfcentre.co.uk

LOCATION: One mile from
Foyle Bridge heading
for Moville turn left.

SECRETARY: Margaret Lapsley.

ARCHITECT: Frank Ainsworth.

PROFESSIONAL: Derek Morrison

Sean Young

NO.	MEDAL YARDS	GEN. YARDS	PAR	S.I.	NO.	MEDAL YARDS	GEN. YARDS	PAR	S.I.
1	397	381	4	6	10	375	353	4	5
2	536	526	5	10	11	382	359	4	11
3	186	166	3	12	12	359	335	4	15
4	430	423	4	2	13	178	168	3	13
5	172	163	3	14	14	501	472	5	7
6	405	394	4	4	15	439	419	4	1
7	389	378	4	16	16	352	336	4	17
8	150	141	3	18	17	539	499	5	9
9	412	406	4	8	18	441	409	4	3
OUT	3,077	2,977	35		IN	3,566	3,354	37	
					TOTAL	6,678	6,312	72	
	STANDARD SCRATCH						72	71	

Course Information: Par 71; SSS 71; Length 6,643 Yards.
Visitors: Welcome at any time. Guaranteed tee times due to
computerised booking system. **Opening Hours:** Dawn – Dusk. **Juveniles:**
Handicap 15 and under anytime, otherwise with an adult. **Green Fees:**
£16, £14 with member weekdays, £19, £17 with member weekends &
Bank Holidays. **Clubhouse Hours:** 8.00am – late. **Clubhouse Dress:**
Informal. **Clubhouse Facilities:** Licensed bar & restaurant with food
available every day, a fully stocked golf shop, lockers and changing rooms.
Open Competitions: Regular open competitions during the Summer.

Course Description:
Foyle consists of an 18 hole par
71 course, nine hole par 3, 25
bay driving range and Golf
Academy with indoor video
teaching facilities. The parkland
course is designed at
championship standard with
water coming into play on three
of the 18 holes.

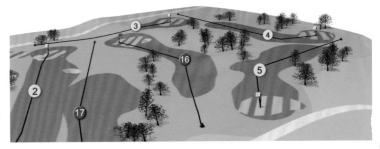

47a Lisnagrot Road, Kilrea,
Londonderry, BT51 5SF.
Tel: (028) 2954 0044.
www.kilreagolfclub.co.uk

Course Information:

Par 68; SSS 68; Length 5,494 yards. **Visitors:** Visitors are welcome at any time, though should avoid Tuesdays and Saturdays when competitions normally take place. **Societies:** Welcome. **Opening Hours:** Sunrise – sunset. **Green Fees:** Weekdays £12.50, weekdays with members £10, weekend £15, weekend with member £12.50. **Juveniles:** Welcome. **Clubhouse Hours:** 8.00am – 12.00 midnight. **Clubhouse Dress:** Dress code - neat casual. **Clubhouse Facilities:** Brand new Clubhouse opened in Spring 2002 offering changing facilities, snacks and light bites and a comfortable lounge to reflect on the day's game. Restaurant opening hours, menu and contact details are on the club website.

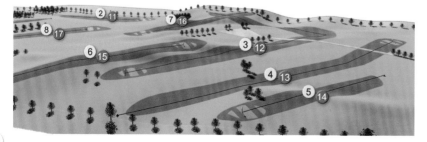

NO.	YARDS	PAR	S.I.	NO.	YARDS	PAR	S.I.
1	334	4	5	10	344	4	6
2	147	3	13	11	147	3	14
3	443	4	1	12	443	4	2
4	323	4	17	13	323	4	18
5	201	3	7	14	201	3	8
6	290	4	11	15	290	4	12
7	210	3	3	16	210	3	4
8	323	4	9	17	323	4	10
9	476	5	15	18	476	5	16
OUT	2,747	34		IN	2,747	34	
				TOTAL	5,494	68	
				STANDARD SCRATCH		68	

LOCATION: Situated half a mile to the south west of the town.

HON. SECRETARY: Noel McMullan.

Course Description:

The original undulating inland course, is one of the driest to be found. Recent extensions to the course, whilst reclaimed from bogland, are also well drained, and the course is often open when others have succumbed to the Irish climate. Extended in recent years to 5504 yards long (par 68), it is longer than the typical 9-hole course. Despite the extra length, accuracy is still required off the tee to give a fighting chance of par at most holes. Generally, the course has tight fairways and small greens.

Shanemullagh, Castledawson,
Co. Londonderry,
BT45 8DE.
Tel: (028) 7946 8468
Email: moyolapark@btconnect.com
Web: www.moyolapark.com

LOCATION: 40 miles north of
Belfast, via M2.

PROFESSIONAL: Bob Cockroft.
Tel: (028) 7946 8830

SECRETARY: Michael Gribbon.

CATERING: Tel: (028) 7946 8270

ARCHITECT: Don Patterson.

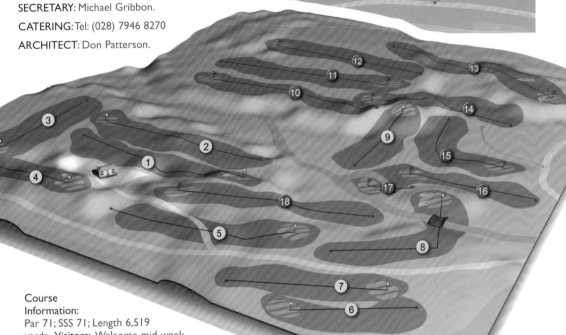

Course
Information:
Par 71; SSS 71; Length 6,519
yards. **Visitors:** Welcome mid-week.
Weekends by prior arrangement. Prior booking
for all tee times advisable. **Opening Hours:** Dawn –
Dusk Monday – Sunday. **Avoid:** Tuesday and Wednesday
evenings in Summer; Saturday in Winter. **Ladies:** Welcome. **Green
Fees:** £20 Mon – Thur (£12 with member); £25 Friday; £30
Weekend and bank holidays. **Juveniles:** Mon – Fri; after 4.30pm on
Sat / Sun. Lessons by prior arrangement. **Clubhouse Hours:**
12noon – 11pm. Full clubhouse facilities. **Clubhouse Facilities:**
12noon – 9pm. A la carte by prior arrangement. Buggies available
for hire. **Clubhouse Dress:** Smart/casual, no denims. **Open
Competitions:** Open Week – July; usually monthly in summer
(mixed opens).

NO.	WHITE YARDS	YELLOW YARDS	PAR	S.I.	NO.	WHITE YARDS	YELLOW YARDS	PAR	S.I.
1	438	406	4	7	10	348	341	4	12
2	418	409	4	5	11	377	370	4	4
3	346	303	4	13	12	200	191	3	10
4	152	140	3	15	13	494	476	5	18
5	521	515	5	17	14	417	404	4	2
6	430	423	4	3	15	320	312	4	14
7	391	387	4	11	16	177	167	3	6
8	421	410	4	1	17	128	128	3	16
9	379	363	4	9	18	562	554	5	8
OUT	3,496	3,356	36		IN	3,023	2,943	35	
					TOTAL	6,519	6,299	71	
					STANDARD SCRATCH	71	70		

Course Description:
The course demands long accurate
driving on most holes and the
strategic use of large mature trees
emphasises the need for well placed
approach shots. The 8th hole is a
ninety degree dog-leg which features
a difficult pitch shot to the green
across the Moyola River.

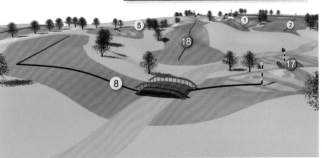

Portstewart

117 Strand Road, Portstewart, Co. L/Derry.
Tel: (028) 7083 2015 Web: www.portstewartgc.co.uk.

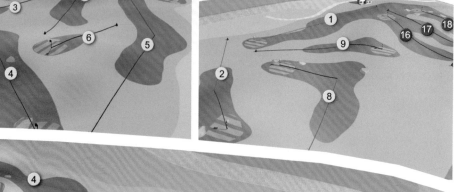

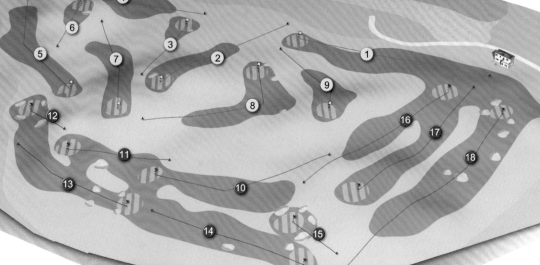

NO.	BLUE YARDS	WHITE YARDS	PAR	S.I.	NO.	BLUE YARDS	WHITE YARDS	PAR	S.I.
1	427	417	4	11	10	407	396	4	10
2	366	360	4	7	11	390	376	4	4
3	218	205	3	13	12	167	154	3	18
4	538	522	5	5	13	498	487	5	16
5	461	449	4	1	14	493	469	5	12
6	143	135	3	15	15	168	159	3	14
7	516	475	5	17	16	418	389	4	6
8	427	411	4	3	17	436	428	4	2
9	361	350	4	9	18	461	389	4	8
OUT	3,457	3,324	36		IN	3,438	3,247	36	
					TOTAL	6,895	6,571	72	
					STANDARD SCRATCH		72	71	

Course Information: Par 72; SSS 73; Length 6,895 yards (Strand Course). Par 64; Length 4,730 yards. (Old Course). Par 68; Length 5,725 yards. (Riverside Course). **Visitors:** Booking necessary. **Avoid:** Weekends and Bank Hols. **Ladies:** Priority on Wednesdays. **Green Fees:** Strand Course – £70 Mon–Fri; £90 Weekends. Old Course – £10 Mon–Fri; £15 Sat / Sun. Riverside Course – £20 Mon–Fri; £25 Weekends & Bank Holidays. **Juveniles:** Must be accompanied by an adult. Lessons by prior arrangements. Club Hire & Caddy trolleys available. **Clubhouse Hours:** All day everyday. **Clubhouse Facilities:** Bar / Bar Food. **Clubhouse Dress:** Casual/Neat. **Open Competitons:** Open Week 7th – 14th July.

LOCATION: Four miles north west of Coleraine on the north coast.

Course Description: Difficult, but open links course giving magnificent views of Donegal Hills, the rolling Atlantic, Strand Beach and the River Bann, especially from the 1st, 5th and 12th tees. Greens are fast and true. The Strand Course has hosted many championships. An outstanding test.

MANAGER: Michael Moss. Tel: (028) 7083 2015 / 3839.

PROFESSIONAL: Alan Hunter.
Tel: (028) 7083 2601. Fax: (028) 7083 4097.
Email: bill@portstewartgc.co.uk

Radisson Roe Park Hotel and Golf Resort, Roe Park.
Limavady, Co. Londonderry. BT49 9LB.
Tel: (028) 7772 2222. Fax: (028) 7772 2313.

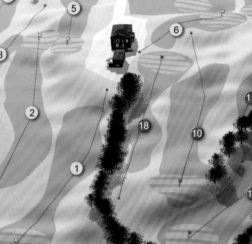

Course Description: This 18 hole parkland course takes full advantage of a beautiful riverside estate setting, with Lough Foyle and the Inishowen Peninsula providing a dramatic backdrop. Water comes into play on five holes, and with a challenging par four 18th to finish, the golfer can enjoy the game to the full.

Course Information: Par 70; SSS 71; Length 6,324 Yards. Visitors: Welcome. **Opening Hours:** 8am – Dusk. Avoid: Weekends 8 – 10.30am and 1 – 2pm (members only). Ladies: Welcome. Juveniles: Permitted. Green Fees: £25 midweek (£18.50 with member), £30 Sat/Sun (£18.50 with member). Hotel residents £20. **Coach House Hours:** Open every day from 10.00am until late. **Coach House Dress:** Smart casual. **Coach House Facilities:** International menu available all day in the Coach House. Flood-lit and covered Driving Range open to the public. Golf Acadamy & full leisure facilities on site. 4 Star luxury hotel on site.

GOLF / LEISURE MANAGER: Jim Cullen. Tel: (028) 7776 0105.

ARCHITECT: Frank Ainsworth.

PROFESSIONAL: Shaun Devenney. Tel: (028) 7776 0105.

NO.	MEDAL YARDS	GEN. YARDS	PAR	S.I.	NO	MEDAL YARDS	GEN. YARDS	PAR	S.I.
1	409	397	4	8	10	420	381	4	3
2	560	498	5	12	11	340	328	4	7
3	210	199	3	16	12	165	153	3	17
4	521	503	5	14	13	414	403	4	1
5	394	383	4	2	14	327	322	4	13
6	139	128	3	18	15	278	266	4	15
7	391	378	4	6	16	498	482	5	9
8	398	390	4	4	17	234	204	3	11
9	160	150	3	10	18	425	419	4	5
OUT	3,182	3,026	35		IN	3,101	2,958	35	
TOTAL						6,283	5,984	70	
STANDARD SCRATCH							70	69	

LOCATION:
One mile west of Limavady, adjacent to Roe Valley Country Park.

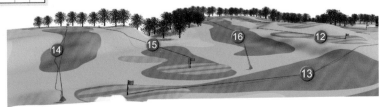

Onomy, Castleblayney, Co. Monaghan.
TEL: (042) 9740451
castleblayney@golfnet.ie
www.castleblayneygolfclub.com

LOCATION: Hope Castle Estate, Castleblayney.

SECRETARY: Raymond Kernan.
Tel: (042) 9740451

ARCHITECT: R.J. Browne.

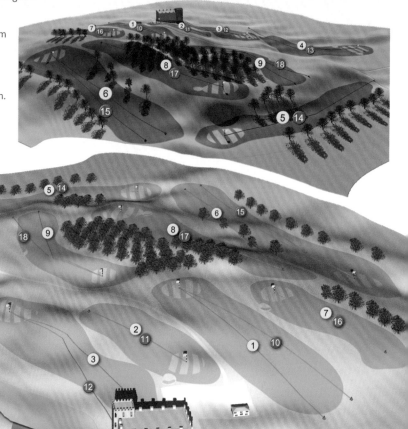

NO.	YARDS	PAR	S.I.	NO.	YARDS	PAR	S.I.
1	336	4	3	10	356	4	5
2	186	3	17	11	170	3	11
3	302	4	7	12	335	4	7
4	381	4	5	13	381	4	3
5	315	4	9	14	325	4	13
6	389	4	13	15	389	4	1
7	126	3	15	16	126	3	17
8	317	4	11	17	317	4	15
9	311	4	1	18	316	4	9
OUT	2,663	34		IN	2,715	34	
				TOTAL	5,378	68	
			STANDARD SCRATCH		66		

Course Information:
Par 68; SSS 66; Length 5,378 yards. **Visitors:** Welcome at all times. **Opening Hours:** Sunrise – sunset. **Ladies:** Welcome Thursdays. **Green Fees:** €12 Mon – Fri; €15 Sat / Sun / all Public Holidays. **Juveniles:** Monday, Tuesday, Thursday, Friday up to 5.00pm; weekends after 6.00pm. **Clubhouse Hours:** Daylight hours in summer. **Clubhouse Dress:** Casual but neat. **Clubhouse Facilities:** Restaurant and bar facilities everyday all day. Restaurant in Hope Castle. **Open Competitions:** Open Week in June.

Course Description:
The course enjoys a scenic setting beside lake and forest. Hilly in character yet convenient (approx. 500 yards) to town centre the course is enjoyable for all levels of handicappers.

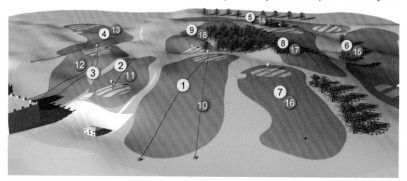

Co. Monaghan. Tel: (047) 56017

LOCATION: Scotshouse Road, Clones.

HON. SECRETARY: PJ McCague.

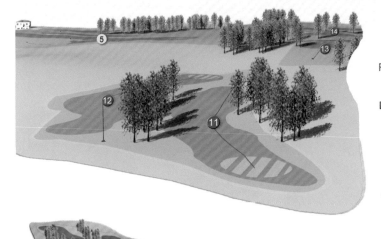

Course Information:
Par 69; SSS 69; Length 5,549 yards.
Visitors: Welcome at all times.
Opening Hours: Sunrise – sunset.
Ladies: Welcome. **Green Fees:** €30.
Juveniles: Up to 5pm Weekdays.
After 6pm Weekends. **Clubhouse
Hours:** 10am – 11.30pm. Caddy
cars and buggies for hire.
Clubhouse Dress: Informal.
Clubhouse Facilities: Full
clubhouse facilities, evening meals,
snacks, etc. **Open Competitions:**
Phone club for details.

Course Description:
The course is usually playable all year round. It
is parkland and set in Hilton Park estate and with its
hills, forts, lakes and streams provides a very scenic
backdrop for a good test of golf.

NO.	WHITE METRES	YELLOW METRES	PAR	S.I.	NO.	WHITE METRES	YELLOW METRES	PAR	S.I.
1	161	150	3	16	10	426	415	5	17
2	414	405	5	18	11	370	352	4	3
3	159	148	3	14	12	204	173	3	9
4	321	310	4	6	13	366	353	4	5
5	370	350	4	4	14	382	370	4	1
6	383	360	4	2	15	129	121	3	15
7	344	323	4	10	16	347	332	4	13
8	324	314	4	12	17	336	327	4	11
9	179	161	3	8	18	334	325	4	7
OUT	2,655	2,521	34		IN	2,894	2,668	35	
					TOTAL	5,549	5,189	69	
					STANDARD SCRATCH	69	69		

Nuremore

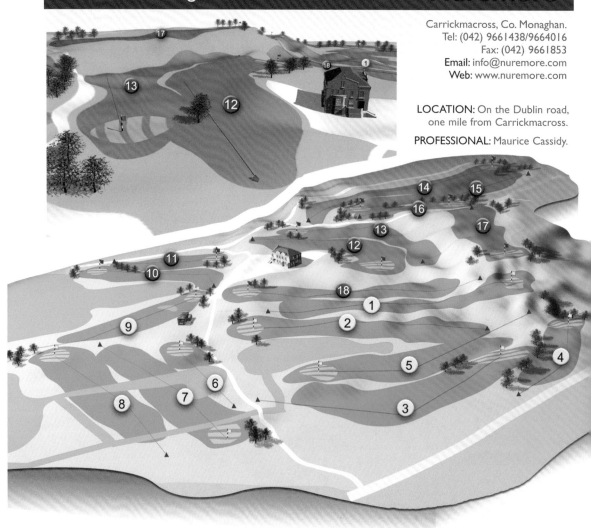

Carrickmacross, Co. Monaghan.
Tel: (042) 9661438/9664016
Fax: (042) 9661853
Email: info@nuremore.com
Web: www.nuremore.com

LOCATION: On the Dublin road, one mile from Carrickmacross.

PROFESSIONAL: Maurice Cassidy.

Course Information:
Par 71; SSS 69; Length 5,870 metres. **Visitors:** Welcome everyday. **Opening Hours:** Daylight hours. **Avoid:** Prior arrangement is preferred. **Green Fees:** €35 Weekdays, €45 weekends. **Clubhouse Dress:** Casual. **Clubhouse Facilities:** Full bar and dining facilities available. **Open Competitions:** Open Week – August.

Course Description:
Panoramic views over counties Monaghan, Cavan, Louth, Armagh and Meath.

NO.	MEDAL YARDS	GEN. YARDS	PAR	S.I.	NO.	MEDAL YARDS	GEN. YARDS	PAR	S.I.
1	374	361	4	7	10	308	289	4	16
2	443	431	5	17	11	157	145	3	12
3	370	358	4	1	12	365	313	4	4
4	151	139	3	15	13	351	339	4	8
5	369	357	4	3	14	513	475	5	6
6	169	157	3	9	15	493	447	5	10
7	330	318	4	5	16	124	112	3	18
8	328	316	4	11	17	294	272	4	14
9	334	322	4	13	18	397	385	4	2
OUT	2,868	2,759	35		IN	3,002	2,777	36	
					TOTAL	5,870	5,536	71	
	STANDARD SCRATCH					69			

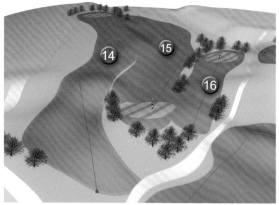

Cootehill Road, Monaghan,
Co. Monaghan.
Tel: (047) 81316.

LOCATION: Two miles south
of Monaghan town on the
Cootehill Road.

SECRETARY: Jimmie McKenna.

ARCHITECT: Des Smith Golf
Design Ltd.

PROFESSIONAL: Ciaran Smyth.
Tel: (047) 71222.

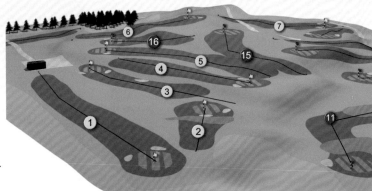

Course Description:
The club has recently
undergone an extensive
development from a
shortish nine hole course to
a 6,000 yard eighteen hole
course.

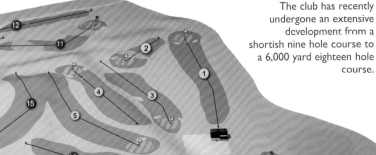

NO.	METRES	PAR	S.I.	NO.	METRES	PAR	S.I.
1	470	5	12	10	310	4	13
2	157	3	10	11	331	4	6
3	393	4	5	12	333	4	2
4	269	4	16	13	118	3	14
5	387	4	1	14	343	4	7
6	336	4	8	15	348	4	4
7	348	4	3	16	160	3	11
8	112	3	15	17	372	4	9
9	440	5	18	18	280	4	17
OUT	2,912	36		IN	2,595	34	
				TOTAL	5,507	70	
				STANDARD SCRATCH	68		

Course Information:
Par 70; SSS 68; Length 5,605 metres. **Visitors:** Welcome –
at all times subject to availabilty, booking essential. **Opening Hours:** Sunrise –
sunset. **Ladies:** Welcome at all times – competition on Wednesdays. **Green Fees:** €30
Mon-Fri, €40 Sat/Sun/Holidays. With member €20 Mon-Fri, €30 Sat/Sun/Holidays.
Juveniles/students half price. Special rates available for socities/groups of 16 or more
people. **Clubhouse Hours:** Mon – Sun in Summer time; 12 noon – 12 pm; Mon – Sun; Full clubhouse
facilities. **Clubhouse Dress:** Smart/casual.

Clubhouse Facilities: Full
catering available from
12.30pm (except
Mondays); large
parties by prior
arrangement. Pro
shop open -
Mon-Fri 8.30-
6.30. Golf buggies
available, book in
advance. Electric
trolleys for hire. **Open
Competitions:** Open
Week – July; Open Weekends –
April, May, June & August.

Aughnacloy Golf Club,
99 Tullyvar Road, Aughnacloy, Co. Tyrone.
Tel: (028) 8555 7050

Course Description:

9 hole inland course situated close
to the Ballygawley roundabout.
Includes a driving range.

NO.	METRES	PAR	S.I.	NO.	METRES	PAR	S.I.
1	328	4	5	10	493	5	4
2	228	4	15	11	200	4	16
3	402	4	3	12	392	4	2
4	299	4	9	13	296	4	8
5	133	3	13	14	156	3	6
6	268	4	7	15	145	3	10
7	478	5	11	16	458	5	14
8	358	4	1	17	380	5	12
9	109	3	17	18	99	3	18
OUT	2,603	35		IN	2,581	35	
				TOTAL	5,184	71	
				STANDARD SCRATCH	69		

Driving Range

LOCATION:
Co. Tyrone.

SECRETARY: S.J. Houston

Course Information:

Par 71; SSS 69; Length 5,184 metres. Visitors:
Welcome. Opening Hours: All day. Ladies:
Welcome. Green Fees: Mon – Fri £12; Sat
/Sun £15. Special rates for golfing societies.
Juveniles: Welcome. Clubhouse Hours: 9.00
a.m.– late. Clubhouse Dress: Casual.
Clubhouse Facilities: Bar, changing room, pool,
meals. Open Competitions: Several. Contact
club for details.

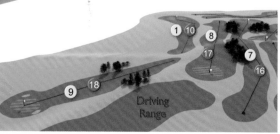

Driving Range

Course Description:
Parkland course in a beautiful secluded rural setting with large undulating greens. Bounded on one side by the river Blackwater and maintained to a high standard. The club house is in a tastefully restored stone built corn mill.

Benburb Valley Golf Course, Maydown Road, Benburb. BT71 7LJ
Tel: (028) 3754 9868

LOCATION: 8 miles from Armagh & Dungannon. 8 miles from M1 junction 14.

ARCHITECT: Ann O'Hagan.

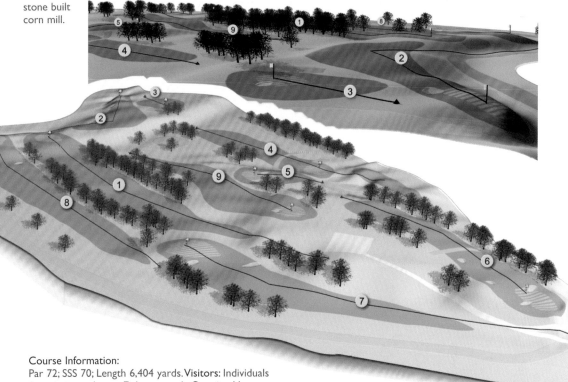

Course Information:
Par 72; SSS 70; Length 6,404 yards. Visitors: Individuals & societies welcome 7 days a week. Opening Hours: Dawn – Dusk. Green Fees: £11 Mon – Fri; £14 Sat.Sun/Holidays. Juveniles: Welcome at weekend. Clubhouse Hours: 12 noon – 12 midnight. Clubhouse Dress: Smart/Casual. Clubhouse Facilities: Full pub and restaurant open to the public. Private function room with bar and food, for societies. Open Competitions: Phone for details.

NO.	MEDAL YARDS	GEN. YARDS	PAR	S.I.	NO.	MEDAL YARDS	GEN. YARDS	PAR	S.I.
1	518	508	5	17	10	518	508	5	18
2	347	338	4	13	11	347	338	4	14
3	134	128	3	3	12	134	128	3	4
4	403	331	4	11	13	403	331	4	12
5	147	140	3	7	14	147	140	3	8
6	350	341	4	9	15	350	341	4	10
7	333	322	4	1	16	333	322	4	2
8	546	520	4	15	17	546	520	5	16
9	424	413	4	5	18	424	413	4	6
OUT	3,202	3,041	36		IN	3,202	3,041	36	
					TOTAL	6,404	6,082	72	
					STANDARD SCRATCH	70	70		

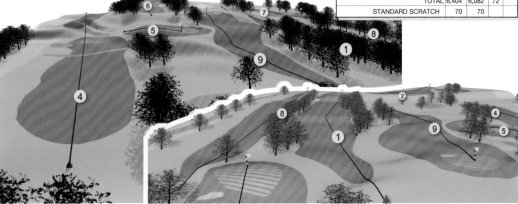

34 Springfield Lane, Dungannon, Co. Tyrone BT70 1QX. Tel: (028) 8772 2098.

GOLF SHOP: Tel: (028) 8772 7485.

RESTAURANT: Tel: (028) 8772 9995.

LOCATION: 40 miles west of Belfast. 1 mile from Dungannon off B43 Donaghmore Road.

SECRETARY: Mr S. T. Hughes.

Course Description:
The Dungannon Golf Club founded in 1890 is a parkland course with tree-lined fairways. Here, golf is flourishing with a membership of about 600. A challenging and pleasant course and today the visitor could reiterate the entry in the old handbook that the greens are 'very good'.

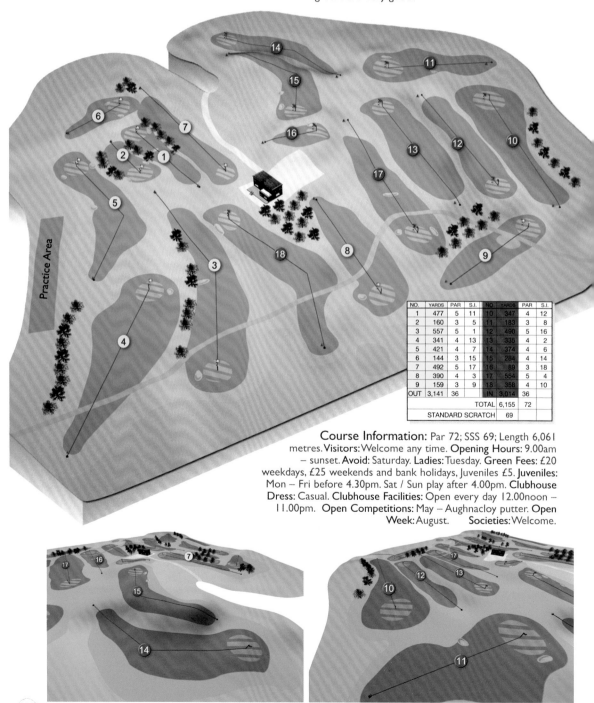

NO.	YARDS	PAR	S.I.	NO.	YARDS	PAR	S.I.
1	477	5	11	10	347	4	12
2	160	3	5	11	183	3	8
3	557	5	1	12	490	5	16
4	341	4	13	13	335	4	2
5	421	4	7	14	374	4	6
6	144	3	15	15	284	4	14
7	492	5	17	16	89	3	18
8	390	4	3	17	554	5	4
9	159	3	9	18	358	4	10
OUT	3,141	36		IN	3,014	36	
				TOTAL	6,155	72	
				STANDARD SCRATCH	69		

Course Information: Par 72; SSS 69; Length 6,061 metres. **Visitors:** Welcome any time. **Opening Hours:** 9.00am – sunset. **Avoid:** Saturday. **Ladies:** Tuesday. **Green Fees:** £20 weekdays, £25 weekends and bank holidays, Juveniles £5. **Juveniles:** Mon – Fri before 4.30pm. Sat / Sun play after 4.00pm. **Clubhouse Dress:** Casual. **Clubhouse Facilities:** Open every day 12.00noon – 11.00pm. **Open Competitions:** May – Aughnacloy putter. **Open Week:** August. **Societies:** Welcome.

1 Kiln Street, Ecclesville Demesne, Fintona,
Co. Tyrone.
Tel: (028) 8284 1480. Fax: (028) 8284 1480.

LOCATION: 8 miles from Omagh.

HON. SECRETARY: Raymond Scott.

SECRETARY/MANAGER: Patricia McNabb.

Course Description:
An attractive parkland course, its main feature
being a trout stream which meanders through
the course causing many problems for
badly executed shots. Rated one of
the top nine hole courses
in the province.

NO.	METRES	PAR	S.I.	NO.	METRES	PAR	S.I.
1	301	4	7	10	261	4	14
2	412	4	1	11	371	4	2
3	257	4	17	12	264	4	18
4	156	3	13	13	178	3	4
5	460	5	11	14	460	5	10
6	400	4	3	15	474	5	16
7	444	5	9	16	311	4	8
8	135	3	15	17	145	3	12
9	368	4	5	18	368	4	6
OUT	2,933	36		IN	2,832	36	
				TOTAL	5,765	72	
	STANDARD SCRATCH				70		

Course Information:
Par 72; SSS 70; Length 5,766 metres. Visitors:
Welcome Mon – Fri. Sat by arrangement.
Opening Hours: Daylight. **Ladies:** Welcome
Tuesdays. **Green Fees:** £10 weekdays, £15
weekends, bank holidays; £10 with member.
Juveniles: Welcome. Saturday & Sunday by
prior arrangement only. **Clubhouse Dress:**
Casual. **Clubhouse Facilities:** Full clubhouse
facilities. Meals on request. **Open
Competitions:** Telephone club for details.

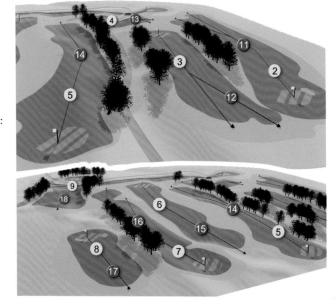

Killymoon

200 Killymoon Road, Cookstown,
Co. Tyrone BT80 8TW.
Tel/Fax: (028) 86763762
Email: killymoongolf@btconnect.com

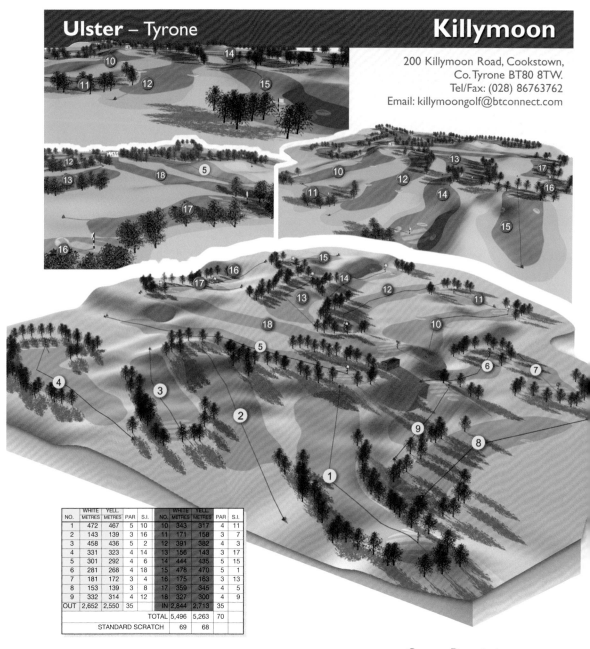

NO.	WHITE METRES	YELL. METRES	PAR	S.I.	NO.	WHITE METRES	YELL. METRES	PAR	S.I.
1	472	467	5	10	10	343	317	4	11
2	143	139	3	16	11	171	158	3	7
3	458	436	5	2	12	391	382	4	3
4	331	323	4	14	13	156	143	3	17
5	301	292	4	6	14	444	435	5	15
6	281	268	4	18	15	478	470	5	1
7	181	172	3	4	16	175	163	3	13
8	153	139	3	8	17	359	345	4	5
9	332	314	4	12	18	327	300	4	9
OUT	2,652	2,550	35		IN	2,844	2,713	35	
					TOTAL	5,496	5,263	70	
	STANDARD SCRATCH					69	68		

Course Information: Par 70; SSS 69; Length 6,202 yrds. **Visitors:** Welcome Tuesday to Friday all day, Saturday and Sunday. Must have current handicap. Members only Saturday before 3pm. **Ladies:** Have priority on Thursdays. **Green Fees:** £28 Sat & Sun, Mon £16 Tue & Fri £22. **Juveniles:** £7-11 Society rates available. **Clubhouse Dress:** Smart and casual. **Clubhouse Facilities:** Full catering and bar facilities available. **Open Competitions:** Take place in August (mostly seniors) Handicap Certificate required for open competitions.

Course Description:
A parkland course set on high ground with the soil being a sandy consistency. The 1st is the most picturesque hole, which is a dog leg skirting the woods of Killymoon Castle.

LOCATION: South end of Cookstown, 1 mile from Dungannon roundabout.

HON. SECRETARY: Tony McCann. Tel: (028) 8676 3762 / 2976
PROFESSIONAL: Gary Chambers
GOLF SHOP: (028) 8676 3460.

Newtownstewart

38 Golf Course Road, Newtownstewart,
Omagh, Co. Tyrone BT78 4HU.
Tel: (028) 8166 1466. Fax: (028) 8166 2506.
Email: newtown.stewart@lineone.net
www.globalgolf.com/newtownstewart

LOCATION: 2 miles west of Newtownstewart.

SECRETARY: Lorraine Donnell

Tel: (028) 8166 1466.

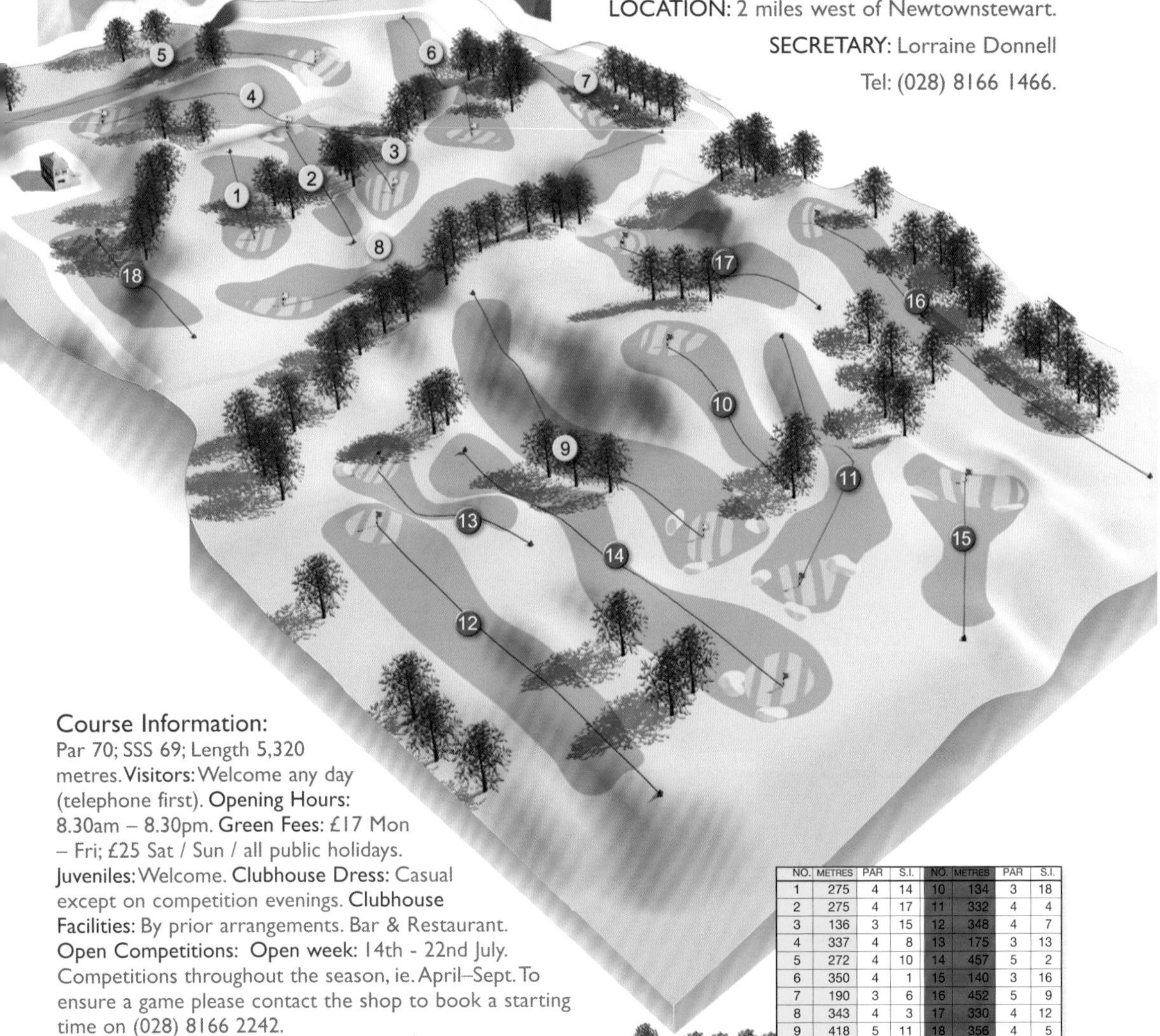

Course Information:

Par 70; SSS 69; Length 5,320 metres. Visitors: Welcome any day (telephone first). **Opening Hours:** 8.30am – 8.30pm. **Green Fees:** £17 Mon – Fri; £25 Sat / Sun / all public holidays. **Juveniles:** Welcome. **Clubhouse Dress:** Casual except on competition evenings. **Clubhouse Facilities:** By prior arrangements. Bar & Restaurant. **Open Competitions:** Open week: 14th - 22nd July. Competitions throughout the season, ie. April–Sept. To ensure a game please contact the shop to book a starting time on (028) 8166 2242.

Course Description:

Newtownstewart, although only an hour and a half from Belfast lies in a different world in the west of Tyrone. The course is positioned at the confluence of the Strule and the Glenelly rivers and at the foot of the Sperrin Mountains.

NO.	METRES	PAR	S.I.	NO.	METRES	PAR	S.I.
1	275	4	14	10	134	3	18
2	275	4	17	11	332	4	4
3	136	3	15	12	348	4	7
4	337	4	8	13	175	3	13
5	272	4	10	14	457	5	2
6	350	4	1	15	140	3	16
7	190	3	6	16	452	5	9
8	343	4	3	17	330	4	12
9	418	5	11	18	356	4	5
OUT	2,596	35		IN	2,724	35	
				TOTAL	5,320	70	
				STANDARD SCRATCH		69	

Omagh

83a Dublin Road, Omagh, Co. Tyrone, BT78 1HQ.
Tel: (028) 8224 3160 / 8224 1442

HON. SECRETARY: Brian Gallagher.

SECRETARY: Florence Caldwell.

ARCHITECT: Don Patterson.

LOCATION: 1 mile from town centre on main Omagh – Dublin Rd.

Course Description:
Attractive course with four of the holes bordering the River Drumragh. The course is split on either side by the Dublin road.

NO.	WHITE METRES	GREEN METRES	PAR	S.I.	NO.	MEDAL METRES	GEN. METRES	PAR	S.I.
1	324	316	4	5	10	169	139	3	12
2	281	283	4	17	11	257	250	4	18
3	198	188	3	11	12	305	280	4	4
4	467	440	5	13	13	135	116	3	14
5	377	348	4	1	14	390	385	4	2
6	506	483	5	7	15	484	471	4	8
7	335	322	4	9	16	305	298	3	6
8	380	362	4	3	17	164	155	4	10
9	310	361	4	15	18	273	268	5	16
OUT	3,003	3,178	37		IN	2,460	2,362	35	
					TOTAL	5,364	5,638		
	STANDARD SCRATCH					68	70		

Course Information:
Par 71; SSS 70; Length 5,650 metres. **Visitors:** Individuals or societies welcome. **Avoid:** Tuesdays and Saturdays. **Ladies:** Ladies have priority on the 1st Tee all day Tuesday. **Green Fees:** £15 Mon – Fri (£10 with member) ; £20 Sat / Sun (£15 with member). O.A.P and students £7.50 weekdays and £10 weekends. Reduced rates for societies. **Clubhouse Hours:** 11.30am – 1.30pm and 4.30pm – 11.00pm. **Clubhouse Dress:** Casual / neat. **Clubhouse Facilities:** Bar snacks available. Full catering by arrangement with caterer. **Open Competitions:** Various Open Days, (telephone for details).

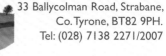

33 Ballycolman Road, Strabane,
Co. Tyrone, BT82 9PH.
Tel: (028) 7138 2271/2007

LOCATION: 1 mile from Strabane
on the Dublin Road.

CLUB SECRETARY: Claire Keys.

ARCHITECT: Desmond Hackett.

E-mail: strabanegc@btconnect.com

Course Information:

Par 69; SSS 69; Length 5,610 metres.

Visitors: Welcome. Telephone appointment advisable.

Opening Hours: 8.00am – dusk. **Avoid:** Saturday. **Ladies:** Tuesday.

Green Fees: £15 Monday – Friday; (£12 with member); £18 Sat / Sun/ Public holidays (£15 with member). Societies by arrangement. **Juveniles:** Welcome. Caddy service available by prior arrangement. Buggy & Trolly hire available Under 18's not allowed in clubhouse. Handicap Certificate required for competition. **Clubhouse Hours:** Mon – Fri 2pm – 11pm, Saturday 11am – 11pm, Sunday 12noon – 10pm. **Clubhouse Dress:** Informal but respectable. **Clubhouse Facilities:** Catering by arrangement only. Full bar.

Open Competitions: Many throughout the year, telephone for details.

Course Description:

Rolling parkland intersected by the River Mourne, which runs alongside the 9th fairway, making the 9th one of the most picturesque and feared holes. The course is at the foothills of the Sperrin Mountains which provide an attractive back-drop to the river falls. Agreed by professionals and low handicapped players as an excellent test of golf.

NO.	MEDAL METRES	GEN. METRES	PAR	S.I.	NO.	MEDAL METRES	GEN. METRES	PAR	S.I.
1	338	328	4	7	10	455	445	5	14
2	144	134	3	13	11	362	349	4	2
3	424	414	4	1	12	135	125	3	18
4	380	370	4	5	13	357	345	4	8
5	466	456	5	9	14	369	323	4	6
6	300	290	4	17	15	287	277	4	16
7	155	145	3	15	16	182	161	3	12
8	171	161	3	11	17	393	383	4	4
9	346	291	4	3	18	346	336	4	10
OUT	2,724	2,589	34		IN	2,886	2,734	35	
					TOTAL	5,610	5,323	69	
					STANDARD SCRATCH		71		

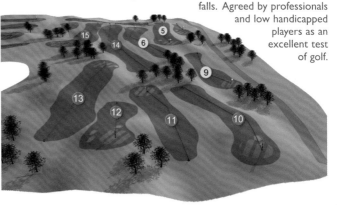

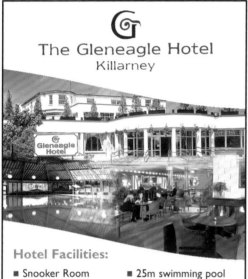

Munster

Dromoland Castle Golf Club, County Clare.

A Provincial Introduction by Jack Magowan

Morrissey's pub in Doonbeg has a board outside which says "Good food, good beer, good cheer on tap here."

It's the oldest of five pubs in a remote parish of 250 people, few of whom would have known a pitching wedge from a putter until Greg Norman was seduced by the most spectacular stretch of linksland unclaimed by golf.

That was in the winter of 1997. Today, designer Norman's first course in the U.K. or Ireland is a must-play masterpiece, links' golf at its very best halfway between two of Ireland's other great shrines, Ballybunion and Lahinch.

Norman promised something different at Doonbeg, and has surely delivered. "Americans think I'm crazy, but I just love

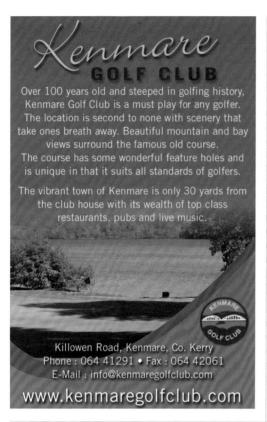
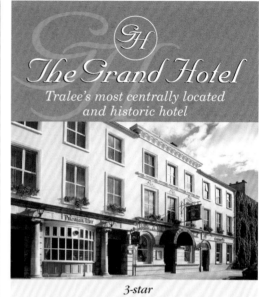

▲

The distinctive pot bunkers of Doonbeg in County Clare. The course is the brainchild of Greg Norman and this modern day 'Mona Lisa' is fast becoming a must-play venue on any golfing pilgrimage.

the idea of hitting a two-iron under the wind, even if it only travels a hundred yards" beams Greg, who built this Co. Clare gem by feel, not by a yardage book, and it shows.

"The quirkiness of some holes is appealing", says Ryder Cup star, Padraig Harrington. "That bunker in the middle of the 12th green sums up the course. Nobody but Greg Norman would have had the courage to do something like this."

Tom Friedman, of *Golf Digest*, likened his round there to a walk on the moon.

"If they sodded the Sea of Tranquility with fescue grass, threw sand into pot bunkers created by all those meteorities, and laid out 18 greens in some craters and plateaus, you'd have Doonbeg," writes Tom. "All that would be missing would be a tall Guinness and the pounding Atlantic."

The dunes along Doughmore Bay are massive, and Norman has weaved a wonderful tapestry through most of them.

The hole I like best is the 15th. It is set in an amphitheatre of 60-feet high sand hills, and after the drama of the more intimidating than tough one-shot 14th, this is a hole to remember on a great new links built to withstand the challenge of time and technology.

Be warned, however, don't expect much change out of £130/€190 (caddy extra) to play Norman's modern-day "Mona Lisa". The whole £150/€220 million package here is

Photograph courtesy of Old Head Golf Club.

▲
Scenic views over the Atlantic Ocean from the 4th at Old Head Golf Course, Kinsale, County Cork. With the ever-changing sea breezes, the course provides a stern test to all golfers.

one of affluence, from the course to the new oceanside clubhouse and cottages, plus 56-suite lodge, all five-star.

Ireland's south-west is as closely linked to golf as Blarney is to the Stone.

Nobody knows for sure who designed Ballybunion; only that God could have had a hand in it, so natural are some of the seaside holes among the wildest terrain in the game.

Not punishingly long at 6,600 yards, but a test of every shot in the bag, maybe some not in it.

Tom Watson was Ballybunion's club captain in millennium year 2000, yet isn't the only great player to have had a love affair with the old course. The late James Bruen was only 17 years old when he won the Irish Amatuer championship there before sharing the glory of Britian's famous Walker Cup triumph in 1938 at St. Andrews.

"Not even Hogan or Cotton's game had more dramatic

KILLARNEY ROYAL

"Overall outstanding service with a positive attitude. I would recommend it to anyone looking for a small hotel with charm and loads of hospitality" ...Peter Zummo

Perfect base for walking, golf and touring. 24 Air-conditioned Bedrooms and 5 Junior Suites designed in a country classical style. 4 star RAC. Privately owned by the Scally family.

College Street, Killarney, Co. Kerry
Tel: (064) 31853 Fax: (064) 34001
info@killarneyroyal.ie
www.killarneyroyal.ie

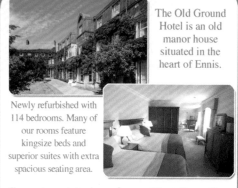

appeal than Bruen's," the author of Masters of Golf, Pat Ward-Thomas, used to say.

Jimmy's style was entirely his own. He would draw the clubhead back in an outside-to-in loop, then whip it through the ball with animal ferocity. Anybody who didn't know him might have scoffed, but not for long. No course, however long or difficult, was safe from attack when James teed it up.

All great courses are remorseless in the face of sloppy play, and Waterville, Tralee, and the Old Head of Kinsale are clearly no exception.

Tralee was Arnold Palmer's first creation outside the United States.

Film buffs will drool over the landscape for 'Ryan's Daughter', and if the scenery is more spectacular than the golf course, that's only because it is mind-blowing. As, indeed, is the postcard setting of Lahinch, now back to former glory after a costly make-over.

John Burke was Lahinch's first golfing son, and just about everybody within a 10-mile radius of the town plays the game. There were tears in many an Irish eye when the club's famous goats had to be put down as a safety-first measure at the height of the foot-and-mouth scare some years ago, but the billies are back, and still a match for the clubhouse wall barometer that doesn't work.

The instrument has no hands; just a card telling you "See Goats". If they are grazing close to the clubhouse, that's a weather warning – wind and rain on the horizon. Away from the clubhouse and it'll be a bright and clear day, no raingear needed.

Don't bank on it. Once an American visitor, happy that the goats were nicely placed, set off in short sleeves and Bermuda

▲

Fota Island Golf Course, County Cork, where the woodlands are woven into a challenging par 71 championship course featuring strategically placed bunkers and water hazards.

▲
Waterville Golf Links, County Kerry, combines sand dunes gorse and native grasses, firm fairways, sod faced bunkers and subtle putting surfaces all intertwined by the ever changing weather.

shorts for a round that was soon washed out by a thunder shower.

"What happened?," he frowned. "How could your goats have got it so badly wrong?"

"Sorry, your honour," said the barman. "We've just had a delivery of new goats!"

To play golf at Waterville is to slide into a blissful vacuum, and Adare, Fota Island, Dromoland Castle and the Old Head of Kinsale all string out, too, like green pearls on a jeweller's tray.

Tom Kane invested about €22 million of his own money on a luxurious Adare Complex, and has never looked back. Tiger Woods is an occasional visitor, and seems to enjoy a Trent Jones' course that features probably the biggest man-built lake in Irish golf, a huge 14-acre spread for which the heavy-duty polythene alone cost nearly half-a-million dollars.

There's also wood and water everywhere at Fota Island, scene of two Irish Opens already, but you'll not see too many trees on the Old Head. Built on a cliff-top promontory surrounded by the ocean on all sides, this has got to be one of the mind-numbing courses in the game, and the toughest in wind.

It's also a bird-watchers' paradise with guillemots, cormorants even falcons, soaring overhead and always a distraction.

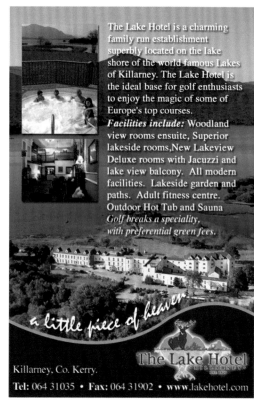

Photograph courtesy of Dromland Castle Golf Club.

▲

Trees and water abound at Dromland Castle Golf Club in County Clare and at the 9th they are in abundance, where water protects almost half the green.

Off the championship tees, the Old Head spans over 7,000 yards, but every hole has six tees in all. Go there with your game in good shape. You'll not find it on this Atlantic headland.

I was at Killarney in '71 when the late Dr Billy O'Sullivan buried a bottle of expensive champagne at the birth of the Killeen course. Now there are three courses of outstanding beauty there, all as busy as Piccadilly Circus most of the year. Be sure to book a tee-off time.

And for Waterville, too, another stunning test of championship golf, or the magnificent monster, as Sam Snead once labelled it.

Like Ballybunion New, a younger brother of the celebrated Old Course, Waterville builds up to a crescendo of great finishing holes, one of them, the eleventh, ranked among the most exciting long holes anywhere.

No golfer passes through Cork city without playing one of over 20 fine courses in the county, and where better to relax and eat well than at Dromoland Castle, or Shannon, or Woodstock, all within a short drive of one another near the airport.

Jay Connolly, a major player in the Wall Street team that bought Waterville from the Mulcahy's, once said his life revolved around the things he liked most – golf, fishing and sharing a pint or two with nice people.

"And Ireland is a great place to do all of that," he added warmly.

Glynns of Ennis is one of Irelands leading coach hire companies. We are an established family-run Irish Coach and Chauffeur drive business situated in the West of Ireland, close to Lahinch, Doonbeg and Ballybunion golf courses. Over the years we have built up a professional team of drivers, office and maintenance staff to ensure the highest standards of customer care and satisfaction.

Our Range of Executive Coaches, Midi Coaches, Mini Vans and Luxury Cars are Approved and Star Rated Annually by The Irish Tourist Board.

Knocknaderry, Tulla Rd, Ennis, Co. Clare
Tel: (065) 682 8234 • Fax: (065) 684 0678
Email: info@glynnscoaches.com
Web: www.glynnscoaches.com

Fáilte Ireland
Approved to Fáilte Ireland Standards

Coach Tourism & Transport Council

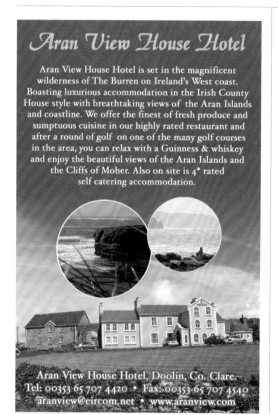

John Burke

by Jack Magowan

Think of Lahinch and one name springs instantly to mind. John Burke, eight times a national champion, is remembered almost with reverence all over County Clare as the golfer with Bobby Jones' built in rhythm and unbeatable in a wind.

Back then, they called Burke the 'Lion of Lahinch'. Until he won a Walker Cup blazer, nobody had ever heard of the sleepy little town from which it would have taken half a day to make a telephone call to Dublin. This was the famous Brookline (Mass) match in which two British golfers badly mauled in the first day foursomes, refused to play in the singles. Instead, the pair decided to see off Boston's nightlife, leaving a note for their team captain to say they were not available.

Such downright insolence and lack of discipline wouldn't be tolerated today, but this was 1932 when the old school tie brigade had a bigger influence in the selection of both Cup teams then the ability to break par.

Burke was the greatest natural player of his day

Burke had wrists of steel, and the constitution of an ox. Even on the coldest day, he rarely wore anything warmer than an open-necked shirt, and in the end, this probably cost him his career in the game. Soon after his 58th and last international match in '49, he went to see his doctor complaining of a back ache. Sadly, it was worse than that, much worse. He had an incurable form of rheumatism, and would spend all of 12 years in a wheelchair before he died.

In Fred Daly's book, Burke was the greatest natural player of his day, "he had every shot in the bag, even some not in it," Fred used to say. "Nobody before Christy O'Connor could disguise a shot better, or hit a driver off the fairway with more skill and confidence."

Such was John's domination as an eleven times winner of the South of Ireland championship that the hoteliers of Lahinch actually wrote asking him not to play in the event. He was frightening off holiday golfers, they said, and bad for business.

Jack Westland, against whom Burke fought back from five down at lunch to snatch a half in their Cup singles, used to tease John about being Ireland's best story-teller, "If only somebody would interpret for me!"

▲
John Burke, eight times a national champion, is remembered almost with reverence all over County Clare as the golfer with Bobby Jones' built in rhythm and unbeatable in a wind.

Killarney Killeen

by Jack Magowan

Golfing aristocrat, Viscount Castlerosse, played poker with Churchill, wrote a popular gossip column for the Express, ate and drank to excess, and died in his sleep at the age of 52.

Killarney Golf and Fishing Club will always be a monument to the big man's vision and energy, but, sadly, few there remember him, only stories of his rare wit and electric personality, like when he found his ball half buried in a bunker tight against the lip.

the 18th at Mahony's Point was "the best one-shot hole in the world"

Castlerosse glanced heavenward, then called out in Mock agony: "Please, God, come down and help me play this shot and don't let your Son come down, this is no job for a boy!"

Killarney is where a golfer slides into a vacuum, blissfully aware that if the phone rings, the call will not be for him. Drink in the scenery and make your best swing. The setting exhausts superlatives, not just on one, but three courses.

▲
The 315 metres, par 4, second at Killarney Killeen with stunning views over Lough Leane.

Killeen is the club's flagship course, re-opened in 2006 after a two million euro face-lift, it was given eighteen new greens and upgraded to classic proportions.

To the late Henry Longhurst, of TV fame, the 18th at Mahony's Point was "the best one-shot hole in the world", but the short tenth on Killeen would now run it close.

Killarney is where a golfer slides into a vacuum, blissfully aware that if the phone rings, the call will not be for him.

"It's probably the signature hole in an inviting cocktail of great holes", says club manager, Tom Prendergast, the dynamo in an engine-room staff of nearly 50.

It was in their centenary year of 1993 that visitors' green fees at Killarney topped IR£750,000, an all-time Irish club record. Now, they are close to the Euro equivilant of twice that, a welcome boost not only for the club, but golf and tourism generally.

Changed times, when Gary Player first played there half a century ago, he shot 84 on a day in which the tournament field was pelted by hailstones the size of golf balls, and revenue from green fees that season had slumped to just over £1,000!

It was in 1991/92 that Nick Faldo won back to back Irish Opens at Killarney, where Britain's top lady golfers later celebrated a historic victory over America in the Curtis Cup. To sample the charm and challenge of Killeen costs €120 (about £85), with Mahony's point and Lackabane proportionately less.

▲
The MacGillycuddy Reeks, Ireland's highest mountain range makes a spectacular backdrop for the par 4 eighth hole.

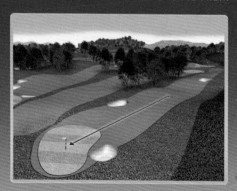

Golf Clubs in Munster – Page Index

Numbers above refer to the page number of each course with approximate geographical location shown on the map below.

Email: Links@doonbeggolfclub.com **Web:** www.doonbeggolfclub.com

Doonbeg Golf Club, Doonbeg, Co. Clare.
Tel: (065) 9055600
Fax: (065) 9055247

Course Information: Par 72; SSS 74; Length 6,870 yards, meters 6,249. **Visitors:** Are welcome. **Opening Hours:** 7.00am – end of daylight. **Avoid:** 11.00am – 2.00pm. **Green Fees:** Mon-Thur, €190. Fri-Sun €200. Twilight rate After 4pm €100 Residents Rate Mon-Sun €150 **Clubhouse Hours:** 7.00am – end of daylight. **Clubhouse Dress:** Smart casual. **Clubhouse Facilities:** Locker facilities, snack bar, fully stocked golf shop.

Course Description:
From arguably the best opening hole in golf, which is set amidst an amphitheatre of natural dunes, to the intoxicating 18th, which plays along the shore of Doughmore Bay, Doonbeg Golf Club features an ebb and flow of holes that will remain indelibly etched in your mind. The course routing maximizes the natural vistas of Doonbeg's dramatic setting while leading golfers along a 1.5 mile stretch of pristine Atlantic coast.

NO.	BLUE YARDS	WHITE YARDS	PAR	S.I.	NO.	BLUE YARDS	WHITE YARDS	PAR	S.I.
1	566	544	5	3	10	573	539	5	2
2	426	409	4	11	11	152	141	3	16
3	361	327	4	17	12	388	365	4	10
4	592	536	5	5	13	500	451	5	4
5	373	331	4	7	14	111	106	3	18
6	370	285	4	9	15	405	397	4	12
7	227	195	3	13	16	205	186	3	14
8	582	542	5	1	17	424	401	4	6
9	175	157	3	15	18	437	383	4	8
OUT	3,672	3,326	37		IN	3,195	2,969	35	
					TOTAL	6,870	6,295	72	
					STANDARD SCRATCH		74	71	

LOCATION: On the N67, between Kilkee and Milton Malbay.

GENERAL MANAGER: Joe Russell.

HEAD PROFESSIONAL: Brian Shaw.

ARCHITECT: Greg Norman.

Course Description:

Dromoland has had an extensive makeover & redesign in Spring 2004, now playing 600 yards longer with considerable alterations to greens, tees and some exciting new layouts. The great strength of the course was the maturity of the parkland setting, however Kirby and Carr have now added a championship edge to the design and produced a real test of skill with their new creation.

Newmarket-on-Fergus, Co. Clare.
Tel: (061) 368144. Fax: (061) 368498.
Email: golf@dromoland.ie
Web: www.dromoland.ie

SECRETARY: John O'Halloran. Tel: (061) 368444.

ARCHITECT: Ron Kirby & JB Carr.

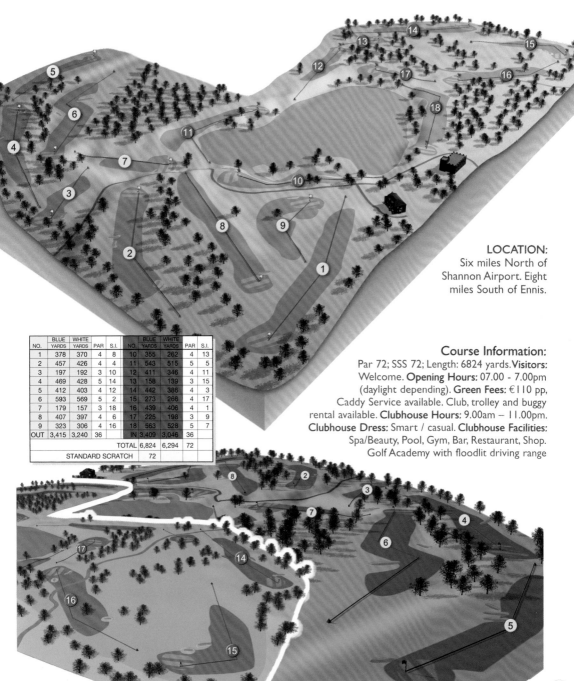

LOCATION:
Six miles North of Shannon Airport. Eight miles South of Ennis.

NO.	BLUE YARDS	WHITE YARDS	PAR	S.I.	NO.	BLUE YARDS	WHITE YARDS	PAR	S.I.
1	378	370	4	8	10	355	262	4	13
2	457	426	4	4	11	543	515	5	5
3	197	192	3	10	12	411	346	4	11
4	469	428	5	14	13	158	139	3	15
5	412	403	4	12	14	442	386	4	3
6	593	569	5	2	15	273	266	4	17
7	179	157	3	18	16	439	406	4	1
8	407	397	4	6	17	225	198	3	9
9	323	306	4	16	18	563	528	5	7
OUT	3,415	3,240	36		IN	3,409	3,046	36	
					TOTAL	6,824	6,294	72	
		STANDARD SCRATCH				72			

Course Information:

Par 72; SSS 72; Length: 6824 yards. **Visitors:** Welcome. **Opening Hours:** 07.00 - 7.00pm (daylight depending). **Green Fees:** €110 pp, Caddy Service available. Club, trolley and buggy rental available. **Clubhouse Hours:** 9.00am – 11.00pm. **Clubhouse Dress:** Smart / casual. **Clubhouse Facilities:** Spa/Beauty, Pool, Gym, Bar, Restaurant, Shop. Golf Academy with floodlit driving range

East Clare Golf Club, Coolreagh, Bodyke. Co. Clare.
Tel: (061) 921322. Fax: (061) 921717.

Web: www.eastclare.com

Email: eastclaregolfclub@eircom.net

Course Information: Par 71; SSS 71; Length 5,922 metres. **Visitors:** Pay as you play. **Opening Hours:** As clubhouse. **Ladies:** Welcome. **Juveniles:** Permitted. **Green Fees:** Weekdays €30; weekends €35. **Clubhouse Hours:** Winter 9am – 4.30pm; Summer 7.30am – 10pm. **Weekly Open Days:** Tuesday & Thursday. **Clubhouse Dress:** Informal. **Clubhouse Facilities:** Full catering.

Open Competitions: Every Thurs from April to mid Sept.

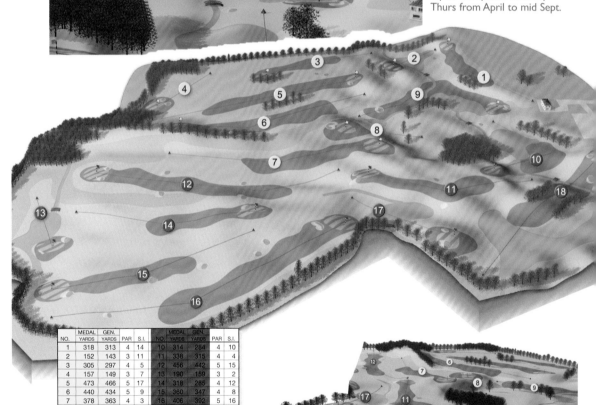

NO.	MEDAL YARDS	GEN. YARDS	PAR	S.I.	NO.	MEDAL YARDS	GEN. YARDS	PAR	S.I.
1	318	313	4	14	10	314	284	4	10
2	152	143	3	11	11	338	315	4	4
3	305	297	4	5	12	456	442	5	15
4	157	149	3	7	13	190	159	3	2
5	473	466	5	17	14	318	285	4	12
6	440	434	5	9	15	360	347	4	8
7	378	363	4	3	16	406	392	5	16
8	121	115	3	18	17	158	139	3	13
9	386	386	4	1	18	369	357	4	6
OUT	2,730	2,666	35		IN	2,909	2,720	36	
					TOTAL	5,639	5,386	71	
					STANDARD SCRATCH		71		

ARHITECT: Arthur Spring.

LOCATION: One and a half miles from Bodyke Village.

SEC MANAGER: M.L O'HANLON. Tel: (061) 921322.

Course Description:

All weather challenging parkland 18-hole course with special water features, designed with the players satisfaction, comfort and safety in mind.

Munster – Clare
Ennis

Drumbiggle, Ennis, Co. Clare.
Tel: (065) 6824074
Fax: (065) 6841848
Email: info@ennisgolfclub.com
Web: www.@ennisgolfclub.com

LOCATION: One mile west of town.

HON SECRETARY: Mike Butler.

MANAGER: Pat McCarthy.

Course Information: Par 71; SSS 69; Length 5,612 metres. **Visitors:** Welcome Mon – Fri. **Opening Hours:** 9.00am – sunset. **Avoid:** Tuesday after 3.00pm. **Green Fees:** €35. **Juveniles:** Welcome (half green fee if playing with an adult). Club Hire available; Caddy service available by prior arrangements. Telephone appointment required. **Clubhouse Hours:** 9.00am – 11.00pm. **Clubhouse Dress:** Casual. **Clubhouse Facilities:** Snacks and á la carte. **Open Competitions:** Open Week August. Handicap Certificate required for Open Competitions.

Course Description:
Rolling parkland course with tree-lined narrow fairways. The course overlooks the town of Ennis to the east and the green cliffs of Clare to the west.

NO.	METRES	PAR	S.I.	NO.	METRES	PAR	S.I.
1	312	4	5	10	351	4	12
2	114	3	18	11	310	5	2
3	305	4	13	12	420	5	2
4	270	4	15	13	158	3	16
5	333	4	7	14	383	4	3
6	419	4	1	15	299	4	6
7	140	3	17	16	176	3	14
8	360	4	4	17	304	4	8
9	492	5	9	18	486	5	10
OUT	2,745	35		IN	2,867	36	
				TOTAL	5,612	71	
	STANDARD SCRATCH				69		

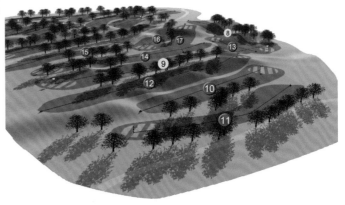

Kilkee Golf Club, East End,
Kilkee, Co. Clare.
Tel: (065) 905 6048
Fax: (065) 905 6977
Email: kilkeegolfclub@eircom.net
Web: www.kilkeegolfclub.ie

SECRETARY/MANAGER: Michael Culligan.

ARCHITECT: Eddie Hackett.

Course Description:
Kilkee Golf Club is proud of its 18 hole Links. Situated on the edge of the Atlantic Ocean in a most spectacular setting overlooking Moore Bay and its famous horse-shoe beach.

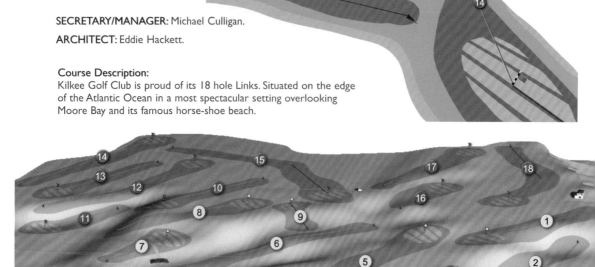

Course Information:
Par 69; SSS 68; Length 5,862 yards. **Visitors:** Welcome.
Opening Hours: Sunrise – sunset.
Ladies: Welcome. **Green Fees:** From €25; Half price with member. **Juveniles:** Welcome. Clubs and trolleys for hire; Caddy service available. **Clubhouse Hours:** 9.00am – closing.
Clubhouse Dress: Casual.
Clubhouse Facilities: Comfortable bar / snack bar, Restaurant with view over Kilkee Bay and Golf shop. **Open Competitions:** During June, July and August. Handicap Certificate required for Open Competitions.

NO.	YARDS	PAR	S.I.	NO.	YARDS	PAR	S.I.
1	329	4	9	10	274	4	18
2	425	5	5	11	159	3	10
3	249	4	17	12	461	5	8
4	155	3	7	13	366	4	6
5	391	4	1	14	425	5	14
6	363	4	3	15	377	4	2
7	132	3	11	16	122	3	16
8	313	4	13	17	360	4	4
9	146	3	15	18	335	4	12
OUT	2,503	34		IN	2,879	36	
				TOTAL	5,382	70	
				STANDARD SCRATCH		69	

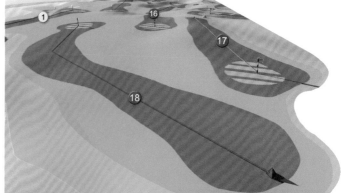

Parknamoney, Ennis Road,
Kilrush, Co. Clare.
Tel: (065) 905 1138
Fax: (065) 905 2633
Email: info@kilrushgolfclub.com
Web: www.kilrushgolfclub.com

LOCATION: One mile on Kilrush – Ennis Road.

SECRETARY/MANAGER: Denis Nagle.
Tel: (087) 623 7557

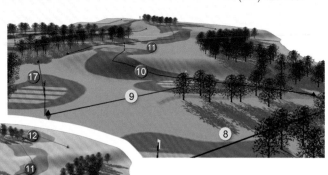

Course Information:

Par 68; SSS 70; Length 4,850 metres.
Visitors: Welcome. **Ladies:** Welcome Thursdays.
Green Fees: €40 Mon – Fri; €45 Sat/Sun & Bank Holidays;
€45 Husband & Wife. **Juveniles:** Welcome if accompanied by
an adult. Club Hire available. Buggy available for hire.
Clubhouse Hours: Daylight hours. **Clubhouse Dress:** Casual.
Clubhouse Facilities: Spacious new clubhouse opened
in 2001. Bar & Restaurant open all year
round. **Open Competitions:** Various
throughout the year, contact club for more
details.

Course Description:

Course with scenic view overlooking
Shannon Estuary. Particularly challenging Par
3 especially the 9th hole. The Par 5's will
prove very demanding to any golfer.
Further developments to both
clubhouse and
course recently
completed. Also, an
18 hole course
was opened in
July 1994.

NO.	CHAMP YARDS	MEDAL YARDS	PAR	S.I.	NO.	CHAMP YARDS	MEDAL YARDS	PAR	S.I.
1	324	313	4	5	10	285	263	4	15
2	348	324	4	9	11	421	416	4	1
3	442	438	4	2	12	338	327	4	13
4	136	127	3	18	13	504	450	5	17
5	402	391	4	4	14	176	161	3	8
6	349	338	4	11	15	505	490	5	6
7	490	483	5	14	16	398	388	4	3
8	166	158	3	16	17	196	184	3	10
9	168	159	3	7	18	338	326	4	12
OUT	2,825	2,731	34		IN	3,161	3,005	36	
					TOTAL	5,986	5,736	70	
					STANDARD SCRATCH		70	68	

Lahinch, Co Clare. Tel: (065) 7081003 Fax: (065) 7081592
Email: info@lahinchgolf.com
Web: www.lahinchgolf.com

SECRETARY: Alan Reardon.

PROFESSIONAL: Robert McCavery.

Tel: (065) 7081408

ARCHITECT: Dr Alastair MacKenzie.

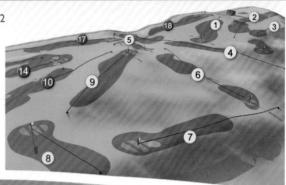

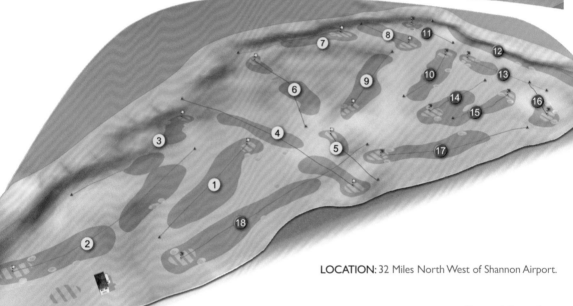

LOCATION: 32 Miles North West of Shannon Airport.

NO.	BLUE YARDS	WHITE YARDS	PAR	S.I.	NO.	BLUE YARDS	WHITE YARDS	PAR	S.I.
1	385	375	4	4	10	445	428	4	1
2	512	498	5	14	11	138	133	3	17
3	151	148	3	16	12	475	457	4	7
4	428	416	4	2	13	273	267	4	11
5	482	476	5	12	14	452	447	4	13
6	155	150	3	18	15	468	440	4	3
7	399	383	4	6	16	198	195	3	15
8	350	348	4	10	17	440	412	4	5
9	403	395	4	8	18	535	500	5	9
OUT	3,265	3,189	36		IN	3,422	3,279	35	
						TOTAL	6,687	6,468	
					STANDARD SCRATCH		73	71	

Course Information:
Par 72; SSS 74; Length 6,950 yards (Old Course). **Visitors:** Welcome most days – booking is necessary. **Opening Hours:** Sunrise – sunset. **Ladies:** Welcome. **Green Fees:** €155 per round, **Juveniles:** Welcome. **Clubhouse Hours:** 8am – 11pm approx. summertime. **Clubhouse Dress:** Casual, but smart. **Clubhouse Facilities:** Full clubhouse facilities; lessons available by prior arrangements; club hire and caddy service available, but cannot be guaranteed. **Open Competitions:** South of Ireland Amateur Open Championship – July.

Course Description:
Lahinch is steeped in history and has such famous holes as 'Dell' and 'Klondyke'. The features of this famous course are carved out of natural terrain. The Old Course is the permanent home of the South of Ireland Open Amateur Championship, first played in 1895 and which annually attracts the cream of Ireland's amateur golfers to play for this most coveted title and the magnificent trophy which goes with it.

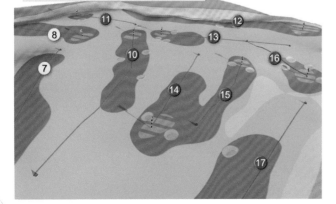

Lahinch, Co Clare. Tel: (065) 7081003 Fax: (065) 7081592

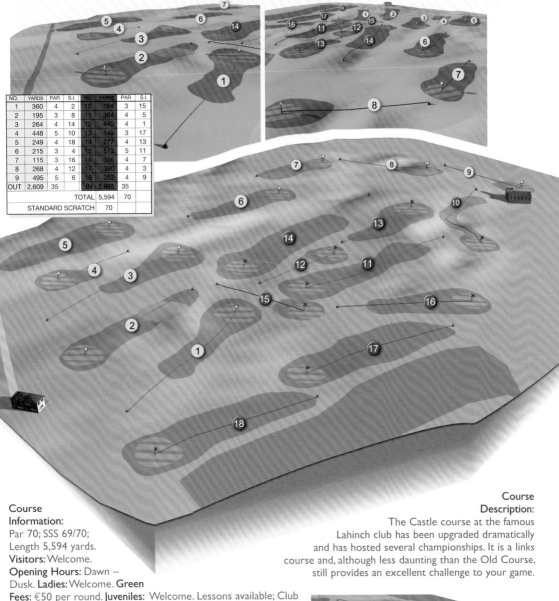

NO.	YARDS	PAR	S.I.	NO.	YARDS	PAR	S.I.
1	360	4	2	10	164	3	15
2	195	3	8	11	364	4	5
3	264	4	14	12	440	4	1
4	448	5	10	13	149	3	17
5	249	4	18	14	277	4	13
6	215	3	4	15	513	5	11
7	115	3	16	16	336	4	7
8	268	4	12	17	390	4	3
9	495	5	6	18	352	4	9
OUT	2,609	35		IN	2,985	35	
				TOTAL	5,594	70	
				STANDARD SCRATCH		70	

Course Information:

Par 70; SSS 69/70; Length 5,594 yards. **Visitors:** Welcome. **Opening Hours:** Dawn – Dusk. **Ladies:** Welcome. **Green Fees:** €50 per round. **Juveniles:** Welcome. Lessons available; Club Hire available; Caddy service available. **Clubhouse Hours:** 8.00am – 11.00pm summertime. **Clubhouse Facilities:** Lunches, dinners and snacks. Full clubhouse facilities. **Open Competitions:** Intermediate Scratch Trophy – May.

LOCATION: 300yds from Lahinch village.

SECRETARY: Alan Reardon.

PROFESSIONAL: Robert McCavery.

Tel: (065) 81408

Email: info@lahinchgolf.com

Web: www.lahinchgolf.com

Course Description:

The Castle course at the famous Lahinch club has been upgraded dramatically and has hosted several championships. It is a links course and, although less daunting than the Old Course, still provides an excellent challenge to your game.

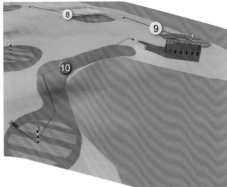

Shannon Airport, Shannon, Co. Clare.
Tel: (061) 471 849 Fax: (061) 471 507
Email: shannongolfclub@eircom.net
Web: www.shannongolfclub.ie

GENERAL MANAGER: Michael Corry.

PROFESSIONAL: Artie Pyke.

ARCHITECT: John D. Harris.

LOCATION: 200 yds beyond Airport
terminal building.

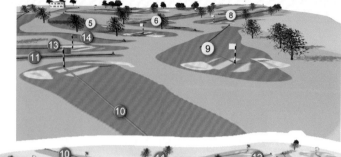

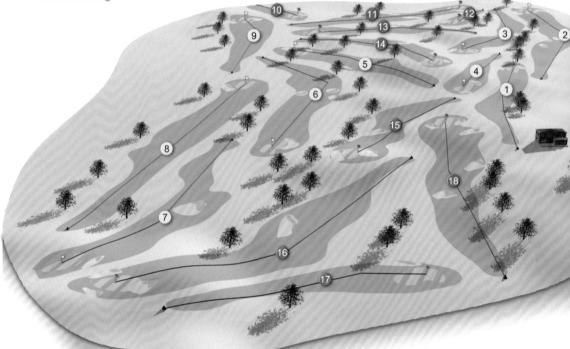

Course Information:

Par 72; SSS 72: Length 6,763 yards.
Visitors: Welcome at all times, subject to availability.
Opening Hours: Dawn to dusk. Avoid: Sunday. **Ladies:** Welcome
Tuesdays. **Green Fees:** €50 Weekday; €60 Weekends. 50% Reductions
with members. €25 early bird before 9.30am Mon- Fri **Juveniles:** Must
be accompanied by an adult. Lessons by prior arrangement. Club Hire
available. Caddy service available by prior arrangement; telephone
appointment required. **Clubhouse Hours:** Summer; 11.00am – 10.00pm.
Winter; 11.00am – 6.00pm. **Clubhouse Dress:** Casual. No shorts.
Clubhouse Facilities: Full bar and catering facilities available throughout
the year. Advisable to book for 4 or more people. **Open Competitions:**
Open Singles each Wednesday.

Course Description:

American styled golf course with plenty of
water hazards and bunkers. Tree lined
fairways demand accurate tee shots. The
greens are largely protected by mounds and
bunkers. Course is flat and presents a superb
challenge for every category of golfer. The
par 3, 17th hole is the signature hole with a
carry of 185 yds over the Shannon estuary.

NO.	MEDAL YARDS	GEN. YARDS	PAR	S.I.	NO.	MEDAL YARDS	GEN. YARDS	PAR	S.I.
1	393	382	4	5	10	172	156	3	18
2	507	497	5	13	11	343	338	4	16
3	433	415	4	3	12	216	180	3	8
4	180	167	3	11	13	338	331	4	10
5	331	321	4	17	14	372	345	4	14
6	515	504	5	9	15	403	397	4	2
7	393	369	4	7	16	394	385	4	4
8	575	501	5	15	17	219	213	3	6
9	472	455	4	1	18	507	492	5	12
OUT	3,799	3,611	38		IN	3,071	2,837	34	
					TOTAL	6,763	6,448	72	
				STANDARD SCRATCH		72	71		

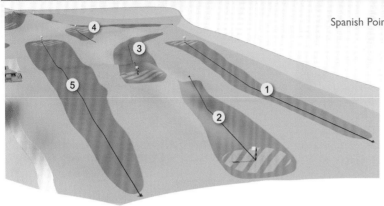

Spanish Point, Miltown Malbay, Co. Clare.
Tel: (065) 708 4198

LOCATION: Two miles from
Miltown Malbay.

SECRETARY MANAGER:
Dave Fitzgerald.
Tel: (065) 708 4219

Course Description:
This links course overlooks the picturesque golden
beach at Spanish Point. Playable all year it is renowned
for its unique six Par 3's and three Par 4's. The strong
Atlantic winds can make life difficult, but it is
both fun to play and a challenge for
any golf enthusiast.

Course Information:
Par 64; SSS 63; Length 4624 metres. **Visitors:**
Welcome (restrictions on Sundays). **Opening
Hours:** Sunrise – Sunset. **Green Fees:**
Weekdays €25, Weekends €30. €15 with
member. **Juveniles:** Welcome if accompanied
by adult. Juveniles under 14 are not allowed
after 5pm or on Sat / Sun. **Clubhouse Hours:**
10.00am – 11.00pm (summer); full clubhouse
facilities. **Clubhouse Dress:** Casual.
Clubhouse Facilities: Sandwiches and light
snacks available in bar everyday during the
summer. **Open Competitions:** Open
Weekend – May. Intermediate Scratch Cup
in September. Handicap certificate required
for Open Competitions.

NO.	METRES	PAR	S.I.	NO.	METRES	PAR	S.I.
1	307	4	13	10	307	4	8
2	180	3	9	11	180	3	12
3	371	4	7	12	371	4	6
4	205	3	5	13	205	3	4
5	387	4	1	14	387	4	18
6	339	4	3	15	339	4	10
7	287	4	11	16	287	4	16
8	100	3	15	17	100	3	14
9	136	3	17	18	136	3	2
OUT	2,312	32		IN	2,312	32	
				TOTAL	4,624	64	
	STANDARD SCRATCH				63		

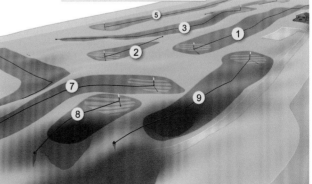

LOCATION: Approx 2 miles from the centre of Ennis off the Lahinch Road (N85).

SECRETARY: Avril Guerin.

ARCHITECT: Dr. Arthur Spring.

Woodstock Golf &
Country Club, Shanaway
Road. Ennis, Co. Clare.
Tel: (065) 6829463. Fax: (065) 6820304.
Email: woodstock.ennis@eircom.net
Web: www.woodstockgolfclub.com

Course Information: Par 71; SSS 71; Length 6429 yards, 5879 metres. **Visitors:** Visitors are welcome all days including weekends, but are advised to avoid members time at weekend. Members time up until 9.30am. **Opening Hours:** 8.00am until dusk. **Ladies:** No restrictions. Have priority on Tuesdays and Sundays. **Green Fees:** €42 Mon – Fri; €45 Sat / Sun / Bank Holidays Groups of 20 or more €32 early bird specials. **Juveniles:** Must be accompanied by an adult. **Clubhouse Hours:** 9.00am until closing time. **Clubhouse Dress:** Informal but neat. **Clubhouse Facilities:** Club shop. Caddy cars and caddies on request. Full bar and bar menu all day everyday. Restaurant and Sunday lunch and weekend nights. Tel: (065) 6841661. **Open Competitions:** Every Wednesday (Apr-Oct) & Bank Holiday Weekends.

NO.	MEDAL METRES	GEN. METRES	PAR	S.I.	NO.	MEDAL METRES	GEN. METRES	PAR	S.I.
1	366	356	4	3	10	427	410	5	16
2	344	334	4	11	11	162	148	3	12
3	379	358	4	5	12	456	423	5	14
4	172	163	3	15	13	372	346	4	2
5	450	423	5	13	14	181	161	3	6
6	170	161	3	7	15	276	272	4	18
7	391	373	4	1	16	377	356	4	4
8	170	134	3	9	17	343	330	4	10
9	469	451	5	17	18	359	340	4	8
OUT	2,911	2,753	35		IN	2,953	2,786	36	
					TOTAL	5,864	5,539	71	
		STANDARD SCRATCH					71	69	

Course Description:

The course is championship standard with greens maintained to the highest standard. It is built on 155 acres of free draining soil and is playable all year round. The course is challenging, yet is built so that it may be enjoyed by all categories of golfers. All who visit Woodstock will be sure of a warm welcome.

Bandon

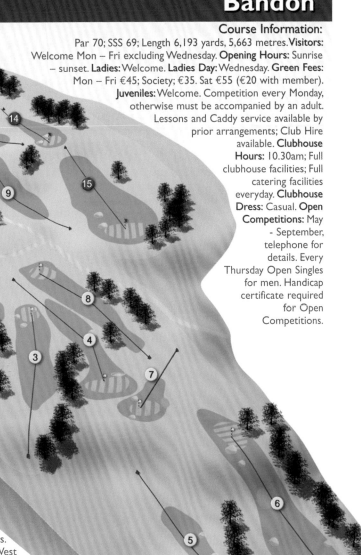

Course Information:
Par 70; SSS 69; Length 6,193 yards, 5,663 metres. **Visitors:** Welcome Mon – Fri excluding Wednesday. **Opening Hours:** Sunrise – sunset. **Ladies:** Welcome. **Ladies Day:** Wednesday. **Green Fees:** Mon – Fri €45; Society; €35. Sat €55 (€20 with member). **Juveniles:** Welcome. Competition every Monday, otherwise must be accompanied by an adult. Lessons and Caddy service available by prior arrangements; Club Hire available. **Clubhouse Hours:** 10.30am; Full clubhouse facilities; Full catering facilities everyday. **Clubhouse Dress:** Casual. **Open Competitions:** May - September, telephone for details. Every Thursday Open Singles for men. Handicap certificate required for Open Competitions.

Castlebernard,
Bandon, Co. Cork.
Tel: (023) 41111/42224.
Fax: (023) 44690.
www.bandongolfclub.com

Course Description:
Beautiful parkland course which some consider difficult due to the sloping fairways. It is one of a few eighteen hole course in West Cork.

SECRETARY: Donal Murphy.
PROFESSIONAL: Paddy O'Boyle.

LOCATION: Two miles west of Bandon Town.

NO.	MEDAL METRES	GEN. METRES	PAR	S.I.	NO.	MEDAL METRES	GEN. METRES	PAR	S.I.
1	296	284	4	16	10	417	390	4	3
2	440	429	4	2	11	115	115	3	17
3	381	370	4	6	12	406	401	4	11
4	369	349	4	12	13	451	418	4	5
5	432	400	4	10	14	427	417	4	1
6	454	449	4	4	15	528	515	5	9
7	192	185	3	14	16	345	335	4	13
8	501	491	5	18	17	330	325	4	15
9	357	346	4	8	18	193	183	3	7
OUT	3,422	3,303	36		IN	3,212	3,099	35	
					TOTAL	6,634	6,402	71	
					STANDARD SCRATCH		72	71	

Bantry Bay

Bantry, West Cork
Tel: (027) 50579 / 53773.
Email: info@bantrygolf.com
Website: www.bantrygolf.com

LOCATION: One mile
from Bantry on
Glengarriff Road, N71.

NO.	MEDAL METRES	GEN. METRES	PAR	S.I.	NO.	MEDAL METRES	GEN. METRES	PAR	S.I.
1	145	138	3	15	10	387	371	4	5
2	463	457	5	16	11	501	486	5	8
3	345	340	4	11	12	416	402	4	1
4	383	378	4	7	13	144	128	3	17
5	307	301	4	13	14	387	364	4	6
6	396	382	4	2	15	358	354	4	12
7	292	283	4	10	16	437	431	4	3
8	397	362	4	4	17	188	176	3	9
9	126	115	3	18	18	445	423	5	14
OUT	2,854	2,756	35		IN	3,263	3,135	36	
					TOTAL	6,117	5,891	71	
					STANDARD SCRATCH		70		

SECRETARY/MANAGER: John O'Sullivan.

Course Information:

Par 71; SSS 70; Length 6,117 metres. **Visitors:**
Contact: (027) 50579 / 53773 for times of play.
Opening Hours: 8.00am – sunset. Avoid: Days of
major competitions. Prior arrangement for
societies. **Green Fees:** Weekdays €35-40,
weekends €40-45; Group of 15+ Jun-Sept €30-
€35; Oct-Mar €25-€30. **Juveniles:** Welcome. Club
Hire available; caddy cars & buggy's available;
telephone appointment required. **Clubhouse
Hours:** 9.00am – sunset during summer months.
Clubhouse Dress: Casual. **Clubhouse Facilities:**
Bar and catering available.

Course Description:

Bantry Park is considered an interesting and
difficult course. Several plantations are steadily
coming into play, and are making the course
more intriguing.

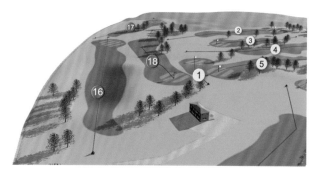

Filane, Castletownbere,
Co. Cork.
Tel: (027) 70700
Web: www.berehavengolf.com

LOCATION: 3 miles from
Castletownbere
on the Glengarriff road.

HON. SECRETARY:
J. J. McLaughlin.

NO.	METRES	PAR	S.I.	NO.	METRES	PAR	S.I.
1	310	4	11	10	270	4	14
2	442	5	17	11	360	4	4
3	351	4	7	12	370	4	2
4	385	4	3	13	410	5	18
5	291	4	15	14	291	4	10
6	146	3	9	15	146	3	16
7	384	4	1	16	329	4	6
8	149	3	5	17	135	3	12
9	166	3	13	18	186	3	8
OUT	2,624	34		IN	2,497	34	
				TOTAL	5,121	68	
	STANDARD SCRATCH		64				

Course Description:
A scenic sea-side links set on the edge of West Cork in a beautiful and quiet location. Water is a feature of the course both visually and in play. The latter features three holes where water comes into play, and require tee shots over the water. A new clubhouse was completed in 1994 which has other tourist facilities such as a caravan park, picnic area tennis courts and shingle beach.

Course Information:
Par 68; SSS 65; Length 5,184 metres. **Visitors:** Welcome at anytime. **Opening Hours:** 8am – Dark. **Ladies:** Welcome (no restrictions). **Green Fees:** €20 midweek, €25 at weekends. **Juveniles:** Welcome; €10; If busy must be accompanied by adult. Club Hire available. **Clubhouse Hours:** 11.00 – 11.30pm in season, otherwise at weekends 12.00 noon – 11.00pm. **Clubhouse Dress:** Casual. **Clubhouse Facilities:** Full facilities including showers and saunas. **Open Competitions:** Paddy Crowley Memorial – July; Open Week – July / August.

Blarney Golf Resort
Tower
Co. Cork
Tel: (021) 4516472 Fax: (021) 4516453
www.ramadablarney.com

LOCATION: Country Retreat just 8 miles from Cork City **DIRECTOR OF GOLF:** David O'Sullivan

Course Description:

Course makes full use of beautiful Shournagh Valley which features a magnificent protected woodland some stunning scenery. A range of tees ensures that everyone is well catered for.

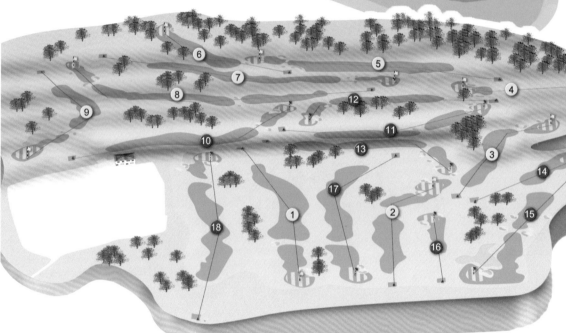

Course Information:

Par 71; SSS 71; Length 6518 Yards. Visitors Welcome. **Opening Hours:** 8am- Sunset, pro shop 8am-7pm, food served 12pm-10pm. **Avoid:** None. **Green Fees:** juveniles/seniors €25, Mon-Thur €55, Fri-Sun €65, Peak season. **Clubhouse Facilities:** Full catering changing rooms, sauna **Clubhouse Dress:** Dresscode applies, no metal spikes.

NO.	BLUE YARDS	WHITE YARDS	PAR	S.I.	NO.	MEDAL YARDS	GEN. YARDS	PAR	S.I.
1	388	384	4	16	10	413	404	4	7
2	169	162	3	5	11	452	434	4	2
3	292	263	4	18	12	393	354	4	6
4	168	162	3	9	13	400	397	4	14
5	361	352	4	11	14	174	169	3	12
6	396	386	4	10	15	450	444	4	3
7	601	598	5	4	16	332	312	4	17
8	509	504	5	15	17	379	373	4	13
9	383	375	4	8	18	452	445	4	1
OUT	3267	3186	36		IN	3445	3332	35	
					TOTAL	3712	6518	71	
					STANDARD SCRATCH	71	71		

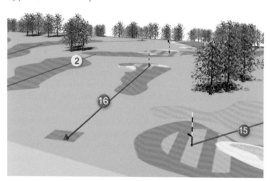

Charleville Golf Club,
Charleville, Co. Cork.
Tel: (063) 81257.
Fax: (063) 81274.

LOCATION: On main road from Cork to Limerick.

Email: info@charlevillegolf.com
www.charlevillegolf.com

SECRETARY: Pat Nagle.

HON. SECRETARY:
Tony Murphy.

WEST COURSE

NO.	YARDS	PAR	S.I.	NO.	YARDS	PAR	S.I.
1	335	4	13	10	370	4	8
2	155	3	18	11	362	4	4
3	369	4	1	12	303	4	15
4	379	4	9	13	533	5	10
5	344	4	5	14	350	4	14
6	373	4	11	15	376	4	6
7	374	4	3	16	158	3	17
8	383	4	7	17	481	5	12
9	162	3	16	18	437	4	2
OUT	2,874	34		IN	3,370	37	
				TOTAL	6,244	71	
				STANDARD SCRATCH		69	

Course Information: West Course: Par 71; SSS 69; Length 6,244 yards. East Course: Par 72; SSS 72; Length 6,902 yards. **Visitors:** Welcome. **Opening Hours:** 9am – sunset. Weekends telephone in advance. Avoid major competitions. **Ladies:** Welcome. **Green Fees:** €25 Mondays (except bank hols); €40 Tue – Fri; €50 weekends. **Juveniles:** Welcome. **Clubhouse Hours:** 9.00am – 12.00 midnight. **Clubhouse Dress:** Casual/neat. **Clubhouse Facilities:** Full bar and catering available. **Open Competitions:** Tuesdays Mar - Nov. Open Singles on Tue, Ladies Competitions Thursdays. Please telephone for details. (entry fee for open competitions; €20 incl green fees.)

Course Description: Both of Charleville's attractive and well maintained parkland courses are located in the foothills of the scenic Ballyhoura Mountains, in the heart of Ireland's Golden Vale. This 18 hole championship course, renowned for its lush fairways and excellent greens, offers relaxed and uncrowded golf in peaceful surroundings.

EAST COURSE

NO.	YARDS	PAR	S.I.	NO.	YARDS	PAR	S.I.
1	404	4	9	10	404	4	10
2	537	5	7	11	537	5	8
3	178	3	17	12	178	3	18
4	421	4	11	13	421	4	2
5	324	4	5	14	324	4	16
6	407	4	11	15	407	4	12
7	358	4	13	16	358	4	14
8	429	4	5	17	429	4	6
9	393	4	3	18	393	4	4
OUT	3,451	36		IN	3,451	36	
				TOTAL	6,902	72	
				STANDARD SCRATCH		72	

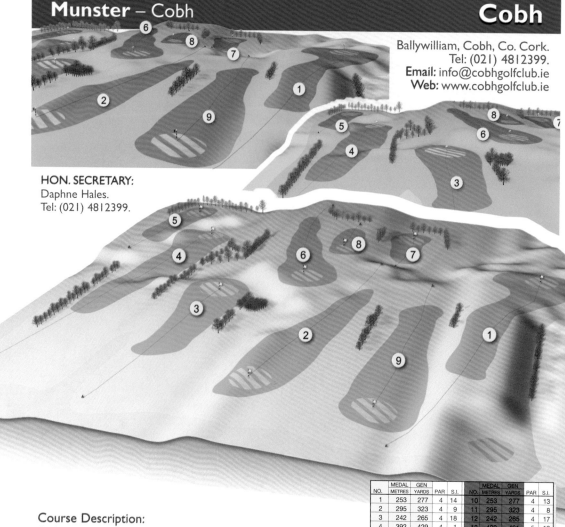

Ballywilliam, Cobh, Co. Cork.
Tel: (021) 4812399.
Email: info@cobhgolfclub.ie
Web: www.cobhgolfclub.ie

HON. SECRETARY:
Daphne Hales.
Tel: (021) 4812399.

Course Description:
A pleasant course on the outskirts of Cobh, noted for the short 7th hole which is a real card wrecker, with the out-of-bounds only feet away from the back of the green and all down along the right-hand side.

Course Information:
Par 67; SSS 64; Length 4,386 meters. **Visitors:** Welcome. Telephone appointment required for weekend play. **Opening Hours:** 9.00am – sunset. **Avoid:** Tuesdays. **Ladies:** Welcome Tuesdays. **Green Fees:** €20 per round (18 holes), €10 per round (18 holes) with full member (maximum of 2 paying green fees members). **Juveniles:** Welcome. **Clubhouse Hours:** 12 noon – 11.30pm. **Clubhouse Dress:** Casual but smart. **Clubhouse Facilities:** Full catering and bar facilities. **Open Competitions:** Mixed Foursomes every Wednesday evening 5.30pm (phone club for timesheet). Saturday Open Mixed Foursomes-Apr-Sept (phone club for timesheet).

NO.	MEDAL METRES	GEN YARDS	PAR	S.I.	NO.	MEDAL METRES	GEN YARDS	PAR	S.I.
1	253	277	4	14	10	253	277	4	13
2	295	323	4	9	11	295	323	4	8
3	242	265	4	18	12	242	265	4	17
4	392	429	4	1	13	422	461	5	12
5	157	172	3	11	14	157	172	3	10
6	375	410	4	3	15	375	410	4	2
7	152	166	3	5	16	152	166	3	4
8	143	156	3	7	17	143	156	3	6
9	264	289	4	16	18	264	289	4	15
OUT	2,273	2,487	33		IN	2,303	2,519	34	
					TOTAL	4,576	5,006	67	
					STANDARD SCRATCH	67	67		

LOCATION: One mile from Cobh.

COURSE MANAGER: Steve McCormack.

ARCHITECT: Eddie Hackett.

Plans for new 18 hole development underway. Due for completion 2008. Course may differ from map. Contact club for further details.

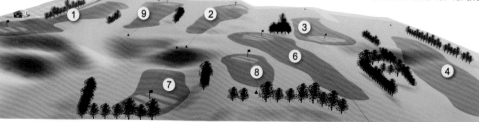

Little Island, Co. Cork.
Tel: (021) 4353451. Fax: (021) 4353410.
Email: corkgolfclub@eircom.net
Web: www.corkgolfclub.ie

NO.	MEDAL YARDS	GEN. YARDS	PAR	S.I.	NO.	MEDAL YARDS	GEN. YARDS	PAR	S.I.
1	340	335	4	8	10	374	358	4	2
2	460	442	5	16	11	454	450	5	15
3	244	244	4	18	12	289	286	4	11
4	411	402	4	1	13	157	149	3	13
5	510	504	5	6	14	397	380	4	4
6	300	272	4	14	15	383	366	4	7
7	169	158	3	10	16	323	315	4	17
8	379	374	4	3	17	360	335	4	9
9	178	170	3	12	18	387	370	4	5
OUT	2,991	2,901	36		IN	3,124	3,009	36	
					TOTAL	6,115	5,910		
					STANDARD SCRATCH		72		

ARCHITECT:
Alister MacKenzie.

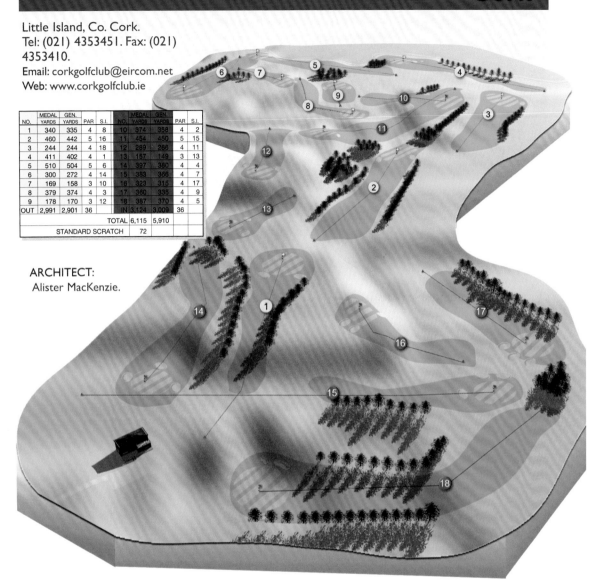

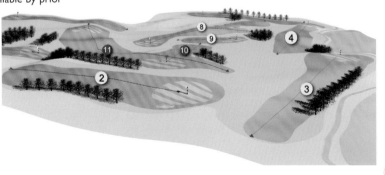

Course Information: Par 72; SSS 72; Length 6632 yards; 6,115 metres. Visitors: Welcome Mon / Tues / Wed / Fri except from 12.30pm – 2.00pm or after 4pm. Sat-Sun from 2pm. Opening Hours: Sunrise – sunset. Avoid: Thursday Ladies Day. Green Fees: €85 Mon – Fri; €95 Sat / Sun. Juveniles: Welcome. Lessons available by prior arrangement; Club Hire available, buggie hire, Caddy service available. Clubhouse Hours: Sunrise – sunset. Clubhouse Dress: Smart / casual. Clubhouse Facilities: Full bar and catering.

LOCATION: Five miles East of Cork City on N25 Rosslare Road.

Course Description: Not many clubs have such an attractive setting for a golf course with parkland running down to a rocky outcrop of land reaching out into Lough Mahon. An excellent championship test and one of the most attractive courses in Ireland.

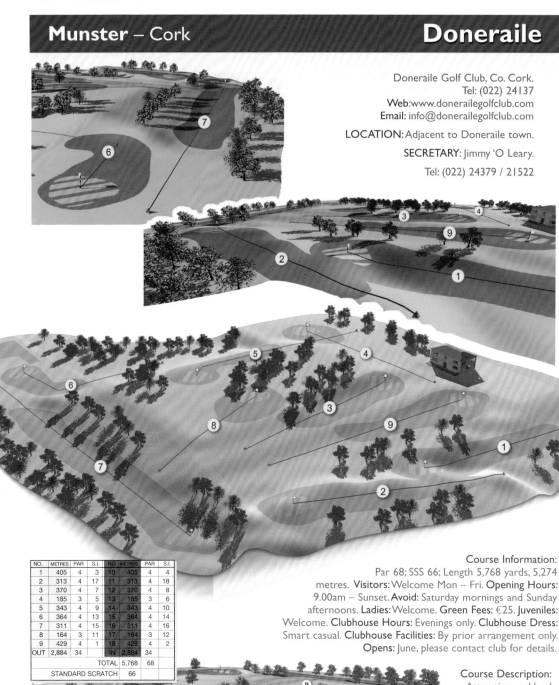

Doneraile Golf Club, Co. Cork.
Tel: (022) 24137
Web:www.donerailegolfclub.com
Email: info@donerailegolfclub.com

LOCATION: Adjacent to Doneraile town.

SECRETARY: Jimmy 'O Leary.

Tel: (022) 24379 / 21522

NO.	METRES	PAR	S.I.	NO.	METRES	PAR	S.I.
1	405	4	3	10	405	4	4
2	313	4	17	11	313	4	18
3	370	4	7	12	370	4	8
4	185	3	5	13	185	3	6
5	343	4	9	14	343	4	10
6	364	4	13	15	364	4	14
7	311	4	15	16	311	4	16
8	164	3	11	17	164	3	12
9	429	4	1	18	429	4	2
OUT	2,884	34		IN	2,884	34	
				TOTAL	5,768	68	
				STANDARD SCRATCH	66		

Course Information:
Par 68; SSS 66; Length 5,768 yards, 5,274 metres. Visitors: Welcome Mon – Fri. Opening Hours: 9.00am – Sunset. Avoid: Saturday mornings and Sunday afternoons. Ladies: Welcome. Green Fees: €25. Juveniles: Welcome. Clubhouse Hours: Evenings only. Clubhouse Dress: Smart casual. Clubhouse Facilities: By prior arrangement only. Opens: June, please contact club for details.

Course Description:
Attractive parkland course with many old oak, lime and beech trees. Deep and wide river valley which must be crossed twice in each nine holes. The Par 3 8th hole is a real gem. It is one of the nicest nine hole courses in the country.

Maryborough Hill, Douglas,
Co. Cork.
Tel: (021) 489 5297
Web: www.douglasgolfclub.ie

Course Information:
Par 72; SSS 71; Length; 5,972 metres. **Visitors:**
Welcome. **Opening Hours:** 7.00am – dusk. **Ladies:** Welcome.
Green Fees: Mon - Fri €45; Weekends €50. **Juveniles:** Must be
accompanied by an adult. **Clubhouse Hours:** 9.00am –
11.30pm. **Clubhouse Dress:** Smart.

Course Description:
A newly reconstructed golf course with a warm
welcome to play on your next visit to Cork. Please
contact the course at the number above to arrange a
Tee Time.

NO.	BLUE METRES	WHITE METRES	PAR	S.I.	NO.	BLUE YARDS	WHITE YARDS	PAR	S.I.
1	352	324	4	2	10	311	293	4	15
2	344	281	4	8	11	346	346	4	9
3	456	445	5	18	12	358	352	4	5
4	152	138	3	14	13	352	318	4	13
5	337	308	4	4	14	374	345	4	1
6	352	342	4	6	15	134	117	3	17
7	167	148	3	12	16	381	348	4	3
8	450	434	5	16	17	363	350	4	7
9	290	290	4	10	18	453	428	5	11
OUT	2,900	2,710	36		IN	3,072	2,897	36	
					TOTAL	5,972	5,607	72	
					STANDARD SCRATCH		71		

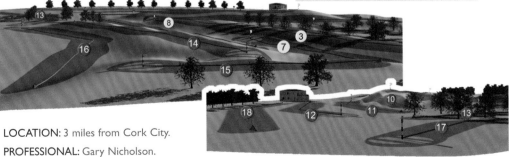

LOCATION: 3 miles from Cork City.
PROFESSIONAL: Gary Nicholson.
SECRETARY/MANAGER: Ronan Burke.

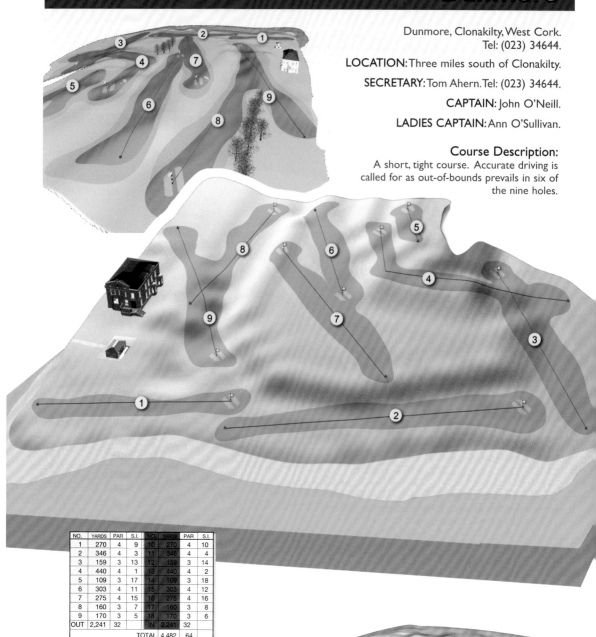

Dunmore, Clonakilty, West Cork.
Tel: (023) 34644.

LOCATION: Three miles south of Clonakilty.

SECRETARY: Tom Ahern. Tel: (023) 34644.

CAPTAIN: John O'Neill.

LADIES CAPTAIN: Ann O'Sullivan.

Course Description:
A short, tight course. Accurate driving is called for as out-of-bounds prevails in six of the nine holes.

NO.	YARDS	PAR	S.I.	NO.	YARDS	PAR	S.I.
1	270	4	9	10	270	4	10
2	346	4	3	11	346	4	4
3	159	3	13	12	159	3	14
4	440	4	1	13	440	4	2
5	109	3	17	14	109	3	18
6	303	4	11	15	303	4	12
7	275	4	15	16	275	4	16
8	160	3	7	17	160	3	8
9	170	3	5	18	170	3	6
OUT	2,241	32		IN	2,241	32	
				TOTAL	4,482	64	
				STANDARD SCRATCH		61	

Course Information:
Par 64; SSS 61; Length 4,464 yards, 4,080 metres. **Visitors:** Welcome avoid Saturday & Sunday mornings. **Opening Hours:** Sunrise – sunset. **Ladies:** Welcome. **Green Fees:** €25. **Juveniles:** Welcome every day – must be accompanied by an adult after 6.00pm in summer. Handicap Certificate required in competitions. **Clubhouse Hours:** 9.00am – 11.00pm. **Clubhouse Dress:** Casual. **Clubhouse Facilities:** In Hotel attached to course – usual trading hours. **Open Competitions:** First week of August.

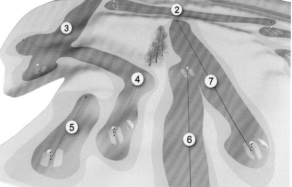

Gortacrue, Midleton, Co. Cork.
Tel: (021) 4631687.
Fax: (021) 4613695.

Course Information: Par 69; SSS 67; Length 5,774 metres. **Visitors:** Welcome. **Opening Hours:** 6.00am – 9.00pm. **Avoid:** Saturday morning and afternoon; Sunday morning. **Ladies:** Welcome. **Green Fees:** €30 Mon-Fri. €35 Weekends. **Juveniles:** Welcome. **Clubhouse Hours:** 9am – 11pm. **Clubhouse Dress:** Casual. **Clubhouse Facilities:** Bar snacks, tea and coffee. **Additional Facilities:** Pro Shop. Driving Range. **Open Competitions:** Contact club for details.

LOCATION: Two miles outside Midleton.

SECRETARY: Maurice Moloney.

ARCHITECT: E. Hackett.

NO.	MEDAL METRES	GEN. METRES	PAR	S.I.	NO.	MEDAL METRES	GEN. METRES	PAR	S.I.
1	176	153	3	3	10	261	251	4	14
2	329	309	4	5	11	325	289	4	8
3	333	313	4	9	12	336	316	4	2
4	343	313	4	1	13	328	300	4	4
5	160	150	3	7	14	142	127	3	10
6	302	287	4	17	15	441	411	5	16
7	130	120	3	15	16	128	128	3	18
8	316	290	4	11	17	480	450	5	12
9	496	470	5	13	18	181	161	3	6
OUT	2,585	2,405	34		IN	2,622	2,433	35	
					TOTAL	5,774	4,838	69	
					STANDARD SCRATCH	67	65		

Course Description:

A fine eighteen hole course, very tight as many trees planted in past years, are now coming into play. A new clubhouse opened in May 1992.

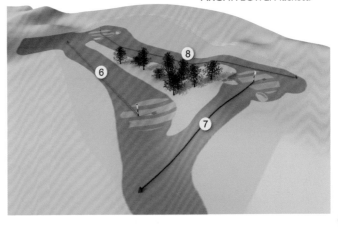

Corrin, Fermoy, Co. Cork.
Tel: (025) 31472.

Course Information:

Par 70; SSS 70; Length 5825 metres. **Visitors:** Welcome.
Opening Hours: 8.30am – sunset. **Green Fees:** Mon – Fri; €20
Sat / Sun & holidays; €30. **Juveniles:** Welcome before 5.00pm.
Must be accompanied by an adult. **Clubhouse Hours:**
10.00am – 11.30pm. **Clubhouse Dress:** Smart/Neat.
Clubhouse Facilities: 10.00am – 11.30pm. **Open
Competitions:** Various throughout the year telephone for
details. Open Singles every Wednesday.

SECRETARY:
Kathleen Murphy.

Course Description:

Heathland course with undulating terrain approximately 700ft above sea level. Plenty of scope with wide fairways. There are two distinct nine holes bisected by a road and the average width of fairways is 25 yards.

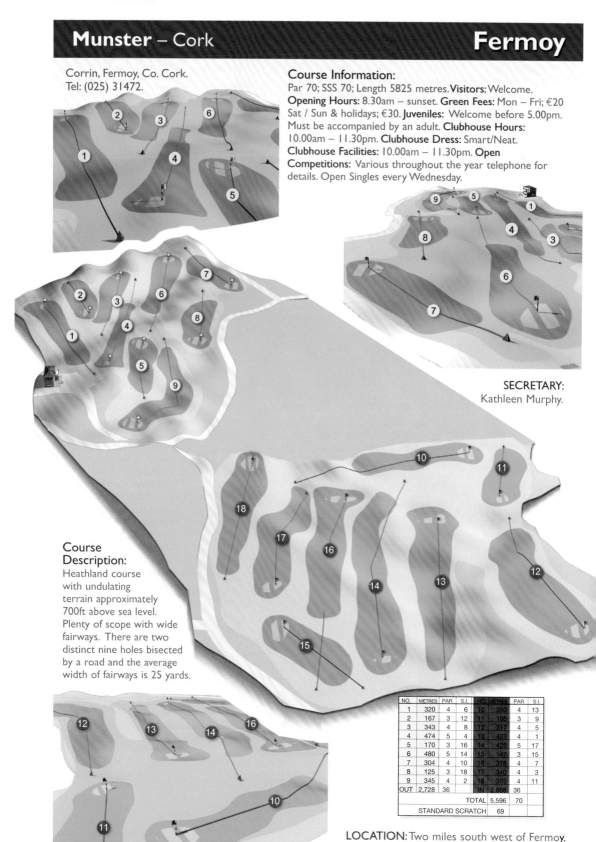

NO.	METRES	PAR	S.I.	NO.	METRES	PAR	S.I.
1	320	4	6	10	350	4	13
2	167	3	12	11	155	3	9
3	343	4	8	12	317	4	5
4	474	5	4	13	423	4	1
5	170	3	16	14	425	5	17
6	480	5	14	15	147	3	15
7	304	4	10	16	378	4	7
8	125	3	18	17	340	4	3
9	345	4	2	18	333	4	11
OUT	2,728	36		IN	2,868	36	
				TOTAL	5,596	70	
				STANDARD SCRATCH		69	

LOCATION: Two miles south west of Fermoy.

ARCHITECT: Commander Harris.

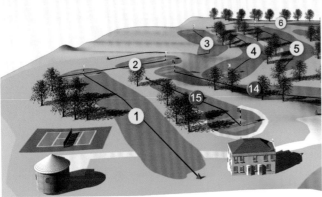

Fernhill Golf & Country Club,
Carrigaline, Co. Cork.
Tel: (021) 437 2226
E-mail: info@fernhillgolfhotel.com
Website: www.fernhillgolfhotel.com

LOCATION: 7 miles south of
Cork City on N28.

MANAGER: Ciaran Young.

ARCHITECT: Mr. Bowes.

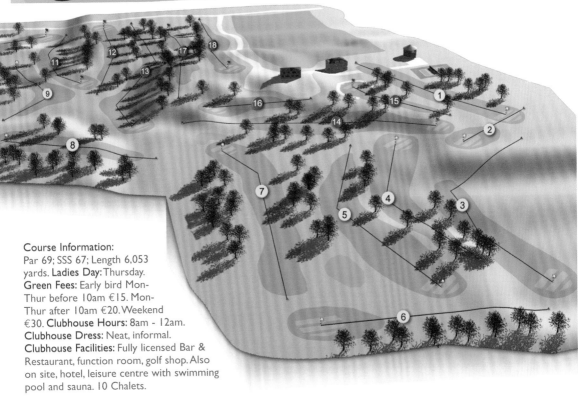

Course Information:
Par 69; SSS 67; Length 6,053
yards. **Ladies Day:** Thursday.
Green Fees: Early bird Mon-
Thur before 10am €15. Mon-
Thur after 10am €20. Weekend
€30. **Clubhouse Hours:** 8am - 12am.
Clubhouse Dress: Neat, informal.
Clubhouse Facilities: Fully licensed Bar &
Restaurant, function room, golf shop. Also
on site, hotel, leisure centre with swimming
pool and sauna. 10 Chalets.

Course Description:
18 hole tree lined course with a great variety of holes. The
par 3's in particular, are very demanding, requiring accurate
tee-shots if the greens are to be reached. The undulating
greens require a sure putting touch.

NO.	METRES	PAR	S.I.	NO.	METRES	PAR	S.I.
1	336	4	11	10	144	3	9
2	168	3	8	11	324	4	13
3	414	4	2	12	371	4	5
4	394	4	4	13	480	5	15
5	385	4	7	14	400	4	3
6	315	4	12	15	250	3	14
7	180	3	6	16	158	3	10
8	318	4	16	17	492	5	17
9	277	4	18	18	360	4	1
OUT	2,787	34		IN	2,979	35	
				TOTAL	5,766	69	
	STANDARD SCRATCH					67	

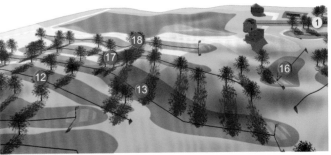

Fota Island Resort, Fota Island, Co. Cork.
Tel: 353 (0) 21 488 3700.
Fax: 353 (0) 21488 3871
Email: reservations@fotaisland.ie
Web: www.fotaisland.ie

Course Information: Par 71; SSS 73; Length 6,927 yards. **Visitors:** Welcome. **Opening Hours:** 8.30am-5pm. **Ladies:** Welcome everyday. **Green Fees:** €75 to €120. **Juveniles:** Welcome - student rate midweek. **Clubhouse Hours:** From 8.30am. **Clubhouse Dress:** Smart / Casual. **Clubhouse Facilities:** Full restaurant and bar.

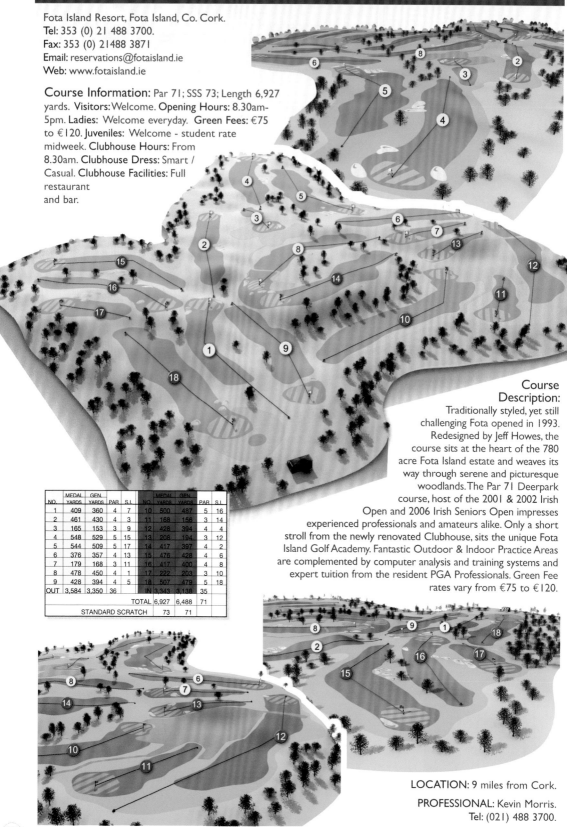

NO.	MEDAL YARDS	GEN YARDS	PAR	S.I.	NO.	MEDAL YARDS	GEN YARDS	PAR	S.I.
1	409	360	4	7	10	500	487	5	16
2	461	430	4	3	11	168	156	3	14
3	165	153	3	9	12	428	394	4	4
4	548	529	5	15	13	208	194	3	12
5	544	509	5	17	14	417	397	4	2
6	376	357	4	13	15	476	428	4	6
7	179	168	3	11	16	417	400	4	8
8	478	450	4	1	17	222	203	3	10
9	428	394	4	5	18	507	479	5	18
OUT	3,584	3,350	36		IN	3,343	3,138	35	
					TOTAL	6,927	6,488	71	
					STANDARD SCRATCH	73	71		

Course Description:

Traditionally styled, yet still challenging Fota opened in 1993. Redesigned by Jeff Howes, the course sits at the heart of the 780 acre Fota Island estate and weaves its way through serene and picturesque woodlands. The Par 71 Deerpark course, host of the 2001 & 2002 Irish Open and 2006 Irish Seniors Open impresses experienced professionals and amateurs alike. Only a short stroll from the newly renovated Clubhouse, sits the unique Fota Island Golf Academy. Fantastic Outdoor & Indoor Practice Areas are complemented by computer analysis and training systems and expert tuition from the resident PGA Professionals. Green Fee rates vary from €75 to €120.

LOCATION: 9 miles from Cork.

PROFESSIONAL: Kevin Morris.
Tel: (021) 488 3700.

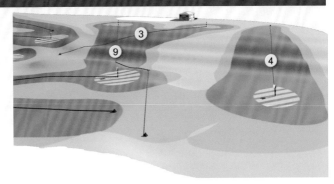

Frankfield, Cork
Tel: (021) 436 3124.
LOCATION: Two miles from Cork
Airport; Three miles from Cork City.

Course Information: Par 68; SSS 65; Length 5137 yards; 4697 metres. **Visitors:** Welcome. **Opening Hours:** 9.00am – Dusk. **Avoid:** Sat / Sun morning, after 2.00pm Thursdays & major competitions. **Ladies:** Welcome. **Green Fees:** Mon-Fri €15; Sat-Sun/Bank Holiday €18; Junior 14 to 18 €10; Student €12. **Juveniles:** Welcome. Must be accompanied by an adult. **Clubhouse Hours:** 10.30am – 11.00pm. **Clubhouse Dress:** Casual. **Clubhouse Facilities:** Lunches and snacks available at all times. Lunches Mon – Fri.

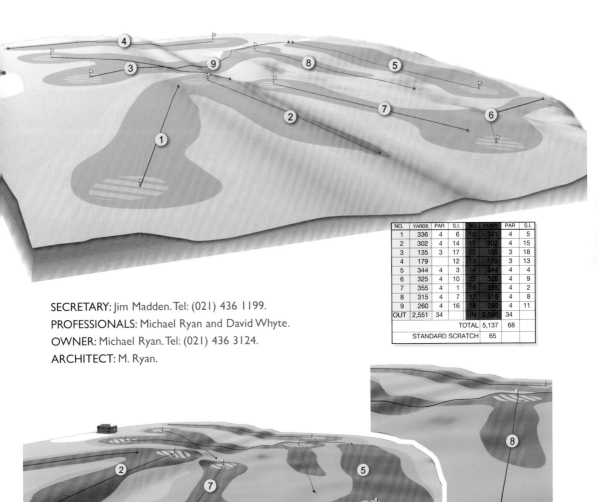

SECRETARY: Jim Madden. Tel: (021) 436 1199.
PROFESSIONALS: Michael Ryan and David Whyte.
OWNER: Michael Ryan. Tel: (021) 436 3124.
ARCHITECT: M. Ryan.

NO.	YARDS	PAR	S.I.	NO.	YARDS	PAR	S.I.
1	336	4	6	10	341	4	5
2	302	4	14	11	302	4	15
3	135	3	17	12	135	3	18
4	179		12	13	179	3	13
5	344	4	3	14	344	4	4
6	325	4	10	15	325	4	9
7	355	4	1	16	355	4	2
8	315	4	7	17	315	4	8
9	260	4	16	18	290	4	11
OUT	2,551	34		IN	2,586	34	
					TOTAL	5,137	68
				STANDARD SCRATCH		65	

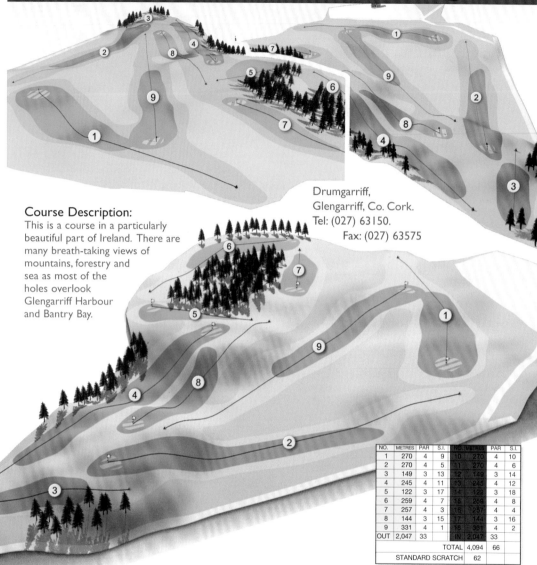

Course Description:
This is a course in a particularly beautiful part of Ireland. There are many breath-taking views of mountains, forestry and sea as most of the holes overlook Glengarriff Harbour and Bantry Bay.

Drumgarriff,
Glengarriff, Co. Cork.
Tel: (027) 63150.
Fax: (027) 63575

NO.	METRES	PAR	S.I.	NO.	METRES	PAR	S.I.
1	270	4	9	10	270	4	10
2	270	4	5	11	270	4	6
3	149	3	13	12	149	3	14
4	245	4	11	13	245	4	12
5	122	3	17	14	122	3	18
6	259	4	7	15	259	4	8
7	257	4	3	16	257	4	4
8	144	3	15	17	144	3	16
9	331	4	1	18	331	4	2
OUT	2,047	33		IN	2,047	33	
				TOTAL	4,094	66	
			STANDARD SCRATCH		62		

LOCATION: One mile from Glengarriff Village.
SECRETARY: Noreen Deasy. Tel: (027) 63150.

Course Information:
Par 66; SSS 62; Length 4477 yards; 4094 metres. **Visitors:** Welcome at all times. **Opening Hours:** 9.00am – sunset. **Ladies:** Welcome. **Green Fees:** Weekday €20 (€10 with menber); Weekend €25 (€15 with member). **Juveniles:** Welcome accompanied by adult. Club Hire available; Caddy service and cars available by prior arrangement. **Clubhouse Hours:** 10.30am – 11.30pm. **Clubhouse Dress:** Casual. **Clubhouse Facilities:** Bar snacks available all week. Full catering available by prior arrangement. **Open Competitions:** Phone club for details.

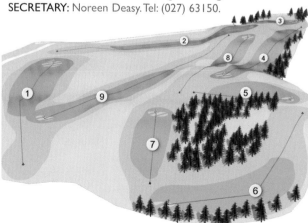

Clash, Little Island, Co. Cork. **Tel:** (021) 435 3094.
Fax: (021) 435 4408.
Email: hpoint@iol.ie
Web: www.harbourpointgolfclub.com

Course Description: Harbour Point on the banks of the River Lee has a particular rustic charm. Little Island by its topography and setting has all the natural gifts required for a great golf course. Championship golf course with each fairway tree lined and each green intricately contoured. It is a complex with an in-built 21 bay, all weather and flood-lit driving range positioned in acres of ground between the 5th & 9th holes.

NO.	MEDAL METRES	GEN. METRES	PAR	S.I.	NO.	MEDAL METRES	GEN. METRES	PAR	S.I.
1	310	280	4	11	10	341	333	4	6
2	176	169	3	7	11	450	442	5	16
3	337	312	4	17	12	197	189	3	4
4	498	490	5	5	13	353	345	4	10
5	180	173	3	9	14	351	330	4	8
6	421	413	4	3	15	341	333	4	12
7	411	403	4	1	16	360	352	4	2
8	345	323	4	13	17	134	127	3	14
9	467	459	5	15	18	430	422	5	18
OUT	3,145	3,022	36		IN	2,957	2,873	36	
					TOTAL	6,102	5,895	72	
					STANDARD SCRATCH	70	71		

Course Information:
Par 72; SSS 72; Length 6,102 metres. **Visitors:** Always welcome. Telephone appointment required. **Opening Hours:** 8am – 5pm. **Avoid:** Sunday before 11am. **Green Fees:** €27 Mon, Wed-Fri, before 11am, €35 after 1pm. Sat-Sun, €43pp. **Juveniles:** Welcome. **Clubhouse Hours:** 8am – 12 midnight. **Clubhouse Dress:** Neat. **Clubhouse Facilities:** Full Restaurant and Bar. **Catering hours:** 10.00am – 6.00pm (winter). 10.00am – 9.00pm (summer). Golf Society and green fees welcome.

LOCATION: Seven km from City Centre.

GENERAL MANAGER: Aylmer Barrett.

PROPRIETOR: Joe Scally.

379

Fairy Hill Golf Club, Kanturk, Boyle, Co. Cork. Tel: (029) 50534. Fax: (029) 20951

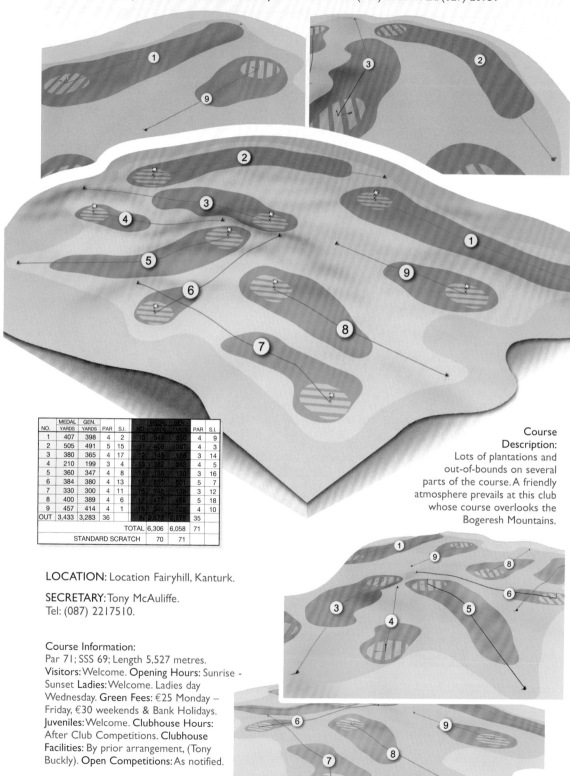

NO.	MEDAL YARDS	GEN. YARDS	PAR	S.I.	NO.	MEDAL YARDS	GEN. YARDS	PAR	S.I.
1	407	398	4	2	10	348	330	4	9
2	505	491	5	15	11	408	397	4	3
3	380	365	4	17	12	145	138	3	14
4	210	199	3	4	13	382	343	4	5
5	360	347	4	8	14	135	130	3	16
6	384	380	4	13	15	511	501	5	7
7	330	300	4	11	16	146	139	3	12
8	400	389	4	6	17	477	468	5	18
9	457	414	4	1	18	348	328	4	10
OUT	3,433	3,283	36		IN	2,873	2,775	35	
					TOTAL	6,306	6,058	71	
					STANDARD SCRATCH	70	71		

Course Description:
Lots of plantations and out-of-bounds on several parts of the course. A friendly atmosphere prevails at this club whose course overlooks the Bogeresh Mountains.

LOCATION: Location Fairyhill, Kanturk.

SECRETARY: Tony McAuliffe.
Tel: (087) 2217510.

Course Information:
Par 71; SSS 69; Length 5,527 metres.
Visitors: Welcome. **Opening Hours:** Sunrise - Sunset **Ladies:** Welcome. Ladies day Wednesday. **Green Fees:** €25 Monday – Friday, €30 weekends & Bank Holidays. **Juveniles:** Welcome. **Clubhouse Hours:** After Club Competitions. **Clubhouse Facilities:** By prior arrangement, (Tony Buckly). **Open Competitions:** As notified.

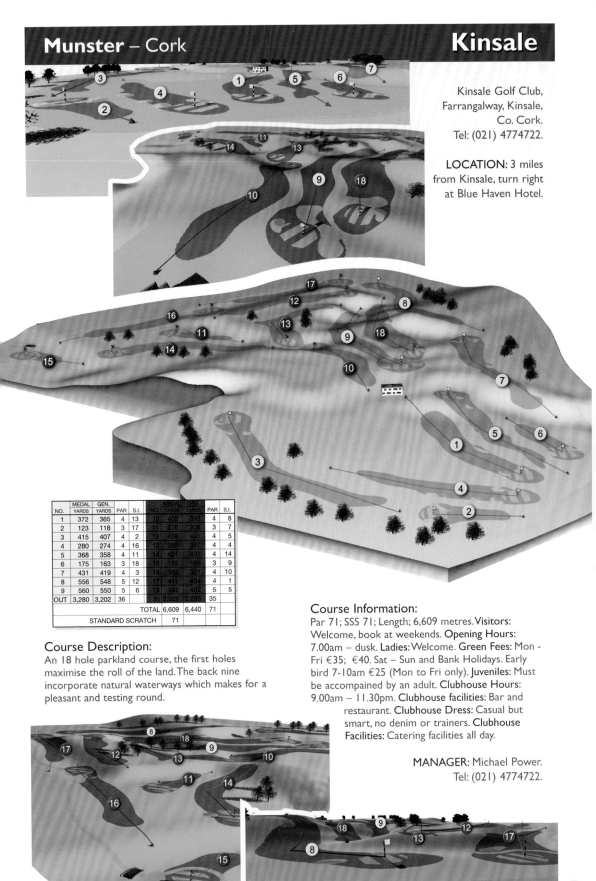

Kinsale Golf Club,
Farrangalway, Kinsale,
Co. Cork.
Tel: (021) 4774722.

LOCATION: 3 miles
from Kinsale, turn right
at Blue Haven Hotel.

NO.	MEDAL YARDS	GEN. YARDS	PAR	S.I.	NO.	MEDAL YARDS	GEN. YARDS	PAR	S.I.
1	372	365	4	13	10	405	398	4	8
2	123	118	3	17	11	216	206	3	7
3	415	407	4	2	12	436	431	4	5
4	280	274	4	16	13	393	387	4	4
5	368	358	4	11	14	421	401	4	14
6	175	163	3	18	15	183	168	3	9
7	431	419	4	3	16	383	361	4	10
8	556	548	5	12	17	411	404	4	1
9	560	550	5	6	18	492	482	5	5
OUT	3,280	3,202	36		IN	3,329	3,238	35	
					TOTAL	6,609	6,440	71	
					STANDARD SCRATCH		71		

Course Description:
An 18 hole parkland course, the first holes
maximise the roll of the land. The back nine
incorporate natural waterways which makes for a
pleasant and testing round.

Course Information:
Par 71; SSS 71; Length; 6,609 metres. Visitors:
Welcome, book at weekends. **Opening Hours:**
7.00am – dusk. **Ladies:** Welcome. **Green Fees:** Mon -
Fri €35; €40. Sat – Sun and Bank Holidays. Early
bird 7-10am €25 (Mon to Fri only). **Juveniles:** Must
be accompanied by an adult. **Clubhouse Hours:**
9.00am – 11.30pm. **Clubhouse facilities:** Bar and
restaurant. **Clubhouse Dress:** Casual but
smart, no denim or trainers. **Clubhouse
Facilities:** Catering facilities all day.

MANAGER: Michael Power.
Tel: (021) 4774722.

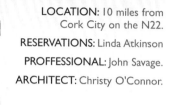

LOCATION: 10 miles from Cork City on the N22.

RESERVATIONS: Linda Atkinson

PROFFESSIONAL: John Savage.

ARCHITECT: Christy O'Connor.

Course Description:
Parkland course with water featuring at several holes. Play one of the top three golf courses in the Cork area.

Clashanure, Ovens, Co. Cork.
Tel: (021) 733 1721
Email: reservations@leevalleygcc.ie
Website: www.leevalleygcc.ie

Course Information:

Par 72; SSS 72; Length 6,725 yards. **Avoid:** Saturday & Sunday til noon. **Opening Hours:** 7am - 6pm (depending on daylight). **Green Fees:** Monday €35 Tues-Thurs €50, Fri-Sun €60, Midweek earlybird (exc Wed) €35 (before 10am)weekdays, €48 weekends. Group and society rates available, Golf & food packages available. **Clubhouse Dress:** Neat informal. **Clubhouse Facilities:** Bar and full restaurant. **Open Competitions:** Regular throughout the year. Specialise in corporate events. 19 seater Lee Valley coach available.

NO.	MEDAL YARDS	GEN. YARDS	PAR	S.I.	NO.	MEDAL YARDS	GEN. YARDS	PAR	S.I.
1	363	345	4	11	10	347	324	4	18
2	344	331	4	7	11	549	522	5	6
3	179	165	3	13	12	178	166	3	16
4	528	504	5	15	13	379	358	4	10
5	475	457	4	1	14	407	389	4	12
6	169	153	3	17	15	538	525	5	4
7	451	436	4	3	16	171	160	3	14
8	528	511	5	9	17	407	394	4	2
9	315	303	4	5	18	399	381	4	8
OUT	3,352	3,205	36		IN	3,373	3,219	36	
					TOTAL	6,725	6,424	72	
					STANDARD SCRATCH		72	70	

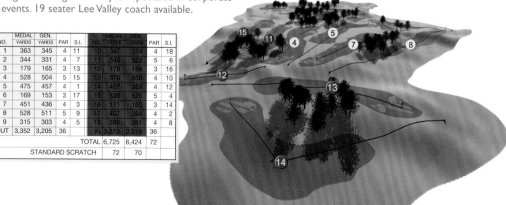

Course Description:

Lisselan is one of the most challenging and picturesque courses to be played anywhere in the country. The new Par 72 layout (nine holes played from different tee boxes) consists of 4 par 5, 4 par 3 and 10 par 4 holes. The course will challenge golfers of all skill levels as golfers must plot their route from tee to green surrounded by the glorious Lisselan Gardens and River Argideen.

Lisselan Golf Club, Clonakilty, West Cork
Tel: (023) 33249 Fax: (023) 34605
Email: info@lisselan.com   Web: www.lisselan.com

SECRETARY: Denis McSweeney.
CAPTAIN: Philip Ward.
PRO: Trevor Kingston.

Course Information:

Visitors: Welcome at all times.
Opening Hours: 8.00am to dusk, seven days a week. **Green Fees:** 9 hole: weekdays €17.50, weekends €20. 18 hole: weekdays €27.50, weekends €30. Group discount available.
Juveniles: Welcome, under 18 discount.
Clubhouse Facilities: Bag and trolley hire available, booking is required.

LOCATION: Course entrance directly of the N71 (from Cork) on left hand side of road (signposted either side).

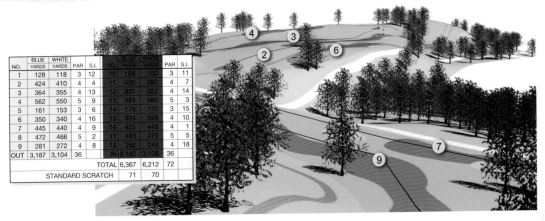

NO.	BLUE YARDS	WHITE YARDS	PAR	S.I.	NO.	BLUE YARDS	WHITE YARDS	PAR	S.I.
1	128	118	3	12	10	155	150	3	11
2	424	410	4	4	11	400	390	4	7
3	364	355	4	13	12	331	322	4	14
4	562	550	5	9	13	593	582	5	3
5	161	153	3	6	14	179	170	3	15
6	350	340	4	16	15	334	326	4	10
7	445	440	4	9	16	453	448	4	1
8	472	466	5	2	17	483	475	5	5
9	281	272	4	8	18	252	245	4	18
OUT	3,187	3,104	36		IN	3,180	3,108	36	
					TOTAL	6,367	6,212	72	
					STANDARD SCRATCH		71	70	

Macroom

Lackaduve, Macroom, Co. Cork.
Tel: (026) 41072. Fax: (026) 41391.
Web: www.macroomgolfclub.com
Email: mcroomgc@iol.ie

LOCATION: On grounds of Castle Demesne in the centre of the town.

HON. SECRETARY: Michael O'Mahoney.

MANAGER: Cathal O' Sullivan.

Course Description:
An undulating scenic 18 hole parkland course within the town and constructed around the River Sullane. Natural water hazards are a major feature of the course on the back nine. Situated on the main Cork / Killarney Road with entrance through castle gates.

NO.	METRES	PAR	S.I.	NO.	METRES	PAR	S.I.
1	429	5	14	10	437	5	15
2	114	3	11	11	130	3	13
3	344	4	1	12	292	4	10
4	290	4	18	13	159	3	7
5	298	4	8	14	300	4	6
6	162	3	4	15	239	4	17
7	412	4	2	16	277	4	16
8	329	4	12	17	450	5	9
9	360	4	5	18	343	4	3
OUT	2,763	35		IN	2,627	36	
				TOTAL	5,390	71	
				STANDARD SCRATCH		70	

Course Information:
Par 71; SSS 70; Length 5574 metres. **Visitors:** Welcome but it is advisable to phone in advance. **Opening Hours:** Sunrise – sunset. **Avoid:** Days of major competitions. **Ladies:** Ladies day Wed. Ladies full membership. **Green Fees:** €35 Mon – Fri; €40 at weekends & Bank Holidays. Early Bird up to 11am Mon-Thur €20. €15 juveniles/student. **Juveniles:** Cannot play after 6.00pm or at weekends. Caddy service and buggies available by prior arrangement. Telephone appointment is required. **Clubhouse Hours:** 9am – 11.30pm. **Clubhouse Dress:** Casual. **Open Competitions:** Open Week: 28th-4th June.

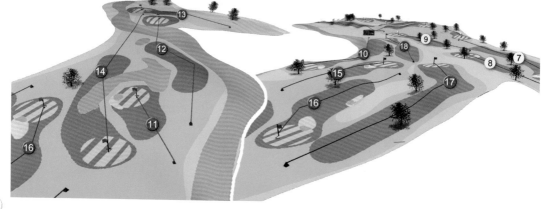

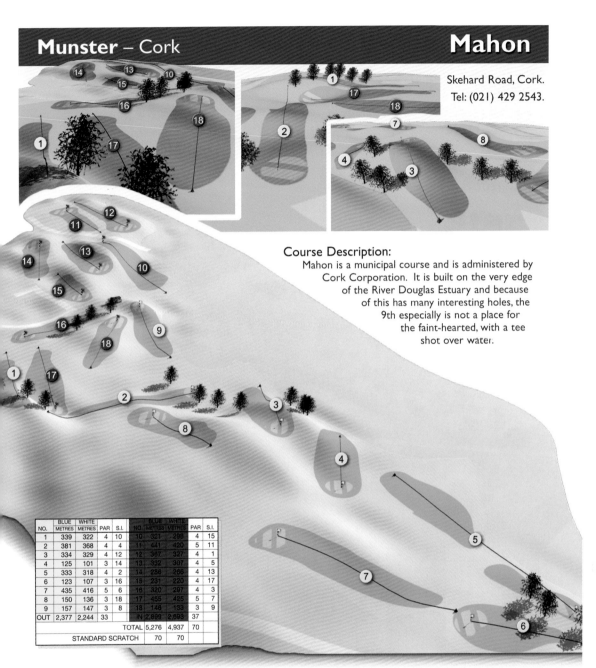

Skehard Road, Cork.
Tel: (021) 429 2543.

Course Description:

Mahon is a municipal course and is administered by Cork Corporation. It is built on the very edge of the River Douglas Estuary and because of this has many interesting holes, the 9th especially is not a place for the faint-hearted, with a tee shot over water.

NO.	BLUE METRES	WHITE METRES	PAR	S.I.	NO.	BLUE METRES	WHITE METRES	PAR	S.I.
1	339	322	4	10	10	321	298	4	15
2	381	368	4	4	11	441	420	5	11
3	334	329	4	12	12	367	327	4	1
4	125	101	3	14	13	332	307	4	5
5	333	318	4	2	14	286	266	4	13
6	123	107	3	16	15	231	220	4	17
7	435	416	5	6	16	320	297	4	3
8	150	136	3	18	17	455	425	5	7
9	157	147	3	8	18	146	133	3	9
OUT	2,377	2,244	33		IN	2,899	2,693	37	
					TOTAL	5,276	4,937	70	
		STANDARD SCRATCH				70	70		

Course Information:

Par 70; SSS 66; Length 5,192 metres. Visitors: Welcome. Should ring in advance. Opening Hours: Sunrise - Sunset. Avoid: Fri/Sat & Sun mornings. Juniors & Seniors discouraged at weekends Ladies: Welcome. Green Fees: €26 Mon - Fri; €30 Sat & Sun; Pensioners, Students and Juveniles €12.50/€13 Mon - Fri. Juveniles: Welcome. Club hire available. Clubhouse Dress: Casual. Clubhouse Facilities: Bar and catering facilities available at the Blackrock Inn. Tel: (021) 4291006.

EMAIL: mahon-golf@leisureworldcork.com

LOCATION: Skehard Road (Three miles from city).

HON. SECRETARY: Harry Kidney Tel: (021) 429 2543.

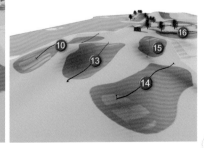

Ballyellis, Mallow, Co Cork.
Tel: (022) 21145.
Fax: (022) 42501.
Email: mallowgolfclubmanager@eircom.net
Web: www.mallowgolfclub.net

SECRETARY / MANAGER: David Curtin. Tel: (022) 21145.

PROFESSIONAL: Sean Conway. Tel: (022) 43424.

ARCHITECT: Commander John D. Harris.

LOCATION: One mile from
centre of Mallow town on the
Killavullen Road.

NO.	MEDAL METRES	GEN. METRES	PAR	S.I.	NO.	MEDAL METRES	GEN. METRES	PAR	S.I.
1	367	359	4	7	10	393	381	4	6
2	174	166	3	9	11	155	145	3	12
3	448	439	5	11	12	496	490	5	8
4	172	167	3	15	13	379	356	4	2
5	347	339	4	3	14	287	273	4	16
6	462	440	5	13	15	351	345	4	4
7	413	388	4	1	16	116	107	3	18
8	435	428	5	17	17	446	435	5	14
9	339	333	4	5	18	180	173	3	10
OUT	3,157	3,059	37		IN	2,803	2,710	35	
					TOTAL	5,960	5,796	72	
					STANDARD SCRATCH	72	71		

Course Information:
Par 72; SSS 72; Length 5,960 metres. **Visitors:** Welcome to play on
weekdays but pre-booking is essential. **Opening Hours:** 8am to late
evening. **Avoid:** Saturday and Sunday. Prior arrangement is essential.
Green Fees: Phone club for details. Caddy car
hire available by prior arrangment. **Clubhouse
Hours:** 9.00am – 11.00pm. **Clubhouse Dress:**
Clean, causal dress. No Denims. **Clubhouse
Facilities:** 4 all weather flood-lit tennis courts,
2 squash courts, snooker room, television
lounge and sauna. Snacks at all times. Full bar and
catering facilities. **Open Competitions:** Open week,
5th – 9th June.

Course Description:
This majestic parkland course, with
exceptional views of both the Mushera and the
distant Galtee mountains, boasts an idyllic rural
setting. Set in the heart of the Blackwater Valley,
Mallow's undulating treelined fairways transport the
golfer from tee to green, and provide an enjoyable
testing round of golf.

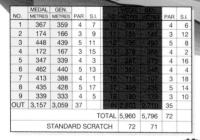

Mitchelstown

Gurrane, Mitchelstown, Co. Cork.
Tel: (025) 24072
Web: www.michelstown-golf.com

LOCATION: One mile on Limerick Road from Mitchelstown.

SECRETARY: Denis Gorey.

Course Description:
A reasonably level course which appears easy, but should not be under estimated. The main attraction to visitors of this delightful parkland championship course are the nearby Galtee Mountains. Additional holes open.

NO.	MEDAL METRES	GEN. METRES	PAR	S.I.	NO.	MEDAL METRES	GEN. METRES	PAR	S.I.
1	451	434	5	5	10	485	445	5	14
2	348	348	4	11	11	103	150	3	12
3	137	126	3	17	12	359	349	4	2
4	357	340	4	1	13	353	333	4	6
5	376	358	4	3	14	143	126	3	16
6	482	455	5	15	15	284	272	4	4
7	365	353	4	7	16	325	314	4	18
8	490	450	5	9	17	175	175	3	8
9	152	135	3	13	18	328	328	4	10
OUT	3,158	2,999	37		IN	2,615	2,494	34	
				TOTAL	5,773	5,493	71		
				STANDARD SCRATCH	71	70			

Course Information:
Par 67; SSS 66; Length 5,148 metres. **Visitors:** Welcome. **Opening Hours:** Sunrise – sunset. **Green Fees:** €25 Mon - Fri, €30 Sat - Sun. **Juveniles:** Welcome. Must be accompanied by an adult after 6.00pm. **Clubhouse Hours:** 9.00am – 11.30pm. **Clubhouse Dress:** Casual. **Clubhouse Facilities:** Bar, Snacks available. No lessons currently available. **Open Competitions:** Contact clubhouse or website for details.

Parkgariffe, Monkstown, Co. Cork.
Tel: (021) 4841376 **Fax:** (021) 4863452
Email: office@monkstowngolfclub.com.

Course Information:

Par 70; SSS 69; Length 6,199 yards; 5,669 metres. **Visitors:** Welcome. Telephone bookings in advance advisable. **Opening Hours:** 8.00am – sunset. **Avoid:** Tues (Ladies Day); Wed afternoon; Sat / Sun mornings. **Green Fees:** €50 Mon – Thurs; €43 Fri / Sun. Reductions for societies, €20 with member. **Juveniles:** Must be accompanied by an adult. Lessons available by prior arrangements; Club Hire and Caddy cars available; telephone appointment advisable. **Clubhouse Hours:** 8.00am – 11.30pm. **Clubhouse Dress:** Casual. No denims or sneakers. **Clubhouse Facilities:** Breakfast, Lunch, Dinner, a la carte. Last orders 9.00pm; Tel: (021) 486 3913. Bar open 12.00 noon – 11.30pm. **Open Competitions:** Intermediate, Junior and Senior Scratch Cups.

LOCATION: Seven miles from City.

NO.	MEDAL METRES	GEN. METRES	PAR	S.I.	NO.	MEDAL METRES	GEN. METRES	PAR	S.I.
1	181	167	3	10	10	305	284	4	13
2	344	330	4	6	11	344	340	4	5
3	513	490	5	14	12	299	287	4	15
4	230	230	4	18	13	159	144	3	17
5	316	286	4	4	14	377	350	4	3
6	166	158	3	12	15	470	455	5	11
7	284	273	4	16	16	172	185	3	9
8	361	347	4	2	17	392	370	4	1
9	360	344	4	8	18	369	350	4	7
OUT	2,755	2,625	35		IN	2,887	2,745	35	
					TOTAL	5,642	5,370	70	
					STANDARD SCRATCH		69		

SECRETARY: Hilary Madden.
Tel: (021) 486 3910.

PROFESSIONAL: Mr B. Murphy.
Tel: (021) 486 3912.

ARCHITECTS: Peter O'Hare and Tom Carey.

Course Description:

A testing parkland course where, because of many trees and bunkers, accuracy is at a premium. All greens are well protected. From the first nine there are many scenic views of Cork Harbour, and on the back nine, water features on four holes.

LOCATION: Eight miles north west of Cork City; Two miles west of Blarney.

MANAGER: Hugo Gallagher.

PROFESSIONAL: M. Lehane.

Carrigrohane, Co. Cork.
Tel: (021) 4385297.
Fax: (021) 4516860.

Course Description:
Undulating on three levels. The 6th hole could be described as good a Par 3 as will be found anywhere. Last four holes provide a most challenging finish, the last two crossing a river. Precise clubbing and accuracy are demanded on this course.

Course Information: Par 71; SSS 70; Length 5,808 metres. **Visitors:** Welcome: Mon & Tue all day; Wed up to 10.30am; Thurs from 1.30pm; Fri up to 4.00pm; Sat / Sun enquire. Telephone in advance each day. **Avoid:** Members hours 12.30 – 1.30pm daily. **Opening Hours:** 9.00am – sunset. **Green Fees:** €40 midweek. €50 Sat / Sun (if available). Early Bird: Mon, Tue, Fri up to 10am €30. **Juveniles:** Welcome. Lessons available by prior arrangement; Club Hire available; telephone in advance at all times. **Clubhouse Hours:** 9.00am - 11.30pm. **Clubhouse Dress:** Neat / casual. **Clubhouse Facilities:** Full catering and bar. **Open Competitions:** Senior, Junior and Intermediate Scratch Cups.

NO.	MEDAL METRES	GEN. METRES	PAR	S.I.	NO.	MEDAL METRES	GEN. METRES	PAR	S.I.
1	385	372	4	2	10	322	292	4	15
2	243	241	4	18	11	361	344	4	11
3	356	348	4	8	12	158	144	3	13
4	444	435	5	10	13	373	351	4	5
5	339	329	4	6	14	448	433	5	17
6	182	172	3	4	15	152	152	3	9
7	425	415	5	16	16	391	348	4	3
8	165	152	3	12	17	406	377	4	1
9	309	285	4	14	18	354	352	4	7
OUT	2,848	2,749	36		IN	2,960	2,771	35	
					TOTAL	5,808	5,520	71	
					STANDARD SCRATCH	71	70		

Old Head

Old Head Golf Links, Kinsale, Co. Cork.
Tel: (021) 477 8444
Email: info@oldhead.com
Web: www.oldhead.com

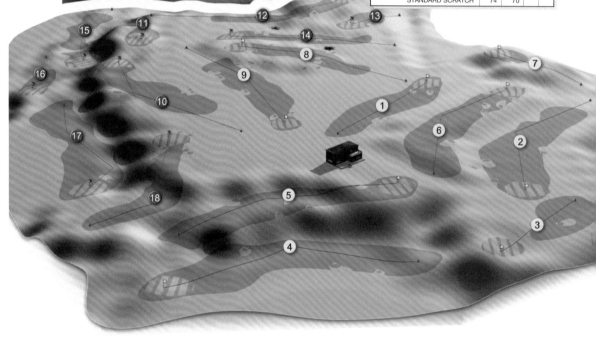

NO.	MEDAL YARDS	GEN. YARDS	PAR	S.I.	NO.	MEDAL YARDS	GEN. YARDS	PAR	S.I.
1	446	418	4	2	10	515	494	5	15
2	406	388	4	10	11	198	178	3	13
3	180	176	3	18	12	564	554	5	9
4	427	423	4	12	13	256	227	3	5
5	430	409	4	6	14	452	426	4	1
6	495	485	5	14	15	342	330	4	17
7	188	179	3	8	16	195	183	3	11
8	549	520	5	16	17	632	606	5	7
9	475	451	4	4	18	460	419	4	3
OUT	3,596	3,449	36		IN	3,619	3,419	36	
					TOTAL	7,215	6,868	72	
					STANDARD SCRATCH	74	70		

Course Information:
Par 72; SSS 74; Length 7,215 yards. **Visitors:** Welcome at all times, subject to pre-booking. **Opening Hours:** 8am – 10pm. **Green Fees:** €295 all week. **Juveniles:** Welcome - over 12 yrs with handicap. **Clubhouse Hours:** 8am – 10pm. **Clubhouse Dress:** Smart/casual, denim jeans and sneakers prohibited. **Clubhouse Facilities:** Bar/Restaurant and Golf Shop.

LOCATION: 7 miles south of Kinsale town.

DIRECTOR OF GOLF: Danny Brassil.

Course Description:
The links is situated on an Atlantic promontory rising hundreds of feet high above dramatic cliffs, surrounded by the ocean on all sides and commanding the most spectacular views. Every hole has a minimum of six tees – providing a test for all category of players.

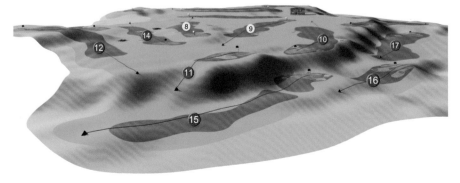

Raffeen Creek

Ringaskiddy, Co. Cork.
Tel: (021) 457 2624
Email: raffeengca@eircom.net
Web: www.raffeencreekgolfclub.com

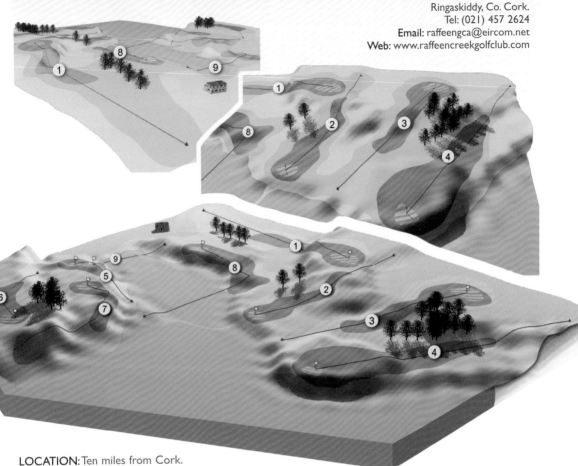

LOCATION: Ten miles from Cork.
SECRETARY: Frank Wiley. Tel: (021) 451 2624
ARCHITECT: E. Hackett.

Course Information:
Par 70; SSS 68; Length 5,575 yards, 5,098 metres. **Visitors:** Welcome. **Opening Hours:** Sunrise – sunset. **Avoid:** Competition times; Sat / Sun mornings. **Ladies:** Welcome Mon – Fri. **Green Fees:** €20 Mon – Fri, €30 Sat-Sun, €15 with a member, €15 student, Society weekday €20 Weekend €25. **Juveniles:** Welcome Tues-Fri up to 6.00pm, €10. Telephone appointment required. **Clubhouse Hours:** 10.00am – 11.30pm. **Clubhouse Dress:** Casual. **Clubhouse Facilities:** Snacks available. Food served daily 12am-2.30pm. **Open Week:** June

Course Description:
A scenic course whose special features are tough over-water shots. Straight, accurate play will get best results. The 8th and 9th are two fearsome holes with the Lake coming into play.

NO.	MEDAL METRES	GEN. METRES	PAR	S.I.	NO.	MEDAL METRES	GEN. METRES	PAR	S.I.
1	370	361	4	2	10	370	361	4	1
2	286	277	4	18	11	286	277	4	17
3	349	340	4	6	12	349	340	4	5
4	450	441	5	12	13	450	441	5	11
5	113	107	3	14	14	113	107	3	13
6	262	253	4	16	15	262	253	4	15
7	305	296	4	4	16	305	296	4	3
8	285	276	4	8	17	285	276	4	7
9	129	120	3	10	18	129	120	3	9
OUT	2,549	2,471	35		IN	2,549	2,471	35	
					TOTAL	5,098	4,942	70	
					STANDARD SCRATCH	68	67		

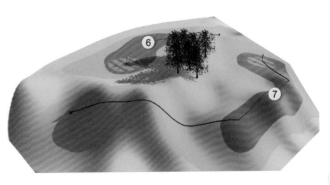

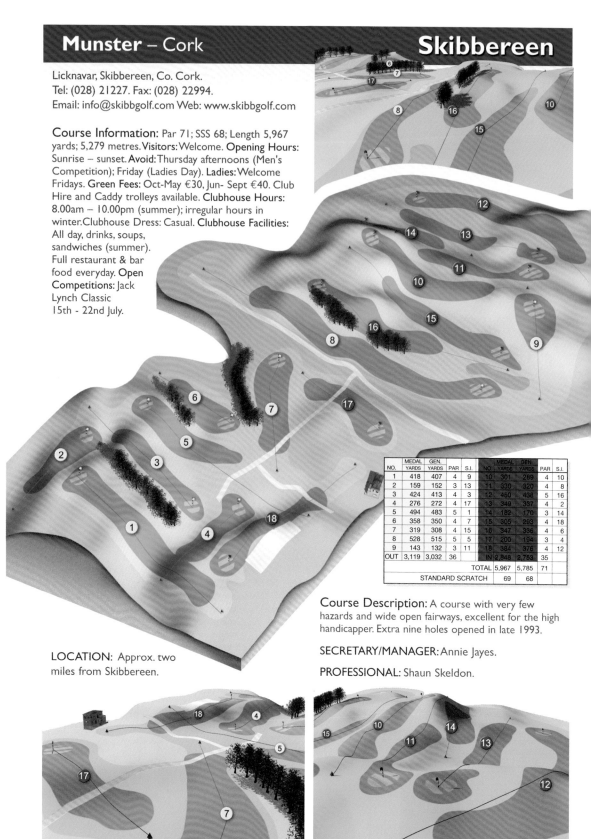

Munster – Cork

Skibbereen

Licknavar, Skibbereen, Co. Cork.
Tel: (028) 21227. Fax: (028) 22994.
Email: info@skibbgolf.com Web: www.skibbgolf.com

Course Information: Par 71; SSS 68; Length 5,967 yards; 5,279 metres. **Visitors:** Welcome. **Opening Hours:** Sunrise – sunset. **Avoid:** Thursday afternoons (Men's Competition); Friday (Ladies Day). **Ladies:** Welcome Fridays. **Green Fees:** Oct-May €30, Jun- Sept €40. Club Hire and Caddy trolleys available. **Clubhouse Hours:** 8.00am – 10.00pm (summer); irregular hours in winter. **Clubhouse Dress:** Casual. **Clubhouse Facilities:** All day, drinks, soups, sandwiches (summer). Full restaurant & bar food everyday. **Open Competitions:** Jack Lynch Classic 15th - 22nd July.

NO.	MEDAL YARDS	GEN. YARDS	PAR	S.I.	NO.	MEDAL YARDS	GEN. YARDS	PAR	S.I.
1	418	407	4	9	10	301	289	4	10
2	159	152	3	13	11	330	320	4	8
3	424	413	4	3	12	450	438	5	16
4	276	272	4	17	13	349	337	4	2
5	494	483	5	1	14	182	170	3	14
6	358	350	4	7	15	305	293	4	18
7	319	308	4	15	16	347	336	4	6
8	528	515	5	5	17	200	194	3	4
9	143	132	3	11	18	384	376	4	12
OUT	3,119	3,032	36		IN	2,848	2,753	35	
					TOTAL	5,967	5,785	71	
					STANDARD SCRATCH	69	68		

Course Description: A course with very few hazards and wide open fairways, excellent for the high handicapper. Extra nine holes opened in late 1993.

SECRETARY/MANAGER: Annie Jayes.

PROFESSIONAL: Shaun Skeldon.

LOCATION: Approx. two miles from Skibbereen.

Knockaveryy, Youghal,
Co. Cork.
Tel: (024) 92787.
Fax: (024) 92641.
Pro Shop: (024) 92590.

Course Description:

Meadowland course offering panoramic views of Youghal Bay and Blackwater estuary. It is enjoyable for high handicap golfers while still offering a good test for the low handicap golfer.

Course Information:

Par 72; SSS 69; Length 6,175 metres. Visitors: Welcome every day except Wednesday; telephone appointment required for weekends. Opening Hours: 9.00am – sunset. Green Fees: €30 Mon – Fri; €40 Sat / Sun. Clubhouse Hours: 9.30am – 11.30pm. Variable in winter months. Clubhouse Dress: Casual. Clubhouse Facilities: Snacks available at all times; full meals served from 10.30am – 9.00pm. Open Competitions: First two weeks in August and weekends during summer.

SECRETARY: Margaret O'Sullivan. PROFESSIONAL: Liam Burns.

ARCHITECT: Commander Harris.

NO.	C'SHIP METRES	MEDAL METRES	PAR	S.I.	NO.	C'SHIP METRES	MEDAL METRES	PAR	S.I.
1	273	252	4	17	10	376	359	4	4
2	448	438	5	15	11	326	320	4	18
3	368	353	4	7	12	299	289	4	16
4	398	390	4	5	13	151	140	3	14
5	316	309	4	11	14	378	369	4	2
6	378	373	4	1	15	332	322	4	12
7	476	460	5	13	16	180	174	3	10
8	172	157	3	9	17	346	340	4	6
9	381	371	4	3	18	378	373	4	8
OUT	3,210	3,103	37		IN	2,766	2,686	35	
					TOTAL	5,976	5,789		
					STANDARD SCRATCH			71	71

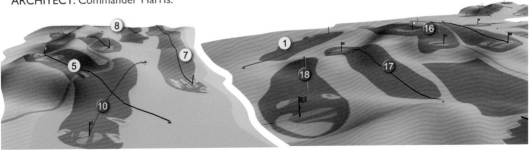

Ardfert Golf Club,
Sackville, Ardfert,
Tralee, Co. Kerry.
Tel: (066) 713 4744
Fax: (066) 713 4744
ardfelftgolfcentre@hotmail.com

LOCATION: 6 miles
from Tralee.

SECRETARY:
Kathleen O'Loughlin/
Tess Meehan.

PROFESSIONAL:
John Sugrue.

NO.	YARDS	PAR	S.I.	NO.	YARDS	PAR	S.I.
1	180	3	10	10	188	3	9
2	338	4	14	11	362	4	13
3	537	5	2	12	547	5	1
4	352	4	6	13	360	4	5
5	306	4	16	14	320	4	15
6	343	4	4	15	355	4	3
7	452	5	18	16	465	5	17
8	163	3	12	17	180	3	11
9	130	3	8	18	155	3	7
OUT	2,775	35		IN	2,927	35	
				TOTAL	5,702	70	
				STANDARD SCRATCH		67	

Course Information:
Par 70; SSS 67; Length 5,118
Yards. **Visitors:** Welcome.
Opening Hours: 9am – sunset.
Ladies: Welcome. **Juveniles:** Welcome,
lessons available. **Green Fees:** €20 for 9
holes. €30 for 18 holes. **Clubhouse Hours:**
9.00am – 9.30pm. **Clubhouse Dress:** Casual.
Clubhouse. **Facilities:** Tea, coffee & light snacks
available everyday.

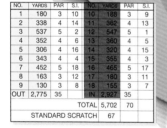

Course Description:
A nine hole parkland course
greatly complimented by the
scenic countryside, with a
river and lake featured in its
design. It has 12 all weather
driving range bays, lessons
available by appointment. Club
hire is also available.

Ballybunion, Co. Kerry. Tel: (068) 27146

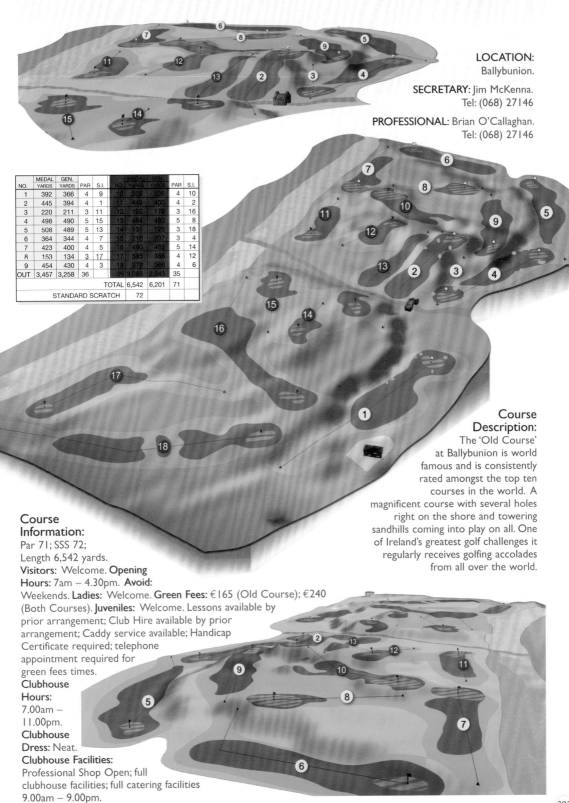

LOCATION:
Ballybunion.

SECRETARY: Jim McKenna.
Tel: (068) 27146

PROFESSIONAL: Brian O'Callaghan.
Tel: (068) 27146

NO.	MEDAL YARDS	GEN. YARDS	PAR	S.I.	NO.	MEDAL YARDS	GEN. YARDS	PAR	S.I.
1	392	366	4	9	10	358	336	4	10
2	445	394	4	1	11	449	400	4	2
3	220	211	3	11	12	192	178	3	16
4	498	490	5	15	13	484	480	5	8
5	508	489	5	13	14	131	125	3	18
6	364	344	4	7	15	216	207	3	4
7	423	400	4	5	16	490	482	5	14
8	153	134	3	17	17	385	368	4	12
9	454	430	4	3	18	379	366	4	6
OUT	3,457	3,258	36		IN	3,085	2,943	35	
					TOTAL	6,542	6,201	71	
					STANDARD SCRATCH		72		

Course Description:
The 'Old Course' at Ballybunion is world famous and is consistently rated amongst the top ten courses in the world. A magnificent course with several holes right on the shore and towering sandhills coming into play on all. One of Ireland's greatest golf challenges it regularly receives golfing accolades from all over the world.

Course Information:
Par 71; SSS 72; Length 6,542 yards.
Visitors: Welcome. **Opening Hours:** 7am – 4.30pm. **Avoid:** Weekends. **Ladies:** Welcome. **Green Fees:** €165 (Old Course); €240 (Both Courses). **Juveniles:** Welcome. Lessons available by prior arrangement; Club Hire available by prior arrangement; Caddy service available; Handicap Certificate required; telephone appointment required for green fees times.

Clubhouse Hours:
7.00am – 11.00pm.

Clubhouse Dress: Neat.

Clubhouse Facilities:
Professional Shop Open; full clubhouse facilities; full catering facilities 9.00am – 9.00pm.

Ballybunion, Co Kerry. Tel: (068) 27146 Fax: (068) 27387
Email: bbgolfc@iol.ie
Web: www.ballybuniongolfclub.ie

LOCATION: Ballybunion.

SECRETARY: Jim McKenna.

PROFESSIONAL: Brian O'Callaghan.

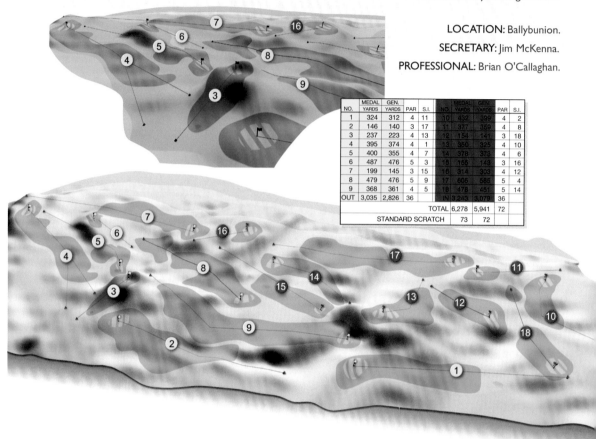

NO.	MEDAL YARDS	GEN. YARDS	PAR	S.I.	NO.	MEDAL YARDS	GEN. YARDS	PAR	S.I.
1	324	312	4	11	10	432	399	4	2
2	146	140	3	17	11	377	359	4	8
3	237	223	4	13	12	154	141	3	18
4	395	374	4	1	13	350	325	4	10
5	400	355	4	7	14	378	373	4	6
6	487	476	5	3	15	155	143	3	16
7	199	145	3	15	16	314	303	4	12
8	479	476	5	9	17	605	585	5	4
9	368	361	4	5	18	478	451	5	14
OUT	3,035	2,826	36		IN	3,243	3,079	36	
					TOTAL	6,278	5,941	72	
					STANDARD SCRATCH	73	72		

Course Information:
Par 72; SSS 73; Length 6,278 yards. **Visitors:** Welcome. **Opening Hours:** 7.00am – 5.30pm. **Avoid:** Weekends. **Ladies:** Welcome. **Green Fees:** Cashen Course - €110 Euro per round. Both Courses €240 Euro (same day). **Juveniles:** Welcome. Lessons available by prior arrangement; Club Hire available by prior arrangement; Caddy service available; Handicap Certificate required; telephone appointment required for green fee times. **Clubhouse Hours:** 7.00am – 11.00pm. **Clubhouse Dress:** Neat. **Clubhouse Facilities:** Professional Shop open; full clubhouse facilities; full catering facilities 9.00am - 9.00pm.

Course Description:
The 'Cashen Course' at Ballybunion was designed by Robert Trent Jones and is every bit as demanding - if not more - than the 'Old Course'. Both courses enjoy the benefit of the Atlantic coastline. The remote location of the course is instrumental in reducing the number of casual players leaving those on 'pilgrimage' with more solitude.

Beaufort Golf Course, Churchtown, Beaufort, Killarney. Co. Kerry.

Tel: (064) 44440. Fax: (064) 44752.

Email: beaufortgc@eircom.net

LOCATION: Seven miles west of Killarney, just off the N72W.

SECRETARY: Colm Kelly.

PROFESSIONAL: Keith Coveney.

Course Information:
Par 71; SSS 72; Length 6,587 yards. Visitors: At Weekends avoid 1pm – 2pm (members only). **Opening Hours:** 7.30am until darkness. **Juveniles:** Permitted. **Green Fees:** €50 weekdays, €60 weekends. Society Rates available on request. **Clubhouse Hours:** 7.30am-11pm. **Clubhouse Dress:** Informal but neat. **Clubhouse Facilities:** Bar food.

Course Description:
Parkland, 6,587 Yds. Par 71. Situated in the centre of South West Ireland's golfing mecca. Just five miles from the world famous Killarney Golf Club. Course is surrounded by Kerry mountains and the back nine is dominated by the ruins of Castle Core.

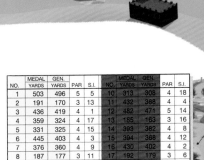

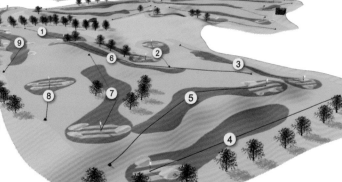

NO.	MEDAL YARDS	GEN. YARDS	PAR	S.I.	NO.	MEDAL YARDS	GEN. YARDS	PAR	S.I.
1	503	496	5	5	10	313	308	4	18
2	191	170	3	13	11	432	388	4	4
3	436	419	4	1	12	482	471	5	14
4	359	324	4	17	13	185	163	3	16
5	331	325	4	15	14	393	382	4	8
6	445	403	4	3	15	394	368	4	12
7	376	360	4	9	16	430	402	4	2
8	187	177	3	11	17	192	179	3	6
9	509	500	5	7	18	429	392	4	10
OUT	3,337	3,174	36		IN	3,250	3,053	35	
					TOTAL	6,587	6,227	71	
					STANDARD SCRATCH		72	70	

Castlegregory Golf & Fishing Club, Stradbally, Castlegregory, Co. Kerry.
Tel: (066) 7139444.

LOCATION: 2 miles west of Castlegregory.

Course Description:
9 hole links course, 1 par 5 and 3 par 3's. Scenically situated between a fresh water lake and the sea.

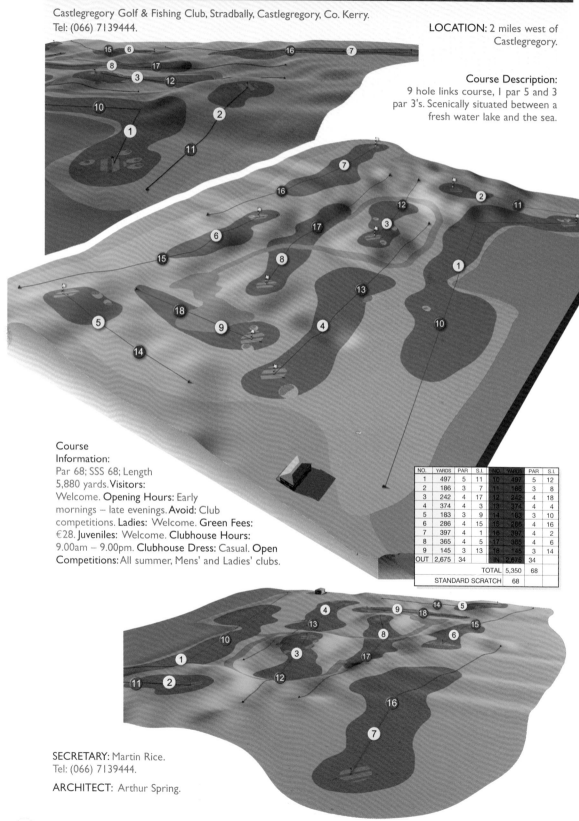

Course Information:
Par 68; SSS 68; Length 5,880 yards. Visitors: Welcome. **Opening Hours:** Early mornings – late evenings. Avoid: Club competitions. **Ladies:** Welcome. **Green Fees:** €28. Juveniles: Welcome. **Clubhouse Hours:** 9.00am – 9.00pm. **Clubhouse Dress:** Casual. **Open Competitions:** All summer, Mens' and Ladies' clubs.

NO.	YARDS	PAR	S.I.	NO.	YARDS	PAR	S.I.
1	497	5	11	10	497	5	12
2	186	3	7	11	186	3	8
3	242	4	17	12	242	4	18
4	374	4	3	13	374	4	4
5	183	3	9	14	183	3	10
6	286	4	15	15	286	4	16
7	397	4	1	16	397	4	2
8	365	4	5	17	365	4	6
9	145	3	13	18	145	3	14
OUT	2,675	34		IN	2,675	34	
				TOTAL	5,350	68	
				STANDARD SCRATCH		68	

SECRETARY: Martin Rice.
Tel: (066) 7139444.

ARCHITECT: Arthur Spring.

LOCATION: Two miles from Castleisland.

HON. SECRETARY:
Eamonn O'Connell.

SECRETARY/MANAGER:
Michael Coote.

ARCHITECT: Dr. A Spring.

Dooneen, Castle Island,
Co Kerry.
Tel: (066) 7141709.
Fax: (066) 7142090.
Email: managercastleislandgolfclub@eircom.net
Web: www.castleislandgolfclub.com

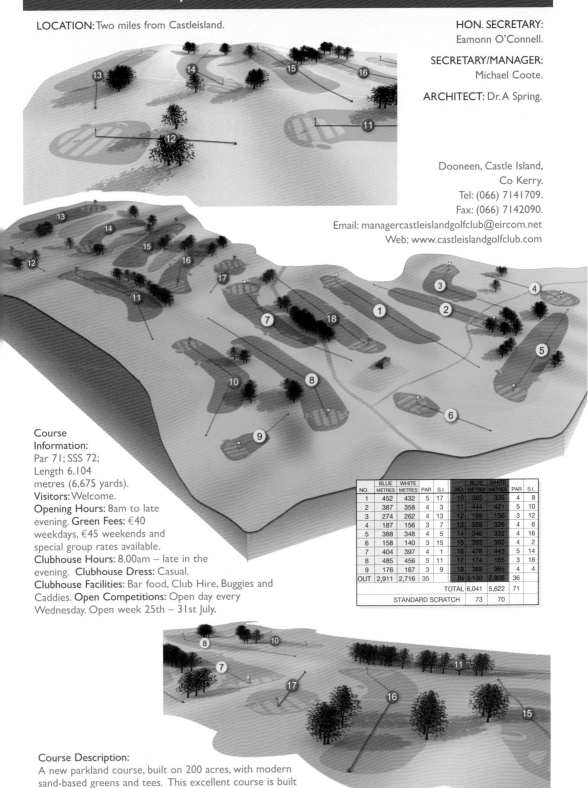

Course Information:
Par 71; SSS 72;
Length 6,104
metres (6,675 yards).
Visitors: Welcome.
Opening Hours: 8am to late
evening. **Green Fees:** €40
weekdays, €45 weekends and
special group rates available.
Clubhouse Hours: 8.00am – late in the
evening. **Clubhouse Dress:** Casual.
Clubhouse Facilities: Bar food, Club Hire, Buggies and
Caddies. **Open Competitions:** Open day every
Wednesday. Open week 25th – 31st July.

NO.	BLUE METRES	WHITE METRES	PAR	S.I.	NO.	BLUE METRES	WHITE METRES	PAR	S.I.
1	452	432	5	17	10	385	336	4	8
2	387	358	4	3	11	444	421	5	10
3	274	262	4	13	12	169	156	3	12
4	187	156	3	7	13	355	326	4	6
5	388	348	4	5	14	346	332	4	16
6	158	140	3	15	15	393	362	4	2
7	404	397	4	1	16	476	443	5	14
8	485	456	5	11	17	174	165	3	18
9	176	167	3	9	18	388	365	4	4
OUT	2,911	2,716	35		IN	3,130	2,906	36	
					TOTAL	6,041	5,622	71	
					STANDARD SCRATCH	73	70		

Course Description:
A new parkland course, built on 200 acres, with modern
sand-based greens and tees. This excellent course is built
to the highest championship standards, that allows it to be
played throughout the year.

Ballyoughterach, Ballyferriter, Co. Kerry.
Tel: (066) 9156 255/408 Fax: (066) 9156409
Email: dinglegc@iol.ie.
Web: www.dinglelinks.com

LOCATION Dingle Penisula.

HON. SECRETARY: Risteard Mac Liam.

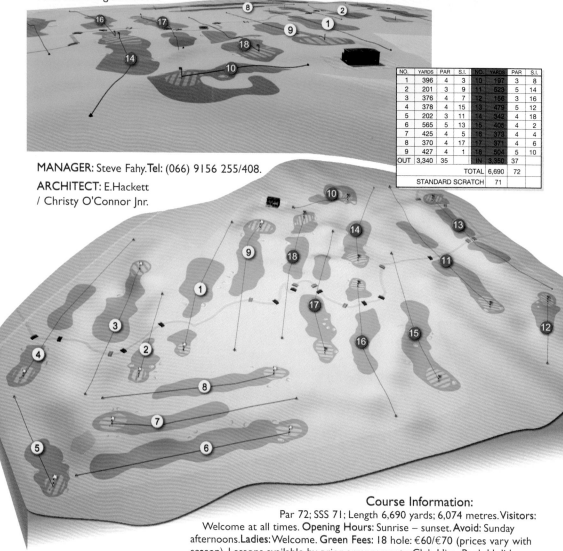

NO.	YARDS	PAR	S.I.	NO.	YARDS	PAR	S.I.
1	396	4	3	10	197	3	8
2	201	3	9	11	523	5	14
3	376	4	7	12	156	3	16
4	378	4	15	13	479	5	12
5	202	3	11	14	342	4	18
6	565	5	13	15	405	4	2
7	425	4	5	16	373	4	4
8	370	4	17	17	371	4	6
9	427	4	1	18	504	5	10
OUT	3,340	35		IN	3,350	37	
				TOTAL	6,690	72	
				STANDARD SCRATCH	71		

MANAGER: Steve Fahy. Tel: (066) 9156 255/408.

ARCHITECT: E.Hackett
/ Christy O'Connor Jnr.

Course Information:

Par 72; SSS 71; Length 6,690 yards; 6,074 metres. **Visitors:** Welcome at all times. **Opening Hours:** Sunrise – sunset. **Avoid:** Sunday afternoons. **Ladies:** Welcome. **Green Fees:** 18 hole: €60/€70 (prices vary with season). Lessons available by prior arrangements; Club Hire, Bank Holidays €75. **Juveniles:** Welcome (accompanied by adult June – August). **Clubhouse Hours:** 8.00am – 9.00pm; Professional Shop open. **Clubhouse Dress:** Casual. **Clubhouse Facilities:** Full clubhouse facilities everyday. Trolly & Cart hire available. **Open Competitions:** Toyota Open 22nd / 23rd July.

Course Description:

A links course with wind proving a big factor as it sweeps in from the Atlantic Ocean. The design of the course uses the natural terrain and has the advantage of the area's marvellous turf. A setting for traditional golf with panoramic surroundings.

Course Description:

Dooks – a word derived from Gaelic 'drumhac' meaning sand-bank – is a testing 18 hole links situated in one of the most picturesque corners of the Ring of Kerry. The golf course is laid out on one of three stretches of sand-dunes at the head of picturesque Dingle Bay.

Dooks, Glenbeigh, Co. Kerry.
Tel: (066) 9768205/9768200. Fax: (066) 9768476.
Email: office@dooks.com

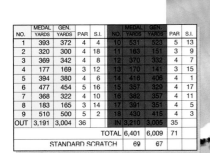

NO.	MEDAL YARDS	GEN. YARDS	PAR	S.I.	NO.	MEDAL YARDS	GEN. YARDS	PAR	S.I.
1	393	372	4	4	10	531	523	5	13
2	320	300	4	18	11	163	151	3	9
3	369	342	4	8	12	370	332	4	7
4	177	169	3	12	13	170	141	3	15
5	394	380	4	6	14	416	406	4	1
6	477	454	5	16	15	357	329	4	17
7	368	322	4	10	16	382	357	4	11
8	183	165	3	14	17	391	351	4	5
9	510	500	5	2	18	430	415	4	3
OUT	3,191	3,004	36		IN	3,210	3,005	35	
				TOTAL	6,401	6,009	71		
				STANDARD SCRATCH		69	67		

Course Information:

Par 71; SSS 68; Length 6,401 yards. Visitors: Welcome. Opening Hours: Sunrise - sunset. Avoid: Sundays. Ladies: Welcome. Caddy service available; Handicap Certificate required. Green Fees: €58 all week, pre-booking advisable. Clubhouse Hours: 9.00am – 11.00pm. Clubhouse Dress: Casual. Clubhouse Facilities: 11.00am – 7.00pm. Open Competitions: By invitation.

LOCATION: Four miles from Killorglin.

SECRETARY: Declan Mangan.
Tel: (066) 9768205.

Kenmare, Co. Kerry. Tel: (064) 41291 Fax:(064) 42061
Email: info@kenmaregolfclub.com
Web: www.kenmaregolfclub.com

LOCATION: Turn left at top of town.

GENERAL MANAGER:
Joy Clifford. Tel: (064) 41291

SECRETARY (for bookings): Donna Harrington.

Course Description:

Outstanding eighteen holes, it is picturesque and mainly
very sheltered which leaves it playable in all kinds of
weather. It also has the advantage of being sited in one
of Ireland's areas of outstanding scenery.

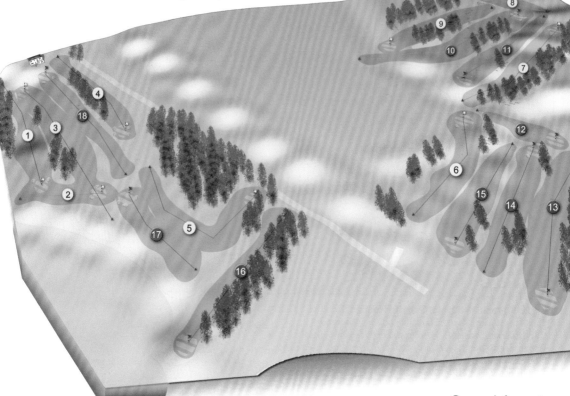

Course Information:

Par 71/70; SSS 69/68; Length 6,053 yards. **Visitors:** Welcome any
time. Booking in advance is advisable (especially weekends). **Opening Hours:** Everyday, peak time
May – Sept 6am – 7pm. Off peak time 9am-6pm. **Juveniles:** Welcome, to be accompanied by adult.
Green Fees: €50 Mon-Sat, €55 Sun. Juveniles/with member - 1/2 price. Club hire €15; Caddy trolley
€2.50. **Clubhouse Hours:** 8.00am (peak time). **Clubhouse Dress:** Casual but neat. **Clubhouse
Facilities:** Tea, coffee & snacks. **Open Competitions:** Many throughout the year, contact: (064) 41291
for details.

NO.	METRES	PAR	S.I.	NO.	METRES	PAR	S.I.
1	341	4	11	10	511	5	4
2	172	3	7	11	370	4	16
3	406	4	1	12	198	3	8
4	308	4	15	13	401	4	2
5	348	4	3	14	346	4	10
6	325	4	5	15	305	4	18
7	453	5	17	16	378	4	12
8	183	3	9	17	198	3	6
9	472	5	13	18	338	4	14
OUT	3,008	36		IN	3,048	35	
				TOTAL	6,053	71	
	STANDARD SCRATCH				69		

Munster – Kerry

Killarney (Killeen)

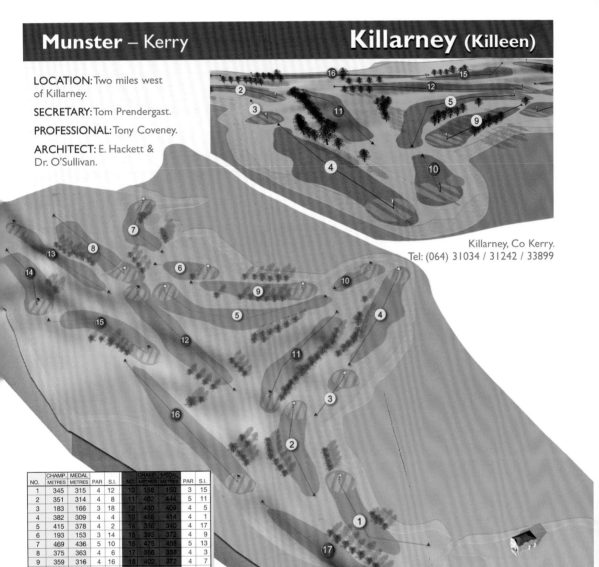

LOCATION: Two miles west of Killarney.

SECRETARY: Tom Prendergast.

PROFESSIONAL: Tony Coveney.

ARCHITECT: E. Hackett & Dr. O'Sullivan.

Killarney, Co Kerry.
Tel: (064) 31034 / 31242 / 33899

NO.	CHAMP. METRES	MEDAL METRES	PAR	S.I.	NO.	CHAMP. METRES	MEDAL METRES	PAR	S.I.
1	345	315	4	12	10	158	150	3	15
2	351	314	4	8	11	462	444	5	11
3	183	166	3	18	12	430	409	4	5
4	382	309	4	4	13	458	414	4	1
5	415	378	4	2	14	356	340	4	17
6	193	153	3	14	15	393	372	4	9
7	469	436	5	10	16	475	458	5	13
8	375	363	4	6	17	356	338	4	3
9	359	316	4	16	18	402	372	4	7
OUT	3,072	2,750	35		IN	3,494	3,297	37	
					TOTAL	6,566	6,047	72	
					STANDARD SCRATCH	73	71		

Course Description:

The second of three courses at Killarney Golf & Fishing Club the 'Killeen' is parkland, the same as its' sister courses. The main characteristics are narrow, tree-lined fairways and of course some of the holes are adjacent to the beautiful Lough Leane.

E-Mail: reservations@killarney-golf.com
Web: www.killarney-golf.com

Course Information:

Par 72; SSS 73; Length 6,566 metres. (Killeen course). **Visitors:** Welcome. **Opening Hours:** 7.30am – 6.00pm. **Ladies:** Welcome. **Green Fees:** Available on request from the secretary. Certificate of Handicap required. **Juveniles:** Welcome. Lessons available; Club Hire available; Caddy service available. **Clubhouse Hours:** 7.30am – 11.30pm. **Clubhouse Dress:** Casual. **Clubhouse Facilities:** Lunches and full dinners all day. Major re-construction was carried out on the Killeen Course during 2005. All tees and greens have been brought up to U.S.G.A. specifications. The cost of the project was €2.2m.

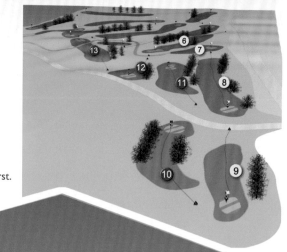

Mahony's Point, Killarney, Co. Kerry.
Tel: (064) 31034 / 31242 / 33899
E-mail: reservations@killarney-golf.com
Web: www.killarney-golf.com

LOCATION: Two miles west of Killarney.

SECRETARY: Tom Prendergast.
Tel: (064) 31034 Fax: (064) 33065

PROFESSIONAL: Tony Coveney. Tel: (064) 31615

ARCHITECT: Sir Guy Campbell & Henry Longhurst.

Course Information:

Par 72; SSS 72;
Length 6,164 metres
(Mahony's Point). Visitors:
Welcome. Opening Hours:
7.30am – 6.00pm. Ladies:
Welcome every day. Green Fees:
Available on request from the secretary.
Certificate of Handicap required. Juveniles:
Welcome to play every day. Clubhouse Hours:
7.30am – 11.30pm. Clubhouse Dress: Casual.
Clubhouse Facilities: Professional shop. Lunches and
dinners all day.

Course Description:

Three excellent parkland courses occupying a site of
great natural beauty. The courses are adjacent to Lough
Leane, with the mountains of Kerry rising on the other
side of the lake. An additional
eighteen holes were
completed in 1971 and the
new holes were mixed with
the old to form the
'Killeen' and Mahony's
Point' courses.

NO.	MEDAL METRES	GEN. METRES	PAR	S.I.	NO.	MEDAL METRES	GEN. METRES	PAR	S.I.
1	341	316	4	12	10	344	336	4	10
2	404	386	4	1	11	428	411	4	6
3	431	395	4	5	12	215	167	3	18
4	141	137	3	15	13	435	435	5	12
5	448	439	5	9	14	344	344	4	1
6	360	347	4	3	15	251	246	4	16
7	169	157	3	11	16	463	435	5	8
8	532	495	5	7	17	373	340	4	4
9	296	288	4	17	18	179	182	3	14
OUT	3,122	2,960	36		IN	3,030	2,876	36	
					TOTAL	6,152	5,836	72	
					STANDARD SCRATCH		72	70	

Killarney, Co Kerry.
Tel: (064) 31034/ 32142/33899.
Email: reservations@killarney-golf.com
Web: www.killarney-golf.com

Course Information:
Par 72; Length 6,410 metres. **Visitors:**
Welcome. **Opening Hours:** 7.30am –
6.00pm. **Green Fees:** Available on request
from the secretary, certificate of Handicap
required. **Juveniles:** Welcome. **Ladies:**
Welcome. **Clubhouse Dress:** Casual.

SECRETARY:
Tom Prendergast.
Tel: (064) 31034

PROFESSIONAL:
Tony Coveney
Tel: (064) 31615

ARCHITECT:
Donald Steel.

Course Description:
The third course at Killarney Golf &
Fishing Club - Lackabane - is parkland.
The main characteristics are undulating
fairways with the lake adjacent to the
3rd green and to the 11th & 12th holes.
Views of the mountains and surrounding
woods are breathtaking.

NO.	MEDAL YARDS	GEN. YARDS	PAR	S.I.	NO.	MEDAL YARDS	GEN. YARDS	PAR	S.I.
1	413	391	4	4	10	395	355	4	7
2	477	446	5	16	11	502	497	5	9
3	248	222	4	18	12	324	308	4	13
4	382	359	4	12	13	384	360	4	5
5	204	184	3	6	14	161	146	3	15
6	433	416	4	2	15	389	358	4	3
7	543	507	5	8	16	180	150	3	17
8	164	152	3	14	17	484	464	5	11
9	336	307	4	10	18	411	391	4	1
OUT	3,200	2,984	36		IN	3,210	3,027	36	
					TOTAL	6,410	6,011	72	
					STANDARD SCRATCH	72	72		

Killorglin

Killorglin Golf Club, Stealroe, Killorglin. Co. Kerry. Tel: (066) 9761979 Fax: (066) 9761437
Email: kilgolf@iol.ie
Web: www.killorglingolf.ie

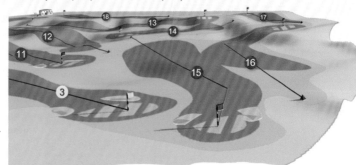

LOCATION: Two miles from Killorglin, on Tralee Road, 14 miles from Killarney.

SECRETARY: Billy Dodd.

RESERVATIONS: Billy / Emma / James.

ARCHITECT: Eddie Hackett.

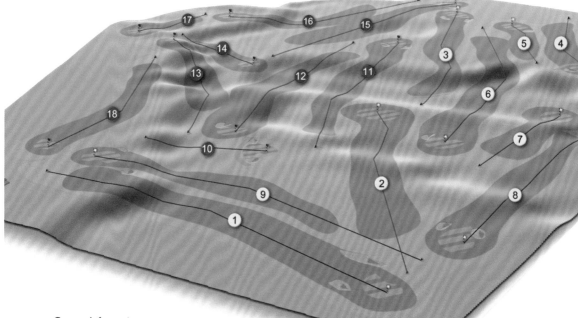

Course Information:

Par 72; SSS 71; Length 6,467 yards.
Visitors: Welcome at all times. **Opening Hours:** Sunrise - sunset. **Ladies:** Welcome all times. **Green Fees:** Mon - Sun €35. **Juveniles:** Welcome if accompanied by an adult. Lessons by prior arrangement. **Clubhouse Hours:** 8.30am – 11.30pm. **Clubhouse Dress:** Neat / casual. **Clubhouse Facilites:** Pro-shop, Bar and full restaurant facilities, societies welcome - special rate on request. Caddies available by prior arrangement. For reservations tel: Billy, James, Emma.
Open Competitions: June

NO.	MEDAL YARDS	GEN. YARDS	PAR	S.I.	NO.	MEDAL YARDS	GEN. YARDS	PAR	S.I.
1	476	450	5	15	10	187	173	3	14
2	417	404	4	3	11	496	483	5	10
3	525	462	5	9	12	504	474	5	12
4	293	267	4	17	13	376	329	4	4
5	194	149	3	13	14	187	166	3	16
6	401	385	4	7	15	511	473	5	8
7	208	184	3	11	16	417	373	4	2
8	416	350	4	1	17	136	127	3	18
9	388	378	4	5	18	335	326	4	6
OUT	3,318	3,029	36		IN	3,149	2,924	36	
					TOTAL	6,467	5,953	72	
					STANDARD SCRATCH		71		

Course Description:

Eddie Hackett has made marvellous use of the dramatic physical features of the land in providing golf shots that are delightful & challenging. It offers a new & exciting challenge to visiting golfers.

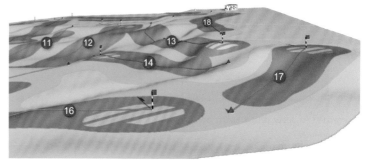

Feale View, Listowel, Co Kerry.
Tel: (068) 21592 Fax: (068) 23387
Email: listowelgc@eircom.net

LOCATION: Within town boundary, on the N69 scenic drive from Shannon.

SECRETARY: Caroline Barrett.

HON. SECRETARY:
Kevin Barry.

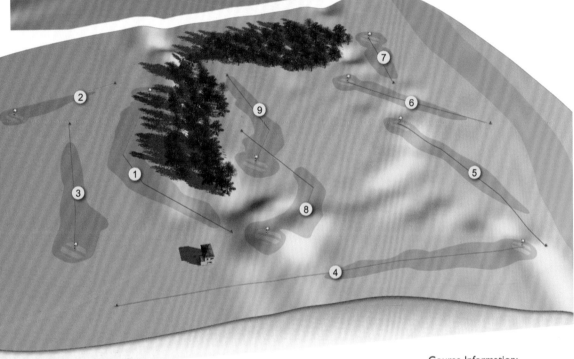

Course Description:
The course is dominated by a towering wood which runs like a spine through its middle. The exciting opening downhill par 4 exposes the major feature of the course, the splendid 'Silver River Feale'.

Course Information:
Par 72; SSS 68; Length 5,728 yards. **Visitors:** Welcome. **Opening Hours:** 8.00am – sunset. **Ladies:** Welcome. **Green Fees:** €15 for 9 holes, €20 for 18 holes, 10% reduction for Societies. **Juveniles:** Welcome. **Clubhouse Hours:** 8.00am – sunset. **Clubhouse Dress:** Neat. **Clubhouse Facilities:** Changing facilities, snack bar and drying room for fishermen. Clubs, trolleys and caddies for hire. Fishing equipment arranged.

NO.	YARDS	PAR	S.I.	NO.	YARDS	PAR	S.I.
1	322	4	4	10	331	4	3
2	326	4	10	11	339	4	9
3	173	3	14	12	191	3	13
4	321	4	12	13	329	4	11
5	370	4	2	14	383	4	1
6	315	4	16	15	340	4	15
7	169	3	8	16	182	3	7
8	489	5	18	17	502	5	17
9	316	4	6	18	330	4	5
OUT	2,801	35		IN	2,927	35	
				TOTAL	5,728	70	
				STANDARD SCRATCH		68	

Parknasilla Great Southern
Hotel, Sneem, Co. Kerry.
Tel: (064) 45122

LOCATION: Parknasilla.

SECRETARY: Mr. M. Walsh.
Tel: (064) 45233

Course Information:
Par 69; SSS 68; Length 5,284 metres. Visitors: Welcome. Opening
Hours: 8.00am – 7.00pm. Ladies: Welcome. Green Fees: €25 – 9
holes; €35 – 18 holes. Juveniles: Welcome. Club Hire available; Caddy
service available by prior arrangment; telephone appointment
required. Clubhouse Dress: Casual. Clubhouse Facilities: Full catering
facilities at hotel, a half mile away. Open Competitions: Small
competitions throughout the year.

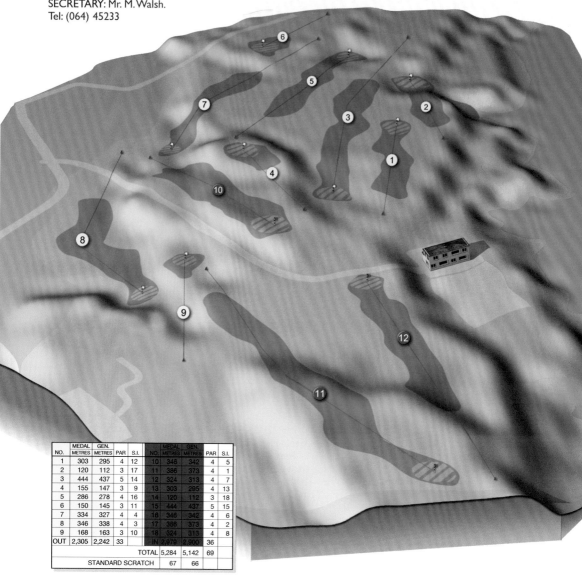

NO.	MEDAL METRES	GEN. METRES	PAR	S.I.	NO.	MEDAL METRES	GEN. METRES	PAR	S.I.
1	303	295	4	12	10	346	342	4	5
2	120	112	3	17	11	386	373	4	1
3	444	437	5	14	12	324	313	4	7
4	155	147	3	9	13	303	295	4	13
5	286	278	4	16	14	120	112	3	18
6	150	145	3	11	15	444	437	5	15
7	334	327	4	4	16	346	342	4	6
8	346	338	4	3	17	386	373	4	2
9	168	163	3	10	18	324	313	4	8
OUT	2,305	2,242	33		IN	2,979	2,900	36	
					TOTAL	5,284	5,142	69	
					STANDARD SCRATCH		67	66	

Course Description:
Well laid out course in beautiful
scenery overlooking Kenmare Bay.
The course is part of the Parknasilla
Great Southern Hotel and golfers
have the added advantage of having
these facilities available to them.

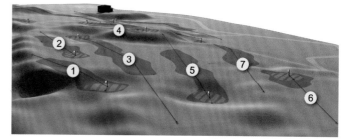

Ring of Kerry Golf & Country Club,
Templenoe,
Kenmare,
Co. Kerry.
Tel: (064) 42000

LOCATION: 4 miles from Kenmare.

GENERAL MANAGER: Ed Edwards.

ARCHITECT: Eddie Hackett.

Course Description:
One of the newest additions to the Co. Kerry circuit, with panoramic views of Kenmare Bay from every hole. Described as 'world class' in Ireland, its extensive drainage and irrigation systems ensure a year round facility. Situated 25 miles from Killarney & 4 miles from Kenmare, this is a popular course in the Kingdom of Kerry. Designed to test serious golfers from the back tees and provide equal enjoyment for all from the more forward ones. Recently voted 2nd in "10 of the best views in British Isles golf" by Today's Golfer, Included in Top 100 Favourite Irish Courses as voted by Golf Digest readers, Dec 05 & awarded Gold Medal by HSBC Regional course rankings Mar 06

Course Information:
Par 72; SSS 73; Length 6,814 yards. Visitors: All day every day. Opening Hours: Sunrise to sunset. Ladies: No restrictions. Green Fees: €90 weekends, €80 Mon-Fri. Juveniles: Welcome. Must be accompanied by an adult. Clubhouse Hours: 8am – 10.30pm. Clubhouse Dress: Smart/Casual (no denim). Clubhouse Facilities: Club, trolley and cart hire available, driving range and putting green. Full dining and bar facilities.

NO.	BLUE YARDS	WHITE YARDS	PAR	S.I.	NO.	BLUE YARDS	WHITE YARDS	PAR	S.I.
1	386	351	4	6	10	450	428	4	3
2	374	350	4	2	11	531	501	5	15
3	162	148	3	14	12	386	366	4	9
4	592	532	5	12	13	233	208	3	7
5	448	413	5	18	14	433	404	4	1
6	367	363	4	4	15	425	385	4	11
7	186	162	3	10	16	472	450	5	17
8	428	422	4	8	17	435	397	4	5
9	307	288	4	16	18	205	185	3	13
OUT	3,250	3,324	36		IN	3,570	3,324	36	
					TOTAL	6,820	6,353	72	
					STANDARD SCRATCH		72	72	

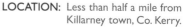

Ross Golf Club, Ross Road, Killarney, Co. Kerry.
Tel: (064) 31125 Fax: (064) 31860

LOCATION: Less than half a mile from Killarney town, Co. Kerry.

SECRETARY: John Looney.

PROFESSIONAL: Alan O'Meara.

ARCHITECT: Roger Jones.
Tel: (064) 31125

Course Description:

Attractive setting in mountains, lakes and woodlands with Ross Castle and the Flesk river adjacent. Situated less than half a mile from Killarney town.

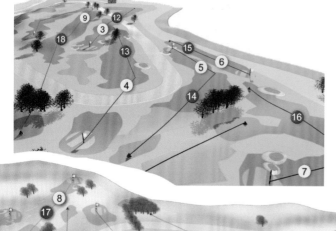

Course Information:

Par 72; SSS 73; Length 6450 yards. **Visitors:** Welcome. **Opening Hours:** 8.00am to sunset. **Avoid:** Sunday mornings. **Green Fees:** €16 for 9 holes & €25 per person for 18 holes. **Students:** €12 for 9 holes and €18 per person for 18 holes. **Juveniles:** €9 for 9 holes & €14 for 18 holes. **Earlybird & Twilight:** €13 for 9 holes and €20 for 18 holes before 9am and after 6pm. **Clubhouse Hours:** 8.00am – sunset. **Clubhouse Dress:** Clean attire. **Clubhouse Facilities:** Pro shop and snack bar, licensed bar.

NO.	MEDAL YARDS	GEN. YARDS	PAR	S.I.	NO.	MEDAL YARDS	GEN. YARDS	PAR	S.I.
1	340	317	4	6	10	340	317	4	5
2	537	495	5	12	11	537	495	5	11
3	410	396	4	8	12	410	396	4	7
4	401	377	4	4	13	401	377	4	3
5	395	377	4	2	14	395	377	4	1
6	116	96	3	18	15	116	96	3	17
7	271	264	4	16	16	271	264	4	15
8	154	133	3	14	17	154	133	3	13
9	600	531	5	10	18	600	531	5	9
OUT	3,225	2,988	36		IN	3,225	2,988	36	
					TOTAL	6,450	5,976	72	
					STANDARD SCRATCH	73	71		

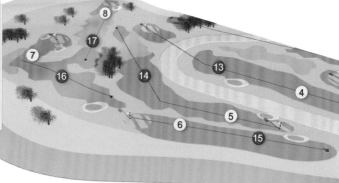

Tralee

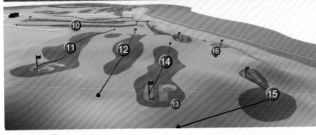

West Barrow, Ardfert, Co. Kerry.
Tel: (066) 7136379. **Fax:** (066)7136008.
Email: Info@traleegolfclub.com
Web: www.traleegolfclub.com

LOCATION: Barrow.

GENERAL MANAGER: Anthony Byrne.

PROFESSIONAL: David Power.

ARCHITECT: Arnold Palmer.

Course Description:

Challenging course with the first nine relatively flat holes, set on cliff top; the second nine by contrast are built on dunes. The course is set amidst the beautiful scenery associated with the Kerry region. Tralee is the first Arnold Palmer designed course in Europe.

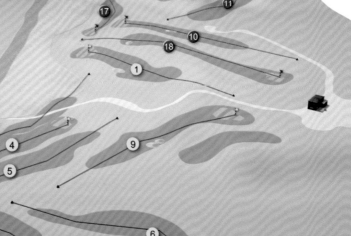

Course Information:

Par 71; SSS 73; Length 6,252 metres. **Visitors:** Welcome up to 3.00pm, May – October. Limited green fees Weds / Weekends. **Opening Hours:** Mon, Tue, Thur, Fri 7.30am - 2.30pm. Saturdays 10.00am - 1.30pm. Sunday members only. Wednesdays, May & Sept only, 7.30am - 10.30am. **Members:** Wed (June, July & August) and all Sun. **Green Fees:** €170 per person. **Juveniles:** Welcome. Must be accompanied by an adult after 6pm. Caddy service available by prior arrangment; Handicap Certificate required. Telephone appointment required. **Clubhouse Hours:** 7.30am – 10pm (summer); 9am – 5.30pm (winter). Golf Shop open. **Clubhouse Dress:** Smart/ Casual – no beach wear or jeans. **Clubhouse Facilities:** Lunch, dinner, snacks available all day everyday.

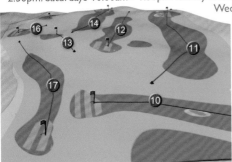

NO.	MEDAL METRES	GEN. METRES	PAR	S.I.	NO.	MEDAL METRES	GEN. METRES	PAR	S.I.
1	368	355	4	12	10	385	370	4	9
2	542	516	5	2	11	530	514	5	13
3	183	140	3	14	12	417	400	4	1
4	388	366	4	8	13	145	139	3	15
5	391	374	4	4	14	367	361	4	5
6	389	383	4	10	15	273	287	4	17
7	142	135	3	18	16	181	152	3	11
8	354	339	4	6	17	323	304	4	7
9	451	443	5	16	18	422	403	4	3
OUT	3,209	3,051	36		IN	3,043	2,910	35	
					TOTAL	6,252	5,961	71	
					STANDARD SCRATCH		73	71	

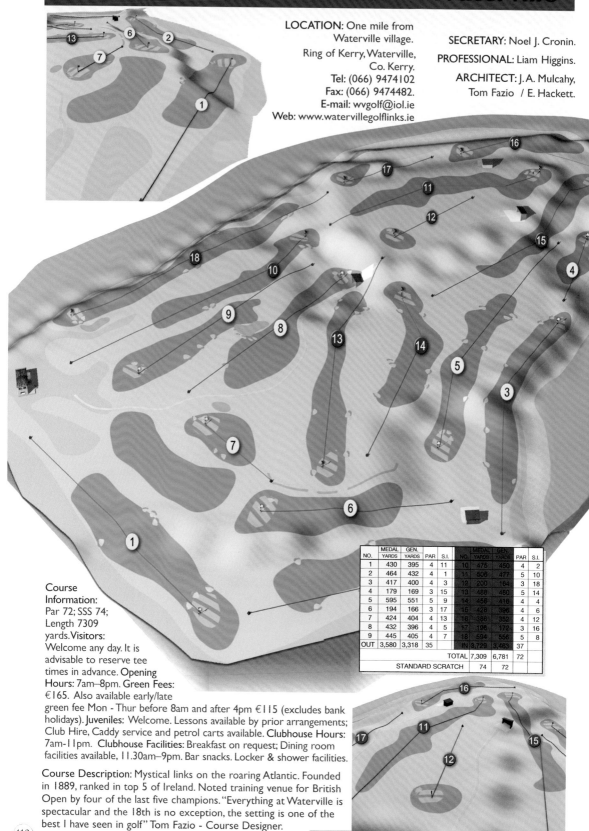

LOCATION: One mile from Waterville village.
Ring of Kerry, Waterville, Co. Kerry.
Tel: (066) 9474102
Fax: (066) 9474482.
E-mail: wvgolf@iol.ie
Web: www.watervillegolflinks.ie

SECRETARY: Noel J. Cronin.
PROFESSIONAL: Liam Higgins.
ARCHITECT: J. A. Mulcahy, Tom Fazio / E. Hackett.

NO.	MEDAL YARDS	GEN. YARDS	PAR	S.I.	NO.	MEDAL YARDS	GEN. YARDS	PAR	S.I.
1	430	395	4	11	10	475	450	4	2
2	464	432	4	1	11	506	477	5	10
3	417	400	4	3	12	200	164	3	18
4	179	169	3	15	13	488	460	5	14
5	595	551	5	9	14	456	418	4	4
6	194	166	3	17	15	428	396	4	6
7	424	404	4	13	16	386	352	4	12
8	432	396	4	5	17	196	172	3	16
9	445	405	4	7	18	594	556	5	8
OUT	3,580	3,318	35		IN	3,729	3,463	37	
					TOTAL	7,309	6,781	72	
					STANDARD SCRATCH	74	72		

Course Information:
Par 72; SSS 74; Length 7309 yards. Visitors: Welcome any day. It is advisable to reserve tee times in advance. Opening Hours: 7am–8pm. Green Fees: €165. Also available early/late green fee Mon - Thur before 8am and after 4pm €115 (excludes bank holidays). Juveniles: Welcome. Lessons available by prior arrangements; Club Hire, Caddy service and petrol carts available. Clubhouse Hours: 7am–11pm. Clubhouse Facilities: Breakfast on request; Dining room facilities available, 11.30am–9pm. Bar snacks. Locker & shower facilities.

Course Description: Mystical links on the roaring Atlantic. Founded in 1889, ranked in top 5 of Ireland. Noted training venue for British Open by four of the last five champions. "Everything at Waterville is spectacular and the 18th is no exception, the setting is one of the best I have seen in golf" Tom Fazio - Course Designer.

Abbeyfeale Golf Club, Abbeyfeale Co. Limerick.
Tel: (068) 32033. Fax: (068) 51871
Email: abbeyfealegolf@eircom.net
www.abbeyfealegolf.ie

Course Description:
Recognised as having some tough Par-3's. All holes are well protected by water hazards, bunkers and trees. This 9 hole course will provide a challange to golfers of all categories.

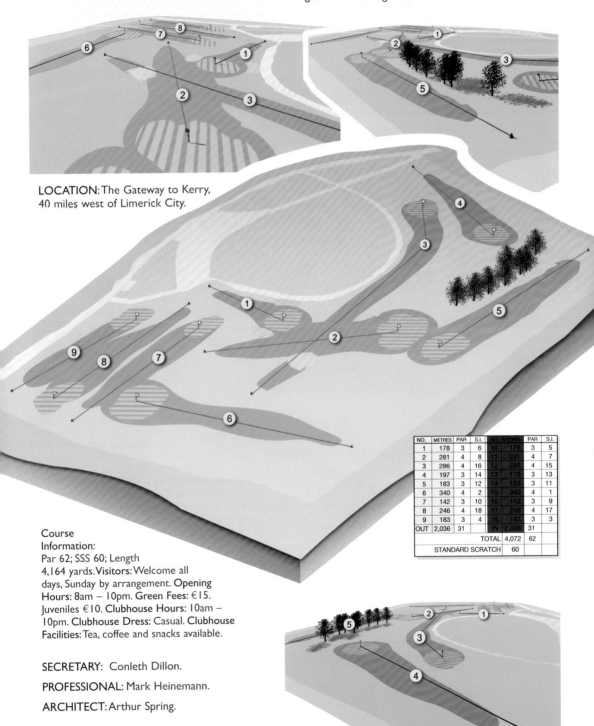

LOCATION: The Gateway to Kerry, 40 miles west of Limerick City.

Course Information:
Par 62; SSS 60; Length 4,164 yards. Visitors: Welcome all days, Sunday by arrangement. Opening Hours: 8am – 10pm. Green Fees: €15. Juveniles €10. Clubhouse Hours: 10am – 10pm. Clubhouse Dress: Casual. Clubhouse Facilities: Tea, coffee and snacks available.

SECRETARY: Conleth Dillon.

PROFESSIONAL: Mark Heinemann.

ARCHITECT: Arthur Spring.

NO.	METRES	PAR	S.I.	NO.	METRES	PAR	S.I.
1	178	3	6	10	178	3	5
2	281	4	8	11	281	4	7
3	286	4	16	12	286	4	15
4	197	3	14	13	179	3	13
5	183	3	12	14	183	3	11
6	340	4	2	15	340	4	1
7	142	3	10	16	142	3	9
8	246	4	18	17	246	4	17
9	183	3	4	18	183	3	3
OUT	2,036	31		IN	2,036	31	
				TOTAL	4,072	62	
				STANDARD SCRATCH		60	

Adare Manor Hotel & Golf Resort,
Adare, Co. Limerick.
Tel: (061) 605 274 Fax: (061) 605 271
Email: golf@adaremanor.com

ARCHITECT: Robert Trent Jones Snr.

Course Description:
New course opened in 1995 in the grounds of Adare
Manor and 1999 saw the opening of a 18,000 sq ft
state of the art clubhouse and accommodation
facility. The championship course measures 7,453
yards off the Championship tees. The design of
the course which originally had four tees on each
holes has now been lenghened, with the
construction of new tees on ten holes (and the
Maigue River which creates a sense of beauty
and challenge) ensures that every level of
golfer will enjoy their game.

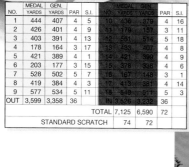

**Course
Information:**
Visitors: Welcome.
Opening Hours: 7.30am
– Dark (summer). 8am –Dark
(winter). **Green Fees:** €75 - €130
Contact course for further green fee
information. Club Hire €40 per round.
Caddy service: €40 per bag. **Drive carts:** €45, 18
holes, €25, 9 holes. **Clubhouse Dress:** Smart casual.
Clubhouse Facilities: Full clubhouse facilities in our 18,000
sq ft complex, along with 25 townhouses and 11 clubhouse
bedrooms& 46 Villas. Practice facilities available. Soft
spikes only.

NO.	MEDAL YARDS	GEN. YARDS	PAR	S.I.	NO.	MEDAL YARDS	GEN. YARDS	PAR	S.I.
1	444	407	4	5	10	436	379	4	16
2	426	401	4	9	11	179	157	3	11
3	403	391	4	13	12	561	514	5	18
4	178	164	3	17	13	433	407	4	8
5	421	389	4	1	14	421	399	4	9
6	203	177	3	15	15	378	336	4	6
7	528	502	5	7	16	167	148	3	1
8	419	384	4	3	17	413	381	4	14
9	577	534	5	11	18	548	511	5	3
OUT	3,599	3,358	36		IN	3,526	3,232	36	
					TOTAL	7,125	6,590	72	
					STANDARD SCRATCH	74	72		

Adare Manor

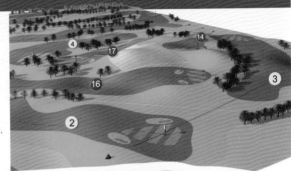

Adare, Co. Limerick. Tel: (061) 396204.

Course Description:
The original and more traditional course in Adare, founded in 1900, is called Adare Manor but is not the new championship course in the grounds of Adare Manor Hotel. Adare is a parkland course, which is particularly scenic. The Abbey and Desmond Castle are unique features to the course. There are three Par 5's and six Par 3's over the eighteen holes. The fairways are narrow and well maintained.

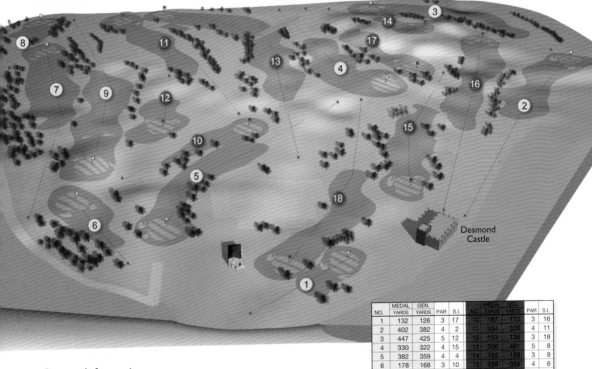

Desmond Castle

Course Information:
Par 69; SSS 69; Length 5,764 yards. **Visitors:** Welcome. Booking required for weekends. **Opening Hours:** 9am-sunset. **Green Fees:** €40 all week. Juveniles: Welcome, but accompanied by an adult. Club Hire available; Caddy service available by prior arrangements (summer months). **Clubhouse Hours:** 10.00am closing time. **Clubhouse Dress:** Casual – no shorts or sports wear. **Clubhouse Facilities:** Full catering. **Open Competitions:** June & August.

NO.	MEDAL YARDS	GEN. YARDS	PAR	S.I.	NO.	MEDAL YARDS	GEN. YARDS	PAR	S.I.
1	132	126	3	17	10	187	170	3	16
2	402	382	4	2	11	334	325	4	11
3	447	425	5	12	12	153	136	3	18
4	330	322	4	15	13	506	491	5	8
5	382	359	4	4	14	195	169	3	9
6	178	168	3	10	15	358	354	4	6
7	383	366	4	5	16	424	414	4	1
8	210	190	3	7	17	284	271	4	14
9	494	472	5	13	18	365	347	4	3
OUT	2,958	2,810	35		IN	2,806	2,698	34	
					TOTAL	5,764	5,508	69	
					STANDARD SCRATCH		69	67	

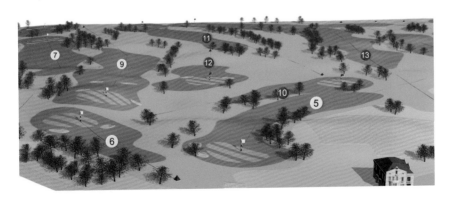

LOCATION:
Ten miles from Limerick City.

SECRETARY:
T.P. Healy

Golf Links Road,
Castletroy, Co. Limerick.
Tel: (061) 335753. Fax: (061) 335373
Email: cgc@iol.ie
Web: www.castletroygolfclub.ie

LOCATION: Less than 3 miles from Limerick City off N7 to Dublin.
COURSE ARCHITECT: Eddie Connaughton

GENERAL MANAGER: Patrick Keane.
Tel: (061) 335753.

Course Description: A mature parkland course which has been popular with visitors throughout the years. In 2006 the new courses opened after extensive re-development. All tee box and green complexes have been redesigned and with the addition of fairway bunkering and water features throughout the course, it offers a challenge to golfers of all standards. Well maintained fairways demanding accuracy off the tee. The long Par 5 6th hole is set into water while the Par 3 14th Hole features a panoramic view from the tee with the green surrounded by water. The picturesque 18th is a stern test to finish with the green guarded by bunkers on both sides.

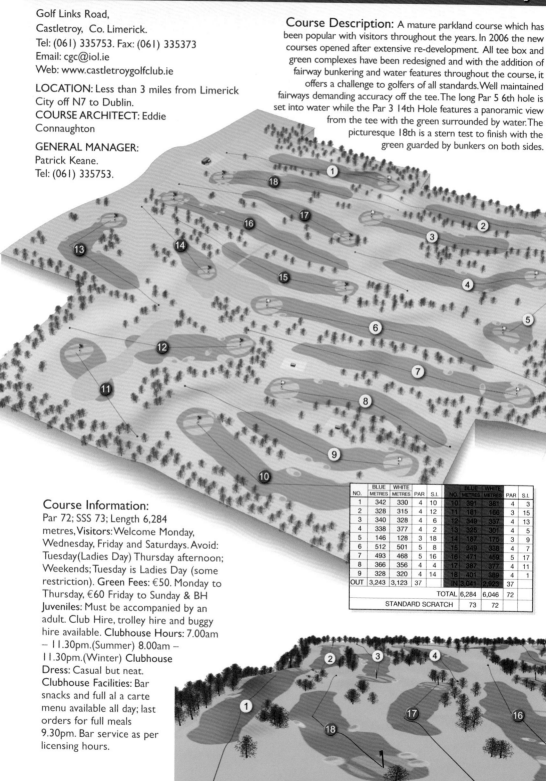

Course Information:
Par 72; SSS 73; Length 6,284 metres, Visitors: Welcome Monday, Wednesday, Friday and Saturdays. Avoid: Tuesday(Ladies Day) Thursday afternoon; Weekends; Tuesday is Ladies Day (some restriction). Green Fees: €50. Monday to Thursday, €60 Friday to Sunday & BH Juveniles: Must be accompanied by an adult. Club Hire, trolley hire and buggy hire available. **Clubhouse Hours:** 7.00am – 11.30pm.(Summer) 8.00am – 11.30pm.(Winter) **Clubhouse Dress:** Casual but neat. **Clubhouse Facilities:** Bar snacks and full al a carte menu available all day; last orders for full meals 9.30pm. Bar service as per licensing hours.

NO.	BLUE METRES	WHITE METRES	PAR	S.I.	NO.	BLUE METRES	WHITE METRES	PAR	S.I.
1	342	330	4	10	10	391	381	4	3
2	328	315	4	12	11	181	166	3	15
3	340	328	4	6	12	349	337	4	13
4	338	377	4	2	13	325	301	4	5
5	146	128	3	18	14	187	175	3	9
6	512	501	5	8	15	349	338	4	7
7	493	468	5	16	16	471	459	5	17
8	366	356	4	4	17	387	377	4	11
9	328	320	4	14	18	401	389	4	1
OUT	3,243	3,123	37		IN	3,041	2,923	37	
					TOTAL	6,284	6,046	72	
					STANDARD SCRATCH		73	72	

Course Information:

Par 72; SSS 71; Length 6,525 yards; 5,932 metres. Course Record: T. Woods (64). Visitors: Welcome by booking. Opening Hours: 8.30am – sunset. Avoid: Tuesday and weekends. Ladies Day: Tuesdays. Lessons available by prior arrangements; Club Hire and Caddy service available by prior arrangements; telephone appointment advisable. Green Fees: €50 Mon-Fri, €70 weekends. Clubhouse Hours: 9.30am – 11.00pm; full clubhouse facilities. Clubhouse Dress: Casual. Clubhouse Facilities: Full service from 11.00am. Open Competitions: Mainly holiday weekends and first week in August.

Ballyclough, Limerick. Tel: (061) 414083/415146.

LOCATION: Three miles South of Limerick City.

SECRETARY: Pat Murray. Tel: (061) 415146.

PROFESSIONAL: Lee Harington. Tel: (061) 412492.

NO.	MEDAL METRES	GEN. METRES	PAR	S.I.	NO.	MEDAL METRES	GEN. METRES	PAR	S.I.
1	303	297	4	9	10	397	379	4	2
2	439	426	5	15	11	341	331	4	11
3	427	419	4	1	12	372	370	4	6
4	349	337	4	5	13	281	270	4	17
5	158	149	3	16	14	140	132	3	14
6	466	456	5	7	15	344	297	4	4
7	378	362	4	3	16	305	287	4	10
8	120	107	3	18	17	344	318	4	8
9	450	438	5	13	18	318	312	4	12
OUT	3,090	2,991	37		IN	2,842	2,696	35	
					TOTAL	5,932	5,687	72	
					STANDARD SCRATCH		71	70	

Course Description:

A parkland course with tree lined fairways located in pleasant surroundings, situated on a hill overlooking the city of Limerick. T. Woods and Mark O'Meara Hon. life members and frequent visitors to the club.

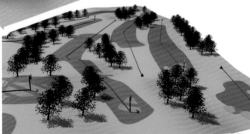

Limerick County

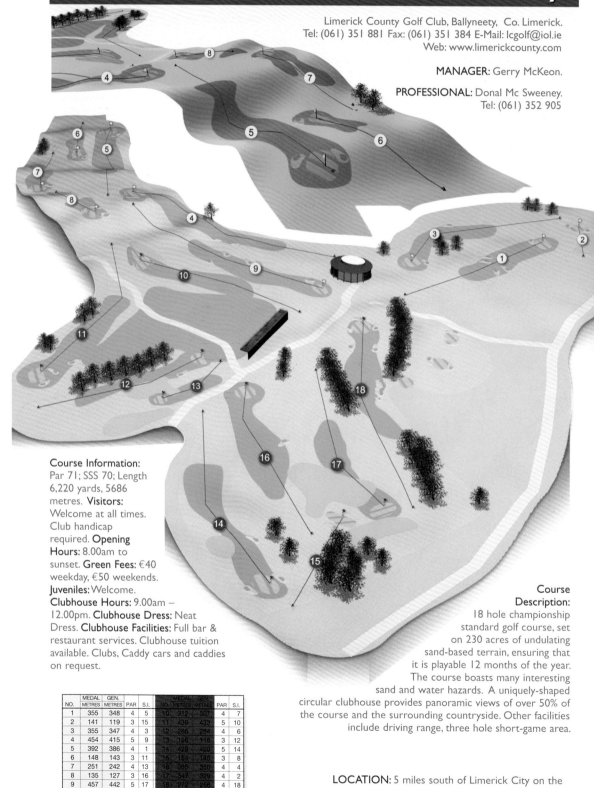

Limerick County Golf Club, Ballyneety, Co. Limerick.
Tel: (061) 351 881 Fax: (061) 351 384 E-Mail: lcgolf@iol.ie
Web: www.limerickcounty.com

MANAGER: Gerry McKeon.

PROFESSIONAL: Donal Mc Sweeney.
Tel: (061) 352 905

Course Information:
Par 71; SSS 70; Length 6,220 yards, 5686 metres. **Visitors:** Welcome at all times. Club handicap required. **Opening Hours:** 8.00am to sunset. **Green Fees:** €40 weekday, €50 weekends. **Juveniles:** Welcome. **Clubhouse Hours:** 9.00am – 12.00pm. **Clubhouse Dress:** Neat Dress. **Clubhouse Facilities:** Full bar & restaurant services. Clubhouse tuition available. Clubs, Caddy cars and caddies on request.

Course Description:
18 hole championship standard golf course, set on 230 acres of undulating sand-based terrain, ensuring that it is playable 12 months of the year. The course boasts many interesting sand and water hazards. A uniquely-shaped circular clubhouse provides panoramic views of over 50% of the course and the surrounding countryside. Other facilities include driving range, three hole short-game area.

LOCATION: 5 miles south of Limerick City on the R512, direction Kilmallock.

ARCHITECT: Des Smyth & Associates.

NO.	MEDAL METRES	GEN. METRES	PAR	S.I.	NO.	MEDAL METRES	GEN. METRES	PAR	S.I.
1	355	348	4	5	10	312	307	4	7
2	141	119	3	15	11	439	433	5	10
3	355	347	4	3	12	285	264	4	6
4	454	415	5	9	13	125	118	3	12
5	392	386	4	1	14	429	420	5	14
6	148	143	3	11	15	154	145	3	8
7	251	242	4	13	16	385	350	4	4
8	135	127	3	16	17	347	329	4	2
9	457	442	5	17	18	272	266	4	18
OUT	2,688	2,569	35		IN	2,729	2,633	36	
					TOTAL	5,417	5,202	71	
					STANDARD SCRATCH	70	70		

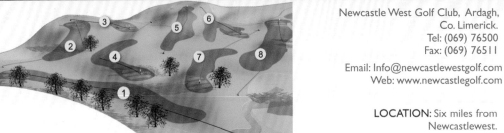

Newcastle West Golf Club, Ardagh,
Co. Limerick.
Tel: (069) 76500
Fax: (069) 76511

Email: Info@newcastlewestgolf.com
Web: www.newcastlegolf.com

LOCATION: Six miles from
Newcastlewest.

SECRETARY: Eamonn Cregan.

ARCHITECT: A. Spring.

NO.	BLUE YARDS	WHITE YARDS	PAR	S.I.	NO.	BLUE YARDS	WHITE YARDS	PAR	S.I.
1	465	456	5	16	10	184	170	3	15
2	356	345	4	12	11	399	387	4	3
3	191	166	3	10	12	358	348	4	7
4	338	310	4	14	13	344	330	4	17
5	414	387	4	12	14	514	504	5	13
6	187	163	3	2	15	414	407	4	9
7	378	368	4	8	16	407	377	4	1
8	506	495	5	18	17	183	187	3	11
9	370	350	4	6	18	435	411	4	5
OUT	3,205	3,040	36		IN	3,239	3,101	35	
					TOTAL	6,444	6,141	71	
	STANDARD SCRATCH						70	69	

Course Information:
Par 71; SSS 73; Length 5,905 metres. **Visitors:**
Welcome. **Opening Hours:** 9.00am – sunset. **Avoid:**
Saturday and Sunday mornings. **Ladies Day:** Play any day.
Green Fees: €35 Mon–Fri, €45 Sat/Sun. **Clubhouse
Hours:** 11.00am – 11.00pm. **Clubhouse Dress:** Casual.
Clubhouse Facilities: Full meals, snacks & Golf Shop.
Open Competitions: Open Week, June & Bank Holiday
weekends. Wednesday open Singles.

Course Description:
Set in 150 acres of unspoilt rolling
west Limerick countryside.
Newcastle West comprises an 18
hole championship course built to
the highest standards on sandy
soil which is playable all the year
round. A practice ground and
floodlit driving range are included.

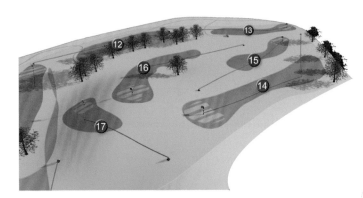

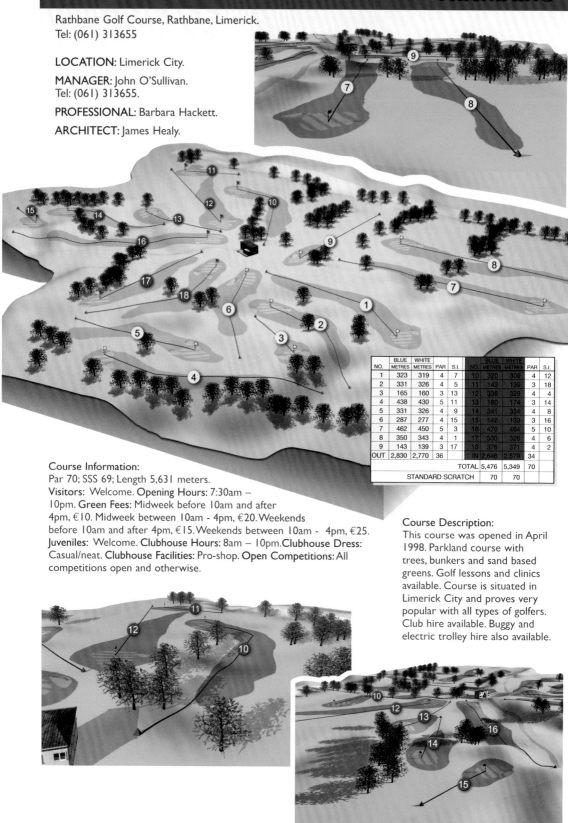

Rathbane Golf Course, Rathbane, Limerick.
Tel: (061) 313655

LOCATION: Limerick City.

MANAGER: John O'Sullivan.
Tel: (061) 313655.

PROFESSIONAL: Barbara Hackett.

ARCHITECT: James Healy.

NO.	BLUE METRES	WHITE METRES	PAR	S.I.	NO.	BLUE METRES	WHITE METRES	PAR	S.I.
1	323	319	4	7	10	320	309	4	12
2	331	326	4	5	11	143	139	3	18
3	165	160	3	13	12	338	329	4	4
4	438	430	5	11	13	180	174	3	14
5	331	326	4	9	14	341	334	4	8
6	287	277	4	15	15	142	133	3	16
7	462	450	5	3	16	476	464	5	10
8	350	343	4	1	17	330	326	4	6
9	143	139	3	17	18	376	371	4	2
OUT	2,830	2,770	36		IN	2,646	2,579	34	
					TOTAL	5,476	5,349	70	
					STANDARD SCRATCH	70	70		

Course Information:
Par 70; SSS 69; Length 5,631 meters.
Visitors: Welcome. **Opening Hours:** 7:30am –
10pm. **Green Fees:** Midweek before 10am and after
4pm, €10. Midweek between 10am - 4pm, €20. Weekends
before 10am and after 4pm, €15. Weekends between 10am - 4pm, €25.
Juveniles: Welcome. **Clubhouse Hours:** 8am – 10pm. **Clubhouse Dress:**
Casual/neat. **Clubhouse Facilities:** Pro-shop. **Open Competitions:** All
competitions open and otherwise.

Course Description:
This course was opened in April
1998. Parkland course with
trees, bunkers and sand based
greens. Golf lessons and clinics
available. Course is situated in
Limerick City and proves very
popular with all types of golfers.
Club hire available. Buggy and
electric trolley hire also available.

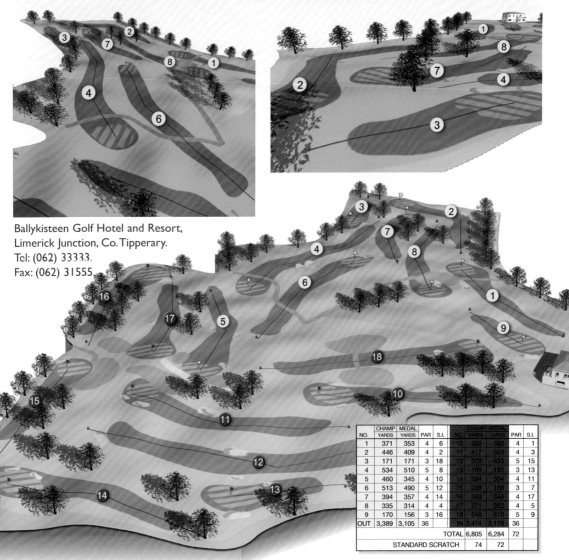

Ballykisteen Golf Hotel and Resort,
Limerick Junction, Co. Tipperary.
Tel: (062) 33333.
Fax: (062) 31555.

NO.	CHAMP YARDS	MEDAL YARDS	PAR	S.I.	NO.	CHAMP YARDS	MEDAL YARDS	PAR	S.I.
1	371	353	4	6	10	392	392	4	1
2	446	409	4	2	11	417	393	4	3
3	171	171	3	18	12	509	493	5	15
4	534	510	5	8	13	169	155	3	13
5	460	345	4	10	14	394	354	4	11
6	513	490	5	12	15	226	168	3	7
7	394	357	4	14	16	389	346	4	17
8	335	314	4	4	17	371	382	4	5
9	170	156	3	16	18	546	516	5	9
OUT	3,389	3,105	36		IN	3,414	3,179	36	
					TOTAL	6,805	6,284	72	
					STANDARD SCRATCH		74	72	

LOCATION: Centrally located on the M24 – two miles from Tipperary Town and within a twenty minute drive of Limerick City.

PGA APPROVED: James Harris.

GENERAL MANAGER: George Graham.

ARCHITECT: Des Smyth.

Course Information:
Par 72; SSS 74; Length 6,805 yards. **Green Fees:** €40 Mon - Thur, €50 Fri - Sun. **Juveniles:** Club Hire available, Caddy service available. Fully equipped Professional Shop, group and individual tuition and a floodlit Driving Range.
Clubhouse Facilities: Elegant restaurant and bar – open to the general public all day every day. Societies welcome, membership available.

Course Description: A parkland course, nestled in emerald green countryside in the heart of the Golden Vale. A very interesting and clever design has made this a course suitable to the high and low handicap golfer.

Email: golf@ballykisteenhotel.com
Web: www.ballykisteenhotel.com

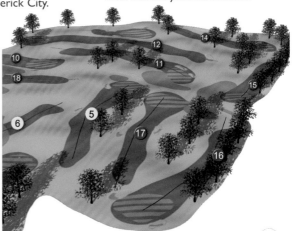

Kilcommon, Cahir, Co. Tipperary. Tel: (052) 41474.
Email: management@cahirparkgolfclub.com
www.cahirparkgolfclub.com

LOCATION: One mile from
town centre.

SECRETARY/MANAGER:
Michael Duggan.

ARCHITECT: E. Hackett.

NO.	MEDAL YARDS	GEN. YARDS	PAR	S.I.	NO.	MEDAL YARDS	GEN. YARDS	PAR	S.I.
1	388	381	4	10	10	410	404	4	3
2	355	348	4	14	11	512	506	5	13
3	191	184	3	4	12	409	404	4	1
4	336	329	4	12	13	381	375	4	7
5	185	174	3	16	14	501	495	5	11
6	493	486	5	8	15	338	332	4	15
7	439	421	4	2	16	96	91	3	17
8	360	354	4	6	17	384	378	4	5
9	152	148	3	18	18	387	378	4	9
OUT	2,899	2,825	34		IN	3,419	3,361	37	
					TOTAL	6,318	6,186	71	
					STANDARD SCRATCH	71	70		

Course Information:
Par 71; SSS 71; Length
5,805 metres. **Visitors:**
Welcome. **Opening Hours:** Sunrise –
sunset. **Avoid:** Major club competition days.
Sat/Sun in June/Aug. **Green Fees:** €30 Monday to
Friday, Weekends €35 (18 holes). **Juveniles:** Welcome
at times when course is available. **Clubhouse Hours:**
10.30am – 11.00pm. **Clubhouse Dress:** Casual.
Clubhouse Facilities: Full clubhouse facilites, tea coffee,
snacks & lunches daily.

Course Description:
Prime parkland, part of old Cahir Park
Estate. Sloping down to the River Suir
which runs along the right hand side of the
7th hole, this hole is rated as one of the
most difficult on the course. Holes 8 and
16 involve playing across the River Suir.

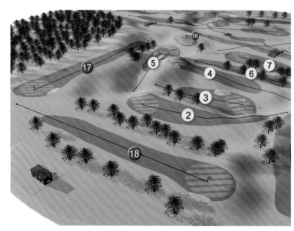

Garravoone, Carrick-On-Suir, Co. Tipperary.
Tel: (051) 640047.
Email: info@carrickgolfclub.com
www.carrickgolfclub.com

LOCATION: 1 mile from Carrick-On-Suir on Dargarvan Road.

MANAGER: Aidan Murphy.

ARCHITECT: E. Hackett.

Course Description:

Carrick on Suir is a scenic 18 hole course on elevated ground close to the town. The Comeragh Mountains are on one side as a backdrop to the first five holes and the River Suir in the valley winds its way to the sea at Waterford. The scenery will keep the golfer occupied if the game is not going to plan.

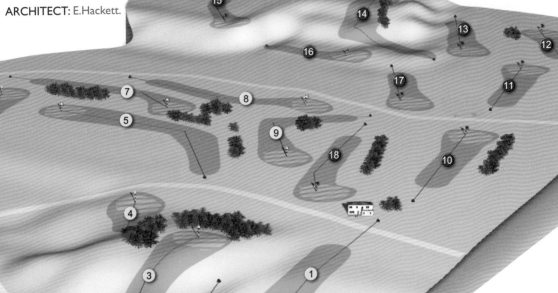

NO.	YARDS	PAR	S.I.	NO.	YARDS	PAR	S.I.
1	367	4	8	10	351	4	3
2	166	3	16	11	447	5	15
3	297	4	2	12	373	4	1
4	154	3	18	13	329	4	7
5	497	5	6	14	439	5	17
6	180	3	4	15	321	4	13
7	332	4	12	16	167	3	9
8	335	4	14	17	418	4	5
9	495	5	10	18	338	4	11
OUT	2,823	35		IN	3,188	37	
				TOTAL	6,011	72	
				STANDARD SCRATCH		70	

Course Information:

Par 72; SSS 70; Length 6,061 metres. **Visitors:** Welcome Mon – Sat. **Opening Hours:** Sunrise – sunset. **Avoid:** Mon – Wed in summer after 5pm. **Ladies Day:** Wednesday. **Green Fees:** €25 Mon – Fri; (€20 with member) €30 weekends (€25 with member) Group discounts. Caddy service available. **Juveniles:** Welcome, telephone appointment required. **Clubhouse Hours:** 10am – 11pm Mon – Fri; 9am – 11pm Sat / Sun (summer); Sat / Sun 9am – 9pm (winter). **Clubhouse Dress:** Casual but neat. **Catering Facilities:** Full catering available. **Open Competitions:** Open Week, July

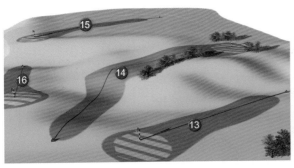

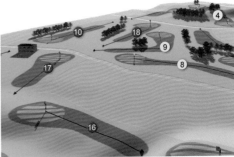

Lyneanearla, Mountain Road, Clonmel, Co. Tipperary.
Tel: (052) 24050. Fax: (052) 83349.

LOCATION: 3 miles from Clonmel.
SECRETARY / MANAGER: Aine Myles-Keating.
PROFESSIONAL: Robert Hayes.
ARCHITECT: Eddie Hackett.

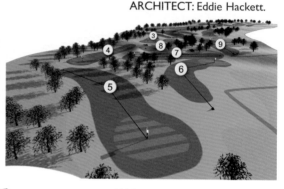

Web: www.clonmelgolfclub.com
Email: cgc@indigo.ie

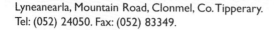

Course Information:
Par 72; SSS 71; Length 6,347 yards.
Opening Hours: 8am – 10pm.
Visitors: Welcome. **Green Fees:** €30
Mon – Fri; €35 Sat, Sun & Bank Hols (with member €20 anytime). Ladies: Welcome.
Juveniles: Welcome. Lessons by prior arrangement. Club Hire available. Telephone appointment required for societies. Motorised buggies available. Clubhouse Hours: 8.30am – 11pm. Clubhouse Dress: Casual. Clubhouse Facilities: Bar open every day; Catering – Light lunch and sandwiches. Lunch and dinner by prior arrangements.
Open Competitions: Open Day - Tuesday during the Summer Months. **Open Week:** 14th- 22nd July **Specials:** Suir Valley Golf Experience - Three rounds of golf for €60 Monday to Friday. Play Clonmel, Carrick & Cahir Park Golf Club. Tickets valid for 12 months from date of purchase.

NO.	WHITE YARDS	GREEN YARDS	PAR	S.I.	NO.	WHITE YARDS	GREEN YARDS	PAR	S.I.
1	374	363	4	12	10	383	371	4	11
2	395	384	4	4	11	490	465	5	13
3	140	131	3	18	12	299	287	4	17
4	493	460	5	14	13	421	405	4	1
5	370	352	4	10	14	185	178	3	3
6	365	353	4	6	15	377	347	4	7
7	335	323	4	16	16	418	406	4	5
8	452	439	5	2	17	184	174	3	9
9	177	162	3	8	18	489	468	5	15
OUT	3,101	2,967	36		IN	3,246	3,101	36	
					TOTAL	6,347	6,068	72	
					STANDARD SCRATCH		70		

Course Description:
Clonmel is a very pleasant inland course with lots of open space and plenty of variety. There is a stream that crosses three fairways and has the advantage of a picturesque setting on the scenic slopes of the pine and fir covered Comeragh Mountains overlooking the plains of Tipperary.

Course Information: Par 72; SSS 72; Length 6,009 metres. Visitors: Welcome Mon-Fri Avoid: Weekends. Opening Hours: Sunrise-sunset. Green Fees: €30 per18 holes. Juveniles: Welcome. Clubhouse Hours: 10am-11pm. Clubhouse Dress: Casual. Clubhouse Facilities: Full catering available. Open Competitions: Open week-1st week in June; Semi-opens -most Bank Holiday Weekends.

Course Description: Re-development completed in 2001. New design is a very fair test for every golfer irrespective of ability or experience. New sand-based greens, guarded by intimidating bunkers, are a challenge for even the most fastidious of putters. Excellent drainage and firm surfaces allows play all year round.

Beechwood, Nenagh, Co. Tipperary.
Tel: (067) 31476

Email: neaghgolfclub@eircom.net
www.neaghgolfclub.com

NO.	MEDAL YARDS	GEN. YARDS	PAR	S.I.	NO.	MEDAL YARDS	GEN. YARDS	PAR	S.I.
1	374	337	4	8	10	326	290	4	15
2	362	340	4	18	11	129	120	3	17
3	457	430	5	6	12	460	417	5	5
4	360	354	4	12	13	314	286	4	3
5	387	366	4	14	14	339	301	4	9
6	177	156	3	2	15	178	138	3	11
7	460	426	5	10	16	399	382	4	1
8	155	146	3	16	17	463	440	5	13
9	309	276	4	4	18	360	349	4	7
OUT	3,041	2,931	36		IN	2,968	2,703	36	
					TOTAL	6,152	5,870	72	
					STANDARD SCRATCH		72	71	

ARCHITECT: Patrick Merrigan.

HON SECRETARY: Alice Varley.

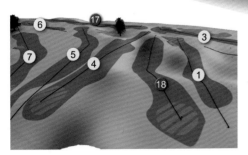

LOCATION: 4 miles from town, on Old Birr Road.

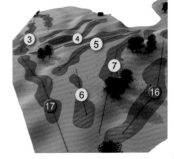

Munster – Tipperary

Roscrea

LOCATION: 2 miles east of Roscrea on the N7.

SECRETARY: S. Crofton.

Derryvale, Roscrea. Co. Tipperary.
Tel: (0505) 21130
Email roscreagolf@eircom.net

Course Description:
A fine 18 hole course with some excellent Par 3's. The last six holes are particularly challenging.

NO.	YARDS	PAR	S.I.	NO.	YARDS	PAR	S.I.
1	266	4	16	10	448	5	9
2	436	5	14	11	180	3	17
3	362	4	6	12	447	5	11
4	313	4	12	13	410	4	1
5	365	4	4	14	159	3	15
6	151	3	10	15	381	4	3
7	473	5	8	16	335	4	5
8	109	3	18	17	190	3	7
9	371	4	2	18	332	4	13
OUT	2,846	36		IN	2,852	35	
				TOTAL	5,708	71	
	STANDARD SCRATCH					70	

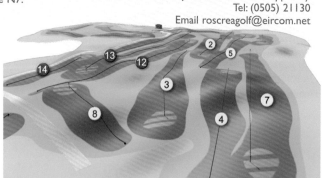

Course Information:
Par 71; SSS 70; Length 5,708 metres. **Visitors:** Welcome Sundays by arrangement. **Opening Hours:** 8am to dusk. **Ladies Day:** Tuesdays. **Green Fees:** €30 Mon – Fri. €35 Sat / Sun. **Juveniles:** Welcome although must be accompanied by an adult. Club Hire and Caddy trolleys available. **Clubhouse Hours:** 10.30am – 11.30pm. **Clubhouse Dress:** Casual but neat. **Clubhouse Facilities:** Full bar and catering. **Open Competitions:** Open week, June. Bank Holiday weekends. Open every Wednesday (Men) April to October.and pool.

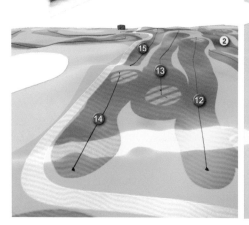

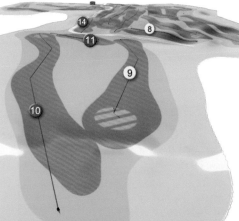

Couse Information:
Par 67; SSS 64; Length 4,846
Yards. **Visitors:** Welcome.
Opening Hours: Dawn – Dusk.
Green Fees: €15 weekdays; €20
weekends, Bank Holidays. €5
Clubhire. **Clubhouse Facilities:**
Full catering, á la carte, Bar.
Catering & Bar Tel: (052)
30876. **Open Competitions:**
Regular open competitions
throughout the season. Regular
Open Singles on Mondays,
April-September.

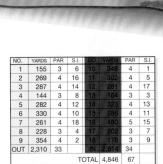

NO.	YARDS	PAR	S.I.	NO.	YARDS	PAR	S.I.
1	155	3	6	10	348	4	1
2	269	4	16	11	302	4	5
3	287	4	14	12	281	4	17
4	144	3	8	13	164	3	3
5	282	4	12	14	323	4	13
6	330	4	10	15	286	4	11
7	261	4	18	16	480	5	15
8	228	3	4	17	202	3	7
9	354	4	2	18	178	3	9
OUT	2,310	33		IN	2,614	34	
				TOTAL	4,846	67	
				STANDARD SCRATCH		64	

Clonacody, Lisronagh
Clonmel, Co. Tipperary.
Tel: (052) 32213
Fax: (052) 32040
Email: info@slievenamongolfclub.com
Web: www.slievenamongolfclub.com

Course Description:
Slievenamon is a flat but tight
parkland course, with tree-lined
fairways and carefully positioned
greens. It is a splendid
18 hole golf course
overlooked by the
beautiful Slievenamon.

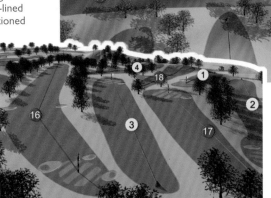

LOCATION: 6km outside
Clonmel.

PRESIDENT: Kevin Lalor.

SECRETARY:
Brendan Kenny.

Templemore

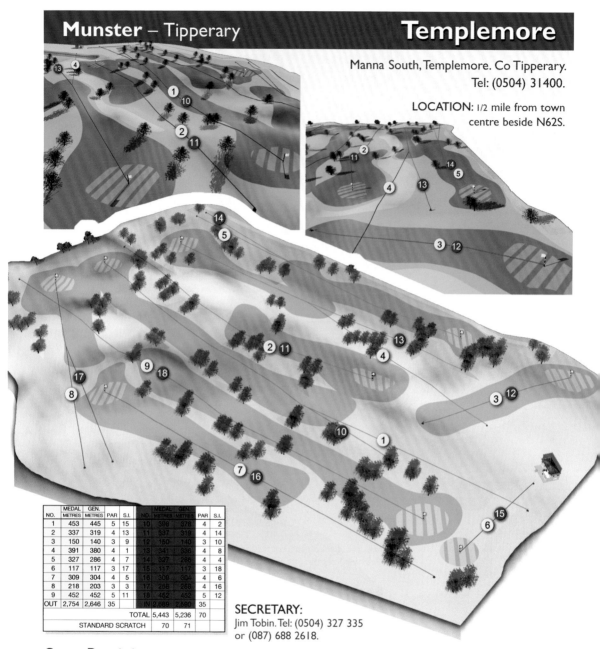

Manna South, Templemore. Co Tipperary.
Tel: (0504) 31400.

LOCATION: 1/2 mile from town centre beside N62S.

NO.	MEDAL METRES	GEN. METRES	PAR	S.I.	NO.	MEDAL METRES	GEN. METRES	PAR	S.I.
1	453	445	5	15	10	398	378	4	2
2	337	319	4	13	11	337	319	4	14
3	150	140	3	9	12	150	140	3	10
4	391	380	4	1	13	341	330	4	8
5	327	286	4	7	14	327	286	4	4
6	117	117	3	17	15	117	117	3	18
7	309	304	4	5	16	309	304	4	6
8	218	203	4	3	17	258	268	4	16
9	452	452	5	11	18	452	452	5	12
OUT	2,754	2,646	35		IN	2,689	2,590	35	
					TOTAL	5,443	5,236	70	
					STANDARD SCRATCH		70	71	

SECRETARY:
Jim Tobin. Tel: (0504) 327 335
or (087) 688 2618.

Course Description:

This course provides a pleasant test of golf, starting with a 442 metre Par 5. The course has five Par 3's, finishing with a very good Par 5 at the 9th and 18th. It has a very compact layout requiring only short walks from green to tees.

Course Information:

Par 70; SSS 69 (White), 68 (Green); Length 5,443 metres.
Visitors: Welcome Mon – Sun. **Opening Hours:** 8.00am – sunset.
Ladies: Welcome. **Green Fees:** €15 per day Mon – Fri. €20 per day Sat, Sun & Bank Holidays. €10 if playing with a member. Special Society Rates apply, contact secretary Societys welcome all day Mon-Fri; Sat up to 11.30am. **Juveniles:** Welcome. **New Members:** Welcome – apply Honorary Secretary. **Clubhouse Hours:** 8.00am – sunset. **Clubhouse Dress:** Casual. **Clubhouse Facilities:** By prior arrangement. **Open Competitions:** Open week July.

LOCATION: One mile from Thurles town.

HON. SECRETARY:
Michael O'Sullivan.

PROFESSIONAL: Sean Hunt.
Tel: (0504) 21983

ARCHITECT: Lionel Hewson.

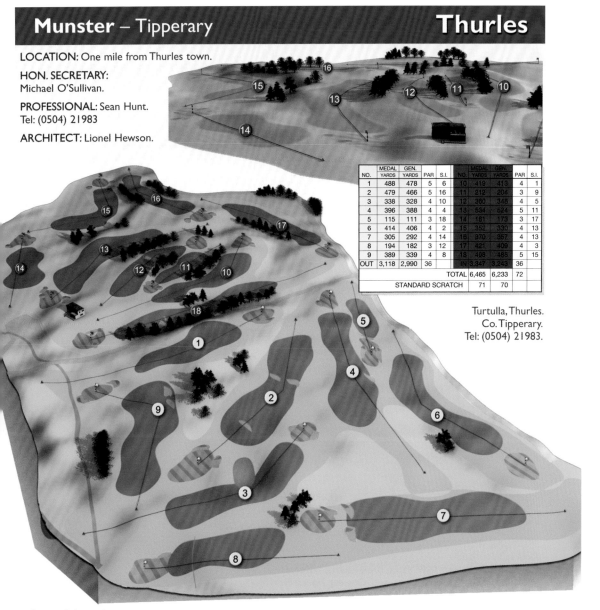

NO.	MEDAL YARDS	GEN. YARDS	PAR	S.I.	NO.	MEDAL YARDS	GEN. YARDS	PAR	S.I.
1	488	478	5	6	10	419	413	4	1
2	479	466	5	16	11	212	204	3	9
3	338	328	4	10	12	360	348	4	5
4	396	388	4	4	13	534	524	5	11
5	115	111	3	18	14	181	173	3	17
6	414	406	4	2	15	352	330	4	13
7	305	292	4	14	16	370	357	4	13
8	194	182	3	12	17	421	409	4	3
9	389	339	4	8	18	498	485	5	15
OUT	3,118	2,990	36		IN	3,347	3,243	36	
					TOTAL	6,465	6,233	72	
					STANDARD SCRATCH	71	70		

Turtulla, Thurles.
Co. Tipperary.
Tel: (0504) 21983.

Course Information:
Par 72; SSS 71; Length 6,456 yards, 5,904 metres. **Visitors:** Welcome. **Opening Hours:** 9.00am – 11.30pm. **Ladies:** Welcome. **Avoid:** Limited availablity at weekends. **Green Fees:** €35 Mon-Thur, €40 Fri-Sun. **Juveniles:** Welcome, Club Hire available; caddy service and lessons available by prior arrangement, telephone appointment required. **Clubhouse Hours:** 10.00am – 11.00pm. Full clubhouse facilities which include two championship squash courts. **Clubhouse Dress:** Casual. **Clubhouse Facilities:** Snacks at all times; full meals as ordered. **Open Competitions:** Open Week, July / Aug; Junior Scratch Cup, July; Inter. Scratch Cup, Sept. Munster Youth Cup, April and Irish Senior Ladies Close, April.

Course Description:
Fine parkland course, with the main features being the four excellent Par 3 holes and the fearsome 18th with the out-of-bounds all the way down the left. Unusual beginning to your round with two Par 5's in a row.

County Tipperary Golf & Country Club, Dundrum, Co. Tipperary.
Tel: (062) 71717. Fax: (062) 71718.
For further information log onto www.dundrumhousehotel.com

NO.	BLUE YARDS	WHITE YARDS	PAR	S.I.	NO.	CHAMP YARDS	MEDAL YARDS	PAR	S.I.
1	388	350	4	10	10	464	427	4	3
2	367	349	4	12	11	510	483	5	7
3	198	186	3	6	12	170	144	3	17
4	366	336	4	18	13	582	558	5	5
5	343	304	4	14	14	424	399	4	15
6	178	160	3	16	15	366	345	4	13
7	561	539	5	4	16	424	357	4	11
8	419	326	4	8	17	387	367	4	9
9	470	427	4	2	18	464	450	4	1
OUT	3,290	2,977	35		IN	3,793	3,470	37	
					TOTAL	7,083	6,447	72	
					STANDARD SCRATCH	72	72		

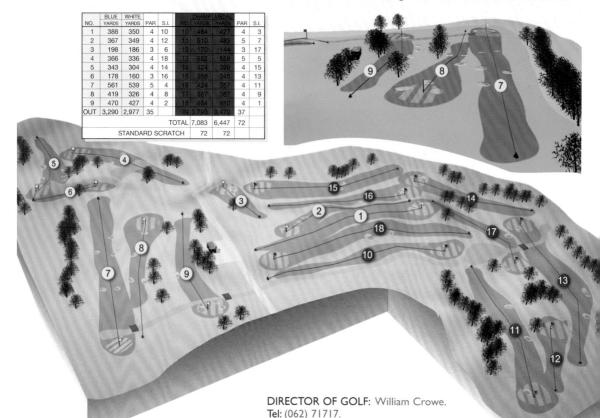

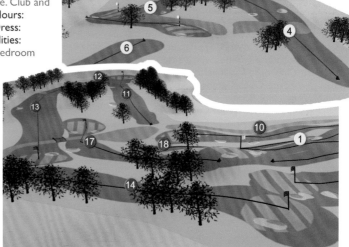

DIRECTOR OF GOLF: William Crowe.
Tel: (062) 71717.

SECRETARY: Marie Lacey.

Course Information:
Par 72; SSS 74; Length 7,083 yards, 6,400 metres. **Visitors:**
Welcome anytime (societies included). **Opening Hours:** 8am
– sunset. **Ladies:** Welcome. **Weekends:** Advisable to
book in advance. **Green Fees:** €50 midweek,
€60 weekends. **Juveniles:** Welcome. Club and
Buggy Hire available. **Clubhouse Hours:**
11.00am – 11.00pm. **Clubhouse Dress:**
Informal but neat. **Clubhouse Facilities:**
Restaurant and bar everyday. 90 bedroom
hotel. **Open Competitions:** Open
Week, 4th - 12th Aug.
Men's Open Singles Every
Monday, Apr-Oct.

Course Description:
An attractive parkland
course, playable all year
round, that has some
interesting holes and
made more intresting
by mature woodland
rivers and streams.

Knocknagranagh, Co. Waterford.
Tel: (058) 41605/43310. Fax: (058) 44113.
Email: dungarvangc@eircom.net
Web: www.dungarvangolfclub.com

LOCATION: Dungarvan 2 miles. On N25 route.
SECETARY/MANAGER: Irene Lynch.
ARCHITECT: Maurice Fives.
Resident PGA Professional: David Hayes

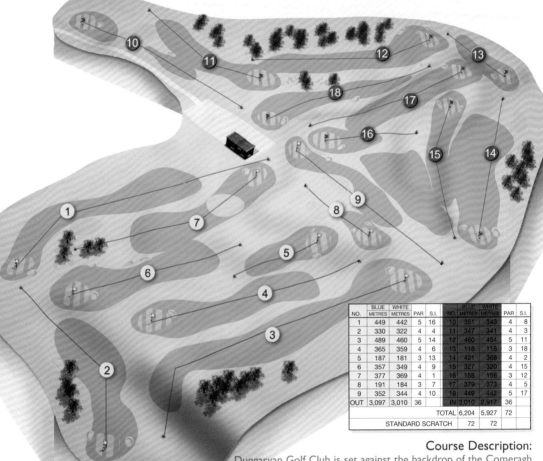

NO.	BLUE METRES	WHITE METRES	PAR	S.I.	NO.	BLUE METRES	WHITE METRES	PAR	S.I.
1	449	442	5	16	10	351	343	4	8
2	330	322	4	4	11	347	341	4	3
3	489	460	5	14	12	460	454	5	11
4	365	359	4	6	13	118	118	3	18
5	187	181	3	13	14	421	368	4	2
6	357	349	4	9	15	327	320	4	15
7	377	369	4	1	16	158	158	3	12
8	191	184	3	7	17	379	373	4	5
9	352	344	4	10	18	449	442	5	17
OUT	3,097	3,010	36		IN	3,010	2,917	36	
					TOTAL	6,204	5,927	72	
					STANDARD SCRATCH	72	72		

Course Description:

Dungarvan Golf Club is set against the backdrop of the Comeragh Mountains and runs adjacent to Dungavan Bay. This 6,785 yd Par 72 championship course has been architecturally designed with nine lakes and man-made hazards strategically placed to test all levels of golfer.

Course Information:

Par 72; SSS 73; Length 6,785 yards; 6,204 metres. **Visitors:** Welcome. **Opening Hours:** 7.00am – sunset. **Green Fees:** Mon – Fri €32, Weekends €44. **Juveniles:** Welcome. **Clubhouse Hours:** 9am – 12pm. **Clubhouse Dress:** Neat at all times. **Clubhouse Facilities:** Include light meals & full dining room service. Resident PGA Professional. Snooker room. **Open Competitions:** Open weeks, July and September.

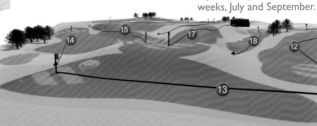

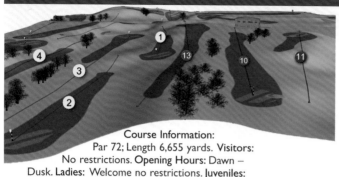

Course Information:
Par 72; Length 6,655 yards. **Visitors:** No restrictions. **Opening Hours:** Dawn – Dusk. **Ladies:** Welcome no restrictions. **Juveniles:** Welcome. **Green Fees:** From €30 Weekdays; €35 Weekends & Bank Holidays. **Clubhouse Hours:** 9am – 12pm. **Clubhouse Dress:** Neat / casual. **Clubhouse Facilities:** Full bar, light snacks full meals available all day in season. Club Hire, caddy trolleys and golf cart available for hire. **Open Competitions:** Fourball every Tuesday. Open Week 24th June to 2nd July.

Dunmore East Golf Club,
Dunmore East,
Co. Waterford.
Tel: (051) 383151

LOCATION: Ten miles from Waterford City in Dunmore East village.

SECRETARY: Sadie Whittle.
Tel: (051) 383151

ARCHITECT: William Henry Jones.

Course Description:
This 18 hole course overlooks the village of Dunmore East with panoramic views of the bay and harbour. The course offers challenging golf, in idyllic surroundings, with five holes on the waters edge, and shots 15 & 16 are played over inlets into the cliffs.

NO.	BLUE METRES	WHITE METRES	PAR	S.I.	NO.	BLUE METRES	WHITE METRES	PAR	S.I.
1	321	290	4	9	10	375	365	4	10
2	303	284	4	17	11	363	308	4	4
3	485	449	5	13	12	486	440	5	16
4	455	406	5	15	13	530	447	5	6
5	357	320	4	3	14	180	180	3	8
6	380	354	4	5	15	390	230	4	2
7	160	139	3	7	16	101	91	3	18
8	384	350	4	1	17	300	292	4	14
9	370	335	4	11	18	130	120	3	12
OUT	3,215	2,927	37		IN	2,855	2,473	35	
					TOTAL	6,076	5,400	72	
					STANDARD SCRATCH	70	69		

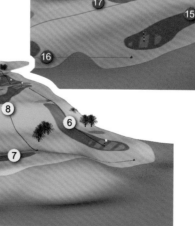

Faithlegg Golf Club, Faithlegg House, Co. Waterford. Tel: (051) 382000 Fax: (051) 382010
Email: golf@fhh.ie **Web:** www.faithlegg.com

LOCATION: Six miles from Waterford City, from Waterford take Dunmore East road for Cheekpoint village.

DIR. OF GOLF: Derry Kiely

Tel: (051) 382000

ARCHITECT: Patrick Merrigan.

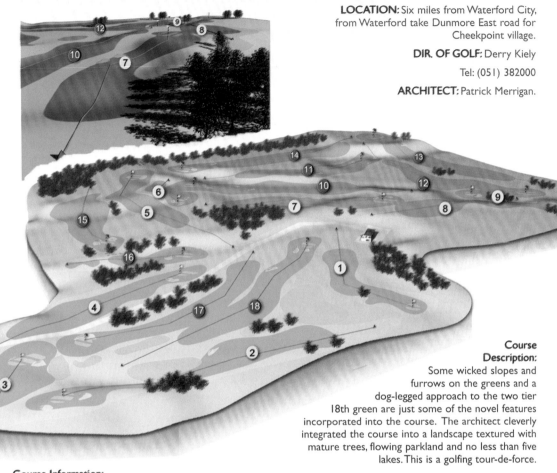

Course Description:
Some wicked slopes and furrows on the greens and a dog-legged approach to the two tier 18th green are just some of the novel features incorporated into the course. The architect cleverly integrated the course into a landscape textured with mature trees, flowing parkland and no less than five lakes. This is a golfing tour-de-force.

Course Information:
Par 72; SSS 72; Length 6,629 yards. **Visitors:** Welcome. Societies always welcome, corporate event specialists. **Opening Hours:** 8am – sunset. **Green Fees:** Mon – Thurs €50, Fri – Sun & Bank Holidays €65; Residents Mon – Thurs €40, Fri – Sun & Bank Holidays €52. **Juveniles:** Permitted. **Clubhouse Hours:** Summer; 9.00am-Close. Winter; 10.00am-Close. **Clubhouse Dress:** Neat, casual. **Clubhouse Facilities:** Full bar and catering facilities available, mens & ladies locker rooms, Pro-Shop. Club, caddy cars and buggies available for hire. **Open Competitions:** Contact clubhouse for details.

NO.	BLUE YARDS	WHITE YARDS	PAR	S.I.	NO.	BLUE YARDS	WHITE YARDS	PAR	S.I.
1	290	280	4	18	10	487	474	5	17
2	494	485	5	10	11	420	397	4	5
3	154	131	3	16	12	438	418	4	3
4	350	330	4	14	13	493	485	5	13
5	418	408	4	2	14	510	501	5	9
6	205	195	3	6	15	367	357	4	15
7	420	401	4	8	16	166	156	3	11
8	388	356	4	4	17	432	397	4	1
9	153	145	3	12	18	444	419	5	7
OUT	2,872	2,731			IN	3,757	3,604		
					TOTAL	6,629	6,335		
					STANDARD SCRATCH	72	70		

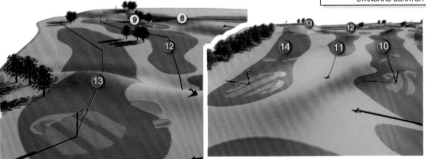

LOCATION: Three miles East of Dungarvan.

PRESIDENT: Declan Kiely.

SECRETARY: Dave Clark.

CAPTAIN: Brian Gaynor.

Gold Coast Golf Club, Ballinacourty, Dungarvan, Co. Waterford.
Tel: (058) 44055 **Fax:** (058) 43378
Web: www.goldcoastgolfclub.com

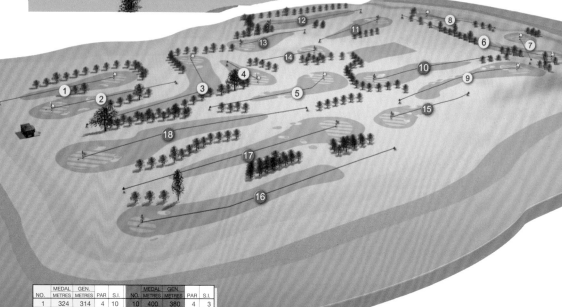

NO.	MEDAL METRES	GEN. METRES	PAR	S.I.	NO.	MEDAL METRES	GEN. METRES	PAR	S.I.
1	324	314	4	10	10	400	380	4	3
2	319	310	4	8	11	337	320	4	17
3	456	446	5	16	12	353	335	4	11
4	165	153	3	14	13	339	323	4	15
5	380	365	4	2	14	197	180	3	9
6	449	438	5	12	15	361	344	4	5
7	150	144	3	18	16	480	468	5	13
8	175	160	3	4	17	430	405	4	1
9	346	332	4	6	18	510	496	5	7
OUT	2,764	2,662	35		IN	3,407	3,251	37	
					TOTAL	6,171	5,913	72	
					STANDARD SCRATCH		72	71	

Course Information:
Par 72; SSS 72; Length 6,171 metres. **Visitors:** Welcome.
Opening Hours: Sunrise – sunset. **Avoid:** Advisable to book in advance for weekends. **Ladies:** Welcome. **Green Fees:** Mon – Fri €35, Sat – Sun €45. **Juveniles:** Welcome. Club and trolly Hire available.
Clubhouse Hours: 8.00am – 12.00pm. **Clubhouse Dress:** Casual, neat.
Clubhouse Facilities: Hotel & catering services, including leisure centre & swimming pool on site.

Course Description:
A parkland course bordered by Atlantic Ocean with a scenic background of Dungarvan Bay and Comeragh Mountains.

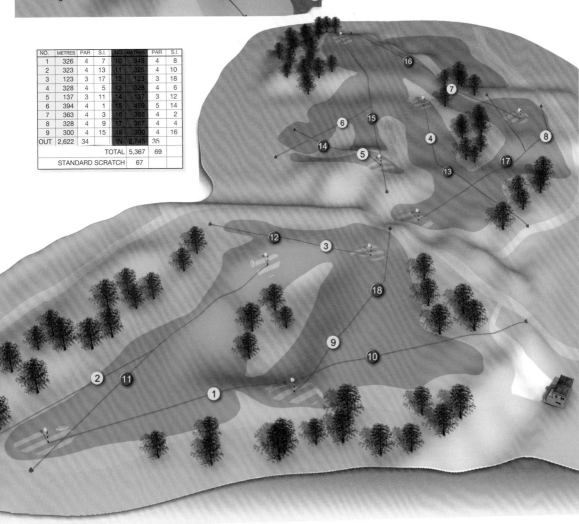

Lismore Golf Club, Ballyin, Lismore,
Co. Waterford.
Tel: (058) 54026
www.lismoregolf.org

LOCATION: 1Km north of town, off R.666.
SECRETARY: Katherine Moynihan.
Tel: (058) 54026

NO.	METRES	PAR	S.I.	NO.	METRES	PAR	S.I.
1	326	4	7	10	343	4	8
2	323	4	13	11	325	4	10
3	123	3	17	12	123	3	18
4	328	4	5	13	328	4	6
5	137	3	11	14	137	3	12
6	394	4	1	15	459	5	14
7	363	4	3	16	363	4	2
8	328	4	9	17	367	4	4
9	300	4	15	18	300	4	16
OUT	2,622	34		IN	2,745	35	
				TOTAL	5,367	69	
				STANDARD SCRATCH		67	

Course Information:
Par 69; SSS 68; Length 5,367 metres. **Visitors:** More than welcome.
Opening Hours: Dawn – dusk. **Avoid:** Saturdays and Sundays. **Ladies Day:**
Wednesday. **Green Fees:** €20 everyday including bank holidays. **Juveniles:**
Accompanied by an adult. **Clubhouse Hours:** 9.00am – close. **Clubhouse**
Dress: Neat / Casual. **Clubhouse Facilities:** Bar, snacks, changing rooms.
Open Competitions: Open day every Friday. Open Competitions on all
Bank Holidays - phone club for details.

Course Description:
Undulating parkland course
with mature hardwood
trees, on the estate of
Lismore Castle, in the
Blackwater Valley.

Tramore

Newtown Hill, Tramore. Co Waterford.
Tel: (051) 386 170.
Fax: (051) 390 961.

LOCATION:
On the Dungarvan
coast road.
MANAGER: David Murray.
PROFESSIONAL: Deirdre Brennan

NO.	MEDAL METERS	GEN. METERS	PAR	S.I.	NO.	MEDAL METERS	GEN. METERS	PAR	S.I.
1	365	365	4	6	10	174	174	3	16
2	455	455	5	15	11	366	333	4	4
3	155	155	3	11	12	315	315	4	10
4	344	344	4	3	13	366	325	4	7
5	294	294	4	12	14	406	367	4	1
6	159	159	3	17	15	117	117	3	18
7	367	367	4	8	16	500	500	5	9
8	371	371	4	2	17	348	322	4	5
9	506	506	5	13	18	449	449	5	14
OUT	3,016	3,016	36		IN	3,039	2,902	36	
					TOTAL	6,055	5,918	72	
					STANDARD SCRATCH		71		

Course Description:
18 hole championship course with generous
fairways. In a recent survey, by Sports
Columnist John Cowyn, two holes — the
4th and the 6th were rated in the top
eighteen in Ireland.

Course Information:
Par 72; SSS 71; Length 5,918 metres. **Green
Fees:** €45 Mon – Thurs. €60 Fri-Sat. **Visitors:**
Welcome, lessons available by prior
arrangements; Club Hire and Caddy service
available; telephone appointments required.
Clubhouse Hours: 11.00am – 11.30pm.
Clubhouse Dress: Casual but neat. **Open
Competitions:** Open Weeks 17th Aug –
2nd Sept

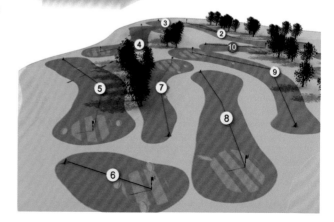

Waterford Castle

Waterford Castle Golf Club, The Island,
Ballinakill, Waterford.
Tel: (051) 871633
Fax: (051) 871634
Email: golf@waterfordcastle.com
Web: www.waterfordcastle.com

Course Information:
Par 72; SSS 73; Length 6,231 Metres.
Visitors: Welcome. **Opening Hours:** 8am –
dusk. **Avoid:** 8.30am – 10.30am (Sat & Sun).
Ladies: Welcome. **Juveniles:** Permitted with
adult. **Green Fees:** €52 midweek. €62 weekends.
Clubhouse Hours: 8am-dusk. **Clubhouse Dress:**
Casual, no jeans etc. **Clubhouse Facilities:** Bar
snacks available. Full meals with pre-
booking. **Open Competitions:**
Open week: July.

NO.	MEDAL METRES	GEN. METRES	PAR	S.I.	NO.	MEDAL METRES	GEN. METRES	PAR	S.I.
1	385	361	4	9	10	160	152	3	12
2	176	154	3	5	11	346	318	4	14
3	372	346	4	1	12	415	397	4	2
4	356	338	4	3	13	463	427	5	16
5	475	432	5	15	14	343	306	4	8
6	337	320	4	17	15	488	454	5	18
7	193	176	3	7	16	187	173	3	4
8	452	443	5	13	17	368	344	4	6
9	381	360	4	11	18	353	326	4	10
OUT	3,128	2,930	36		IN	3,103	2,897	36	
					TOTAL	6,231	5,827	72	
	STANDARD SCRATCH					73	71		

Course Description:
Ireland's only true island golf
course. A unique 310-acre island
golf course surrounded by the river
Suir and accessed by private ferry.
A mature parkland course and a
commendable test of golf.

LOCATION: Waterford City.

DIRECTOR OF GOLF: Micheal Garland.

ARHITECT: Des Smyth & Associates.

West Waterford

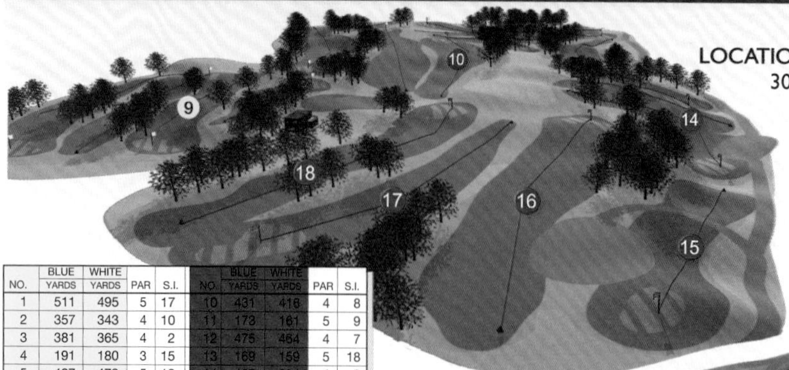

LOCATION: 3 miles from Dungarvan, 30 miles from Waterford City.

SECRETARY/MANAGER: Tom Whelan.

ARCHITECT: Eddie Hackett.

NO.	BLUE YARDS	WHITE YARDS	PAR	S.I.	NO.	BLUE YARDS	WHITE YARDS	PAR	S.I.
1	511	495	5	17	10	431	418	4	8
2	357	343	4	10	11	173	161	5	9
3	381	365	4	2	12	475	464	4	7
4	191	180	3	15	13	169	159	5	18
5	487	472	5	12	14	407	394	4	3
6	404	392	4	6	15	333	322	3	11
7	383	371	4	13	16	523	511	4	16
8	361	349	4	14	17	424	405	4	5
9	233	219	3	4	18	469	455	4	1
OUT	3,308	3,186	36		IN	3,404	3,287	37	
					TOTAL	6,712	6,473	72	
					STANDARD SCRATCH	72	72		

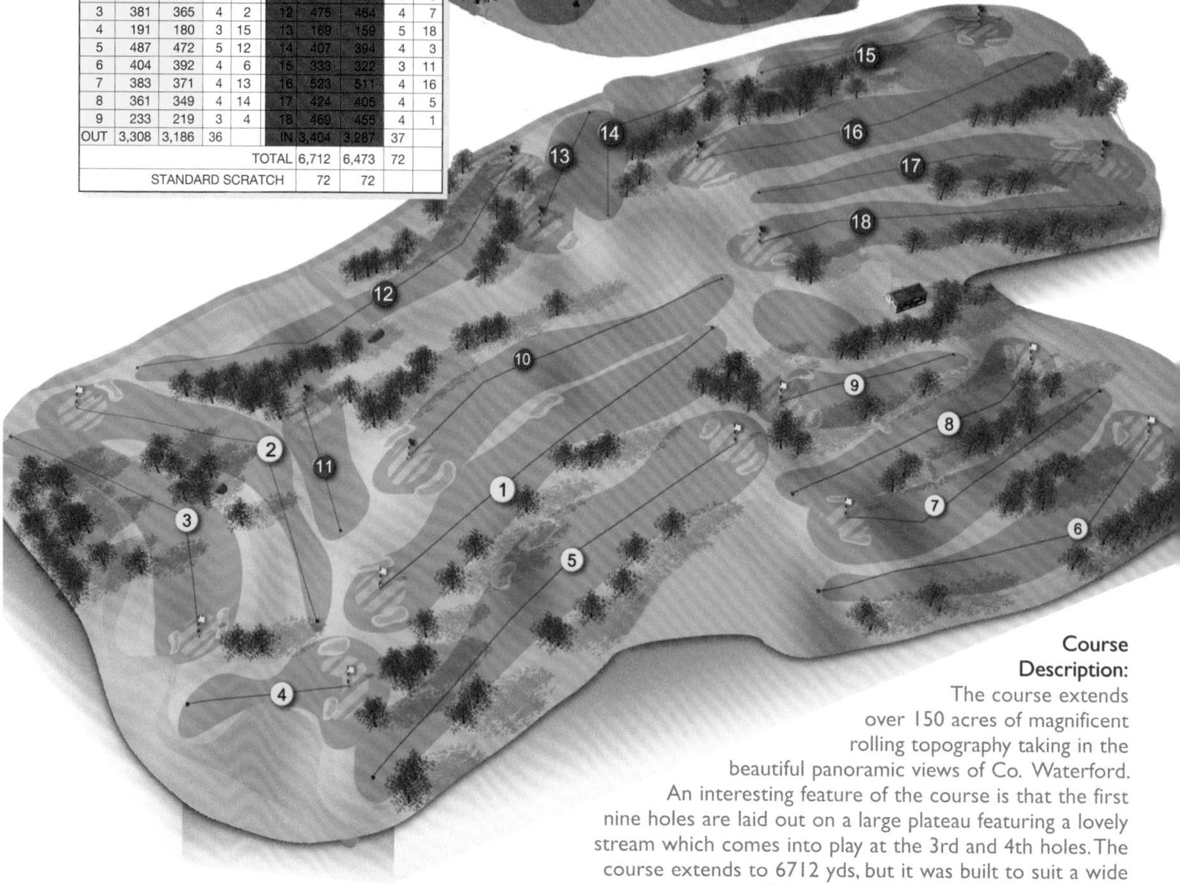

Course Description:

The course extends over 150 acres of magnificent rolling topography taking in the beautiful panoramic views of Co. Waterford. An interesting feature of the course is that the first nine holes are laid out on a large plateau featuring a lovely stream which comes into play at the 3rd and 4th holes. The course extends to 6712 yds, but it was built to suit a wide range of players with a minimum interference to the natural characteristics and vegetation. Playable all year round.

Course Information:

Par 72; SSS 72: Length 6,712 yards. **Visitors:** Welcome. **Opening Hours:** Sunrise – sunset. **Green Fees:** €32 Mon – Fri. €44 Sat / Sun / Bank Holidays. Discount for societies. **Juveniles:** Welcome. Clubs and caddy cars available for hire. **Clubhouse Hours:** 8.00am – sunset. **Clubhouse Dress:** Casual / neat. **Clubhouse Facilities:** Full bar & catering facilities all day, every day.

Dungarvan, Co. Waterford. Tel: (058) 43216 Fax: (058) 44343
Email: info@westwaterfordgolf.com **Web:** www.westwaterfordgolf.com

LOCATION: Only minutes from Waterford City Centre.

SECRETARY: Margaret Murray, Geraldine Fitzgerald.

ARCHITECT: Eddie Hackett.

Waterford Municipal Golf Course,
Williamstown, Co. Waterford.
Tel: (051) 853131
Fax: (051) 843690

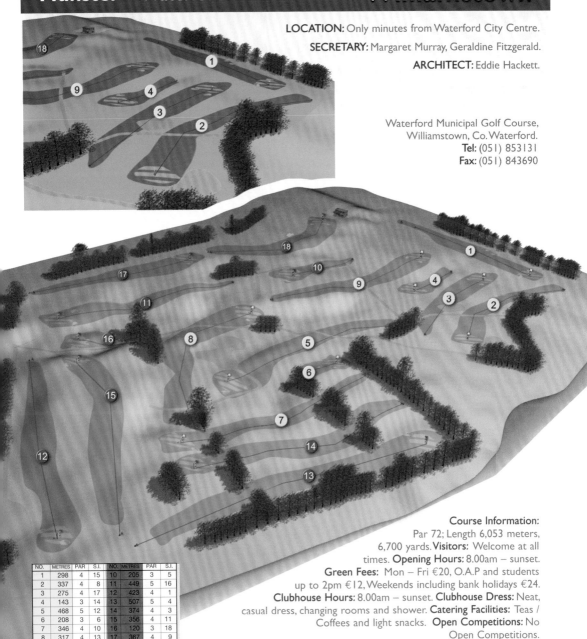

NO.	METRES	PAR	S.I.	NO.	METRES	PAR	S.I.
1	298	4	15	10	205	3	5
2	337	4	8	11	449	5	16
3	275	4	17	12	423	4	1
4	143	3	14	13	507	5	4
5	468	5	12	14	374	4	3
6	208	3	6	15	356	4	11
7	346	4	10	16	120	3	18
8	317	4	13	17	367	4	9
9	475	5	7	18	385	4	2
OUT	2,867	36		IN	3,186	36	
				TOTAL	6,053	72	
				STANDARD SCRATCH		72	

Course Information:

Par 72; Length 6,053 meters, 6,700 yards. **Visitors:** Welcome at all times. **Opening Hours:** 8.00am – sunset. **Green Fees:** Mon – Fri €20, O.A.P and students up to 2pm €12, Weekends including bank holidays €24. **Clubhouse Hours:** 8.00am – sunset. **Clubhouse Dress:** Neat, casual dress, changing rooms and shower. **Catering Facilities:** Teas / Coffees and light snacks. **Open Competitions:** No Open Competitions.

Course Description:

Combines excellent golfing facilities in beautiful countryside, yet it is only minutes from the centre of the city. Existing land features are used to the maximum to create a beautiful and challenging environment for golfers. Obstacles include sand traps and water traps.

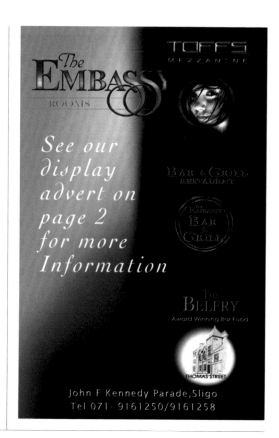

Connacht

MAYO SLIGO LEITRIM ROSCOMMON GALWAY

A Provincial Introduction by Jack Magowan

Bernhard Langer once dropped in unannounced for 18 holes, and stayed two weeks. It was the home club of a six-time Walker Cup giant, and where Nobel prize-winner Yeats, a founder member, had his first sexual experience on the nearby beach. The aristocrat of old golf courses, for sure, that may bite off a piece of every great links you've ever played.

County Sligo is where Cecil Ewing invented the game's half-to-three-quarter swing. He was a huge man, humorous and opinionated, with hands the size of dinner plates, and a profile to match Ben Bulben's.

Nobody loved an audience as much as Cecil, whose favourite party piece was to challenge somebody at the bar, or dinner table to a match over the last three holes of his beloved Rosses Point course, and he wouldn't have taken 'no' for an answer.

If the reply had been "Thank you, Cecil, you're much too

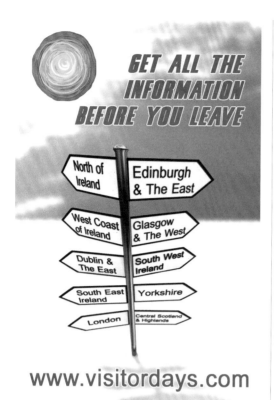
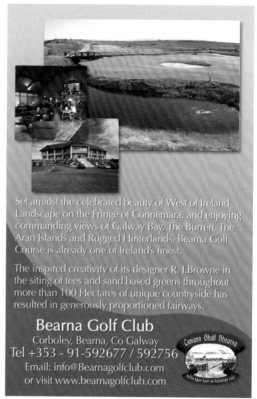

good," a compromise was soon forthcoming. "OK, I'll play left-handed, and you right-handed," he would tease, but nine times out of ten the result would be the same – he won!

When the wind blows at the Point, the only hiding place is in the clubhouse, Ewing used to say, but be sure to play the 14th hole first. It's a double dog-leg of 400 yards that seems to puzzle even the best of golfers.

"I wouldn't know how to play this hole, except badly," said one with a hint of frustration.

Ask Christy O'Connor Senior for his vote on Sligo's finest hole, and he'll not hesitate. It will be the 17th, which he knows would be talked about in the same reverential tones as the 'Road Hole' at St. Andrews were it not so isolated in a corner of Ireland.

What a pity they haven't found a substitute for the second hole there. If it was in Switzerland, they would probably install a ski-lift. It's the only weak hole on a links that compares with Ireland's classiest, and there are close to thirty of them.

If it wasn't the sea, air and scenery that captivated Ryder Cup ace Langer, it could only have been the loudest silence in the game.

Was it the late Henry Cotton who said after an all-too-brief visit to Connacht: "Here you leave chaos behind, forget all the world's agonies, and think only about things that don't matter. Try defining the Irish, and you come up with the same old hoary mix – charm, wit, originality, and a thirst for partying like people possessed."

Neither Connemara nor Carne were on the map when Cotton called, but Westport and Castlebar were, and the welcome there tripped him up.

▲
The 18th green at Connemara finishes a long 6,600 metre course with long meandering fairways. Superb location sandwiched between the Atlantic Ocean and the impressive Twelve Bens Mountains.

ASHFORD CASTLE

EXCELLENCE SINCE 1828

Set on the shores of Lough Corrib, this magnificent undulating parkland course with mature trees, hundreds of years old and generous greens, is a challenging par 70 which is very user friendly.

This nine hole course measuring 3,000 yards is exclusive and complimentary to the guests of the hotel and designed in a way that everyone – beginning and advanced golfers, female or male are all very welcome.

There is club hire and tuition facilities for ladies and gents in this tranquil location which is perfect for learning the wonderful game of golf at your leisure.

Ashford Castle has established itself as a premiere venue for golf and corporate entertainment.

If you would like some information on our new *"VIP Golf Programme"* please contact golf Pro Tom Devereux.

Cong, Co. Mayo, Ireland.
Tel: 353 94 9546003
Fax: 353 94 9546260
e-mail: ashford@ashford.ie
Website: www.ashford.ie
Booking in the
U.S.A.: 1 800 346 7007

Enniscrone, Co Sligo
Tel 096-36297
Fax 096-36657

Email : enniscronegolf@eircom.net
www.enniscronegolf.com

Enniscrone is one of Ireland's finest links golf courses set in scenic splendour in Killala Bay. Originally designed by the great Eddie Hackett – Enniscrone's reputation as a top class venue has been embellished with the addition of six new holes threading a path through the mountainous dunes. The new holes, expertly designed by famous course architect Donald Steele, add an exciting dimension to the 27 hole layout. Adoption of the relinquished six holes together with the development of three new holes on adjoining land has provided the Club with a further quality nine hole course.

Par/SSS 73/73 • Yards 6948 • Type Links
Holes 27

Green Fees
Mon – Fri €55
Sat / Sun / Bk.Hol €70

Photograph courtesy of Enniscrone Golf Club.

Have you ever been to Belmullet?. That's where Carne is; in the back of beyond. Or as *Golf World* so aptly put it in their choice of Britain's top ten new courses some years ago; "It's not the sort of place you pop into on the way to somewhere else."

That such a great links is still underplayed puzzles us all. Some holes on this haunted moonscape are truly majestic, and there's the odd one or two that may push the realms of respectability too far. But it's a wonderful challenge, and fun to play.

"We motored to Belmullet,
The local name for Carne;
The sand dunes there are massive,
Big as an elephant barn!"

The gifts of the Irish, they say, have enriched other nations more than their own, but in golf it's different.

The piano in the lounge of the Connemara club was a gift from a German diplomat who came for a fishing holiday, but never got the rod and line out of his car. Instead, he hired a set of golf clubs and had a ball in the company of some of most hospitable people on earth.

Like Waterville, Connemara has Eddie Hackett's name written all over it, and, like Waterville, the second nine there are better than the first. In fact, the last six holes at Clifden is as tough a finishing stretch as there is anywhere, a veritable no-man's land of sand and wilderness, so remote in places that even the sheep look lonely.

Another of Hackett's low-budget miracles must be Enniscrone, near Ballina. Once a good links, but now a great links after a Donald Steel make-over that highlights six new holes, all of them quite memorable. The first hole is what used to be the old 16th, and arguably the hardest opening hole in Ireland.

▲
The 9th green at Enniscrone Course in County Sligo looks out across a sandy beach to the Atlantic Ocean. The 6,700 yards links is situated in the scenic Killala Bay area.

Shannon Oaks Hotel & Country Club

The Shannon Oaks Hotel & Country Club in the bustling village of Portumna, Co. Galway is the perfect location for a Golfing break. Our Award Winning White Flag Leisure Centre, the traditional & comfortable oak décor, the choice of two restaurants on site and an abundance of activities locally makes. Portumna the perfect spot for everyone. Golf courses in the area include Portumna, Ballinasloe, Loughrea, Gort, East Clare, Nenagh and Birr.

Portuma Co. Galway, Ireland
Tel (090) 9741 777 Fax: (090) 9741 357
Int Tel: (+353 90) 9741 777 Int. Fax (+353 90 0 9741 357
email: sales@shannonoaks.ie   www.shannonoaks.ie
RAC ★★★★

Nick Faldo's own private island, and course-to-be, is within a short boat ride of Enniscrone, where a round of golf is a lot like lovemaking, writes Michael Konik. "When it's good it's great, and when it's not so great, it still ain't bad!"

Westport has hosted the Irish Amateur Championship, and makes a fuss of visiting golfers in a town where a comfortable bed is not expensive, and there are plenty of them.

After a benign start, the course picks up momentum, with the long 15th the pinnacle hole. The tee-shot here is not for the faint-hearted, not with a carry over an inlet of Clew Bay that must be all of 170 yards.

Again, the welcome at Westport has been known to trip up the unsuspecting guest, so go prepared.

No two golf courses play the same, and in the west of Ireland they are all different. From Achill to Athlone, to the sylvan setting of Athenry – they're all nature's own design, a playground for those who like to compliment their golf with scenery and atmosphere.

Ashford Castle on the shores of Lough Corrib is best known for a hotel that can provide almost hedonistic levels of self-indulgence, yet if the nine-hole course there was a restaurant, it too, would have a five-star rosette. As Henry Longhurst once wrote, Irish golf has that indefinable something which makes you relive again and again the days you played there.

Don't take Henry's word for it. Go and see for yourself.

▲

Galway Bay course plays over undulating ground overlooking Galway Bay with views across the famous bay to the equally famous Burren. Trees and gorse come into play throughout the course along with several tiered greens.

Cecil Ewing

by Jack Magowan

a man's man, feisty, opinionated, and funny among friends

▲
Cecil Ewing was a giant in Irish golf and not just in size, he was capped by his country over 90 times.

For two generations, the toughest competitor in amateur golf was a giant 17-stone Irishman who played in a trance, he concentrated so hard.

There's a portrait of him in the clubhouse at County Sligo, where the ball he played for a thrilling victory in the first Walker Cup match Britain ever won is proudly displayed.

A legend is never born out of one performance, however, and Cecil Ewing was capped six times against the Americans and by his country over 90 times; won both Irish Open and Close titles before twice captaining the international side to success in the European championship; reached the final of the 'West' a staggering 18 times (winning ten of them) before drawing the curtain on a long and chequered career as president of the world's oldest Golfing Union.

Was there anything in golf Cecil didn't do, and well? Ewing was a man's man, feisty, opinionated, and funny among friends. Nobody loved an audience as much as Cecil, whose favourite party piece was to challenge a visitor to a match over the last three holes of his beloved Rosses Point links. If the reply was "no thanks, you're too good," Cecil would suggest a compromise. "Ok, I'll play left-handed and you right-handed." he would tease. And nine times out of ten the result would be the same – he won!

For two generations, the toughest competitor in amateur golf was a giant 17-stone Irishman who played in a trance, he concentrated so hard.

Ewing, who was at his best in wind and rough weather, had a gift for making the game look easy. On the course, a surly, almost arrogant foe; off the course, a warm and entertaining companion whom the Edwards' brothers, Brendan especially, greatly admired.

"Once, he could have hit the ball past any of us, amateur or professional, but a serious illness forced him to trade power for precision," recalls Ulster's Branch secretary. "He was a demon putter who always had a Churchillian desire to engage the enemy. As Ireland's non-playing captain, he got the best out of everybody."

Ewing was an honourary member of nearly 20 clubs, Royal Portrush and Portmarnock among them and died in 1973 aged 63. His daughter, Ann (Bradshaw), was president of the Irish Ladies Golf Union. Cecil's dad, Tom, was also a fine golfer off a one-handicap, and his grandfather a founder member of the famous Sligo club.

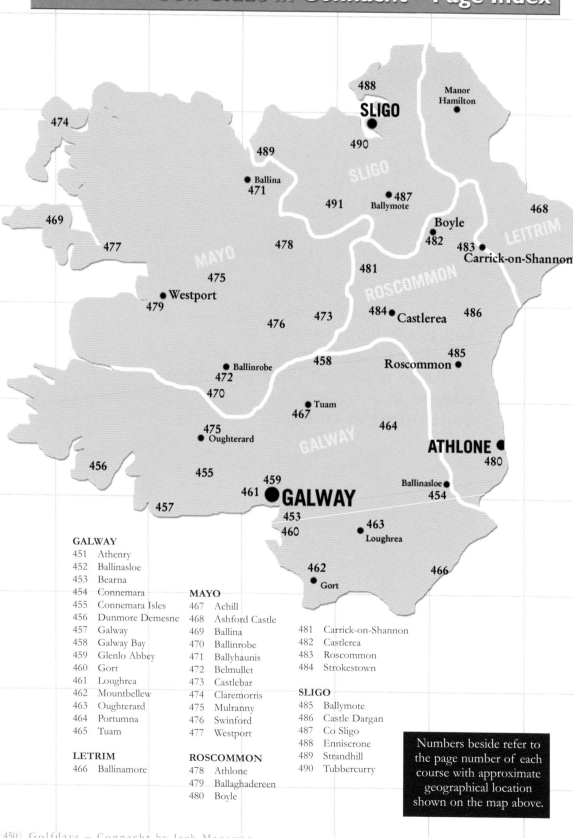

474

SLIGO
488
490

Manor Hamilton

489

Ballina
471

491
487
Ballymote

SLIGO

468

469

Boyle
482
483
Carrick-on-Shannon

LEITRIM

477

478

481

ROSCOMMON

MAYO

475

484 Castlerea
486

Westport
479

476
473

485
Roscommon

Ballinrobe
472
470

458

485

Tuam
467

464

ATHLONE
480

475
Oughterard

GALWAY

456

455

461 459 GALWAY

Ballinasloe
454

457

453
460

463
Loughrea

462
Gort

466

GALWAY
451 Athenry
452 Ballinasloe
453 Bearna
454 Connemara
455 Connemara Isles
456 Dunmore Demesne
457 Galway
458 Galway Bay
459 Glenlo Abbey
460 Gort
461 Loughrea
462 Mountbellew
463 Oughterard
464 Portumna
465 Tuam

LETRIM
466 Ballinamore

MAYO
467 Achill
468 Ashford Castle
469 Ballina
470 Ballinrobe
471 Ballyhaunis
472 Belmullet
473 Castlebar
474 Claremorris
475 Mulranny
476 Swinford
477 Westport

ROSCOMMON
478 Athlone
479 Ballaghadereen
480 Boyle

481 Carrick-on-Shannon
482 Castlerea
483 Roscommon
484 Strokestown

SLIGO
485 Ballymote
486 Castle Dargan
487 Co Sligo
488 Enniscrone
489 Strandhill
490 Tubbercurry

Numbers beside refer to
the page number of each
course with approximate
geographical location
shown on the map above.

Course Description:

This eighteen hole parkland course sports two ruined forts amidst dense wooded backdrop. It was extended from a nine hole to an eighteen hole course in 1991 taking on a completely different layout, but not detracting from its sylvan setting.

LOCATION: 5 miles from Athenry town. 8 miles from Galway.

SECRETARY/MANAGER: Padraig Flattery.

ARCHITECT: Eddie Hackett.

Athenry Golf Club, Palmerstown, Oranmore, Co. Galway.
Tel: (091) 794466.
Web: www.athenrygolfclub.net
Email: athenrygc@eircom.net

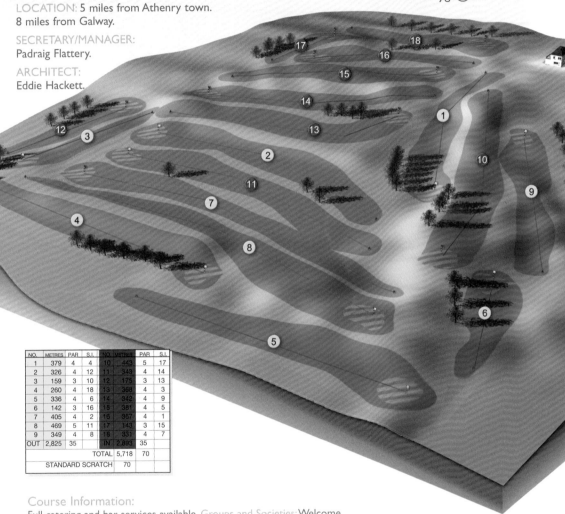

NO.	METRES	PAR	S.I.	NO.	METRES	PAR	S.I.
1	379	4	4	10	443	5	17
2	326	4	12	11	343	4	14
3	159	3	10	12	175	3	13
4	260	4	18	13	368	4	3
5	336	4	6	14	342	4	9
6	142	3	16	15	381	4	5
7	405	4	2	16	367	4	1
8	469	5	11	17	143	3	15
9	349	4	8	18	331	4	7
OUT	2,825	35		IN	2,893	35	
				TOTAL	5,718	70	
	STANDARD SCRATCH					70	

Course Information:

Full catering and bar services available. Groups and Societies: Welcome. Groups of 16+ €25 Green Fee. Green Fees: Weekday €35 per day, Weekend €40 per day. Facilities: Professional tuition, practice ground, club hire. Open Days: Every Tuesday and all Bank Holiday Weekends.

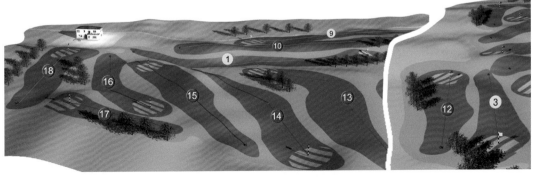

Ballinasloe

Rossgloss, Ballinasloe, Co. Galway. Tel: (090)96 42126. Fax: (090)96 42126.

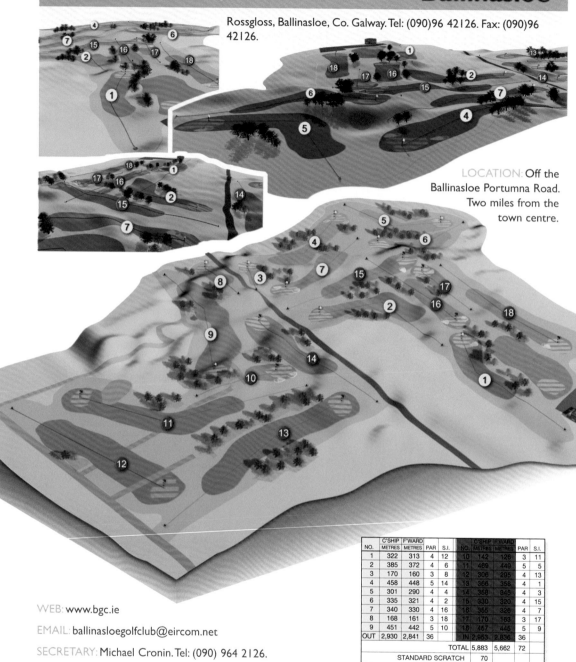

LOCATION: Off the Ballinasloe Portumna Road. Two miles from the town centre.

WEB: www.bgc.ie

EMAIL: ballinasloegolfclub@eircom.net

SECRETARY: Michael Cronin. Tel: (090) 964 2126.

ARCHITECT: Eddie Connaughton.

NO.	C'SHIP METRES	F'WARD METRES	PAR	S.I.	NO.	C'SHIP METRES	F'WARD METRES	PAR	S.I.
1	322	313	4	12	10	142	126	3	11
2	385	372	4	6	11	469	449	5	5
3	170	160	3	8	12	306	295	4	13
4	458	448	5	14	13	366	358	4	1
5	301	290	4	4	14	358	345	4	3
6	335	321	4	2	15	330	320	4	15
7	340	330	4	16	16	355	328	4	7
8	168	161	3	18	17	170	163	3	17
9	451	442	5	10	18	457	445	5	9
OUT	2,930	2,841	36		IN	2,953	2,836	36	
					TOTAL	5,883	5,662	72	
					STANDARD SCRATCH		70		

Course Information:

Par 72; SSS 70; Length 5,865 Metres. Visitors: Welcome. Opening Hours: 8am – Dusk. Avoid: Major Sunday competitions. Ladies: Welcome anyday. Green Fees: €25 Mon–Fri. €30 Sat & Sun; Societies €20 Mon–Fri, €25 Sat & Sun. Clubhouse Dress: Neat and tidy. Clubhouse Facilities: Full catering facilities Monday to Sunday. Open Competitions: Phone club for details.

Course Description:

Ballinasloe Golf Club was established on the Cloncarty Estate, now Garbally College, in 1894. Originally a nine hole parkland course, major redevelopment of the club was undertaken in 1970 and the course was extended to eighteen holes in 1984. The course is invariably playable all year round.

Bearna

Bearna Golf & CountryClub, Corboley, Barna, Co. Galway.

Tel: (091) 592 677 / 592 756 Fax: (091) 592 674
Bar&Restaurant: (091) 592 866 / 592 328
E-mail: info@bearnagolfclub.com
Web Page: www.bearnagolfclub.com

MANAGER: Michael Meade

NO.	MEDAL METRES	GEN. METRES	PAR	S.I.	NO.	MEDAL METRES	GEN. METRES	PAR	S.I.
1	388	375	4	3	10	362	315	4	8
2	450	403	5	17	11	350	328	4	4
3	356	345	4	11	12	450	440	5	12
4	350	340	4	5	13	120	115	3	18
5	196	175	3	9	14	330	305	4	14
6	405	345	4	1	15	345	338	4	2
7	510	470	5	13	16	350	336	4	6
8	180	168	3	15	17	460	425	5	16
9	402	365	4	7	18	170	158	3	10
OUT	3,237	2,986	36		IN	2,937	2,760	36	
				TOTAL	6,174	5,746	72		
				STANDARD SCRATCH	73	72			

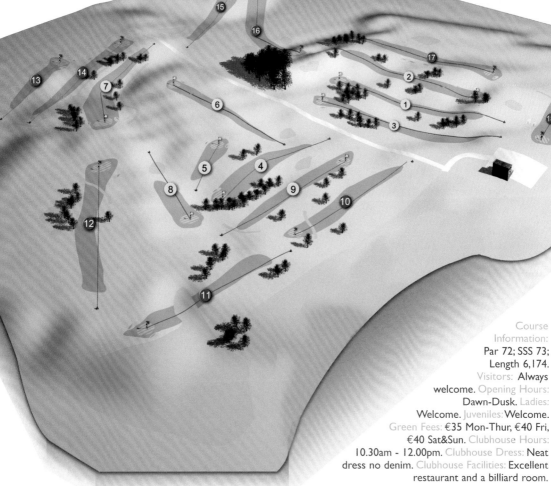

Course Information:
Par 72; SSS 73;
Length 6,174.
Visitors: Always
welcome. Opening Hours:
Dawn-Dusk. Ladies:
Welcome. Juveniles: Welcome.
Green Fees: €35 Mon-Thur, €40 Fri,
€40 Sat&Sun. Clubhouse Hours:
10.30am - 12.00pm. Clubhouse Dress: Neat
dress no denim. Clubhouse Facilities: Excellent
restaurant and a billiard room.

Course Description:

Set amidst the celebrated beauty of the West Ireland landscape, Bearna Golf Course is already being hailed as one of Irelands finest golf courses. The inspired creativity of its designer R.J. Browne in the siting of tees and sand-based greens has resulted in generously proportioned fairways, many elevated tee-boxes and some splendid carries. The thirteenth and eighteenth holes boast unique water features that will test even the most accomplished golfers.

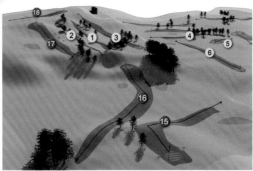

Ballyconneely, Co. Galway. Tel: (095) 23502 Fax: (095) 23662
Email: links@iol.ie www.connemaragolflinks.com

Course Description:
Situated on the edge of the Atlantic Ocean in a spectacular setting with the Twelve Bens Mountains in the background, this championship course is a challenge as good as any golfer would wish for. Established in 1973 the course has a popular reputation with big hitters, who relish the long meandering fairways.

LOCATION: Nine miles from Clifden.

PROFESSIONAL: Hugh O'Neil

ARHITECT:
Eddie Hackett.

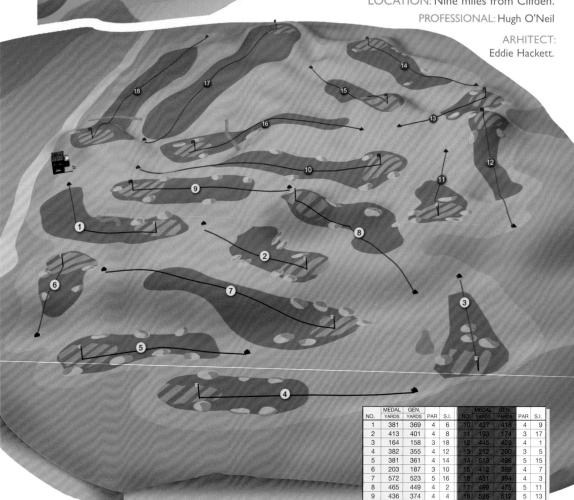

NO.	MEDAL YARDS	GEN. YARDS	PAR	S.I.	NO.	MEDAL YARDS	GEN. YARDS	PAR	S.I.
1	381	369	4	6	10	427	418	4	9
2	413	401	4	8	11	193	174	3	17
3	164	158	3	18	12	445	429	4	1
4	382	355	4	12	13	212	200	3	5
5	381	361	4	14	14	513	498	5	15
6	203	187	3	10	15	412	389	4	7
7	572	523	5	16	16	431	394	4	3
8	465	449	4	2	17	499	475	5	11
9	436	374	4	4	18	526	512	5	13
OUT	3,397	3,177	35		IN	3,658	3,489	37	
					TOTAL	7,055	6,666	72	
					STANDARD SCRATCH		71		

SECRETARY/MANAGER: Richard Flaherty.

Course Information: Par 72; SSS 73; Length 7,055 metres. Visitors: Welcome. Opening Hours: Dawn – Dusk. Avoid: Sunday mornings. Green Fees: Weekends: Nov-Mar €35/€40 Apr+Oct €50/€60. May €60. June-Sept €60/€70. Lessons available by prior arrangement. Club hire and caddy car available. Golf carts available. Juveniles: Welcome but may not play weekends, Bank Holidays or Open Weeks. Handicap Certificate required. Clubhouse Hours: 8am – 11pm. Clubhouse Dress: Casual (no spikes). Clubhouse Facilities: Bar Snacks & a la carte restaurant. Open Competitions: Open Weeks, June & Sept. Handicap required for competitions.

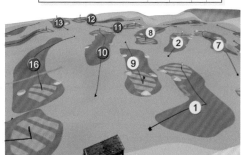

Connemara Isles

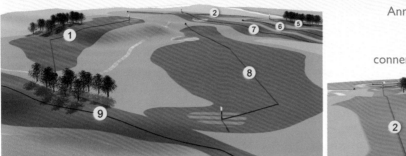

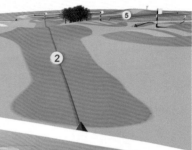

Annaghvane, Bealadanoan,
Co. Galway.
Tel: (091) 572498
connemaraisles@eircom.net

Course Information:

Par 70; SSS 67; Length 4770 metres.
Visitors: Welcome (appreciated if able to contact office). Opening Hours: 9.30am – 11.30pm. Avoid: Sunday afternoon. Ladies: Welcome any day. Green Fees: Weekdays €20; €25 Saturday & Sunday (€20 with member). Clubhouse Hours: 9.30am – 11.30pm. Clubhouse Dress: Informal / casual. Clubhouse Facilities: Full bar, catering available by arrangement. Open Competitions: 2nd and 3rd June. Open Week 5th - 12th August, contact club for details.

LOCATION: Annaghvaan Island, Leitir Moir via Causeway from Beal A'Daingin.

SECRETARY/MANAGER: Tony Lynch. Tel: (091) 572 498.

ARCHITECT: Craddock & Ruddy.

NO.	YARDS	PAR	S.I.	NO.	YARDS	PAR	S.I.
1	314	4	12	10	314	4	12
2	340	4	5	11	340	4	5
3	170	3	9	12	170	3	9
4	280	4	18	13	280	4	18
5	380	5	6	14	380	5	6
6	165	3	16	15	165	3	16
7	282	4	14	16	282	4	14
8	425	5	13	17	425	5	13
9	165	3	3	18	165	3	3
OUT	2,521	35		IN	2,521	35	
				TOTAL	5,042	70	
				STANDARD SCRATCH		67	

Course Description:

Unique Island course located in the heart of the Connemara Gaeltacht. The course is distractingly beautiful – where ocean inlets and rocky outcrops provide natural hazards, demanding steady nerves. After the game relax in the friendly atmosphere of Ireland's only thatched clubhouse, which is warmed by an open fire.

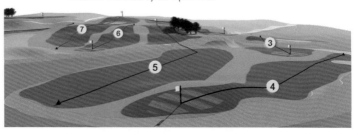

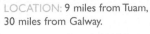

LOCATION: 9 miles from Tuam, 30 miles from Galway.

SECRETARY: Fergal O' Malley.
Tel: (087) 8139433

Course Bookings: Tel: (087) 8134433,

COURSE DESIGNER: Eddie Hackett.

COURSE BUILDER: Peter Casbalt.

Dunmore Demesne Golf Club,
Dunmore, Co.Galway.
Tel: (093) 38709.
Email: ddgc@ddgc.ie

NO.	METRES	PAR	S.I.	NO.	METRES	PAR	S.I.
1	306	4	3	10	306	4	4
2	294	4	13	11	294	4	14
3	332	4	1	12	332	4	2
4	136	3	11	13	136	3	12
5	475	5	7	14	475	5	8
6	125	3	17	15	125	3	18
7	308	4	15	16	306	4	16
8	341	4	5	17	341	4	6
9	322	4	9	18	322	4	10
OUT	2,639	35		IN	2,639	35	
				TOTAL	5,278	70	
				STANDARD SCRATCH	68		

Course Description:
A short but difficult course located in mature parkland. Rewards accuracy and skill around the greens. 5th tee features a spectacular view of the entire course. Unique in that the 1st tee is located within 200 metres of the town centre.

Course Information:
Par 70; SSS 68; Length 5,278 metres. Visitors: Welcome. Opening Hours: 8.30am – darkness. Green Fees: €15. Clubhouse Hours: 8.30am onward. Clubhouse Dress: Informal. Clubhouse Facilities: Dressing room & showers only. Open Competitions: First week in August 2007. Green Fees & Societies welcome.

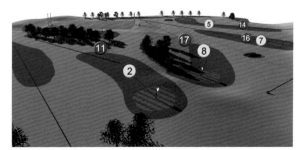

Galway Golf Club, Blackrock, Galway.
Tel: (091) 522 033

LOCATION: 3 miles west of Galway city.

SECRETARY: Padraic Fahy.
Tel: (091) 522 033 (office).

PROFESSIONAL: Don Wallace
Tel: (091) 523 038

NO.	MEDAL YARDS	GEN. YARDS	PAR	S.I.	NO.	MEDAL YARDS	GEN. YARDS	PAR	S.I.
1	275	287	4	17	10	378	398	4	4
2	129	142	3	11	11	171	188	3	12
3	373	394	4	5	12	453	474	5	14
4	348	354	4	9	13	115	125	3	18
5	399	403	4	1	14	352	382	4	8
6	386	396	4	3	15	350	362	4	6
7	460	475	5	13	16	379	389	4	2
8	318	343	4	15	17	308	314	4	16
9	173	185	3	7	18	349	363	4	10
OUT	2,861	2,979	35		IN	2,855	2,995	35	
					TOTAL	5,716	5,974	70	
					STANDARD SCRATCH	71	70		

Course Information:
Par 70; SSS 71; Length
5,974 Metres. Visitors: Welcome.
Opening Hours: 8am – Dusk. Avoid: Tuesday, Saturday
and Sunday. Ladies: Welcome. Green Fees: €50
weekdays, €60 weekends. Clubhouse Hours: 9am –
11pm. Clubhouse Dress: Clean and presentable clothes.
Clubhouse Facilities: At all times.

Course Description:
A tight tree lined course. Some tiered greens make it
very important to accurately place your drives and a
good short game is necessary to score well. The course
has excellent views of Galway Bay, The Burren and the
Arran Islands.

457

LOCATION: Six miles south
of Galway City.

PROFESSIONAL:
Eugene O'Connor.
Tel: (091) 790 711 (Ext. 1)

ARCHITECT:
Christy O'Connor Jnr.

Galway Bay Golf & Country Club, Renville,
Oranmore, Co. Galway.
Tel: (091) 790 711/2
Fax: (091) 792 510
E-mail: info@galwaybaygolfresort.com
Web: www.galwaybaygolfresort.com

NO.	MEDAL METRES	GEN. METRES	PAR	S.I.	NO.	MEDAL METRES	GEN. METRES	PAR	S.I.
1	506	486	5	14	10	411	367	4	5
2	409	362	4	2	11	377	348	4	7
3	387	370	4	10	12	400	372	4	1
4	155	136	3	16	13	162	148	3	15
5	336	323	4	8	14	501	464	5	13
6	481	434	5	12	15	172	160	3	17
7	138	126	3	18	16	496	481	5	11
8	418	386	4	6	17	349	323	4	9
9	400	374	4	4	18	439	423	4	3
OUT	3,230	2,997	36		IN	3,307	3,094	36	
					TOTAL	6,537	6,091	72	
					STANDARD SCRATCH		73	71	

Course Description:
Christy O'Connor Jnr, Ryder & World
cup player, designed this 18 hole course to
highlight and preserve the ancient historic
features of the Renville Peninsula. The
spectacular setting on Galway Bay is
distractingly beautiful and the cleverly
designed mix of holes presents a real golfing
challenge which demands total
concentration. See website for on-line
booking. Hosted European Tour West
of Ireland Open 1999.

Course Information:
Par 72; Length 6,537 metres. Visitors: Welcome.
Opening Hours: 8am – 7pm. Ladies: Welcome.
Green Fees: €55 weekdays, €70 weekends &
bank hols; Nov–Mar: €35 weekdays, €40
weekends & bank hols. Group discounts
available, tel for details.
Clubhouse Hours: 8am –
11pm. Clubhouse Dress:
Informal. Clubhouse Facilities:
Flamme Bay Restaurant, Spike /
Seafood Bar & Cocktail Bar –
all day.

Galway Bay Golf Club
closed for developmet.
Opening Late 2008.

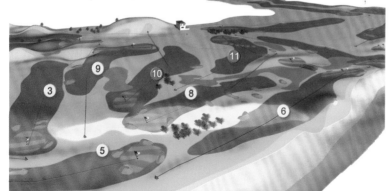

Glenlo Abbey Golf Course, Bushypark, Galway.
Tel: (091) 519698
Email: glenlo@iol.ie
Web: www.glenlo.com

LOCATION: 2.5 miles from
Galway city.

DIRECTOR OF GOLF/SECRETARY:
Mr. Bill Daley.

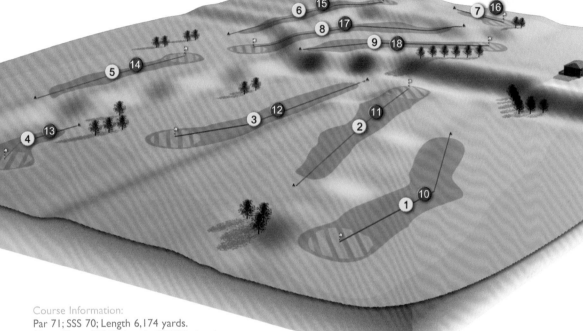

Course Information:
Par 71; SSS 70; Length 6,174 yards.
Green Fees: €20 Midweek, €25 Weekend.
Juveniles: Welcome. Clubhouse Hours: Dawn to Dusk.
(Timesheet daily). Clubhouse Dress: Neat dress essential, no
denims. Clubhouse Facilities: 5 star Hotel facilities on site.
Pro on site, floodlit Driving Range. Open Competitions:
Thursday Open Day €15. Open Week: Jul 31st - Aug 7th.

Course Description:
Lakeside - 9 hole - double green layout. Very
picturesque and a good challenge, in a particularly
attractive part of the country.

NO.	MEDAL YARDS	GEN. YARDS	PAR	S.I.	NO.	MEDAL YARDS	GEN. YARDS	PAR	S.I.
1	365	362	4	15	10	413	386	4	8
2	430	396	4	3	11	430	397	4	2
3	399	388	4	9	12	361	350	4	16
4	163	137	3	17	13	179	151	3	6
5	370	342	4	7	14	366	337	4	14
6	416	404	4	1	15	470	458	5	10
7	204	194	3	13	16	177	167	3	18
8	492	477	5	11	17	492	478	5	12
9	383	365	4	5	18	404	386	4	4
OUT	3,246	3,065	35		IN	3,292	3,109	36	
					TOTAL	6,538	6,174	71	
					STANDARD SCRATCH		70	71	

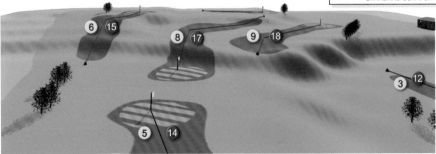

LOCATION: Kilmacduagh Road, Gort.

HON. SECRETARY: John Skehill. Tel: (091) 632244.

ARCHITECT: Christy O'Connor Jnr.

Gort Golf Club, Castlequarter,
Gort, Co. Galway.
Tel: (091) 632244.
Fax: (091) 632387.

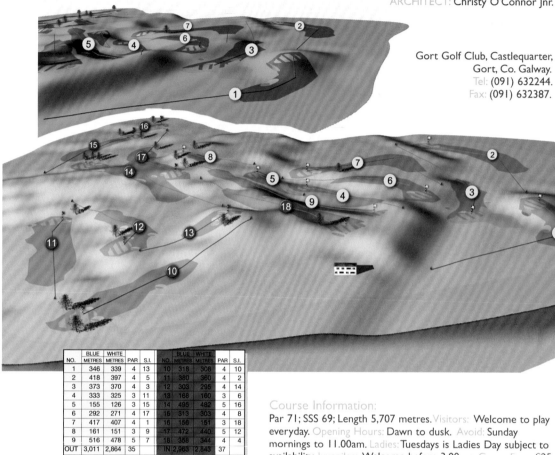

NO.	BLUE METRES	WHITE METRES	PAR	S.I.	NO.	BLUE METRES	WHITE METRES	PAR	S.I.
1	346	339	4	13	10	318	308	4	10
2	418	397	4	5	11	380	360	4	2
3	373	370	4	3	12	303	295	4	14
4	333	325	3	11	13	168	160	3	6
5	155	126	3	15	14	495	482	5	16
6	292	271	4	17	15	313	303	4	8
7	417	407	4	1	16	156	151	3	18
8	161	151	3	9	17	472	440	5	12
9	516	478	5	7	18	358	344	4	4
OUT	3,011	2,864	35		IN	2,963	2,843	37	
					TOTAL	5,707	5,477	71	
		STANDARD SCRATCH						70	69

Course Information:

Par 71; SSS 69; Length 5,707 metres. Visitors: Welcome to play everyday. Opening Hours: Dawn to dusk. Avoid: Sunday mornings to 11.00am. Ladies: Tuesdays is Ladies Day subject to availability. Juveniles: Welcome before 3.00pm. Green Fees: €25 Weekdays, €30 Weekends. Clubhouse Hours: 10.00am – 11.30pm. Clubhouse Dress: Casual. Clubhouse Facilities: Light snacks. Open Competitions: Open Week June & August

Course Description:

A parkland course opened in 1996. Set in an area of rare beauty, surrounded by world famous Burren, Coole Woods & Aughty mountains.
A course for every club in your bag.

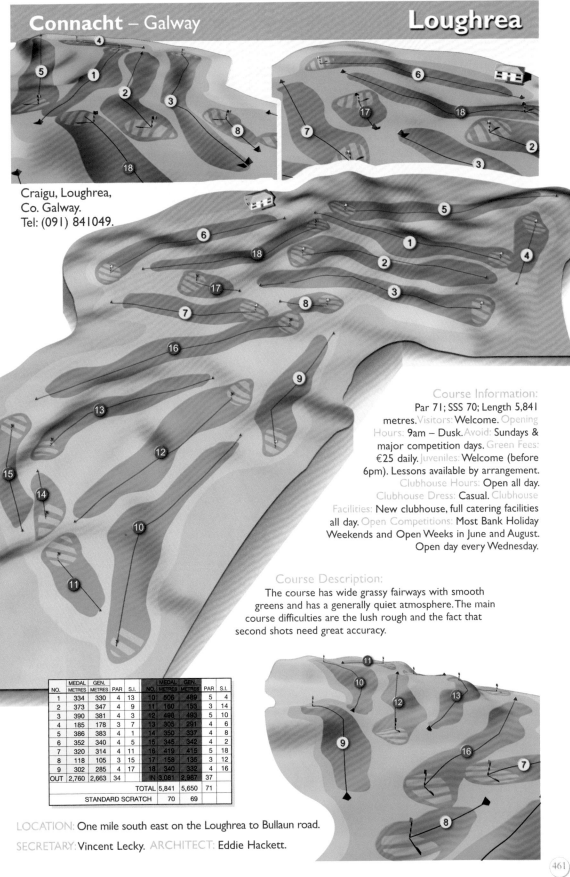

Craigu, Loughrea,
Co. Galway.
Tel: (091) 841049.

Course Information:
Par 71; SSS 70; Length 5,841
metres. Visitors: Welcome. Opening
Hours: 9am – Dusk. Avoid: Sundays &
major competition days. Green Fees:
€25 daily. Juveniles: Welcome (before
6pm). Lessons available by arrangement.
Clubhouse Hours: Open all day.
Clubhouse Dress: Casual. Clubhouse
Facilities: New clubhouse, full catering facilities
all day. Open Competitions: Most Bank Holiday
Weekends and Open Weeks in June and August.
Open day every Wednesday.

Course Description:
The course has wide grassy fairways with smooth
greens and has a generally quiet atmosphere. The main
course difficulties are the lush rough and the fact that
second shots need great accuracy.

NO.	MEDAL METRES	GEN. METRES	PAR	S.I.	NO.	MEDAL METRES	GEN. METRES	PAR	S.I.
1	334	330	4	13	10	506	489	5	4
2	373	347	4	9	11	160	153	3	14
3	390	381	4	3	12	498	493	5	10
4	185	178	3	7	13	305	291	4	6
5	386	383	4	1	14	350	337	4	8
6	352	340	4	5	15	345	342	4	2
7	320	314	4	11	16	419	415	5	18
8	118	105	3	15	17	158	135	3	12
9	302	285	4	17	18	340	332	4	16
OUT	2,760	2,663	34		IN	3,081	2,987	37	
				TOTAL	5,841	5,650	71		
		STANDARD SCRATCH				70	69		

LOCATION: One mile south east on the Loughrea to Bullaun road.

SECRETARY: Vincent Lecky. ARCHITECT: Eddie Hackett.

Mountbellew Golf Club, Mountbellew,
Ballinasloe, Co. Galway.
Tel: (0905) 79259 / 79274
Fax: (090) 967 9405

LOCATION: Ballinasloe
17 miles,
Galway 30 miles and
Roscommon 20 miles.

HON. SECRETARY:
Joe Keane.
Tel: (0905) 79274

CHAIRPERSON:
Michael Dollan.

Course
Information:
Par 69; SSS 66; Length
5,143 metres. Visitors:
Welcome to play, no special
arrangements required. Opening Hours:
Daylight hours. Avoid: Saturday afternoons
(Ladies competitions). Green Fees: €15 every day;
€60 per weekly ticket. Clubhouse Hours: 3.00pm – 9.00pm.
Clubhouse Dress: Informal. Clubhouse Facilities: Light snacks
in bar. Outings catered for by arrangement. Open
Competitions: Open Week – June.

NO.	METRES	PAR	S.I.	NO.	METRES	PAR	S.I.
1	155	3	17	10	181	3	8
2	312	4	9	11	296	4	14
3	146	3	13	12	123	3	18
4	295	4	11	13	326	4	6
5	302	4	5	14	325	4	2
6	391	4	1	15	434	5	16
7	314	4	7	16	306	4	12
8	318	4	3	17	321	4	4
9	290	4	15	18	308	4	10
OUT	2,523	34		IN	2,620	35	
				TOTAL	5,143	69	
				STANDARD SCRATCH	66		

Course Description:
Parkland course in sylvan setting.
Ideal for a casual, leisurely round
or a day of golf. Generous
fairways on all holes with
the greens always in
good condition.

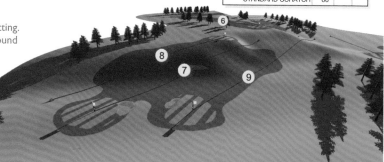

Oughterard

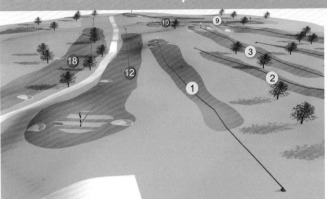

HON. SECRETARY: Michael Heaney.
Tel: (091) 552131

PROFESSIONAL: Michael Ryan.
Tel: (091) 552626.

ARCHITECT: Patrick Merrigan.

Gortreevagh, Oughterard, Co. Galway.
Tel: (091) 552131 Fax: (091) 552733
Email: oughterardgc@eircom.net
Web: www.oughterardgolf.com

LOCATION: Fifteen miles west of Galway
City, en route to Connemara.

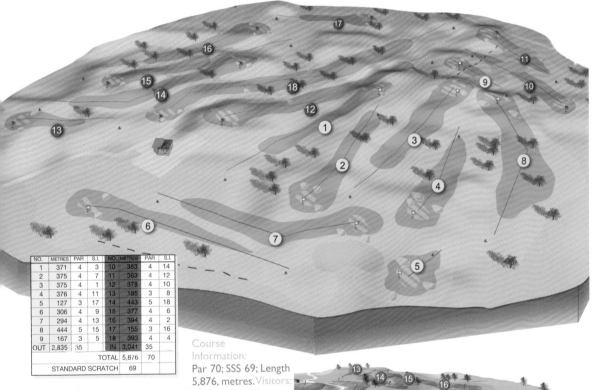

NO.	METRES	PAR	S.I.	NO.	METRES	PAR	S.I.
1	371	4	3	10	353	4	14
2	375	4	7	11	363	4	12
3	375	4	1	12	378	4	10
4	376	4	11	13	185	3	8
5	127	3	17	14	443	5	18
6	306	4	9	15	377	4	6
7	294	4	13	16	394	4	2
8	444	5	15	17	155	3	16
9	167	3	5	18	393	4	4
OUT	2,835	35		IN	3,041	35	
				TOTAL	5,876	70	
				STANDARD SCRATCH		69	

Course Information:
Par 70; SSS 69; Length 5,876, metres. Visitors:
Welcome. Restricted at weekends, due to competitions.
Opening Hours: Sunrise – sunset. Avoid: Telephone in
advance. Ladies: Wednesday. Green Fees: €35 standard
(€20 with member), societies €25 per person. €60
husband & wife, €20 student. Junior €15. Clubhouse
Hours: 8.00am –12.00pm (except Winter). Full clubhouse
facilities. Clubhouse Dress: Neat, casual, no jeans.
Clubhouse Facilities: Breakfast from 8.00am – 10.30am; full
dinner menu everyday all day until 10.00pm. Open
Competitions: Open Week 5th - 8th June. Open Day, every
Tuesday between Apr and Sept, €20.
Course Description:
A beautiful and mature championship parkland
course on the shores of Lough Corrib,
Oughterard is renowned for its friendly and
welcoming atmosphere. Always in pristine
condition with a variety of trees and shrubs to
punish wayward shots to otherwise generous
and lush fairways.

LOCATION: Less than two miles west of Portumna on the Woodford Road.

CAPTAIN: Tony Coen.

Course Description:

Located in Portumna Forest Park, this is a very attractive woodland course with plenty of mature trees. Deer can sometimes be found on the course. The finishing Par 3 hole is the most difficult of the round, playing to an elevated green.

Portumna, Co. Galway. Tel: (090) 974 1059 Fax: (090) 974 1798
Email: portumna@eircom.net
Web: www.portumnagolfclub.ie

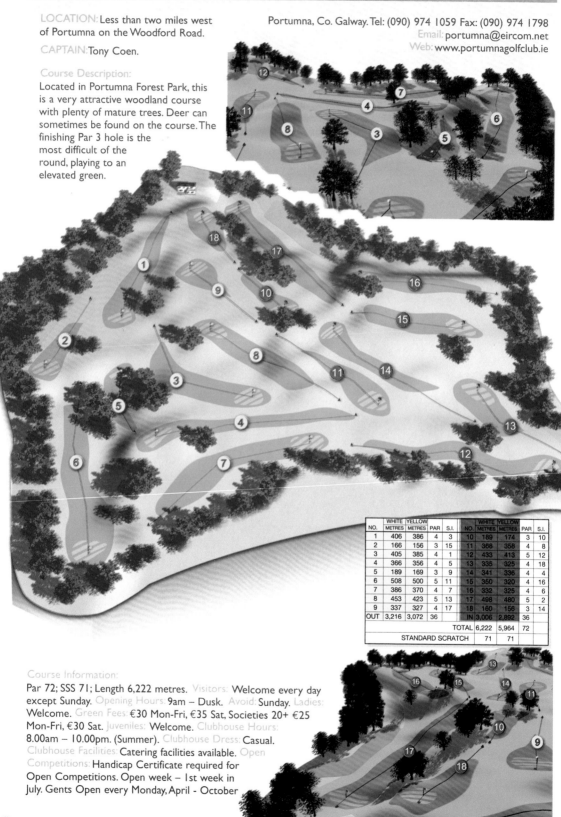

NO.	WHITE METRES	YELLOW METRES	PAR	S.I.	NO.	WHITE METRES	YELLOW METRES	PAR	S.I.
1	406	386	4	3	10	189	174	3	10
2	166	156	3	15	11	368	358	4	8
3	405	385	4	1	12	433	413	5	12
4	366	356	4	5	13	335	325	4	18
5	189	169	3	9	14	341	336	4	4
6	508	500	5	11	15	350	320	4	16
7	386	370	4	7	16	332	325	4	6
8	453	423	5	13	17	498	480	5	2
9	337	327	4	17	18	160	156	3	14
OUT	3,216	3,072	36		IN	3,006	2,892	36	
					TOTAL	6,222	5,964	72	
					STANDARD SCRATCH	71	71		

Course Information:

Par 72; SSS 71; Length 6,222 metres. Visitors: Welcome every day except Sunday. Opening Hours: 9am – Dusk. Avoid: Sunday. Ladies: Welcome. Green Fees: €30 Mon-Fri, €35 Sat, Societies 20+ €25 Mon-Fri, €30 Sat. Juveniles: Welcome. Clubhouse Hours: 8.00am – 10.00pm. (Summer). Clubhouse Dress: Casual. Clubhouse Facilities: Catering facilities available. Open Competitions: Handicap Certificate required for Open Competitions. Open week – 1st week in July. Gents Open every Monday, April - October

Tuam Golf Club, Barnacurragh, Tuam, Co. Galway.
Tel: (093) 28993Fax: (093) 26003
Web: www.tuamgolfclub.com
Email: tuamgolfclub.com

LOCATION: Twenty miles north of Galway.

ADMINISTRATOR: Mary Burns.

PROFESSIONAL: Larry Smyth.
Tel: (093) 24091

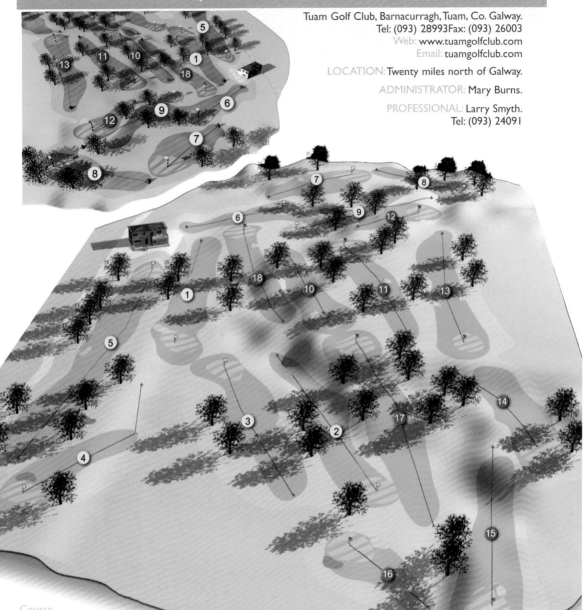

Course
Information:
Par 72; SSS 71; Length
6,045 Metres. Visitors: Welcome.
Opening Hours: 7.30am – Midnight. Avoid:
Saturday mornings and Sundays. Ladies: Welcome
Tuesdays. Green Fees: €30 all week, (weekends in Summer
have limited availability. Lessons available, groups on request Club Hire,
Caddy service, buggies. Clubhouse Hours: 11.00am-11.30pm.
Clubhouse Dress: Casual, no denim. Clubhouse Facilities: Full bar,
restaurant and catering facilities everyday in peak season. Off season,
call club for details. Open Competitions: Open Weekends: March &
June Open week: July

Course Description:
Fine parkland course. The fairways are guarded by plantations
and trees, with greens well bunkered. Tuam recently completed
their new clubhouse development.

NO.	CHAMP METRES	MEDAL METRES	PAR	S.I.	NO.	CHAMP METRES	MEDAL METRES	PAR	S.I.
1	368	361	4	5	10	331	311	4	18
2	469	464	5	15	11	340	335	4	14
3	384	374	4	3	12	183	172	3	6
4	312	307	4	9	13	478	468	5	16
5	484	454	5	13	14	309	303	4	8
6	172	166	3	11	15	346	326	4	4
7	381	358	4	1	16	152	142	3	12
8	133	131	3	17	17	486	456	5	10
9	349	339	4	7	18	368	358	4	2
OUT	3,052	2,954	36		IN	2,993	2,871	36	
					TOTAL	6,045	5,825	72	
					STANDARD SCRATCH	71	70		

Ballinamore Golf Club,
Ballinamore, Co. Leitrim
Tel: (074) 964 4346.

Course Description:

Redesigned by Arthur Spring with new sand based
greens well bunkered with water coming into play
on 1st and 2nd fairways. The Canal comes into play
on the 1st, 2nd, 6th and 7th holes. A warm and
friendly atmosphere awaits you at Ballinamore.

LOCATION: Two miles
north west of Ballinamore.

Course Information:

Par 70; SSS 68; Length 5,514
metres. Visitors: Welcome except
on Captain's or President's Day.
Opening Hours: 8am-sunset. Ladies:
Welcome. Green Fees: €20. Clubhouse
Hours: 9.00am – 11.00pm. Clubhouse
Dress: Casual. Clubhouse Facilities:
Catering facilities – soup and
sandwiches. Open Competitions: Open
Week and certain weekends.

SECRETARY/MANAGER:

Eileen Blessing.

NO.	METRES	PAR	S.I.	NO.	METRES	PAR	S.I.
1	316	4	7	10	316	4	8
2	177	3	5	11	177	3	6
3	362	4	3	12	362	4	4
4	330	4	9	13	330	4	10
5	318	4	13	14	318	4	14
6	433	5	15	15	433	5	16
7	121	3	17	16	121	3	18
8	367	4	1	17	367	4	2
9	333	4	11	18	333	4	12
OUT	2,757	35		IN	2,757	35	
				TOTAL	5,192		
				STANDARD SCRATCH	68		

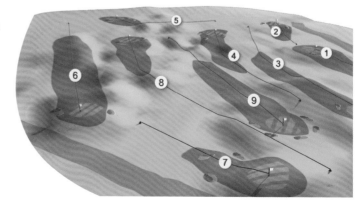

LOCATION: Keel, Achill.
SECRETARY/MANAGER: Michael McGinty.

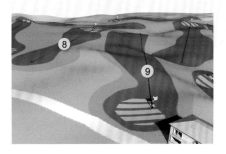

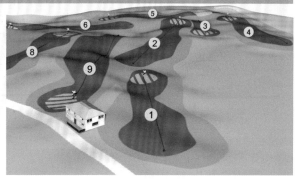

Achill Golf Club, Keel, Co. Mayo.
Tel: (098) 43456.
Fax: (098) 43265.
web: achillgolfclub.com
Email: achillgolfclub@eircom.net

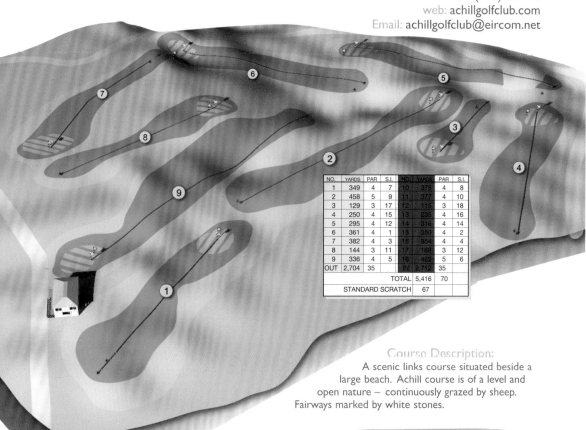

NO.	YARDS	PAR	S.I.	NO.	YARDS	PAR	S.I.
1	349	4	7	10	375	4	8
2	458	5	9	11	377	4	10
3	129	3	17	12	115	3	18
4	250	4	15	13	235	4	16
5	295	4	12	14	316	4	14
6	361	4	1	15	350	4	2
7	382	4	3	16	354	4	4
8	144	3	11	17	168	3	12
9	336	4	5	18	422	5	6
OUT	2,704	35		IN	2,712	35	
				TOTAL	5,416	70	
				STANDARD SCRATCH		67	

Course Description:

A scenic links course situated beside a
large beach. Achill course is of a level and
open nature – continuously grazed by sheep.
Fairways marked by white stones.

Course Information:

Par 70; SSS 67; Length 5,416
metres. Visitors: Welcome. Opening
Hours: Dawn – Dusk. Ladies: Welcome.
Green Fees: Weekday €15, Weekend €20.
Juveniles: Must be accompanied by an adult (under
14's). Clubhouse Hours: Same as course. Clubhouse
Dress: Casual. Open Competitions: Various competitions throughout
year, handicap certificate required, please contact club for details.

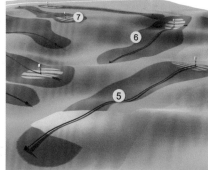

Cong, Co. Mayo.
Tel: (094) 954 6003
Fax: (094) 954 6260
E-mail: ashford@ashford.ie
Website: www.ashford.ie

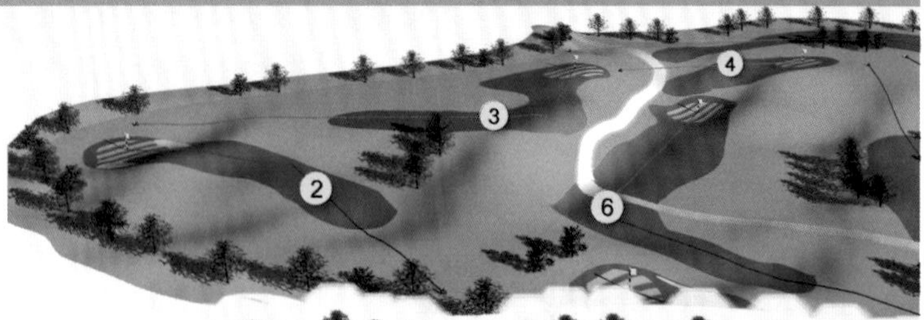

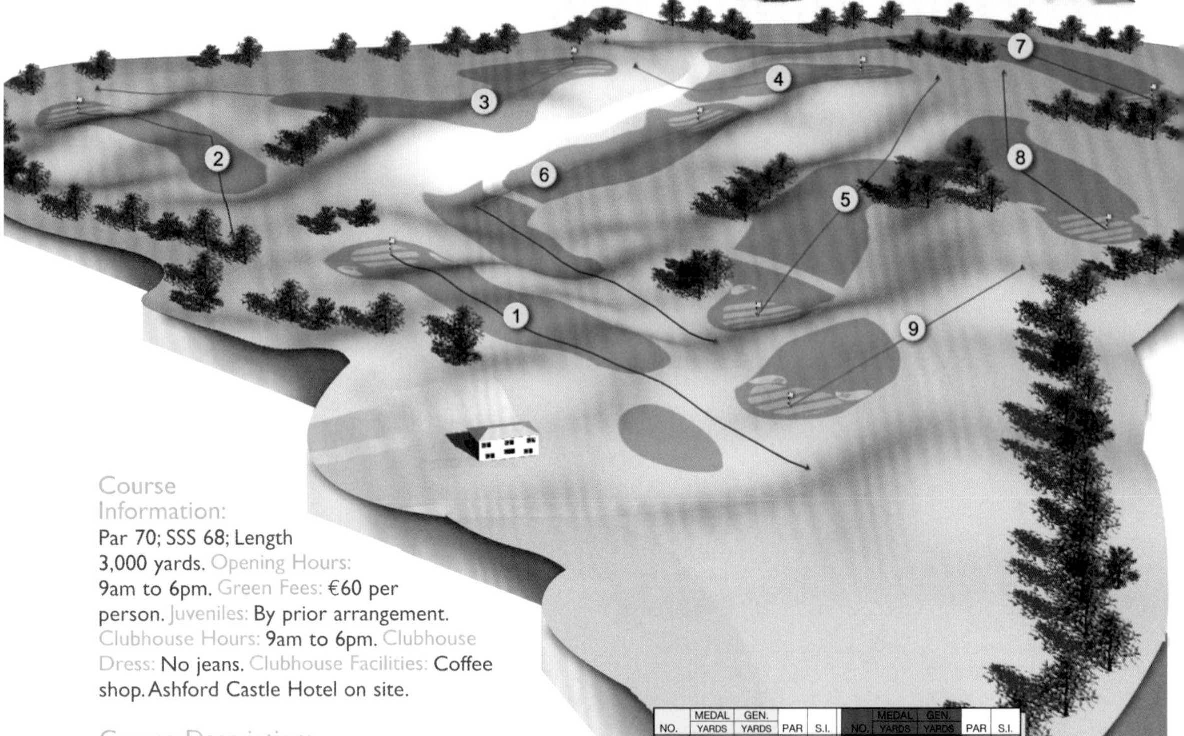

Course Information:

Par 70; SSS 68; Length 3,000 yards. Opening Hours: 9am to 6pm. Green Fees: €60 per person. Juveniles: By prior arrangement. Clubhouse Hours: 9am to 6pm. Clubhouse Dress: No jeans. Clubhouse Facilities: Coffee shop. Ashford Castle Hotel on site.

Course Description:

Beautiful matured 9 hole golf course set on the shores of Lough Corrib, with panoramic views of Ashford Castle, where some of the world's top professionals have stayed and played.

PROFESSIONAL: Tom Devereux

ARCHITECT: Eddie Hackett.

NO.	MEDAL YARDS	GEN. YARDS	PAR	S.I.	NO.	MEDAL YARDS	GEN. YARDS	PAR	S.I.
1	273	320	4	14	10	273	320	4	13
2	246	340	4	6	11	246	340	4	5
3	321	391	4	1	12	321	391	4	2
4	130	136	3	17	13	130	136	3	18
5	284	384	4	7	14	284	384	4	8
6	343	494	5	10	15	343	494	5	9
7	231	381	4	3	16	231	381	4	4
8	200	289	4	12	17	200	289	4	11
9	133	161	3	16	18	133	161	3	15
OUT	2,253	2,996	35		IN	2,253	2,996	35	
					TOTAL	4,506	5,992	70	
	STANDARD SCRATCH					68	68		

Mossgrove, Shanaghy, Ballina, Co. Mayo.
Tel: (096) 21050. Fax: (096) 21718.
LOCATION: Bonniconlon Rd, Ballina.
1.5 KM from town centre.
SECRETARY: Dick Melrose.

Course Description:
Ballina Golf Club offers a scenic parkland course in
the West of Ireland. Situated in the heart of the
unspoiled May Valley region, of great natural beauty
and only minutes from Ballina Town. Lush fairways
with manicured green, guarded by water hazards and
bunkers create an interesting and fair golf
course.

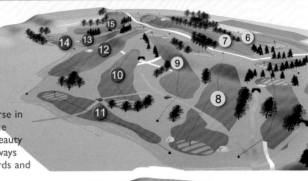

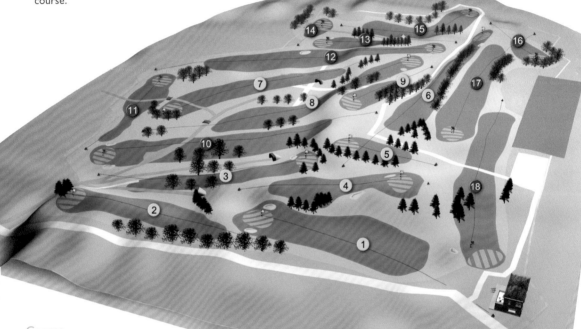

Course
Information:
Par 71; SSS 69; Length 6,103
yards. Visitors: Welcome. Opening
Hours: 8am –10pm (summer); 9am – 6pm
(winter). Avoid: Sunday mornings. Green Fees: Mon to
Fri €30. Sat & Sun / Bank Holidays €40. Husband & Wife €50,
With a member €15. Juveniles: Welcome. Clubhouse Hours: 9am –11pm.
Clubhouse Dress: Neat / Casual. Clubhouse Facilities: Restaurant and bar,
kitchen, locker rooms, pro shop, parking. Open Competitions: Whit
Weekend; Open Weekend – August. Handicap Certificate required for
Open Competitions.

NO.	MEDAL YARDS	GEN. YARDS	PAR	S.I.	NO.	MEDAL YARDS	GEN. YARDS	PAR	S.I.
1	372	360	4	12	10	414	377	4	8
2	304	290	4	16	11	260	245	4	17
3	343	330	4	13	12	509	490	5	4
4	312	283	4	18	13	354	307	4	11
5	213	194	3	3	14	139	130	3	15
6	489	483	5	14	15	365	327	4	10
7	416	340	4	1	16	187	180	3	7
8	517	506	5	6	17	438	425	4	2
9	202	189	3	5	18	341	322	4	9
OUT	3,168	2,975	36		IN	3,007	2,803	35	
					TOTAL	6,175	5,778	71	
					STANDARD SCRATCH	69	68		

Ballinrobe Golf Club, Cloonacastle,
Ballinrobe, Co. Mayo.
Tel: (094) 954 1118.
info@ballinarobegolfclub.com
www.ballinarobegolfclub.com

LOCATION: **30 miles from
Galway. 20 miles from Castlebar
and Westport.**

SECRETARY/MANAGER:
John McMahon.

ARCHITECT: Eddie Hackett.

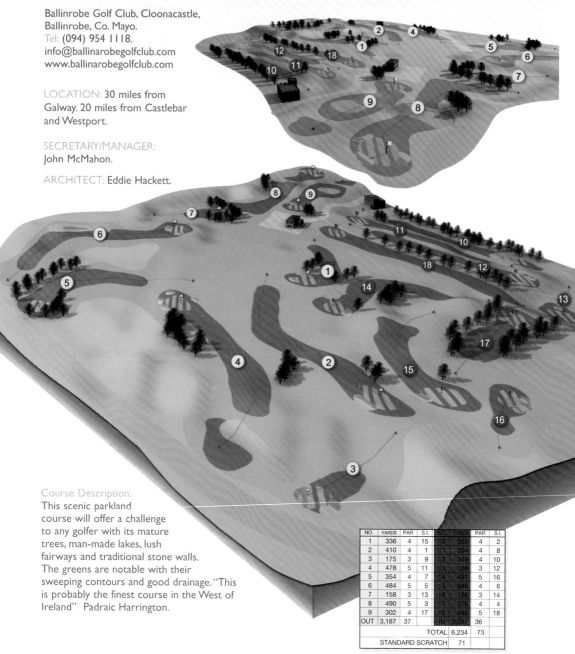

Course Description:
This scenic parkland
course will offer a challenge
to any golfer with its mature
trees, man-made lakes, lush
fairways and traditional stone walls.
The greens are notable with their
sweeping contours and good drainage. "This
is probably the finest course in the West of
Ireland" Padraic Harrington.

NO.	YARDS	PAR	S.I.	NO.	YARDS	PAR	S.I.
1	336	4	15	10	365	4	2
2	410	4	1	11	364	4	8
3	175	3	9	12	348	4	10
4	478	5	11	13	156	3	12
5	354	4	7	14	491	5	16
6	484	5	5	15	348	4	6
7	158	3	13	16	156	3	14
8	490	5	3	17	376	4	4
9	302	4	17	18	443	5	18
OUT	3,187	37		IN	3,047	36	
				TOTAL	6,234	73	
				STANDARD SCRATCH		71	

Course Information:
Par 73; SSS 73; Length 6,234 metres. Visitors: Welcome.
Opening Hours: 8am – Sunset. Avoid: Sunday and Tuesday
evenings. Ladies: Welcome. Green Fees: €33 Sat, €45 Sun,
€28 Midweek, €20 Fri. Juveniles: Welcome. Clubhouse
Hours: 9am – 11pm (June – August). Clubhouse Dress:
Casual. Clubhouse Facilities: The clubhouse is a fully
restored 250 year old estate house. Which offers golfers a
restaurant with full bar, comfortable and well appointed
changing rooms with a new pro shop on site. Open
Competitions: 25th June - Sunday 1st July

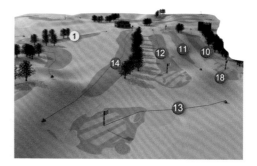

Coolnaha, Co. Mayo. Tel: (0907) 30014.

LOCATION: 2 miles north of Ballyhaunis on the Charlstown Road. 7 miles from Horan International Airport.

SECRETARY: Lorena Freely
MANAGER: Tom Prenty.

NO.	METRES	PAR	S.I.	NO.	METRES	PAR	S.I.
1	355	4	3	10	369	4	2
2	324	4	9	11	334	4	8
3	437	5	11	12	409	5	18
4	354	4	1	13	350	4	4
5	271	4	17	14	285	4	16
6	153	3	15	15	149	3	14
7	342	4	5	16	327	4	6
8	148	3	13	17	146	3	10
9	385	4	7	18	347	4	12
OUT	2,747	35		IN	2,696	35	
				TOTAL	5,443	70	
				STANDARD SCRATCH		70	

Course Description:

An interesting parkland course situated close to the famous Knock Shrine. The main features of Ballyhaunis are its pleasant elevated greens protected with well positioned bunkers.

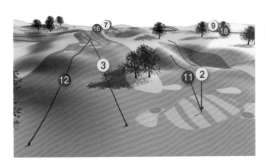

Course Information:

Par 70; SSS 69; Length 5,801 yards, 5,413 metres. Visitors: Welcome at all times. Opening Hours: 9.00am – sunset. Avoid: Members competitions on Sundays & Thursdays. Ladies: Welcome Thursdays. Green Fees: €20 per day. Juveniles: Welcome (Handicap Certificate required). Must be off the course by 3.00pm unless accompanied by an adult. Caddy service available by prior arrangement summer only. Clubhouse Hours: Licencing hours. Clubhouse Dress: Casual. During presentations – jacket and tie. Clubhouse Facilities: Full catering facilities by prior arrangement. Snacks available normally. Open Competitions: Various competitions throughout the year, handicap certificate required, call club for details.

Carne Golf Links, Carne, Belmullet, Co. Mayo.
Tel: (097) 82292. Fax: (097) 81477.
Web: carnegolflinks.com Email: carngolf@iol.ie

Course Description:

This new exciting links has a natural setting of considerable beauty. Splendid sand dunes on ancient commonage. Elevated tees and plateau greens exploit the magnificent backdrops over Blacksod Bay. Voted No.5 in Ireland by *Golf World* January 2000.

Course Information:

Par 72; SSS 72; Length 6,119 metres. Visitors: Welcome anytime. Green Fees: €60 per day Mon - Fri. €60 per round Sat/Sun. Club Facilities: Practice range, Caddy and Car Hire. Clubhouse Facilities: Bar and restaurant.

LOCATION: On the Mullet Peninsula near Belmullet, Co. Mayo. 2.5KM from Belmullet.

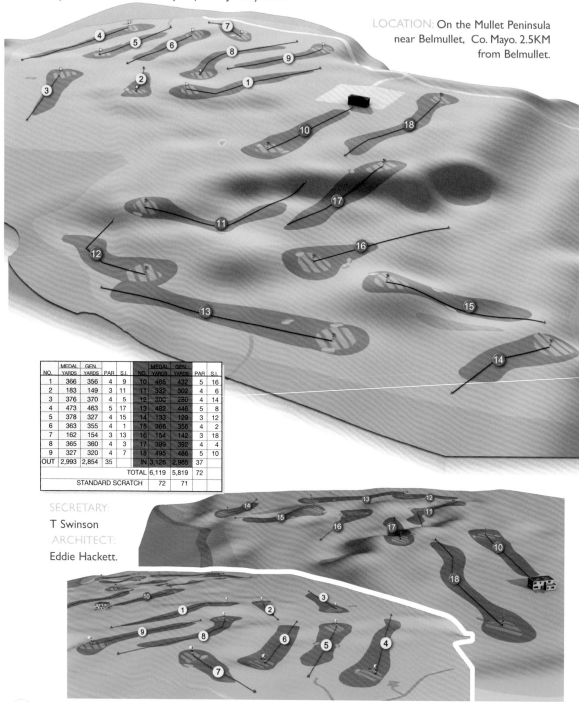

NO.	MEDAL YARDS	GEN. YARDS	PAR	S.I.	NO.	MEDAL YARDS	GEN. YARDS	PAR	S.I.
1	366	356	4	9	10	465	432	5	16
2	183	149	3	11	11	332	302	4	6
3	376	370	4	5	12	300	280	4	14
4	473	463	5	17	13	482	446	5	8
5	378	327	4	15	14	133	129	3	12
6	363	355	4	1	15	366	356	4	2
7	162	154	3	13	16	154	142	3	18
8	365	360	4	3	17	399	392	4	4
9	327	320	4	7	18	495	486	5	10
OUT	2,993	2,854	35		IN	3,126	2,965	37	
					TOTAL	6,119	5,819	72	
					STANDARD SCRATCH	72	71		

SECRETARY:
T Swinson
ARCHITECT:
Eddie Hackett.

LOCATION: **2 miles from Castlebar.**

SECRETARY: **Paul Kilcourse**

Mobile: **087 819535**

Castlebar Golf Club, Rocklands, Castlebar, Co. Mayo.
Tel: (094) 90 21649. Fax: (094) 90 26088.
info@castlebargolfclub.ie
www.castlebargolfclub.ie

NO.	MEDAL YARDS	GEN. YARDS	PAR	S.I.	NO.	MEDAL YARDS	GEN. YARDS	PAR	S.I.
1	298	283	4	15	10	141	127	3	18
2	199	153	3	7	11	437	432	5	16
3	436	410	5	13	12	158	137	3	10
4	286	258	4	4	13	358	342	4	12
5	359	350	4	4	14	383	370	4	4
6	171	141	3	3	15	364	350	4	6
7	361	315	4	11	16	145	131	3	14
8	498	459	5	5	17	422	418	4	2
9	419	405	4	1	18	467	423	5	8
OUT	3,027	2,774	36		IN	2,875	2,730	35	
					TOTAL	5,902	5,504	71	
					STANDARD SCRATCH		71	70	

Course Information:

Par 71; SSS 71; Length 5,907 Metres. Visitors: Welcome.
Opening Hours: Sunrise – Sunset, Please phone golf club for times of play. Avoid: Club competitions & Sunday. Green Fees: €25 Mon - Thurs, €32 Fri/Sat/Sun, €40 Husband/ Wife, Student/Junior/Juvenile Mon - Thur €15; Fri/Sun €20, For society rates contact Secretary on 087-2267936. Juveniles: Must be accompanied by an adult. Clubhouse Dress: Casual. Clubhouse Facilities: Catering facilities, snacks. Open Competitions: Last week of July.

Course Description:

Situated just 1.5 miles from Castlebar, the capital of County Mayo, Castlebar Golf Club is a parklands course of 18 holes, redesigned and redeveloped in 2001. The course is now one of Connacht's premiere golf courses. With a balanced mix of length and clever hole design, Castlebar Golf is now a must-play course for visitors to the region.

Claremorris Golf Club, Castlemagarrett,
Claremorris, Co. Mayo.
Tel: (094) 9371527. Fax: (094) 9372919.

Email: info@claremorrisgolfclub.com
Web: www.claremorrisgolfclub.com

LOCATION: Galway Road, 2 miles from town.

SECRETARY / MANAGER: Christina Rush (094) 9371527.

HON. SECRETARY: Willie Feeley.

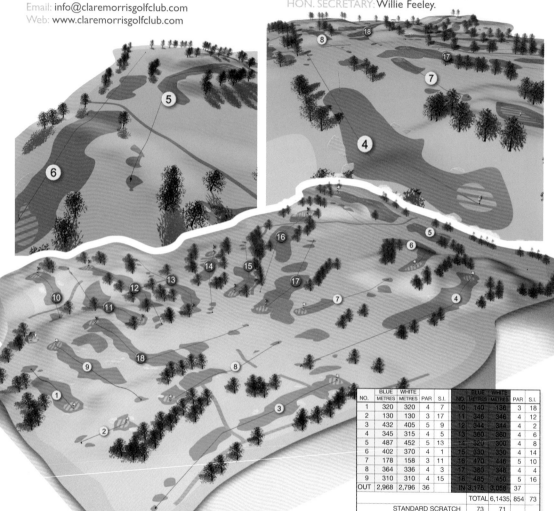

NO.	BLUE METRES	WHITE METRES	PAR	S.I.	NO.	BLUE METRES	WHITE METRES	PAR	S.I.
1	320	320	4	7	10	140	136	3	18
2	130	130	3	17	11	346	346	4	12
3	432	405	5	9	12	344	344	4	2
4	345	315	4	5	13	360	360	4	6
5	487	452	5	13	14	320	300	4	8
6	402	370	4	1	15	330	330	4	14
7	178	158	3	11	16	470	446	5	10
8	364	336	4	3	17	380	346	4	4
9	310	310	4	15	18	485	450	5	16
OUT	2,968	2,796	36		IN	3,175	3,058	37	
					TOTAL	6,1435	854	73	
	STANDARD SCRATCH					73	71		

Course Description:

An 18 Hole Championship parkland Course designed to
the highest standards by Tom Craddock (designer of the
Druid's Glen) Claremorris consists of many eye-catching water
features, bunkers, trees and wooded backgrounds. It has been highly
praised by golfers of all descriptions for its layout, the variations on each
hole, the eye-catching features and above all the excellent quality of the
sand based greens.

Course Information:

Par 73; SSS 71; Length 6,143 metres.
Visitors: Welcome to play at any time.
Avoid: Competitions for members. Ladies: Welcome.
Juveniles: Welcome. Green Fees: Weekdays – €32
Weekends and Bank Holidays – €40, with a member
€20. Clubhouse Dress: Casual. Clubhouse Facilities:
Catering and bar facilities. Open Competitions: Open
Week August 6th - 13th. Open Day every Thursday.

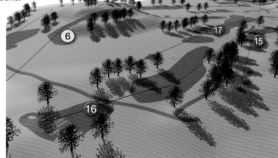

Mulranny Golf Course, Mulranny, Westport,
Co. Mayo. Tel: (098) 36262

LOCATION: 18 miles outside of Westport on
the Newport road. Signposted on the left just as
you enter Mulranny.

HON. SECRETARY: Noel Grealis.

HON. TREASURER: Ciaran Moran.

Course Information:
Par 71; SSS 69; Length 5,729 metres.
Visitors: Welcome. Course opening hours:
Daylight hours. Clubhouse opening hours:
9.00pm-11.30pm (Summer). Clubhouse dress: Neat and
casual, no denim, no mobile phones allowed on course or in
clubhouse. Green Fees: Midweek €15, weekends €20, for
opens €10. Facilities: Full catering facilities (July and August),
club hire and practice area also available. Competitions: Pre
booking for open tournaments 14 days in advance.

NO.	METRES	PAR	S.I.	NO.	METRES	PAR	S.I.
1	426	5	18	10	455	5	16
2	358	4	4	11	346	4	9
3	313	4	13	12	310	4	12
4	400	4	1	13	384	4	2
5	381	4	6	14	440	5	15
6	183	3	8	15	151	3	14
7	340	4	5	16	370	4	3
8	146	3	10	17	137	3	11
9	275	4	17	18	312	4	7
OUT	2,824	35		IN	2,905	36	
				TOTAL	5,729	71	
				STANDARD SCRATCH		69	

Course Description:
Mulranny Golf Club is one of the oldest
courses in Connacht. This is an unique
experience of links golf set on the shores
of the Atlantic Ocean, where the powerful
winds can make play exceptionally
challenging. Other hazards the golfer may
encounter are the cows and sheep that
roam the course. Set in one of the most
scenic parts of Ireland, golf here is a
tranquil and beautiful experience on this
wild and original golf course. The greens
are also truly great to putt on. Mulranny
prides itself on a warm West of Ireland
welcome that is extended to all visitors.

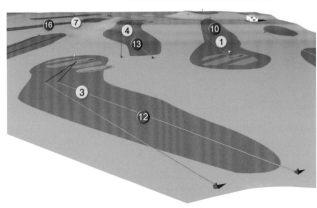

Swinford Golf Club, Barbazon Park, Swinford, Co. Mayo.
Tel/Fax: (094) 92 51378.
LOCATION: Beside Swinford town.

Course Description:

There are quite a number of trees on the course which adds considerably to the difficulty of wayward shots.

Course Information:

Par 70; SSS 68; Length 5,542 metres. Visitors: Welcome everyday. Opening Hours: All day everyday. Ladies: Welcome. Green Fees: €15 per day. Juveniles: Permitted. Clubhouse Hours: Open all day. Clubhouse Dress: Casual. Clubhouse Facilities: Bar. Catering by request. Open Competitions: Open weekends: on bank holidays. Open Week; 27th July - 4th Aug. Handicap certificate required.

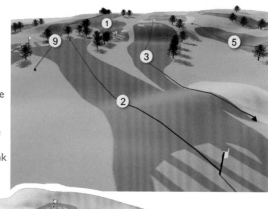

NO.	METRES	PAR	S.I.	NO.	METRES	PAR	S.I.
1	271	4	17	10	271	4	18
2	358	4	1	11	358	4	2
3	344	4	6	12	344	4	7
4	159	3	10	13	159	3	11
5	447	5	14	14	447	5	15
6	342	4	3	15	342	4	4
7	309	4	12	16	309	4	13
8	184	3	5	17	137	3	16
9	314	4	8	18	314	4	9
OUT	2,728	35		IN	2,517	35	
				TOTAL	5,245	70	
				STANDARD SCRATCH		68	

HON SECRETARY:
Tom Regan.
Tel/Fax: (094) 92 51378.
HEAD GROUNDSMAN:
Michael Farrelly.

Carrowholly, Westport, Co. Mayo.
Tel: (098) 28262
Web: www.westportgolfclub.com
Email: info@westportgolfclub.com

LOCATION: 2¹/₂ miles from Westport town.

MANAGER: Paul O'Neill.
Tel: (098) 28262/27070

PROFESSIONAL: Alex Mealia.
Tel: (098) 28262

ARCHITECT: Fred Hawtree.

NO.	MEDAL YARDS	GEN. YARDS	PAR	S.I.	NO.	MEDAL YARDS	GEN. YARDS	PAR	S.I.
1	348	335	4	14	10	500	498	5	13
2	342	330	4	8	11	434	420	4	3
3	164	152	3	16	12	231	220	3	5
4	496	488	5	18	13	449	439	4	1
5	356	343	4	12	14	191	180	3	11
6	455	445	4	4	15	560	494	5	9
7	520	511	5	10	16	363	350	4	15
8	472	436	4	2	17	335	333	4	17
9	204	196	3	6	18	560	550	5	7
OUT	3,357	3,236	36		IN	3,623	3,484	37	
					TOTAL	7,086	6,653		
					STANDARD SCRATCH		73		

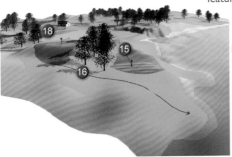

Course Description:

Situated on the shores of Clew Bay and set in 260 acres of parkland, Westport offers golfers a memorable challenge. The course commands a wonderful view of Clew Bay and is dominated by the Holy Mountain, Croagh Patrick. The best known hole on this course is the Par 5 fifteenth which reaches 580 yards (535 metres) and features a long carry from the tee over an inlet of Clew Bay. Designed by the noted golf architect Fred Hawtree, who also designed the new course at St Andrews.

Course Information:

Par 73; SSS 72; Length 6,653 yards. Visitors: Welcome (phone first). Opening Hours: Sunrise to sunset. Avoid: Competition days. Ladies: Welcome. Green Fees: Weekdays – €38/€45; weekends & Bank Holidays – €42/€55. Special rates for societies. Juveniles: Welcome. Lessons and Caddy service available by prior arrangement. Club hire available. Clubhouse Hours: 9.00am – 11.30pm. Clubhouse Dress: Informal. Clubhouse Facilities: Catering facilities – meals available 9am – 10pm. Open Competitions: Every Wednesday (April-September) Open Week Aug 4th - Aug 11th.

Athlone Golf Club, Hodson Bay,
Athlone, Co. Roscommon.
Tel: (090) 649 2073
Fax: (090) 649 4080

LOCATION: 6 km from Athlone off
the N6 to Roscommon on the shores
of Lough Ree.

HON. SECRETARY: Paddy O'Boyle.
Tel: (090) 649 2073

PROFESSIONAL: Kevin Grealey.
Tel: (090) 644 6008

NO.	MEDAL MEDAL	GEN. CHAMP.	PAR	S.I.	NO.	MEDAL MEDAL	GEN. CHAMP.	PAR	S.I.
1	343	338	4	11	10	172	172	3	13
2	140	140	3	7	11	390	365	4	10
3	389	377	4	15	12	478	454	5	12
4	398	387	4	4	13	396	396	4	3
5	532	520	5	9	14	326	326	4	14
6	177	151	3	8	15	300	293	4	16
7	425	417	5	17	16	421	407	4	1
8	390	390	4	5	17	139	107	3	18
9	400	377	4	2	18	361	361	4	6
OUT	3,194	3,097	36		IN	2,981	2,881	35	
					TOTAL	6,175	5,978	71	
					STANDARD SCRATCH		72	71	

Course
Information:
Par 71; SSS 71;
Length 5,854 yards.
Visitors: Welcome.
Opening Hours: 7.30am –
10.00pm. Ladies Day: Tuesday. Green
Fees: €30 Mon – Fri; €35 Sat / Sun / Bank
Holidays. Juveniles: Must play with an adult
before 3.30pm. Special times on noticeboard.
Lessons available by prior arrangements. Club Hire
available. Caddy service available by prior arrangements.
Handicap Certificate required. Clubhouse Hours: 7.30am –
11.30pm. Clubhouse Dress: Casual – tailored shorts. Clubhouse
Facilities: Full catering facilities available, restaurant hours 9.30am
– 10.00pm open all year round. Locker rooms, practice ground,
putting green, driving range, pro shop, buggies, trolleys, club hire
and tuition. Open Competitions: Open Week first week in June;
Lough Ree Open July and August.

Course Description:
A testing 18 hole parkland course that has
recently added to its stature by installing 18
USGA greens and four new water feature
holes to its course. Would be high up in the
order as one of the best inland courses in
the country. With an elevated clubhouse has
probably one of the best scenic views of
Lough Ree and River Shannon in the country.

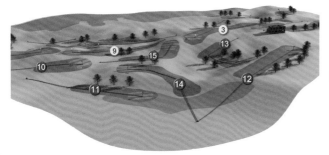

Aughalustia, Ballaghadereen, Co. Roscommon.
Tel: (094) 986 0295
www.ballaghadereen.com

LOCATION: Three mile from Ballaghadereen town.
SECRETARY: Pat Coen. Tel: (094) 986 1092.
CAPTAIN: John Freeman.
LADY CAPTAIN: Susan Kiernan.

NO.	METRES	PAR	S.I.	NO.	METRES	PAR	S.I.
1	307	4	14	10	307	4	15
2	312	4	9	11	312	4	8
3	348	4	2	12	435	5	13
4	347	4	3	13	336	4	4
5	166	3	7	14	129	3	17
6	436	5	16	15	383	4	1
7	154	3	11	16	154	3	12
8	245	4	18	17	300	4	10
9	334	4	5	18	334	4	6
OUT	2,649	35		IN	2,690	35	
				TOTAL	5,339	70	
				STANDARD SCRATCH	70		

Course Description:
A relatively flat course but
trees that are maturing are becoming
a great asset both visually and also coming
into play. A trip to the rough can quite easily cost a
shot. The 5th hole in particular requires great accuracy
to a very small green, well protected with bunkers.

Course Information: Par 70; SSS 698;
Length 5,840 yards. Visitors: Welcome at all
times. Opening Hours: 9.00am – Dusk.
Ladies: Welcome. Green Fees: €15 daily.
Handicap Certificate required for open
competitions. Juveniles: Welcome. Must be off
the course by 6.00pm. Clubhouse Hours:
Saturday and Sunday evenings. Clubhouse
Dress: Casual. Clubhouse Facilities: Bar.
Catering by prior arrangement. Open
Competitions: Open Week July 23rd - 30th.
May - Aug Open Saturday.

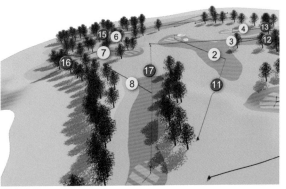

Boyle Golf Club, Knockadoobrusna, Boyle, Co. Roscommon.
Tel: (071) 966 2594

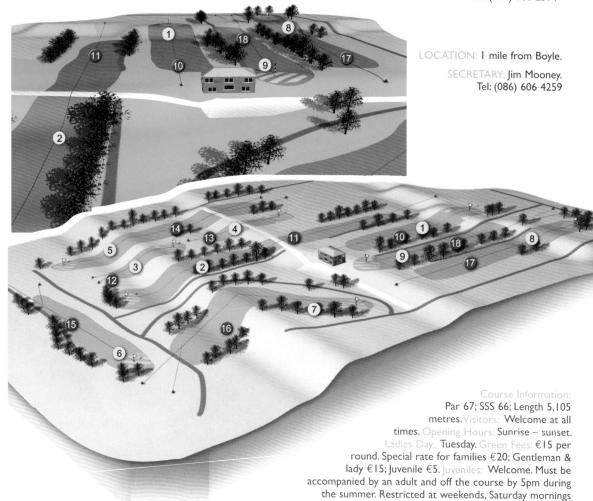

LOCATION: I mile from Boyle.

SECRETARY: Jim Mooney.
Tel: (086) 606 4259

Course Information:

Par 67; SSS 66; Length 5,105 metres. Visitors: Welcome at all times. Opening Hours: Sunrise – sunset. Ladies Day: Tuesday. Green Fees: €15 per round. Special rate for families €20; Gentleman & lady €15; Juvenile €5. Juveniles: Welcome. Must be accompanied by an adult and off the course by 5pm during the summer. Restricted at weekends, Saturday mornings 10am – 12 noon only. Clubhouse Hours: 4.00pm – midnight. Clubhouse Dress: Casual. Clubhouse Facilities: Catering facilities: bar snacks. Open Competitions: Open Week 15th-23rd July, Open Weekend 29th-30th April, Open Day every Thursday evening (April-October only).

Course Description:

A feature of the course is the views of Lough Key, Curlew Mountains, Sligo Mountain and the Mayo Mountains from the 8th green and 2nd tee. The course is also within easy reach of Lough Key and Forest Park, Boyle.

NO.	METRES	PAR	S.I.	NO.	METRES	PAR	S.I.
1	259	4	15	10	259	4	16
2	430	4	1	11	482	5	12
3	144	3	9	12	155	3	8
4	128	3	17	13	128	3	18
5	339	4	11	14	377	4	2
6	203	3	5	15	168	3	10
7	300	4	7	16	306	4	6
8	313	4	3	17	313	4	4
9	306	4	13	18	304	4	14
OUT	2,422	33		IN	2,492	34	
				TOTAL	4,914	67	
				STANDARD SCRATCH		66	

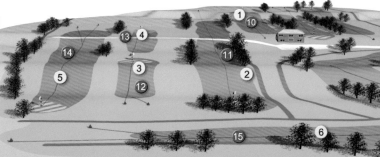

Woodbrook, Carrick-on-Shannon, Co. Leitrim.
Tel: (071) 9667015
ckgc@eircom.net   www.carrickgolfclub.ie

LOCATION: On N4 route, four miles west of Carrick-on-Shannon to Sligo.

Course Information:
Par 70; SSS 68; Length 5,787 metres. Visitors: Welcome at all times (book online at www.carrickgolfclub.ie.) Opening Hours: Daylight hours. Ladies: Welcome. Green Fees: €35 Weekday, €40 Weekend. Clubhouse Dress: Informal. Clubhouse hours: 11am-close. Clubhouse Facilities: Full bar and restaurant serving hot meals & cold snacks. Open Competitions: Open Tuesday, every Tuesday May-Oct. Open Week, Aug 19-Aug 26th 2007. Golf Classic June 2nd-4th 2007.

General Manager: Chris Lowe.

NO.	BLUE METRES	WHITE METRES	PAR	S.I.	NO.	BLUE METRES	WHITE METRES	PAR	S.I.
1	319	309	4	11	10	198	167	3	8
2	419	396	4	5	11	300	300	4	12
3	389	373	4	3	12	370	331	4	2
4	482	482	5	15	13	195	175	3	4
5	148	148	3	13	14	431	431	5	14
6	312	312	4	17	15	323	305	4	18
7	502	462	5	7	16	325	325	4	6
8	193	168	3	9	17	184	162	3	16
9	397	365	4	1	18	320	312	4	10
OUT	3,161	3,015	36		IN	2,626	2,508	34	
					TOTAL	5,787	5,523	70	
					STANDARD SCRATCH	70	68		

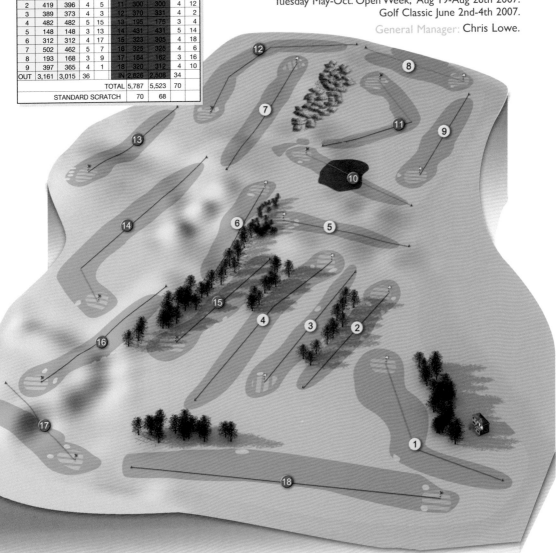

Course Description:
A pleasant 18 hole inland course overlooking the River Shannon, with two new tee-boxes right on the edge of the river. Philip Reid writing in the Irish Times in July 02 said "Carrick can rightly claim to have one of the finer inland courses in Ireland."

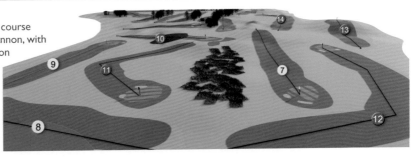

Clonailis, Castlerea, Co. Roscommon.
Tel: (094) 962 0068 / Fax: (090) 962 1214.

LOCATION: Town of Castlerea. Between Castlebar and Roscommon.

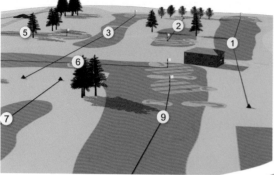

SECRETARY/MANAGER:
E. O'Laughlan.
Tel: (094) 962 0072

CAPTAIN:
Sean Naughton.

NO.	YARDS	PAR	S.I.	NO.	YARDS	PAR	S.I.
1	314	4	12	10	314	4	12
2	340	3	5	11	340	3	5
3	170	4	9	12	170	4	9
4	280	4	18	13	280	4	18
5	380	3	6	14	380	3	6
6	165	3	16	15	165	3	16
7	282	4	14	16	282	4	14
8	425	4	13	17	425	4	13
9	165	5	3	18	165	5	3
OUT	2,521	35		IN	2,521	35	
					TOTAL	5,042	70
				STANDARD SCRATCH	67		

Course Information:
Par 68; SSS 66; Length 4,974 metres. Visitors: Welcome. Opening Hours: Sunrise – sunset. Ladies: Welcome. Green Fees: €20. Juveniles: Welcome. Caddy service available by prior arrangement. Trolleys for hire. Clubhouse Hours: 10.30am to closing time. Bar open from 5pm weekdays and all day weekends. Clubhouse Dress: Casual. Clubhouse Facilities: By prior arrangment. Open Competitions: Open Week June & August. Handicap Certificate required for Open Competitions.

Course Description:
This is a short parkland course with three Par 3 holes. River comes into play on 4th, 5th and 8th holes. Narrow fairways make accuracy important, although the light rough does not cause too much frustration for errant shots.

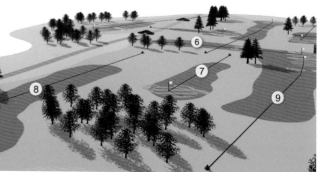

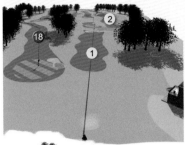

Roscommon Golf Club, Mote Park, Roscommon, Co Roscommon. Tel: (090) 6626382. Fax: (090) 6626043. Email: rosgolfclub@eircom.net

LOCATION: Roscommon Town.

SECRETARY: Marina Dolan CAPTAIN: Eddie Miley.

NO.	YARDS	PAR	S.I.	NO.	YARDS	PAR	S.I.
1	285	4	13	10	404	4	1
2	343	4	6	11	124	3	18
3	300	4	14	12	465	5	10
4	466	5	9	13	132	3	17
5	363	4	4	14	365	4	5
6	149	3	16	15	357	4	7
7	418	4	12	16	458	5	11
8	408	4	2	17	329	4	15
9	163	3	8	18	384	4	3
OUT	2,895	36		IN	3,006	35	
				TOTAL	5,901	70	
				STANDARD SCRATCH		70	

Course Information:

Par 72; SSS 70; Length 5,901 metres. Visitors: Welcome to play any time. Tuesdays and Sundays by arrangement. Opening Hours: Sunrise – sunset. Avoid: Summer evenings. Ladies Day: Tuesday. Green Fees: €30 Weekdays; €35 Weekends. Weekly tickets on request, and society rates available. Clubhouse Hours: 11am – midnight. Clubhouse Dress: Informal but neat. Clubhouse Facilities: Bar and catering available everyday. Open Competitions: Open Days: Every Wednesday, April - September.

Course Description:

Roscommon is one of the more challenging golf tests in the Midlands and West. With a standard scratch score of 70, it requires long and accurate hitting on some holes, while others will test the short game skills of the golfer.

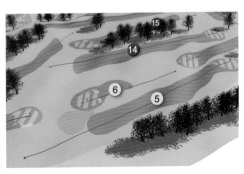

Strokestown

Strokestown,
Co. Roscommon.
Tel: (071) 963 3528.

LOCATION: 12 miles
from Longford

Course Information:
Par 70; SSS 66; Length 5,256 metres.
Visitors: Welcome. Opening Hours: Dawn – Dusk. Ladies: Welcome.
Green Fees: €15 all week. Clubhouse Dress: Casual.

Course Description:
Newly established 9 hole, parkland course
with scenic setting. New clubhouse added
in 2004.

HON SECRETARY:
Liam Glover.

NO.	YARDS	PAR	S.I.	NO.	YARDS	PAR	S.I.
1	378	4	3	10	378	4	4
2	337	4	5	11	337	4	6
3	135	3	15	12	135	3	16
4	355	4	1	13	355	4	2
5	119	3	13	14	119	3	14
6	304	4	11	15	304	4	12
7	352	4	7	16	352	4	8
8	245	4	9	17	245	4	10
9	403	5	17	18	403	5	18
OUT	2,628	35		IN	2,628	35	
				TOTAL	5,256	70	
				STANDARD SCRATCH			

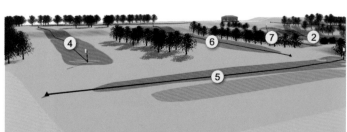

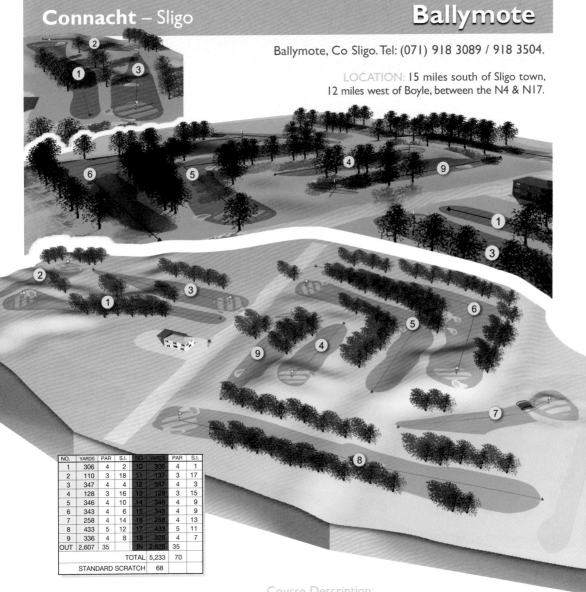

Ballymote, Co Sligo. Tel: (071) 918 3089 / 918 3504.

LOCATION: 15 miles south of Sligo town, 12 miles west of Boyle, between the N4 & N17.

NO.	YARDS	PAR	S.I.	NO.	YARDS	PAR	S.I.
1	306	4	2	10	306	4	1
2	110	3	18	11	137	3	17
3	347	4	4	12	347	4	3
4	128	3	16	13	128	3	15
5	346	4	10	14	346	4	9
6	343	4	6	15	343	4	9
7	258	4	14	16	258	4	13
8	433	5	12	17	433	5	11
9	336	4	8	18	328	4	7
OUT	2,607	35		IN	2,626	35	
				TOTAL	5,233	70	
			STANDARD SCRATCH		68		

Course Information:

Par 70; SSS 68; Length 5,302 metres. Visitors: Welcome at all times (some restrictions Jul & Aug). Opening Hours: Dawn – Dusk. Ladies: Welcome. Green Fees: €20 per day. Clubhouse Dress: Casual. Clubhouse Facilities: Practice putting green, practice range, training bunker & training net. Buggies available for hire. Open Competitions: Contact club for details.

Course Description:

The Club is based one mile outside the town on the Castlebaldwin Road. The course offers a fine test of golf over undulating parkland.

PRESIDENT: Alfie Parke.
HON SECRETARY: John McCarrick.
SECRETARY/MANAGER: John. O'Connor.

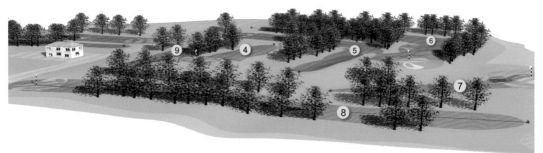

Castle Dargan Estate, Ballygawley, Co. Sligo
Tel: (071) 911 8080
Fax: (071) 911 8090

CLUB CAPTAIN: Dermot Flynn.
HON. SECRETARY: Michael Callaghan.
CLUB MANAGER: David O'Donovan
PROFESSIONAL: Xavier Medas.

NO.	BLUE YARDS	WHITE YARDS	PAR	S.I.	NO.	BLUE YARDS	WHITE YARDS	PAR	S.I.
1	406	379	4	7	10	478	429	5	14
2	507	452	5	9	11	147	132	3	10
3	121	117	3	17	12	390	367	4	18
4	383	373	4	5	13	192	166	3	16
5	419	414	4	1	14	471	436	4	4
6	493	474	5	15	15	262	259	4	12
7	176	173	3	13	16	422	417	4	8
8	454	409	4	3	17	439	431	4	6
9	538	517	5	11	18	455	435	4	2
OUT	3,497	3,308	37		IN	3,257	3,095	35	
					TOTAL	6,754	6,403	72	
					STANDARD SCRATCH		72	71	

Email: golf@castledargan.com
Web: www.castledargan.com

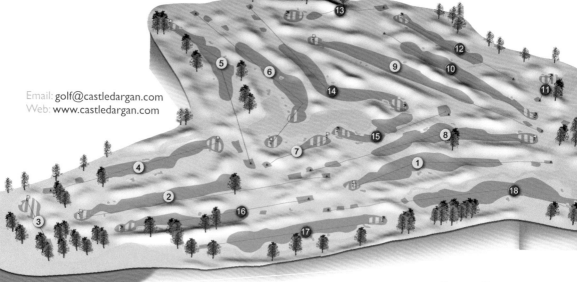

Course Information:
Par 72; ; Length 6,754 yards. Visitors: Welcome.
Opening Hours: 8am - 8pm (seasonal opening times).
Juniors: Over 16yrs full green fees payable.
Green Fees: Non-resident Summer (April-October): Mon -
Thur €65, Fri - Sun €75. Golf Club Dress: Dress code in
operation. Golfers are required to wear soft spikes. (service
available). Additional Facilities: Short game, practice area and
putting green. Golf Shop stocking all major brands. Trolley,
Buggy & Club Hire all available.

Course Description:
This 18 hole Championship Golf Course is
built to USGA specifications. The natural
tumbling terrain compliments the design of
this beautiful 170 acres of rolling parkland,
6754 yards Par 72 Golf Course, situated in
the North West. Our Golf Resort offers a
unique and exclusive opportunity, combining
timeless opulence with modern sophistication
to offer an unrivalled resort experience in
Yeat's Land of Hearts Desire.

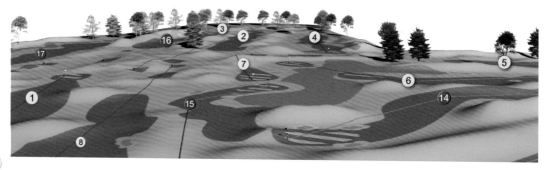

County Sligo Golf Club,
Rosses Point, Co Sligo.
Tel: (071) 9177186/9177134
Fax: (071) 9177460

LOCATION: Eight km. west of Sligo.

SECRETARY: Teresa Banks. Tel: (071) 9177134

PROFESSIONAL: Jim Robinson. Tel: (071) 9177171

ARCHITECT: Colt & Allison.

MANAGER: Hugh O'Neill.

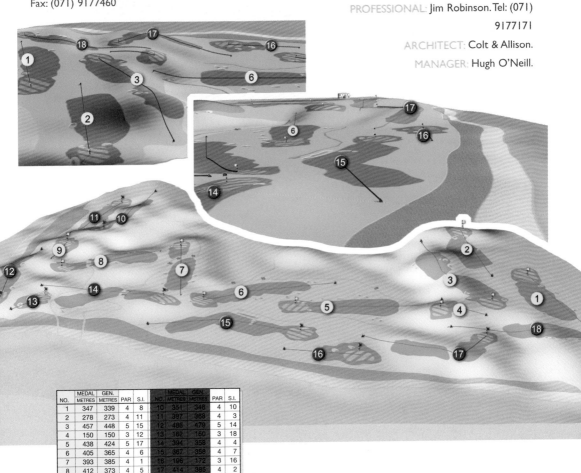

NO.	MEDAL METRES	GEN. METRES	PAR	S.I.	NO.	MEDAL METRES	GEN. METRES	PAR	S.I.
1	347	339	4	8	10	351	348	4	10
2	278	273	4	11	11	397	368	4	3
3	457	448	5	15	12	486	479	5	14
4	150	150	3	12	13	162	150	3	18
5	438	424	5	17	14	394	358	4	4
6	405	365	4	6	15	367	358	4	7
7	393	385	4	1	16	196	172	3	16
8	412	373	4	5	17	414	385	4	2
9	153	140	3	13	18	336	325	4	9
OUT	3,033	2,897	36		IN	3,103	2,943	35	
					TOTAL	6,136	5,840	71	
					STANDARD SCRATCH		72		

Course Information:
Par 71; SSS 72; Length 6,043 metres.
Visitors: Welcome to play, except during major championship competitions.
Opening Hours: Daylight. Avoid: Advisable to check tee time available before travel. Ladies: Welcome. Green Fees: Mon-Thur €70, Fri/Sat/ Sun/Bank Holidays €85; Lessons available by prior arrangement. Club Hire available. Caddy service available by prior arrangement.
Clubhouse Hours: 8.00am - 11.30pm.
Clubhouse Dress: Neat/Casual.
Clubhouse Facilities: Full facilities. Snacks during day, a la carte after 6pm, and any other requirements by arrangement.
Open Competitions: Open week August. Handicap Certificate required. 9 holes Bowmore Course.

Course Description:
Situated under the shadow of famous Benbulben, the County Sligo Golf Club, or Rosses Point as it is more popularly known, is one of Ireland's great championship links. Home of the West of Ireland Championship held each year since 1923. Set among vast sand dunes on the cliffs overlooking three large beaches. Constant winds are an added factor to its many challenges, not least of which are some of its elevated tees. A burn meanders through the course and comes into play on a number of holes.

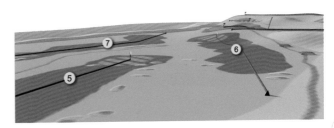

LOCATION: Ballina Road, south of Enniscrone.

SECRETARY/MANAGER: Micheal Staunton.

ARCHITECT: E. Hackett/ Donald Steel.

HON. SECRETARY: Brian Casey.
Tel: (096) 36414

PROFESSIONAL:
Charles McGoldrick.

Enniscrone Golf Club, Enniscrone, Co. Sligo.
Tel: (096) 36297 Fax: (096) 36657
Email: enniscronegolf@eircom.net
web: www.enniscronegolf.com

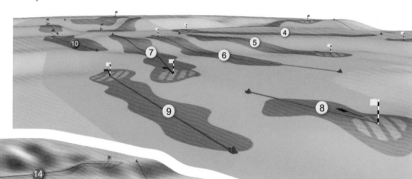

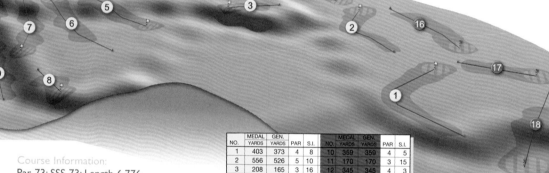

Course Information:

Par 73; SSS 73; Length 6,776 yards. Visitors: Always welcome. (telephone at weekends). Opening Hours: Sunrise – sunset. Avoid: Bank Holidays & Sunday between 7.00am – 11.00am and 1.00pm – 4.00pm. Ladies: Welcome. Green Fees: €55 weekdays, €70 weekends, Monday - Friday €40 societies (16 or more people). Juveniles: Must be accompanied by an adult. Club Hire is available. Caddy service and lessons available by prior arrangements. Telephone appointment required. Clubhouse Hours: Open at all times. Clubhouse Dress: Casual but neat. Clubhouse Facilities: Catering facilities: snacks at all times. Meals by arrangement. Open Competitions: Open Week 26th-30th June.

NO.	MEDAL YARDS	GEN. YARDS	PAR	S.I.	NO.	MEDAL YARDS	GEN. YARDS	PAR	S.I.
1	403	373	4	8	10	359	359	4	5
2	556	526	5	10	11	170	170	3	15
3	208	165	3	16	12	345	345	4	3
4	523	523	5	12	13	350	338	5	13
5	450	450	4	2	14	542	542	4	7
6	395	395	4	4	15	421	373	5	1
7	534	524	5	14	16	514	514	3	11
8	170	170	3	18	17	149	149	4	17
9	395	382	4	6	18	400	400	3	9
OUT	3,634	3,508	37		IN	3,250	3,190	36	
					TOTAL	6,884	6,698	73	
					STANDARD SCRATCH			72	

Course Description:

This links, on the shore of Killala Bay, is one of the many marvellous tests of golf which can be found in Ireland. The quality of the golf is matched by the surroundings, with the Ox Mountains close at hand. Killala Bay reaches out to the broad Atlantic within miles of sandy beaches surrounding the course. "This is certainly a course not to be missed... the club is very keen to encourage visitors, so a warm welcome is assured" (GolfWorld). During 2007 Enniscrone was a venue for the Irish Close Championships and the West of Ireland Championship. Now a 27 hole championship complex.

Strandhill Golf Club, Strandhill, Co. Sligo.
Tel: (071) 91 68188. Fax: (071) 91 68811.
Email: strandhillgc@eircom.net
Web: www.strandhillgc.com

Course Description:

Strandhill is a links course, playable all year round and situated in a most scenic area with views of Knocknarea and Benbulben Mountains. It has some very interesting holes, with the final three providing a sting in the tail.

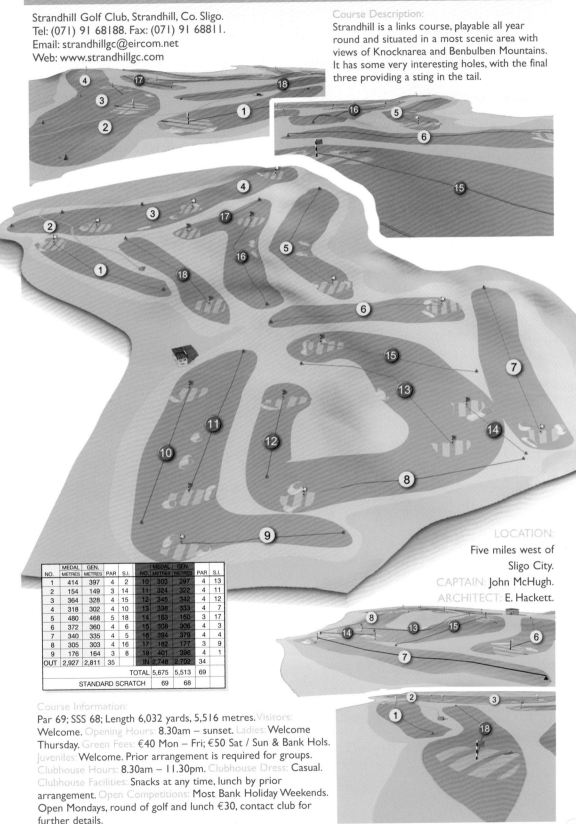

NO.	MEDAL METRES	GEN. METRES	PAR	S.I.	NO.	MEDAL METRES	GEN. METRES	PAR	S.I.
1	414	397	4	2	10	303	297	4	13
2	154	149	3	14	11	324	322	4	11
3	364	328	4	15	12	345	342	4	12
4	318	302	4	10	13	338	333	4	7
5	480	468	5	18	14	163	150	3	17
6	372	360	4	6	15	308	306	4	3
7	340	335	4	5	16	394	379	4	4
8	305	303	4	16	17	182	177	3	9
9	176	164	3	8	18	401	396	4	1
OUT	2,927	2,811	35		IN	2,748	2,702	34	
					TOTAL	5,675	5,513	69	
					STANDARD SCRATCH		69	68	

LOCATION:
Five miles west of Sligo City.
CAPTAIN: John McHugh.
ARCHITECT: E. Hackett.

Course Information:

Par 69; SSS 68; Length 6,032 yards, 5,516 metres. Visitors: Welcome. Opening Hours: 8.30am – sunset. Ladies: Welcome Thursday. Green Fees: €40 Mon – Fri; €50 Sat / Sun & Bank Hols. Juveniles: Welcome. Prior arrangement is required for groups. Clubhouse Hours: 8.30am – 11.30pm. Clubhouse Dress: Casual. Clubhouse Facilities: Snacks at any time, lunch by prior arrangement. Open Competitions: Most Bank Holiday Weekends. Open Mondays, round of golf and lunch €30, contact club for further details.

Tubbercurry, Co. Sligo. Tel: (071) 9185849.

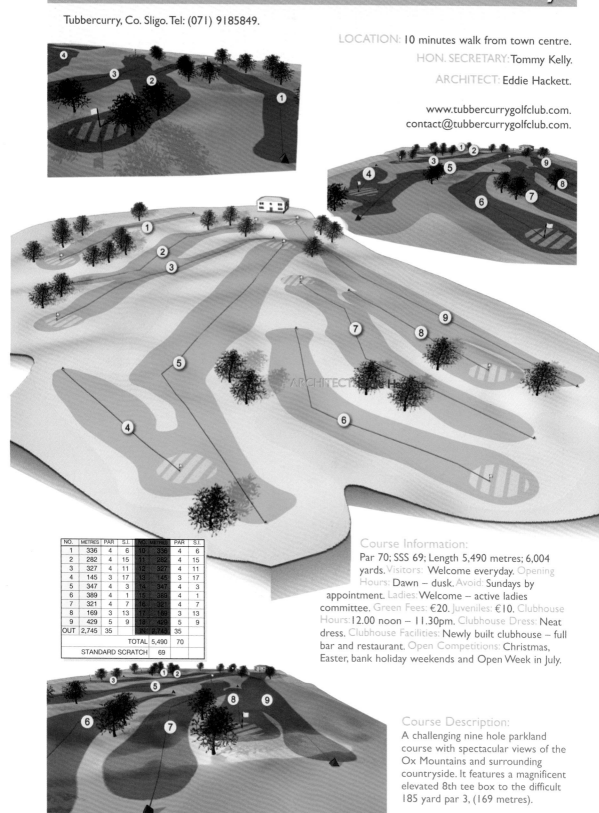

LOCATION: 10 minutes walk from town centre.

HON. SECRETARY: Tommy Kelly.

ARCHITECT: Eddie Hackett.

www.tubbercurrygolfclub.com.
contact@tubbercurrygolfclub.com.

NO.	METRES	PAR	S.I.	NO.	METRES	PAR	S.I.
1	336	4	6	10	336	4	6
2	282	4	15	11	282	4	15
3	327	4	11	12	327	4	11
4	145	3	17	13	145	3	17
5	347	4	3	14	347	4	3
6	389	4	1	15	389	4	1
7	321	4	7	16	321	4	7
8	169	3	13	17	169	3	13
9	429	5	9	18	429	5	9
OUT	2,745	35		IN	2,745	35	
				TOTAL	5,490	70	
				STANDARD SCRATCH		69	

Course Information:

Par 70; SSS 69; Length 5,490 metres; 6,004 yards. Visitors: Welcome everyday. Opening Hours: Dawn – dusk. Avoid: Sundays by appointment. Ladies: Welcome – active ladies committee. Green Fees: €20. Juveniles: €10. Clubhouse Hours: 12.00 noon – 11.30pm. Clubhouse Dress: Neat dress. Clubhouse Facilities: Newly built clubhouse – full bar and restaurant. Open Competitions: Christmas, Easter, bank holiday weekends and Open Week in July.

Course Description:

A challenging nine hole parkland course with spectacular views of the Ox Mountains and surrounding countryside. It features a magnificent elevated 8th tee box to the difficult 185 yard par 3, (169 metres).

Advertiser Index

Golf Course Index

Notes

Keep up to date with golf courses in Ireland at
www.golfdays.com